Introduction to Java™ Programming

Third Edition

Y. Daniel Liang
Armstrong Atlantic State University
Department of Computer Science

Prentice Hall
Upper Saddle River, New Jersey 07458
http://www.prenhall.com

Library of Congress Cataloging-in-Publication Data

Liang, Y. Daniel.
Introduction to Java Programming/ Y. Daniel Liang.—3rd ed,
p. cm.
Includes bibliographical references and index.
ISBN 0-13-031997-X
1. Java (Computer program language) I. Title
QA76.73.J38 L52 2001
005.13'3—dc21 00-061970
CIP

Vice president and editorial director, ECS: *Marcia Horton*
Publisher: *Alan R. Apt*
Associate editor: *Toni D. Holm*
Editorial assistant: *Amy Todd*
Marketing manager: *Jennie Burger*
Production editor: *Pine Tree Composition*
Executive managing editor: *Vince O'Brien*
Managing editor: *David A. George*
Art director: *Heather Scott*
Art Editor: *Adam Velthaus*
Assistant art director: *John Christiana*
Manufacturing manager: *Trudy Pisciotti*
Manufacturing buyer: *Dawn Murrin*
Vice president and director of production and manufacturing, ESM: *David W. Riccardi*
Cover image: *Photodisc PD*

The author and publisher of this book have used their best efforts in preparing this book. These efforts include the development, research, and testing of the theories to determine their effectiveness.

Printed in the United States of America
10 9 8 7 6

ISBN 0-13-031997-X

Prentice-Hall International (UK) Limited, *London*
Prentice-Hall of Australia Pty. Limited, *Sydney*
Prentice-Hall Canada Inc., *Toronto*
Prentice-Hall Hispanoamericana, S.A., *Mexico*
Prentice-Hall of India Private Limited, *New Delhi*
Prentice-Hall of Japan, Inc., *Tokyo*
Pearson Education Asia Pte. Ltd., *Singapore*
Editora Prentice-Hall do Brasil, Ltda., *Rio de Janeiro*

ABOUT THE AUTHOR

Y. Daniel Liang is the author of four successful Java books. He has taught over 40 Java courses to the university students and corporate employees.

Dr. Liang is currently a Yamacyaw professor of software engineering in the Department of Computer Science at Armstrong Atlantic State University, Savannah, Georgia. He can be reached via the Internet at **liangjava@yahoo.com,** or **liang@armstrong.edu.**

ACKNOWLEDGMENTS

I am grateful to the readers of the previous editions, both students and instructors, who offered comments, suggestions, bug reports, and praise. Their enthusiastic support prompted the third edition, which incorporates many of their fine contributions. Without supportive readers and instructors, this edition would not have been possible.

Students and faculty at Armstrong Atlantic State University and at Purdue University at Fort Wayne have been great supporters of this ongoing project. I would like to thank Ray Greenlaw of Armstrong Atlantic State University for his support of incorporating Java into the CS curriculum, and for his tireless efforts of building a first-class computer science undergraduate program.

This book has benefited from the previous editions of my *Introduction to Java Programming*. I would like to acknowledge the following people who helped produce the previous editions: Hao Wu, Greg Geller, Michael Willig, Russell Minnich, Balaram Nair, Ben Stonebraker, C-Y Tang, Bertrand I-P Lin, Maw-Shang Chang, Ruay-Shiung Chang, Mike Sunderman, Fen English, James Silver, Mark Temte, Bob Sanders, Marta Partington, Tom Cirtin, Songlin Qiu, Tim Tate, Carolyn Linn, Alfonso Hermida, Nathan Clement, Eric Miller, Chris Barrick, John Etchison, Louisa Klucznik, Angela Denny, Randy Haubner, Robin Drake, Betsy Brown, and Susan Kindel.

For this edition, I would like to thank Alan Apt, Toni Holm, Jennie Burger, Cindy Szollose, Jake Warde, and their colleagues at Prentice-Hall for organizing and managing this project, and Patty Donovan, Robert Milch, Dan Boilard, Dana Smith, and their colleagues at Pine Tree Composition for helping to produce the book.

As always, I am indebted to my wife, Samantha, for love, support, and encouragement.

To Samantha, Michael, and Michelle

PREFACE

To the Instructor

There are three popular strategies in teaching Java. The first is to mix Java applets and graphics programming with object-oriented programming concepts. The second is to introduce object-oriented programming from the start. The third strategy is a step-by-step approach, first laying a sound foundation on programming concepts, control statements, and methods, then introducing object-oriented programming, and finally moving on to graphical user interface (GUI), applets, internationalization, multithreading, multimedia, I/O, and networking.

The first strategy, starting with GUI and applets, seems attractive, but requires substantial knowledge of object-oriented programming and a good understanding of the Java event-handling model; thus, students may never fully understand what they are doing. The second strategy is based on the notion that the objects should be introduced first because Java is an object-oriented programming language. This notion, however, does not strike a chord with students. From the more than 40 Java courses I have taught, I have concluded that introducing primary data types, control structures, and methods prepares students to learn object-oriented programming. Therefore, this text adopts the third strategy, first proceeding at a steady pace through all the necessary and important basic concepts, then moving to object-oriented programming, and then to using the object-oriented approach to build interesting GUI applications and applets with multithreading, multimedia, I/O, and networking.

The book is suited for both beginning and advanced students, depending on how it is used. This book has been used in a two-semester freshman programming course and a one-semester course in Java as a second language. It has also been used for a short training course for experienced programmers. Computer science departments, engineering departments, and management information systems departments around the world have used this book at various levels. For students with no programming experience, the emphasis should be on Part I of the book, particularly on writing the loops. You could spend the entire semester of four credit hours just on the first six chapters of the book.

The Instructor's Manual on CD-ROM is available for instructors using this book. It contains the following resources:

- Microsoft PowerPoint slides for lectures.
- Answers to review questions.
- Source code for the examples in the book.
- The new edition provides 45% more programming exercises. Instructor's Solutions are provided in the Instructor's Manual. Students will have access to the solutions of even-numbered exercises.

To obtain the Instructor's Manual, contact your Prentice-Hall sales representative.

Instructors may request sample exams directly from the author.

Microsoft PowerPoint slides, answers to review questions, solutions to even-numbered programming exercises, and source code for the examples in the book are also available at the book's companion Web site at **www.cs.armstrong.edu/liang/intro3e.html** and **www.prenhall.com/liang**

Pedagogical Features of the Book

Introduction to Java Programming Third Edition uses the following elements to get the most out of the material:

- **Objectives** lists what students should have learned from the chapter. This will help them to determine whether they have met the objectives after completing the chapter.
- **Introduction** opens the discussion with a brief overview of what to expect from the chapter.
- Programming concepts are taught by representative **Examples**, carefully chosen and presented in an easy-to-follow style. Each example is described, and includes the source code, a sample run, and an example review. The source code of the examples is contained in the companion CD-ROM.
- Each program is complete and ready to be compiled and executed. The sample run of the program is captured from the screen to give students a live presentation of the example. Reading these examples is much like entering and running them on a computer.
- **Chapter Summary** reviews the important subjects that students should understand and remember. It helps them to reinforce the key concepts they have learned in the chapter.
- **Review Questions** help students to track their progress and evaluate their learning.
- **Programming Exercises** at the end of each chapter provide students with opportunities to apply the skills on their own. The trick of learning programming is practice, practice, and practice. To that end, the book provides a large number of exercises.
- **Notes** and **Tips** are inserted throughout the text to offer valuable advice and insight on important aspects of program development.

NOTE

Provides additional information on the subject and reinforces important concepts.

Tip
Teaches good programming style and practice, and helps students steer away from the pitfalls of programming errors.

What's New in This Edition

This book expands and improves upon the second edition of *Introduction to Java Programming.* The major changes are as follows:

- The use of UML enhances the treatment of object-oriented design and programming. UML graphical notations are used to describe classes and their relationships throughout the book.
- Beginning with Chapter 8, "Getting Started with Graphics Programming," all the AWT user interface components are replaced with state-of-the-art Swing components.
- Chapter 12, "Internationalization," is brand-new. It introduces date, time, and number formatting, and the development of Java programs for international audiences.
- Several new case studies are provided to give more examples for learning the fundamentals of programming, such as writing loops.
- Nonessential sections are marked optional and can be skipped or covered later with no adverse effect on the students' understanding of subsequent chapters. These sections include such topics as recursion, advanced layout managers, and resource bundles.
- Several new appendices provide readers with additional background information.

To the Student

There is nothing more important to the future of computing than the Internet. There is nothing more exciting on the Internet than Java. A revolutionary programming language developed by Sun Microsystems, Java has become the de facto standard for cross-platform applications and programming on the World Wide Web.

Before Java, the Web was used primarily for viewing static information on the Internet using HTML, a marked-up language for document layout and for linking documents over the Internet. Java programs can be embedded in an HTML page and downloaded by Web browsers to bring live animation and interactive applications to Web clients.

Java is a full-featured, general-purpose programming language that is capable of developing robust mission-critical applications. In the last three years, Java has gained enormous popularity and has quickly become the most popular and successful programming language. Today, it is used not only for Web programming, but also for developing standalone applications. Many companies that once considered Java to be more hype than substance are now using it to create distributed applications accessed by customers and partners across the Internet. For every new project being developed today, companies are asking how they can use Java to make their work easier.

Java's Design and Advantages

Java is an object-oriented programming language. Object-oriented programming is a favored programming approach that has replaced traditional procedure-based programming techniques. An object-oriented language uses abstraction, encapsulation, inheritance, and polymorphism to provide great flexibility, modularity, and reusability for developing software.

Java is platform-independent. Its programs can run on any platform with a Java Virtual Machine, a software component that interprets Java instructions and carries out associated actions.

Java is distributed. Networking is inherently built-in. Simultaneous processing can occur on multiple computers on the Internet. Writing network programs is treated as simple data input and output.

Java is multithreaded. Multithreading is the capability of a program to perform several tasks simultaneously, such as downloading a video file while playing the video at the same time. Multithreading is particularly useful in graphical user interfaces (GUI) and network programming. Multithread programming is smoothly integrated in Java. In other languages, you can only enable multithreading by calling procedures that are specific to the operating system.

Java is secure. Computers become vulnerable when they are connected with other computers. Viruses and malicious programs can damage your computer. Java is designed with multiple layers of security that ensure proper access to private data and restrict access to disk files.

Java's Versatility

Stimulated by the promise of writing programs once and running them anywhere, Java has become the most important programming language. IBM, Sun, and Apple, and many other vendors are working to integrate the Java Virtual Machine with their operating systems so that Java programs can run directly and efficiently on the native machine. Java programs run on full-featured computers, and also on consumer electronics and appliances.

Because of its great potential to unite existing legacy applications written on different platforms so that they can run together, Java has been perceived as a universal front end for the enterprise database. The leading database companies, IBM, Oracle, Sybase, and Informix, have extended their commitment to Java by integrating it into their products. Oracle, for example, enables Java applications to run on its server, and to deliver a complete set of Java-based development tools supporting the integration of current applications with the Web.

Learning Java

To the first time programmers, learning Java is like learning any high-level programming languages. The foundation of learning programming is to develop critical skills of formulating programmatic solutions for the programs and to translate the solutions into programs using the selection statements, loops, and methods.

Applying the concept of abstraction in the design and implementation of software projects is the key to developing software. The overriding objective of this book, therefore, is to teach students to use many levels of abstraction in solving problems and to see problems in small and in large.

Students with no programming experience should take a slow-pace approach in Part I of the book. I recommend you to complete all the exercises in Chapter 3 and 4 before moving to Chapter 5. Students new to object-oriented programming may need some time to become familiar with the concept of objects and classes. Once the principles are mastered, programming in Java is easy and productive. Students who know object-oriented programming languages like C++ and Smalltalk will find it easier to learn Java. In fact, you will find that Java is simpler than C++ and Smalltalk in many aspects.

Organization of the Book

This book is divided into four parts that, taken together, form a comprehensive introductory course on Java programming. Because knowledge is cumulative, the early chapters provide the conceptual basis for understanding Java and guide students through simple examples and exercises; subsequent chapters progressively present Java programming in detail, culminating with the development of comprehensive Java applications. The appendixes contain a mixed bag of topics, including an HTML tutorial.

Part I: Fundamentals of Programming

The first part of the book is a stepping stone that will prepare you to embark on the journey of learning Java. You will begin to know Java, and will learn how to write simple Java programs with primitive data types, control statements, and methods.

Chapter 1, "Introduction to Java," gives an overview of the major features of Java: object-oriented programming, platform-independence, Java bytecode, security, performance, multithreading, and networking. The chapter also introduces how to create, compile, and run Java applications and applets. Simple examples of writing applications and applets are provided, along with a brief anatomy of programming structures.

Chapter 2, "Primitive Data Types and Operations," introduces primitive data types, operators, and expressions. Important topics include identifiers, variables, constants, assignment statements, primitive data types, operators, and shortcut operators. Java programming style and documentation are also addressed.

Chapter 3, "Control Statements," introduces decision and repetition statements. Java decision statements include various forms of `if` statements, and the `switch` statement. Java repetition statements include the `while` loop, the `do` loop, and the `for` loop. The keywords `break` and `continue` are discussed.

Chapter 4, "Methods," introduces method creation, calling methods, passing parameters, returning values, method overloading, and recursion. Applying the concept of abstraction is the key to developing software. The chapter also introduces the use of method abstraction in problem-solving. The `Math` class for performing basic math operations is introduced.

Part II: Object-Oriented Programming

In the book's second part, object-oriented programming is introduced. Java is a class-centric, object-oriented programming language that uses abstraction, encapsulation, inheritance, and polymorphism to provide great flexibility, modularity, and reusability in developing software. You will learn programming with objects and classes, arrays and strings, and class inheritance.

Chapter 5, "Programming with Objects and Classes," begins with objects and classes. The important topics include defining classes, creating objects, using constructors, passing objects to methods, instance and class variables, and instance and class methods, analyzing relationships among classes, and using the UML graphical notations to describe classes. Several examples are provided to demonstrate the power of the object-oriented programming approach. Students will learn the benefits (abstraction, encapsulation, and modularity) of object-oriented programming from these examples. There are more than 500 predefined Java classes grouped in several packages. Starting with this chapter, students will gradually learn how to use Java classes to develop their own programs. The classes `String`, `StringBuffer`, and `StringTokenizer` for storing and processing strings are introduced.

Chapter 6, "Class Inheritance," teaches how an existing class can be extended and modified as needed. Inheritance is an extremely powerful programming technique, further extending software reusability. Java programs are all built by extending predefined Java classes. The major topics include defining subclasses, using the keywords `super` and `this`, using the modifiers `protected`, `final` and `abstract`, polymorphism and dynamic binding, and casting objects. This chapter introduces the `Object` class, which is the root of all Java classes. You will learn to use abstract classes, and interfaces.

Chapter 7, "Arrays and Vectors," explores an important structure: arrays for processing data in lists and tables. You will learn how to declare, initialize, and copy arrays. You will also learn how to use wrapper classes to encapsulate primitive data type values in objects for use in generic programming. This chapter introduces the `Vector` class, which can be used to store an unspecified number of elements.

Part III: Graphics Programming

The third part of the book introduces Java graphics programming. Major topics include event-driven programming, creating graphical user interfaces, and writing applets. You will learn the architecture of Java graphics programming API and use the user interface components to develop graphics applications and applets.

Chapter 8, "Getting Started with Graphics Programming," introduces the concepts of Java graphics programming using Swing components. Topics include the Swing class hierarchy, event-driven programming, frames, panels, and simple layout managers (`FlowLayout`, `GridLayout`, and `BorderLayout`). The chapter also introduces drawing geometric figures in the graphics context.

Chapter 9, "Creating User Interfaces," introduces the user interface components: buttons, labels, text fields, text areas, combo boxes, lists, check boxes, radio buttons, menus, scrollbars, and scroll panes. Today's client/server and Web-based applications use a graphical user interface (GUI, pronounced "goo-ee"). Java has a rich set of classes to help you build GUIs.

Chapter 10, "Applets and Advanced Graphics," takes an in-depth look at applets, discussing applet behavior and the relationship between applets and other Swing classes. Applets are a special kind of Java class that can be executed from the Web browser. Students will learn how to convert applications to applets, and vice versa, and how to run programs both as applications and as applets. The chapter also introduces two advanced layout mangers (`CardLayout` and `GridBagLayout`) and the use of no layout. Advanced examples of handling mouse and keyboard events are provided. You will learn how to package and deploy Java applications and applets.

Part IV: Developing Comprehensive Projects

The book's final part is devoted to several advanced features of Java programming. You will learn how to use these features to develop comprehensive programs; for example, using exception handling to make your program robust, using multithreading to make your program more responsive and interactive, incorporating sound and images to make your program user-friendly, using input and output to manage and process a large quantity of data, and creating client/server applications with Java networking support.

Chapter 11, "Exception Handling," teaches students how to define exceptions, throw exceptions, and handle exceptions so that their programs can either continue to run or terminate gracefully in the event of runtime errors. The chapter discusses predefined exception classes, and gives examples of creating user-defined exception classes.

Chapter 12, "Internationalization," introduces the development of Java programs for international audiences. You will learn how to format dates, numbers, currencies, and percentages for different regions, countries, and languages. You will also learn how to use resource bundles to define which images and strings are used by a component depending on the user's locale and preferences.

Chapter 13, "Multithreading," introduces threads, which enable the running of multiple tasks simultaneously in one program. Students will learn how to use the `Thread` class and the `Runnable` interface to launch separate threads. The chapter also discusses thread states, thread priority, thread groups, and the synchronization of conflicting threads.

Chapter 14, "Multimedia," teaches how to incorporate sound and images to bring live animation to Java programs. Various techniques for smoothing animation are introduced.

Chapter 15, "Input and Output," introduces input and output streams. Students will learn the class structures of I/O streams, byte and character streams, file I/O streams, data I/O streams, print streams, delimited I/O, random file access, and interactive I/O.

Chapter 16, "Networking," introduces network programming. Students will learn the concept of network communication, stream sockets, client/server programming, and reading data files from the Web server.

Appendixes

This part of the book covers a mixed bag of topics. Appendix A lists Java keywords. Appendix B gives tables of ASCII characters and their associated codes in decimal and in hex. Appendix C shows the operator precedence. Appendix D summarizes Java modifiers and their usage. Appendix E introduces number systems and conversions among binary, decimal, and hex numbers. Appendix F introduces HTML basics. Appendix G lists UML Graphical Notations for describing classes and their relationships. Appendix H introduces packages for grouping classes. Appendix I gives a JBuilder 3.5 tutorial. Finally, Appendix J provides a glossary of key terms used in the text.

Companion Web Site for the Book

The companion Web site for the book can be accessed from **www.cs.armstrong.edu/liang/intro3e.html** or **www.prenhall.com/liang**. The Web site contains the following resources:

- Microsoft PowerPoint slides for lectures
- Answers to review questions
- Solutions to even-numbered programming exercises
- Source code for the examples in the book
- Interactive on-line self test
- How to obtain and install Java 2 SDK v1.3
- A JBuilder 4 Tutorial
- Java Data Structures
- Errata
- FAQs

CONTENTS AT A GLANCE

TABLE OF CONTENTS

APPENDIXES

PART I

Fundamentals of Programming

By now you have heard a lot about Java and are anxious to start writing Java programs. The first part of the book is a stepping stone that will prepare you to embark on the journey of learning Java. You will begin to know Java and will develop fundamental programming skills. Specifically, you will learn how to write simple Java programs with primitive data types, control statements, and methods.

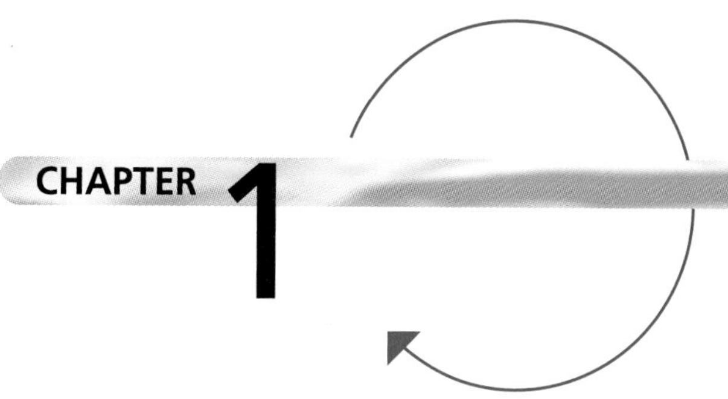

Introduction to Java

Objectives

- Learn about Java and its history.
- Become familiar with the Java development and runtime environment.
- Create Java programs; compile and run Java programs.
- Write a simple Java application.
- Write a simple Java applet. (Optional)
- Understand the relationship between Java and the World Wide Web.

Introduction

By now you have heard quite a lot about the exciting Java programming language. It must seem as if Java is everywhere! Your local bookstores are filled with Java books. There are articles about Java in every major newspaper and magazine. It is impossible to read a computer magazine without coming across the magic word *Java*. You must be wondering why Java is so hot. The answer is that it enables users to deploy applications on the Internet. In fact, this is its main distinguishing characteristic. The future of computing will be profoundly influenced by the Internet, and Java promises to remain a big part of that future. Java is *the* Internet programming language.

You are about to begin an exciting journey, learning a powerful programming language. Java is cross-platform, object-oriented, network-based, and multimedia-ready. After its inception in May 1995, Java quickly became an attractive language for developing Internet applications. This chapter introduces Java and its programming features, followed by simple examples of Java applications and applets.

The History of Java

Java was developed by a team led by James Gosling at Sun Microsystems, a company best known for its Sun workstations. Originally called *Oak*, it was designed in 1991 for use in embedded consumer electronic applications. In 1995, renamed *Java*, it was redesigned for developing Internet applications. Java programs can be embedded in HTML pages and downloaded by Web browsers to bring live animation and interaction to Web clients.

The power of Java is not limited to Web applications, for it is a general-purpose programming language. It has full programming features and can be used to develop standalone applications. Java is inherently object-oriented. Although many object-oriented languages began strictly as procedural languages, Java was designed from the start to be object-oriented. Object-oriented programming (OOP) is a popular programming approach that is replacing traditional procedural programming techniques.

NOTE

One of the central issues in software development is how to reuse code. Object-oriented programming provides great flexibility, modularity, clarity, and reusability through method abstraction, class abstraction, and class inheritance—all of which you'll learn about in this book.

Characteristics of Java

Java has gained enormous popularity. Java's rapid rise and wide acceptance can be traced to its design and programming features, particularly its promise that you can write a program once and run the program anywhere. As stated in the Java-language white paper by Sun, Java is *simple*, *object-oriented*, *distributed*, *interpreted*, *robust, secure, architecture-neutral, portable, high-performance, multithreaded,* and *dynamic.* Let's analyze these often-used buzzwords.

Java Is Simple

No language is simple, but Java is a bit easier than the popular object-oriented programming language C++, which was the dominant software-development language before Java. Java is partially modeled on C++, but greatly simplified and improved. For instance, pointers and multiple inheritance often make programming complicated. Java replaces the multiple inheritance in C++ with a simple language construct called an *interface,* and eliminates pointers.

Java uses automatic memory allocation and garbage collection, whereas C++ requires the programmer to allocate memory and collect garbage. Also, the number of language constructs is small for such a powerful language. The clean syntax makes Java programs easy to write and read. Some people refer to Java as "C++––" because it is like C++, but with more functionality and fewer negative aspects.

Java Is Object-Oriented

Computer programs are instructions to the computers. You tell a computer what to do through programs. Without programs, a computer is an empty machine. Computers do not understand human languages. So you need to use computer languages to communicate with computers. There are over one hundred programming languages. The most popular languages are:

COBOL (COmmon Business Oriented Language)
FORTRAN (FORmula TRANslation)
BASIC (Beginner All-purpose Symbolic Instructional Code)
Pascal (Named for Blaise Pascal)
Ada (Named for Ada Lovelace)
C (Whose developer designed B first)
Visual Basic (Basic-like visual language developed by Microsoft)
Delphi (Pascal-like visual language developed by Borland)
C++ (an object-oriented language, based on C)

Each language was designed with a specific purpose. COBOL was designed for business applications and now is used primarily for business data processing. FORTRAN was designed for mathematical computations and is used mainly for numeric computations. BASIC, as its name suggests, was designed to be learned and used easily. Ada was developed at the direction of the Department of Defense, and is mainly used in defense projects. C is popular among system software projects like writing compilers and operating systems. Visual Basic and Delphi are for rapid application development. C++ is the C language with object-oriented features.

All of these languages except C++ are known as *procedural programming language.* Software systems developed using procedural programming language are based on the paradigm of procedures. Object-oriented programming models the real world in terms of objects. Everything in the world can be modeled as an object. A circle is an object, a person is an object, and a window's icon is an object. Even a mortgage can be perceived as an object. A Java program is object-oriented because programming in Java is centered on creating objects, manipulating objects, and making objects work together.

Part I, "Fundamentals of Programming," introduces primitive data types and operations, control statements, and methods. These are the fundamentals for all programming languages. You will learn object-oriented programming in Part II, "Object-Oriented Programming." Object-oriented programming provides great flexibility, modularity, and reusability. For years, object-oriented technology was perceived as elitist, requiring a substantial investment in training and infrastructure. Java has helped object-oriented technology enter the mainstream of computing. Its simple, clean syntax makes programs easy to write and read. Java programs are quite *expressive* in terms of designing and developing applications.

Java Is Distributed

Distributed computing involves several computers working together on a network. Java is designed to make distributed computing easy. Since networking capability is inherently integrated into Java, writing network programs is like sending and receiving data to and from a file. For example, Figure 1.1 shows three programs running on three different systems; the three programs communicate with each other to perform a joint task.

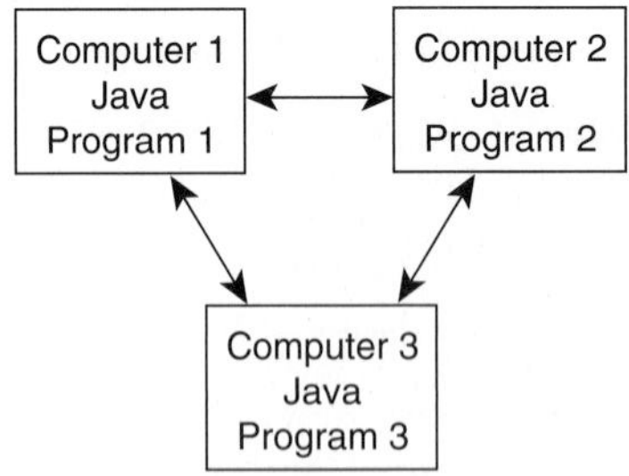

Figure 1.1 *Java programs can run on different systems that work together.*

Java Is Interpreted

You need an interpreter to run Java programs. The programs are compiled into Java Virtual Machine code called *bytecode*. The bytecode is machine-independent and can run on any machine that has a Java interpreter, as shown in Figure 1.2.

Usually, a compiler, such as C++ compiler, translates a program in a high-level language to machine code. The code can only run on the native machine. If you run the program on other machines, it has to be recompiled on the native machine. For instance, if you compile a C++ program in Windows, the executable code generated by the compiler can only run on the Windows platform. With Java, you compile the source code once, and the bytecode generated by a Java compiler can run

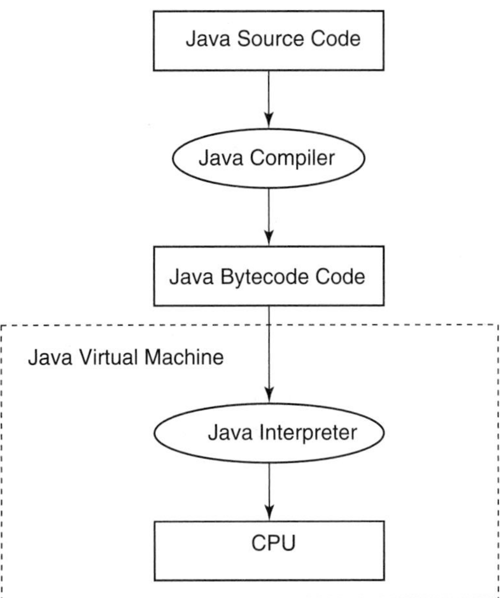

Figure 1.2 *The Java interpreter executes Java bytecode.*

on any platform with a Java interpreter. The Java interpreter translates the bytecode into the machine language of the target machine.

Java Is Robust

Robust means *reliable*. No programming language can ensure complete reliability. Java puts a lot of emphasis on early checking for possible errors, because Java compilers can detect many problems that would first show up at execution time in other languages. Java has eliminated certain types of error-prone programming constructs found in other languages. It does not support pointers, for example, thereby eliminating the possibility of overwriting memory and corrupting data.

Java has a runtime exception-handling feature to provide programming support for robustness. Java forces the programmer to write the code to deal with exceptions. Java can catch and respond to an exceptional situation so that the program can continue its normal execution and terminate gracefully when a runtime error occurs.

Java Is Secure

As an Internet programming language, Java is used in a networked and distributed environment. If you download a Java applet (a special kind of program) and run it on your computer, it will not damage your system because Java implements several security mechanisms to protect your system against harm caused by stray programs. The security is based on the premise that *nothing should be trusted*.

Java Is Architecture-Neutral

The most remarkable feature of Java is that it is *architecture-neutral*, also known as platform-independent. With a Java Virtual Machine (JVM), you can write one program that will run on any platform, as shown in Figure 1.3.

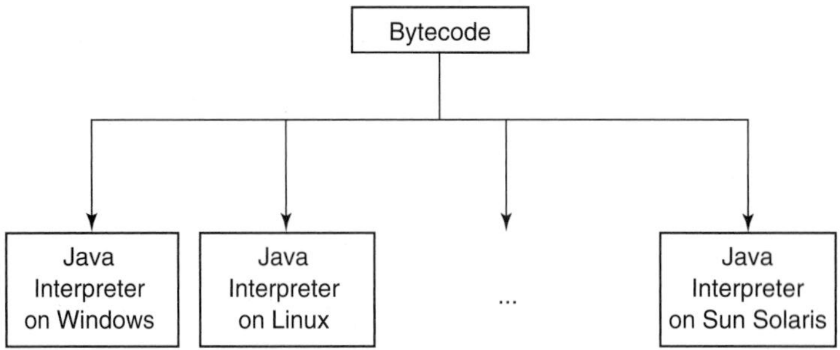

Figure 1.3 *Java bytecode can be executed on a platform that has a JVM.*

Java's initial success derived from its Web programming capability. You can run Java applets from a Web browser, but Java is for more than just writing Web applets. You can also run standalone Java applications directly from operating systems, using a Java interpreter. Today, software vendors usually develop multiple versions of the same product to run on different platforms (Windows, OS/2, Macintosh, and various UNIX, IBM AS/400, and IBM mainframes). Using Java, developers need to write only one version to run on all platforms.

Java Is Portable

Java programs can be run on any platform without being recompiled, making them very portable. Moreover, there are no platform-specific features in the Java language. In some languages, such as Ada, the largest integer varies on different platforms. But in Java, the size of the integer is the same on every platform, as is the behavior of arithmetic. The fixed size of numbers makes the program portable.

The Java environment is portable to new hardware and operating systems. In fact, the Java compiler itself is written in Java.

Java's Performance

Java's performance is sometimes criticized. The execution of the bytecode is never as fast as it would be with a compiled language, such as C++. Because Java is interpreted, the bytecode is not directly executed by the system, but is run through the interpreter. However, the speed is more than adequate for most interactive applications, where the CPU is often idle, waiting for input or for data from other sources.

CPU speed has increased dramatically in the past few years, and this trend will continue. There are many ways to improve performance. Users of the earlier Sun

Java Virtual Machine (JVM) have certainly noticed that Java is slow. However, the new JVM is significantly faster. The new JDK uses the technology known as just-in-time compilation, as shown in Figure 1.4. It compiles bytecode into native machine code, stores the native code, and reinvokes the native code when its bytecode is executed. Sun recently developed the Java HotSpot Performance Engine, which includes a compiler for optimizing the frequently used code. The HotSpot Performance Engine can be plugged into a JVM to dramatically boost its performance.

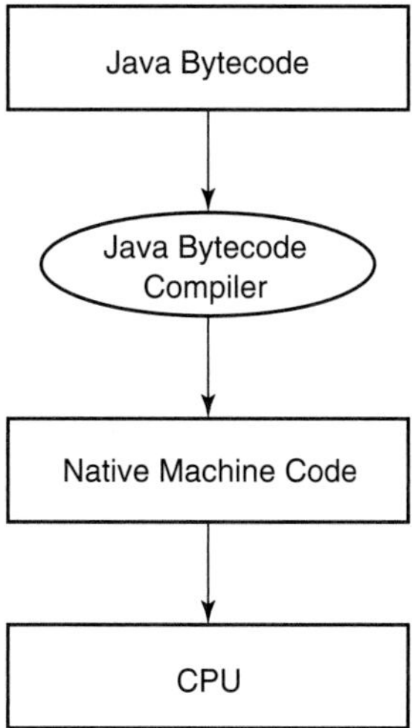

Figure 1.4 *Just-in-time compiler compiles bytecode to the native machine code.*

Java Is Multithreaded

Multithreading is a program's capability to perform several tasks simultaneously. For example, downloading a video file while playing the video would be considered multithreading. Multithread programming is smoothly integrated in Java, whereas in other languages, you have to call operating system-specific procedures to enable multithreading.

Multithreading is particularly useful in graphical user interface (GUI) and network programming. In GUI programming, there are many things going on at the same time. A user can listen to an audio recording while surfing a Web page. In network programming, a server can serve multiple clients at the same time. Multithreading is a necessity in visual and network programming.

Java Is Dynamic

Java was designed to adapt to an evolving environment. You can freely add new methods and properties to a class without affecting its clients. For example, in the `Circle` class, you can add a new data property to indicate the color of the circle, and a new method to obtain the circumference of the circle. The original client program that uses the `Circle` class remains the same. Also, at runtime Java loads classes as they are needed.

Java and the World Wide Web

The World Wide Web is an electronic information repository that can be accessed on the Internet from anywhere in the world. You can use the Web to book a hotel room, buy an airline ticket, register for a college course, download the *New York Times*, chat with friends, and listen to live radio. There are countless activities you can do on the Internet. Today, many people spend a good part of their computer time surfing the Web for fun and profit.

The Internet is the infrastructure of the Web. The Internet has been around for more than thirty years, but has only recently become popular. The colorful World Wide Web is the major reason for its popularity.

The primary authoring language for the Web is Hypertext Markup Language (HTML). HTML is a markup language: a simple language for laying out documents, linking documents on the Internet, and bringing images, sound, and video alive on the Web. However, it cannot interact with the user except through simple forms. Web pages in HTML essentially are static and flat.

Java programs can run from a Web browser. Because Java is a full-blown programming language, you can make programs responsive and interactive with users. Java programs that run from a Web page are called *applets*. Applets use a modern graphical user interface, including buttons, text fields, text areas, option buttons, and so on. Applets can respond to user events, such as mouse movements and keystrokes.

Figure 1.5 shows an applet in an HTML page, and Figure 1.6 shows the HTML source. The source contains an applet tag, and the applet tag specifies the Java applet. The HTML source can be seen by choosing View, Page Source from the Netscape 6 Web Browser.

NOTE

For a demonstration of Java applets, visit **www.javasoft.com/applets/**. This site contains a rich Java resource as well as links to other cool applet demo sites.

The Java Language Specification

Computer languages have strict rules of usage. You must follow the rules when writing programs or else the computer will be unable to understand them. Sun Microsystems, the originator of Java, intends to retain control of this important new computer language—and for a very good reason: to prevent it from losing its unified standards. The complete reference of Java standards can be found in *Java Language Specification, Second Edition,* by James Gosling, Bill Joy, and Guy Steele (Addison-Wesley, 2000).

The Java language specification is a technical definition of the language that includes syntax, constructs, and the *application programmer interface* (API), which contains predefined classes. The Java language syntax and constructs are stable, but

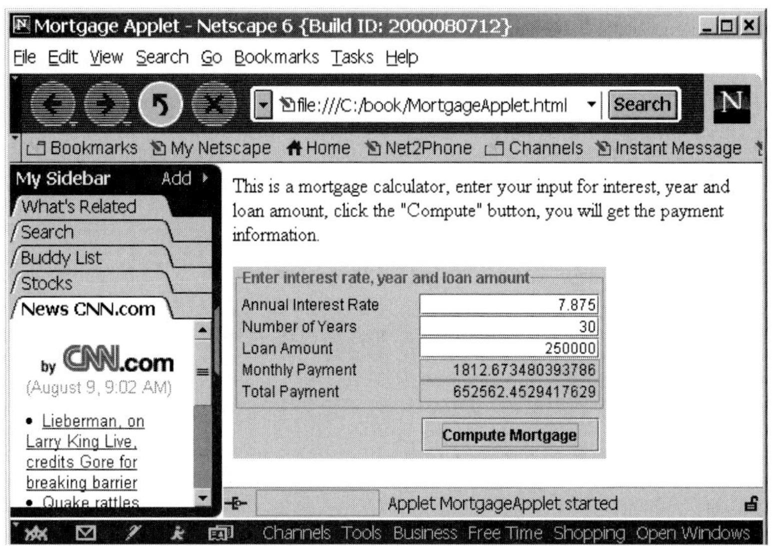

Figure 1.5 *A Java applet for computing a mortgage is embedded in an HTML page. The user can find the mortgage payment by using this applet.*

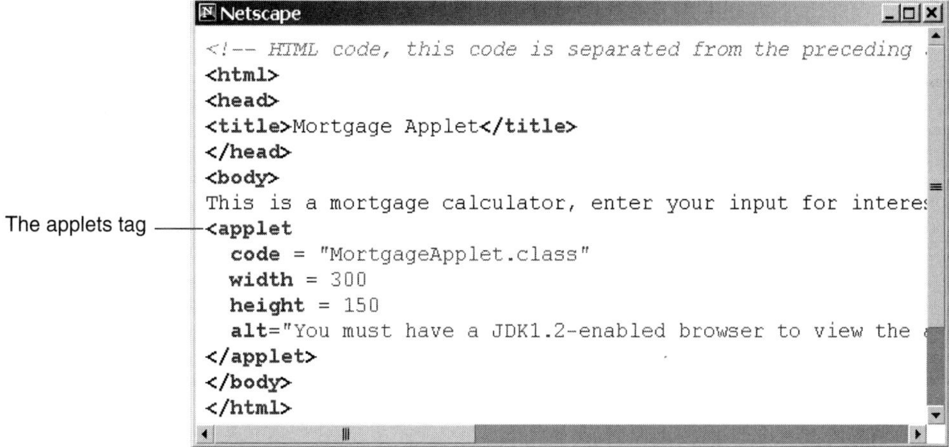

Figure 1.6 *The HTML source that contains the applet shows the tag specifying the Java applet.*

the API is still expanding. At the JavaSoft Web site (**www.javasoft.com**), you can view the language specification and the latest version and updates to the Java API.

Sun releases each version of Java with a Java Development Toolkit, known as JDK. This is a primitive command-line tool set that includes software libraries, a compiler for compiling Java source code, an interpreter for running Java bytecode, and an applet viewer for testing Java applets, as well as other useful utilities.

NOTE

Sun announced the Java 2 name in December 1998, just as it released JDK 1.2. Java 2 is the overarching brand that applies to the latest Java technology. JDK 1.2 was the first version of the Java Development Toolkit that supported the Java 2 technology. This book is based on the latest version, JDK 1.3. The official name for JDK 1.3 is Java 2 SDK v 1.3. SDK stands for Software Development Toolkit. Since most Java programmers are familiar with the name JDK, this book uses the names Java SDK and JDK interchangeably.

Java Development Tools

JDK consists of a set of separate programs for developing and testing Java programs, each of which is invoked from a command line. Besides JDK, there are more than a dozen Java development packages on the market today. The major development tools are

JBuilder by Inprise/Borland (**www.inprise.com**)
Visual J++ by Microsoft (**www.microsoft.com**)
Visual Café by WebGain (**www.webgain.com**)
Forte by Sun (**www.javasoft.com**)
Visual Age for Java by IBM (**www.ibm.com**)

These tools provide an *integrated development environment* (IDE) for rapidly developing Java programs. Editing, compiling, building, debugging, and online help are integrated in one graphical user interface. Just enter source code in one window or open an existing file in a window, then click a button, menu item, or function key to compile the source code.

The use of development tools makes it easy and productive to develop Java programs. However, you have to devote considerable time to learn how to use a development tool. The advantage of learning Java with JDK command-line tools is that you can completely concentrate on the Java language, and not be intimidated by the sophisticated tools.

Java Applications

Java programs can be of two types: *applications* or *applets*. Applications are standalone programs. This includes any program written with a high-level language. Applications can be executed from any computer with a Java interpreter. Applets are special kinds of Java programs that can run directly from a Java-compatible Web browser. Applets are suitable for deploying Web projects.

Let's begin with a simple Java application program that displays the message "Welcome to Java!" on the console.

Example 1.1 A Simple Application

This program shows how to write a simple Java application and demonstrates the compilation and execution of an application.

```
Comments →  // Welcome.java: This application program prints Welcome to Java!
            public class Welcome  ← Class Name
            {
Main Method→  public static void main(String[] args)
signature     {
                System.out.println("Welcome to Java!"); ← String
              }
            }
```

Example Review

In this program, `println("Welcome to Java!")` is actually the statement that prints the message. So why use the other statements in the program? Because computer languages have rigid styles and strict syntax, and you need to write code that the Java compiler understands.

Every Java program must have at least one class. Each class begins with a class declaration that defines data and methods for the class. In this example, the class name is `Welcome`.

The class contains a method named `main`. The `main` method in this program contains the `println` statement. The `main` method is invoked by the interpreter.

Creating, Compiling, and Executing a Java Program

Before your program can be executed, you have to first create the program and then compile it. This process is repetitive, as shown in Figure 1.7. If your program has compilation errors, you have to fix them by modifying the program, then recompile it. If your program has runtime errors or does not produce the correct result, you have to modify the program, recompile it, and execute it again.

You can use a text editor to create a file to store Java source code. This file must end with the extension .java and should have the exact same name as the public class name. For example, the file for the source code in Example 1.1 should be named **Welcome.java**, since the public class name is `Welcome`.

To compile the program is to translate the Java source code into Java bytecode using a program called the *compiler*. The Java compiler is bundled in JDK 1.3. To install JDK 1.3 on your system, please refer to the companion Web site at **www.cs.armstrong.edu/liang/intro3e.html** or **www.prenhall.com/liang**.

The following command compiles **Welcome.java**.

```
javac Welcome.java
```

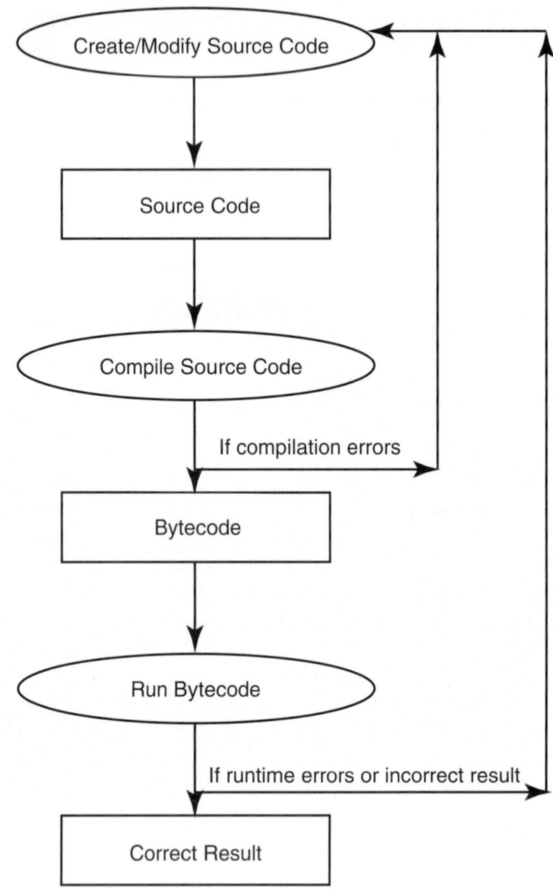

Figure 1.7 *The Java programming development process consists of creating/modifying source code, compiling, and executing programs.*

NOTE

Java source programs are case-sensitive. It would be wrong, for example, to replace `main` in the program with `Main`. Program filenames are case-sensitive on UNIX and generally not case-sensitive on PCs, but JDK treats filenames as case-sensitive on any platform. If you try to compile the program using `javac welcome.java`, you will get a file-not-found error.

If there are no syntax errors, the *compiler* generates a file named **Welcome.class**. This file is not an object file as generated by other high-level language compilers. This file is called the *bytecode*. The bytecode is similar to machine instructions, but is architecture-neutral and can run on any platform that has the Java interpreter and runtime environment. This is one of Java's primary advantages: Java bytecode can run on a variety of hardware platforms and operating systems.

To execute a Java program is to run the program's bytecode. You can execute the bytecode on any platform with a Java interpreter.

The following command runs the bytecode:

```
java Welcome
```

Figure 1.8 shows the **javac** command for compiling Welcome.java. The compiler generated the Welcome.class file. This file is executed using the **java** command.

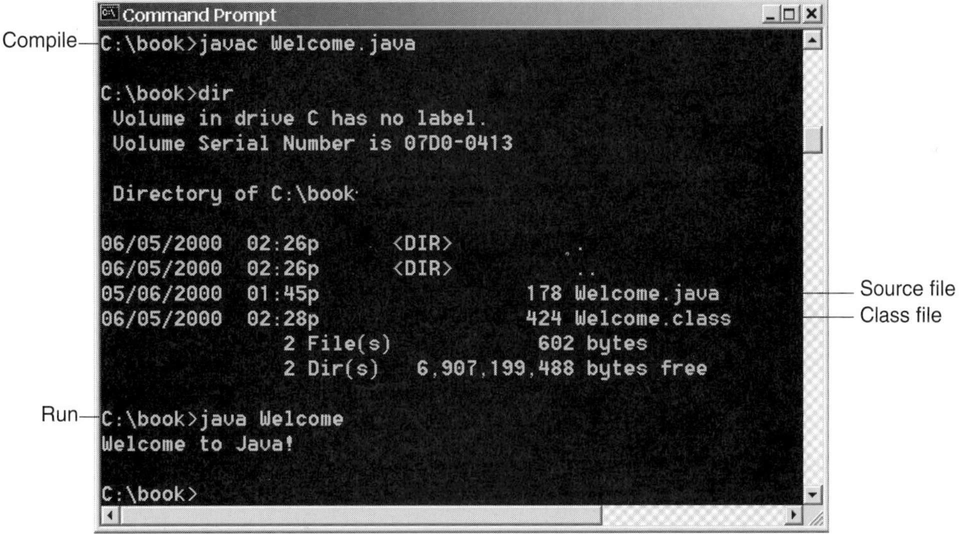

Figure 1.8 *The output of Example 1.1 displays a message: Welcome to Java!*

NOTE

Do not use the extension .class in the command line when executing the program. The Java interpreter assumes that the first argument in the command is the filename and then fetches **filename.class** to execute. It would fetch **filename.class.class** if you used Java **filename.class** in the command line.

Anatomy of the Application Program

The application program in Example 1.1 has the following components:

- Comments
- Reserved words
- Modifiers
- Statements
- Blocks
- Classes
- Methods
- The `main` method

To build a program, you need to understand these basic elements. The following sections explain each of them.

Comments

The first line in the program is a *comment*, which documents what the program is and how the program is constructed. Comments help programmers and users to communicate and understand the program. Comments are not programming statements and are ignored by the compiler. In Java, comments are preceded by two slashes (`//`) in a line, or enclosed between `/*` and `*/` in multiple lines. When the compiler sees `//`, it ignores all text after `//` in the same line. When it sees `/*`, it scans for the next `*/` and ignores any text between `/*` and `*/`.

Here are examples of the two types of comments:

```
// This application program prints Welcome to Java!
/* This application program prints Welcome to Java! */
```

NOTE

In addition to the two comment styles, // and /*, Java supports comments of a special type, referred to as *javadoc comments.* javadoc comments begin with /** and end with */. They are used for documenting classes and data and methods. They can be extracted into an HTML file using JDK's `javadoc` command. For more information, visit

java.sun.com/products/jdk/javadoc/index.html

Reserved Words

Reserved words or *keywords* are words that have a specific meaning to the compiler and cannot be used for other purposes in the program. For example, when the compiler sees the word `class`, it understands that the word after `class` is the name for the class. Other reserved words in Example 1.1 are `public`, `static`, and `void`. Their use will be introduced later in the book.

TIP

Because Java is case-sensitive, `public` is a reserved word, but `Public` is not. Nonetheless, for clarity and readability, it would be best to avoid using reserved words in other forms. (See Appendix A, "Java Keywords.")

Modifiers

Java uses certain reserved words called *modifiers* that specify the properties of the data, methods, and classes and how they can be used. Examples of modifiers are `public` and `static`. Other modifiers are `private`, `final`, `abstract`, and `protected`. A `public` datum, method, or class can be accessed by other programs. A `private` datum or method cannot be accessed by other programs. Modifiers are discussed in Chapter 5, "Programming with Objects and Classes."

Statements

A *statement* represents an action or a sequence of actions. The statement `println("Welcome to Java!")` in the program in Example 1.1 is a statement to display the greeting "Welcome to Java!" Every statement in Java ends with a semicolon (;).

The following lines of code are statements:

```
x = 5;
x = x + 5;
```

The first statement assigns `5` to the variable `x`, and the second adds `5` to the variable `x`.

Blocks

Braces in a program form a *block* that groups components of a program. In Java, each block begins with an open brace ({) and ends with a closing brace (}). Each class has a *class block* that groups the data and methods of the class. Each method has a *method block* that groups the statements in the method. Blocks can be *nested*, meaning that one block can be placed within another, as shown in the following code.

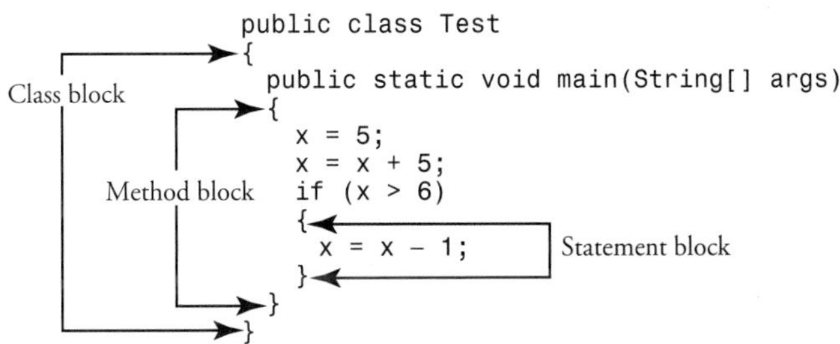

Classes

The *class* is the essential Java construct. A class is a template or blueprint for objects. To program in Java, you must understand classes and be able to write and use them. The mystery of the class will continue to be unveiled throughout this book. For now, though, understand that a program is defined by using one or more classes. Every Java program has at least one class, and programs are contained inside a class definition enclosed in blocks. The class can contain data declarations and method declarations.

Methods

What is `System.out.println`? It is a *method*: a collection of statements that performs a sequence of operations to display a message on the console. `println` is predefined as part of the standard Java language. It can be used even without fully understanding the details of how it works. It is used by invoking a calling statement with string arguments. The string arguments are enclosed within parentheses.

In this case, the argument is `"Welcome to Java!"`. You can call the same `println` method with a different argument to print a different message.

The *main* Method

You can create your own method. Every Java application must have a user-declared `main` method that defines where the program begins. The `main` method provides the control of program flow. The Java interpreter executes the application by invoking the `main` method.

The `main` method looks like this:

```
public static void main(String[] args)
{
  // Statements;
}
```

NOTE

You are probably wondering about such points as why the `main` method is declared this way. Your questions cannot be fully answered yet. For the time being, you will just have to accept that this is how things are done. You will find the answers in the coming chapters.

Java Applets (Optional)

Applications and applets share many common programming features, although they differ slightly in some aspects. For example, every application must have a `main` method, which is invoked by the Java interpreter. Java applets, on the other hand, do not need a `main` method. They run within the Web browser environment. Example 1.2 demonstrates the applet that displays the same message, "Welcome to Java!"

Example 1.2 A Simple Applet

This program shows how to write a simple Java applet and demonstrates the compilation and execution of an applet.

```
/* WelcomeApplet.java: This is an example of Java applets */
import java.awt.Graphics;

public class WelcomeApplet extends java.applet.Applet
{
  public void paint(Graphics g)
  {
    g.drawString("Welcome to Java!",10,10);
  }
}
```

Example Review

Applets run in a graphical environment. You need to display everything, including text, in graphical mode, and Java provides the `drawString` method to display text in a graphics context in an applet.

The `drawString("Welcome to Java!", 10, 10)` method draws the string `"Welcome to Java!"` on a line. The baseline of the first character, *W*, in the string is displayed at the location `(10, 10)`. The drawing area of the applet is measured in pixels, with `(0,0)` at the upper-left corner, as shown in Figure 1.9.

Figure 1.9 *The message string "Welcome to Java!" is drawn at (10, 10).*

Compiling an Applet

You use the **javac** command to compile all Java programs, whether they are applications or applets, and the Java interpreter to run applications. However, applets are executed by a Web browser from an HTML file. You need to create an HTML file to tell the browser where to get the Java applet and how to run it.

Creating an HTML File

To run an applet, embed HTML tags that refer to the applet within a Web page. HTML is a script language that presents static documents on the Web. HTML uses tags to instruct the Web browser how to render a Web page. HTML contains a tag called `<applet>` that incorporates applets into a Web page.

The following HTML file contains a tag to invoke **WelcomeApplet.class**:

```
<html>
<head>
<title>Welcome Java Applet</title>
</head>
<body>
<applet
  code = "WelcomeApplet.class"
  width = 200
  height = 50>
</applet>
</body>
</html>
```

A tag is an instruction to the Web browser. The browser interprets the tags and decides how to display or otherwise treat the subsequent contents of the HTML document. Tags are enclosed inside brackets; the first word in a tag is called the *tag name*, which describes tag functions. Tags can have additional attributes, sometimes with values after an equals sign, which further define the tag's action. For example, in the following tag, `<applet>` is the tag name and `code`, `width`, and `height` are the attributes:

```
<applet
  code="WelcomeApplet.class"
  width = 100
  height = 40>
</applet>
```

The `width` and `height` attributes specify the rectangular viewing area of the applet.

Most tags have a *start tag* and a corresponding *end tag*. The tag has a specific effect on the region between the start tag and the end tag. For example, `<applet...>...</applet>` tells the browser to display an applet. An end tag is always the start tag's name preceded by a slash.

An HTML document begins with the `<html>` tag, which declares that the document is written in HTML. Each document has two parts, a *head* and a *body*, defined by `<head>` and `<body>` tags, respectively. The head part contains the document title using the `<title>` tag and other parameters the browser can use when rendering the document, and the body part contains the actual contents of the document. The header is optional.

HTML files can be created and saved as text files by using a text editor. For more information, refer to Appendix F, "An HTML Tutorial."

Viewing Applets

Assume that the HTML file in Example 1.2 is named `WelcomeApplet.html`. You now can use a Web browser to view it. The result is displayed in Figure 1.10.

Applets can run from a Web browser on any platform. For example, the same applet can run on a Windows-based PC or on a UNIX workstation.

Applet Viewer Utility

You can also view a Java applet using Java's Applet Viewer. Using this utility, you do not need to start a Web browser. Applet Viewer functions as a browser. It is a valuable utility to test an applet before deploying it on a Web site. The following command invokes **WelcomeApplet.html** (see Figure 1.11). Its output is shown in Figure 1.12.

```
appletviewer WelcomeApplet.html
```

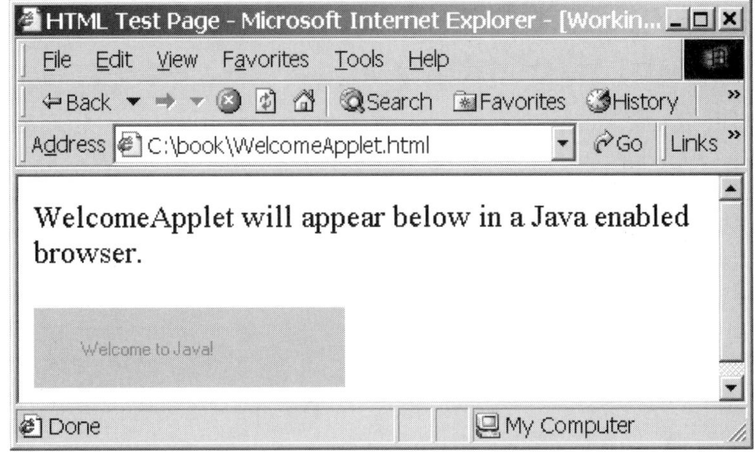

Figure 1.10 *The message "Welcome to Java!" is drawn on the browser.*

Figure 1.11 *The appletviewer command runs a Java applet in the Applet Viewer utility.*

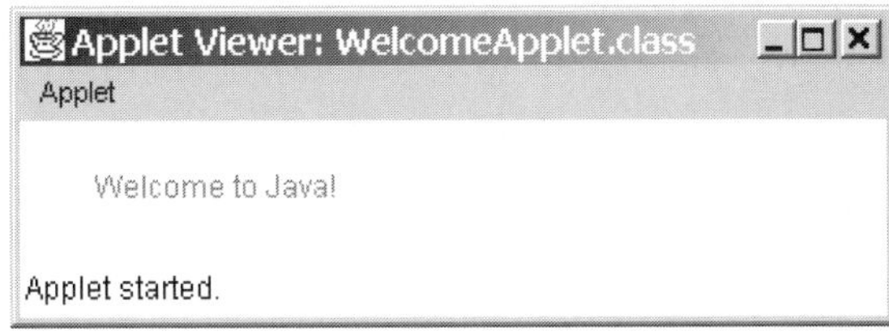

Figure 1.12 *The WelcomeApplet program is running from the Applet Viewer as if it were running in a Web browser.*

Anatomy of the Applet Program (Optional)

Let's take a closer look at the program in Example 1.2 and examine its components: the `import` statement, the `Graphics` class, the `extends` keyword, the `paint` method, the `drawString` method, and the class instance. As you have seen, applications and applets have much in common. Indeed, an applet is merely a special kind of Java program with certain characteristics that make it run from a Web browser. The components mentioned here are also used in other Java programs.

The *import* Statement

The first line after the comment in Example 1.2 is an `import` statement. The `import` statement tells the compiler to include existing Java programs in the current program. In this case, the existing program is `java.awt.Graphics`. You can use the operations in `java.awt.Graphics` in your program rather than rewriting the code. This is an example of software *reusability*; that is, the same program is written once and used by many other people without rewriting it.

Java code is organized into packages and classes. Classes are inside packages, and packages are libraries of Java code that contain all kinds of operations ready for you to import and use. Java provides standard packages, such as `java.awt`, that come with the compiler. Users can create their own packages. `Graphics` is a class contained in the `java.awt` package. (See Chapter 8, "Getting Started with Graphics Programming," for more information.)

Class Instance

The `g` in the `paint(Graphics g)` method is called an *instance* for the class `Graphics`. An instance is a concrete object of the class. `g` can access the methods defined in `Graphics`. `drawString` is a method in `Graphics`, which now can be used in `g` by a call, such as `g.drawString("Welcome to Java!", 10, 10)`. This is exactly the way object-oriented programming works. You can create an instance from a class and invoke the methods in the instance without knowing how the methods are implemented.

The *paint* Method and the *Graphics* Class

An applet may use the `paint` method to display graphics like this:

```
public void paint(Graphics g)
{
  // TODO: What to paint...
}
```

You write statements in this method to tell the Web browser what should be displayed.

Because the Web is a graphical environment, everything, including text, needs to be displayed as a graphic. The Java `Graphics` class provides operations for drawing objects, such as text strings, lines, rectangles, ovals, arcs, and polygons. The drawing area is a rectangle measured in pixels with `(0, 0)` at its upper-left corner. The following is another example:

```
public void paint(Graphics g)
{
  g.drawLine(10, 10, 50, 30);
  g.drawRect(10, 20, 20, 30);
  g.drawString("Welcome to Java", 30, 10);
}
```

The `drawLine(10, 10, 50, 30)` method draws a line from `(10, 10)` to `(50, 30)`. The `drawRect(10, 20, 20, 30)` method draws a rectangle of width `20` and height `30`; the upper-left corner of the rectangle is at `(10, 20)`. The `drawString("Welcome to Java", 30, 10)` method draws the string `"Welcome to Java"` at `(30, 10)`. See Figure 1.13 for the drawings.

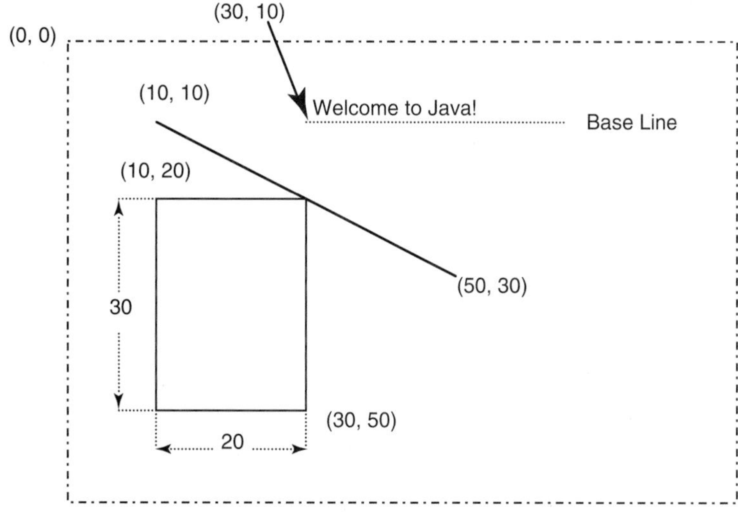

Figure 1.13 *The string* `Welcome to Java!` *is drawn at* `(30, 10)`*; a line is drawn from* `(10, 10)` *to* `(50, 30)`*; and a rectangle is drawn with its upper-left corner at* `(10, 20)` *with width of* `20` *and height of* `30`.

The *extends* Keyword and Class Inheritance

The class definition in Example 1.2 is different from the class definition in Example 1.1; Example 1.2 has an extra keyword, `extends`, which tells the compiler that the class to be defined is an extension of an existing class. In this case, the class

WelcomeApplet extends the existing class Applet. The extended class WelcomeApplet inherits all functionality and properties from class Applet. This is an example of *inheritance*, another software-engineering concept. Inheritance complements and extends software reusability, which will be introduced in Chapter 6, "Class Inheritance."

Applet is a class in the package java.applet. You could add the statement import java.applet.Applet at the beginning of the program and directly extend Applet, as follows:

```
import java.awt.Graphics;
import java.applet.Applet;

public class WelcomeApplet extends Applet
{
  public void paint(Graphics g)
  {
    g.drawString("Welcome to Java!",10,10);
  }
}
```

The import java.applet.Applet statement imports the Applet class so that you can use it in the program without explicitly referencing Applet as java.applet.Applet.

Applications Versus Applets (Optional)

You probably have many questions, such as whether it is necessary to write two programs—one for the application and one for the applet, and when to use applications and when to use applets. To answer these questions, it is important to understand the similarities and differences between applications and applets.

Much of the code for applications and applets is the same, but there are differences in the code dealing with their running environments. Applications run as standalone programs, as do programs written in any high-level language. Applets, however, must run from inside a Web browser. If your program is not required to run from a Web browser, choose applications. Developing Java applications is slightly quicker than developing applets because you do not need to create an HTML file and load it from a Web browser to view the results.

For security reasons, the following limitations are imposed on applets to prevent destructive programs from damaging the system on which the browser is running:

- Applets are not allowed to read from, or write to, the file system of the computer. Otherwise, they could damage the files and spread viruses.
- Applets are not allowed to run any programs on the browser's computer. Otherwise, they might call destructive local programs and damage the local system on the user's computer.
- Applets are not allowed to establish connections between the user's computer and any other computer, except for the server where the applets are stored.

This restriction prevents the applet from connecting the user's computer to another computer without the user's knowledge.

However, applications can directly interact with the computer on which they are running without these limitations. Applications can be used to develop fully functional software. In fact, applications can use the same graphical features used for applets, although applications would require slightly more effort in order to create the browser environment.

In general, you can convert a Java applet to run as an application without loss of functionality. However, an application cannot always be converted to run as an applet, due to the security limitations imposed on the applets. In Chapter 10, "Applets and Advanced Graphics," you will learn how to convert between applications and applets.

Chapter Summary

In this chapter, you learned about Java and the relationship between Java and the World Wide Web. Java is an Internet programming language, and since its inception in 1995, it has quickly become a premier language for building fully portable Java applications and applets.

Java is platform-independent, meaning that you can write a program once and run it anywhere. Java is a simple, object-oriented programming language with built-in graphics programming, input and output, exception handling, networking, and multithreading support.

Java source files end with the .java extension. Every class is compiled into a separate file called a bytecode that has the same name as the class and ends with the .class extension.

Every Java program is a class definition. The keyword `class` introduces a class definition. The contents of the class are included in a block. A block begins with an open brace (`{`) and ends with a closing brace (`}`). A class contains at least one method. A Java application must have a `main` method. The `main` method is the entry point where the application program starts when it is executed.

A Java applet always extends the `Applet` class. The keyword `extends` enables new classes to inherit from existing class definitions. The `import` statement loads classes required to compile a Java program.

Modifiers are the keywords that specify how classes and methods can be accessed. A Java applet must be a `public` class so that a Web browser can access it.

Web browsers control the execution of Java applets. You must create an HTML file with an `<applet>` tag to specify the bytecode file (with the extension .class) for the applet, and the width and height of the applet viewing area in pixels.

The JVM in the Web browser calls the `paint` method to display graphics in the applet's viewing area. The coordinates of the viewing area are measured in pixels with

`(0, 0)` at the upper-left corner. The `drawString` method draws a string at a specified location in the viewing area.

Review Questions

1.1 Briefly summarize the history of Java.

1.2 Java is object-oriented. What are the advantages of object-oriented programming?

1.3 Can Java run on any machine? What is needed to run Java on a computer?

1.4 What are the input and output of a Java compiler?

1.5 List some Java development tools. Are Visual J++ and JBuilder different languages from Java, or are they dialects or extensions of Java?

1.6 What is the relationship between Java and HTML?

1.7 Explain the concept of keywords. List some Java keywords you learned in this chapter.

1.8 Is Java case-sensitive? What is the case for Java keywords?

1.9 What is the Java source filename extension, and what is the Java bytecode filename extension?

1.10 What is the command to compile a Java program?

1.11 What is the command to run a Java application?

1.12 What is a comment? What is the syntax for a comment in Java? Is the comment ignored by the compiler?

1.13 What is the statement to display a string on the console?

1.14 What is the `import` statement for?

1.15 What is `Graphics`, and what is the `paint` method?

1.16 What are the differences between applications and applets? How do you run an application, and how do you run an applet? Is the compilation process different for applications and applets?

1.17 What is the applet viewer?

1.18 Is a lot of work needed to convert between applications and applets?

1.19 List some security restrictions on applets.

Programming Exercises

1.1 Create a source file containing a Java program. Perform the following steps to compile the program and run it (see "Compiling a Java Program" earlier in this chapter):

1. Create a file named **Welcome.java** for Example 1.1. You can use any editor that will save your file in text format.
2. Compile the source file.
3. Run the bytecode.
4. Replace "Welcome to Java" with "My first program" in the program; save, compile, and run the program. You will see the message "My first program" displayed.
5. Replace `main` with `Main`, and recompile the source code. The compiler returns an error message because the Java program is case-sensitive.
6. Change it back, and compile the program again.
7. Instead of the command `javac Welcome.java`, use `javac welcome.java`.

   What happens?
8. Instead of the command `java Welcome`, use `java Welcome.class`.

   What happens? (The interpreter searches for `Welcome.class.class`.)

1.2 Create an HTML file that invokes a Java applet to display Welcome to Java! from a Web browser, as follows:

1. Create a program named WelcomeApplet.java for Example 1.2.
2. Create an HTML file named **WelcomeApplet.html**, as shown in Example 1.2.
3. Compile WelcomeApplet.java.
4. View **WelcomeApplet.html** from your Web browser.
5. At your operating system command prompt, type the following to view the applet:

   ```
   appletviewer WelcomeApplet.html
   ```
6. Replace the following `drawString` statement:

   ```
   g.drawString("Welcome to Java!", 10, 10);
   ```

   with the following:

   ```
   g.drawString("Another Message!", 10, 10);
   ```
7. Recompile, view, and find out what is new this time.

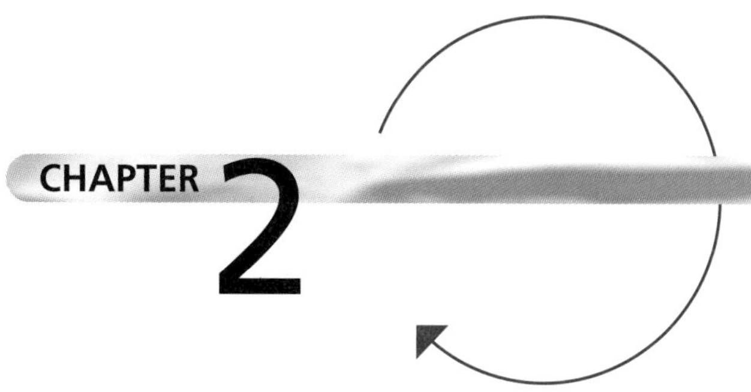

Primitive Data Types and Operations

Objectives

- Write simple Java programs.
- Understand identifiers, variables, and constants.
- Use assignment statements.
- Know Java primitive data types: `byte`, `short`, `int`, `long`, `float`, `double`, `char`, and `boolean`.
- Use Java operators and write Java expressions.
- Become familiar with Java documentation, programming style, and naming conventions.
- Understand syntax errors, runtime errors, and logic errors.
- Debug errors. (Optional)

Introduction

In the preceding chapter, you learned how to create, compile, and run a Java program. In this chapter, you will be introduced to Java primitive data types and related subjects, such as variables, constants, data types, operators, and expressions. You will learn how to write programs using primitive data types.

Writing Simple Programs

To begin, let's look at a simple program that computes the area of a circle. The program reads in the radius of the circle and displays its area. The program will use variables to represent the circle and the area, and will use an expression to compute the area.

Writing this program involves designing algorithms and data structures, as well as translating algorithms into programming codes. An *algorithm* describes how a problem is solved in terms of the actions to be executed, and it specifies the order in which the actions should be executed. Algorithms can help the programmer to plan a program before writing it in a programming language. An algorithm is often described by means of a pseudocode.

The algorithm for this program can be described as follows:

1. Read in the radius.
2. Compute the area using the following formula:

   $$area = radius \times radius \times \pi$$

3. Display the area.

Many of the problems you will meet when taking an introductory course in programming using this text can be described with simple, straightforward algorithms. As your education progresses, and you take courses on data structures, algorithm design, and analysis, you will encounter complex problems that have sophisticated solutions. You will need to design accurate, efficient algorithms with appropriate data structures in order to solve such problems.

Data structures involve data representation and manipulation. Java provides basic data types for representing integers, floating-point numbers, characters, and Boolean types. Java also supports array and string types as objects. Some advanced data structures, such as stacks and hashing, are already supported by Java.

To novice programmers, coding is a daunting task. When you *code*, you translate the algorithm into a programming language understood by the computer. You already know that every Java program begins with a class declaration in which the keyword `class` is followed by the class name. Assume that you have chosen `ComputeArea` as the class name. The outline of the program would look like this:

```
public class ComputeArea
{
  // Data and methods to be given later
}
```

As you know, every application must have a main method that controls the execution of the program. So the program is expanded as follows:

```
public class ComputeArea
{
  public static void main(String[] args)
  {
    // Step 1: Read in radius

    // Step 2: Compute area

    // Step 3: Display the area
  }
}
```

The program needs to read the radius entered by the user from the keyboard. You should consider two important issues next:

- Reading the radius.
- Storing the radius in the program.

Let's address the second issue first. In order to store the radius, the program needs to declare a symbol called a *variable*, which represents the radius in the program. Variables are used to store data and computational results in the program.

Choose descriptive names like `radius` for radius and `area` for area. To let the compiler know what `radius` and `area` are, specify their data types, indicating whether they are integer, float, or others. Declare `radius` and `area` as double-precision, floating-point numbers. The program can be expanded as follows:

```
public class ComputeArea
{
  public static void main(String[] args)
  {
    double radius;
    double area;

    // Step 1: Read in radius

    // Step 2: Compute area

    // Step 3: Display the area
  }
}
```

The program declares `radius` and `area` as double variables. The reserved word `double` indicates that `radius` and `area` are double-precision floating-point values stored in the computer.

The first step is to read in `radius`. Reading a number is not a simple matter at this time. Java does not provide a method for reading a number from the keyboard. For convenience, this book provides a class named `MyInput` that contains three methods named `readDouble`, `readInt`, and `readString` for reading, respectively, floating-point numbers, integer numbers, and strings from the keyboard.

The second step is to compute area by assigning the expression radius*radius*3.14159 to area.

In the final step, print area on the console by using the System.out.println method.

The program is completed in Example 2.1. The result is shown in Figure 2.1.

Example 2.1 Computing the Area of a Circle

This program lets the user enter the radius for a circle and then computes the area. Finally, it displays the area.

```
// ComputeArea.java: Compute the area of a circle
public class ComputeArea
{
  // Main method
  public static void main(String[] args)
  {
    double radius;
    double area;

    // Prompt the user to enter radius
    System.out.print("Enter radius: ");
    radius = MyInput.readDouble();

    // Compute area
    area = radius*radius*3.14159;

    // Display results
    System.out.println("The area for the circle of radius " +
      radius + " is " + area);
  }
}
```

Comments (// ComputeArea.java …), *Class Name* (ComputeArea), *Main Method Signature* (public static void main(String[] args)), *Data Type* (double), *Variable* (radius), *End of a Statement* (;), *Assignment* (=), *Expression* (radius*radius*3.14159), *Concatenation* (+)

```
// MyInput.java: Contain the methods for reading int, double, and
// string values from the keyboard
import java.io.*;

public class MyInput
{
  // Read a string from the keyboard
  public static String readString()
  {
    BufferedReader br
      = new BufferedReader(new InputStreamReader(System.in), 1);

    // Declare and initialize the string
    String string = " ";

    // Get the string from the keyboard
    try
    {
      string = br.readLine();
    }
    catch (IOException ex)
    {
      System.out.println(ex);
    }
```

```
      // Return the string obtained from the keyboard
      return string;
    }

    // Read an int value from the keyboard
    public static int readInt()
    {
      return Integer.parseInt(readString());
    }

    // Read a double value from the keyboard
    public static double readDouble()
    {
      return Double.parseDouble(readString());
    }
  }
```

Example Review

To test this program, create two files, one named ComputeArea.java for the `ComputeArea` class, and the other named MyInput.java for the `MyInput` class. Compile the programs and fix any errors. A sample run of the program is shown in Figure 2.1.

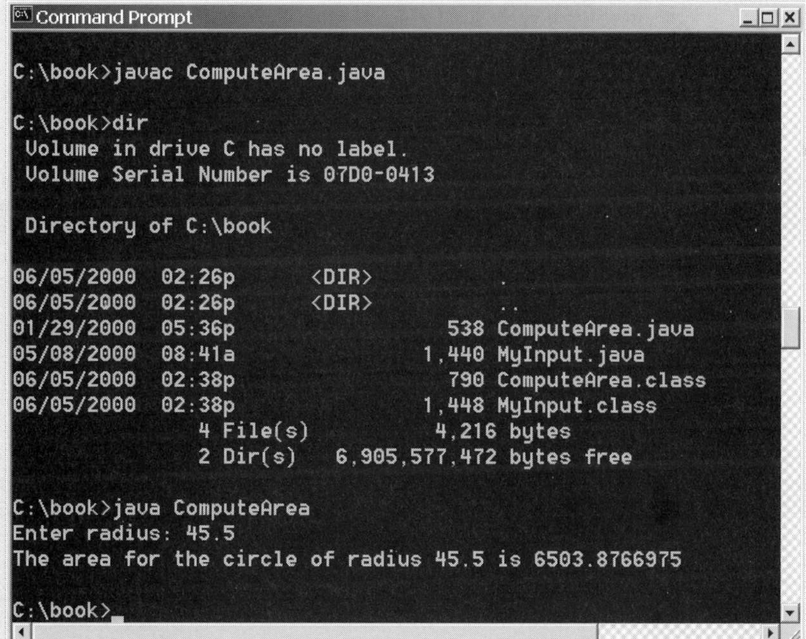

Figure 2.1 *The program receives the radius from the keyboard and displays the area of the circle.*

continues

Example 2.1 continued

The methods defined in the `MyInput` class are `readInt`, `readDouble` and `readString`. You will learn the details of implementing these methods in Chapter 15, "Input and Output." These methods are available for use in the `ComputeArea` class because `MyInput` is compiled, and its `bytecode` is stored in the same directory as the `ComputeArea` class. If you get a compilation error indicating that `MyInput` is not defined, make sure that `MyInput.java` is in the directory with `ComputeArea.java`.

When the `readDouble`, `readInt`, or `readString` method is executed, the computer waits for the input from the keyboard until the Enter key is pressed. The `readDouble` and `readInt` methods return a numeric value, and the `readString` method returns a string. From now on, you can use the `readDouble` and `readInt` methods in other programs to read numeric values and the `readString` method to read a string from the keyboard.

The program uses `print` and `println` methods to display a string to the console. These two methods are identical except that the `println` method moves to the next line after displaying the string, but the print method does not advance to the next line when completed.

The plus sign (+) in the `System.out.println("The area for the circle of radius " + radius + " is " + area)` statement means to concatenate strings if one of the operands is a string. If both operands are numbers, the `+` operator will add these two numbers.

Suppose `i = 1` and `j = 2`, what is the output of the following statement?

```
System.out.println("i+j is " + i + j);
```

The output is "i+j is 12" because `"i+j is "` is concatenated with `i` first. To force `i + j` to be executed first, enclose `i + j` in the parentheses, as follows:

```
System.out.println("i+j is " + (i + j));
```

NOTE

Each class in Java is compiled into a separate bytecode file with the extension .class. As shown in Figure 2.1, MyInput.class is the bytecode file for the `MyInput` class, and ComputeArea.class is the bytecode file for the `ComputeArea` class.

NOTE

The `readInt` method expects an integer and the `readDouble` method expects a floating-point value from the keyboard. A runtime error would occur if your input were incorrect.

Identifiers

Just as every entity in the real world has a name, you need to choose names for the things you will refer to in your programs. Programming languages use special symbols called *identifiers* to name such programming entities as variables, constants, methods, classes, and packages. Here are the rules for naming identifiers:

- An identifier must start with a letter, an underscore (_), or a dollar sign ($).
- An identifier cannot contain operators, such as +, –, and so on.
- An identifier cannot be a reserved word. (See Appendix A, "Java Keywords," for a list of reserved words.)
- An identifier cannot be `true`, `false`, or `null`.
- An identifier can be of any length.

For example, `$2`, `ComputeArea`, `area`, `radius`, and `readInt` are legal identifiers, while `2A` and `d+4` are illegal identifiers. Illegal identifiers do not follow the rules. The Java compiler detects illegal identifiers and reports syntax errors.

TIP

Identifiers are used for naming variables, constants, methods, classes, and packages. Descriptive identifiers make programs easy to read. Since Java is case-sensitive, X and x are two different identifiers.

Variables

Variables are used to store data—input, output, or intermediate data. In the program in Example 2.1, `radius` and `area` are variables of double-precision, floating-point type. You can assign any float value to `radius` and `area`, and the value of `radius` and `area` can be reassigned. For example, you can write the following code to compute the area for different radii:

```
// Compute the first area
radius = 1.0;
area = radius*radius*3.14159;
System.out.println("The area is " + area + " for radius " + radius);

// Compute the second area
radius = 2.0;
area = radius*radius*3.14159;
System.out.println("The area is " + area + " for radius " + radius);
```

Declaring Variables

Variables are used to represent many different types of data. To use a variable, you declare it and tell the compiler the name of the variable as well as what type of data it represents. This is called a *variable declaration*. Declaring a variable tells the compiler to allocate appropriate memory space for the variable based on its data type. The syntax for declaring a variable is as follows:

```
datatype variableName;
```

Here are some examples of variable declarations:

```
int x;           // Declare x to be an integer variable;
double radius;   // Declare radius to be a double variable;
char a;          // Declare a to be a character variable;
```

The examples use data types `int`, `double`, and `char`. You will be introduced to additional data types, such as `byte`, `short`, `long`, `float`, `char`, and `boolean`, in this chapter.

Assignment Statements

After a variable is declared, you can assign a value to it by using an *assignment statement.* The syntax for the assignment statement is as follows:

```
variable = value;
variable = expression;
```

For example, consider the following code:

```
x = 1;             // Assign 1 to variable x;
radius = 1.0;      // Assign 1.0 to variable radius;
a = 'A';           // Assign 'A' to variable a;
x = 5*(3/2)+3*2;   // Assign the value of the expression to x;
```

Tip

In an assignment statement, the data type of the variable on the left must be compatible with the data type of the value on the right. For example, `x = 1.0` would be illegal because the data type of `x` is `int`. You cannot assign a `double` value (`1.0`) to an `int` variable without using type casting. Type casting is introduced in the section "Numeric Type Conversion."

The variable name must be on the left. Thus, `1 = x` would be wrong.

An *expression* represents a computation involving values, variables, and operators. As an example, consider this code:

```
area = radius*radius*3.14159;
```

The variable on the left can also be used in the expression on the right. For example,

```
x = x + 1;
```

In this assignment statement, `x + 1` is assigned to `x`. If `x` is `1` before the statement is executed, then `x` becomes `2` after the statement is executed.

TIP

The Java assignment statement uses the equals sign (=), not :=, which is often used in other languages.

Declaring and Initializing Variables in One Step

Variables often have initial values. You can declare a variable and initialize it in one step. For example, consider the following code:

```
int x = 1;
```

This is equivalent to the next two statements:

```
int x;
x = 1;
```

TIP

A variable must be declared before it can be assigned a value. A variable must be assigned a value before it can be used.

Whenever possible, declare a variable and assign its initial value in one step. This makes the program easy to read.

Constants

The value of a variable may change during the execution of the program. A constant represents permanent data that never changes. In our `ComputeArea` program, π is a constant. If you use it frequently, you don't want to keep typing 3.14159; instead, you can define a constant for π. Here is the syntax for declaring a constant:

```
final datatype CONSTANTNAME = VALUE;
```

The word `final` is a Java keyword which means that the constant cannot be changed. For example, in the `ComputeArea` program, you could define π as a constant and rewrite the program as follows:

```
// ComputeArea.java: Compute the area of a circle
public class ComputeArea
{
  // Main method
  public static void main(String[] args)
  {
    double radius;
    double area;
    final double PI = 3.14159; // Declare a constant

    // Prompt the user to enter radius
    System.out.print("Enter radius: ");
    radius = MyInput.readDouble();

    // Compute area
    area = radius*radius*PI;

    // Display results
```

```
        System.out.println("The area for the circle of radius " +
          radius + " is " + area);
      }
    }
```

TIP

A constant must be declared and initialized before it can be used. You cannot change the constant's value once it is declared.

Numeric Data Types

Every data type has a *domain* (range) of values. The compiler allocates memory space to store each variable or constant according to its data type. Java provides several primitive data types for numerical values, characters, and Boolean values. In this section, numeric data types are introduced.

Java has six numeric types: four for integers and two for floating-point numbers. Table 2.1 lists the six numeric data types, their domains, and their storage sizes.

TABLE 2.1 Numeric Data Types

Name	*Domain (Range)*	*Storage Size*
`byte`	-2^7 (−128) to 2^7-1 (127)	8-bit signed
`short`	-2^{15} (−32768) to $2^{15}-1$ (32767)	16-bit signed
`int`	-2^{31} (−2147483648) to $2^{31}-1$ (2147483647)	32-bit signed
`long`	-2^{63} to $2^{63}-1$ (i.e. −9223372036854775808 to 9223372036854775807)	64-bit signed
`float`	–3.4E38 to 3.4E38 (6 to 7 significant digits of accuracy)	32-bit IEEE 754
`double`	–1.7E308 to 1.7E308 (14 to 15 significant digits of accuracy)	64-bit IEEE 754

Numeric Operators

Standard arithmetic operators for numerical data types include addition (+), subtraction (–), multiplication (*), division (/), and modulus (%). For examples, see the following code:

```
int i1 = 34 + 1;              // i1 becomes 35
double d1 = 34.0 - 0.1;       // d1 becomes 33.9
long  i2 = 300*30;            // i2 becomes 9000
double d2 = 1.0/2.0;          // d2 becomes 0.5
int i3 = 1/2;                 // i3 becomes 0; Note the result is
                              // the integer part of the division
byte i4 = 20%3;               // i4 becomes 2; Note the result is
                              // the remainder after the division
```

The result of integer division is an integer. For example, 5/2 = 2, not 2.5. The fraction part is truncated.

The % operator yields the remainder after division. Therefore 7%3 yields 1 and 20%3 yields 2. This operator is often used for integers, but also can be used with floating-point values.

The + and − operators can be both unary and binary. A *unary* operator has only one operand, and a *binary* operator has two operands. For example, the − operator in −5 can be considered as a unary operator to negate number 5, whereas the − operator in 4 − 5 is a binary operator for subtracting 5 from 4.

Numeric Literals

A *literal* is a primitive type value that appears directly in the program. For example, 34, 1,000,000, and 5.0 are literals in the following statements:

```
int i = 34;

long l = 1000000;

double d = 5.0;
```

Floating-point literals are written with a decimal point. By default, a floating-point literal is treated as a `double` type value. For example, 5.0 is considered a `double` value, not a `float` value. You can make a number a `float` or a `double` by appending the letter `f`, `F`, `d`, or `D`. For example, you can use `100.2f` or `100.2F` for a `float` number, and `100.2d` or `100.2D` for a `double` number. A floating-point literal can also be written in scientific notation; for example, 1.23456e+2, which is equivalent to $1.23465 \times 10^2 = 123.456$.

Shortcut Operators

Very often the current value of a variable is used, modified, and then reassigned back to the same variable. For example, consider the following code:

```
i = i + 8;
```

This statement is equivalent to

```
i += 8;
```

The += is called a *shortcut operator*. The common shortcut operators are shown in Table 2.2.

TABLE 2.2 Shortcut Operators

Operator	*Name*	*Example*	*Equivalent*
`+=`	`Addition Assignment`	`i+=8`	`i = i+8`
`-=`	`Subtraction Assignment`	`f-=8.0`	`f = f-8.0`
`*=`	`Multiplication Assignment`	`i*=8`	`i = i*8`
`/=`	`Division Assignment`	`i/=8`	`i = i/8`
`%=`	`Modulus Assignment`	`i%=8`	`i = i%8`

There are two more shortcut operators for incrementing and decrementing a variable by 1. This is handy because that's often how much the value needs to be changed. These two operators are ++ and --. They can be used in prefix or suffix notation. For example:

x++ is equivalent to x = x+1;

++x is equivalent to x = x+1;

x-- is equivalent to x = x-1;

--x is equivalent to x = x-1;

The increment operator ++ and the decrement operator -- can be applied to all integer and floating-point types. These operators are often used in loop statements. A loop statement is a structure that controls how many times an operation or a sequence of operations is performed in succession. This structure, and the subject of loop statements, is introduced in Chapter 3, "Control Statements." The prefix (++x, --x) and suffix (x++, x--) are different when they occur in an expression. If the operator is prefixed to the variable, the variable is first incremented or decremented by 1, then used in the expression. If the operator is a suffix to the variable, the variable is used in the expression first, then incremented or decremented by 1. Therefore, the prefixes ++x and --x are referred to, respectively, as the *preincrement operator* and the *predecrement operator*; and the suffixes x++ and x-- are referred to, respectively, as the *postincrement operator* and the *postdecrement operator*. The following code illustrates this:

```
int i=10;
int newNum;
newNum = 10*i++;
```

In this case, `i++` is evaluated after the entire expression `(10*i++)` is evaluated. If `i++` is replaced by `++i`, `++i` is evaluated before the entire expression is evaluated. So `newNum` is 100 for the first case and 110 for the second case. In both cases, `i` is incremented by 1.

Here is another example:

```
double x = 1.0;
double y = 5.0;
double z = x-- + (++y);
```

After all three lines are executed, y becomes 6.0, z becomes 7.0, and x becomes 0.0.

TIP

Shortcut operators originally came from C. They were inherited by C++ and adopted by Java. Using shortcut operators makes expressions short, but it also makes them complex and difficult to read. Avoid using shortcut operators in long expressions that involve many operators.

Numeric Type Conversion

Sometimes it is necessary to mix numerical values of different types in a computation. Consider the following statements:

```
byte i = 100;
```

```
long l = i*3+4;
double f = i*3.1+l/2;
```

Are these statements correct? Java allows binary operations on numerical variables and sometimes on values of different types. When performing a binary operation involving two operands of different types, Java automatically converts the less accurate operand to the type of the other, more accurate operand. For example, if one operand is `int` and the other is `float`, the `int` operand is converted to `float`, since `float` is more accurate than `int`. If one of the operands is of the type `double`, the other is converted to `double`, since `double` has the best accuracy among all numerical types. Thus the result of 1/2 is 0, and the result of 1.0/2 is 0.5.

You can always assign a less accurate value to a more accurate variable, such as assigning a `long` value to a `float` variable. You cannot, however, assign a more accurate value to a variable of less accuracy unless you use *type casting*. Casting is an operation that converts a value of one data type into a value of another data type. Casting a variable of a type with small range to a variable of a type with larger range is known as *widening a type*. Casting a variable of a type with large range to a variable of a type with smaller range is known as *narrowing a type*. Narrowing a type must be performed explicitly.

The syntax for casting gives the target type in parentheses, followed by the variable's name or the value to be cast. The code that follows is an example.

```
float f = (float)10.1;
int i = (int)f;
```

In the first line, the `double` value 10.1 is cast into a `float` variable. In the second line, `i` has a value of 10; the fractional part in `f` is truncated. Be careful when using casting. Lost information might lead to inaccurate results, as shown in this example:

```
int i = 256;
byte b = (byte)i;
```

So what is `b`? The numbers are represented in binary in the computer. Appendix E, "Number Systems," introduces number representations in the computer. The binary representation for `i` ($256 = 2^8$) is 100000000. Since an integer has four bytes and the last byte of `i` is 00000000, which is assigned to `b`, as shown in Figure 2.2. Thus, `b` becomes 0, which is totally distorted. To ensure correctness, you can test whether the value is in the correct target type range (see Table 2.1) before performing casting, using an if satement. The if statement will be introduced in Chapter 3, "Control Statements".

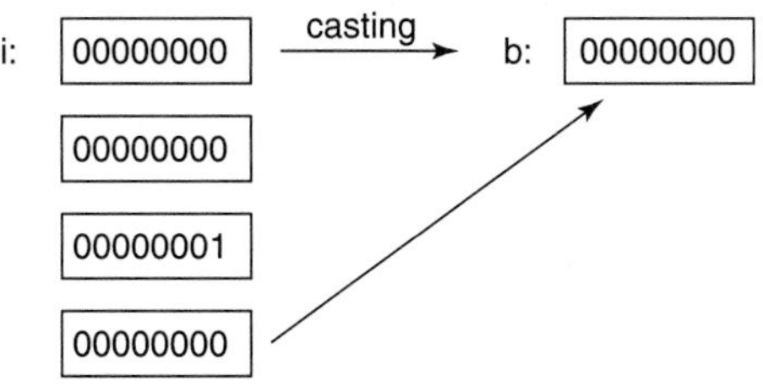

Figure 2.2 *An integer* `i` *is casted into a byte* `b`.

TIP

Casting is necessary if you are assigning a more accurate value to a less accurate variable, such as assigning a `double` value to an `int` variable. A compilation error would occur if casting were not used in these situations.

Character Data Type

The character data type, `char`, is used to represent a single character.

A character value is enclosed within single quotation marks. For example, consider the following code:

```
char letter = 'A';
char numChar = '4';
```

The first statement assigns character `A` to the `char` variable `letter`. The second statement assigns numerical character `4` to the `char` variable `numChar`.

The `char` type only represents one character. To represent a string of characters, use a data structure called `String`. For example, the line of code below declares the message to be a string that has an initial value of "Welcome to Java!"

```
String message = "Welcome to Java!";
```

`String` is discussed in more detail in Chapter 5, "Programming with Objects and Classes."

TIP

A string must be enclosed in quotation marks. A literal character is a single character enclosed in single quotation marks.

Java characters use *Unicode*, a 16-bit encoding scheme established by the Unicode Consortium to support the interchange, processing, and display of written texts in the world's diverse languages. (See the Unicode Web site at **www.unicode.org** for more information.) Unicode takes two bytes, preceded with \u, expressed in four hexadecimal numbers that run from `'\u0000'` to `'\uFFFF'`. For example, the Unicode for Taipei in Chinese is \u6077 \u6079.

Most computers use ASCII code. Unicode includes ASCII code with `'\u0000'` to `'\u00FF'` corresponding to the 128 ASCII characters. (See Appendix B, "The ASCII Character Set," for a list of ASCII characters and their decimal and hexadecimal codes.) You can use ASCII characters like `'X'`, `'1'`, and `'$'` in a Java program as well as Unicodes. For example, the following statements are equivalent:

```
char letter = 'A';

char letter = '\u0041';
```

Both statements assign character `A` to `char` variable `letter`.

You can use casting to convert a character to a numerical code, and vice versa. For example, to obtain a character's decimal code, use a casting like this:

```
int decimalCode = (int)'0';
```

The variable `decimalCode` becomes `48`.

Java also allows you to use the escape sequence for special characters. An escape sequence begins with the backslash character (\) followed by a character, which has a special meaning to the compiler. Some of the commonly used special characters are listed in Table 2.3.

TABLE 2.3 Examples of Special Characters

Description	*Character Escape Sequence*	*Unicode*
Backspace	`\b`	`\u0008`
Tab	`\t`	`\u0009`
Linefeed	`\n`	`\u000A`
Carriage return	`\r`	`\u000D`
Backslash	`\\`	`\u005C`
Single Quote	`\'`	`\u0027`
Double Quote	`\"`	`\u0022`

Suppose you want to print a quoted message like this:

```
He said "Java is fun"
```

You should write a statement as follows:

```
System.out.println("He said \"Java is fun\"");
```

boolean Data Type

The `boolean` data type comes from Boolean algebra. The domain of the `boolean` type consists of two literal values: `true` and `false`. For example, the following line of code assigns `true` to the variable `lightsOn`.

```
boolean lightsOn = true;
```

The operators associated with Boolean values are *comparison operators* and *Boolean operators*. Comparison operators, also known as *relational operators*, can be used in expressions that result in a Boolean value. Table 2.4 contains a list of comparison operators.

TIP

The equality comparison operator is two equals signs (==), not a single equals sign (=). The latter symbol is for assignment.

TABLE 2.4 Comparison Operators

Operator	*Name*	*Example*	*Answer*
`<`	less than	`1 < 2`	`true`
`<=`	less than or equal to	`1 <= 2`	`true`
`>`	greater than	`1 > 2`	`false`
`>=`	greater than or equal to	`1 >= 2`	`false`
`==`	equal to	`1 == 2`	`false`
`!=`	not equal to	`1 != 2`	`true`

Boolean operators, also known as *logical operators*, operate on Boolean values to create a new Boolean value. Table 2.5 contains a list of Boolean operators.

TABLE 2.5 Boolean Operators

Operator	*Name*	*Description*
`!`	not	logical negation
`&&`	and	logical conjunction
`||`	or	logical disjunction
`^`	exclusive or	logical exclusion

These operators are demonstrated by the examples that follow. In the examples, the variables `width` and `height` contain the values of 1 and 2, respectively.

Table 2.6 defines the not (!) operator. The not (!) operator negates `true` to `false` and `false` to `true`. For example, `!(width == 3)` is `true` because `(width == 3)` is `false`.

TABLE 2.6 Truth for Operator `!`

Operand	*!Operand*
`true`	`false`
false	true

Table 2.7 defines the and (`&&`) operator. The and (`&&`) of two Boolean operands is `true` if and only if both operands are `true`. For example, `(width == 1) && (height > 1)` is `true` because `(width == 1)` and `(height > 1)` are both `true`.

TABLE 2.7 Truth for Operator `&&`

Operand1	*Operand2*	*Operand1* `&&` *Operand2*
`false`	`false`	`false`
`false`	`true`	`false`
`true`	`false`	`false`
`true`	`true`	`true`

Table 2.8 defines the or (`||`) operator. The or (`||`) of two Boolean operands is `true` if at least one of the operands is `true`. For example, `(width > 1) || (height == 2)` is `true` because `height == 2` is `true`.

TABLE 2.8 Truth for Operator `||`

Operand1	*Operand2*	*Operand1* `||` *Operand2*
`false`	`false`	`false`
`false`	`true`	`true`
`true`	`false`	`true`
`true`	`true`	`true`

Table 2.9 defines the exclusive or (`^`) operator. The exclusive or (`^`) of two Boolean operands is `true` if and only if two operands have different Boolean values. For example, `(width > 1) ^ (height == 2)` is `true` because `(width > 1)` is `false` and `(height == 2)` is `true`.

TABLE 2.9 Truth for Operator `^`

Operand1	*Operand2*	*Operand1* `^` *Operand2*
`false`	`false`	`false`
`false`	`true`	`true`
`true`	`false`	`true`
`true`	`true`	`false`

When evaluating `p1 && p2`, Java first evaluates `p1`, then evaluates `p2` if `p1` is `true`; if `p1` is `false`, `p2` is not evaluated. When evaluating `p1 || p2`, Java first evaluates `p1`, then evaluates `p2` if `p1` is `false`; if `p1` is `true`, `p2` is not evaluated. Therefore, `&&` is referred to as the *conditional and* operator, and `||` is referred to as the *conditional or* operator.

Java also provides the `&` and `|` operators. The `&` operator works identically to the `&&` operator, and the `|` operator works identically to the `||` operator with one exception: the `&` and `|` operators always evaluate both operands. Therefore, `&` is referred to as the *unconditional and* operator, and `|` is referred to as the *unconditional or* operator. In some rare situations, you can use the `&` and `|` operators to guarantee that the right operand is evaluated regardless of whether the left operand is `true` or `false`. For example, the expression `(width < 2) & (height-- < 2)` guarantees that `(height-- < 2)` is evaluated. Thus, the variable `height` will be decremented regardless of whether `width` is less than 2 or not.

TIP

Avoid using the `&` and `|` operators. The benefits of the `&` and `|` operators are marginal. Using the `&` and `|` operators makes the program difficult to read and could cause errors. For example, the expression `(x != 0) & (100/x)` results in a runtime error if x is `0`.

NOTE

As shown in the preceding section, a char value can be cast into an `int` value, and vice versa. A Boolean value, however, cannot be cast into a value of other types, and vice versa.

Operator Precedence

Operator precedence determines the order in which expressions are evaluated. Suppose that you have this expression:

```
3 + 4*4 > 5*(4+3) - i++
```

What is its value? How does the compiler know the execution order of the operators? The expression in the parentheses is evaluated first. (Parentheses can be nested, in which case the expression in the inner parentheses is executed first.) When evaluating an expression without parentheses, the operators are applied in the order shown in Table 2.10, which contains the operators you have learned in this section. (See Appendix C, "Operator Precedence Chart," for a complete list of Java operators and their precedence.) Operators are applied from left to right if they are in the same order.

TABLE 2.10 Operator Precedence Chart

Precedence	*Operator*
Highest Order	casting
↓	++ and – – (prefix)
	! (not)
	*, /, %
	+, –
	<, <=, >, >=
	==, !=
	& (Unconditional AND)
	^ (Exclusive OR)
	¦ (Unconditional OR)
	&&
↓	¦¦
Lowest Order	=, +=, –=, *=, /=, %=

TIP

You can use parentheses to force an evaluation order as well as to make a program easy to read.

Case Studies

In the preceding sections, you learned about variables, constants, primitive data types, operators, and expressions. You are now ready to use them to write interesting programs. This section presents two examples: computing mortgage payments, and breaking a sum of money down into its smaller units.

Example 2.2 Computing Mortgages

This example shows you how to write a program that computes mortgage payments. The program will let the user enter the interest rate, number of years, and loan amount, and then will compute the monthly payment and the total payment. Finally, it will display the monthly and total payments.

The formula to compute the monthly payment is as follows:

$$\frac{loanAmount \times monthlyInterestRate}{1 - \dfrac{1}{(1 + monthlyInterestRate)^{numOfYears \times 12}}}$$

The mortgage calculation program follows, and the output is shown in Figure 2.3.

```
// ComputeMortgage.java: Compute mortgage payments
public class ComputeMortgage
{
  // Main method
  public static void main(String[] args)
  {
    double annualInterestRate;
    int numOfYears;
    double loanAmount;

    // Enter annual interest rate
    System.out.println(
      "Enter yearly interest rate, for example 8.25: ");
    annualInterestRate = MyInput.readDouble();

    // Obtain monthly interest rate
    double monthlyInterestRate = annualInterestRate/1200;

    // Enter number of years
    System.out.println(
      "Enter number of years as an integer, for example 5: ");
    numOfYears = MyInput.readInt();

    // Enter loan amount
    System.out.println("Enter loan amount, for example 120000.95: ");
    loanAmount = MyInput.readDouble();

    // Calculate payment
    double monthlyPayment = loanAmount*monthlyInterestRate/
```

continues

Example 2.2 continued

```
      (1 - 1/(Math.pow(1 + monthlyInterestRate, numOfYears*12)));
    double totalPayment = monthlyPayment*numOfYears*12;

    // Display results
    System.out.println("The monthly payment is " + monthlyPayment);
    System.out.println("The total payment is " + totalPayment);
  }
}
```

```
C:\book>java ComputeMortgage
Enter yearly interest rate, for example 8.25:
8
Enter number of years as an integer, for example 5:
30
Enter loan amount, for example 120000.95:
250000
The monthly payment is 1834.411434698445
The total payment is 660388.1164914402

C:\book>
```

Figure 2.3 *The program receives annual interest rate, years, and loan amount, then displays the monthly payment and total payment.*

Example Review

Each new variable in a method must be declared once and only once. Choose the most appropriate data type for the variable. For example, `numOfYears` is best declared as `int`, although it could be declared as `long`, `float`, or `double`.

The methods for reading numbers from the keyboard, `readInt` and `readDouble`, are defined in the `MyInput` class. Make sure MyInput.class is placed in the same directory with ComputeMortgage.class, so you can invoke these two methods in the `ComputeMortgage` class.

The method for computing b^p in the `Math` class is `pow(b, p)`. The `Math` class, which comes with the Java runtime system, is available to all Java programs. The `Math` class is introduced in Chapter 4, "Methods."

NOTE

The monthly payment and total payment are not displayed in currency format. You could modify the program so that it only displays two digits after the decimal point. A better solution, however, is to use the `NumberFormat` class, which is introduced in Chapter 12, "Internationalization."

Example 2.3 Computing Change

This example shows you how to write a program that classifies a given amount of money into its smaller monetary units. The program will let the user enter an amount as a double value representing a total in dollars and cents, and will output a report listing the monetary equivalent in dollars, quarters, dimes, nickels, and pennies.

Your program should report the maximum number of dollars, then the maximum number of quarters, and so on, in this order.

The program follows, and the output is shown in Figure 2.4.

```
// ComputeChange.java: Break down an amount into smaller units
public class ComputeChange
{
  // Main method
  public static void main(String[] args)
  {
    double amount; // Amount entered from the keyboard

    // Receive the amount entered from the keyboard
    System.out.println(
      "Enter an amount in double, for example 11.56");
    amount = MyInput.readDouble();

    int remainingAmount = (int)(amount*100);

    // Find the number of one dollars
    int numOfOneDollars = remainingAmount/100;
    remainingAmount = remainingAmount%100;

    // Find the number of quarters in the remaining amount
    int numOfQuarters = remainingAmount/25;
    remainingAmount = remainingAmount%25;

    // Find the number of dimes in the remaining amount
    int numOfDimes = remainingAmount/10;
    remainingAmount = remainingAmount%10;

    // Find the number of nickels in the remaining amount
    int numOfNickels = remainingAmount/5;
    remainingAmount = remainingAmount%5;

    // Find the number of pennies in the remaining amount
    int numOfPennies = remainingAmount;

    // Display results
    System.out.println("Your amount " + amount + " consists of ");
    System.out.println(numOfOneDollars + "\t dollars");
    System.out.println(numOfQuarters + "\t quarters");
    System.out.println(numOfDimes + "\t dimes");
    System.out.println(numOfNickels + "\t nickels");
    System.out.println(numOfPennies + "\t pennies");
  }
}
```

continues

Example 2.3 continued

```
C:\book>java ComputeChange
Enter an amount in double, for example 11.56
11.56
Your amount 11.56 consists of
11      dollars
2       quarters
0       dimes
1       nickels
1       pennies

C:\book>
```

Figure 2.4 *The program receives an amount in decimals and breaks it into singles, quarters, dimes, nickels, and pennies.*

Example Review

The program extracts the maximum number of singles from the total amount and obtains the remaining amount in the variable `remainingAmount`. It then extracts the maximum number of quarters from `remainingAmount` and obtains a new `remainingAmount`. Continuing the same process, the program finds the maximum number of dimes, nickels, and pennies in the remaining amount.

The variable `amount` stores the amount entered from the keyboard. This variable is not changed because the amount has to be used at the end of the program to display the results. The program introduces the variable `remainingAmount` to store the changing `remainingAmount`.

The variable `amount` is a `double` decimal representing dollars and cents, it is converted to an `int` variable `remainingAmount`, which represents all cents. For instance, if `amount` is 11.56, then the initial `remainingAmount` is 1156. The division operator yields the integer part of the division. So 1156/100 is 11. The remainder operator obtains the remainder of the division. So 1156%100 is 56.

The tab character `\t` prints eight spaces in the `System.out.print` method.

One serious problem with this example is the possible loss of precision when casting a `double` amount to an `int remainingAmount`. This could lead to an inaccurate result. There are two ways to fix the problem. One is to enter the amount as an `int` value representing cents (see Exercise 2.4); the other is to read the decimal number as a string and extract the dollars part and cents part separately as `int` values. Processing strings will be introduced in Chapter 5, "Programming with Objects and Classes."

As shown in Figure 2.4, 0 dimes, 1 nickels, and 1 pennies are displayed in the result. It would be better not to display 0 dimes, and to display 1 nickel and 1 penny using the singular words. You will learn how to modify this program using the selection statements in the next chapter (see Exercise 3.1).

Programming Style and Documentation

Programming style deals with the appearance of your program. If you were to write an entire program on one line, it would compile and run properly, but doing this would be bad programming style because the program would be hard to read. Documentation consists of explanatory remarks and comments for the program. Programming style and documentation are as important as coding. Good programming style and appropriate documentation reduce the chance of errors and make programs easy to read. Some guidelines for Java programming style and documentation are given below.

Appropriate Comments

You should include a summary at the beginning of the program to explain what the program does, its key features, its supporting data structures, and any unique techniques it uses. In a long program, you should also include comments to introduce each major step and to explain anything that is difficult to read. It is important to make your comments concise so that you do not crowd the program or make it difficult to read.

Naming Conventions

Make sure that the meanings of the descriptive names you choose for variables, constants, classes, and methods are straightforward. Names are case-sensitive. Listed below are the conventions for naming variables, methods, and classes.

- For variables and methods, always use lowercase. If the name consists of several words, concatenate them into one, making the first word lowercase and capitalizing the first letter of each subsequent word in the name; for example, the variables `radius` and `area` and the method `readDouble`.
- For class names, capitalize the first letter of each word in the name; for example, the class name `ComputeArea`.
- All letters in constants should be capitalized, and underscores should be used between words; for example, the constant `PI` and constant MAX_VALUE.

TIP

It is important to become familiar with the naming conventions. Understanding them will help you to understand Java programs. If you stick with the naming conventions, other programmers will be more willing to accept your program.

TIP

Do not choose class names that are already used in the Java standard packages. For example, since the `Math` class is defined in Java, you should not name your class Math.

Proper Indentation and Spacing

A consistent indentation style makes programs clear and easy to read. Indentation is used to illustrate structural relationships among the program's components or statements. Java can read the program even if all of the statements are in a straight line, but it is easier to read and maintain code that is aligned properly. You should indent each subcomponent or statement *two* spaces more than the structure within which it is nested.

Spacing lines should be used to separate segments of the code to make the program easier to read.

Block Styles

A block is a group of statements surrounded by braces. A block can be written in many ways. For example, the following are equivalent:

```
public class Test
{
  public static void main(String[] args)
  {
    System.out.println("Block Styles");
  }
}

public class Test {
  public static void main(String[] args) {
    System.out.println("Block Styles");
  }
}
```

The former is referred to as the *next-line* style, and the latter, as the *end-of-line* style. In the next-line style, the open brace and the closing brace are on the same column; thus it is easy to see the beginning and end of the block. That is why the next-line block style is used in this book.

Programming Errors

Programming errors are unavoidable, even for experienced programmers. Errors can be categorized into three types: *compilation errors*, *runtime errors*, or *logic errors*.

Compilation Errors

Errors that occur during compilation are called *compilation errors* or *syntax errors*. Compilation errors result from errors in code construction, such as mistyping a keyword, omitting some necessary punctuation, or using an opening brace without a corresponding closing brace. These errors are usually easy to detect, because the compiler tells you where they are and the reasons for them. For example, compiling the following program results in a compilation error, as shown in Figure 2.5.

```
// The program contains syntax errors
public class ShowSyntaxErrors
{
  public static void main(String[] args)
  {
```

```
    i = 30;
    System.out.println(i+4);
  }
}
```

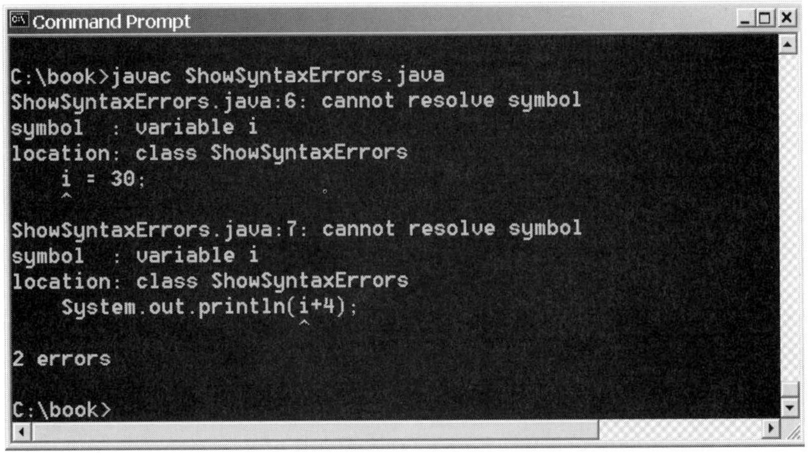

```
C:\book>javac ShowSyntaxErrors.java
ShowSyntaxErrors.java:6: cannot resolve symbol
symbol  : variable i
location: class ShowSyntaxErrors
    i = 30;
    ^
ShowSyntaxErrors.java:7: cannot resolve symbol
symbol  : variable i
location: class ShowSyntaxErrors
    System.out.println(i+4);
                       ^
2 errors

C:\book>
```

Figure 2.5 *The compiler detects a syntax error: Undefined variable* `i`*, at lines 6 and 7 in the source code.*

Both errors are a result of not declaring variable `i`. A single error will often display many lines of compilation errors. Therefore, it is a good practice to start debugging from the top line and work downward. Fixing errors that occur earlier may fix cascading errors that occur later in the program.

Runtime Errors

Runtime errors are errors that cause a program to terminate abnormally. Runtime errors occur while an application is running if the environment detects an operation that is impossible to carry out. Input errors are typical runtime errors.

An *input error* occurs when the user enters an unexpected input value that the program cannot handle. For instance, if the program expects to read in a number, but instead the user enters a string, this causes data-type errors to occur in the program. To avoid the input error, the program prompts the user to enter the correct type of values. It may display a message like "Please enter an integer" before reading an integer from the keyboard.

Another common source of runtime errors is division by zero. This happens when the divisor is zero for integer divisions. For instance, the following program would cause a runtime error, as shown in Figure 2.6.

```
// Program contains runtime errors
public class ShowRuntimeErrors
{
```

```
    public static void main(String[] args)
    {
      int i = 1 / 0;
    }
  }
```

```
C:\book>java ShowRuntimeErrors
Exception in thread "main" java.lang.ArithmeticException: / by zero
        at ShowRuntimeErrors.main(ShowRuntimeErrors.java:5)

C:\book>
```

Figure 2.6 *The runtime error causes the program to terminate.*

Logic Errors

Logic errors occur when a program doesn't perform the way it was intended to. Errors of this kind occur for many different reasons. For example, suppose you wrote the following program to display a message reporting whether a number is between 1 and 100, inclusively.

```
// program contains a logic errors
public class ShowLogicErrors
{
  // Determine if a number is between 1 and 100 inclusively
  public static void main(String[] args)
  {
    // Prompt the user to enter a number
    System.out.println("Please enter an integer");
    int number = MyInput.readInt();

    // Display the result
    System.out.println("The number is between 1 and 100, " +
      "inclusively? " + ((1 < number) && (number < 100)));
  }
}
```

The program does not have syntax errors or runtime errors, but it does not print the correct result for the number 1, as shown in Figure 2.7.

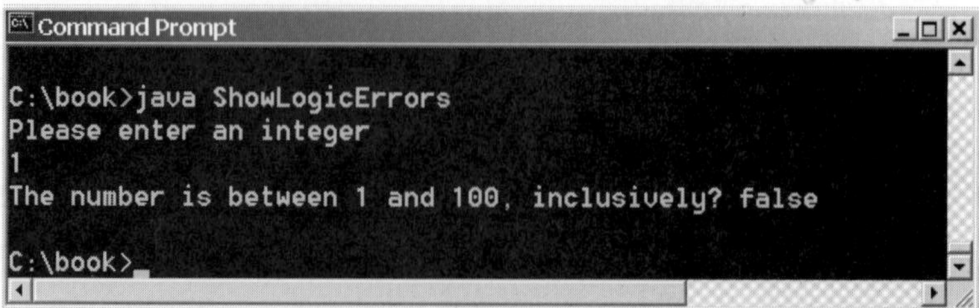

Figure 2.7 *The logic error causes the program to produce an incorrect result.*

The error is in the Boolean expression in the `println` statement. It should be as follows:

```
((1 <= number) && (number <= 100))
```

Debugging (Optional)

In general, syntax errors are easy to find and easy to correct because the compiler gives indications as to where the errors came from and why they are there. Runtime errors are not difficult to find either, since the Java interpreter displays them on the console when the program aborts. Finding logic errors, on the other hand, can be very challenging.

Logic errors are called *bugs*. The process of finding and correcting errors is called *debugging*. A common approach to debugging is to use a combination of methods to narrow down to the part of the program where the bug is located. You can *hand trace* the program (that is, catch errors by reading the program), or you can insert print statements in order to show the values of the variables or the execution flow of the program. This approach might work for a short, simple program. But for a large, complex program, the most effective approach for debugging is to use a debugger utility.

JDK includes a command-line debugger (jdb), which is invoked with a class name. jdb is itself a Java program, running its own copy of the Java interpreter. All the Java IDE tools like JBuilder, Visual J++, and Visual Café include integrated debuggers. The debugger utilities let you follow the execution of a program. They vary from one system to another, but they all support most of the following helpful features:

- **Executing a single statement at a time:** The debugger allows you to execute one statement at a time so that you can see the effect of each statement.
- **Tracing into or stepping over a method:** If a method is being executed, you can ask the debugger to enter the method and execute one statement at a time in the method, or you can ask it to step over the entire method. You should step over the entire method if you know the method works. For example, you should always step over the system-supplied methods, such as `System.out.println`.
- **Setting breakpoints:** You can also set a breakpoint at a specific statement. Your program pauses when it reaches a breakpoint, and the line with the breakpoint is displayed. You can set as many breakpoints as you want. Breakpoints are particularly useful when you know where your programming error starts. You can set a breakpoint at that line and have the program execute until it reaches the breakpoint.
- **Displaying variables:** The debugger lets you select several variables and display their values. As you trace through a program, the content of a variable is continuously updated.

- **Using call stacks:** The debugger lets you trace all of the method calls and lists all pending methods. This feature is helpful when you need to see a large picture of the program-execution flow.
- **Modifying variables:** Some debuggers enable you to modify the value of a variable when debugging. This is convenient when you want to test a program with different samples but do not want to leave the debugger.

NOTE

The debugger is an indispensable, powerful tool that boosts your programming productivity. However, it could take some time to become familiar with it. I recommend that beginning Java programmers using this book insert print statements to trace the programs.

Chapter Summary

In this chapter, you learned about data representation, operators, and expressions. These are the fundamental elements needed to construct Java programs. You also learned about programming errors, debugging, and programming styles. These are all important concepts and should be fully understood before you apply them.

Identifiers are used for naming programming entities, such as variables, constants, methods, classes, and packages. Variables are symbols that represent data. The value of a variable can be changed with an assignment statement. All variables must be declared with an identifier and a type before they can be used. An initial value must be assigned to a variable before it is referenced.

The equals sign (`=`) is used to assign a value to a variable. A statement with an equals sign is called an assignment statement. When a value is assigned to a variable, it replaces the previous value of the variable, which is destroyed.

A constant is a symbol representing a value in the program that is never changed. Sometimes it is called a constant variable. You cannot assign a new value to a constant.

Java provides four integer types (`byte`, `short`, `int`, `long`) that represent integers of four different sizes, and two floating-point types (`float`, `double`) that represent float numbers of two different sizes. Character type (`char`) represents a single character, and `boolean` type represents a `true` or `false` value. These are called primitive data types. Java's primitive types are portable across all computer platforms. When they are declared, the variables of these types are created and assigned memory space.

Java provides operators that perform numerical operations: `+` (addition), `-` (subtraction), `*` (multiplication), `/` (division), and `%` (modulus). Integer division (`/`) yields an integer result. The modulus operator (`%`) yields the remainder of the division.

The increment operator (`++`) and the decrement operator (`--`) increment or decrement a variable by 1. If the operator is prefixed to the variable, the variable is first incremented or decremented by 1, then used in the expression. If the operator is a suffix to the variable, the variable is used in the expression first, then incremented or decremented by 1.

In a computation involving different types of numerical values, numbers are converted to a unifying type. The unifying type is chosen according to the data type of the operands in the following order: `double`, `float`, `long`, `int`, `short`, `byte`. You can assign a value of a lower order to a variable of a higher order. However, an explicit casting operator must be used if you assign a value of a higher order (for instance, `double`) to a variable of a lower order (for instance, `int`).

The operators in arithmetic expressions are evaluated in the order determined by the rules of operator precedence. Parentheses can be used to force the order of evaluation to occur in any sequence.

Review Questions

2.1 Are the following identifiers valid?

```
applet, Applet, a++, --a, 4#R, $4, #44, apps
```

2.2 Declare the following:

- An `int` variable with an initial value of `0`.
- A `long` variable with an initial value of `10000`.
- A `float` variable with an initial value of `3.4`.
- A `double` variable with an initial value of `34.45`.
- A `char` variable with an initial value of `4`.
- A `boolean` variable with an initial value of `true`.

2.3 Assume that `int a = 1` and double `d = 1.0`, and that each expression is independent. What are the results of the following expressions?

```
a = 46/9;

a = 46%9+4*4-2;

a = 45+43%5*(23*3%2);

a = 45+45*50%a--;

a = 45+1+45*50%(--a);

d = 1.5*3+(++d);

d = 1.5*3+d++;

a %= 3/a+3;
```

2.4 Find the largest and smallest `byte`, `short`, `int`, `long`, `float`, and `double`. Which of these data types requires the least amount of memory?

2.5 Can different types of numeric values be used together in a computation?

2.6 Describe Unicode and ASCII code.

2.7 Can the following conversions involving casting be allowed? If so, find the converted result.

```
char c = 'A';
i = (int)c;

boolean b = true;
i = (int)b;

float f = 1000.34f;
int i = (int)f;

double d = 1000.34;
int i = (int)d;

int i = 1000;
char c = (char)i;

int i = 1000;
boolean b = (boolean)i;
```

2.8 What is the result of 25/4? How would you rewrite the expression if you wanted the result to be a floating-point number?

2.9 Are the following statements correct? If so, show the printout.

```
System.out.println("the output for 25/4 is " + 25/4);

System.out.println("the output for 25/4.0 is " + 25/4.0);
```

2.10 What does an explicit conversion from a `double` to an `int` do with the fractional part of the double value?

2.11 How would you write the following arithemetic expression in Java?

$$\frac{4}{3(r + 34)} - 9(a + bc) + \frac{3 + d(2 + a)}{a + bd}$$

2.12 List six comparison operators.

2.13 Show the result of the following Boolean expressions if the result can be determined.

```
(true) && (3 > 4)

!(x > 0) && (x > 0)

(x > 0) || (x < 0)

(x != 0) || (x == 0)

(x >= 0) || (x < 0)

(x != 1) == !(x = 1)
```

2.14 Write a Boolean expression that evaluates to `true` if the number is between 1 and 100.

2.15 Write a Boolean expression that evaluates `true` if the number is between 1 and 100 or the number is negative.

2.16 Are the following expressions correct?

```
x > y > 0

x = y && y

x /= y

x or y

x and y

(x != 0) || (x = 0)
```

2.17 How do you denote a comment line? a comment paragraph?

2.18 Describe compilation errors, runtime errors, and logic errors.

2.19 What are the naming conventions for class names, method names, constants, and variables? Which of the following items can be a constant, a method, a variable, or a class according to Java naming conventions?

```
MAX_VALUE, Test, read, readInt
```

2.20 Suppose x is 1, what is x after the evaluation of the following expression?

```
(x > 1) & (x++ > 1)
```

2.21 Suppose x is 1, what is x after the evaluation of the following expression?

```
(x > 1) && (x++ > 1)
```

Programming Exercises

2.1 Write a program that converts Fahrenheit to Celsius. The formula for the conversion is as follows:

```
celsius = (5/9)*(fahrenheit-32)
```

Your program reads a Fahrenheit degree in double from the keyboard, then converts it to Celsius and displays the result on the console.

(Hint: In Java, 5/9 is 0. So you need to write 5.0/9 in the program to obtain the correct result.)

2.2 Write a program to compute the volume of a cylinder. Your program reads in radius and length, and computes volume using the following formulas:

```
area = radius*radius*π

volume = area*length
```

2.3 Write a program to display "Welcome to Java!" in large block letters, each letter made up of the same character it represents. The letter should be six printed lines. For example, *W* is displayed as follows:

2.4 Rewrite Example 2.3, "Computing Changes," to fix possible loss of accuracy when converting a `double` value to an `int` value. Enter the input as an integer whose last two digits represent the cents. For example, the input 1156 represents 11 dollars and 56 cents.

2.5 Write a program that reads an integer between 0 and 1000 and summarizes all the digits in the integer. For example, if an integer is 932, the sum of all its digits is 14.

(Hint: Use the % operator to extract digits and use the / operator to remove the extracted digit. For instance, 932%10 = 2 and 932/10 = 93.)

2.6 Write a program that reads a double number and checks if the number is between 1 and 1000. If you input is 5, your output should be like this:

```
The number 5 between 1 and 1000 is true.
```

If you input is 2000, your output should be like thie:

```
The number 2000 between 1 and 1000 is false.
```

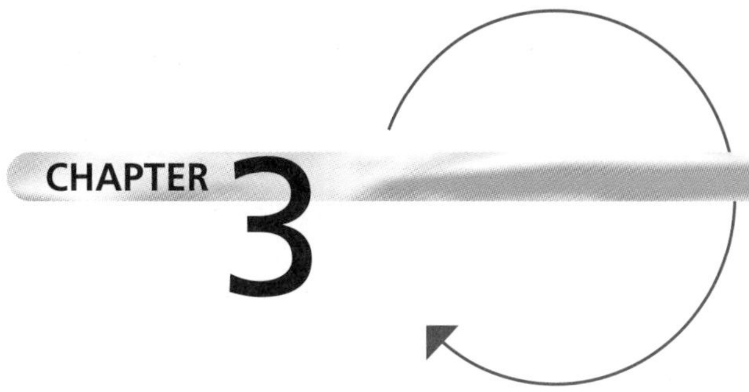

Control Statements

Objectives

- Understand the concept of program control.
- Use selection statements to control the execution of a program.
- Use loop statements to control the repetition of statements.
- Understand and use the keywords `break` and `continue`.

Introduction

Program control can be defined as specifying the order in which statements are executed in a program. The programs that you have written so far execute statements in sequence. Often, however, you are faced with situations in which you must provide alternative steps.

In Chapter 2, "Primitive Data Types and Operations," if you entered a negative input for `radius` in Example 2.1, "Computing the Area of a Circle," for instance, the program would print an invalid result. If the radius is negative, you don't want the program to compute the area. Like all high-level programming languages, Java provides selection statements that let you choose actions with two or more alternative courses. You can use the selection statements in the following pseudocode to rewrite Example 2.1:

```
if the radius is negative
  the program displays a message indicating a wrong input;
else
  the program computes the area and displays the result;
```

Like other high-level programming languages, Java provides loop statements in order to control the repeated execution of statements. Suppose that you need to print the same message a hundred times. It would be tedious to have to write the message over and over again. Java provides a powerful control structure called a *loop*, which controls how many times an operation or a sequence of operations is performed in succession. Using a loop statement, you can simply tell the computer to print the message a hundred times without actually coding the print statement a hundred times. Java has three types of loop statements: `while` loops, `do` loops, and `for` loops.

In this chapter, you will learn various selection and loop control statements.

Selection Statements

This section introduces various selection statements. Java has several types of `if` statements: simple `if` statements, `if . . . else` statements, nested `if` statements, `switch` statements, and conditional expressions.

Simple *if* Statements

A simple `if` statement executes an action only if the condition is `true`. The syntax for a simple `if` statement is as follows:

```
if (booleanExpression)
{
  statement(s);
}
```

The execution flow chart is shown in Figure 3.1.

If the `booleanExpression` evaluates as `true`, the statements in the block are executed. For example, see the following code:

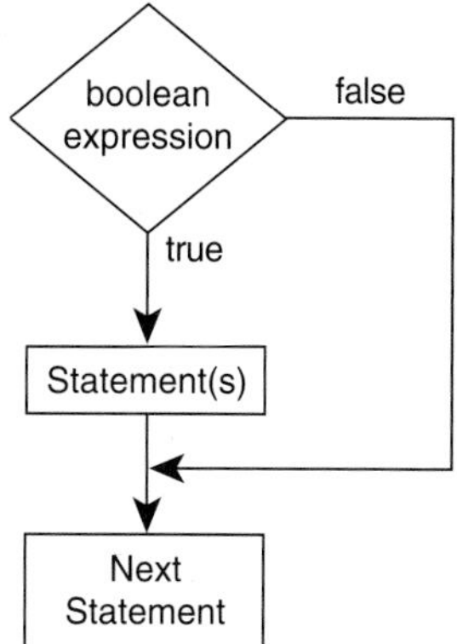

Figure 3.1 *An* `if` *statement executes statements if the* `booleanExpression` *evaluates as* `true`.

```
if (radius >= 0)
{
  area = radius*radius*PI;
  System.out.println("The area for the circle of radius " +
    radius + " is " + area);
}
```

If the value of `radius` is greater than or equal to 0, then the `area` is computed and the result is displayed; otherwise, the two statements in the block will not be executed.

TIP

Adding a semicolon at the end of the if clause is a common mistake, as follows:

```
if (radius >= 0);
{
  area = radius*radius*PI;
  System.out.println("The area for the circle of radius " +
    radius + " is " + area);
}
```

TIP

The `booleanExpression` is always enclosed in parentheses for all forms of the `if` statement. For example, the outer parentheses in the following if statement are required.

```
if ((i >= 0) && (i <= 10))
{
  system.out.println("i is an integer between 0 and 10");
}
```

The curly braces can be omitted if they enclose a single statement. For example:

```
if ((i >= 0) && (i <= 10))
  system.out.println("i is an integer between 0 and 10");
```

TIP

I strongly suggest the use of curly braces to avoid programming errors. If you modify the code by adding new statements in the `if` statement, you will have to insert the curly braces if they are not already in place. Forgetting the curly braces when they are needed for grouping multiple statements is a common programming error.

if . . . else Statements

A simple `if` statement takes an action if the specified condition is `true`. If the condition is `false`, nothing is done. But what if you want to take alternative actions when the condition is `false`? You can use an `if . . . else` statement. The actions that an `if . . . else` statement specifies differ based on whether the condition is `true` or `false`.

Here is the syntax for this type of statement:

```
if (booleanExpression)
{
  statement(s)-for-the-true-case;
}
else
{
  statement(s)-for-the-false-case;
}
```

The flow chart of the `if . . . else` statement is shown in Figure 3.2.

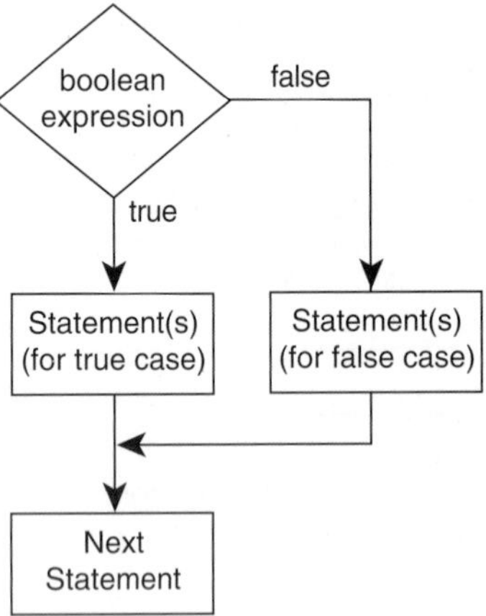

Figure 3.2 *An* `if . . . else` *statement executes statements for the* `true` *case if the* `boolean` *expression evaluates as* `true`*; otherwise, statements for the* `false` *case are executed.*

If the `booleanExpression` evaluates as `true`, the `statement(s)` for the true case is executed; otherwise, the `statement(s)` for the false case is executed. For example, consider the following code:

```
if (radius >= 0)
```

```
{
  area = radius*radius*PI;
  System.out.println("The area for the circle of radius " +
    radius + " is " + area);
}
else
{
  System.out.println("Negative input");
}
```

If `radius >= 0` is `true`, `area` is computed and displayed; if it is `false`, the message `"Negative input"` is printed.

As usual, the curly braces can be omitted if there is only one statement within them. The curly braces enclosing the `System.out.println("Negative input")` statement can therefore be omitted in the preceding example.

Nested *if* Statements

The statement in an `if` or `if . . . else` statement can be any legal Java statement—including another `if` or `if . . . else` statement. The inner `if` statement is said to be *nested* inside the outer `if` statement. The inner `if` statement can contain another `if` statement; in fact, there is no limit to the depth of the nesting. For example, the following is a nested `if` statement:

```
if (i > k)
{
  if (j > k)
    System.out.println("i and j are greater than k");
}
else
  System.out.println("i is less than or equal to k");
```

The `if (j > k)` statement is nested inside the `if (i > k)` statement.

The nested `if` statement can be used to implement multiple alternatives. The statement given below, for example, assigns a letter grade to the variable `grade` according to the score, with multiple alternatives.

```
if (score >= 90.0)
  grade = 'A';
else
  if (score >= 80.0)
    grade = 'B';
  else
    if (score >= 70.0)
      grade = 'C';
    else
      if (score >= 60.0)
        grade = 'D';
      else
        grade = 'F';
```

The execution of this `if` statement proceeds as follows. The first condition `(score >= 90.0)` is tested. If it is `true`, the grade becomes `'A'`. If it is `false`, the second condition `(score >= 80.0)` is tested. If the second condition is `true`, the grade becomes `'B'`. If that condition is `false`, the third condition and the rest of the conditions (if necessary) continue to be tested until a condition is met or all of the conditions prove to be `false`. If all of the conditions are `false`, the grade becomes `'F'`. Note that a condition is tested only when all of the conditions that come before it are `false`.

The preceding `if` statement is equivalent to the following:

```
if (score >= 90.0)
  grade = 'A';
else if (score >= 80.0)
  grade = 'B';
else if (score >= 70.0)
  grade = 'C';
else if (score >= 60.0)
  grade = 'D';
else
  grade = 'F';
```

In fact, this is the preferred writing style for multiple alternative `if` statements. This style avoids deep indentation and makes the program easy to read.

NOTE

The `else` clause matches the most recent `if` clause in the same block. For example, the following statement

```
// Determine leap year
if (year % 4 == 0)
  if (year % 100 != 0)
    System.out.println(year + " is a leap year");
else if (year % 400 == 0)
  System.out.println(year + " is a leap year");
```

is equivalent to

```
// Determine leap year
if (year % 4 == 0)
  if (year % 100 != 0)
    System.out.println(year + " is a leap year");
  else if (year % 400 == 0)
    System.out.println(year + " is a leap year");
```

To force the `else` clause to match the first `if` clause, you must rewrite the statement:

```
// Determine leap year
if (year % 4 == 0)
{
  if (year % 100 != 0)
    System.out.println(year + " is a leap year");
}
else if (year % 400 == 0)
  System.out.println(year + " is a leap year");
```

Example 3.1 Using Nested `if` Statements

In Example 2.2, "Computing Mortgages," you built a program that reads annual mortgage interest rate, number of years, and loan amount and computes mortgage payments. In this example, assume that the annual interest rate depends on the number of years.

Suppose that you have three different interest rates: 7.25 percent for 7 years, 8.5 percent for 15 years, and 9 percent for 30 years. The program prompts the user to enter a loan amount and the number of years for the mortgage, then finds the annual interest rate according to the number of years. The program finally displays the monthly payment amount and the total amount paid. Figure 3.3 shows a sample run of the program.

```
// TestIfElse.java: Test if-else statements
public class TestIfElse
{
  // Main method
  public static void main(String[] args)
  {
    double annualInterestRate = 0;
    int numOfYears;
    double loanAmount;

    // Enter number of years
    System.out.print(
      "Enter number of years (7, 15 and 30 only): ");
    numOfYears = MyInput.readInt();

    // Find interest rate based on year
    if (numOfYears == 7)
      annualInterestRate = 7.25;
    else if (numOfYears == 15)
      annualInterestRate = 8.50;
    else if (numOfYears == 30)
      annualInterestRate = 9.0;
    else
    {
      System.out.println("Wrong number of years");
      System.exit(0);
    }

    // Obtain monthly interest rate
    double monthlyInterestRate = annualInterestRate/1200;

    // Enter loan amount
    System.out.print("Enter loan amount, for example 120000.95: ");
    loanAmount = MyInput.readDouble();

    // Compute mortgage
    double monthlyPayment = loanAmount*monthlyInterestRate/
      (1-(Math.pow(1/(1+monthlyInterestRate), numOfYears*12)));
    double totalPayment = monthlyPayment*numOfYears*12;

    // Display results
    System.out.println("The monthly payment is " + monthlyPayment);
    System.out.println("The total payment is " + totalPayment);
  }
}
```

continues

Example 3.1 continued

```
C:\book>java TestIfElse
Enter number of years (7, 15 and 30 only): 30
Enter loan amount, for example 120000.95: 250000
The monthly payment is 2011.5565423619532
The total payment is 724160.3552503032

C:\book>
```

Figure 3.3 *The program in Example 3.1 validates the input year, obtains the interest rate according to the year, receives the loan amount, and displays the monthly payment and the total payment.*

Example Review

The program receives the year and assigns the annual interest rate: 7.25 percent for 7 years, 8.5 percent for 15 years, and 9 percent for 30 years. If the number of years is not 7, 15, or 30, the program displays `Wrong number of years`.

Note that an initial value of 0 is assigned to `annualInterestRate`. A syntax error would occur if it had no initial value because all of the other statements that assign values to `annualInterestRate` are within the `if` statement. The compiler thinks that these statements may not be executed and therefore reports a syntax error.

switch Statements

The `if` statement in Example 3.1 makes selections based on a single `true` or `false` condition. There are three cases for assigning interest rates, which depend on the number of years. To fully account for all the cases, nested `if` statements were used. Clearly, overuse of the nested `if` statement makes the program difficult to read. Java provides a `switch` statement to handle multiple conditions efficiently. You could write the following `switch` statement to replace the nested `if` statement in Example 3.1:

```
switch (numOfYears)
{
  case 7:  annualInterestRate = 7.25;
           break;
  case 15: annualInterestRate = 8.50;
           break;
  case 30: annualInterestRate = 9.0;
           break;
  default: System.out.println("Wrong number of years");
}
```

The flow chart of the preceding `switch` statement is shown in Figure 3.4.

This statement checks to see whether the number of years matches the value 7, 15, or 30, in that order. If matched, the corresponding statement is executed; if not matched, a message is displayed. Here is the full syntax for the `switch` statement:

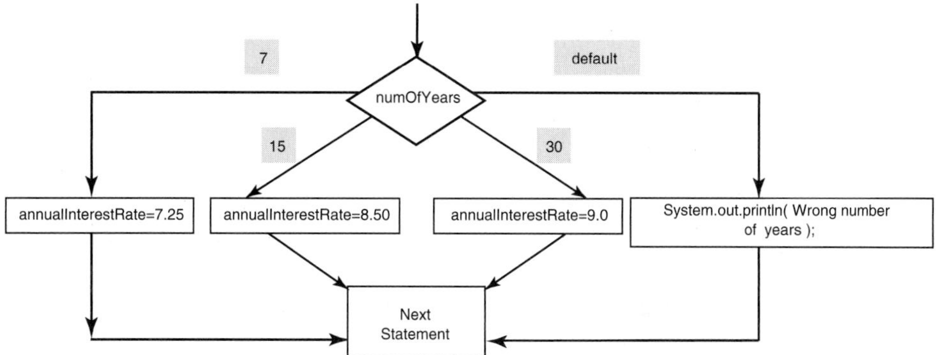

Figure 3.4 *The* `switch` *statement obtains the interest rate according to numOfYears.*

```
switch (switch-expression)
{
  case value1: statement(s)1;
               break;
  case value2: statement(s)2;
               break;
  ...
  case valueN: statement(s)N;
               break;
  default:     statement(s)-for-default;
}
```

The `switch` statement observes the following rules:

- The `switch-expression` must yield a value of `char`, `byte`, `short`, or `int` type and must always be enclosed in parentheses.
- The `value1 . . . valueN` must have the same data type as the value of the `switch-expression`. The resulting statements in the `case` statement are executed when the value in the `case` statement matches the value of the `switch-expression`. (Each `case` statement is executed in sequential order.)
- The keyword `break` is optional. The `break` statement terminates the entire `switch` statement. If the `break` statement is not present, the next `case` statement will be executed.
- The default case, which is optional, can be used to perform actions when none of the specified cases is `true`. The default case always appears last in the `switch` block.

TIP

Do not forget to use a `break` statement when one is needed. For example, the following code always displays `Wrong number Of Years` regardless of what `numOfYears` is. Suppose the `numOfYears` is 15. The statement `annualInterestRate = 8.50` is executed, then the statement `annualInterest Rate = 9.0`, and finally the statement `System.out.println("Wrong number of years")`.

```
switch (numOfYears)
{
  case 7:  annualInterestRate = 7.25;
  case 15: annualInterestRate = 8.50;
  case 30: annualInterestRate = 9.0;
  default: System.out.println("Wrong number of years");
}
```

Conditional Expressions

You might want to assign a value to a variable that is restricted by certain conditions. For example, the following statement assigns 1 to y if x is greater than 0, and −1 to y if x is less than or equal to 0.

```
if (x > 0)
  y = 1
else
  y = -1;
```

Alternatively, you can use a conditional expression as follows to achieve the same result.

```
y = (x > 0) ? 1 : -1;
```

Conditional expressions are in a completely different style, with no explicit `if` in the statement. The syntax is shown below:

```
variable = booleanExpression ? expression1 : expression2;
```

This is equivalent to the following:

```
if (booleanExpression)
  variable = expression1;
else
  variable = expression2;
```

For another example, suppose you want to assign the larger number between variable `num1` and `num2` to `num3`. You can simply write a statement using the conditional expression as follows:

```
num3 = (num1 > num2) ? num1 : num2;
```

NOTE

The symbols `?` and `:` appear together in a conditional expression. They form a conditional operator, also known as a *ternary operator*. This is the only ternary operator in Java.

Loop Statements

Loops are structures that control repeated executions of a block of statements. The part of the loop that contains the statements to be repeated is called the *loop body*. A one-time execution of a loop body is referred to as an *iteration of the loop*. Each loop contains a loop `continue-condition`, a Boolean expression that controls the execution of the body. After each iteration, the `continue-condition` is reevaluated. If the condition is `true`, the body is repeated. If the condition is `false`, the loop terminates.

The concept of looping is fundamental to programming. Java provides three types of loop statements: the `while` loop, the `do` loop, and the `for` loop.

The *while* Loop

The syntax for the `while` loop is as follows:

```
while (continue-condition)
{
  // Loop-body;
}
```

The curly braces can be omitted for the `while` loop and other loops, if the loop body contains only one statement. The `while` loop flow chart is shown in Figure 3.5.

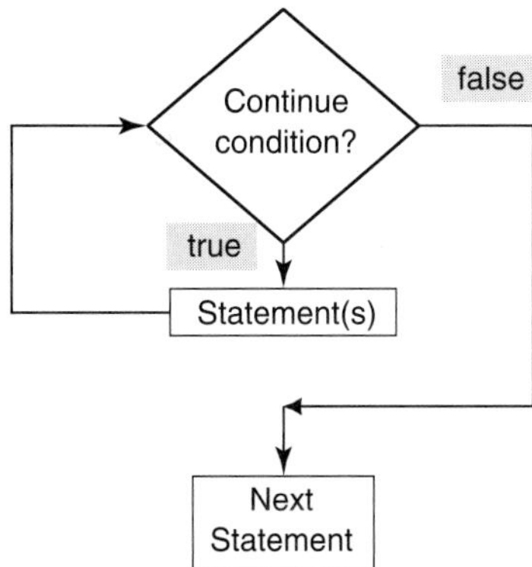

Figure 3.5 *The* `while` *loop repeatedly executes the statements in the loop body when* `continue-condition` *evaluates as* `true`.

The `continue-condition`, a Boolean expression, must appear inside the parentheses. It is always evaluated before the loop body is executed. If its evaluation is `true`, the loop body is executed; if its evaluation is `false`, the entire loop terminates and the program control turns to the statement that follows the `while` loop. For example, the following `while` loop prints `Welcome to Java!` 100 times.

```
int i = 0;
while (i < 100)
{
  System.out.println("Welcome to Java!");
  i++;
}
```

The flow chart of the previous statement is shown in Figure 3.6.

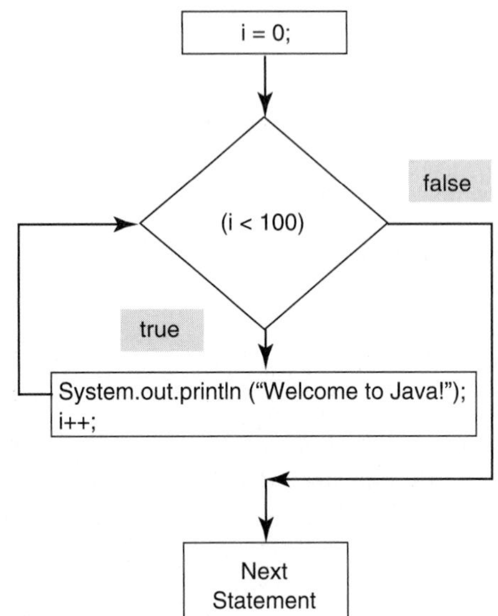

Figure 3.6 *The* `while` *loop repeatedly executes the statements in the loop body for 100 times.*

The variable `i` is initially 0. The loop checks whether `(i < 100)` is true. If so, it executes the loop body to print the message `Welcome to Java!` and increments `i` by 1. It repeatedly executes the loop body until `(i < 100)` becomes false. When `(i < 100)` is false, the loop terminates and the next statement after the loop statement is executed.

Example 3.2 Using `while` Loops

This example reads and calculates an unspecified number of integers. The input 0 signifies the end of the input.

The program's sample run is shown in Figure 3.7.

```
// TestWhile.java: Test the while loop
public class TestWhile
{
  // Main method
  public static void main(String[] args)
  {
    int data;
    int sum = 0;

    // Read an initial data
    System.out.println("Enter an int value");
    data = MyInput.readInt();

    // Keep reading data until the input is 0
```

```
      while (data != 0)
      {
        sum += data;

        System.out.println(
          "Enter an int value, the program exits if the input is 0");
        data = MyInput.readInt();
      }

      System.out.println("The sum is " + sum);
    }
  }
```

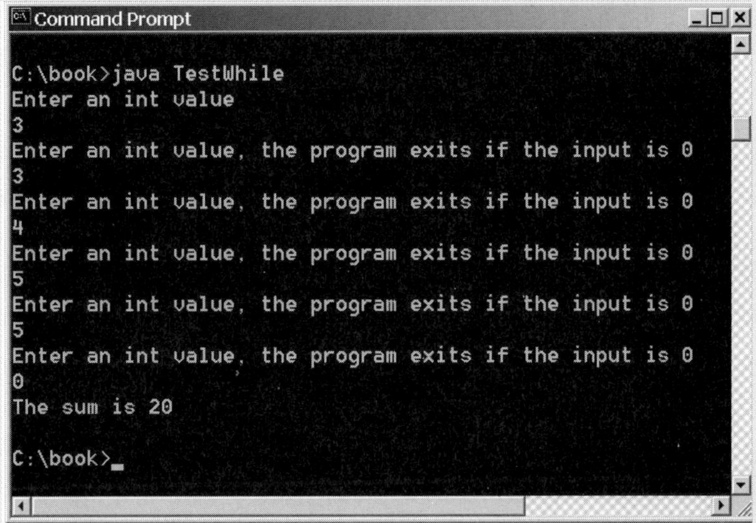

Figure 3.7 *Example 3.2 uses a* `while` *loop to add an unspecified number of integers.*

Example Review

If `data` is not 0, it is added to the sum and the next input data is read. If `data` is 0, the loop body is not executed and the `while` loop terminates.

Note that if the first input read is 0, the loop body never executes, and the resulting `sum` is 0.

TIP

Make sure that the `continue-condition` eventually becomes `false` so that the program will terminate.

Don't use floating-point values for equality checking in a loop control. Since floating-point values are approximations, using them could result in imprecise counter values and inaccurate results. This example uses `int` value for `data`. If a floating-point type value is used for `data`, `(data != 0)` may be `true` even though `data` is 0.

The *do* Loop

The do loop is a variation of the while loop. Its syntax is given below:

```
do
{
  // Loop body;
} while (continue-condition)
```

Its execution flow chart is shown in Figure 3.8.

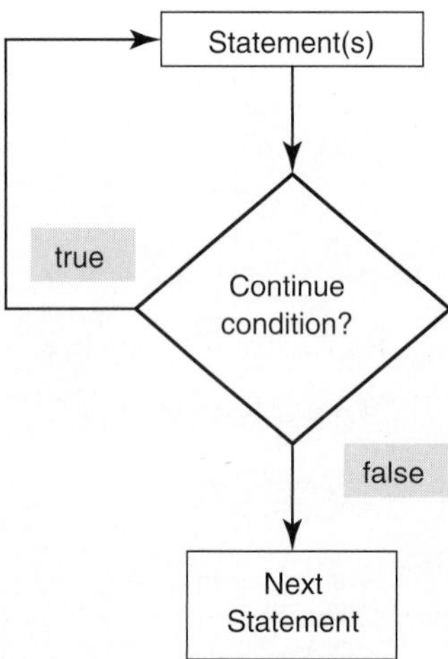

Figure 3.8 *The* do *loop executes the loop body first, and then checks the* continue-condition *to determine whether to continue or terminate the loop.*

The loop body is executed first. Then the continue-condition is evaluated. If the evaluation is true, the loop body is executed again; if it is false, the do loop terminates. The major difference between a while loop and a do loop is the order in which the continue-condition is evaluated and the loop body is executed. The while loop and the do loop have equal expressive power. Sometimes it is more convenient to choose one over the other. For example, you can rewrite Example 3.2 as follows:

```
// TestDo.java: Test the do loop
public class TestDo
{
  // Main method
  public static void main(String[] args)
  {
    int data;
    int sum = 0;

    do
    {
      data = MyInput.readInt();
      sum += data;
    } while (data != 0);

    System.out.println("The sum is " + sum);
  }
}
```

TIP

I recommend the do loop if you have statements inside the loop that must be executed at least once, as in the case of the do loop in the preceding TestDo program. These statements must appear before the loop as well as inside the loop if you are using a while loop.

The *for* Loop

Often you write the loop in the following common form:

```
i = initialValue;  // Initialize loop control variable
while (i < endValue)
{
  // Loop body
  ...
  i++; // Adjust loop control variable
}
```

The for loop can be used to simplify the above loop as follows:

```
for (i = initialValue; i < endValue; i++)
{
  // Loop body
  ...
}
```

In general, the syntax of the for loop is as follows:

```
for (control-variable-initializer; continue-condition;
     adjustment-statement)
{
  // Loop-body;
}
```

The flow chart of the for loop is shown in Figure 3.9.

The for loop statement starts with the keyword for, followed by the three control elements, which are enclosed by parentheses, and the loop body, which is inside curly braces. The control elements, which are separated by semicolons, control how many times the loop body is executed and when the loop terminates. The following for loop prints Welcome to Java! 100 times:

```
int i;
for (i = 0; i<100; i++)
{
  System.out.println("Welcome to Java!");
}
```

The flow chart of the statement is shown in Figure 3.10.

The first element, i = 0, initializes the control variable, i. The control variable tracks how many times the loop body has been executed. The adjustment statement changes the value of the variable.

The next element, i < 100, which is the continue-condition, is a Boolean expression. The expression is evaluated at the beginning of each iteration. If the continue-condition is true, execute the loop body. If it is false, the loop terminates and the program control turns to the line following the loop.

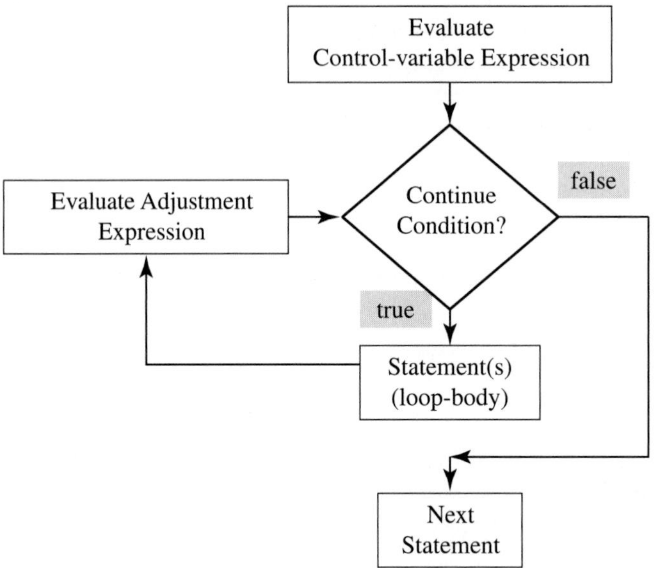

Figure 3.9 *The* `for` *loop initializes the control variable, and then repeatedly executes the statements in the loop body, and evaluates the adjustment expression when the* `continue-condition` *evaluates as* `true`.

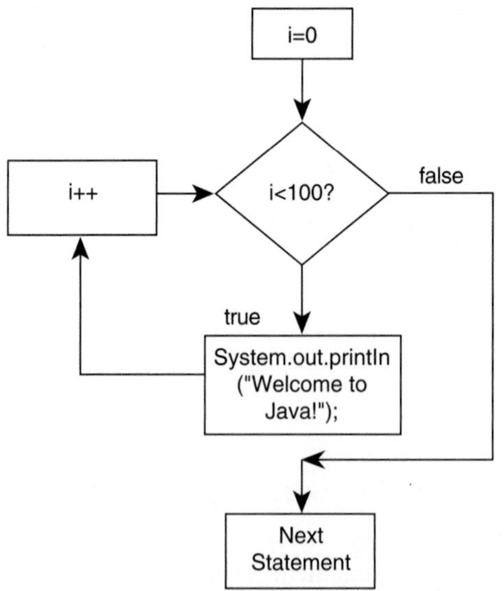

Figure 3.10 *The* `for` *loop initializes* `i` *to* `0`*, and then repeatedly executes the* `println` *statement, and evaluates* `i++` *when* `i` *is less than* `100`.

The adjustment statement, `i++`, is a statement that adjusts the control variable. This statement is executed after each iteration. Usually, an adjustment statement either increments or decrements the control variable. Eventually, the value of the control variable forces the `continue-condition` to become `false`.

The loop control variable can be declared and initialized in the for loop. Here is an equivalent statement for the preceding example:

```
for (int i = 0; i<100; i++)
{
  System.out.println("Welcome to Java!");
}
```

If there is only one statement in the loop body, as in this example, the curly braces can be omitted.

NOTE

control-variable-initializer, adjustment-statement in a for loop can be any statement, or can be omitted. Therefore, the following statement is correct.

```
for (int i=1; i<100; System.out.println(i++));
```

If continue-condition is omitted, it implies the condition is rue. Thus the statement given below, which is an infinite loop, is correct.

```
for ( ; ; ) { }
```

Nevertheless, I recommend that you use the following equivalent loop to avoid confusions.

```
while (true) { }
```

Example 3.3 Using for Loops

This example computes the summation of a series that starts with 0.01 and ends with 1.0. The numbers in the series will increment by 0.01, as follows: 0.01+0.02+0.03 and so on. The output of this program appears in Figure 3.11.

```
// TestSum.java: Compute sum = 0.01 + 0.02 + … + 1;
public class TestSum
{
  // Main method
  public static void main(String[] args)
  {
    // Initialize sum
    float sum = 0;

    // Keep adding 0.01 to sum
    for (float i=0.01f; i <= 1.0f; i = i+0.01f)
      sum += i;

    // Display result
    System.out.println("The summation is " + sum);
  }
}
```

Example Review

The for loop repeatedly adds the control variable i to the sum. This variable, which begins with 0.01, is incremented by 0.01 after each iteration. The loop terminates when i exceeds 1.0.

continues

Example 3.3 continued

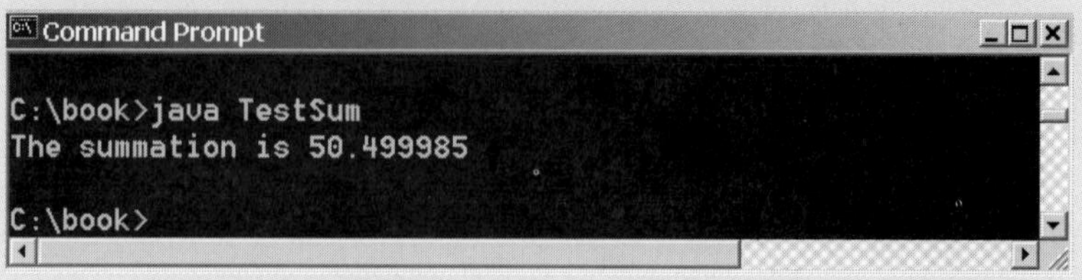

```
C:\book>java TestSum
The summation is 50.499985

C:\book>
```

Figure 3.11 *Example 3.3 uses a* `for` *loop to sum a series from 0.01 to 1 in increments of 0.01.*

From this example, you can see that a control variable can be a `float` type. In fact, it can be any numeric data type.

You may have noticed that the answer is not precise. This is because computers use a fixed number of bits to represent floating-point numbers, and thus cannot represent some floating-point numbers exactly. If you change `float` in the program to `double`, you will see a slight improvement in precision because a double variable takes 64 bits, whereas a float variable takes 32 bits.

TIP

Always use semicolons rather than commas to separate the control elements in the `for` loop header. Using commas in the `for` loop header is a common mistake.

Do not change the value of the control variable inside the `for` loop, even though it is perfectly legal to do so. Changing the value makes the program difficult to understand and could lead to subtle errors.

Example 3.4 Using Nested `for` Loops

The following program uses nested `for` loops to print a multiplication table. Nested loops are composed of an outer loop and one or more inner loops. Each time the outer loop is repeated, the inner loops are reentered, their loop control parameters are reevaluated, and all required iterations are performed. The output of the program is shown in Figure 3.12.

```
// TestMulTable.java: Display a multiplication table
public class TestMulTable
{
  // Main method
  public static void main(String[] args)
  {
    // Display the table heading
    System.out.println("       Multiplication Table");
    System.out.println("----------------------------------");
```

```
      // Display the number title
      System.out.print("  | ");
      for (int j=1; j<=9; j++)
        System.out.print("  " + j);
      System.out.println(" ");

      // Print table body
      for (int i=1; i<=9; i++)
      {
        System.out.print(i+" | ");
        for (int j=1; j<=9; j++)
        {
          // Display the product and align properly
          if (i*j < 10)
            System.out.print("  " + i*j);
          else
            System.out.print(" " + i*j);
        }
        System.out.println();
      }
    }
  }
```

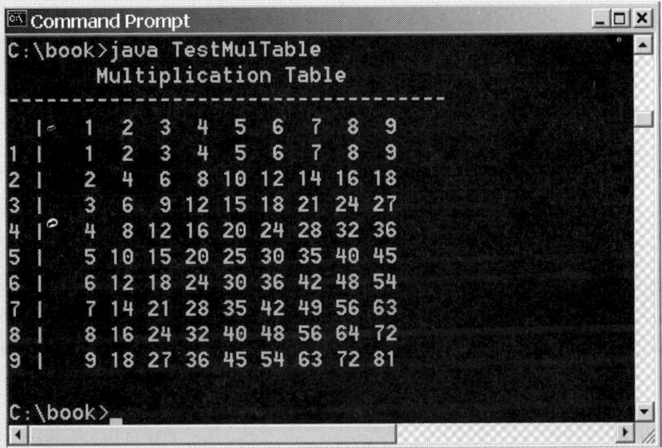

Figure 3.12 *Example 3.4 uses nested* `for` *loops to print a multiplication table.*

Example Review

The program displays a title on the first line, dashes (-) in the second line. The first `for` loop displays the numbers 1 through 9 on the third line.

The next loop is a nested `for` loop with the control variable `i` in the outer loop and `j` in the inner loop. For each `i`, the product `i*j` is displayed on a line in the inner loop, with `j` being 1, 2, 3, . . . , 9. The `if` statement in the inner loop is used so that the product is aligned properly. If the product is a single digit, it is displayed with an extra space before it.

continues

Example 3.4 continued

Tip

The control variable must always be declared inside the control structure of the loop or before the loop. If the variable is declared inside the loop control structure, it cannot be referenced outside of the loop. For example, you cannot reference `i` outside the `for` loop, because it is declared inside the `for` loop.

Note

The three forms of loop statements, `while`, `do`, and `for`, are expressively equivalent; i.e. you can write a loop in any of these three forms. I recommend that you use the one that is most intuitive and comfortable for you. In general, a `for` loop may be used if the number of repetitions is known, as, for example, when you need to print a message 100 times. A `while` loop may be used if the number of repetitions is not known, as in the case of reading the numbers until the input is 0. A `do` loop can be used to replace a while loop if the loop body has to be executed before testing the continue condition.

Using the Keywords *break* and *continue*

Two statements, `break` and `continue`, can be used in loop statements to provide the loop with additional control.

- `break`: This keyword immediately ends the innermost loop that contains it.
- `continue`: This keyword only ends the current iteration. Program control goes to the next iteration of the loop.

You have already used the keyword `break` in a `switch` statement. You can also use `break` and `continue` in any of the three kinds of loop statements.

The diagrams in Figure 3.13 and Figure 3.14 illustrate the functions of `break` and `continue` in a loop statement.

Example 3.5 Testing a `break` Statement

In this example, you will see how a `break` statement affects the results of a program.

```
// TestBreak.java: Test the break keyword in the loop
public class TestBreak
{
  // Main method
  public static void main(String[] args)
```

continues

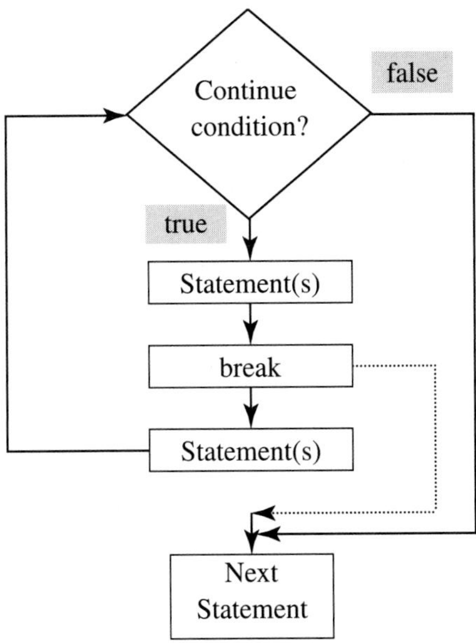

Figure 3.13 *The* `break` *statement forces its containing loop to exit.*

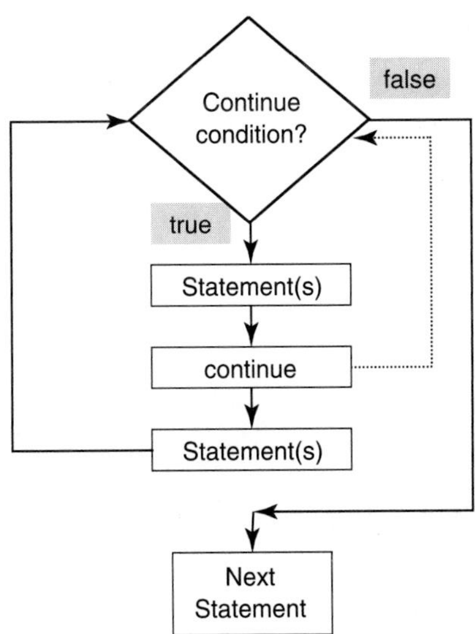

Figure 3.14 *The* `continue` *statement forces the current iteration of the loop to end.*

Example 3.5 continued

```
    {
      int sum = 0;
      int item = 0;

      while (item < 5)
      {
        item ++;
        sum += item;
        if (sum >= 6) break;
      }

      System.out.println("The sum is " + sum);
    }
  }
```

Example Review

Without the `if` statement, this program calculates the sum of the numbers from 1 to 5. But with the `if` statement, the loop terminates when the sum becomes greater than or equal to 6. The output of the program is shown in Figure 3.15.

If you changed the `if` statement as shown below, the output would resemble that in Figure 3.16.

```
if (sum == 5) break;
```

In this case, the `if` condition will never be `true`. Therefore, the `break` statement will never be executed.

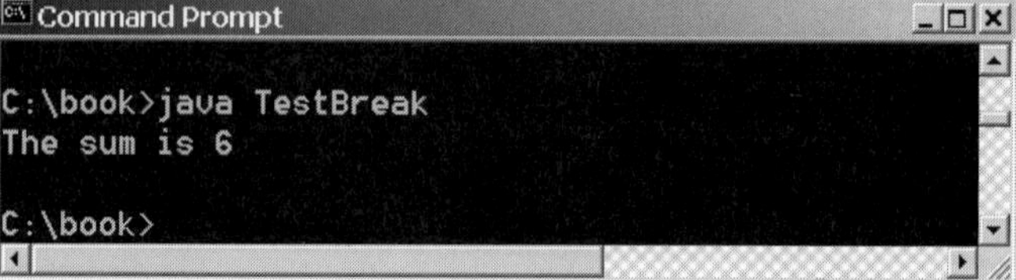

Figure 3.15 *The* `break` *statement in the TestBreak program forces the* `do` *loop to exit when* `sum` *is greater than 6.*

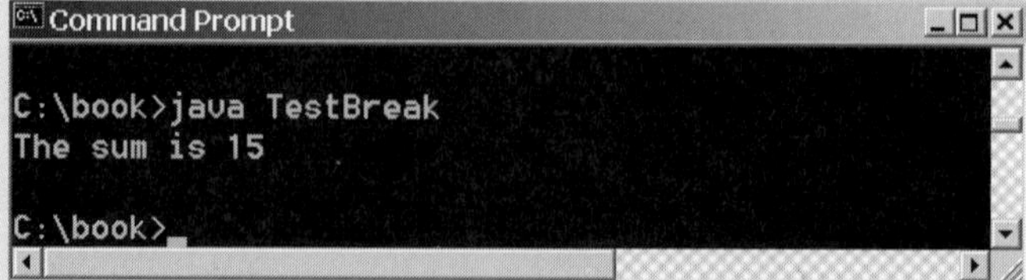

Figure 3.16 *The* `break` *statement is not executed in the modified* `TestBreak` *program because* `sum == 5` *cannot be* `true`.

In this example, you will see the effect of a `continue` statement on a program.

Example 3.6 Using a `continue` Statement

```
// TestContinue.java: Test the continue keyword
public class TestContinue
{
  // Main method
  public static void main(String[] args)
  {
    int sum = 0;
    int item = 0;

    while (item < 5)
    {
      item++;
      if (item == 2) continue;
      sum += item;
    }

    System.out.println("The sum is " + sum);
  }
}
```

Example Review

With the `if` statement in the program, the `continue` statement is executed when `item` becomes 2. The `continue` statement ends the current iteration so that the rest of the statement in the loop body is not executed; therefore, `item` is not added to `sum` when it is 2. The output of the program is shown in Figure 3.17.

Without the `if` statement in the program, the output would look like Figure 3.18.

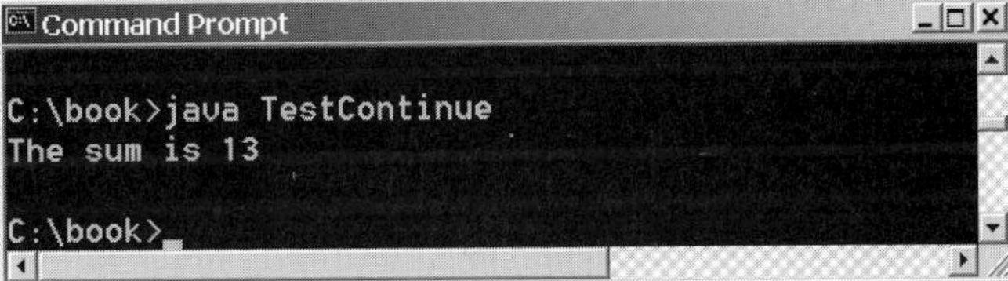

Figure 3.17 *The* `continue` *statement in the* `TestContinue` *program forces the current iteration to end when* `item` *equals 2.*

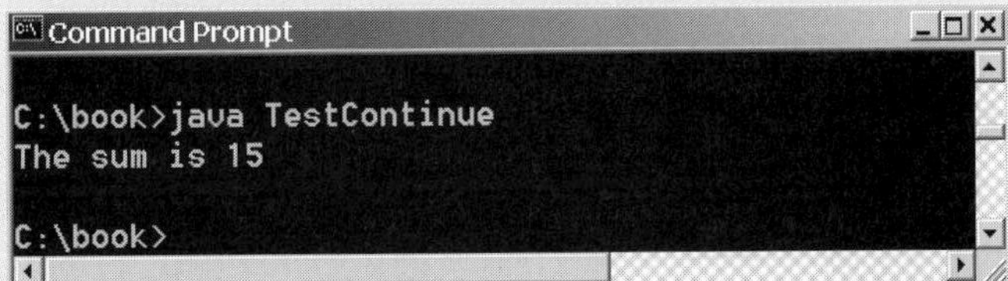

Figure 3.18 *Since the modified* `TestContinue` *program has no* `continue` *statement, every item is added to* `sum`.

Without the `if` statement, all of the items are added to `sum`, including when `item` is 2. Therefore, the result is 15, which is two more than it was with the `if` statement.

continues

Example 3.6 continued

NOTE

The `continue` statement is always inside a loop. In `while` and `do` loops, the loop continue-condition is evaluated immediately after the `continue` statement. In the `for` loop, the adjustment-statement is evaluated, and then the loop continue-condition is evaluated.

NOTE

You can always write a program without using `break` or `continue` in a loop. See Review Question 3.20.

Statement Labels and Breaking with Labels

Every statement in Java can have an optional label, which is an identifier. Labels are often used with the `break` and `continue` statements. You can use the `break` statement with a label to break out of the labeled statement, and use the `continue` statement with a label to break out the current iteration of the labeled loop statement.

For example, the following `break` statement breaks out the outer loop and transfers control to the statement immediately following the outer loop.

```
outer:
  for (int i=1; i<10; i++)
  {
  inner:
    for (int j=1; j<10; j++)
    {
      if (i*j > 50)
        break outer;

      System.out.println(i*j);
    }
  }
```

If you replace `break outer` with `break` in the above statement, the `break` statement would break out of the inner loop and continue to stay inside the outer loop.

Case Studies

Control statements are fundamental in programming. The ability to write control statements is essential in learning Java programming. This section presents three additional examples of the use of selection statements and loops to solve problems.

Example 3.7 Finding the Sales Amount

You have just started a sales job in a department store. Your pay consists of a base salary and a commission. The base salary is $5,000. The following scheme is used to determine the commission rate:

Sales Amount	Commission Rate
$1–$5,000	8 percent
$5,001–$10,000	10 percent
$10,001 and above	12 percent

Your goal is to earn $30,000 in a year. Write a program that will find out the minimum amount of sales you have to generate in order to make $30,000.

Since your base salary is $5,000, you have to make $25,000 on commission to earn $30,000 in a year. What is the sales amount for a $25,000 commission? If you know the sales amount, the commission can be computed as follows:

```
if (salesAmount >= 10001)
  commission = 5000*0.08 + 5000*0.1 + (salesAmount-10000)*0.12;
else if (salesAmount >= 5001)
  commission = 5000*0.08 + (salesAmount-5000)*0.10;
else
  commission = salesAmount*0.08;
```

This suggests that you can try to find the `salesAmount` to match a given `commission` through incremental approximation. For `salesAmount` of $1, find `commission`. If `commission` is less than $25,000, increment `salesAmount` by 1 and find `commission` again. If `commission` is less than $25,000, repeat the process until the commission is greater than $25,000. This is a tedious job for humans, but it is exactly what a computer is good for. You can write a loop and let a computer execute it painlessly.

The complete program is given below, and a sample run of the program is shown in Figure 3.19.

```
// FindSalesAmount.java: Find the sales amount to get the desired
// commission
public class FindSalesAmount
{
  // Main method
  public static void main(String[] args)
  {
    // The commission sought
    final double COMMISSION_SOUGHT = 25000;
    double commission = 0;
    double salesAmount = 1;
```

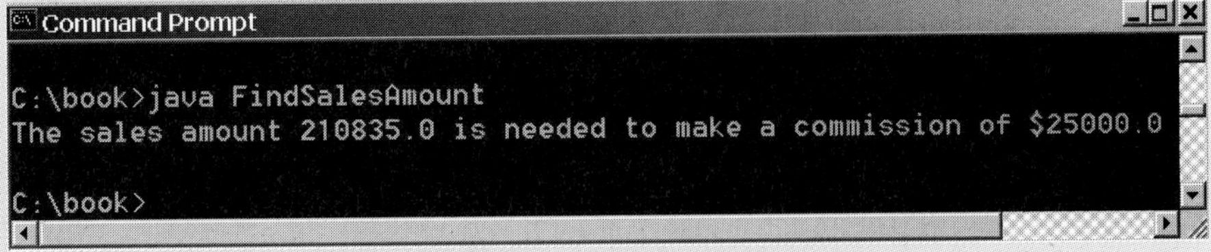

Figure 3.19 *The program finds the sales amount for the given commission.*

continues

Example 3.7 continued

```
    while (commission < COMMISSION_SOUGHT)
    {
      // Compute commission
      if (salesAmount >= 10001)
        commission = 5000*0.08 + 5000*0.1 + (salesAmount-10000)*0.12;
      else if (salesAmount >= 5001)
        commission = 5000*0.08 + (salesAmount-5000)*0.10;
      else
        commission = salesAmount*0.08;

      salesAmount++;
    }

    // Display the sales amount
    System.out.println("The sales amount " + salesAmount +
      " is needed to make a commission of $" + COMMISSION_SOUGHT);
  }
}
```

Example Review

The `while` loop is used to repeatedly compute `commission` for an incremental `salesAmount`. The loop terminates when `commission` is greater than or equal to a constant `COMMISSION_SOUGHT`.

In Exercise 3.11, you will rewrite this program to let the user enter `COMMISSION_SOUGHT` dynamically from the keyboard.

You can improve the performance of this program by using the *binary search* approach. The binary search approach is introduced in Chapter 7, "Arrays and Vectors." A rewrite of this program using a binary search is proposed in Exercise 7.5.

Example 3.8 Displaying a Pyramid of Numbers

In this example, you will use nested loops to print the following output:

```
    1
   212
  32123
 4321234
543212345
```

Your program prints five lines. Each line consists of three parts. The first part comprises the spaces before the numbers; the second part, the leading numbers, such as 3 2 1 on line 3; and the last part, the ending numbers, such as 2 3 on line 3.

You can use an outer loop to control the lines. At the nth row, there are 5 – n leading spaces, the leading numbers are n, n – 1, . . . , 1, and the ending numbers are 2, . . . , n. You can use three separate inner loops to print each part.

The complete program is given below, and a sample run of the program is shown in Figure 3.20.

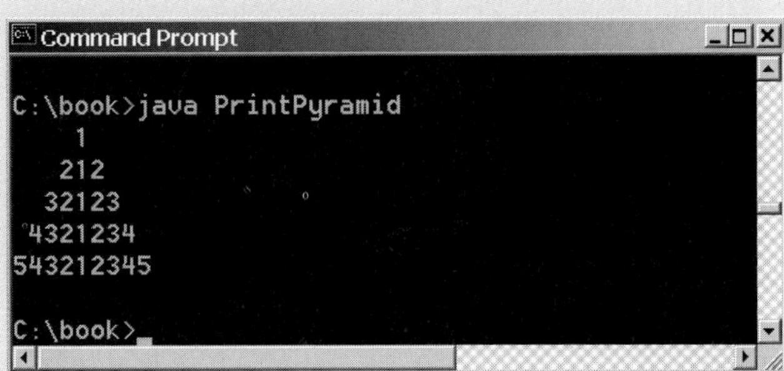

Figure 3.20 *The program uses nested loops to print numbers in a triangular pattern.*

```
// PrintPyramid.java: Print a pyramid of numbers
public class PrintPyramid
{
  // Main method
  public static void main(String[] args)
  {
    for (int row = 1; row < 6; row++)
    {
      // Print leading spaces
      for (int column = 1; column < 6 - row; column++)
        System.out.print(" ");

      // Print leading numbers
      for (int num = row; num >= 1; num--)
        System.out.print(num);

      // Print ending numbers
      for (int num = 2; num <= row; num++)
        System.out.print(num);

      // Start a new line
      System.out.println();
    }
  }
}
```

Example Review

Printing patterns like this one and the ones in Exercises 3.9 and 3.10 is my favorite exercise for practicing loop control statements. The key is to understand the pattern and to describe it using loop control variables.

The last line in the outer loop, `System.out.println()`, does not have any argument in the method. This call has the effect of printing a blank line.

Example 3.9 Displaying Prime Numbers

This example displays the first 50 prime numbers in five lines, each of which contains 10 numbers. An integer greater than 1 is *prime* if its only positive

continues

Example 3.9 continued

divisor is 1 or itself. For example, 2, 3, 5, and 7 are prime numbers, but 4, 6, 8, and 9 are not.

The problem can be broken into the following tasks:

- For number = 2, 3, 4, 5, 6, . . . , test whether the number is prime.
- Determine whether a given number is prime.
- Count the prime numbers.
- Print each prime number, and print 10 numbers per line.

Obviously, you need to write a loop and repeatedly test whether a new number is prime. If the number is prime, increase the count by 1. The count is 1 initially. When the count exceeds 50, the loop terminates. The program is given as shown below. Figure 3.21 contains a sample run of the program.

```
// PrimeNumber.java: Print first 50 prime numbers
public class PrimeNumber
{
  // Main method
  public static void main(String[] args)
  {
    int count = 1; // Count the number of prime numbers
    int number = 2; // A number to be tested for primeness
    boolean isPrime = true;  // Is the current number is prime?

    System.out.println("The first 50 prime numbers are \n");

    // Repeatedly test if a new number is prime
    while (count <= 50)
    {
      // Assume the number is prime
      isPrime = true;

      // Set isPrime to false, if the number is not prime
      for (int divisor = 2; divisor <= number/2; divisor++)
      {
        if (number % divisor == 0)
        // If true, the number is not prime
        {
          isPrime = false;
          break;  // Exit the for loop
        }
      }

      // Print the prime number and increase the count
      if (isPrime)
      {
        if (count%10 == 0)
        {
          // Print the number and advance to the new line
          System.out.println(number);
        }
        else
          System.out.print(number + " ");
```

continues

```
          count++;  // Increase the count
        }

        // Check if the next number is prime
        number++;
      }
    }
  }
```

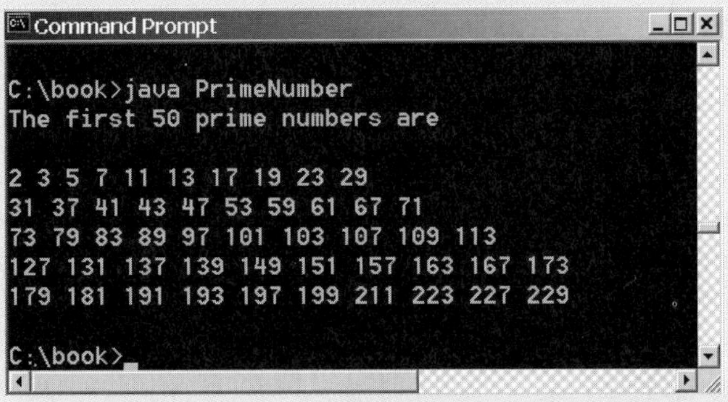

```
C:\book>java PrimeNumber
The first 50 prime numbers are

2 3 5 7 11 13 17 19 23 29
31 37 41 43 47 53 59 61 67 71
73 79 83 89 97 101 103 107 109 113
127 131 137 139 149 151 157 163 167 173
179 181 191 193 197 199 211 223 227 229

C:\book>_
```

Figure 3.21 *The program displays the first 50 prime numbers.*

Example Review

This is a complex example for novice programmers. The key to developing a programmatic solution to this problem, and to many other problems, is to break it into subproblems and develop solutions for each of them. Do not attempt to develop a complete solution in the first trial. Instead, begin by writing the code to determine whether a given number is prime, then expand the program to test whether other numbers are prime in a loop.

To determine whether a number is prime, check whether it is divisible by a number between 2, and number/2, inclusive. If so, it is not a prime number; otherwise, it is a prime number. For a prime number, display it. If the count is divisible by 10, advance to a new line. The program ends when the count becomes 51.

Chapter Summary

Program control specifies the order in which statements are executed in a program. In this chapter, you learned about two types of control statements: selection control and loop control.

Selection statements are used for building selection steps into programs. You learned several forms of selection statements: `if` statements, `if . . . else` statements, nested `if` statements, `switch` statements, and conditional expressions.

The various `if` statements all make control decisions based on a Boolean expression. Based on the `true` or `false` evaluation of that expression, these statements take one of two possible courses. The `switch` statement makes control decisions based on a switch variable of type `char`, `byte`, `short`, `int`, or `boolean`.

You learned three types of repetition statements: the `while` loop, the `do` loop, and the `for` loop. In designing loops, you need to consider both the loop control structure and the loop body.

The `while` loop checks the `continue-condition` first. If the condition is `true`, the loop body is executed; if it is `false`, the loop terminates. The `do` loop is similar to the `while` loop, except that the `do` loop executes the loop body first and then checks the `continue-condition` to decide whether to continue or to terminate.

Since the `while` loop and the `do` loop contain the `continue-condition`, which is dependent on the loop body, the number of repetitions is determined by the loop body. The `while` loop and the `do` loop are often used when the number of repetitions is unspecified.

The `for` loop is generally used to execute a loop body for a predictable number of times; this number is not determined by the loop body. The loop control has three parts. The first is a control variable, which has an initial value. The second is the `continue-condition`, which determines whether the loop body is to be executed. The third part is the adjustment statement, which changes the control variable. Usually, the loop control variable is initialized and changed in the control structure.

You also learned the `break` and `continue` keywords. The `break` keyword immediately ends the innermost loop, which contains the break. The `continue` keyword only ends the current iteration.

Review Questions

3.1 Show the output, if any, of the following code:

```
x = 2;
y = 3;
if (x > 2)
  if (y > 2)
  {
    int z = x + y;
    System.out.println("z is " + z);
  }
else
  System.out.println("x is " + x);
```

3.2 Show the output, if any, of the following code:

```
x = 3;
y = 2;
if (x > 2)
{
  if (y > 2)
  {
    int z = x + y;
    System.out.println("z is " + z);
```

```
    }
  }
  else
    System.out.println("x is " + x);
```

3.3 Can you convert a `switch` statement to an equivalent `if` statement, or vice versa? What are the advantages of using a `switch` statement?

3.4 Write a statement to determine whether an integer i is even or odd.

3.5 What data types are required for a `switch` variable? If the keyword `break` is not used after a case is processed, what is the next statement to be executed?

3.6 What is `y` after the following `switch` statement is executed?

```
x = 3;
switch (x+3)
{
  case 6:  y = 1;
  default: y += 1;
}
```

3.7 Use a `switch` statement to rewrite the following `if` statement:

```
if (a == 1)
  x += 5;
else if (a == 2)
  x += 10;
else if (a == 3)
  x += 16;
else if (a == 4)
  x += 34;
```

3.8 What is `y` after the following statement is executed?

```
x = 0;
y = (x > 0) ? 1 : -1;
```

3.9 How many times is the following loop body repeated? What is the printout of the loop?

```
int i = 1;
while (i < 10)
  if ((i++)%2 == 0)
    System.out.println(i);
```

3.10 What are the differences between a `while` loop and a `do` loop?

3.11 Do the following two statements result in the same value in sum?

```
for (int i=0; i<10; ++i)
{
  sum += i;
}

for (int i=0; i<10; i++)
{
  sum += i;
}
```

3.12 What are the three parts of a `for` loop control? Write a `for` loop that will print the numbers from 1 to 100.

3.13 What does the following statement do?

```
for (;;)
{
  do something;
}
```

3.14 If a variable is declared in the `for` loop control, can it be used after the loop exits?

3.15 Can you convert a `for` loop to a `while` loop? List the advantages of using `for` loops.

3.16 Convert the following `for` loop statement to a `while` loop and to a `do` loop:

```
long sum = 0;
for (int i=0; i<=1000; i++)
  sum = sum + i;
```

3.17 What is the keyword `break` for? Will the following program terminate? If so, give the output.

```
int balance = 1000;
while (true)
{
  if (balance < 9)
    break;
  balance = balance - 9;
}

System.out.println("Balance is " + balance);
```

3.18 What is the keyword `continue` for? Will the following program terminate? If so, give the output.

```
int balance = 1000;
while (true)
{
  if (balance < 9)
    continue;
  balance = balance - 9;
}

System.out.println("Balance is " + balance);
```

3.19 Can you always convert a `while` loop into a `for` loop? Convert the following `while` loop into a `for` loop.

```
int i = 1;
int sum = 0;
while (sum < 10000)
{
  sum = sum + i;
  i++;
}
```

3.20 Rewrite the programs `TestBreak` and `TestContinue` without using `break` and `continue` (see Examples 3.5 and 3.6).

3.21 After the `break outer` statement is executed in the following loop, which statement is executed?

```
outer:
  for (int i=1; i<10; i++)
  {
  inner:
    for (int j=1; j<10; j++)
    {
      if (i*j > 50)
        break outer;

      System.out.println(i*j);
    }
  }

next:
```

a. The statement labeled inner.

b. The statement labeled outer.

c. The statement labeled next.

d. None of the above.

3.22 After the `continue outer` statement is executed in the following loop, which statement is executed?

```
outer:
  for (int i=1; i<10; i++)
  {
  inner:
    for (int j=1; j<10; j++)
    {
      if (i*j > 50)
        continue outer;

      System.out.println(i*j);
    }
  }

next:
```

a. The control is in the outer loop and the next iteration of the outer loop is executed.

b. The control is in the inner loop and the next iteration of the inner loop executed.

c. The statement labeled next.

d. None of the above.

Programming Exercises

3.1 Modify Example 2.3, "Computing Changes." Display the non-zero denominations only. Display singular words for single units like 1 dollar and 1 penny, and display plural words for more than one unit like 2 dollars and 3 pennies.

3.2 Write a program that will sort three integers. The integers are entered from the keyboard and stored in variables `num1`, `num2`, and `num3`, respectively. The program sorts the numbers so that `num1 <= num2 <= num3`.

3.3 Write a program that will compute sales commissions using the same scheme as in Example 3.7. Your program reads the sales amount from the keyboard and displays the result on the console.

3.4 Write a program that will read an unspecified number of integers and determine how many positive and negative values have been read. Your program ends when the input is 0.

3.5 Write a program that will read integers and find the total and average of the input values. Your program ends with the input 0.

3.6 Use a `while` loop to find the smallest `n` such that n^2 is greater than 12000.

3.7 Modify Example 3.9 to print all prime numbers between 2 and 10000. Display 8 prime numbers per line.

3.8 Write a program that reads an integer and displays all its smallest factors. For example, if the input integer is 120, the output should be as follows: 2, 2, 2, 3, 5.

3.9 Write a nested `for` loop that will print the following output:

```
1
1 2
1 2 3
1 2 3 4
1 2 3 4 5
```

3.10 Write a nested `for` loop that will print the following output:

```
                              1
                          1   2   1
                      1   2   4   2   1
                  1   2   4   8   4   2   1
              1   2   4   8  16   8   4   2   1
          1   2   4   8  16  32  16   8   4   2   1
      1   2   4   8  16  32  64  32  16   8   4   2   1
  1   2   4   8  16  32  64 128  64  32  16   8   4   2   1
```

Hint: Here is the pseudocode solution:

```
for the row from 0 to 7
{
  Pad leading blanks in a row using a loop like this:
  for the column from 1 to 7-row
    System.out.print("    ");

  Print left half of the row for numbers 1, 2, 4, up to
  2^row using a look like this:
  for the column from 0 to row
    System.out.print((int)Math.pow(2, column)+"    ");

  Print the right half of the row for numbers
  2^(row-1), 2^(row-2), ..., 1 using a loop like this:
  for (int column=row-1; column>=0; col--)
```

```
      System.out.print((int)Math.pow(2, column) + "    ");

    Start a new line
    System.out.println();
  }
```

The `Math.pow()` method was introduced in Example 2.2. Can you write this program without using it?

3.11 Rewrite Example 3.7 as follows:

- Use a `for` loop instead of a `while` loop;
- Let the user enter COMMISSION_SOUGHT from the keyboard instead of fixing it as a constant.

3.12 You can approximate π by using the following series:

```
π = 4*(1-1/3+1/5-1/7+1/9-1/11+1/13+...)
```

Write a program that will find out how many terms of this series you need to use before you first get 3.14159.

3.13 A *cancellation error* occurs when you are manipulating a very large number with a very small number. The large number may cancel out the smaller number. For example, on some computers the result of 10000.0 + 0.000001 is equal to 10000.0. To avoid cancellation errors and obtain more accurate results, carefully select the order of computation. For example, in computing the following series, you will obtain more accurate results by computing from right to left:

```
1 + 1/2 + 1/3 + ... + 1/n
```

Write a program to compare the results of the summation of the preceding series, computing from left to right and from right to left with `n` = 50000.

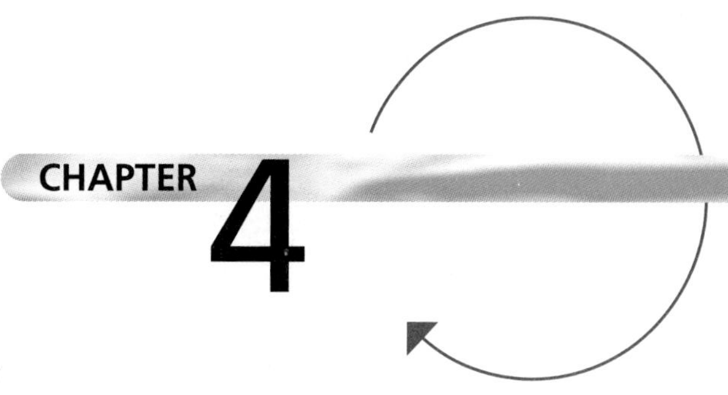

METHODS

Objectives

- Understand and use methods.
- Create and invoke methods.
- Understand the role of arguments in a method.
- Pass parameters of primitive types to a method.
- Understand method overloading.
- Know the concept of method abstraction.
- Become familiar with the `Math` class.
- Use the divide-and-conquer approach to developing programs.
- Become familiar with recursion. (Optional)

Introduction

In Chapter 2, "Primitive Data Types and Operations," and Chapter 3, "Control Statements," you learned about such methods as `println`, which is used to print messages, and `readDouble` and `readInt`, which are used to read `double` and `int` numbers, respectively. A method is a collection of statements that are grouped together to perform an operation. When you call the `println` method, for example, the system actually executes several statements in order to display a message on the console.

This chapter introduces several topics that involve, or are related to, methods. You will learn how to create your own methods with or without return values, invoke a method with or without parameters, overload methods using the same names, write a recursive method that invokes itself, and apply method abstraction in the program design.

Creating a Method

In general, a method has the following structure:

```
modifier returnValueType methodName(list of parameters)
{
  // Method body;
}
```

Let's take a look at a method created to find which of two integers is the maximum. This method, named `max`, has two `int` parameters, `num1` and `num2`, the larger of which is returned by the method. Figure 4.1 illustrates the components of this method.

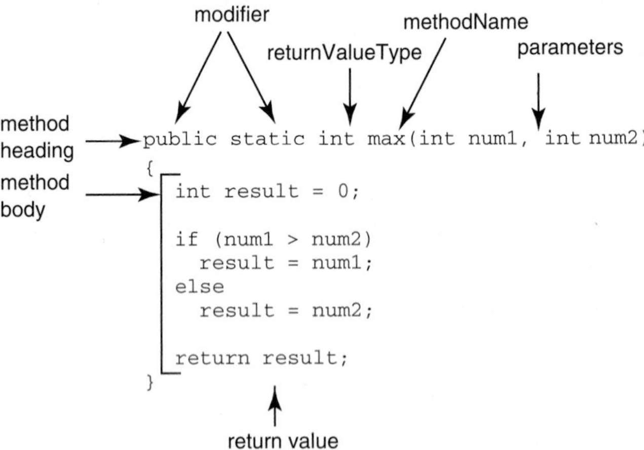

Figure 4.1 *A method declaration consists of a method heading and a method body.*

The method heading specifies the *modifiers, return value type, method name,* and the *parameters* of the method. The modifier, which is optional, tells the compiler how the method should be called. Modifiers are discussed in more depth in Chapter 5, "Programming with Objects and Classes."

A method may return a value. The `returnValueType` is the data type of the value the method returns. If the method does not return a value, the `returnValueType` is the keyword `void`. For example, the `returnValueType` in the `main` method is `void`. All methods except constructors require `returnValueType`. Constructors are introduced in Chapter 5.

A method can have a list of parameters, known as *formal parameters*, in the method specification. When a method is called, its formal parameters are replaced by variables or data, which are referred to as *actual parameters*. Parameters are optional.

The method body contains a collection of statements that define what the method does. The method body of the `max` method simply uses an `if` statement to determine which number is larger and return the value of that number. The keyword `return` is required for nonvoid methods other than those with a `void` return value type. The return statement can also be used in a void method for terminating the method and returning to the method's caller. The method terminates when a `return` statement is executed.

NOTE

In certain other languages, methods are referred to as *procedures* and *functions*. A method with a nonvoid return value type is called a *function*; a method with a `void` return value type is called a *procedure*.

TIP

You need to declare a separate data type for each parameter. For instance, `int num1, num2` should be replaced by `int num1, int num2`.

Calling a Method

In creating a method, you give a definition of what the method is to do. To use a method, you have to call or invoke it. There are two ways to call a method; the choice is based on whether the method returns a value or not.

If the method returns a value, a call to the method is usually treated as a value. For example,

```
int larger = max(3, 4);
```

calls `max(3, 4)` and assigns the result of the method to the variable `larger`. Another example of a call that is treated as a value is

```
System.out.println(max(3,4));
```

which prints the return value of the method call `max(3,4)`.

If the method returns `void`, a call to the method must be a statement. For example, the method `println` returns `void`. The following call is a statement:

```
System.out.println("Welcome to Java!");
```

NOTE

A method with nonvoid return value type can also be invoked as a statement in Java. In this case, the caller simply ignores the return value. In the majority of cases, a call to a method with return value is treated as a value. In some cases, however, the caller is not interested in the return value. For example, many methods in database applications return a Boolean value to indicate whether the operation is successful. You can choose to ignore the return value if you know the operation will always succeed. I recommend, though, that you always treat a call to a method with return value as a value in order to avoid programming errors.

When a program calls a method, program control is transferred to the called method. A called method returns control to the caller when its return statement is executed or when its method-ending right brace is reached.

The example shown below gives the complete program that is used to test the `max` method.

Example 4.1 Testing the `max` Method

This example demonstrates how to create and invoke the `max` method. The output of the program is shown in Figure 4.2.

```
// TestMax.java: demonstrate using the max method
public class TestMax
{
  // Main method
  public static void main(String[] args)
  {
    int i = 5;
    int j = 2;
    int k = max(i, j);
    System.out.println("The maximum between " + i +
      " and " + j + " is " + k);
  }

  // A method for finding a max between two numbers
  static int max(int num1, int num2)
  {
    if (num1 > num2)
      return num1;
    else
      return num2;
  }
}
```

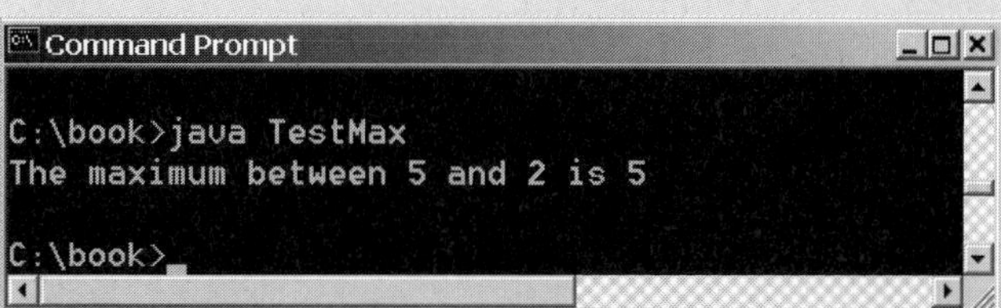

Figure 4.2 *The program invokes* `max(i, j)` *in order to get the maximum value between* `i` *and* `j`.

Example Review

This program contains the `main` method and the `max` method. The `main` method is just like any other method, with one exception: It is invoked by the Java interpreter.

The `main` method's heading is always the same, like the one in this example, with modifiers `public` and `static`, return value type `void`, method name `main`, and parameters `String[] args`. `String[]` indicates that `args` is an array of `String`, a subject addressed in Chapter 7, "Arrays and Vectors."

The statements in `main` may invoke other methods that are defined in the class that contains the `main` method or in other classes. In this example, the `main` method invokes `max(i, j)`, which is defined in the same class with the `main` method.

When the `max` method is invoked, variable `i`'s value 5 is passed to `num1`, and variable `j`'s value 2 is passed to `num2` in the `max` method. The flow of control transfers to the max method. The max method is executed. When one of the `return` statements in the `max` method is executed, the `max` method returns the control to its caller (in this case the caller is the `main` method). This process is illustrated in Figure 4.3.

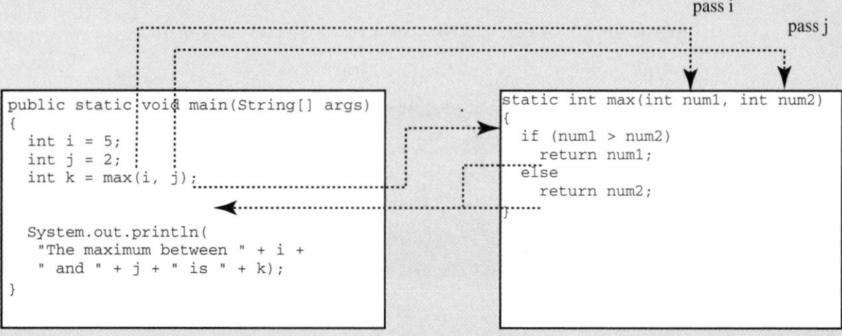

Figure 4.3 *When invoking the* `max` *method, the flow of control transfers to the* `max` *method. Once the* `max` *method is finished, it returns the control back to the caller.*

Passing Parameters

The power of a method is its ability to work with parameters. You can use `println` to print any message and `max` to find the maximum between any two numbers. When calling a method, you need to provide actual parameters, which must be given in the same order as their respective formal parameters in the method specification. This is known as *parameter order association.* For example, the following method prints a message `n` times:

```
void nPrintln(String message, int n)
{
  for (int i=0; i<n;  i++)
    System.out.println(message);
}
```

You can use `nPrintln("Hello", 3)` to print "Hello" three times. The `nPrintln("Hello", 3)` statement passes the actual string parameter, `"Hello"`, to the formal parameter, `message`; passes `3` to `n`; and prints `"Hello"` three times. However, the statement `nPrintln(3, "Hello")` would be wrong. The data type of `3` does not match the data type for the first formal parameter, `message`, nor does the second parameter, `"Hello"`, match the second formal parameter, `n`.

TIP

The actual parameters must match the formal parameters in type, order, and number.

Pass by Value

When invoking a method with parameters, a copy of the value of the actual parameter is passed to the method. This is referred to as *pass by value.* The actual variable outside the method is not affected, regardless of the changes made to the formal parameter inside the method. Let's examine an interesting scenario in the following example, in which the formal parameters are changed in the method, but the actual parameters are not affected.

The program given below shows the effect of pass by value.

Example 4.2 Testing Pass by Value

This program creates a method for swapping two variables. The `swap` method is invoked by passing two actual parameters. Interestingly, after invoking the method, the actual parameters are not changed. The output of the program is shown in Figure 4.4.

```
// TestPassByValue.java: Demonstrate passing values to methods
public class TestPassByValue
{
  // Main method
```

```
    public static void main(String[] args)
    {
      // Declare and initialize variables
      int num1 = 1;
      int num2 = 2;

      System.out.println("Before invoking the swap method, num1 is " +
        num1 + " and num2 is " + num2);

      // Invoke the swap method to attempt to swap two variables
      swap(num1, num2);

      System.out.println("After  invoking the swap method, num1 is " +
        num1 + " and num2 is " + num2);
    }

    // The method for swapping two variables
    static void swap(int n1, int n2)
    {
      System.out.println("    Inside the swap method");
      System.out.println("    Before swapping n1 is " + n1
        + " n2 is " + n2);

      // Swapping n1 with n2
      int temp = n1;
      n1 = n2;
      n2 = temp;

      System.out.println("    After  swapping n1 is " + n1
        + " n2 is " + n2);
    }
  }
```

```
C:\book>java TestPassByValue
Before invoking the swap method, num1 is 1 and num2 is 2
    Inside the swap method
    Before swapping n1 is 1 n2 is 2
    After  swapping n1 is 2 n2 is 1
After  invoking the swap method, num1 is 1 and num2 is 2

C:\book>
```

Figure 4.4 *After invoking the* swap *method, the contents of the actual parameters are not swapped.*

Example Review

Before invoking the swap method, num1 is 1 and num2 is 2. After invoking the swap method, num1 remains to be 1 and num2 remains to be 2. Their values are not swapped by invoking the swap method. As shown in Figure 4.5, the values of the actual parameters num1 and num2 are passed to n1 and n2, but n1 and n2 have their own memory location independent from num1 and num2. Therefore, changes in n1 and n2 do not affect the contents in num1 and num2.

continues

Example 4.2 continued

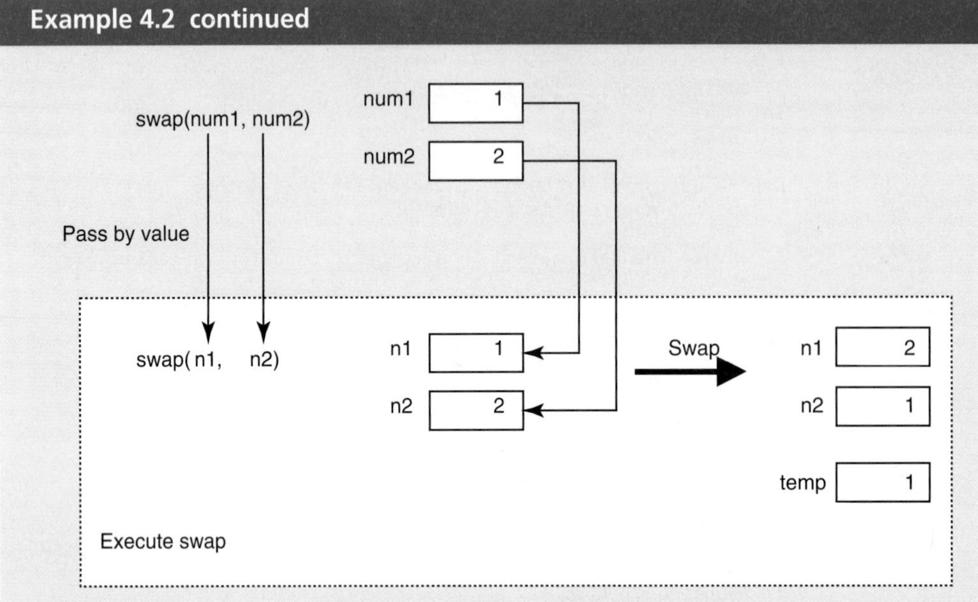

Figure 4.5 *After invoking the* swap *method, the contents of the actual parameters are not swapped.*

Another twist is to change the formal parameter name `n1` in `swap` to `num1`. What effect does this have? No change occurs because it does not matter whether the formal parameter and the actual parameter have the same name. The formal parameter is a local variable in the method with its own memory space. The local variable is allocated when the method is invoked, and it disappears when the method is completed.

Overloading Methods

The `max` method that was used earlier works only with the `int` data type. But what if you need to find which of two floating-point numbers has the maximum value? The solution is to create another method with the same name but with different parameters, as shown in the following code:

```
double max(double num1, double num2)
{
  if (num1 > num2)
    return num1;
  else
    return num2;
}
```

If you call `max` with `int` parameters, the `max` method that expects `int` parameters will be invoked; if you call `max` with `double` parameters, the `max` method that expects `double` parameters will be invoked. This is referred to as *method overloading*;

that is, two methods have the same name but different parameter profiles. The method name along with the parameter profiles is referred to as the *method signature*. The Java compiler determines which method is used based on the method signature.

Example 4.3 Overloading the max Method

In the following program, three methods are created. The first finds the maximum integer; the second finds the maximum double; the third finds the maximum among three double values. All three methods are named max. The output of the program is shown in Figure 4.6.

```
// TestMethodOverloading.java: Demonstrate method overloading
public class TestMethodOverloading
{
  // Main method
  public static void main(String[] args)
  {
    // Invoke the max method with int parameters
    System.out.println("The maximum between 3 and 4 is "
      + max(3, 4));

    // Invoke the max method with the double parameters
    System.out.println("The maximum between 3.0 and 5.4 is "
      + max(3.0, 5.4));

    // Invoke the max method with three double parameters
    System.out.println("The maximum between 3.0, 5.4, and 10.14 is "
      + max(3.0, 5.4, 10.14));
  }

  // Find the max between two int values
  static int max(int num1, int num2)
  {
    if (num1 > num2)
      return num1;
    else
      return num2;
  }

  // Find the max between two double values
  static double max(double num1, double num2)
  {
    if (num1 > num2)
      return num1;
    else
      return num2;
  }

  // Find the max among three double values
  static double max(double num1, double num2, double num3)
  {
    return max(max(num1, num2), num3);
  }
}
```

continues

Example 4.3 continued

```
C:\book>java TestMethodOverloading
The maximum between 3 and 4 is 4
The maximum between 3.0 and 5.4 is 5.4
The maximum between 3.0, 5.4, and 10.14 is 10.14

C:\book>
```

Figure 4.6 *The program invokes three different* `max` *methods*—`max(3, 4)`, `max(3.0, 5.4)`, *and* `max(3.0, 5.4, 10.14)`—*even though they all have the same name.*

Example Review

When calling `max(3, 4)`, the `max` method for finding maximum integers is invoked. When calling `max(3.0, 5.4)`, the `max` method for finding maximum doubles is invoked. When calling `max(3.0, 5.4, 10.14)`, the `max` method for finding maximum among three double values is invoked.

Can you invoke the `max` method with an `int` value and a `double` value such as `max(2, 2.5)`? If so, which of the `max` methods is invoked? The answer to the first question is yes. The answer to the second is that the `max` method for finding the maximum of two `double` values is invoked. The actual parameter 2 is automatically converted into a double value and passed to this method.

You may be wondering why this method is not invoked for the call `max(3, 4)`. The Java compiler first chooses the method that exactly matches the actual parameters. If an exact match cannot be found, it then tries to match actual parameters with formal parameters by automatic casting. In this case, the `max` method for finding the maximum of two integers is the exact match for `max(3, 4)`.

TIP
Overloading methods can make programs clear and more readable. Methods that perform closely related tasks should be given the same name.

NOTE
The overloaded methods must differ in their parameter profiles. You cannot overload methods based on different modifiers or return types.

Method Abstraction

The key to developing software is to apply the concept of abstraction. You will learn many levels of abstractions from this book. *Method abstraction* is defined as separating the use of a method from its implementation. The client can use a method without knowing how the method is implemented. If you decide to change the implementation, the client program will not be affected provided that you don't change the method signature. So the implementation of the method is hidden in a black box from the client, as shown in Figure 4.7.

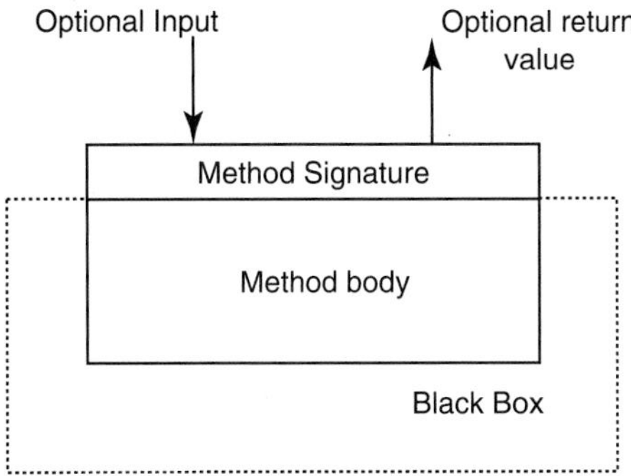

Figure 4.7 *You can think of the method body as a black box that contains the detailed implementation for the method.*

You have already used the method `System.out.print` to display a string, used the method `MyInput.readDouble` to read a double number from the keyboard, and used the method `max` to find the maximum number. You know how to write the code to invoke these methods in your program, but as a user of these methods, you are not required to know how they are implemented.

The *Math* Class

The `Math` class contains the methods needed to perform basic mathematical functions. You have already used the `pow(a, b)` method for computing a^b in Example 2.2, "Computing Mortgages." This section introduces other useful methods in the `Math` class. These methods can be categorized as trigonometric methods, exponent methods, and service methods. Besides methods, the `Math` class provides two useful `double` constants, `PI` and `E` (the base of natural logarithms). You can use these constants as `Math.PI` and `Math.E` in any program.

Trigonometric Methods

The `Math` class contains the following trigonometric methods, among many others:

```
public static double sin(double radians)

public static double cos(double radians)

public static double tan(double radians)

public static double asin(double radians)

public static double acos(double radians)

public static double atan(double radians)
```

Each method has a single `double` parameter, and its return type is `double`. The parameter represents an angle in radians. 1 degree is equal to $\pi/180$ in radians. For example, `Math.sin(Math.PI)` returns the trigonometric sine of π.

Exponent Methods

There are four methods related to exponents in the `Math` class:

```
public static double exp(double a)
// Return e raised to the power of a (e^a)

public static double log(double a)
// Return the natural logarithm of a (ln(a) = log_e(a))

public static double pow(double a, double b)
// Return a raised to the power of b (a^b)

public static double sqrt(double a)
// Return the square root of √a
```

Note that the parameter in the `sqrt` method must not be negative.

The *min, max, abs, round,* and *random* Methods

Other useful methods in the `Math` class are the `min` and `max` methods, the `abs` method, the `round` method, and the random generator `random`.

The `min` and `max` methods are overloaded to return the minimum and maximum numbers between two numbers (`int`, `long`, `float`, or `double`). For example, `max(3.4, 5.0)` returns `5.0`, and `min(3, 2)` returns `2`.

The `abs` method is overloaded to return the absolute value of the number (`int`, `long`, `float`, and `double`). For example, `abs(-3.03)` returns `3.03`.

The `round` method has two overloaded versions. One is for rounding a `float` value to an `int` value, and the other for rounding a `double` value to a `long` value.

The `Math` class also has a powerful method, `random`, which generates a random double floating-point number greater than or equal to 0.0 and less than 1.0 (`0<=Math.random()<1.0`).

Example 4.4 Computing Mean and Standard Deviations

In this example, you will write a program that generates 10 random numbers and computes the mean and standard deviations of these numbers using the following formula:

$$mean = \frac{\sum_{i=1}^{n} x_i}{n}$$

$$deviation = \sqrt{\frac{\sum_{i=1}^{n} x_i^2 - mean}{n - 1}}$$

A sample run of the following program is shown in Figure 4.8.

```
// ComputeMeanDeviation.java: Demonstrate using the math methods
public class ComputeMeanDeviation
{
  // Main method
  public static void main(String[] args)
  {
    int number = 0; // Store a random number
    double sum = 0; // Store the sum of the numbers
    double squareSum = 0; // Store the sum of the squares

    // Create 10 numbers, find its sum, and its square sum
    for (int i=1; i<=10; i++)
    {
      // Generate a new random number
      number = (int)Math.round(Math.random()*1000);
      System.out.println(number);

      // Add the number to sum
      sum += number;

      // Add the square of the number to squareSum
      squareSum += Math.pow(number, 2); // Same as number*number;
    }

    // Find mean
    double mean = sum/10;

    // Find standard deviation
    double deviation = Math.sqrt((squareSum - mean)/(10 - 1));

    // Display result
    System.out.println("The mean is " + mean);
    System.out.println("The standard deviation is " + deviation);
  }
}
```

Example Review

The program demonstrates the use of the math methods `random`, `round`, `pow`, and `sqrt`. The `random` method generates a `double` value that is greater than or equal to 0 and less than 1.0. After multiplying the generated number by 1000, the random number is greater than or equal to 0 and less than 1000.0. The `round` method converts the double number into a `long` value, which is cast into an `int` variable `number`.

Invoking `pow(number, 2)` returns the square of `number`. The `sqrt` method is used to get the square root of a `double` value.

The formula for computing standard deviation used in the example is an approximation of the following formal formula:

continues

Example 4.4 continued

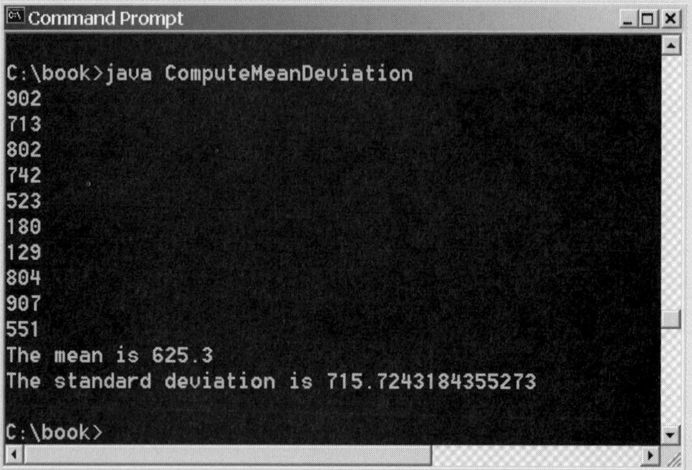

Figure 4.8 *The program finds the mean and standard deviations of 10 random integers.*

$$deviation = \sqrt{\frac{\sum_{i=1}^{n}(x_i - mean)^2}{n - 1}}$$

To use this formula, you have to store the individual numbers using an array so that they can be used after the mean is obtained. See Exercise 7.2 for writing a program to compute the standard deviation using this accurate formula.

Case Studies

Method abstraction hides the details of the implementation of the method from the client who invokes the method. This is known as *information hiding*. The concept of method abstraction can be applied to developing programs. When writing a large program, you can use the "divide and conquer" strategy to decompose a large problem into subproblems. The subproblems can be further decomposed into smaller problems that can be easily managed.

The following example demonstrates the divide-and-conquer approach to the development of programs.

Example 4.5 Displaying Calendars

In this example, a program is created that displays the calendar for a given month of the year. The program prompts the user to enter the year and the month, and then displays the entire calendar for the month, as shown in Figure 4.9.

```
C:\book>java PrintCalendar
Enter full year: 2000
Enter month in number between 1 and 12: 6
       June, 2000
-----------------------------
 Sun Mon Tue Wed Thu Fri Sat
                   1   2   3
   4   5   6   7   8   9  10
  11  12  13  14  15  16  17
  18  19  20  21  22  23  24
  25  26  27  28  29  30

C:\book>
```

Figure 4.9 *After prompting the user to enter the year and the month, the program displays the calendar for that month.*

How would you get started on such a program? Would you start coding immediately? Beginning programmers often start by trying to work out the solution to every detail. Although details are important in the final program, concern for detail in the early stages could block the problem-solving process. To make problem-solving flow as smoothly as possible, this example begins by using method abstraction to isolate details from design and only later implements details.

For this example, the problem is first broken into two subproblems: get input from the user, and print the monthly calendar. At this stage, the creator of the program should be concerned with what the subproblems will achieve, but not with the ways in which they will get input and print the calendar for the month. You can draw a structure chart to help visualize the decomposition of the problems (see Figure 4.10).

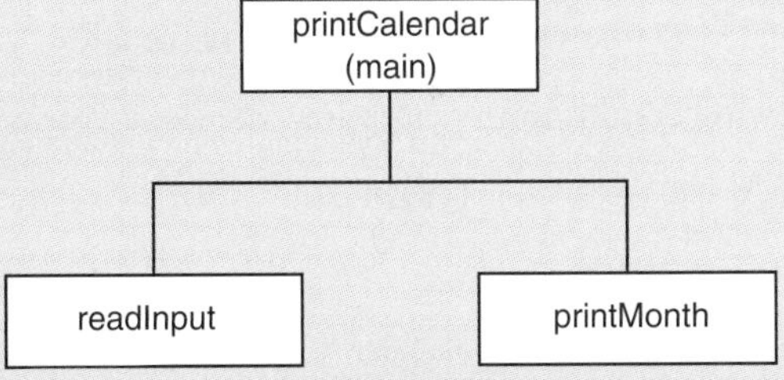

Figure 4.10 *The structure chart shows that the* `printCalendar` *problem is divided into two subproblems:* `readInput` *and* `printMonth`.

continues

Example 4.5 continued

Use `System.out.println(messageString)` to display a message to prompt the user for the year and the month. Then use `MyInput.readInt()` to get the input.

In order to print the calendar for a month, you need to know which day of the week is the first day of the month and how many days the month has. With this information, you can print the title and body of the calendar. Therefore, the print-month problem would be further decomposed into four subproblems: get the start day, get the number of days in the month, print title, and print month body.

How would you get the start day for the first date in a month? There are several ways to find the start day. The simplest approach is to use the `Date` and `Calendar` classes in Chapter 12, "Internationalization." For now, an alternative approach is used. Assume that you know that the start day (`startDay1800 = 3`) for Jan 1, 1800 is Wednesday. You could compute the total number of days (`total NumOfDays`) between Jan 1, 1800, and the first date of the calendar month. The start day for the calendar month is `(totalNumOfDays + startDay1800) % 7`.

To compute the total days (`totalNumOfDays`) between Jan 1, 1800 and the first date of the calendar month, you could find the total number of days between the year 1800 and the calendar year and then figure out the total number of days prior to the calendar in the calendar year. The sum of these two totals is `totalNumOfDays`.

You would also need to know the number of days in a month and in a year. Remember the following:

- January, March, May, July, August, October, and December have 31 days.
- April, June, September, and November have 30 days.
- February has 28 days during a regular year and 29 days during a leap year. A regular year, therefore, has 365 days, while a leap year has 366 days.

Use the following condition to determine whether a year is a leap year:

```
if ((year % 400 == 0) || ((year % 4 == 0) && (year % 100 != 0)))
  return true;
else
  return false;
```

To print a title, use `println()` to display three lines, as shown in Figure 4.11.

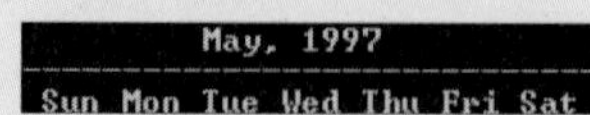

Figure 4.11 *The calendar title consists of three lines: month and year, a dash line, and the names of the seven days of the week.*

To print a body, first pad some space before the start day and then print the lines for every week, as shown for June 2000 (see Figure 4.9).

In general, a subproblem corresponds to a method in the implementation, although some are so simple that this is unnecessary. You would need to decide which modules to implement as methods and which to combine in other methods. Decisions of this kind should be based on whether the overall program will be easier to read as a result of your choice. In this example, the subproblem `readInput` was implemented in the `main` method (see Figure 4.12).

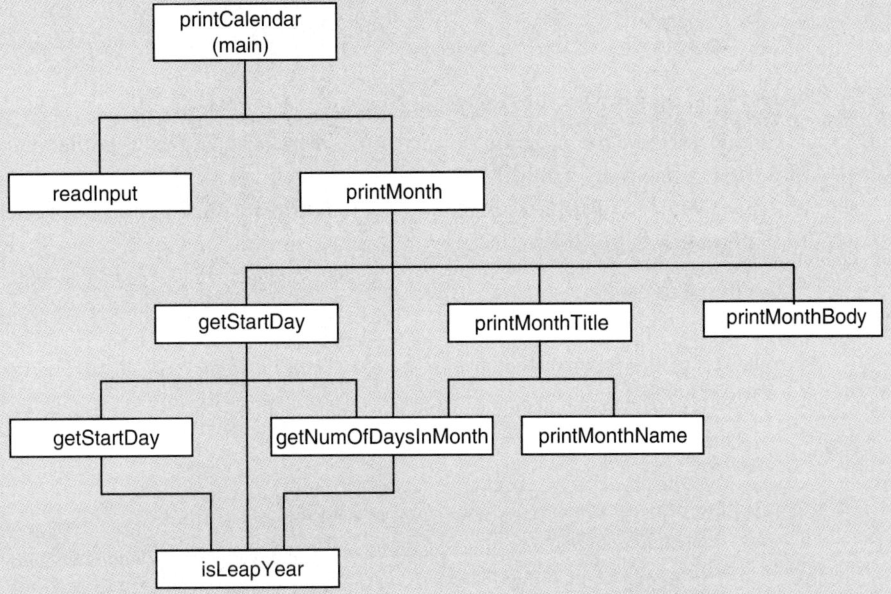

Figure 4.12 *The structure chart shows the hierarchical relationship of the subproblems in the program.*

When implementing the program, use the "top-down" approach. In other words, implement one method in the structure chart at a time—from the top to the bottom. You could use stubs for the methods waiting to be implemented. Implement the `main` method first and then use a stub for the `printMonth` method. For example, let `printMonth` display the year and the month in the stub. Thus, your program may begin like this:

```
// PrintCalendar.java: Print a calendar for a given month in a year
public class PrintCalendar
{
  // Main method
  public static void main(String[] args)
  {
    // The user enters year and month
```

continues

Example 4.5 continued

```
    System.out.print("Enter full year: ");
    int year = MyInput.readInt();
    System.out.print("Enter month in number between 1 and 12: ");
    int month = MyInput.readInt();

    // Print calendar for the month of the year
    printMonth(year, month);
  }

  // Print the calendar for a month in a year
  static void printMonth(int year, int month)
  {
    // Stub
    System.out.println("Year is " + year + " and month is " + month);
  }
}
```

Compile and test the program, and fix any errors. You can now implement the `printMonth` method. For the methods that are invoked from the `printMonth` method, you can again use the stubs. This top-down incremental implementation approach helps isolate the programming errors and makes debugging easy.

The complete program is given as follows:

```
// PrintCalendar.java: Print a calendar for a given month in a year
public class PrintCalendar
{
  // Main method
  public static void main(String[] args)
  {
    // The user enters year and month
    System.out.print("Enter full year: ");
    int year = MyInput.readInt();
    System.out.print("Enter month in number between 1 and 12: ");
    int month = MyInput.readInt();

    // Print calendar for the month of the year
    printMonth(year, month);
  }

  // Print the calendar for a month in a year
  static void printMonth(int year, int month)
  {
    // Get start day of the week for the first date in the month
    int startDay = getStartDay(year, month);

    // Get number of days in the month
    int numOfDaysInMonth = getNumOfDaysInMonth(year, month);

    // Print headings
    printMonthTitle(year, month);

    // Print body
    printMonthBody(startDay, numOfDaysInMonth);
  }

  // Get the start day of the first day in a month
  static int getStartDay(int year, int month)
```

```
{
  // Get total number of days since 1/1/1800
  int startDay1800 = 3;
  long totalNumOfDays = getTotalNumOfDays(year, month);

  // Return the start day
  return (int)((totalNumOfDays + startDay1800) % 7);
}

// Get the total number of days since Jan 1, 1800
static long getTotalNumOfDays(int year, int month)
{
  long total = 0;

  // Get the total days from 1800 to year -1
  for (int i = 1800; i < year; i++)
  if (isLeapYear(i))
    total = total + 366;
  else
    total = total + 365;

  // Add days from Jan to the month prior to the calendar month
  for (int i = 1; i < month; i++)
    total = total + getNumOfDaysInMonth(year, i);

  return total;
}

// Get the number of days in a month
static int getNumOfDaysInMonth(int year, int month)
{
  if (month == 1 || month==3 || month == 5 || month == 7 ||
    month == 8 || month == 10 || month == 12)
    return 31;

  if (month == 4 || month == 6 || month == 9 || month == 11)
    return 30;

  if (month == 2)
    if (isLeapYear(year))
      return 29;
    else
      return 28;

  return 0; // If month is incorrect.
}

// Determine if it is a leap year
static boolean isLeapYear(int year)
{
  if ((year % 400 == 0) || ((year % 4 == 0) && (year % 100 != 0)))
    return true;

  return false;
}

// Print month body
static void printMonthBody(int startDay, int numOfDaysInMonth)
{
  // Pad space before the first day of the month
  int i = 0;
  for (i = 0; i < startDay; i++)
```

continues

Example 4.5 continued

```
        System.out.print("    ");

      for (i = 1; i <= numOfDaysInMonth; i++)
      {
        if (i < 10)
          System.out.print("   " + i);
        else
          System.out.print("  " + i);

        if ((i + startDay) % 7 == 0)
          System.out.println();
      }

      System.out.println();
    }

    // Print the month title, i.e. May, 1999
    static void printMonthTitle(int year, int month)
    {
      System.out.println("         "+getMonthName(month)+", "+year);
      System.out.println("-----------------------------");
      System.out.println(" Sun Mon Tue Wed Thu Fri Sat");
    }

    // Get the English name for the month
    static String getMonthName(int month)
    {
      String monthName = null;
      switch (month)
      {
        case 1: monthName = "January"; break;
        case 2: monthName = "February"; break;
        case 3: monthName = "March"; break;
        case 4: monthName = "April"; break;
        case 5: monthName = "May"; break;
        case 6: monthName = "June"; break;
        case 7: monthName = "July"; break;
        case 8: monthName = "August"; break;
        case 9: monthName = "September"; break;
        case 10: monthName = "October"; break;
        case 11: monthName = "November"; break;
        case 12: monthName = "December";
      }

      return monthName;
    }
  }
```

Example Review

The program does not validate user input. For instance, if the user enters a month not in the range between 1 and 12, or a year before 1800, the program would display an erroneous calendar. To avoid this error, you can simply add an `if` statement to check the input before printing the calendar.

This program can print calendars for a month but could easily be modified to print calendars for a whole year. Although it can only print months after January 1800, it could also be modified to trace the day of a month before 1800.

See Chapter 12, "Internationalization," to find out how to use the `Date` and `Calendar` classes to simplify the program.

NOTE

Method abstraction helps modularize programs in a neat, hierarchical manner. Programs written as collections of concise methods are easier to write, debug, maintain, and modify than would otherwise be the case. This writing style also promotes method reusability.

TIP

When implementing a large program, use the top-down coding approach. Start with the main method, and code and test one method at a time. Do not write the entire program at once. This approach seems to take more time for coding (because you are repeatedly compiling and running the program), but it actually saves time and makes debugging easier.

Recursion (Optional)

You have seen a method calling another method—that is, a statement contained in the method body calling another method. Can a method call itself? And what happens if it does? This section examines these questions and uses three classic examples to demonstrate recursive programming.

Computing Factorials

Recursion, a powerful mathematical concept, is the process of a function calling itself, directly or indirectly. Many mathematical functions are defined using recursion. The factorial of a number `n` can be recursively defined as follows:

```
0! = 1;
n! = n × (n-1)!; n > 0
```

How do you find `n!` for a given `n`? It is easy to find `1!` because you know `0!` and 1! is 1 × 0!. Assuming that you know `(n-1)!`, `n!` can be obtained immediately using `n × (n-1)!`. Thus, the problem of computing `n!` is reduced to computing `(n-1)!`. When computing `(n-1)!`, you can apply the idea recursively until `n` is reduced to 0.

Let `factorial(n)` be the method for computing `n!`. If you call the method with `n=0`, it immediately returns the result. The method knows how to solve the simplest case, which is referred to as the *base case* or the *stopping condition*. If you call the method with `n>0`, it reduces the problem into a subproblem for computing factorial of `n-1`. The subproblem is essentially the same as the original problem, but is slightly simpler or smaller than the original. Because the subproblem has the same property as the original, you can call the method with a different actual parameter, which is referred to as a *recursive call.*

The recursive algorithm for computing `factorial(n)` can be simply described as follows:

```
if (n==0)
  return 1;
else
  return n*factorial(n-1);
```

A recursive call can result in many more recursive calls because the method is dividing a subproblem into new subproblems. For a recursive method to terminate, the problem eventually must be reduced to a stopping case. When it reaches a stopping case, the method returns a result to its caller. The caller then performs a computation and returns the result to its own caller. This process continues until the result is passed back to the original caller. The original problem can now be solved by multiplying `n` with the result of `factorial(n-1)`.

Example 4.6 Computing Factorials

In this example, a recursive method is written for computing a factorial `factorial(n)`, given index `n`. The test program prompts the user to enter `n`.

A sample run of the program is shown in Figure 4.13.

```
// ComputeFactorial.java: Compute factorial of an integer
public class ComputeFactorial
{
  public static void main(String[] args)
  {
    // Prompt the user to enter an integer
    System.out.println("Please enter a nonnegative integer");
    int n = MyInput.readInt();

    System.out.println("Factorial of " + n + " is " + factorial(n));
  }

  // Recursive method for computing factorial of n
  static long factorial(int n)
  {
    if (n == 0) // Stopping condition
      return 1;
    else
      return n*factorial(n-1); // Call factorial recursively
  }
}
```

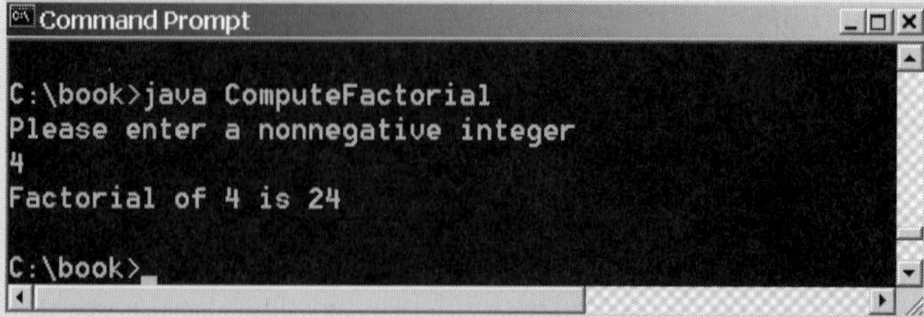

Figure 4.13 *The program prompts the user to enter a non-negative integer and then displays the factorial for the number.*

Example Review

The `factorial` method is essentially a direct translation of the recursive mathematical definition for the factorial into Java code. The call to factorial is recursive, because it calls itself. The parameter passed to `factorial` is decremented until it reaches the base case of 0.

Figure 4.14 illustrates the execution of the recursive calls starting with `n=4`.

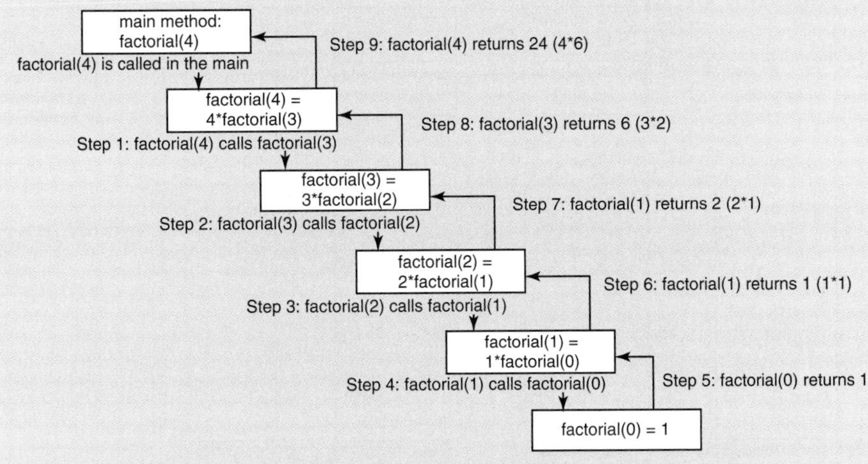

Figure 4.14 *Invoking* `factorial(4)` *spawns recursive calls to* `factorial`.

Each time a method is invoked, the system stores parameters, local variables, and system registers in a space known as a *stack*. When a method calls another method, the caller's stack space is kept intact, and new space is created to handle the new method call. When a method finishes its work and returns to its caller, its associated space is released. The use of stack space for recursive calls is shown in Figure 4.15.

Note

All recursive methods have the following common characteristics:

- One or more base cases (the simplest case) are used to stop recursion.
- Every recursive call reduces the original problem, bringing it increasingly closer to a base case until it becomes that case.

Tip

Infinite recursion can occur if recursion does not reduce the problem in a manner that allows it to eventually converge into the base case.

---

continues

Example 4.6 continued

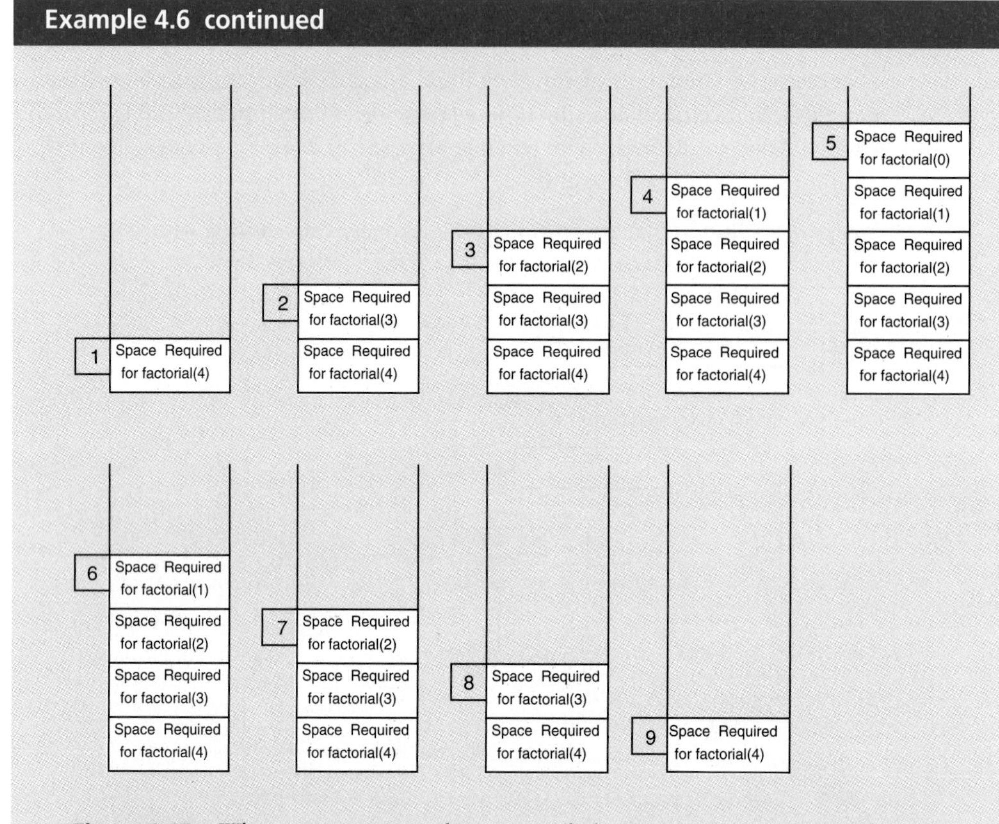

Figure 4.15 *When* `factorial(4)` *is being executed, the* `factorial` *method is called recursively, causing memory space to dynamically change.*

Computing Fibonacci Numbers

In some cases, using recursion enables you to give a natural, straightforward, simple solution to a program that would otherwise be difficult to solve. Consider the well-known Fibonacci series problem. The Fibonacci series

0, 1, 1, 2, 3, 5, 8, 13, 21, 34, . . . ,

begins with 0, and 1, and each subsequent number is the sum of the preceding two numbers in the series. The series can be recursively defined as follows:

```
fib(0) = 0;
fib(1) = 1;
fib(n) = fib(n-2) + fib(n-1); n >= 2
```

The Fibonacci series was named for Leonardo Fibonacci, a medieval mathematician, who originated it to model the growth of the rabbit population. It can be applied in numeric optimization and in various other areas.

How do you find `fib(n)` for a given `n`? It is easy to find `fib(2)` because you know `fib(0)` and `fib(1)`. Assuming that you know `fib(n-2)` and `fib(n-1)`, `fib(n)` can be obtained immediately. Thus, the problem of computing `fib(n)` is reduced to computing `fib(n-2)` and `fib(n-1)`. When computing `fib(n-2)` and `fib(n-1)`, you can apply the idea recursively until `n` is reduced to 0 or 1.

The base case is `n=0` or `n=1`. If you call the method with `n=0` or `n=1`, it immediately returns the result. If you call the method with `n>=2`, it divides the problem into two subproblems for computing `fib(n-1)` and `fib(n-2)` using recursive calls. The recursive algorithm for computing `fib(n)` can be simply described as follows:

```
if ((n==0) || (n==1))
  return n;
else
  return fib(n-1)+fib(n-2);
```

Example 4.7 Computing Fibonacci Numbers

In this example, a recursive method is written for computing a Fibonacci number `fib(n)`, given index `n`. The test program prompts the user to enter index `n`, then calls the method and displays the result.

A sample run of the program is shown in Figure 4.16.

```
// ComputeFibonacci.java: Find a Fibonacci number for a given index
public class ComputeFibonacci
{
  // Main method
  public static void main(String args[])
  {
    // Read the index
    System.out.println("Enter an index for the Fibonacci number");
    int n = MyInput.readInt();
```

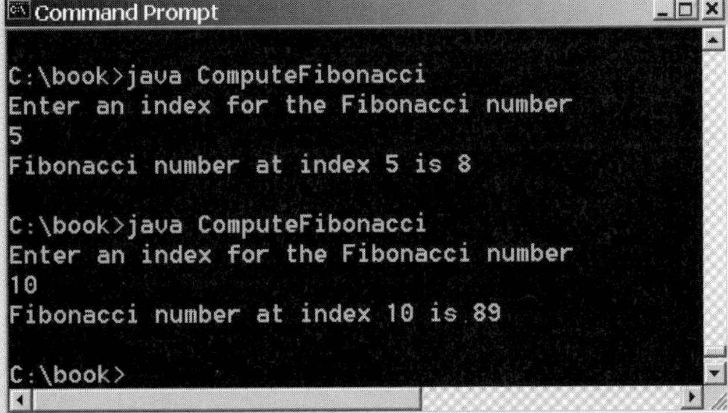

Figure 4.16 *The program prompts the user to enter an index for the Fibonacci number and then displays the number at the index.*

continues

Example 4.7 continued

```
        // Find and display the Fibonacci number
        System.out.println("Fibonacci number at index " + n +
          " is "+fib(n));
      }

      // The method for finding the Fibonacci number
      public static long fib(long n)
      {
        if ((n==0)||(n==1))  // Stopping condition
          return n;
        else  // Reduction and recursive calls
          return fib(n-1) + fib(n-2);
      }
    }
```

Example Review

The implementation of the method is, in fact, very simple and straightforward. The solution is slightly more difficult if you do not use recursion. For a hint on computing Fibonacci numbers using iterations, see Exercise 4.8.

The program does not show the considerable amount of work done behind the scenes by the computer. Figure 4.17, however, shows successive recursive calls for evaluating `fib(4)`. The original method, `fib(4)`, makes two recursive calls—`fib(3)` and `fib(2)`—and then returns `fib(3)+fib(2)`. But in what order are these methods called? In Java, operands are evaluated from left to right. The upper-left corner labels in Figure 4.17 show the order in which methods are called.

As shown in Figure 4.17, there are many duplicated recursive calls. For instance, `fib(2)` is called two times, `fib(1)` is called three times, and `fib(0)` is called two

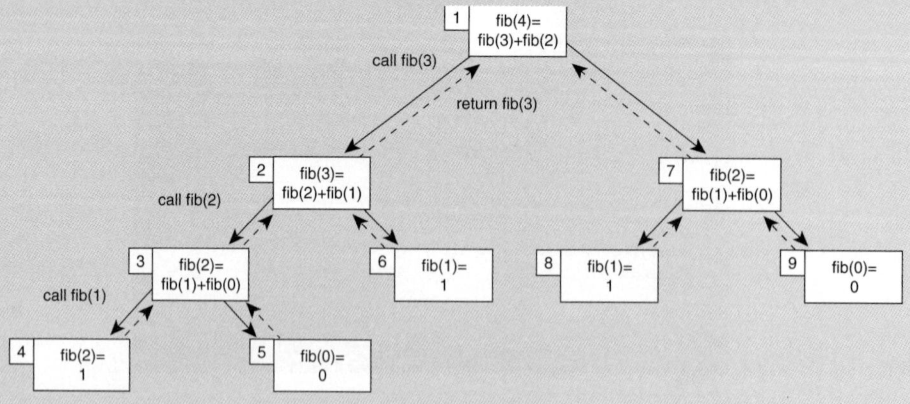

Figure 4.17 *Invoking* `fib(4)` *spawns recursive calls to* `fib`.

times. In general, computing `fib(n)` requires twice as many recursive calls as are needed for computing `fib(n-1)`. As you try larger index values, the number of calls substantially increases.

Besides the large number of recursive calls, the computer requires more time and space to run recursive methods. See Exercise 4.9 for a more efficient method.

The Tower of Hanoi Problem

You have seen a recursive method with a return value. Here is an example of a recursive method with a return type of `void`.

The problem involves moving a specified number of disks of a distinct size from one tower to another while observing the following rules:

- There are *n* disks labeled 1, 2, 3, . . . , *n*, and three towers labeled A, B, and C.
- No disk can be on top of a smaller disk at any time.
- All the disks are initially placed on tower A.
- Only one disk can be moved at a time, and this disk must be the top disk of a tower.

The objective of the problem is to move all the disks from A to B with the assistance of C. For example, if you have three disks, as shown in Figure 4.18, the following steps will move all of the disks from A to B:

1. Move disk 1 from A to B.
2. Move disk 2 from A to C.
3. Move disk 1 from B to C.
4. Move disk 3 from A to B.
5. Move disk 1 from C to A.
6. Move disk 2 from C to B.
7. Move disk 1 from A to B.

In the case of three disks, you can find the solution manually. However, the problem is quite complex for a larger number of disks—even for four. Fortunately, the problem has an inherently recursive nature, which leads to a straightforward recursive solution.

The base case for the problem is `n=1`. If `n=1`, you could simply move the disk from A to B. When `n>1`, you could split the original problem into three subproblems and solve them sequentially.

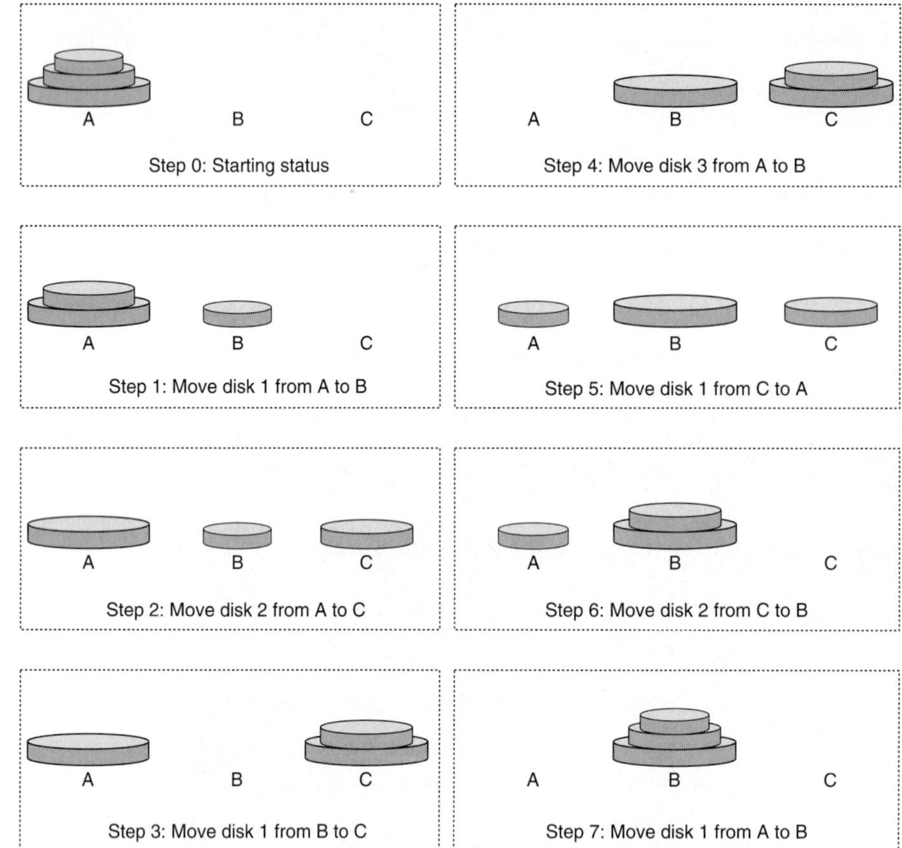

Figure 4.18 *The goal of the Towers of Hanoi problem is to move disks from tower A to tower B without breaking the rules.*

1. Move the first `n-1` disks from A to C with the assistance of tower B.
2. Move disk n from A to B.
3. Move `n-1` disks from C to B with the assistance of tower A.

The following method moves *n* disks from the `fromTower` to the `toTower` with the assistance of the `auxTower`:

```
void moveDisks(int n, char fromTower, char toTower, char auxTower)
```

The algorithm for the method can be described as follows:

```
if (n==1) // Stopping condition
  Move disk 1 from the fromTower to the toTower;
else
{
  moveDisks(n-1, fromTower, auxTower, toTower);
  Move disk n from the fromTower to the toTower;
  moveDisks(n-1, auxTower, toTower, fromTower);
}
```

Example 4.8 Solving the Towers of Hanoi Problem

This example finds a solution for the Towers of Hanoi problem. The program prompts the user to enter the number of disks and invokes the recursive method `moveDisks` to display the solutions to move the disks.

The sample run of the following program appears in Figure 4.19.

```
// TowersOfHanoi.java: Find solutions for the Towers of Hanoi problem
public class TowersOfHanoi
{
  // Main method
  public static void main(String[] args)
  {
    // Read number of disks, n
    System.out.println("Enter number of disks");
    int n = MyInput.readInt();

    // Find the solution recursively
    System.out.println("The moves are:");
    moveDisks(n, 'A', 'B', 'C');
  }

  // The method for finding the solution to move n disks
  // from fromTower to toTower with auxTower
```

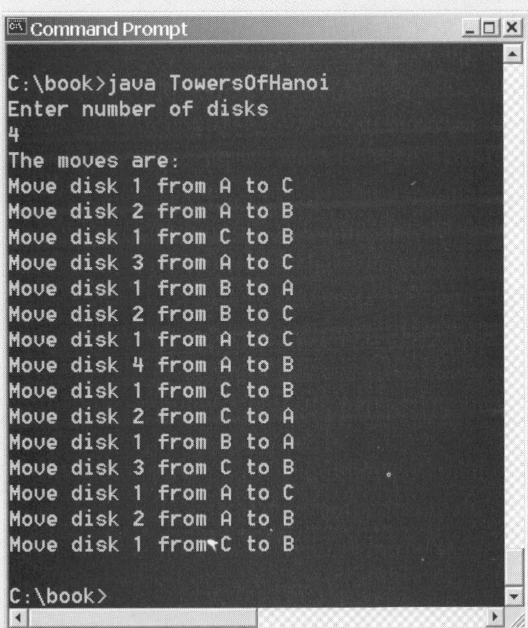

Figure 4.19 *The program prompts the user to enter the number of disks and then displays the steps that must be followed to solve the Towers of Hanoi problem.*

continues

Example 4.8 continued

```
public static void moveDisks(int n, char fromTower,
  char toTower, char auxTower)
{
  if (n==1) // Stopping condition
    System.out.println("Move disk " + n + " from " +
      fromTower+" to " + toTower);
  else
  {
    moveDisks(n-1, fromTower, auxTower, toTower);
    System.out.println("Move disk " + n + " from " +
      fromTower + " to " + toTower);
    moveDisks(n-1, auxTower, toTower, fromTower);
  }
}
}
```

Example Review

This problem is inherently recursive. Using recursion makes it possible to find a natural, simple solution for the problem. It would be difficult to solve it without using recursion.

Consider tracing the program for `n=3`. The successive recursive calls are shown in Figure 4.20. As you can see, writing the program is easier than tracing the recursive calls. The system uses stacks to trace the calls behind the scenes. To some extent, recursion provides a level of abstraction that hides iterations and other details from the user.

The `fib` method in the earlier example returns a value to its caller, but the `moveDisks` method in this example does not return any value to its caller.

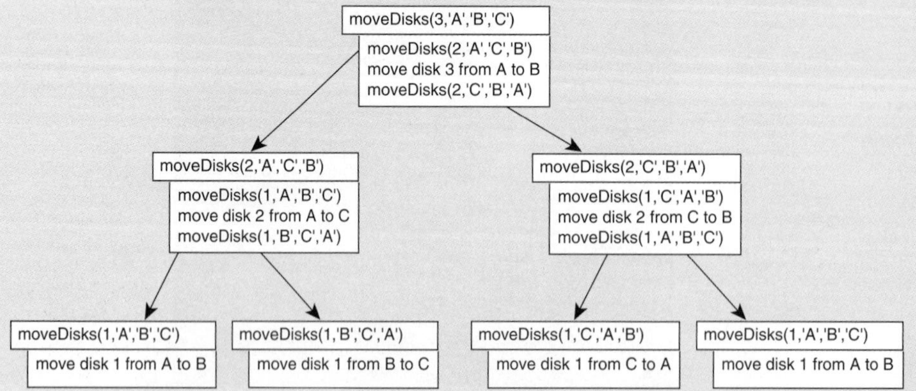

Figure 4.20 *Invoking* `moveDisks(3, 'A', 'B', 'C')` *spawns calls to* `moveDisks` *recursively.*

Recursion versus Iteration

Recursion is an alternative form of program control. It is essentially repetition without a loop control. When you use loops, you specify a loop body. The repetition of the loop body is controlled by the loop control structure. In recursion, the method itself is called repeatedly. The successive recursive calls are handled behind the scenes by the system. There is always a selection statement to control the repetition.

Recursion bears substantial overhead. Each time the program calls a method, the system must assign space for all of the method's local variables and parameters. This can consume considerable memory and requires extra time to manage the additional space.

Any problem that can be solved recursively can be solved nonrecursively with iterations. Recursion has many negative aspects: it uses up too much time and too much memory. Why, then, should you use it? In some cases, using recursion enables you to specify a clear, simple solution that would otherwise be difficult to obtain.

The decision whether to use recursion or iteration should be based on the nature of the problem you are trying to solve and your understanding of the problem. The rule of thumb is to use recursion or iteration to develop an intuitive solution that naturally mirrors the problem. If an iterative solution is obvious, use it. It will generally be more efficient than the recursive option.

NOTE

Your recursive program could run out of memory, causing a runtime error. In Chapter 11, "Exception Handling," you will learn how to handle errors so that the program terminates gracefully when there is a stack overflow.

TIP

If you are concerned about your program's performance, avoid using recursion, because it takes more time and consumes more memory than iteration.

Chapter Summary

Making programs modular and reusable is one of the central goals in software engineering. Java provides many powerful constructs that help to achieve this goal. The method is one such construct.

In this chapter, you have learned how to write reusable methods. You now know how to create a method with a method heading that specifies how it can be used, and a method body that implements it.

You have also learned how to call a method by passing actual parameters that replace the formal parameters in the method specification. The arguments that are passed to a method should have the same number, type, and order as the parameters in the method definition. Outside of the method, the actual values of the primitive parameters that are passed by the value are not affected by the method call.

In addition, you have learned that a method can be overloaded. For example, two methods can have the same name as long as their method parameter profiles differ.

You learned the `Math` class. The `Math` class contains methods that perform trigonometric functions (`sin`, `cos`, `tan`, `acos`, `asin`, `atan`), exponent functions (`exp`, `log`, `pow`, `sqrt`), and some miscellaneous functions (`min`, `max`, `abs`, `round`, `random`). All of these methods operate on `double` values; `min`, `max`, and `abs` can also operate on `int`, `long`, `float`, and `double`.

You are now familiar with the divide-and-conquer strategy. The best way to develop and maintain a large program is to divide it into several subproblems that are individually more manageable than the original problem.

You learned the techniques needed to write recursive methods. Recursion is an alternative form of program control. It can be used to specify simple, clear solutions for inherently recursive problems that would otherwise be difficult to solve.

Review Questions

4.1 What is the purpose of using a method? How do you declare a method? How do you invoke a method?

4.2 What is a return type of a main method?

4.3 What would be wrong with not writing a return statement in a nonvoid method? Can you have a return statement in a void method, such as the following?

```
public static void main(String[] args)
{
  int i;
  while (true)
  {
    i = MyInput.readInt();
    if (i == 0) return;
      System.out.println("i = "+i);
  }
}
```

4.4 What is method overloading? Can you define two methods that have the same name but different parameter types? Can you define two methods in a class that have identical method names and parameter profiles with different return value types or different modifiers?

4.5 How do you pass actual parameters to a method? Can the actual parameter have the same name as its formal parameter?

4.6 What is pass by value? Show the result of the following method call:

```
public class Test
{
  public static void main(String[] args)
  {
    int max = 0;
    max(1, 2, max);
    System.out.println(max);
  }

  public static void max(int value1, int value2, int max)
  {
    if (value1 > value2)
      max = value1;
    else
      max = value2;
  }
}
```

4.7 Show the output of the following program:

```
public class Test
{
  // Main method
  public static void main(String[] args)
  {
    // Initialize times
    int times = 3;
    System.out.println("Before the call, variable times is"
      +times);

    // Invoke nPrintln and display times afterwards
    nPrintln("Welcome to Java!", times);
    System.out.println("After the call, variable times is "
      +times);
  }

  // Print the message n times
  static void nPrintln(String message, int n)
  {
    while (n > 0)
    {
      System.out.println("n = "+n);
      System.out.println(message);
      n--;
    }
  }
}
```

4.8 A call for the method with a `void` return type is always a statement itself, but a call for the method with a nonvoid return type is always a component of an expression. Is this statement true or false?

4.9 Does the `return` statement in the following method cause syntax errors?

```
public static void main(String[] args)
{
  int max = 0;

  if (max != 0)
    System.out.println(max);
  else
    return;
}
```

4.10 In some other languages, you can define methods inside a method. Can you define a method inside a method in Java?

4.11 For each of the following, decide whether a void method or a nonvoid method is the most appropriate implementation:

- Computing a sales commission, given the sales amount and the commission rate.
- Printing a calendar for a month.
- Computing a square root.
- Testing whether a number is even and returning `true` if it is.
- Printing a message a specified number of times.

4.12 Which of the following is a possible output from invoking `Math.random()`?

a. 323.4

b. 0.5

c. 34

d. 1.0

e. None of the above.

4.13 Evaluate the following method calls:

```
Math.sqrt(4)
Math.sin(2*Math.PI)
Math.cos(2*Math.PI)
Math.pow(2, 2)
Math.log(Math.E)
Math.exp(1)
Math.max(2, Math.min(3, 4))
Math.round(-2.5)
Math.round(Math.abs(-2.5))
```

4.14 What is a recursive method?

4.15 Describe the characteristics of recursive methods.

4.16 Show the printout of the following program:

```
public class Test
{
  public static void main(String[] args)
  {
    int sum = xMethod(5);
    System.out.println("Sum is "+sum);
  }

  public static int xMethod(int n)
  {
    if (n==1)
      return 1;
```

```
    else
      return n + xMethod(n-1);
  }
}
```

Programming Exercises

4.1 Write a method to find the ceiling of a double value, and write a method to find its floor. The ceiling of a number `d` is the smallest integer greater than or equal to `d`. The floor of a number `d` is the largest integer less than or equal to `d`. For example, the ceiling of 5.4 is 6, and the floor of 5.4 is 5.

4.2 Write a method to compute the sum of the digits in an integer. Use the following method declaration:

```
public static int sumDigits(long n)
```

For example, `sumDigits(234)` returns 2+3+4=9.

Hint: Use the % operator to extract digits and use the / operator to remove the extracted digit. For instance, 234%10 = 4 and 234/10 = 23. Use a loop to extract and remove the digit repeatedly until all the digits are extracted.

4.3 Write a method to compute future investment value at a given interest rate for a specified number of years. The future investment is determined using the following formula:

```
futureInvestmentValue =
   investmentAmount x (1 + monthlyInterestRate)^(years*12)
```

Use the following method declaration:

```
public static double futureInvestmentValue(double investmentAmount,
                                           double monthlyInterestRate,
                                           int years)
```

For example, `futureInvestmentValue(10000, 0.05, 5)` returns 12833.59.

Hint: Use the `Math.pow(a, b)` method to compute `a` raised to the power of `b`.

4.4 Write a method to convert Celsius to Fahrenheit using the following declaration:

```
public static double celsToFahr(double cels)
```

The formula for the conversion is as follows:

```
Fahrenheit = (9.0/5)*celsius + 32
```

Write a program that uses a `for` loop and calls the `celsToFahr` method in order to produce the following output:

```
Cels. Temp.      Fahr. Temp.
---------------------------
40.00            104.00
39.00            102.20
38.00            100.40
37.00            98.60
36.00            96.80
```

```
35.00          95.00
34.00          93.20
33.00          91.40
32.00          89.60
31.00          87.80
```

4.5 Write a program to print the following table using the `sqrt` method in `Math` class.

```
Number         SquareRoot
--------------------------
0              0.0000
2              1.4142
4              2.0000
6              2.4495
8              2.8284
10             3.1623
12             3.4641
14             3.7417
16             4.0000
18             4.2426
20             4.4721
```

4.6 Write a program that meets the following requirements:

- Declare a method to determine whether an integer is a prime number. Use the following method declaration:

  ```
  public static boolean isPrime(int num)
  ```

  An integer greater than 1 is a *prime number* if its only divisor is 1 or itself. For example, `isPrime(11)` returns `true` and `isPrime(9)` returns `false`.

- Use the `isPrime` method to find first 100 prime numbers, and display every 10 prime numbers in a row as follows:

  2 3 5 7 11 13 17 19 23 29

  31 37 41 43 47 53 59 61 67 71

  73 79 83 89 97 ...

  ...

4.7 You have used the `sqrt` method in the `Math` class in Example 4.4. In this exercise, you will write your own method to compute square roots. The square root of a number, `num`, can be approximated by repeatedly performing a calculation using the following formula:

```
nextGuess = (lastGuess + (num / lastGuess))/2
```

When `nextGuess` and `lastGuess` are almost identical, `nextGuess` is the approximated square root.

The initial guess will be the starting value of `lastGuess`. If the difference between `nextGuess` and `lastGuess` is less than a very small number, such as 0.0001, you can claim that `nextGuess` is the approximated square root of `num`.

4.8 Rewrite Example 4.6 using iterations.

4.9 Write a nonrecursive method to compute Fibonacci numbers.

Hint: To compute `fib(n)` without recursion, you need to obtain `fib(n-2)` and `fib(n-1)` first. Let `f0` and `f1` denote the two previous Fibonacci numbers. The current Fibonacci number would then be `f0+f1`. The algorithm can be described as follows:

```
f0 = 0; // For fib(0)
f1 = 1; // For fib(1)

for (int i=1; i<=n; i++)
{
  currentFib = f0+f1;
  f0 = f1;
  f1 = currentFib;
}

// After the loop, currentFib is fib(n)
```

4.10 Modify Example 4.8 so that the program finds the number of moves needed to move n disks from tower A to B.

4.11 Write a recursive method and a nonrecursive method for the greatest common divisor (GCD). Given two positive integers, the GCD is the largest integer that divides them both. `GCD(m, n)` can be defined as follows:

- `GCD(m, n)` is `n`, if `n` is less than or equal to `m` and `n` divides `m`.
- `GCD(m, n)` is `GCD(n, m)`, if `m` is less than `n`.
- `GCD(m, n)` is `GCD(n, m%n)`, otherwise.

PART II

Object-Oriented Programming

In Part I, "Fundamentals of Programming," you learned how to write simple Java applications using primitive data types, control statements, and methods, all of which are features commonly available in procedural programming languages. Java, however, is a class-centric object-oriented programming language that uses abstraction, encapsulation, inheritance, and polymorphism to provide great flexibility, modularity, and reusability for developing software. In this part of the book you will learn how to define, extend, and work with classes and their objects.

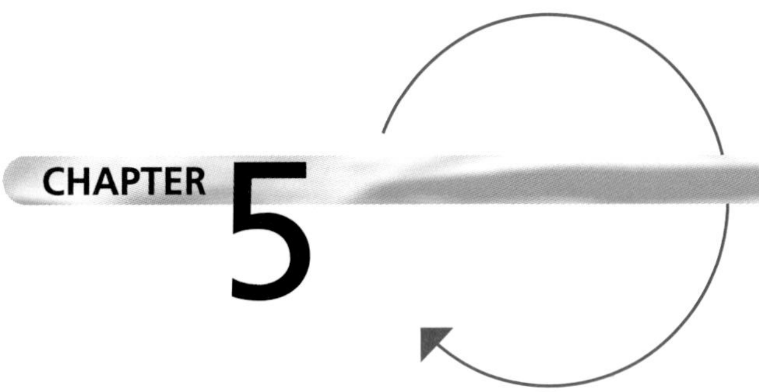

Programming with Objects and Classes

Objectives

- Understand objects and classes and the relationship between them.
- Learn how to define a class and how to create an object of the class.
- Comprehend the roles of constructors.
- Know object references and how to pass objects to methods.
- Understand instance variables and methods.
- Understand class variables, constants, and methods.
- Understand the scope of variables.
- Become familiar with the organization of the Java API.
- Process strings using the `String` class, the `StringBuffer` class, and the `StringTokenizer` class.
- Analyze relationships among classes: association, aggregation, and inheritance.
- Use UML graphical notations to describe classes and objects.

Introduction

Programming in procedural languages like C, Pascal, BASIC, Ada, and COBOL involves choosing data structures, designing algorithms, and translating algorithms into code. An object-oriented language like Java combines the power of procedural languages with an added dimension that provides such benefits as abstraction, encapsulation, reusability, and inheritance.

In procedural programming, data and operations on the data are separate, and this methodology requires sending data to procedures and functions. Object-oriented programming places data and the operations that pertain to them within a single data structure; this approach solves many of the problems inherent in procedural programming because the data and operations are part of the same entity. The object-oriented programming approach organizes programs in a way that more closely models the real world, in which all objects are associated with both attributes and activities. Programming in Java involves thinking in terms of objects; a Java program can be viewed as a collection of cooperating objects.

This chapter introduces the fundamentals of object-oriented programming: declaring classes, creating objects, manipulating objects, and making objects work together.

Objects and Classes

Object-oriented programming (OOP) involves programming using objects. An *object* represents anything in the real world that can be distinctly identified. For example, a student, a desk, a circle, and even a mortgage loan can all be viewed as objects. An object has a state and behavior. The state of an object consists of a set of properties, or fields, and their current values. The behavior of an object is defined by a set of methods. Figure 5.1 shows a diagram of an object with its data fields and methods.

A `Circle` object, for example, has a data field `radius`, which is the property that characterizes a circle. One behavior of a circle is that its area can be computed. A `Circle` object is shown in Figure 5.2.

Classes are constructs that define objects. In a Java class, data are used to describe properties, and methods are used to define behaviors. A class for an object contains a collection of method and data definitions. Here is an example of the class for a circle:

```
class Circle
{
  double radius = 1.0;

  double findArea()
  {
    return radius*radius*3.14159;
  }
}
```

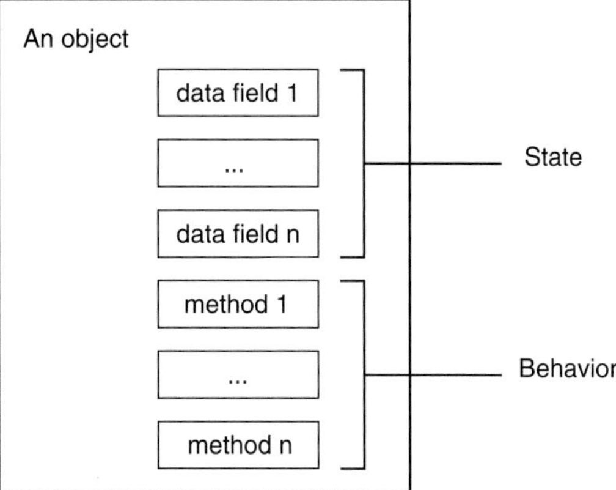

Figure 5.1 *An object contains both state and behavior. The state defines the object, and the behavior defines what the object does.*

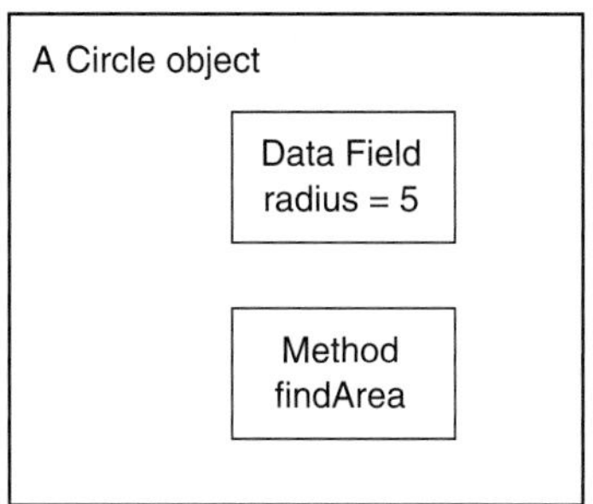

Figure 5.2 *A* `Circle` *object contains the* `radius` *data field and the* `findArea` *method.*

This class is different from all of the other classes you have seen thus far. The `Circle` class does not have a main method. Therefore, you cannot run this class; it is merely a definition used to declare and create `Circle` objects. For convenience, the class that contains the `main` method will be referred to as the *main class* in this book.

A class is a blueprint that defines what an object's data and methods will be. An object is an instance of a class. You can create many instances of a class (see Figure 5.3). Creating an instance is referred to as *instantiation*. The terms *object* and *instance* are often interchangeable. The relationship between classes and objects is analogous to the relationship between apple pie recipes and apple pies. You can make as many apple pies as you want from a single recipe.

NOTE

Figure 5.3 uses the graphical notations adopted in the Unified Modeling Language (UML) to illustrate classes and objects. UML has become the standard for object-oriented modeling. For more information on UML, see

www.rational.com/uml. For a summary of the graphical notations used in this book, see Appendix G, "UML Graphical Notations."

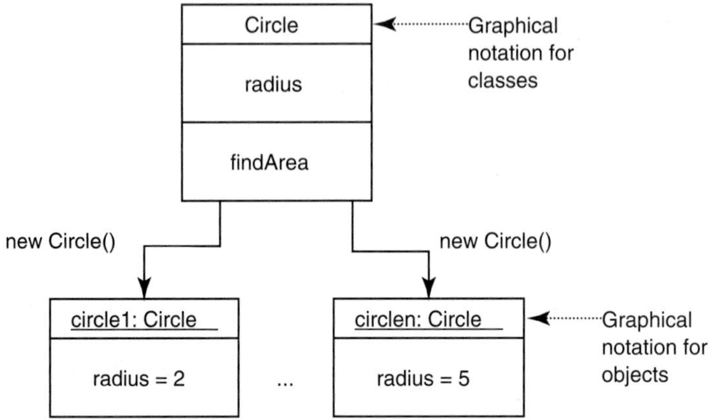

Figure 5.3 *A class can have many different objects.*

Declaring and Creating Objects

In order to declare an object, you must use a variable to represent it (which is similar to declaring a variable for a primitive data type). Here is the syntax for declaring an object:

```
ClassName objectName;
```

The following statement declares the variable `myCircle` to be an instance of the `Circle` class:

```
Circle  myCircle;
```

An object is similar to a variable that has a class type. To create variables of a primitive data type, you simply declare them, as is done in the following line:

```
int i;
```

This statement creates a variable and allocates appropriate memory space for `i`.

However, for object variables, declaring and creating are two separate steps. The declaration of an object simply associates the object with a class, making the object an instance of that class. The declaration does not create the object. To actually create `myCircle`, you need to use the operator `new` in order to tell the computer to create an object for `myCircle` and allocate appropriate memory space for it. Here is the syntax for creating an object:

```
objectName = new ClassName();
```

For example, this statement creates an object, `myCircle`, and allocates memory for it:

```
myCircle = new Circle();
```

You can combine the declaration and instantiation together in one statement using the following syntax:

```
ClassName objectName = new ClassName();
```

Below is an example of creating and instantiating `myCircle` in one step:

```
Circle myCircle = new Circle();
```

Differences between Variables of Primitive Types and Object Types

Every variable represents a memory location that holds a value. For a variable of a primitive type, the value is of the primitive type. For a variable of an object type, the value is a reference to where the object is located. For this reason, a variable of an object type is referred to as a *reference variable*. For example, as shown in Figure 5.4, the value of `int` variable `i` is `int` value 1, and the value of Circle object `c` holds the reference to where the contents of the object `c` are stored in the memory.

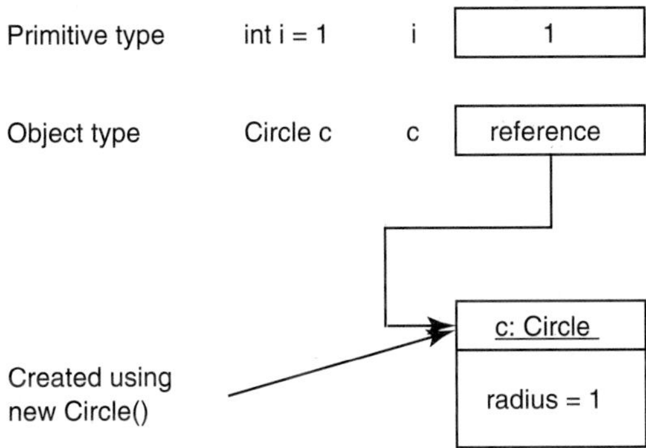

Figure 5.4 *A variable of a primitive type holds the value of the primitive type, and a variable of an object type holds the reference to where the object is stored in the memory.*

When a variable of an object type is declared, the variable holds a special Java value, `null`, which means that the object has not been created. Once an object is created, its reference is assigned to the variable. For example, the statement

```
c = new Circle();
```

creates a `Circle` object by allocating the memory space for the object and assigns its memory reference to the variable `c`.

When you assign one variable into another, the other variable is set to the same value. For a variable of a primitive type, the real value of one variable is assigned to the other variable. For a variable of an object type, the reference of one variable is assigned to the other variable. As shown in Figure 5.5, the assignment statement `i = j` copies the contents of `j` into `i` for primitive variables, and the assignment statement c1 = c2 copies the reference of c2 into c1 for object variables. After the assignment, variable c1 and c2 refer to the same object.

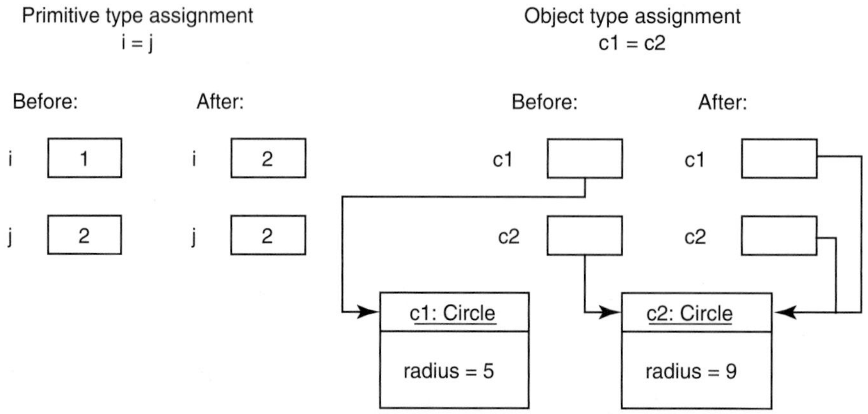

Figure 5.5 *Copying an object variable to another does not make a copy of the object; it merely assigns the reference of one object to the other variable.*

Garbage Collection

As shown in Figure 5.5, after the assignment statement c1 = c2, c1 points to the same object referenced by c2. The object previously referenced by c1 is no longer useful. This object is known as *garbage*. Garbage occupies memory space. The Java runtime system detects garbage and automatically reclaims the space it occupies. This process is known as *garbage collection*.

NOTE

If you know that an object is no longer needed, you can explicitly assign null to a reference variable for the object. The Java VM will automatically collect the space if the object is not referenced by any variable.

Accessing an Object's Data and Methods

After an object is created, its data and methods can be accessed using the following dot notation:

objectName.data—References an object's data

objectName.method—References an object's method

For example, myCircle.radius indicates what the radius of myCircle is, and myCircle.findArea() returns the area of myCircle.

The data field radius is referred to as an *instance variable* because it is dependent on a specific instance. For the same reason, the method findArea is referred to as an *instance method*, because you can only invoke it on a specific instance.

NOTE

You can create an anonymous object without explicitly assigning it to a variable, as shown below:

```
new Circle();
```

This statement creates an anonymous `Circle` object. You cannot access the contents of an anonymous object, since there is no explicit reference to it. Anonymous objects are used in Chapter 8, "Getting Started with Graphics Programming."

Example 5.1 Using Objects

The program in this example creates a `Circle` object from the `Circle` class and uses the data and method in the object. The output of the program is shown in Figure 5.6.

```
// TestCircle.java: Demonstrate creating and using an object
public class TestCircle
{
  // Main method
  public static void main(String[] args)
  {
    Circle myCircle = new Circle();  // Create a Circle object
    System.out.println("The area of the circle of radius "
      + myCircle.radius + " is " + myCircle.findArea());
  }
}

// Define a circle
class Circle
{
  double radius = 1.0;

  // Find the area of this circle
  double findArea()
  {
    return radius*radius*3.14159;
  }
}
```

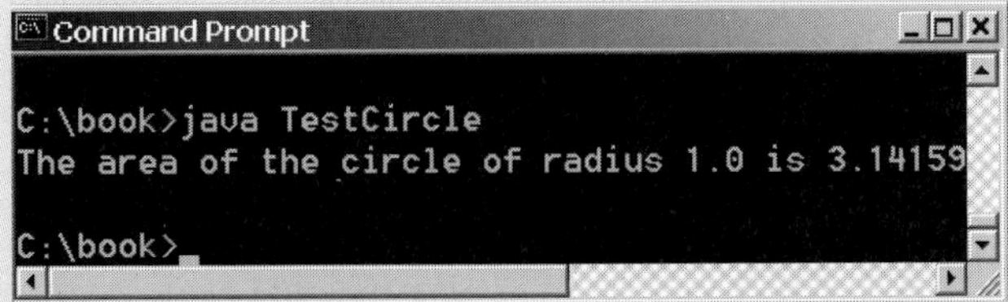

Figure 5.6 *This program creates a* `Circle` *object and displays its* `radius` *and* `area`.

continues

Example 5.1 continued

Example Review

The program contains two classes. The first class, `TestCircle`, is the main class. Its sole purpose is to test the second class, `Circle`. Every time you run the program, the Java runtime system invokes its `main` method in the main class.

You can put the two classes into one file, but only one class in the same file is a public class. Furthermore, the public class must have the same name as the file name. Therefore, the file name is TestCircle.java if both `TestCircle` and `Circle` classes are in the same file.

The main class contains the `main` method that creates an object of the `Circle` class and prints its radius and area. The `Circle` class contains the `findArea` method and the `radius` data field.

To write the `findArea` method in a procedural programming language like Pascal, you would pass radius as argument to the method. But in the object-oriented programming, `radius` and `findArea` are defined in the same class. The `radius` is a data member in the `Circle` class, which is accessible by the `findArea` method. In the procedural programming languages, data and method are separated, but in an object-oriented programming language, data and methods are defined together in a class.

The `findArea` method is an instance method that is always invoked by an instance in which the `radius` is specified.

There are many ways to write Java programs. For instance, you can combine the two classes in the example into one, as follows:

```
public class TestCircle
{
  double radius = 1.0;

  // Find the area of this circle
  double findArea()
  {
    return radius*radius*3.14159;
  }

  // Main method
  public static void main(String[] args)
  {
    // Create a Circle object
    TestCircle myCircle = new TestCircle();
    System.out.println("The area of the circle of radius "
      + myCircle.radius + " is " + myCircle.findArea());
  }
}
```

In this revised program, `radius` and `findArea` are the members of the `TestCircle` class. Since `TestCircle` contains a main method, it can be executed by the Java interpreter. The main method creates `myCircle` to be an instance of `TestCircle` and then displays radius and finds area in `myCircle`.

TIP

You must always create an object before manipulating it. Manipulating an object that has not been created would cause a `NullPointer` exception. Exception handling will be introduced in Chapter 11, "Exception Handling."

NOTE

The default value of a data field is `null` for object type, `0` for numerical type, `false` for `boolean` type, and `'\u0000'` for `char` type. For example, if `radius` is not initialized in the `Circle` class, Java assigns a default value of `0` to `radius`. However, Java assigns no default value to a local variable inside a method. The following code is erroneous because `x` is not initialized:

```
class Test
{
  public static void main(String[] args)
  {
    int x; // x has no default value
    System.out.println("x is " + x);
  }
}
```

Constructors

One problem with the `Circle` class that was just discussed is that all of the objects created from it have the same radius (1.0). Wouldn't it be more useful to create circles with radii of various lengths? Java enables you to define a special method in the class, known as the *constructor*, that can be used to initialize an object's data. You can use a constructor to assign an initial radius when you create an object.

The constructor has exactly the same name as the defining class. Like methods, constructors can be overloaded, making it easier to construct objects with different initial data values. Let's see what happens when the following constructors are added to the `Circle` class:

```
// Construct a circle with the specified radius
Circle(double r)
{
  radius = r;
}

// Construct a circle with the default radius
Circle()
{
  radius = 1.0;
}
```

When creating a new `Circle` object that has a radius of 5.0, you can use the following, which assigns 5.0 to `myCircle.radius`:

```
myCircle = new Circle(5.0);
```

If you create a circle using the following statement, the second constructor is used, which assigns the default radius 1.0 to `myCircle.radius`:

```
myCircle = new Circle();
```

A constructor with no parameters is referred to as a *default constructor*. The second constructor is a default constructor. Now you know why the syntax `ClassName()` is used to create the object. This syntax calls a constructor. A constructor can perform any action like a method, but constructors are designed to perform initializing actions, such as initializing the properties of objects.

Note

Constructors are a special kind of method, with two differences:

- Constructors do not have a return type—not even `void`.
- Constructors are invoked using the new operator when an object is created. Constructors play the role of initializing objects.

Example 5.2 Using Constructors

In this example, a program is written that will use constructors in the `Circle` class to create two objects of different radii. The output of the program is shown in Figure 5.7.

```
// TestCircleWithConstructors.java: Demonstrate constructors
public class TestCircleWithConstructors
{
  // Main method
  public static void main(String[] args)
  {
    // Create a Circle with radius 5.0
    Circle myCircle = new Circle(5.0);
    System.out.println("The area of the circle of radius "
      + myCircle.radius + " is " + myCircle.findArea());

    // Create a Circle with default radius
    Circle yourCircle = new Circle();
    System.out.println("The area of the circle of radius "
      + yourCircle.radius + " is " + yourCircle.findArea());
  }
}

// Circle with two constructors
class Circle
{
  double radius;

  // Default constructor
  Circle()
  {
    radius = 1.0;
  }

  // Construct a circle with a specified radius
  Circle(double r)
  {
    radius = r;
  }
```

```
    // Find area of this circle
    double findArea()
    {
      return radius*radius*3.14159;
    }
  }
```

```
C:\book>java TestCircleWithConstructors
The area of the circle of radius 5.0 is 78.53975
The area of the circle of radius 1.0 is 3.14159

C:\book>
```

Figure 5.7 The program constructs two circles of radii 5 and 1, and displays their radii and areas.

Example Review

The new `Circle` class has two constructors. You can specify a radius or use the default radius to create a `Circle` object. In this example, two objects were created. The constructor `Circle(5.0)` was used to create `myCircle` with a radius of 5.0, and the constructor `Circle()` was used to create `yourCircle` with a default radius of 1.0.

These two objects (`myCircle` and `yourCircle`) have different data but share the same methods. Therefore, you can compute their respective areas by using the `findArea()` method.

NOTE
The data members of the class describe the properties (or state) of an object. The methods of the class describe the behaviors of an object. The data members and the methods can be declared in any order in a class.

NOTE
If a class does not define any constructors explicitly, a default constructor is defined implicitly. If a class defines constructors explicitly, a default constructor does not exist unless it is defined explicitly.

Passing Objects to Methods

Just as you can pass the parameters of primitive types to methods, you can also pass the parameters of object types to methods. The following example passes the `myCircle` object as an argument to the method `printCircle()`:

```
class TestPassingObject
{
  public static void main(String[] args)
  {
    Circle myCircle = new Circle(5.0);
```

```
    printCircle(myCircle);
  }

  public static void printCircle(Circle c)
  {
    System.out.println("The area of the circle of radius "
      + c.getRadius() + " is " + c.findArea());
  }
}
```

There are important differences between passing a value of variables of primitive data types and passing objects.

- Passing a variable of a primitive type means that the value of the variable is passed to a formal parameter. Changing the value of the local parameter inside the method does not affect the value of the variable outside the method.
- Passing an object means that the reference of the object is passed to the formal parameter. Any changes to the local object that occur inside the method body will affect the original object that was passed as the argument.

You will see the difference in the next example.

Example 5.3 Passing Objects as Arguments

In this example, a program is written to pass a `Circle` object and an integer value to the method `printAreas`, which prints a table of areas for radii 1, 2, 3, 4, and 5. The output of the program is shown in Figure 5.8.

```
// TestPassingObject.java: Demonstrate passing objects to methods
public class TestPassingObject
{
  // Main method
  public static void main(String[] args)
  {
    // Create a Circle object with default radius 1
    Circle myCircle = new Circle();

    // Print areas for radius 1, 2, 3, 4, and 5.
    int n = 5;
    printAreas(myCircle, n);

    // See myCircle.radius and times
    System.out.println("\n" + "Radius is " + myCircle.radius);
    System.out.println("n is " + n);
  }

  // Print a table of areas for radius
  public static void printAreas(Circle c, int times)
  {
    System.out.println("Radius \t\tArea");
    while (times >= 1)
    {
      System.out.println(c.radius + "\t\t" + c.findArea());
      c.radius++;
      times--;
    }
  }
}
```

```
C:\book>java TestPassingObject
Radius          Area
1.0             3.14159
2.0             12.56636
3.0             28.27431
4.0             50.26544
5.0             78.53975

Radius is 6.0
n is 5

C:\book>
```

Figure 5.8 *The program passes a circle object* `myCircle` *and an integer value* `n` *as parameters to the* `printAreas` *method, which displays a table of the areas for radii 1, 2, 3, 4, and 5.*

Example Review

The `main` method invokes the `printAreas` method by passing an object `myCircle` and an integer `n` to the `printAreas` method, as shown in Figure 5.9.

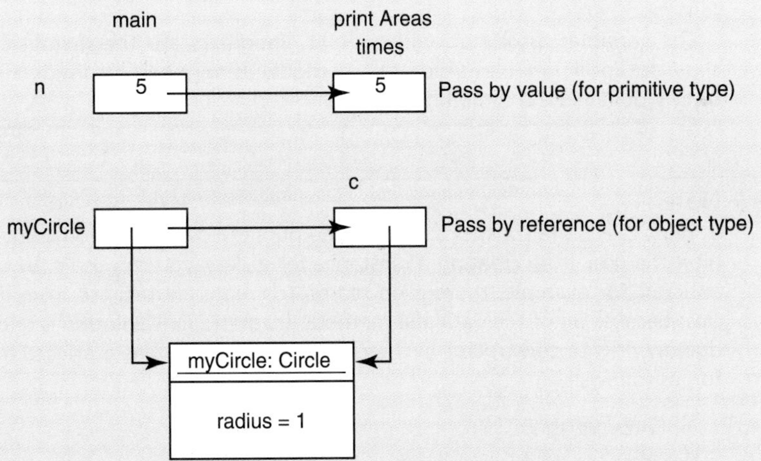

Figure 5.9 *The value of* `n` *is passed to* `times`*, and the reference of* `myCircle` *object is passed to* `c` *in the* `printAreas` *method.*

When passing a parameter of a primitive data type, the value of the actual parameter is passed. In this case, the value of `n` (5) is passed to `times`. Inside the `printAreas` method, the content of `times` is changed, this does not affect the content of `n`. When passing a parameter of an object type, the reference of the object is passed. In this case, `c` contains the reference for object `myCircle`. Therefore, changing properties of the object through `c` inside the `printAreas` method has the same effect as doing so outside the method through variable `myCircle`.

Visibility Modifiers and Accessor Methods

Example 5.3 works fine, but it is not a good practice to let the client modify the properties directly through the object reference. Doing so often causes programming errors that are difficult to debug. To prevent direct modifications of the properties through the object reference, you can declare the property private, using the `private` modifier. Java provides several modifiers that control access to data, methods, and classes. This section introduces the `public`, `private`, and default modifiers.

- **`public:`** Defines classes, methods, and data in such a way that all programs can access them.
- **`private:`** Defines methods and data in such a way that they can be accessed by the declaring class, but not by any other classes.

NOTE

The modifier `private` applies solely to data or methods, not to classes. If `public` or `private` is not used, then by default the classes, methods, and data are accessible by any class in the same package. For information regarding packages, see Appendix H, "Java Packages." Java has another visibility modifier called `protected`, which will be introduced in Chapter 6, "Class Inheritance." Appendix D, "Java Modifiers," contains a table that summarizes all the Java modifiers.

The variables associated with visibility modifiers are the members of the class, not local variables inside the methods. Using modifiers inside a method body would cause a compilation error.

NOTE

In most cases, the constructor should be public. However, if you want to prohibit the user from creating an instance for a class, you can use a private constructor. For example, there is no reason to create an instance from the `Math` class because all of the data and methods are static. One solution is to define a dummy private constructor in the class. The `Math` class has a private constructor, as follows:

```
private Math()
{
}
```

Therefore, the `Math` class cannot be instantiated. The `Math` class comes with the Java system, which was introduced in the section "The `Math` Class" in Chapter 4, "Methods."

The private data fields cannot be accessed by the object through a direct reference. But often the client needs to retrieve and modify the data field. To make the private data fields accessible, you can provide getter methods and setter methods for the private data fields. These methods are referred to as *accessor methods*.

A getter method has the following signature:

```
public returnType getPropertyName()
```

If the `returnType` is `boolean`, the getter method should be defined as follows by convention:

```
public boolean isPropertyName()
```

A setter has the following signature:

```
public void setPropertyName(dataType propertyValue)
```

The example given below demonstrates the use of the `private` modifier and accessor methods.

Example 5.4 Using the `private` Modifier and Accessor Methods

This example declares a new `Circle` class, in which private data are used for the radius, and the accessor methods `getRadius` and `setRadius` are provided for the clients to retrieve and modify the radius. The program creates an instance of the `Circle` class and modifies the radius using the `setRadius` method. The output of the sample run is shown in Figure 5.10.

```
// TestCircleWithPrivateModifier.java: Demonstrate private modifier
public class TestCircleWithPrivateModifier
{
  // Main method
  public static void main(String[] args)
  {
    // Create a Circle with radius 5.0
    Circle myCircle = new Circle(5.0);
    System.out.println("The area of the circle of radius "
      + myCircle.getRadius() + " is " + myCircle.findArea());

    // Increase myCircle's radius by 10%
    myCircle.setRadius(myCircle.getRadius()*1.1);
    System.out.println("The area of the circle of radius "
      + myCircle.getRadius() + " is " + myCircle.findArea());
  }
}

// Declare class Circle with private radius and accessor methods
class Circle
{
  private double radius;

  // Default constructor
  public Circle()
  {
    radius = 1.0;
  }

  // Construct a circle with a specified radius
  public Circle(double r)
  {
    radius = r;
  }
```

continues

Example 5.4 continued

```
    // Getter method for radius
    public double getRadius()
    {
      return radius;
    }

    // Setter method for radius
    public void setRadius(double newRadius)
    {
      radius = newRadius;
    }

    // Find the circle area
    public double findArea()
    {
      return radius*radius*3.14159;
    }
  }
```

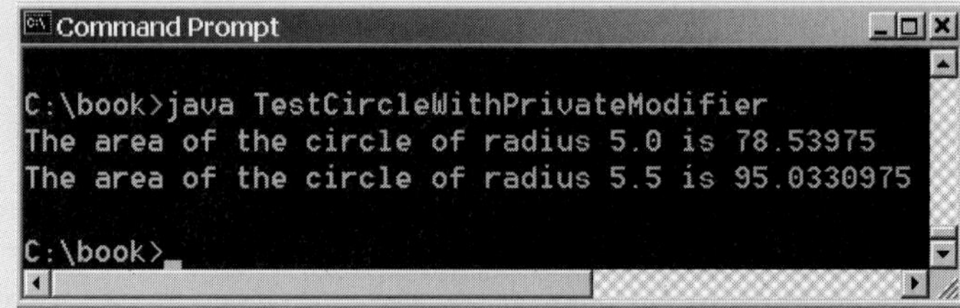

Figure 5.10 *This program creates a* `Circle` *object and uses the getter method to read radius, and the setter method to modify its radius.*

Example Review

The data field `radius` is declared private. Private data can only be accessed within their defining class. You cannot use `myCircle.radius` in the client program. A compilation error would occur if you attempted to access private data from a client.

To access radius, you have to use the `getRadius` method to retrieve the radius and the `setRadius` method to modify the radius.

Class Variables, Constants, and Methods

The variable `radius` in the `Circle` class in the previous examples is known as an *instance variable*. An instance variable is tied to a specific instance of the class; it is not shared among objects of the same class. For example, suppose that you create the following objects:

```
Circle circle1 = new Circle();
Circle circle2 = new Circle(5);
```

The `radius` in `circle1` is independent of the `radius` in `circle2`, and is stored in different memory location. Changes made to `circle1`'s `radius` do not affect `circle2`'s `radius`, and vice versa.

If you want all the instances of a class to share data, use *class variables*. Class variables store values for the variables in a common memory location. Because of this common location, all objects of the same class are affected if one object changes the value of a class variable.

To declare a class variable, put the modifier `static` in the variable declaration. Suppose that you want to track the number of objects of the `Circle` class created, you can define the class variable as follows:

```
static int numOfObjects;
```

Figure 5.11 pictures the instance variables and class variables.

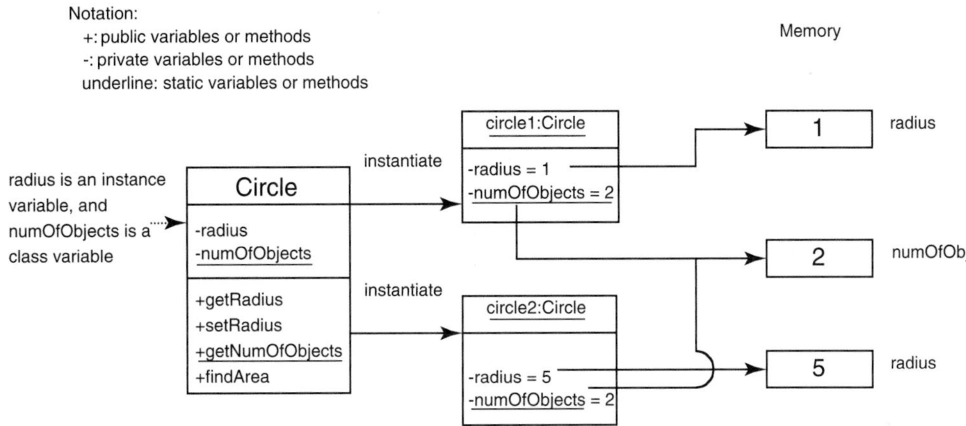

Figure 5.11 *The instance variables, which belong to the instances, have memory storage independent of one other. The class variables are shared by all the instances of the same class.*

To declare a class constant, add the `final` keyword in the above declaration. For example, the constant `PI` in the `Math` class is defined as follows:

```
public final static double PI = 3.14159265358979323846;
```

Instance methods belong to instances and can only be applied after the instances are created. They are called by the following:

```
objectName.methodName();
```

The methods defined in the `Circle` class are instance methods. Java supports class methods as well as class variables. Class methods can be called without creating an instance of the class. To define a class method, put the modifier `static` in the method declaration, as follows:

```
static returnValueType staticMethod();
```

Examples of class methods are the `readDouble()` and the `readInt()` in the class `MyInput`, and all the methods in the `Math` class. In fact, so are all the methods used in Chapters 2, 3, and 4, including the `main` method.

Class methods are called by one of the following syntaxes:

```
ClassName.methodName();

objectName.methodName();
```

For example, `MyInput.readInt()` is a call that reads an integer from the keyboard. `MyInput` is a class, not an object.

NOTE

Instance variables can be accessed from instance methods in a class, but not from a class method in a class. Thus the following code would be wrong.

```
class Foo
{
  int i = 5;

  static void p()
  {
    int j = i; // Wrong because p() is static and i is non-static
  }
}
```

TIP

A method that does not use instance variables can be defined as a class method. This method can be invoked without creating an object of the class.

You should define a constant as `static` data that can be shared by all class objects. Do not change the value of a constant.

Variables that describe common properties of objects should be declared as class variables.

The following example demonstrates how to use instance and class variables and methods, and illustrates the effects of using them.

Example 5.5 Using Instance and Class Variables and Methods

This example adds a class variable `numOfObjects` to track the number of `Circle` objects created. The new `Circle` class can be shown using graphical notations in Figure 5.12.

The `main` method creates two circles, `circle1` and `circle2`, and modifies the instance and class variables. You will see the effect of using instance and class variables after changing the data in the circles. The output of the program is shown in Figure 5.13.

```
// TestInstanceAndClassVariable.java: Demonstrate using instance and
// class variables
public class TestInstanceAndClassVariable
{
```

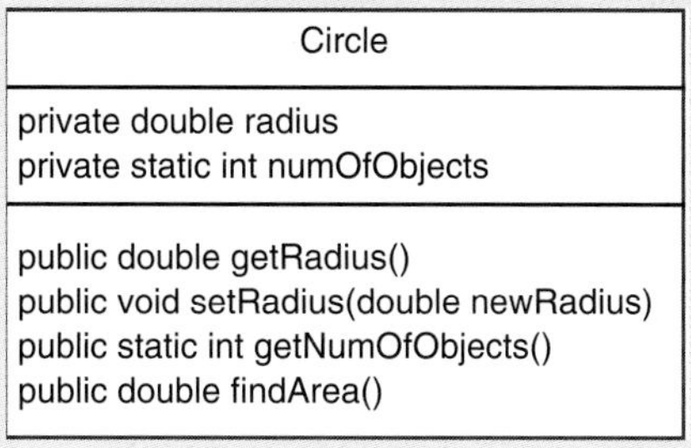

Circle
private double radius private static int numOfObjects
public double getRadius() public void setRadius(double newRadius) public static int getNumOfObjects() public double findArea()

Figure 5.12 *The* `Circle` *class defines instance variable* `radius`, *class variable* `numOfObjects`, *instance methods* `getRadius`, `setRadius`, `findArea`, *and a class method* `getNumOfObjects`.

```
    // Main method
    public static void main(String[] args)
    {
      // Create circle1
      Circle circle1 = new Circle();

      // Display circle1 BEFORE circle2 is created
      System.out.println("Before creating circle2");
      System.out.print("circle1 is : ");
      printCircle(circle1);

      // Create circle2
      Circle circle2 = new Circle(5);

      // Change the radius in circle1
      circle1.setRadius(9);

      // Display circle1 and circle2 AFTER circle2 was created
      System.out.println("\nAfter creating circle2 and modifying " +
        "circle1's radius to 9");
      System.out.print("circle1 is : ");
      printCircle(circle1);
      System.out.print("circle2 is : ");
      printCircle(circle2);
    }

    // Print circle information
    public static void printCircle(Circle c)
    {
      System.out.println("radius (" + c.getRadius() +
        ") and number of Circle objects (" +
        c.getNumOfObjects() + ")");
    }
  }

  // Circle.java: Circle class with instance and class variables
  class Circle
  {
    private double radius;
    private static int numOfObjects = 0;  // Class variable

    // Default constructor
    public Circle()
    {
```

continues

Example 5.5 continued

```
    radius = 1.0;
    numOfObjects++;
  }

  // Construct a circle with a specified radius
  public Circle(double r)
  {
    radius = r;
    numOfObjects++;
  }

  // Getter method for radius
  public double getRadius()
  {
    return radius;
  }

  // Setter method for radius
  public void setRadius(double newRadius)
  {
    radius = newRadius;
  }

  // Getter method for numOfObjects
  public static int getNumOfObjects()
  {
    return numOfObjects;
  }

  // Find circle area
  public double findArea()
  {
    return radius*radius*Math.PI;
  }
}
```

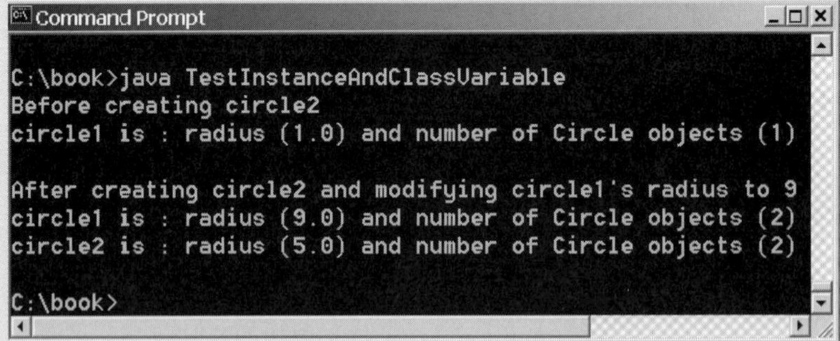

Figure 5.13 *The program uses the instance variable* `radius` *as well as the class variable* `numOfObjects`. *All of the objects share the same* `numOfObjects`.

Example Review

The instance variable `radius` in `circle1` is modified to become 9. This change does not affect the instance variable radius in `circle2`, since these two instance variables are independent. The class variable `numOfObjects` becomes 1 after `circle1` is created, and it becomes 2 after `circle2` is created. This change affects all the instances of the `Circle` class, since the class variable `numOfObjects` is shared by all the instances of the `Circle` class.

Note that `Math.PI` was used to access `PI`, and that `c.numOfObjects` in the `printCircle` method is used to access `numOfObjects`. `Math` is the class name, and `c` is an object of the `Circle` class. To access a constant like `PI`, you can use either the `ClassName.CONSTANTNAME` or the `objectName.CONSTANTNAME`. To access an instance variable like `radius`, you need to use `objectName.variableName`.

TIP

I recommend that you invoke static variables and methods using `ClassName.variable` and `ClassName.method`. This improves readability because the reader can easily recognize the static variables and methods. Thus you should replace `c.getNumOfObjects()` by `Circle.getNumOfObjects()` in this example.

The Scope of Variables

You use an instance variable or a class variable to describe the property of an object. These variables are referred to as *global variables* because they can be accessed by all the methods in the class. A variable declared in a method is referred to as a *local variable*, since it is only used inside a method locally.

The *scope of a variable* is the part of the program where the variable can be referenced. The scope of instance and class variables is the entire class, regardless of where the variables are declared. The instance and class variables can be declared anywhere in the class. For example, you can place the instance variable declaration at the end of the class, and use the variable in the method that is defined earlier in the class, as shown below.

```
class Circle
{
  double findArea()
  {
    return radius*radius*Math.PI;
  }

  double radius = 1;
}
```

NOTE

The data properties and methods are the members of the class. There is no order among them. Therefore, they can be declared in any order in a class.

The scope of a local variable starts from its declaration and continues to the end of the block that contains the variable. A local variable must be declared before it can be used.

You can declare a variable only once as a class member (instance variable or class variable), but you can declare the same variable in a method multiple times in different non-nesting blocks.

For example, in the following program, x is defined as an instance variable and as a local variable in the method.

```
class Foo
{
  int x = 0; // instance variable
  int y = 0;

  Foo()
  {
  }

  void p()
  {
    int x = 1; // local variable
    System.out.println("x = " + x);
    System.out.println("y = " + y);
  }
}
```

What is the printout for `f.p()`, where `f` is an instance of `Foo`? The printout for `f.p()` is 1 for `x` and 0 for `y`, based on the following reasons:

- `x` is declared again in the method `p()` with an initial value of 1.
- `y` is declared outside the method `p()`, but is accessible inside it.

TIP

As demonstrated in the example, it is easy to make mistakes. To avoid confusion, do not declare the same variable names.

Do not declare a variable inside a block and then use it outside the block. Here is an example of a common mistake:

```
for (int i=0; i<10; i++)
{
}

int j = i;
```

The last statement would cause an error because variable `i` is not defined outside of the `for` loop.

NOTE

You can declare a local variable with the same name multiple times in different non-nesting blocks in a method, but you cannot declare a local variable twice in nested blocks. Thus, the following code is correct.

```
public void correctMethod()
{
  int x = 1;
  int y = 1;

  for (int i = 1; i<10; i++) // i is declared
  {
    x += i;
  }

  for (int i = 1; i<10; i++) // i is declared again
  {
    y += i;
  }
}
```

However, the following code would cause a compilation error because x is declared in the for loop body block, which is nested inside the method body block where another x is declared.

```
public void incorrectMethod()
{
  int x = 1;
  int y = 1;

  for (int i = 1; i<10; i++)
  {
    int x = 0;
    x += i;
  }
}
```

The Keyword *this*

If a local variable has the same name as an instance or a class variable, the local variable takes precedence and the same instance or class variable is hidden. Occasionally, you need to reference the hidden instance or class variable in the method. A hidden class variable can be accessed simply by using the `ClassName.classvariable` reference. A hidden instance variable can be accessed by using the keyword `this`, as shown in the following code:

```
class Foo
{
  int i = 5;

  void setI(int i)
  {
    this.i = i;
  }
}
```

The line `this.i = i` means "assign argument `i` to the object's data field `i`."

You can also use the keyword `this` in the constructor. For example, you can redefine the `Circle` class as follows:

```
public class Circle
{
```

```
    private double radius;

    public Circle(double radius)
    {
      this.radius = radius;
    }

    public Circle()
    {
      this(1.0);
    }

    public double findArea()
    {
      return radius*radius*Math.PI;
    }
  }
```

The line `this(1.0)` invokes the constructor with a `double` value argument in the class.

NOTE
Java requires the `this()` statement to appear first in the constructor before any other statements.

Analyzing Relationships Among Objects

By now you have formed some ideas about objects and classes and their programming features. Object-oriented programming is centered on objects; it is particularly involved with getting objects to work together. The first step in object-oriented program development is to identify the objects and establish relationships among them. Since objects are modeled using classes, the relationship among objects of different classes is the same as the relationship among classes. The relationships can be classified into three types: *association*, *aggregation*, and *inheritance*.

Association

Association represents a general binary relationship that describes an activity between two classes. For example, a student taking a course is an association between the `Student` class and the `Course` class, and a faculty member teaching a course is an association between the `Faculty` class and the `Course` class. These associations can be represented in UML graphical notations, as shown in Figure 5.14.

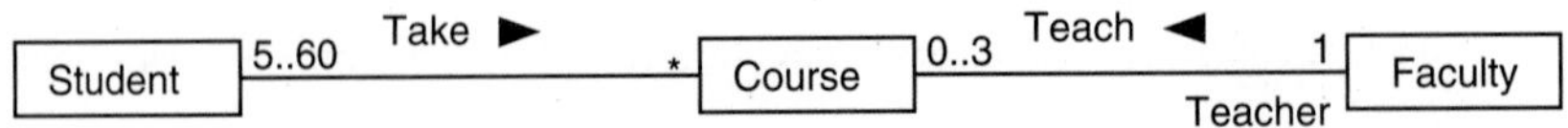

Figure 5.14 *A student may take any number of the courses, and a faculty teaches at most three courses. A course may have 5 to 60 students, and a course is taught by only one faculty.*

An association is illustrated using a solid line between the two classes with an optional label that describes the relationship. In Figure 5.14, the labels are *Take* and *Teach*. Each relationship may have an optional small black triangle that indicates the direction of the relationship. In Figure 5.14, the direction indicates that a student takes a course, as opposed to a course taking a student.

Each class involved in the relationship may have a role name that describes the role played by the class in the relationship. In our example, *teacher* is the role name for `Faculty`.

Each class involved in the association may specify a multiplicity. A multiplicity could be a number or an interval that specifies how many objects of the class are involved in the relationship. The character * means unlimited number of objects, and an interval `1..u` means the number of objects should be between `1` and `u`, inclusive. In our example, each student may take any number of courses, and each course must have at least 5 students and at most 60 students. Each course is taught by only one faculty member, and a faculty member may teach 0 to 3 courses per semester.

Association may exist between objects of the same class. For example, a person may supervise several people. This is illustrated in Figure 15.15.

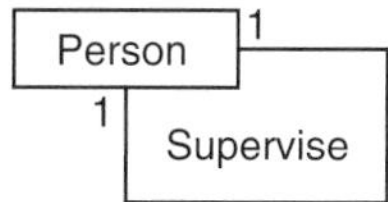

Figure 5.15 *A person may supervise another person.*

Aggregation

Aggregation is a special form of association that represents an ownership relationship between two classes. Aggregation models relationships like has-a, part-of, owns, and employed-by. An object may be owned by several other aggregated objects. If an object is exclusively owned by an aggregated object, the relationship between the object and its aggregated object is referred to as *composition*. For example, a publisher that owns a magazine is a composition between the `Publisher` class and the `Magazine` class, whereas a publisher that has consultants is an aggregation between the `Publisher` class and the `Consultant` class, since a consultant may work for several publishers. In UML, a filled diamond is attached to the `Publisher` class of the association to denote the composition relationship, and an empty diamond is attached to the aggregated class of the association to denote the aggregation relationship, as shown in Figure 5.16.

Inheritance

Inheritance models the is-a relationship between two classes. For example, a student is a person, and a faculty member is a person. You can define a class for `Student`

Figure 5.16 *A magazine is owned by a publisher, and a consultant may work for several publishers.*

that inherits from the `Person` class, and a class for `Faculty` that inherits from the `Person` class. The `Person` class is referred to as a *superclass* of the `Student` class and the `Faculty` class. The `Student` class inherits all the properties and methods from the `Person` class. An empty triangle pointing to the superclass is used to denote the inheritance relationship between two classes involved. As shown in Figure 5.17, classes `Student` and `Faculty` are subclasses of the `Person` class.

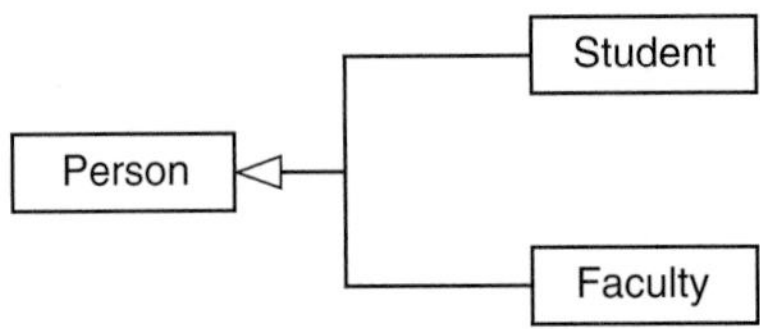

Figure 5.17 *A student is a person, and a faculty is a person.*

Inheritance will be discussed in Chapter 6, "Class Inheritance."

Class Abstraction

In Chapter 4, "Methods," you learned about method abstraction and used it in program development. Java provides many levels of abstraction. Class abstraction means to separate class implementation from the use of the class. The creator of the class provides a description of the class and lets the user know how the class can be used. The user of the class does not need to know how the class is implemented. The details of implementation are encapsulated and hidden from the user. For example, you can create a `Circle` object and find the area of the circle without knowing how the area is computed. There are many real-life examples that illustrate the concept of class abstraction.

Consider building a computer system, for instance. Your personal computer is made up of many components, such as a CPU, CD-ROM, floppy disk, motherboard, fan, and so on. Each component can be viewed as an object that has properties and methods. To get the components to work together, all you need to know is how each component is used and how it interacts with the others. You don't need to know how it works internally. The internal implementation is encapsulated and hidden from you. You can build a computer without knowing how a component is implemented.

This precisely mirrors the object-oriented approach. Each component can be viewed as an object of the class for the component. For example, you might have a class that models all kinds of fans for use on a computer with properties like fan size, speed, and so on, and methods like start, stop, and so on. A specific fan is an instance of this class with specific property values.

Consider paying a mortgage, for another example. A specific mortgage can be viewed as an object of a `Mortgage` class. Interest rate, loan amount, and loan period are its data properties, and computing monthly payment and total payment are its methods. When you buy a house, a mortgage object is created by instantiating the class with your mortgage interest rate, loan amount, and loan period. You can then use the mortgage methods to easily find the monthly payment and total payment of your loan. As a user of the `Mortgage` class, you don't need to know how these methods are implemented.

Case Studies

This section uses two examples to demonstrate identifying classes, analyzing classes, and applying class abstraction in object-oriented program development.

Example 5.6 Borrowing Mortgages

The first example develops classes to model borrowing mortgages. For simplicity, this example does not attempt to build a complete system for storing, processing, and manipulating mortgages for borrowers; instead it focuses on modeling borrowers and the mortgages for the borrowers. To build an object-oriented system, the following steps are usually involved:

1. Identify classes for the system.
2. Describe attributes and methods in each class.
3. Establish relationships among classes.
4. Create classes.

The first step is to identify classes for the system. There are many strategies for identifying classes in a system, one of which is to study how the system works and select a number of use cases, or scenarios. Suppose the system stores borrowers' names, addresses, and mortgages, and displays borrower mortgages. You can at least identify the following classes: `Borrower`, `Name`, `Address`, and `Mortgage`.

The second step is to describe attributes and methods in each of the classes you have identified. The attributes and methods can be illustrated using UML, as shown in Figure 5.18. The `Name` class has properties `firstname`, `mi`, `lastname`, their associated accessor methods, and the `getFullname` method for returning the full name. The `Address` class has properties street, city, state, zip, their associated accessor methods, and the `getAddress` method for returning the full address. The `Mortgage` class has properties `annualInterestRate`, `numOfYears`,

continues

Example 5.6 continued

loanAmount, property accessor methods, monthlyPayment, and totalPayment methods. The Borrower class has properties name, address, and mortgage, their associated accessor methods, and the toString method for displaying complete information about the borrower.

The third step is to establish relationships among the classes. Each borrower borrows a mortgage, has a name, and has an address. So their relationships are illustrated in Figure 5.18.

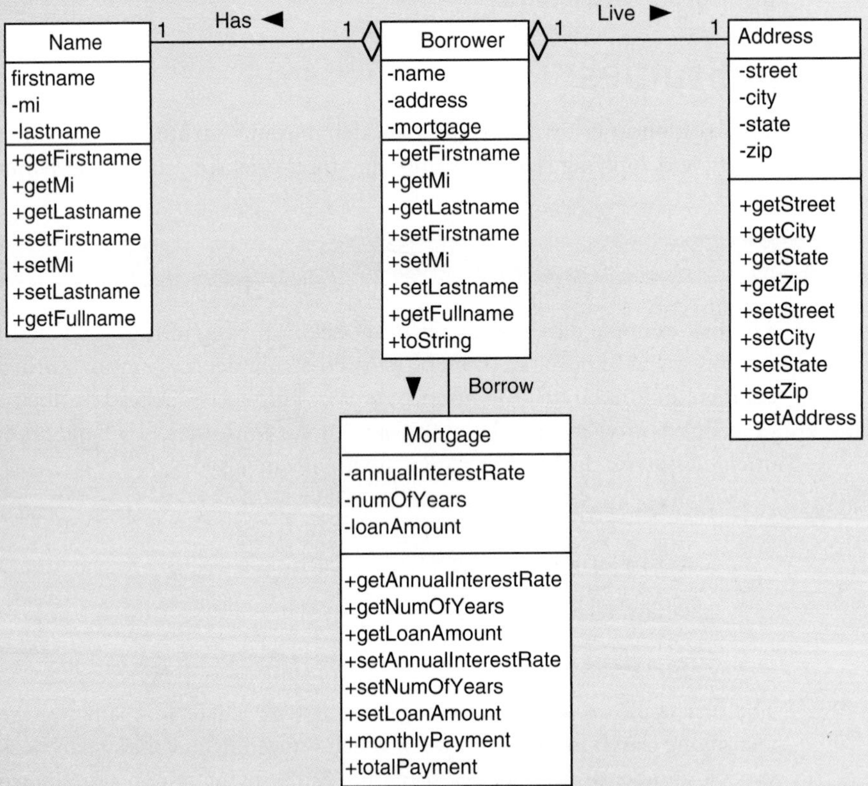

Figure 5.18 *A borrower has a name with an address and borrows a mortgage.*

The fourth step is to write the code for the classes as follows:

```
// Name.java: Encapsulate name information
public class Name
{
  private String firstname;
  private String mi;
  private String lastname;
```

```
  // Default constructor
  public Name()
  {
  }

  // Construct a name with firstname, mi, and lastname
  public Name(String firstname, String mi, String lastname)
  {
    this.firstname = firstname;
    this.mi = mi;
    this.lastname = lastname;
  }

  // Getter method for firstname
  public String getFirstName()
  {
    return firstname;
  }

  // Setter method for firstname
  public void setFirstname(String firstname)
  {
    this.firstname = firstname;
  }

  // Getter method for middlename initial
  public String getMi()
  {
    return mi;
  }

  // Setter method for middlename initial
  public void setMi(String mi)
  {
    this.mi = mi;
  }

  // Getter method for lastname
  public String getLastname()
  {
    return lastname;
  }

  // Setter method for lastname
  public void setLastname(String lastname)
  {
    this.lastname = lastname;
  }

  // Obtain full name
  public String getFullname()
  {
    return firstname + ' ' + mi + ' ' + lastname;
  }
}

// Address.java: Encapsulate address information
public class Address
{
  private String street;
```

continues

Example 5.6 continued

```
private String city;
private String state;
private String zip;

// Default constructor
public Address()
{
}

// Create address with street, city, state, and zip
public Address(String street, String city,
  String state, String zip)
{
  this.street = street;
  this.city = city;
  this.state = state;
  this.zip = zip;
}

// Getter method for street
public String getStreet()
{
  return street;
}

// Setter method for street
public void setStreet(String street)
{
  this.street = street;
}

// Getter method for city
public String getCity()
{
  return city;
}

// Setter method for city
public void setCity(String city)
{
  this.city = city;
}

// Getter method for state
public String getState()
{
  return state;
}

// Setter method for state
public void setState(String state)
{
  this.state = state;
}

// Getter method for zip
public String getZip()
{
  return zip;
}
```

```
  // Setter method for zip
  public void setZip(String zip)
  {
    this.zip = zip;
  }

  // Get full address
  public String getFullAddress()
  {
    return street + '\n' + city + ", " + state + ' ' + zip + '\n';
  }
}

// Mortgage.java: Encapsulate mortgage information
public class Mortgage
{
  private double annualInterestRate;
  private int numOfYears;
  private double loanAmount;

  // Default constructor
  public Mortgage()
  {
  }

  // Construct a mortgage with specified annual interest rate,
  // number of years and loan amount
  public Mortgage(double annualInterestRate, int numOfYears,
    double loanAmount)
  {
    this.annualInterestRate = annualInterestRate;
    this.numOfYears = numOfYears;
    this.loanAmount = loanAmount;
  }

  // Getter method for annualInterestRate
  public double getAnnualInterestRate()
  {
    return annualInterestRate;
  }

  // Setter method for annualInterestRate
  public void setAnnualInterestRate(double annualInterestRate)
  {
    this.annualInterestRate = annualInterestRate;
  }

  // Getter method for numOfYears
  public int getNumOfYears()
  {
    return numOfYears;
  }

  // Setter method for numOfYears
  public void setNumOfYears(int numOfYears)
  {
    this.numOfYears = numOfYears;
  }

  // Getter method for loanAmount
```

continues

Example 5.6 continued

```
  public double getLoanAmount()
  {
    return loanAmount;
  }

  // Setter method for loanAmount
  public void setLoanAmount(double loanAmount)
  {
    this.loanAmount = loanAmount;
  }

  // Find monthly payment
  public double monthlyPayment()
  {
    double monthlyInterestRate = annualInterestRate/1200;
    return loanAmount*monthlyInterestRate/
      (1 - (Math.pow(1/(1 + monthlyInterestRate), numOfYears*12)));
  }

  // Find total payment
  public double totalPayment()
  {
    return monthlyPayment()*numOfYears*12;
  }
}

// Borrower.java: Encapsulate borrower information
public class Borrower
{
  private Name name;
  private Address address;
  private Mortgage mortgage;

  // Default constructor
  public Borrower()
  {
  }

  // Getter method for name
  public Name getName()
  {
    return name;
  }

  // Setter method for name
  public void setName(Name name)
  {
    this.name = name;
  }

  // Getter method for address
  public Address getAddress()
  {
    return address;
  }

  // Setter method for address
  public void setAddress(Address address)
  {
    this.address = address;
  }
```

```
    // Getter method for mortgage
    public Mortgage getMortgage()
    {
      return mortgage;
    }

    // Setter method for mortgage
    public void setMortgage(Mortgage mortgage)
    {
      this.mortgage = mortgage;
    }

    // String representation for borrower
    public String toString()
    {
      return '\n' + name.getFullname() + '\n' +
        address.getFullAddress() + '\n' +
        "Monthly payment is " + mortgage.monthlyPayment() + '\n' +
        "Total payment is " + mortgage.totalPayment();
    }
  }
```

The following is a test program that uses the classes `Name`, `Address`, `Borrower`, and `Mortgage`. The output of the program is shown in Figure 5.19.

```
  // BorrowMortgage.java: Demonstrate using the classes Borrower
  // Name, Address, and Mortgage
  public class BorrowMortgage
  {
    // Main method
    public static void main(String[] args)
    {
      // Create one borrower
      Borrower borrower = new Borrower();

      // Enter the information for the borrower

      // 1. Enter name
      Name name = new Name();
      System.out.print("Enter first name: ");
      String firstname = MyInput.readString();
      name.setFirstname(firstname);

      System.out.print("Enter mi: ");
      String mi = MyInput.readString();
      name.setMi(mi);

      System.out.print("Enter last name: ");
      String lastname = MyInput.readString();
      name.setLastname(lastname);

      // 2. Enter address
      Address address = new Address();
      System.out.print("Enter street: ");
      String street = MyInput.readString();
      address.setStreet(street);

      System.out.print("Enter city: ");
      String city = MyInput.readString();
      address.setCity(city);
```

continues

Example 5.6 continued

```
      System.out.print("Enter state: ");
      String state = MyInput.readString();
      address.setState(state);

      System.out.print("Enter zip: ");
      String zip = MyInput.readString();
      address.setZip(zip);

      // 3. Enter mortgage information
      Mortgage mortgage = new Mortgage();
      System.out.print("Enter annual interest rate (i.e. 7.25): ");
      double annualInterestRate = MyInput.readDouble();
      mortgage.setAnnualInterestRate(annualInterestRate);

      System.out.print("Enter number of years: ");
      int numOfYears = MyInput.readInt();
      mortgage.setNumOfYears(numOfYears);

      System.out.print("Enter loan amount: ");
      double loanAmount = MyInput.readDouble();
      mortgage.setLoanAmount(loanAmount);

      // 4. Set values to the borrower
      borrower.setName(name);
      borrower.setAddress(address);
      borrower.setMortgage(mortgage);

      // Print mortgage information
      System.out.println(borrower.toString());
    }
  }
```

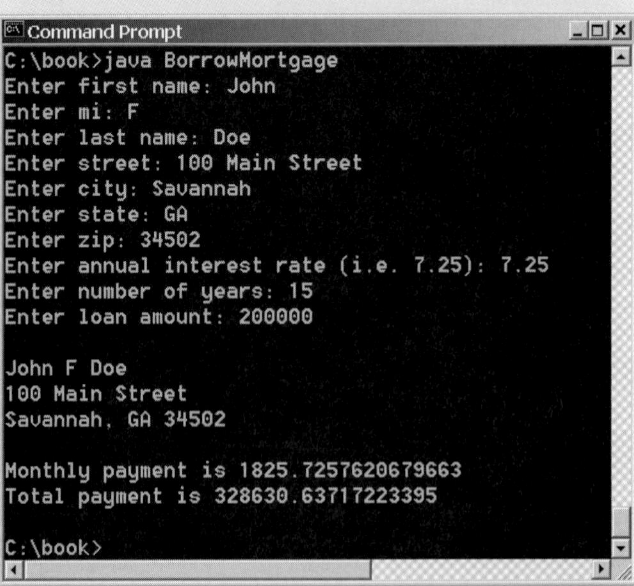

Figure 5.19 *The program obtains name, address, and mortgage, stores the information in a* `Borrower` *object, and displays the information with mortgage payment.*

Example Review

Identifying the objects is very difficult for novice programmers. How do you find the right objects? There is no unique solution to even a simple problem. Software development is more an art than a science. The quality of a program ultimately depends on the programmer's intuition, experience, and knowledge.

Once an object is identified, its properties and methods can be defined by analyzing the requirements and scenarios of the system. It is often a good practice to provide complete accessor methods. These methods may not be needed for your current project, but they may be useful in other projects, since your classes are designed for reuse in future projects.

Establishing relationships among the objects helps you to understand the interactions among objects. An object-oriented system consists of a collection of interrelated, cooperative objects.

Example 5.7 Using the `Rational` Class

In this example, a class for rational numbers is defined. The class provides constructors and addition, subtraction, multiplication, and division methods.

A rational number is a number with a numerator and a denominator in the form a/b, where a is the numerator and b is the denominator. For example, 1/3, 3/4, and 10/4.

A rational number cannot have a denominator of 0, but a numerator of 0 is fine. Every integer `a` is equivalent to a rational number `a/1`. Rational numbers are used in exact computations involving fractions; for example, 1/3 = 0.33333. . . . This number cannot be precisely represented in floating-point format using data type `double` or `float`. To obtain the exact result, it is necessary to use rational numbers.

There are many equivalent rational numbers; for example, 1/3 = 2/6 = 3/9 = 4/12. For convenience, 1/3 is used in this example to represent all rational numbers that are equivalent to 1/3. The numerator and the denominator of 1/3 have no common divisor except 1, so 1/3 is said to be in lowest terms.

To reduce a rational to its lowest terms, you need to find the greatest common divisor, or GCD, of the absolute values of its numerator and denominator, then divide both numerator and denominator by this value. Here is Euclid's famous algorithm for finding the GCD of two `integers` `n` and `d`:

```
t1 = Math.abs(n); t2 = Math.abs(d); // Get absolute value of n and d;
r = t1 % t2; // r is the remainder of t1 divided by t2;
while (r != 0)
```

continues

Example 5.7 continued

```
{
  t1 = t2;
  t2 = r;
  r = t1 % t2;
}

// When r is 0, t2 is the greatest common divisor between t1 and t2
return t2;
```

Based upon the foregoing analysis, the following data and methods are needed in the `Rational` class:

Data field:

- `long numerator`: Represent the numerator of the rational number.
- `long denominator`: Represent the denominator of the rational number.

Methods:

- public Rational add(Rational secondRational)

  Return the addition of this rational with another.

- `public Rational subtract(Rational secondRational)`

  Return the subtraction of this rational with another.

- `public Rational multiply(Rational secondRational)`

  Return the multiplication of this rational with another.

- `public Rational divide(Rational secondRational)`

  Return the division of this rational with another.

- `private long gcd(long n, long d)`

  Return the GCD of two numbers.

Figure 5.20 is an illustration of the `Rational` class.

The `Rational` class is presented below, followed by a test program. Figure 5.21 shows the sample run of the program.

```
// Rational.java: Define a rational number and its associated
// operations such as add, subtract, multiply, and divide
public class Rational
{
  // Data fields for numerator and denominator
  private long numerator = 0;
  private long denominator = 1;

  // Default constructor
  public Rational()
  {
    this(0, 1);
  }
```

```
// Construct a rational with specified numerator and denominator
public Rational(long numerator, long denominator)
{
  long gcd = gcd(numerator, denominator);
  this.numerator = numerator/gcd;
  this.denominator = denominator/gcd;
}

// Find GCD of two numbers
private long gcd(long n, long d)
{
  long t1 = Math.abs(n);
  long t2 = Math.abs(d);
  long remainder = t1%t2;

  while (remainder != 0)
  {
    t1 = t2;
    t2 = remainder;
    remainder = t1%t2;
  }

  return t2;
}

// Getter method for numerator
public long getNumerator()
{
  return numerator;
}

public long getDenominator()
{
  return denominator;
}

// Add a rational number to this rational
public Rational add(Rational secondRational)
{
  long n = numerator*secondRational.getDenominator() +
    denominator*secondRational.getNumerator();
  long d = denominator*secondRational.getDenominator();
  return new Rational(n, d);
}

// Subtract a rational number from this rational
public Rational subtract(Rational secondRational)
{
  long n = numerator*secondRational.getDenominator()
    - denominator*secondRational.getNumerator();
  long d = denominator*secondRational.getDenominator();
  return new Rational(n, d);
}

// Multiply a rational number to this rational
public Rational multiply(Rational secondRational)
{
  long n = numerator*secondRational.getNumerator();
  long d = denominator*secondRational.getDenominator();
  return new Rational(n, d);
}
```

continues

Example 5.7 continued

```
  // Divide a rational number from this rational
  public Rational divide(Rational secondRational)
  {
    long n = numerator*secondRational.getDenominator();
    long d = denominator*secondRational.numerator;
    return new Rational(n, d);
  }

  // Override the toString() method
  public String toString()
  {
    if (denominator == 1)
      return numerator + "";
    else
      return numerator + "/" + denominator;
  }
}

// TestRationalClass.java: Demonstrate using the Rational class
public class TestRationalClass
{
  // Main method
  public static void main(String[] args)
  {
    // Create and initialize two rational numbers r1 and r2.
    Rational r1 = new Rational(4,2);
    Rational r2 = new Rational(2,3);

    // Display results
    System.out.println(r1.toString() + " + " + r2.toString() +
      " = " + (r1.add(r2)).toString());
    System.out.println(r1.toString() + " - " + r2.toString() +
      " = " + (r1.subtract(r2)).toString());
    System.out.println(r1.toString() + " * " + r2.toString() +
      " = " + (r1.multiply(r2)).toString());
    System.out.println(r1.toString() + " / " + r2.toString() +
      " = " + (r1.divide(r2)).toString());
  }
}
```

Example Review

The main method creates two rational numbers, `r1` and `r2`, and displays the results of `r1+r2`, `r1-r2`, `r1xr2`, and `r1/r2`.

The rational number is encapsulated in a `Rational` object. Internally, a rational number is represented in its lowest terms; in other words, the greatest common divisor between the numerator and the denominator is 1.

The `gcd()` method is private; it is not intended for use by clients. The `gcd()` method is only for internal use by the `Rational` class.

The `abs(x)` method is defined in the `Math` class that returns the absolute value of `x`.

Two `Rational` objects can interact with each other to perform add, subtract, multiply and divide operations. To add `Rational` object `r1` with r2, invoke `r1.add(r2)`, which returns a new `Rational` object.

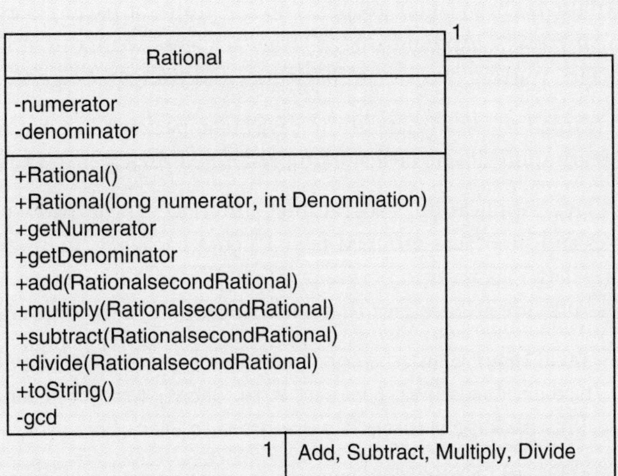

Figure 5.20 *The properties and methods of the* `Rational` *class are illustrated using UML notations.*

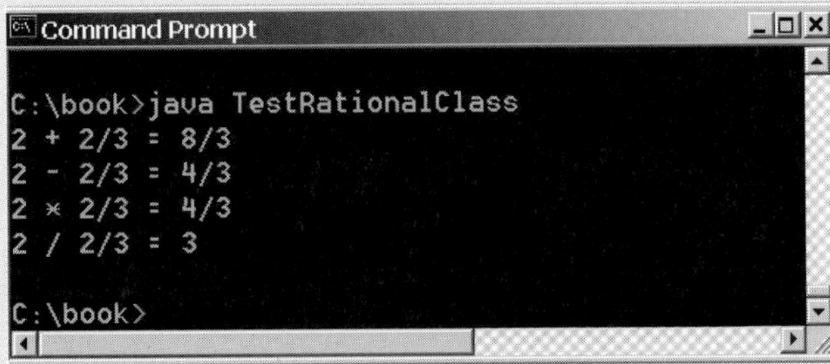

Figure 5.21 *The program creates two instances of the Rational class and displays their addition, subtraction, multiplication, and division by invoking the instance methods.*

The `toString()` method returns a string representation of a `Rational` object in the form `numerator/denominator`, or simply `numerator` if `denominator` is 1.

When you divide rational numbers, what happens if the divisor is zero? In this example, the program would terminate with a runtime exception. You need to make sure that this does not occur when you are using the division method. In Chapter 11, "Exception Handling," you will learn how to deal with the zero divisor case for a `Rational` object.

Java Application Programmer Interface

The Java language comes with a rich set of classes that you can use to build applications. These classes are grouped into packages that provide a convenient way to organize classes. You can put the classes you have developed in packages and distribute them to other people. You can think of packages as libraries to be shared by many users. Appendix H, "Java Packages," contains information on creating packages, putting classes into packages, and using packages.

You learned the `Math` class in the `java.lang` package in Chapter 4, "Methods." You will learn more about Java system predefined packages in the coming chapters.

The Java Application Programmer Interface (Java API) consists of numerous classes and interfaces grouped into 15 core packages, such as `java.lang`, `java.awt`, `java.event`, `javax.swing`, `java.applet`, `java.util`, `java.io`, and `java.net`. These classes provide an interface that allows Java programs to interact with the system.

- **`java.lang:`** Contains core Java classes (such as `Object`, `String`, `System`, `Math`, `Number`, `Character`, `Boolean`, `Byte`, `Short`, `Integer`, `Long`, `Float`, and `Double`). This package is implicitly imported to every Java program.
- **`java.awt:`** Contains classes for drawing geometrical figures, managing component layout, and creating peer-based (so-called heavyweight) components, such as windows, frames, panels, menus, buttons, fonts, lists, and many others.
- **`java.awt.event:`** Contains classes for handling events in graphics programming.
- **`javax.swing:`** Contains the lightweight graphical user interface components.
- **`java.applet:`** Contains classes for supporting applets.
- **`java.io:`** Contains classes for input and output streams and files.
- **`java.util:`** Contains many utilities, such as date, calendar, locale, system properties, vectors, hashing, and stacks.
- **`java.text:`** Contains classes for formatting information, such as date and time, in a number of formatting styles based on language, country, and culture.
- **`java.net:`** Contains classes for supporting network communications.

The `java.lang` is the most fundamental package supporting basic operations. Many of the popular classes in `java.lang` are introduced later in the book. See the following chapters for information on these classes:

- Chapter 6, "Class Inheritance," covers the `Object` class in the `java.lang` package.
- Chapter 7, "Arrays and Vectors," introduces wrapper classes, such as `Integer`, and `Double`, in the `java.lang` package, and the `Vector` class in the `java.util` package.
- Chapter 8, "Getting Started with Graphics Programming," and Chapter 9, "Creating User Interfaces," introduce the classes in the packages `java.awt`,

`java.awt.event`, and `javax.swing`, which are used for drawing geometrical figures, event-driven programming, and creating graphical user interfaces.

- Chapter 10, "Applets and Advanced Graphics," introduces the `Applet` in the `java.applet` package, which is used to program Java applets.
- Chapter 11, "Exception Handling," discusses using the `java.lang.Throwable` class and its subclasses for exception handling.
- Chapter 12, "Internationalization," introduces classes `java.util.Date`, `java.util.Calendar`, `java-util.Timezone` and `java.text.DateFormat` for processing and formatting date and time based on locale.
- Chapter 13, "Multithreading," focuses on the `java.lang.Thread` class and the `java.lang.Runnable` interface, which are used for multithreading.
- Chapter 14, "Multimedia," addresses the use of multimedia by several classes in the packages `java.awt` and `java.applet`.
- Chapter 15, "Input and Output," discusses the use of the classes in the `java.io` package by input and output streams.
- Chapter 16, "Networking," discusses using the classes in the `java.net` package for network programming.

Once you understand the concept of programming, the most important lesson in Java is learning how to use API to develop useful programs. The core Java API will be introduced in the coming chapters. The following sections introduce classes `java.lang.String`, `java.lang.StringBuffer`, and `java.util.StringTokenizer` for storing and processing strings.

The *String* Class

The `java.lang.String` class represents character strings. You have already used string literals, such as the parameter in the `println(String s)` method. The Java compiler actually converts the string literal into a string object and passes it to `println`.

Constructing a String

To create a string explicitly, use a syntax like this one:

```
String newString = new String(s);
```

The argument `s` is a sequence of characters enclosed inside double quotes. The following statement creates a `String` object `message` for the string literal `"Welcome to Java!"`:

```
String message = new String("Welcome to Java!");
```

Since strings are used frequently, Java provides a simple notation for creating a string:

```
String message = "Welcome to Java!";
```

String Comparisons

Often, in a program, you need to compare the contents of two strings. You might attempt to use the == operator, as follows:

```
if (string1 == string2)
  System.out.println("string1 and string2 are the same object");
else
  System.out.println("string1 and string2 are different objects");
```

However, the == operator only checks whether `string1` and `string2` refer to the same object; it does not tell you whether `string1` and `string2` contain the same contents when they are different objects. Therefore, you cannot use the == operator to find out whether two string variables have the same contents. Instead, you should use the `equals()` method for an equality comparison of the contents of objects. The code given below, for instance, can be used to compare two strings.

```
if (string1.equals(string2))
  System.out.println("string1 and string2 have the same contents");
else
  System.out.println("string1 and string2 are not equal");
```

The `compareTo()` method can also be used to compare two strings. For example, see the following code:

```
s1.compareTo(s2)
```

The method returns the value `0` if `s1` is equal to `s2`, a value less than `0` if `s1` is lexicographically less than `s2`, and a value greater than `0` if `s1` is lexicographically greater than `s2`.

The actual value returned from the `compareTo` method depends on the offset of the first two distinct characters in `s1` and `s2` from left to right. For example, suppose `s1` is `"abc"` and `s2` is `"abe"`, and `s1.compareTo(s2)` returns `-2`. The first two characters (`a` versus `a`) from `s1` and `s2` are compared. Because they are equal, the second two characters (`b` versus `b`) are compared. Because they are also equal, the third characters (`c` versus `e`) are compared. Since the character `c` is 2 less than `e`, the comparison returns `-2`.

NOTE

Syntax errors will occur if you compare strings by using comparison operators, such as >, >=, <, or <=. Instead, you have to use `s1.compareTo(s2)`.

The `equals` method returns `true` if two strings are equal, and `false` if they are not equal. The `compareTo` method returns `0`, a positive integer, or a negative integer, depending on whether a string is equal to, greater than, or less than the other string.

The `String` class also provides `equalsIgnoreCase` and `regionMatches` methods for comparing strings. The `equalsIgnoreCase` method ignores the case of the letters when determining whether two strings are equal. The `regionMatches` method compares portions of two strings for equality. For more information, please refer to the Java 2 API documentation.

NOTE

Strings are used frequently in programming. To improve efficiency and save memory, Java Virtual Machine makes a great effort to identify the identical strings and store them in the same memory location, but it does not guarantee that all of the same strings are stored in the same memory location. Therefore, you must use the `equals` method to test whether two strings have the same contents, and the `==` operator to test whether the two strings have the same references (that is, point to the same memory location).

String Concatenation

You can use the `concat` method to concatenate two strings. For example, the following statement concatenates strings `s1` and `s2` into `s3`:

```
String s3 = s1.concat(s2);
```

Since string concatenation is heavily used in programming, Java provides a convenient way to concatenate strings. You can use the plus sign to concatenate two or more strings. For example, the following code combines the strings `message`, `" and "`, and `"HTML!"` into one string:

```
String myString = message + " and " + "HTML!";
```

Recall that you have used the + sign to concatenate a number with a string in the `println` method. A number is converted into a string and then concatenated.

Substrings

`String` is an immutable class. After a string is created, its value cannot be changed individually. For example, you cannot change `"Java"` in `message` to `"HTML"`. So what can you do if you need to change the `message` string? You assign a new string to `message`. The following code illustrates this:

```
message = "Welcome to HTML!";
```

As an alternative, you can use the `substring` method. You extract a substring from a string by using the `substring` method in the `String` class. The `substring` method has two versions:

- `public String substring(int beginIndex, int endIndex)`

  This returns a new string that is a substring of this string. The substring begins at the specified `beginIndex` and extends to the character at index `endIndex - 1`. Thus the length of the substring is `endIndex-beginIndex`. The first character in a Java string has a position of 0.

- `public String substring(int beginIndex)`

This returns a new string that is a substring of this string. The substring begins with the character at the specified index and extends to the end of this string.

For example,

```
String message = "Welcome to Java".substring(0, 10) + "HTML!";
```

The string `message` now becomes `"Welcome to HTML!"`.

String Length and Retrieving Individual Characters in a String

You can get the length of a string by invoking its `length()` method. For example, `message.length()` returns the length of the string `message`.

The `s.charAt(index)` method can be used to retrieve a specific character in a string `s`, where the index is between `0` and `s.length()-1`. For example, `message.charAt(0)` returns the character `W`.

Example 5.8 Checking Palindromes

This example gives a program that checks whether a string is a palindrome: that is, whether it reads the same forward and backward. For example, mom, dad, and atoyota are palindromes.

The program prompts the user to enter a string and reports whether the string is a palindrome. The output of a sample run of the program is shown in Figure 5.22.

```
// CheckPalindrome.java: Check whether a string is a palindrome
public class CheckPalindrome
{
  // Main method
  public static void main(String[] args)
  {
    // Prompt the user to enter a string
    System.out.print("Enter a string: ");
    String s = MyInput.readString();

    if (isPalindrome(s))
    {
      System.out.println(s + " is a palindrome");
    }
    else
    {
      System.out.println(s + " is not a palindrome");
    }
  }

  // Check if a string is a palindrome
  public static boolean isPalindrome(String s)
  {
    // The index of the first character in the string
    int low = 0;

    // The index of the last character in the string
    int up = s.length() - 1;
```

```
    while (low < up)
    {
      if (s.charAt(low) != s.charAt(up))
        return false; // Not a palindrome

      low++;
      up--;
    }

    return true; // The string is a palindrome
  }
}
```

```
C:\book>java CheckPalindrome
Enter a string: toyota
toyota is not a palindrome

C:\book>java CheckPalindrome
Enter a string: atoyota
atoyota is a palindrome

C:\book>
```

Figure 5.22 *The program checks whether a string is a palindrome.*

Example Review

The `isPalindrome` method uses a `while` loop to check whether the first character in the string is the same as the last character. If so, it then checks whether the second character is the same as the second-last character. This process continues until a mismatch is found or all the characters in the string are checked, except for the middle character if the string has an odd number of characters.

This program considers all characters case-sensitive, including spaces and punctuation. In Exercise 5.7, you will rewrite this program in a version that ignores cases, spaces, and punctuation.

The *StringBuffer* Class

The `StringBuffer` class is an alternative to the `String` class. In general, a string buffer can be used wherever a string is used. `StringBuffer` is more flexible than `String`. You can add, insert, or append new contents into a string buffer. However, the value of a string is fixed once the string is created.

Many of the methods in the `StringBuffer` class are synchronized to ensure that the contents of `StringBuffer` are not corrupted when running with multiple threads (Synchronization will be introduced in Chapter 13, "Multithreading"). The `StringBuffer` class provides three constructors:

- `public StringBuffer()`

  Constructs a string buffer with no characters in it and an initial capacity of 16 characters.

- `public StringBuffer(int length)`

  Constructs a string buffer with no characters in it and an initial capacity specified by the `length` argument.

- `public StringBuffer(String string)`

  Constructs a string buffer for the string argument. The initial capacity of the string buffer is 16 plus the length of the string argument.

Appending and Inserting New Contents into a *StringBuffer*

You can append new contents at the end of a string buffer or insert new contents at a specified position in a string buffer.

The `StringBuffer` class provides 10 overloaded methods to append `boolean`, `char`, `char array`, `double`, `float`, `int`, `long`, `String`, and so on, into a string buffer. For example, the following code appends strings and characters into `strBuf` to form a new string, `"Welcome to Java"`.

```
StringBuffer strBuf = new StringBuffer();
strBuf.append("Welcome");
strBuf.append(' ');
strBuf.append("to");
strBuf.append(' ');
strBuf.append("Java");
```

The `StringBuffer` class also contains nine overloaded methods to insert `boolean`, `char`, `char array`, `double`, `float`, `int`, `long`, `String`, and so on, into a string buffer. Consider the following code:

```
strBuf.insert(11, "HTML and ");
```

Suppose `strBuf` contains `"Welcome to Java"` before the `insert()` method is applied. This code inserts `"HTML and "` at position 11 in `strBuf` (just before `J`). The new `strBuf` is `"Welcome to HTML and Java"`.

NOTE

Every string buffer has a capacity. If its capacity is exceeded, the buffer is automatically made larger to accommodate the additional characters.

The *capacity, reverse, length, setLength, charAt,* and *setCharAt* Methods

The `StringBuffer` class provides many other methods for manipulating string buffers. Here are some examples:

- `public int capacity()`

  This method returns the current capacity of the string buffer. The capacity is the number of new characters that can be stored in it.

- `public synchronized StringBuffer reverse()`

  This method reverses the sequence of the string contained in the string buffer.

- `public int length()`

  This method returns the number of characters in the string buffer.

- `public synchronized setLength(int newLength)`

  This method sets the length of the string buffer. If the `newLength` argument is less than the current length of the string buffer, then the string buffer is truncated to contain exactly the number of characters given by the `newLength` argument. If the `newLength` argument is greater than, or equal to, the current length, sufficient null characters (`'\u0000'`) are appended to the string buffer so that `length` becomes the newLength argument. The `newLength` argument must be greater than, or equal to, 0.

- `public synchronized charAt(int index)`

  This method returns the character at a specific index in the string buffer. The first character of a string buffer is at index 0, the next at index 1, and so on, for array indexing. The index argument must be greater than or equal to 0, and less than the length of this string buffer.

- `public synchronized void setCharAt(int index, char ch)`

  This method sets the character at the specified index of the string buffer to `ch`.

Example 5.9 Testing `StringBuffer`

This example gives a program that prints the multiplication table created in Example 3.4, "Using Nested `for` Loops," from Chapter 3. Rather than print one number at a time, the program appends all the elements of the table into a string buffer. After the table is completely constructed in the string buffer, the program prints the entire string buffer on the console once. The output of the program is the same as shown in Figure 3.14.

```
// TestMulTableUsingStringBuffer.java: Demonstrate string buffers
public class TestMulTableUsingStringBuffer
{
  // Main method
  public static void main(String[] args)
  {
    // Create a string buffer
    StringBuffer strBuf = new StringBuffer();

    // Get start time
    long startTime = System.currentTimeMillis();
```

continues

Example 5.9 continued

```
        // Append the title to the buffer
        strBuf.append("        Multiplication Table" + '\n');
        strBuf.append("-----------------------------------" + '\n');

        // Append the number title to the buffer
        strBuf.append("  ¦ ");
        for (int j=1; j<=9; j++)
          strBuf.append("   " + j);
        strBuf.append('\n');

        // Append multiplication table body to the buffer
        for (int i=1; i<=9; i++)
        {
          strBuf.append(i + " ¦ ");
          for (int j=1; j<=9; j++)
          {
            if (i*j < 10)
              strBuf.append("   "+i*j);
            else
              strBuf.append("  "+i*j);
          }

          strBuf.append(" " + '\n');
        }

        // Print the string buffer
        System.out.println(strBuf);

        // Get end time
        long endTime = System.currentTimeMillis();
        System.out.println("Elapsed time is " + (endTime - startTime)
          + " milliseconds");
      }
    }
```

Example Review

The program builds the multiplication table and stores it in the string buffer `strBuf` using the `append` method. The program is the same as used in Example 3.4 except that all the `print` statements in Example 3.4 are replaced by the `strBuf.append` statements.

The `System.out.println(strBuf)` displays the string stored in `strBuf` to the console.

This program should run faster than the one in Example 3.4 because the `print` method is called only once to display the entire table on-screen.

The program uses the static method `currentTimeMillis()` in the `System` class to get the time before and after the operations to obtain the elapsed time for the operations. Thus you can compare the performance of this example with Example 3.4.

Tip

Use `StringBuffer` to construct an output string, and display the whole string once to reduce I/O time and improve performance.

If the string does not require any change, use String rather than StringBuffer. Java can perform some optimizations for String, such as sharing one string among multiple references, because strings do not change after they are created.

The *StringTokenizer* Class

Another useful class related to processing strings is the `java.util.StringTokenizer` class. This class is used to break a string into pieces so that information contained in it can be retrieved and processed. For example, to get all of the words in a string like `"I am learning Java now"`, you can create an instance of the `StringTokenizer` class for the string and then retrieve individual words in the string by using the methods in the `StringTokenizer` class.

How does the `StringTokenizer` class recognize individual words? You can specify a set of characters as delimiters when constructing a `StringTokenizer` object. The delimiters break a string into pieces known as *tokens*.

Listed below are the available constructors for `StringTokenizer`.

- `public StringTokenizer(String s, String delim, boolean returnTokens)`

  This constructor constructs a `StringTokenizer` for string s with specified delimiters. If `returnTokens` is true, the delimiter is returned in a token.

- `public StringTokenizer(String s, String delim)`

  This constructor constructs a `StringTokenizer` for string s with specified delimiters `delim`, and the delimiter is not considered in a token.

- `public StringTokenizer(String s)`

  This constructor constructs a `StringTokenizer` for string s with default delimiters `" \t\n\r"` (a space, tab, new line, and carriage return), and the delimiter is not considered in a token.

You can use the following instance methods in the `StringTokenizer` class.

- `public boolean hasMoreTokens()`

  This method returns `true` if there is any token left in the string.

- `public String nextToken()`

  This method returns the next token in the string.

- `public String nextToken(String delim)`

  This method returns the next token in the string after resetting the delimiter to `delim`.

- `public int countTokens()`

  This method returns the number of tokens remaining in the string tokenizer.

Example 5.10 Testing `StringTokenizer`

In this example, a program is written that will use a string tokenizer to retrieve words from the string `"I am learning Java. Show me how to use StringTokenizer."` and display them on the console. The output of the program is shown in Figure 5.23.

```
// TestStringTokenizer.java: Demonstrate StringTokenizer
import java.util.StringTokenizer;

public class TestStringTokenizer
{
  // Main method
  public static void main(String[] args)
  {
    // Create a string and string tokenizer
    String s =
      "I am learning Java. Show me how to use StringTokenizer.";
    StringTokenizer st = new StringTokenizer(s);

    // Retrieve and display tokens
    System.out.println("The total number of words is " +
      st.countTokens());

    while (st.hasMoreTokens())
      System.out.println(st.nextToken());
  }
}
```

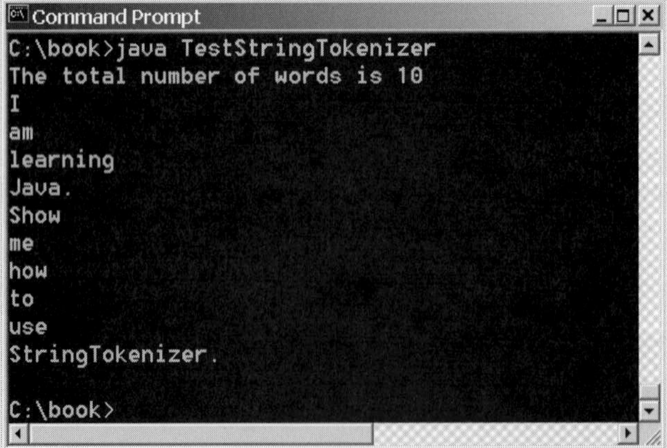

Figure 5.23 *The program uses the* `StringTokenizer` *class to extract tokens from a string.*

Example Review

The `String` class and `StringBuffer` class are in the `java.lang` package, so they are automatically imported. But the `StringTokenizer` class is in the `java.util` package. You need to import the `StringTokenizer` class from the `java.util` package. After all the tokens are read, `st.countTokens()` is `0`.

If you create a `StringTokenizer` instance as follows, the same words will be displayed in the program, but the dot will not be shown:

```
StringTokenizer st = new StringTokenizer(s, ". \n\t\r");
```

Chapter Summary

In this chapter, you learned how to program using objects and classes. You learned how to define classes, create objects, and use objects. You also learned about visibility modifiers, instance variables, class variables, instance methods, and class methods.

A class is a template for objects. It defines the generic properties of objects and provides methods for manipulating them.

An object is an instance of a class. It is declared in the same way as a primitive type variable. You use the `new` operator to create an object, and you use the dot (.) operator to access members of that object.

A constructor is a special method that is called when an object is created. Constructors can be overloaded.

Modifiers specify how the class, method, and data are accessed. You learned about `public`, `private`, and `static` modifiers. A `public` class, method, or data is accessible to all clients. A `private` method or data is only visible inside the class. You should make instance data `private`. You can provide a getter method or a setter method to enable clients to see or modify the data. A class variable or a class method is defined using the keyword `static`.

An instance variable is a variable that belongs to an instance of a class. Its use is associated with individual instances. A class variable is a variable shared by all instances of the same class.

An instance method is a method that belongs to an instance of a class. Its use is associated with individual instances. A class method is a method that can be invoked without using instances.

The scope of a variable is the portion of the program where the variable can be accessed. The scope of an instance or a class variable is the entire class. The scope of a local variable is limited locally to a method. Instance and class variables can be defined anywhere in the class as members of the class, but a local variable in a method must be declared before it can be accessed.

You can use the `this` keyword to reference the members of the class, including the constructors.

You learned to model the relationships among classes using the UML notations. The relationships are association, aggregation, composition, and inheritance. A relationship may exist among objects of the same class.

Strings are objects, encapsulated in the `String` class. You learned how to create and initialize a string, compare strings, concatenate strings, use substrings, and access individual characters in strings.

The `StringBuffer` class can be used to replace the `String` class. The `String` object is immutable, but you can add, insert, or append new contents into a `StringBuffer` object. Use `String` if the string contents do not require any change, and use `StringBuffer` if the string contents change.

The `StringTokenizer` class is used to retrieve and process tokens in a string. You learned the role of delimiters, how to create a string tokenizer from a string, and how to use the `countTokens`, `hasMoreTokens`, and `nextToken` methods to process a string tokenizer.

Review Questions

5.1 Describe the relationship between an object and its defining class. How do you declare a class? How do you declare an object? How do you create an object? How do you declare and create an object in one statement?

5.2 What are the differences between constructors and methods?

5.3 Show the output of the following program:

```
public class Test
{
  public static void main(String[] args)
  {
    Count myCount = new Count();
    int times = 0;

    for (int i=0; i<100; i++)
      increment(myCount, times);

    System.out.println("count is " + myCount.count);
    System.out.println("times is " + times);
  }

  public static void increment(Count c, int times)
  {
    c.count++;
    times++;
  }
}

class Count
{
  public int count;
```

```
    Count(int c)
    {
      count = c;
    }

    Count()
    {
      count = 1;
    }
  }
```

5.4 Show the output of the following program:

```
  public class Test
  {
    public static void main(String[] args)
    {
      Circle circle1 = new Circle(1);
      Circle circle2 = new Circle(2);

      // Attempt to swap circle1 with circle2
      System.out.println("Before swap: circle1 = " +
        circle1.radius +
        " circle2 = " + circle2.radius);
      swap(circle1, circle2);
      System.out.println("After swap: circle1 = " +
        circle1.radius +
        " circle2 = " + circle2.radius);
    }

    public static void swap(Circle x, Circle y)
    {
      System.out.println("Before swap: x = " + x.radius +
        " y = " + y.radius);

      Circle temp = x;
      x = y;
      y = temp;

      System.out.println("After swap: x = " + x.radius +
        " y = " + y.radius);
    }
  }
```

5.5 Suppose that the class `Foo` is defined as follows:

```
  public class Foo
  {
    int i;
    static String s;

    void imethod()
    {
    }

    static void smethod()
    {
    }
  }
```

Let `f` be an instance of `Foo`. Are the following statements correct?

```
System.out.println(f.i);
System.out.println(f.s);
f.imethod();
f.smethod();
System.out.println(Foo.i);
System.out.println(Foo.s);
Foo.imethod();
Foo.smethod();
```

5.6 What is the output of the following program?

```
public class Foo
{
  static int i = 0;
  static int j = 0;

  public static void main(String[] args)
  {
    int i = 2;
    int k = 3;

    {
      int j = 3;
      System.out.println("i + j is " + i+j);
    }

    k = i + j;
    System.out.println("k is "+k);
    System.out.println("j is "+j);
  }
}
```

5.7 What is wrong with the following program?

```
public class ShowErrors
{
  public static void main(String[] args)
  {
    int i;
    int j;

    j = MyInput.readInt();
    if (j > 3)
      System.out.println(i+4);
  }
}
```

5.8 What is wrong with the following program?

```
public class ShowErrors
{
  public static void main(String[] args)
  {
    for (int i=0; i<10; i++);
      System.out.println(i+4);
  }
}
```

5.9 List the modifiers that you learned in this chapter and describe their purposes.

5.10 Describe the role of the `this` keyword.

5.11 What are the types of relationships among classes? Describe the graphical notations for modeling the relationships among classes. What relationship is appropriate for the following classes:

- Company and Employee
- Course and Faculty
- Student and Person
- House and Window
- Account and Savings Account

5.12 Suppose that `s1`, `s2`, and `s3` are three strings, given as follows:

```
String s1 = "Welcome to Java!";
String s2 = s1;
String s3 = "Welcome to Java!";
```

Assume that `s3` and `s1` have different memory location. What are the results of the following expressions?

```
s1 == s2
s2 == s3
s1.equals(s2)
s2.equals(s3)
s1.compareTo(s2)
s2.compareTo(s3)
```

5.13 Suppose that `s1` and `s2` are two strings. Which of the following statements or expressions are incorrect?

```
String s = new String("new string");

String s3 = s1 + s2;

String s3 = s1 - s2;

s1 == s2;

s1 >= s2;

s1.compareTo(s2);

int i = s1.length();

char c = s1(0);

char c = s1.charAt(s1.length());
```

5.14 Declare a `StringTokenizer` for a string s with slash (/) and backslash (\) as delimiters.

5.15 What is the output of the following program?

```
import java.util.StringTokenizer;

class TestStringTokenizer
{
  public static void main(String[] args)
```

```
    {
      //create a string and string tokenizer
      String s = "I/am\learning Java.";
      StringTokenizer st = new StringTokenizer(s, "/\.");

      //retrieve and display tokens
      while (st.hasMoreTokens())
        System.out.print(st.nextToken()+" ");
    }
  }
```

Programming Exercises

5.1 Write a class named `Rectangle` to represent rectangles. The data fields are `width`, `height`, and `color`. Use `double` for `width` and `height`, and `String` for color. Suppose that all rectangles have the same color. Use a class variable for color. You need to provide the accessor methods for the properties and a method `findArea()` for computing the area of the rectangle.

The outline of the class is given as follows:

```
public class Rectangle
{
  private double width = 1;
  private double height = 1;
  private static String color = "white";

  public Rectangle()
  {
  }

  public Rectangle(double width, double height, String color)
  {
  }

  public double getWidth()
  {
  }

  public void setWidth(double width)
  {
  }

  public double getHeight()
  {
  }

  public void setHeight(double height)
  {
  }

  public static String getColor()
  {
  }

  public static void setColor(String color)
  {
  }
```

```
  public double findArea()
  {
  }
}
```

Write a client program to test the class Rectangle. In the client program, create two Rectangle objects. Assign any widths and heights to the two objects. Assign the first object the color red, and the second, yellow. Display both objects' properties and find their areas.

5.2 Write a class named Fan to model the fans. The properties are speed, on, radius, and color. You need to provide the accessor methods for the properties, and the toString method for returning a string consisting of all string values of all the properties in this class. Suppose the fan has three fixed speeds. Use constants 1, 2, and 3 to denote slow, medium, and fast speed.

The outline of the class is given as follows:

```
public class Fan
{
  public static int SLOW = 1;
  public static int MEDIUM = 2;
  public static int FAST = 3;

  private int speed = SLOW;
  private boolean on = false;
  private double radius = 5;
  private String color = "white";

  public Fan()
  {
  }

  public int getSpeed()
  {
  }

  public void setSpeed(int speed)
  {
  }

  public boolean isOn()
  {
  }

  public void setOn(boolean trueOrFalse)
  {
  }

  public double getRadius()
  {
  }

  public void setRadius(double radius)
  {
  }

  public String getColor()
  {
  }
```

```
    public void setColor(String color)
    {
    }

    public String toString()
    {
    }
}
```

Write a client program to test the `Fan` class. In the client program, create a `Fan` object. Assign maximum speed, radius 10, color yellow, and turn it on. Display the object by invoking its `toString` method.

5.3 Write a class named `Account` to model accounts. The properties and methods of the class are shown in Figure 5.24. Interest is compounded monthly.

Account
private int id private double balance private double annualInterestRate
public Account() public Account(int id, double balance, double annualInterestRate)
public int getId() public double getBalance() public double getAnnualInterestRate() public void setId(int id) public void setBalance(double balance) public void setAnnualInterestRate(double annualInterestRate) public double getMonthlyInterest() public void withdraw(double amount) public void deposit(double amount)

Figure 5.24 *The Account class contains properties id, balance, annual interest rate, accessor methods, and the methods for computing interest, withdrawing money, and depositing money.*

Write a client program to test the `Account` class. In the client program, create an `Account` object with account id of 1122, balance of 20000, and an annual interest rate of 4.5%. Use the `withdraw` method to withdraw $2500, use the deposit method to deposit $3000, and print the balance and the monthly interest.

5.4 Write a class named `Stock` to model a stock. The properties and methods of the class are shown in Figure 5.25. The method `changePercent` computes the percent of the change of the current price vs. the previous closing price.

Write a client program to test the `Stock` class. In the client program, create a `Stock` object with stock symbol SUNW, name Sun Microsystems Inc, previous closing price of 100. Set a new current price randomly and display the price change percentage.

5.5 Rewrite the `Rational` class in Example 5.7 with the following additional methods:

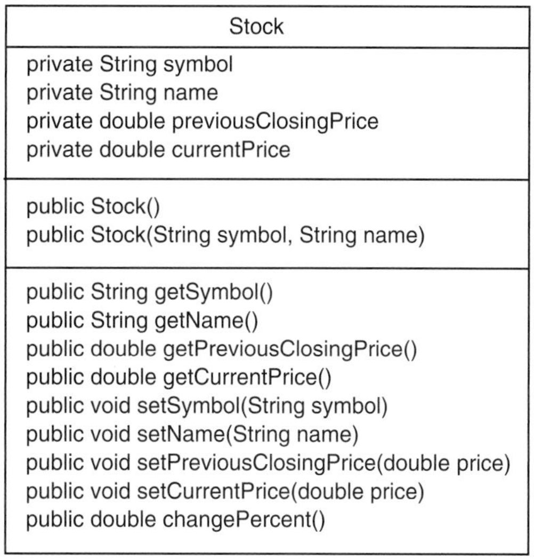

Stock
private String symbol private String name private double previousClosingPrice private double currentPrice
public Stock() public Stock(String symbol, String name)
public String getSymbol() public String getName() public double getPreviousClosingPrice() public double getCurrentPrice() public void setSymbol(String symbol) public void setName(String name) public void setPreviousClosingPrice(double price) public void setCurrentPrice(double price) public double changePercent()

Figure 5.25 *The Stock class contains properties symbol, name, previous closing price, and current price, accessor methods, and the methods for computing price changes.*

```
public boolean lessThan(Rational r)
// Return true if this Rational is < r

public boolean greaterThan(Rational r)
// Return true if this Rational is > r

public boolean equal(Rational r)
// Return true if this Rational is = r

public boolean lessThanOrEqual(Rational r)
// Return true if this Rational is <= r

public boolean greaterThanOrEqual(Rational r)
// Return true if this Rational is >= r

static Rational max(Rational r1, Rational r2)
// Return the larger one
```

Write a client program to test the new `Rational` class.

5.6 Write a program that will compute the following summation series using the `Rational` class.

$1/1 + 1/2 + 1/3 + ... + 1/n$

$1/1 + 1/2 + 1/2^2 + ... + 1/2^n$

5.7 Rewrite Example 5.8, "Checking Palindromes," which checks whether a string is a palindrome. Ignore cases, spaces, and punctuation.

5.8 Write a program that prompts the user to enter two strings and check whether the first string is a substring of the second string.

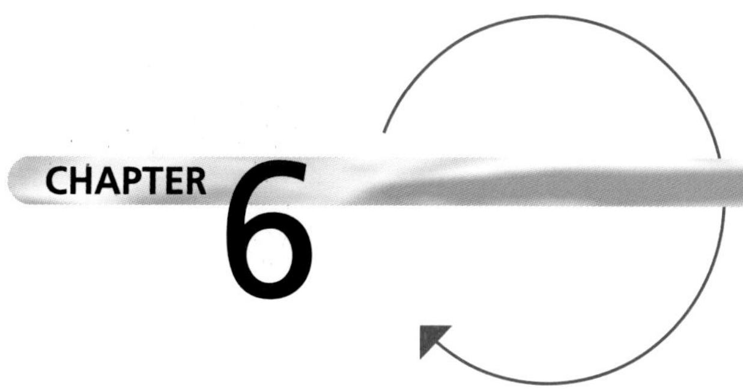

Class Inheritance

Objectives

- Understand the concept of class inheritance and the relationship between superclasses and subclasses.
- Create new classes from existing classes.
- Know how to use the `super` keyword.
- Learn to use three modifiers: `protected`, `final`, and `abstract`.
- Create abstract classes.
- Understand polymorphism and object casting.
- Use interfaces and inner classes.
- Become familiar with program development process and class-design guidelines.

Introduction

With object-oriented programming, you can derive new classes from existing classes. This is called *inheritance*. Inheritance models the is-a relationship. In Chapter 1, "Introduction to Java," you created the `WelcomeApplet` applet by deriving it from the `Applet` class. `WelcomeApplet` is an applet. Inheritance is an important and powerful concept in Java. In fact, every class you define in Java is inherited from an existing class, either explicitly or implicitly. Every class you created in the preceding chapters is actually derived implicitly from the class `Object`.

This chapter introduces the concept of inheritance. Specifically, it discusses superclasses and subclasses, the use of the `super` keyword, the `protected` modifier, the `final` modifier, the `abstract` modifier, polymorphism, casting objects, the interface, and inner classes, and class-design guidelines.

Superclasses and Subclasses

In Java terminology, a class `C1` derived from another class `C2` is called a *subclass*, and `C2` is called a *superclass*. Sometimes a superclass is referred to as a *parent class* or a *base class*, and a subclass is referred to as a *child class*, an *extended class*, or a *derived class*. You can reuse or change the methods defined in the superclasses in the subclass, as well as creating new data and new methods in subclasses. Subclasses usually have more functionality than their superclasses.

NOTE

Contrary to conventional interpretation, a subclass is not a subset of its superclass. In fact, a subclass is usually extended to contain more functions and more detailed information than its superclass.

Example 6.1 Demonstrating Inheritance

To demonstrate inheritance, this example creates a new class for `Cylinder` extended from `Circle`. The `Cylinder` class inherits all the data and methods from the `Circle` class. In addition, the `Cylinder` class has a new data field, `length`, and a new method, `findVolume`.

The relationship of these two classes is shown in Figure 6.1.

The `Cylinder` class can be declared as follows:

```
// Cylinder.java: Class definition for describing Cylinder
public class Cylinder extends Circle
{
  private double length;

  // Default constructor
  public Cylinder()
  {
```

```
    super(); // Invoke the default superclass constructor
    length = 1.0;
  }

  // Construct a cylinder with specified radius and length
  public Cylinder(double r, double l)
  {
    super(r); // Invoke superclass constructor Circle(r)
    length = l;
  }

  // Getter method for length
  public double getLength()
  {
    return length;
  }

  // Find cylinder volume
  public double findVolume()
  {
    return findArea()*length;
  }
}
```

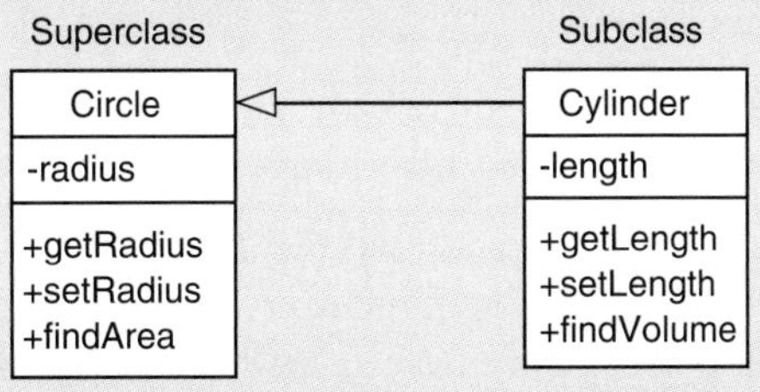

Superclass: Circle	Subclass: Cylinder
-radius	-length
+getRadius +setRadius +findArea	+getLength +setLength +findVolume

Figure 6.1 *The* `Cylinder` *class inherits data and methods from the* `Circle` *class and extends the* `Circle` *class with its own data and methods.*

The test program creates a `Cylinder` object and explores the relationship between the `Cylinder` and `Circle` classes by accessing the data and methods (`radius`, `findArea()`) defined in the `Circle` class and the data and methods (`length`, `findVolume()`) defined in the `Cylinder` class. The output of the program is shown in Figure 6.2.

```
// TestCylinder.java: Use inheritance
public class TestCylinder
{
  public static void main(String[] args)
  {
    // Create a Cylinder object and display its properties
    Cylinder myCylinder = new Cylinder(5.0, 2.0);
    System.out.println("The length is " + myCylinder.getLength());
    System.out.println("The radius is " + myCylinder.getRadius());
    System.out.println("The volume of the cylinder is " +
      myCylinder.findVolume());
    System.out.println("The area of the circle is " +
      myCylinder.findArea());
  }
}
```

continues

Example 6.1 continued

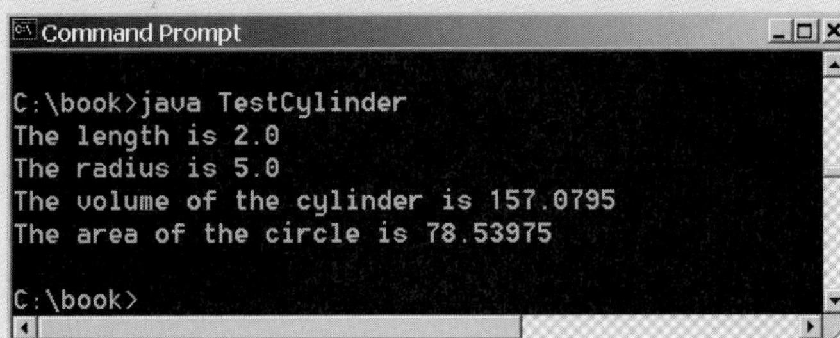

Figure 6.2 *The program creates a* `Cylinder` *object and accesses the data and methods defined in the* `Circle` *class and in the* `Cylinder` *class.*

Example Review

The `Cylinder` class extends the circle class defined in Example 5.4, "Using the `private` Modifier and Accessor Methods," in Chapter 5, "Programming with Objects and Classes."

The reserved word `extends` tells the compiler that the `Cylinder` class is derived from the `Circle` class, thus inheriting data and methods from `Circle`.

The `Cylinder` class extends all the functionality of the `Circle` class. The `myCylinder` object inherits all the data and methods in `Circle`. Therefore, it can access the `getRadius` and `findArea` methods defined in the `Circle` class.

The keyword `super` is used in the constructors. This keyword is discussed in the next section.

Using the *super* Keyword

In Chapter 5, you learned to use the `this` keyword. The `this` keyword refers to the class itself. You can use the keyword `super` to refer to the superclass of the class in which `super` appears. The `super` keyword can be used in two ways:

- To call a superclass constructor.
- To call a superclass method.

Calling Superclass Constructors

The syntax to call a superclass constructor is:

```
super(), or super(parameters);
```

The statement `super()` invokes the default constructor of its superclass and the statement `super(parameters)` invokes the superclass's constructor that matches the `parameters`. The statement `super()` or `super(parameters)` must appear in the first line of the constructor and is the only way to invoke a superclass's constructor. In

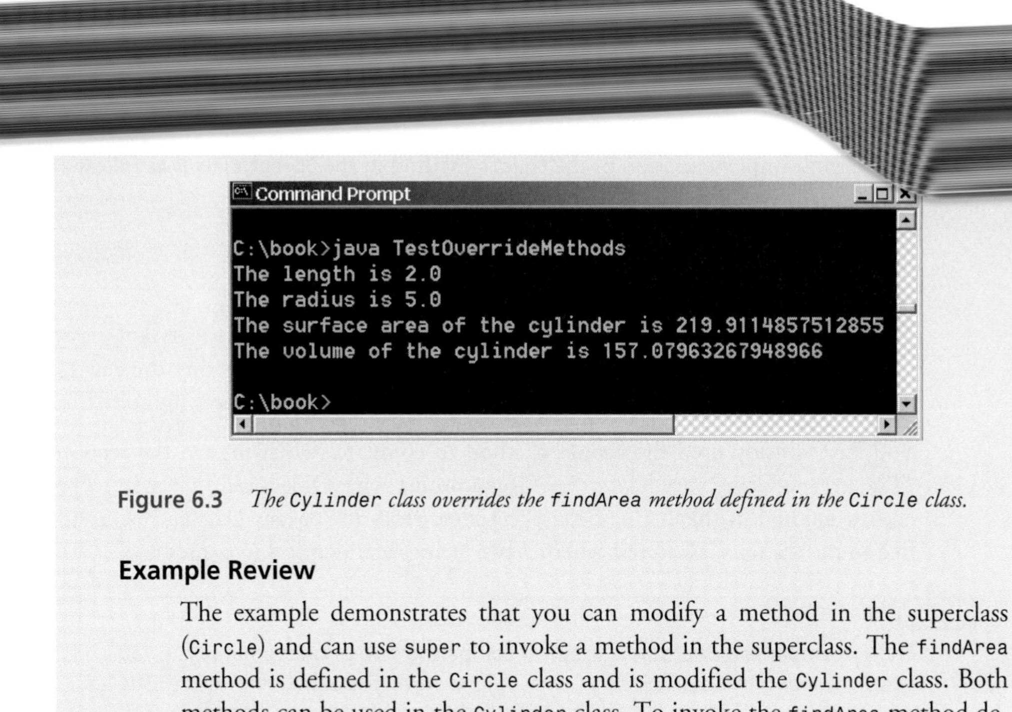

Figure 6.3 *The `Cylinder` class overrides the `findArea` method defined in the `Circle` class.*

Example Review

The example demonstrates that you can modify a method in the superclass (`Circle`) and can use `super` to invoke a method in the superclass. The `findArea` method is defined in the `Circle` class and is modified the `Cylinder` class. Both methods can be used in the `Cylinder` class. To invoke the `findArea` method defined in the `Circle` class, use `super.findArea()`.

A subclass of the `Cylinder` class can no longer access the `findArea` method defined in the `Circle` class because the `findArea` method is redefined in the `Cylinder` class.

The *Object* Class

Every class in Java is descended from the `java.lang.Object` class. If no inheritance is specified when a class is defined, the superclass of the class is `Object`. Classes like `Rational`, `Mortgage`, and `Circle` are implicitly the child classes of `Object` (as are all the main classes you have seen in this book so far). It is important to be familiar with the methods provided by the `Object` class so that you can use them in your classes. Three useful instance methods in the `Object` class are:

- public boolean equals(Object object)
- public String toString()
- public Object clone()

The *equals* Method

The `equals` method tests whether two objects are equal. The syntax to use `equals` is as follows:

```
object1.equals(object2);
```

The variables `object1` and `object2` are of the same class.

The default implementation of the `equals` method in the `Object` class is as follows:

```
public boolean equals(Object obj)
{
  return (this == obj);
}
```

Thus, using the `equals` method is equivalent to the `==` operator in the `Object` class, but it is really intended for the subclasses of the `Object` class to modify the `equals` method to test whether two distinct objects of the same class have the same contents.

You have already used the `equals` method to compare two strings in the section "The `String` Class" in Chapter 5, "Programming with Objects and Classes." The `equals` method in the `String` class is inherited from the `Object` class and is modified in the `String` class to test whether two strings are identical in content.

NOTE

The `==` comparison operator is used for comparing two primitive data type values or for determining whether two objects have the same references. The `equals` method is intended to test whether two objects have the same contents, provided that this method is modified in the defining class of the objects. The `==` operator is stronger than the `equals` method.

The *toString* Method

Invoking `object.toString()` returns a string that represents the value of this `object`. By default, it returns a string consisting of a class name of which the object is an instance, the at sign (@), and a number representing the object. For example, consider the following code:

```
Cylinder myCylinder = new MyCylinder(5.0, 2.0);
System.out.println(myCylinder.toString());
```

This code displays something like `Cylinder@15037e5`. This message is not very helpful or informative. Usually you should overwrite the `toString` method so that it returns a digestible string representation of the object. For example, you can override the `toString` method in the `Cylinder` class:

```
public String toString()
{
  return "Cylinder length = " + length;
}
```

Then `System.out.println(myCylinder.toString())` displays something like the following:

```
Cylinder length = 2
```

TIP

Alternatively, you could write `System.out.println(myCylinder)` instead of `System.out.println(myCylinder.toString())`. The Java compiler automatically translates `myCylinder` into a string by invoking its `toString` method when it is used in the `print` method.

The *clone* Method

Sometimes you need to make a copy of an object. Naturally, you would use the assignment statement, as follows:

```
newObject = someObject;
```

This statement does not create a duplicate object. It simply assigns the reference of `someObject` to `newObject`. To create a new object with separate memory space, you need to use the `clone()` method, as follows:

```
newObject = someObject.clone();
```

This statement copies `someObject` to a new memory location and assigns the reference of the new object to `newObject`.

NOTE
Not all objects can be cloned. For an object to be cloneable, its class must implement the `java.lang.Cloneable` interface. Interfaces are introduced in the section "Interfaces," in this chapter.

NOTE
The `Object` class also contains the `wait` and `notify` methods to control threads, which are used in Chapter 13, "Multithreading."

The *protected* and *final* Modifiers

You have already used the modifiers `static`, `private`, and `public`. Three new modifiers will now be introduced: `protected`, `final`, and `abstract`. The `protected` and `final` modifiers are introduced in this section, and the `abstract` modifier is introduced in the next section. These three modifiers are used with respect to class inheritance.

The *protected* Modifier

The `protected` modifier can be applied on data and methods in a class. A protected datum or a protected method in a public class can be accessed *by any class in the same package or its subclasses*, even if the subclasses are in different packages.

Suppose class `C1` contains a protected datum named `x` in package `p1`, as shown in Figure 6.4. Consider the following scenarios:

1. If class `C2` in package `p2` is a subclass of `C1`, then `x` is accessible in `C2`, since it can be accessed by any subclass of `C1`.

2. If class `C3` in package `p1` contains an instance of `C1` named `c1`, then `x` is visible in `c1`, since `C3` and `C1` are in the same package.

3. If class `C4` in package `p2` contains an instance of `C1` named `c1`, then `x` is not visible in `c1`, because `C4` and `C1` are in different packages.

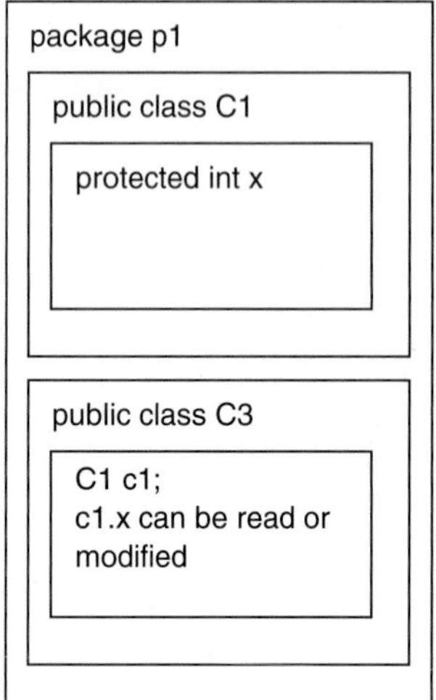

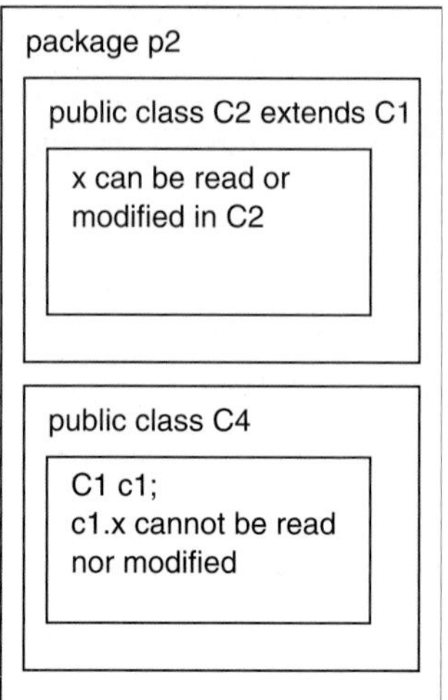

Figure 6.4 *The `protected` modifier can be used to prevent a non-subclass in a different package from accessing the class's data and methods.*

Note

The modifiers `private`, `public`, and `protected` are also known as *visibility modifiers*, which specify how class and class members are accessed. In UML, the symbols +, -, and #, respectively, are used to denote `public`, `private`, and `protected` modifiers.

The *final* Modifier

You have already seen the `final` modifier used in declaring constants. You may occasionally want to prevent classes from being extended. In such cases, use the `final` modifier to indicate that a class is final and cannot be a parent class. The `Math` class, introduced in Chapter 4, "Methods," is a final class. The `String` class, introduced in Chapter 5, "Programming with Objects and Classes," is also a final class.

You also can define a method to be final; a final method cannot be modified by its subclasses.

Note

The modifiers are used on classes and class members (data and methods), except that the `final` modifier can also be used on local variables in a method. A final local variable is a constant inside a method.

Abstract Classes

In the inheritance hierarchy, classes become more specific and concrete *with each new subclass.* If you move from a subclass back up to a superclass, the classes become more general and less specific. Class design should ensure that a superclass shares features with its subclasses. Sometimes a superclass is so abstract that it cannot have any specific instances.

Consider geometric objects. Suppose you want to design the classes to model geometric objects like circles, cylinders, and rectangles. Geometric objects have many common properties and behaviors. Color and weight are examples of common properties. Common behaviors include the fact that their areas and perimeters can be computed. Thus a general class `GeometricObject` can be used to model all the geometric objects. This class contains the properties `color` and `weight`, and the methods `findArea` and `findPerimeter`. A cylinder is a special type of circle, and thus it shares common properties and behaviors with a circle. You can define the `Cylinder` class that extends the `Circle`. Figure 6.5 illustrates the relationship of the classes for geometric objects.

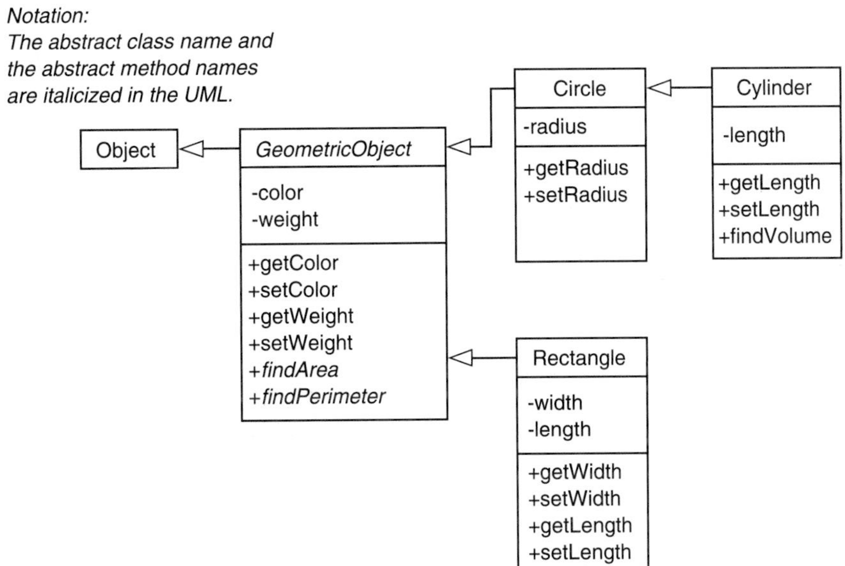

Figure 6.5 *The* `GeometricObject` *class models the common features of the geometric objects.*

The methods `findArea` and `findPerimeter` cannot be implemented in the `GeometricObject` class, because their implementation is dependent on the specific type of geometric object. Such methods are referred to as *abstract methods*. Classes that contains abstract methods are referred to as *abstract classes*. In UML graphic notation, the names of abstract classes and their abstract methods are italicized. The `GeometricObject` class can be defined as follows:

```
// GeometricObject.java: The abstract GeometricObject class
public abstract class GeometricObject
{
  protected String color;
  protected double weight;

  // Default construct
  protected GeometricObject()
```

```
  {
    color = "white";
    weight = 1.0;
  }

  // Construct a geometric object
  protected GeometricObject(String color, double weight)
  {
    this.color = color;
    this.weight = weight;
  }

  // Getter method for color
  public String getColor()
  {
    return color;
  }

  // Setter method for color
  public void setColor(String color)
  {
    this.color = color;
  }

  // Getter method for weight
  public double getWeight()
  {
    return weight;
  }

  // Setter method for weight
  public void setWeight(double weight)
  {
    this.weight = weight;
  }

  // Abstract method
  public abstract double findArea();

  // Abstract method
  public abstract double findPerimeter();
}
```

Abstract classes are like regular classes with data and methods, but you cannot create instances of abstract classes using the `new` operator. Abstract classes always contain abstract methods. An abstract method is a method signature without implementation. Its implementation is provided by its subclasses.

The `GeometricObject` abstract class provides the common features (data and methods) for geometric objects. Because you don't know how to compute areas and perimeters of geometric objects, `findArea` and `findPerimeter` are defined as abstract methods. These methods are to be implemented in the subclasses. The implementation of the classes `Circle`, `Rectangle`, and `Cylinder` is given as follows:

```
// Circle.java: The circle class that extends GeometricObject
public class Circle extends GeometricObject
{
  protected double radius;

  // Default constructor
  public Circle()
```

```
  {
    this(1.0, "white", 1.0);
  }

  // Construct circle with specified radius
  public Circle(double radius)
  {
    super("white", 1.0);
    this.radius = radius;
  }

  // Construct a circle with specified radius, weight, and color
  public Circle(double radius, String color, double weight)
  {
    super(color, weight);
    this.radius = radius;
  }

  // Getter method for radius
  public double getRadius()
  {
    return radius;
  }

  // Setter method for radius
  public void setRadius(double radius)
  {
    this.radius = radius;
  }

  // Implement the findArea method defined in GeometricObject
  public double findArea()
  {
    return radius*radius*Math.PI;
  }

  // Implement the findPerimeter method defined in GeometricObject
  public double findPerimeter()
  {
    return 2*radius*Math.PI;
  }

  // Override the equals() method defined in the Object class
  public boolean equals(Circle circle)
  {
    return this.radius == circle.getRadius();
  }

  // Override the toString() method defined in the Object class
  public String toString()
  {
    return "[Circle] radius = " + radius;
  }
}

// Rectangle.java: The Rectangle class that extends GeometricObject
public class Rectangle extends GeometricObject
{
  protected double width;
  protected double height;

  // Default constructor
  public Rectangle()
  {
    this(1.0, 1.0, "white", 1.0);
  }
```

```
// Construct a rectangle with specified width and height
public Rectangle(double width, double height)
{
  this.width = width;
  this.height = height;
}

// Construct a rectangle with width, height, weight, and color
public Rectangle(double width, double height,
  String color, double weight)
{
  super(color, weight);
  this.width = width;
  this.height = height;
}

// Getter method for width
public double getWidth()
{
  return width;
}

// Setter method for width
public void setWidth(double width)
{
  this.width = width;
}

// Getter method for height
public double getHeight()
{
  return height;
}

// Setter method for height
public void setHeight(double height)
{
  this.height = height;
}

// Implement the findArea method in GeometricObject
public double findArea()
{
  return width*height;
}

// Implement the findPerimeter method in GeometricObject
public double findPerimeter()
{
  return 2*(width + height);
}

// Override the equals method defined in the Object class
public boolean equals(Rectangle rectangle)
{
  return (width == rectangle.getWidth()) &&
    (height ==  rectangle.getHeight());
}

// Override the toString method defined in the Object class
public String toString()
```

```
  {
    return "[Rectangle] width = " + width + " and height = " + height;
  }
}

// Cylinder.java: The new cylinder class that extends the circle
// class
class Cylinder extends Circle
{
  private double length;

  // Default constructor
  public Cylinder()
  {
    super();
    length = 1.0;
  }

  // Construct a cylinder with specified radius, and length
  public Cylinder(double radius, double length)
  {
    this(radius, "white", 1.0, length);
  }

  // Construct a cylinder with specified radius, weight, color, and
  // length
  public Cylinder(double radius,
    String color, double weight, double length)
  {
    super(radius, color, weight);
    this.length = length;
  }

  // Getter method for length
  public double getLength()
  {
    return length;
  }

  // Setter method for length
  public void setLength(double length)
  {
    this.length = length;
  }

  // Find cylinder surface area
  public double findArea()
  {
    return 2*super.findArea()+(2*getRadius()*Math.PI)*length;
  }

  // Find cylinder volume
  public double findVolume()
  {
    return super.findArea()*length;
  }

  // Override the equals method defined in the Object class
  public boolean equals(Cylinder cylinder)
  {
    return (this.radius == cylinder.getRadius()) &&
      (this.length == cylinder.getLength());
  }
```

```
    // Override the toString method defined in the Object class
    public String toString()
    {
      return "[Cylinder] radius = " + radius + " and length "
        + length;
    }
  }
```

The data field `radius` is protected. So it can be referenced by any subclass of `Circle`. The methods `equals` and `toString` are defined in the `Object` class and modified in the classes `Circle`, `Rectangle`, and `Cylinder`. The abstract methods `findArea` and `findPerimeter` defined in the `GeometricObject` class are implemented in the classes `Circle` and `Rectangle`.

NOTE

If a subclass of an abstract superclass does not implement all the abstract methods, it must be declared abstract. In other words, an abstract method cannot be contained in a nonabstract class. In a nonabstract subclass extended from an abstract class, all the abstract methods must be implemented, even if they are not used in the subclass.

NOTE

An abstract class cannot be instantiated using the `new` operator, but you can still define its constructors, which are invoked in the constructors of its subclasses. For instance, The constructors of `GeometricObject` are invoked in the `Circle` class and in the `Rectangle` class.

Polymorphism and Dynamic Binding

An object of a subclass can be used by any code designed to work with an object of its superclass. For example, if a method expects a parameter of the GeometricObject type, can invoke it with a Circle object. A Circle object can be used as both a Circle object and a GeometricObject. This feature is known as *Polymorphism* (a Greek word meaning "many forms.") A method may be defined in a superclass, but is overridden in a subclass. Which implementation of the method is used is dynamically determined by the JVM at runtime. This capability is known as *dynamic binding*.

The example below demonstrates polymorphism and dynamic binding.

Example 6.3 Testing Polymorphism

This example creates two geometric objects, a circle and a rectangle, invokes the `equalArea` method to check whether the two objects have equal area, and invokes the `displayGeometricObject` method to display the objects.

A sample run of the program is shown in Figure 6.6.

```
// TestPolymorhism.java: Demonstrate Polymorphism
public class TestPolymorphism
{
  // Main method
  public static void main(String[] args)
  {
    // Declare and initialize two geometric objects
    GeometricObject geoObject1 = new Circle(5);
    GeometricObject geoObject2 = new Rectangle(5, 3);

    System.out.println("The two objects have the same area? " +
      equalArea(geoObject1, geoObject2));

    // Display circle
    displayGeometricObject(geoObject1);

    // Display rectangle
    displayGeometricObject(geoObject2);
  }

  // A method for comparing the areas of two geometric objects
  static boolean equalArea(GeometricObject object1,
    GeometricObject object2)
  {
    return object1.findArea() == object2.findArea();
  }

  // A method for displaying a geometric object
  static void displayGeometricObject(GeometricObject object)
  {
    System.out.println();
    System.out.println(object.toString());
    System.out.println("The area is " + object.findArea());
    System.out.println("The perimeter is " + object.findPerimeter());
  }
}
```

```
Command Prompt

C:\book>java TestPolymorphism
The two objects have the same area? false

[Circle] radius = 5.0
The area is 78.53981633974483
The perimeter is 31.41592653589793

[Rectangle] width = 5.0 and height = 3.0
The area is 15.0
The perimeter is 16.0

C:\book>
```

Figure 6.6 *The program compares the areas of the objects and displays the properties of the objects.*

continues

Example 6.3 continued

Example Review

The classes GeometricObject, Circle, and Rectangle were presented in the preceding section. The methods findArea() and findPerimeter() defined in the GeometricObject class are overridden in the Circle class and the Rectangle class. The statements

```
GeometricObject geoObject1 = new Circle(5);
GeometricObject geoObject2 = new Rectangle(5, 3);
```

create a new circle and a rectangle, and assign them to variables geoObject1 and geoObject2. These two variables are of the GeometricObject type. These assignments, known as *implicit casting*, are legal, since both circles and rectangles are geometric objects. Casting objects is introduced in the next section.

When invoking equalArea(geoObject1, geoObject2), the findArea method defined in the Circle class is used for object1.findArea(), since geoObject1 is a circle, and the findArea method defined in the Rectangle class is used for object2.findArea(), since geoObject2 is a rectangle.

Similarly, when invoking displayGeometricObject(geoObject1), the methods findArea, findPerimeter, and toString defined in the Circle class are used, and when invoking displayGeometricObject(geoObject2), the methods findArea, findPerimeter, and toString defined in the Rectangle class are used. Which of these methods are invoked is dynamically determined at runtime, depending on the type of the object.

Casting Objects and the *instanceof* Operator

You have already used the casting operator to convert variables of one primitive type to another. Similarly, casting can also be used to convert an object of one class type to another within an inheritance hierarchy. In the preceding section, the statement

```
GeometricObject geoObject1 = new Circle(5);
```

is known as *implicit casting*, which assigns a circle to a variable of the GeometricObject type.

To perform an explicit casting, use a syntax similar to the one used for casting among primitive data types. Enclose the target object type in parentheses and place it before the object to be cast. For example:

```
Circle myCircle = (Circle)myCylinder;
Cylinder myCylinder = (Cylinder)myCircle;
```

The first statement converts myCylinder to its superclass variable myCircle; the second converts myCircle to its subclass variable myCylinder.

It is always possible to convert an instance of a subclass to an instance of a superclass, simply because an instance of a subclass is also an instance of its superclass. For example, an apple is an instance of the `Apple` class, which is a subclass of the `Fruit` class. An apple is always a fruit. Therefore, you can always assign an apple to a variable of the `Fruit` class. For this reason, explicit casting can be omitted in this case. Thus,

```
Circle myCircle = myCylinder;
```

is equivalent to

```
Circle myCircle = (Circle)myCylinder;
```

When converting an instance of a superclass to an instance of its subclass, explicit casting must be used to confirm your intention to the compiler with the (`SubclassName`) cast notation. For the casting to be successful, you must make sure that the object to be cast is an instance of the subclass. If the superclass object is not an instance of the subclass, a runtime exception occurs. For example, if the fruit is an orange, an instance of the `Fruit` class cannot be cast into an instance of the `Apple` class. It is good practice, therefore, to ensure that the object is an instance of another object before attempting a casting. This can be accomplished by using the `instanceof` operator. Consider the following code:

```
Circle myCircle = new Circle();
if (myCircle instanceof Cylinder)
{
  // Perform casting if myCircle is an instance of Cylinder
  Cylinder myCylinder = (Cylinder)myCircle;
  ...
}
```

You may wonder how `myCircle` could become an instance of the `Cylinder` class and why it is necessary to perform casting. There are some cases in which a superclass becomes an instance of a subclass. To fully explore the properties and functions, you need to cast the object to its subclass. This is shown in the following example.

Example 6.4 Casting Objects

This example creates two geometric objects, a circle and a cylinder, and invokes the `displayGeometricObject` method to display the objects. The `displayGeometricObject` method displays the area and perimeter if the object is a circle, and displays area and volume if the object is a cylinder.

A sample run of the program is shown in Figure 6.7.

```
// TestCasting.java: Demonstrate casting objects
public class TestCasting
{
  // Main method
  public static void main(String[] args)
```

continues

Example 6.4 continued

```
  {
    // Declare and initialize two geometric objects
    GeometricObject geoObject1 = new Circle(5);
    GeometricObject geoObject2 = new Cylinder(5, 3);

    // Display circle
    displayGeometricObject(geoObject1);

    // Display cylinder
    displayGeometricObject(geoObject2);
  }

  // A method for displaying a geometric object
  static void displayGeometricObject(GeometricObject object)
  {
    System.out.println();
    System.out.println(object.toString());

    if (object instanceof Cylinder)
    {
      System.out.println("The area is " +
        ((Cylinder)object).findArea());
      System.out.println("The volume is " +
        ((Cylinder)object).findVolume());
    }
    else if (object instanceof Circle)
    {
      System.out.println("The area is " + object.findArea());
      System.out.println("The perimeter is " +
        object.findPerimeter());
    }
  }
}
```

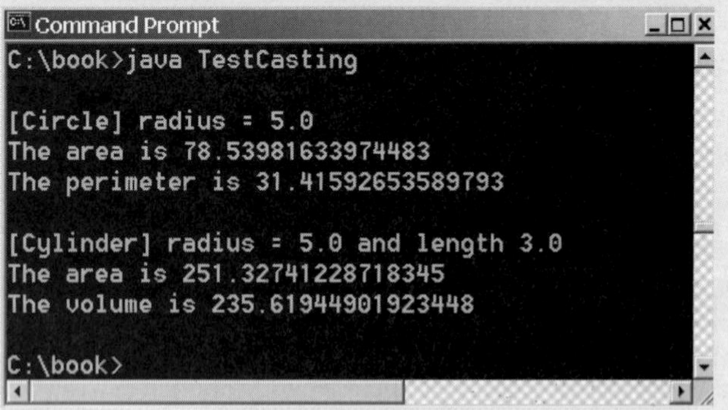

Figure 6.7 *The program creates two objects of* `GeometricObject` *and casts them to subclasses of* `GeometricObject` *in order to use the methods defined in the subclasses* `Circle` *and* `Cylinder`.

Example Review

Casting can only be done when the source object is an instance of the target class. The program uses the `instanceof` operator to ensure that the source object is an instance of the target class before performing a casting.

The program uses implicit casting to assign a `Circle` object to `geoObject1` and a `Cylinder` object to `geoObject2`, and then invokes the `displayGeometricObject` method to display the information on these objects.

In the `displayGeometricObject` method, explicit casting is used to cast the object to `Cylinder` if the object is an instance of `Cylinder`, and the methods `findArea` and `findVolume` are used to display the area and volume for the cylinder.

Explicit casting to `Cylinder` is necessary because the `findVolume` method is available only in the `Cylinder` class. However, explicit casting to `Circle` is not necessary, because the `findArea` method is defined in the `GeometricObject` class and overridden in the `Circle` class. By means of polymorphism, the `findArea` method of the `Circle` is invoked if the geometric object is a circle.

Note that the order in the `if` statement is significant. If it is reversed (for example, testing whether the object is an instance of `Circle` first), then the cylinder will never be cast into `Cylinder` because `Cylinder` is an instance of `Circle`. Try to run the program with the following `if` statement and observe the effect.

```
    if (object instanceof Circle)
    {
      System.out.println("The area is " + object.findArea());
      System.out.println("The perimeter is " +
        object.findPerimeter());
    }
    else if (object instanceof Cylinder)
    {
      System.out.println("The area is " +
        ((Cylinder)object).findArea());
      System.out.println("The volume is " +
        ((Cylinder)object).findVolume());
    }
  }
```

TIP

I recommend that you use the `instanceof` operator to ensure that the source object is an instance of the target class before performing a casting.

Interfaces

Sometimes it is necessary to derive a subclass from several classes, thus inheriting their data and methods. Java, however, does not allow multiple inheritance. If you use the `extends` keyword to define a subclass, it allows only one parent class. With interfaces, you can obtain the effect of multiple inheritance.

An interface is a classlike construct that contains only constants and abstract methods. In many ways, an interface is similar to an abstract class, but an abstract class can contain constants and abstract methods as well as variables and concrete methods.

The syntax to declare an interface is as follows:

```
modifier interface InterfaceName
{
  // Constants declarations;
  // Methods signatures;
}
```

An interface is treated like a special class in Java. Each interface is compiled into a separate bytecode file, just like a regular class. As with an abstract class, you cannot create an instance for the interface using the `new` operator, but in most cases you can use an interface more or less the same way you use an abstract class. For example, you can use an interface as a data type for a variable, as the result of casting, and so on.

Suppose you want to design a generic method to find the maximum of two objects. The objects can be students, circles, or cylinders. Because compare methods are different for different types of objects, you need to define a generic compare method to determine the order of two objects. Then you can tailor the method to compare students, circles, or cylinders. For example, you can use student ID as the key for comparing students, radius as the key for comparing circles, and volume as the key for comparing cylinders. You can use an interface to define a generic `compareTo` method, as follows:

```
// Interface for comparing objects, defined in java.lang
public interface Comparable
{
  public int compareTo(Object o);
}
```

The `compareTo` method determines the order of this object with the specified object `o`, and returns a negative integer, zero, or a positive integer as this object is less than, equal to, or greater than the specified object `o`.

NOTE

The `Comparable` interface has been available since JDK 1.2, and is included in the `java.lang` package.

A generic `max` method for finding the max between two objects can be declared in a class named `Max`, as follows:

```
// Max.java: Find a maximum object
public class Max
{
  // Return the maximum between two objects
  public static Comparable max(Comparable o1, Comparable o2)
  {
    if (o1.compareTo(o2) > 0)
      return o1;
    else
      return o2;
  }
}
```

The `Max` class contains the static method named `max`. To use the `max` method to find a maximum between two objects, implement the `Comparable` interface for the class of these objects. The following example demonstrates how the interface is used.

Example 6.5 Using Interfaces

In this example, a program is written that uses the max method to find a maximum circle between two circles and a maximum cylinder between two cylinders.

The output of the program is shown in Figure 6.8.

```
// TestInterface.java: Use the Comparable interface
// and the generic max method to find max objects
public class TestInterface
{
  // Main method
  public static void main(String[] args)
  {
    // Create two comparable circles
    ComparableCircle circle1 = new ComparableCircle(5);
    ComparableCircle circle2 = new ComparableCircle(4);

    // Display the max circle
    Comparable circle = Max.max(circle1, circle2);
    System.out.println("The max circle's radius is " +
      ((Circle)circle).getRadius());
    System.out.println(circle);

    // Create two comparable cylinders
    ComparableCylinder cylinder1 = new ComparableCylinder(5, 2);
    ComparableCylinder cylinder2 = new ComparableCylinder(4, 5);

    // Display the max cylinder
    Comparable cylinder = Max.max(cylinder1, cylinder2);
    System.out.println();
    System.out.println("cylinder1's volume is " +
      cylinder1.findVolume());
    System.out.println("cylinder2's volume is " +
      cylinder2.findVolume());
    System.out.println("The max cylinder's \tradius is " +
      ((Cylinder)cylinder).getRadius() + "\n\t\t\tlength is " +
      ((Cylinder)cylinder).getLength() + "\n\t\t\tvolume is " +
      ((Cylinder)cylinder).findVolume());
    System.out.println(cylinder);
  }
}

// ComparableCircle is a subclass of Circle, which implements the
// Comparable interface
class ComparableCircle extends Circle implements Comparable
{
  // Construct a CompareCircle with specified radius
  public ComparableCircle(double r)
  {
    super(r);
  }

  // Implement the compareTo method defined in Comparable
  public int compareTo(Object o)
  {
    if (getRadius() > ((Circle)o).getRadius())
      return 1;
    else if (getRadius() < ((Circle)o).getRadius())
      return -1;
```

continues

Example 6.5 continued

```
      else
        return 0;
    }
  }

  // ComparableCylinder is a subclass of Cylinder, which implements the
  // CompareObject interface
  class ComparableCylinder extends Cylinder implements Comparable
  {
    // Construct a CompareCylinder with radius and length
    ComparableCylinder(double r, double l)
    {
      super(r, l);
    }

    // Implement the compareTo method defined in Comparable interface
    public int compareTo(Object o)
    {
      if (findVolume() > ((Cylinder)o).findVolume())
        return 1;
      else if (findVolume() < ((Cylinder)o).findVolume())
        return -1;
      else
        return 0;
    }
  }
```

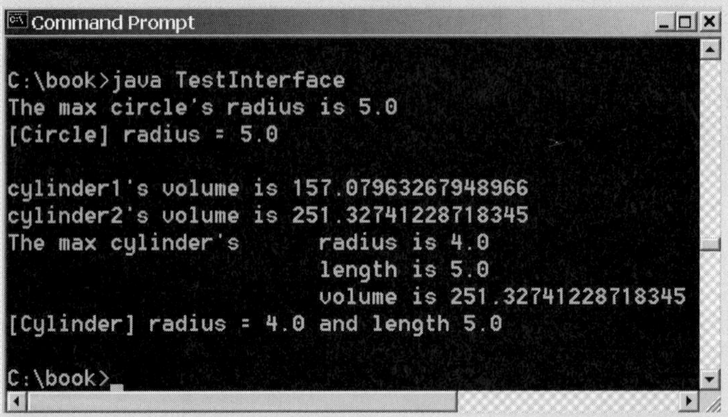

Figure 6.8 *The program displays the maximum circle and maximum cylinder.*

Example Review

The `max` method can be used to find a maximum object between two objects of the `Comparable` type. Any object whose class implements the `Comparable` interface is an instance of the `Comparable` type. The example creates the classes `ComparableCircle` and `ComparableCylinder` in order to utilize the generic `max` method. The relationship of the classes and the interface is shown in Figure 6.9.

The common functionality is to compare objects in this example, but the `compareTo` methods are different for different types of objects. Therefore, the in-

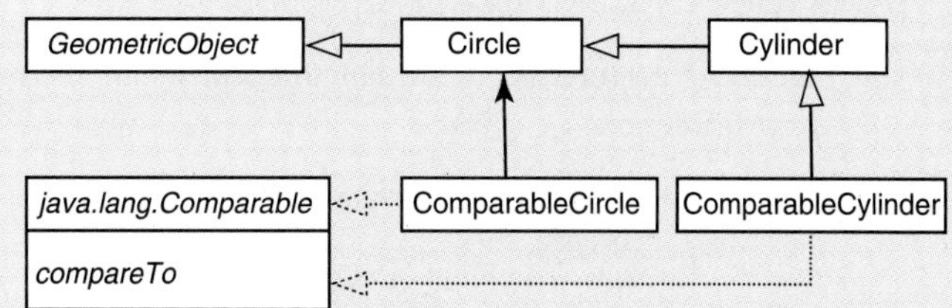

Figure 6.9 *The* `ComparableCircle` *class extends* `Circle` *and implements* `Comparable;` `ComparableCylinder` *extends* `Cylinder` *and implements* `Comparable`.

terface `Comparable` is used to generalize common functionality and leave the detail for the subclasses to implement.

The keyword `implements` in the `ComparableCircle` class indicates that it inherits all data from the `Comparable` interface and implements the methods in the interface.

The `ComparableCircle` class implements the `compareTo` method for comparing the radii of two circles, and the `ComparableCylinder` class implements the `compareTo` method for comparing the cylinders based on their volumes.

The interface `Comparable` is used as a data type for variables `o1` and `o2` in the `max` method, for the variable `o`. When you invoke `max(circle1, circle2)`, you passed `circle1` and `circle2` to `o1` and `o2`. This is implicit casting. The interface `Comparable` is like a superclass for `Circle`. `circle1` is an instance of `Circle`, as well as an instance of `Comparable`. Invoking `max(circle1, circle2)` returns an object of the `Comparable` type and this object's reference is assigned to the variable `o`. To invoke the `getRadius` in the `Circle` class, you have to cast the variable `o` into a `Circle` object, because `getRadius` is not defined in the `Comparable` interface.

The statement `System.out.println(o)` displays `o.toString()`. Since the `toString` method is defined in the `Object` class, it can be accessed by the objects of the `Comparable` type. By means of polymorphism, the `toString` method for the `Circle` method is used if `o` is an instance of `Circle`.

An interface provides another form of generic programming. It would be difficult to use a generic `max` method to find the maximum of the objects without using an interface in this example, because multiple inheritance is necessary to inherit `Comparable` and an object's class, such as `Circle` or `Cylinder`, in the same time.

The `Object` class contains the `equals` method, which is intended for the subclasses of the `Object` class to override in order to compare whether the contents of the objects are the same. Suppose that the `Object` class contains the `compareTo` method as defined in the `Comparable` interface; the new `max` method can be used to compare a list of *any* objects. Whether a `compareTo` method should be included in the `Object` class is debatable. Since the `compareTo` method is not defined in the `Object` class, the `Comparable` interface is created in Java 2 to enable objects to be compared if they are instances of the `Comparable` interface.

Interfaces vs. Abstract Classes

Defining an interface is similar to defining an abstract class. There are, however, a few differences:

- In an interface, the data must be constants; an abstract class can have all types of data.
- Each method in an interface has only a signature without implementation; an abstract class can have concrete methods.
- Since all the methods defined in an interface are abstract methods, Java does not require that you put the `abstract` modifier in the methods in an interface, but you must put the `abstract` modifier before an abstract method in an abstract class.

Java allows only single inheritance for class extension, but multiple extension for interfaces.

For example,

```
public class NewClass extends BaseClass
  implements Interface1, ..., InterfaceN
{ ... }
```

An interface can inherit other interfaces using the `extends` keyword, as follows:

```
public interface NewInterface extends Interface1, ..., InterfaceN
{
  // constants and abstract methods
}
```

A class implementing `NewInterface` must implement the abstract methods defined in `NewInterface`, `Interface1`, . . ., and `InterfaceN`. An interface can only extend other interfaces, but not classes. A class can extend its superclass and implement multiple interfaces.

All classes share a single root—the `Object` class, but there is no single root for interfaces. As shown in Example 6.5, an interface can be used as an abstract class. If a class extends an interface, this interface is like a superclass for the class. You can use an interface as a data type and cast a variable of an interface type to its subclass, and vice versa. For example, suppose that `c` is an instance of `Class2` in Figure 6.10. `c` is also an instance of `Object`, `Class1`, `Interface1`, `Interface1_1`, `Interface1_2`, `Interface2_1`, and `Interface2_2`.

Both interfaces and abstract classes can be used to generalize common features. In what circumstances should an interface or a class be used? In general, a clear is-a relationship should be modeled using classes. For example, a staff member is a person. So their relationship should be modeled using classes. A weak is-a relationship can be modeled using interfaces. For example, all circles are comparable. So you can define a `Circle` class to implement the `Comparable` interface. You should use interfaces to circumvent single inheritance restriction if multiple inheritance is desired. You may use

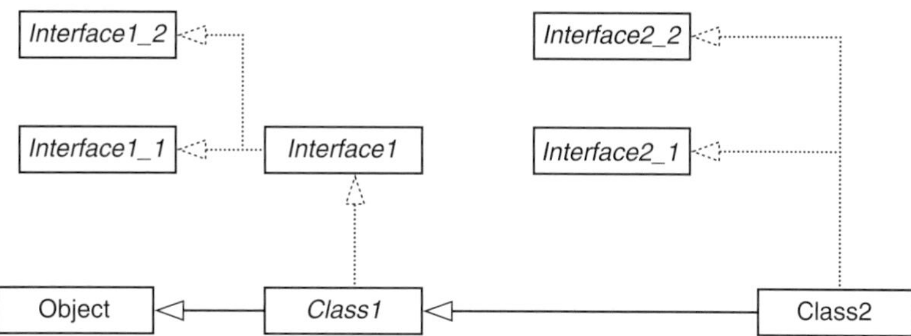

Figure 6.10 *Abstract class* `Class1` *implements* `Interface1`, `Interface1` *extends* `Interface1_1` *and* `Interface1_2`. `Class2` *extends* `Class1` *and implements* `Interface2_1` *and* `Interface2_2`.

abstract classes if single inheritance is sufficient. Generally, it is easier to use an abstract class than an interface, but interfaces are more flexible than abstract classes.

The *Cloneable* Interface

An interface contains constants and abstract methods, but the `Cloneable` interface is a special case. The `Cloneable` interface is defined as follows:

```
public interface Cloneable
{
}
```

This interface is empty. An interface with an empty body is referred to as a *marker interface*. A marker interface does not contain constants or methods, but it has a special meaning to the Java system. The Java system requires a class that implements the `Cloneable` interface to become cloneable. The object of a cloneable class can use the `clone` method defined in the `Object` class to make an identical copy of the object.

The following example demonstrates the `Cloneable` interface and the `clone` method, and shows the effect of object cloning.

Example 6.6 Cloning Objects

In this example, a program is written that uses the `Cloneable` interface to mark classes cloneable and uses the `clone` method to copy objects. The program creates a new class named `CloneableCircle` that extends `Circle` and implements `Cloneable` interface. The main method creates a `CloneableCircle` object, and copies it to a new variable.

The output of the program is shown in Figure 6.11.

```
// TestCloneable.java: Use the TestCloneable interface
// to enable cloning
public class TestCloneable
{
  // Main method
  public static void main(String[] args)
```

continues

Example 6.6 continued

```
  {
    // Declare and create an instance of CloneableCircle
    CloneableCircle c1 = new CloneableCircle(5);
    CloneableCircle c2 = (CloneableCircle)c1.clone();

    System.out.println("After copying c1 to circl2");

    // Check if two variables point to the same object
    if (c1 == c2)
      System.out.println("c1 and c2 reference to the same object");
    else
      System.out.println("c1 and c2 don't point to the same object");

    // Check if two objects are of identical contents
    if (c1.equals(c2))
      System.out.println("c1 and c2 have the same contents");
    else
      System.out.println("c1 and c2 don't have the same contents");

    // Modify c1's radius, name
    c1.setRadius(10);
    c1.getCreator().setFirstname("Michael");
    c1.getCreator().setMi("Z");

    // Display c1 and c2
    System.out.println("\nAfter modifying c1");
    System.out.println("c1 " + c1);
    System.out.println("c2 " + c2);

    System.out.println();
    if (c1 instanceof Cloneable)
    {
      System.out.println("A CloneableCircle object is cloneable");
    }
    else
    {
      System.out.println(c1 + "is not cloneable");
    }

    // Check if a Circle object is cloneable
    Circle c = new Circle();
    if (c instanceof Cloneable)
    {
      System.out.println("A Circle object is cloneable");
    }
    else
    {
      System.out.println("A Circle object is not cloneable");
    }
  }
}

// CloneableCircle is a subclass of Circle, which implements the
// Cloneable interface
class CloneableCircle extends Circle implements Cloneable
{
  // Store the creator of the object
  private Name creator = new Name("Yong", "D", "Liang");

  // Construct a CloneableCircle with specified radius
  public CloneableCircle(double radius)
```

```
    {
      super(radius);
    }

    // Getter method for creator
    public Name getCreator()
    {
      return creator;
    }

    // Setter method for creator
    public void setCreator(Name name)
    {
      creator = name;
    }

    // Override the protected clone method defined in the Object class
    public Object clone()
    {
      try
      {
        return super.clone();
      }
      catch (CloneNotSupportedException ex)
      {
        return null;
      }
    }

    // Override the toString method defined in the Object class
    public String toString()
    {
      return super.toString() + " " + creator.getFullname();
    }
  }
```

```
Command Prompt
C:\book>java TestCloneable
After copying c1 to circl2
c1 and c2 don't point to the same object
c1 and c2 have the same contents

After modifying c1
c1 [Circle] radius = 10.0 Michael Z Liang
c2 [Circle] radius = 5.0 Michael Z Liang

A CloneableCircle objec is cloneable
A Circle object is not cloneable

C:\book>
```

Figure 6.11 *The `clone` method creates a new copy for the cloneable object.*

Example Review

The `CloneableCircle` class overrides the `clone` method defined in the `Object` class. The `clone` method in the `Object` class is defined as follows:

```
protected native Object clone() throws CloneNotSupportedException;
```

continues

Example 6.6 continued

The keyword `native` indicates that this method is not written in Java, but is implemented in JVM for the native platform. The keyword `protected` indicates that this method cannot be directly invoked by an object of the class in a different package. For this reason, the cloneable class must override this method and change the visibility modifier to `public` so that the method can be used in any packages. Since the `clone` method implemented for the native platform in the `Object` class performs the task of cloning objects, the `clone` method in the `CloneableCircle` class simply invokes `super.clone()`. The `clone` method defined in the `Object` class may throw `CloneNotSupportedException`. Thus, `super.clone()` must be placed in a `try/catch` block. Exceptions and the `try/catch` block are introduced in Chapter 11, "Exception Handling."

The `main` method creates a `CloneableCircle` object `c1` and clones `c1` into `c2`. The `clone` method in the `Object` class copies each field from the original object to the target object. If the field is of a primitive type, its value is copied. For example, the value of `radius` (`double` type) is copied from `c1` to `c2`. If the field is of an object, the reference of the field is copied. For example, the field `creator` is of the `Name` class type, the reference of `creator` in `c1` is copied into `c2`. As shown in Figure 6.12, the reference of `creator` in `c1` is copied into `c2`. Therefore, `c1.getCreator() == c2.getCreator()` is true, although `c1 == c2` is false. This is referred to as a *shallow copy* instead of *deep copy*, meaning that if the field is of an object, the reference of the field is copied instead of the contents of the field.

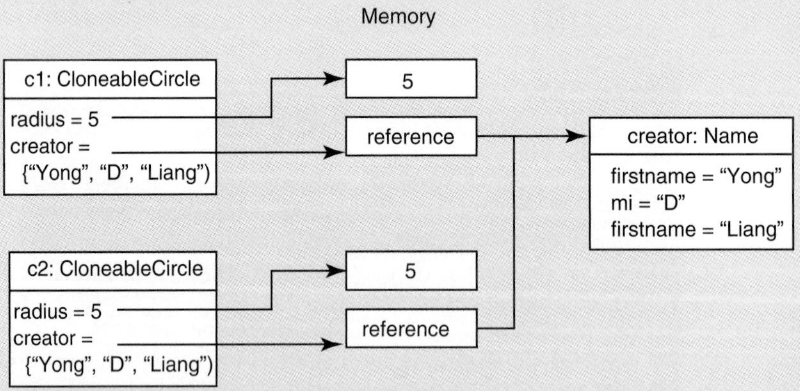

Figure 6.12 *The `clone` method copies the values of primitive type fields and the references of object type fields.*

If you want to perform a deep copy, you can override the `clone` method with custom cloning operations instead of invoking `super.clone()`.

NOTE

An instance of `CloneableCircle` is also an instance of `Cloneable`. This means that you can copy the instance using the `clone` method. Since the `Circle` class does not implement the `Cloneable` interface, an instance of the `Circle` class is not cloneable. If you attempt to copy an instance of the `Circle` class, you would get a `CloneNotSupportedException`. Exceptions will be introduced in Chapter 11, "Exception Handling."

Inner Classes

An *inner class,* or *nested class,* is a class defined within the scope of another class. Here is an example of an inner class:

```
// ShowInnerClass.java: Demonstrate using inner classes
public class ShowInnerClass
{
  private int data;

  // A method
  public void m()
  {
    // Do something
    InnerClass instance = new InnerClass();
  }

  // An inner class
  class InnerClass
  {
    // A method in the inner class
    public void mi()
    {
      // Directly reference data and method defined in its outer class
      data++;
      m();
    }
  }
}
```

The class `InnerClass` is defined inside `ShowInnerClass`. This inner class is just like any regular class, with the following features:

- An inner class can reference the data and methods defined in the outer class in which it nests, so you do not need to pass the reference of the outer class to the constructor of the inner class.
- Inner classes can make programs simple and concise. As you will see in Example 10.8, "The TicTacToe Game," the program is shorter and leaner using inner classes.
- An inner class is only for supporting the work of its containing outer class and is compiled into a class named *`OutClassName$InnerClassName`*`.class`. For example, the inner class `InnerClass` in `ShowInnerClass` is compiled into `ShowInnerClass$InnerClass.class`.

NOTE

The inner class can be further shortened with the use of an anonymous inner class. An anonymous inner class is an inner class without a name. An anonymous inner class combines declaring an inner class and creating an instance of the class in one step. Many Java development tools use inner classes to generate adapters for handling events. Event-driven programming is introduced in Chapter 8, "Getting Started with Graphics Programming."

Software Development Processes

Developing a software project is an engineering process. Software products, no matter how large or how small, have the same developmental phases: requirement specification, analysis, design, implementation, testing, deployment, and maintenance, as shown in Figure 6.13.

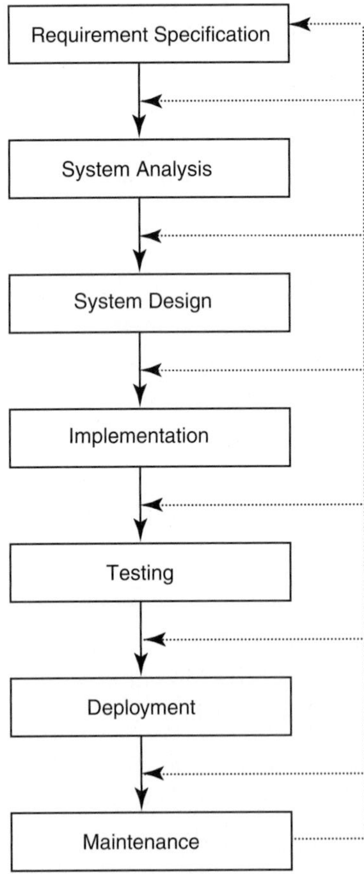

Figure 6.13 *Developing a project involves requirements specification, system analysis, system design, implementation, testing, deployment, and maintenance.*

Requirements specification is a formal process that seeks to understand the problem and document in detail what it needs to do. This phase involves close interaction between users and designers. Most of the examples in this book are simple, and their requirements are clearly stated. In the real world, however, problems are not well defined. You need to study a problem carefully to identify its requirements.

System analysis seeks to analyze the business process in terms of data flow, and to identify the system's input and output. Part of the analysis entails modeling the system's behavior. The model is intended to capture the essential elements of the system and to define services to the system.

System design is the process of designing the system's components. This phase involves the use of many levels of abstraction to decompose the problem into manageable components, identify classes and interfaces, and establish relationships among the classes and interfaces.

Implementation is the process of translating the system design into programs. Separate programs are written for each component, and they are put to work together. This phase requires the use of an object-oriented programming language like Java. The implementation involves coding, testing, and debugging.

Testing ensures that the code meets the requirements specification and weeds out bugs. An independent team of software engineers not involved in design and implementation of the project usually conducts such testing.

Deployment makes the project available for use. For a Java applet, this means installing it on a Web server. For a Java application, install it on the client's computer. The project usually consists of many classes. An effective approach for deployment is to package all the classes into a Java archive file, as will be introduced in the section "Packaging and Deploying Java Projects," in Chapter 10, "Applets and Advanced Graphics."

Maintenance is concerned with changing and improving the product. A software product must continue to perform and improve in a changing environment. This requires periodic upgrades of the product to fix newly discovered bugs and incorporate changes.

TIP

The system should be developed incrementally. Do not attempt to develop the entire project at once. The development process should consist of successive iterations. Each iteration deals with a small part of the system. The iterative process continues until the entire system is developed.

Class-Design Guidelines

The key to object-oriented programming is to model the application in terms of cooperative objects. Carefully designed classes are critical when a project is being developed. There are many levels of abstraction in system design. You have learned method abstraction and have applied it to the development of large programs. Methods are means to group statements. Classes extend abstraction to a higher level and provide a means of grouping methods. Classes do more than just group methods, however; they also contain data fields. Methods and data fields together describe the properties and behaviors of classes.

The power of classes is further extended by inheritance. Inheritance enables a class to extend existing classes without knowing the details of the existing classes. In the development of a Java program, class abstraction is applied to decompose the problem into a set of related classes, and method abstraction is applied to design classes.

Here are some guidelines for designing classes:

- A class should use the `private` modifier to hide its data from direct access by clients. This prevents the clients from damaging the data. A class should also hide methods not intended for client use. The `gcd` method in the `Rational` class in Example 5.7, "Using the `Rational` Class," is private, for example, because it is only for internal use within the class. You can use getter methods and setter methods to provide users with access to the hidden data, but only to hidden data you want the user to see or to modify.

- Provide a public default constructor and override the `equals` method and the `toString` method defined in the `Object` class whenever possible.

- A property that is shared by all the instances of the class should be declared as a class property. For example, the variable `numOfObjects` in Example 5.5, "Using Instance and Class Variables and Methods," is shared by all the objects of the `Circle` class, and therefore is declared as a class variable. A method that is not dependent on a specific instance should be declared as a class method. For instance, the `getNumOfObjects` method in Example 5.5 is not tied to a specific instance of the `Circle` class, and therefore is declared as a class method. The class properties and methods are denoted using the `static` modifier.

- A class should describe a single entity or a set of similar operations. You can use a class for students, for example, but do not combine students and staff in the same class. Since the `Math` class provides mathematical operations, it is natural to group the mathematical methods in one class. A single entity with too many responsibilities can be broken into several classes to separate responsibilities. The `String` class, `StringBuffer` class, and `StringTokenizer` class all deal with strings, for example, but have different responsibilities.

- Group common data fields and operations shared by other classes into a superclass, which is sometimes an abstract class. For example, the classes `Circle`, `Rectangle`, and `Cylinder` share many common data fields and operations, which are grouped into an abstract class `GeometricObject`. You should use inheritance to model the is-a relationship. A student or a faculty member is a person, for example, so `Student` can be designed as a subclass of `Person`.

- Follow standard Java programming style. Choose informative names for classes, data fields, and methods. Always place the data declaration before the constructor, and place constructors before methods. Always provide a constructor and initialize variables to avoid programming errors.

Chapter Summary

In this chapter, you learned about inheritance, an important and powerful concept in object-oriented programming. You can immediately see the benefits of inheritance in Java graphics programming, exception handling, internationalization, multithreading, multimedia, I/O, network programming, and every Java program that inherits and extends existing classes.

You learned how to create a subclass from a superclass by adding new fields and methods. You can also override the methods in the superclass. The keywords `super` and `this` are used to reference superclasses and subclasses, respectively.

You learned how to use the `protected` modifier to allow data and methods to be accessed by its subclasses, even if the subclasses are in different packages.

You learned how to use the `final` modifier to prevent changes to a class, method, or variable. A final class cannot be extended. A `final` method cannot be overridden. A `final` variable is a constant.

You learned how to use the `abstract` modifier to design generic superclasses. An abstract class cannot be instantiated. An abstract method contains only the method description without implementation. Its implementation is provided by subclasses.

You learned the concept of polymorphism and Java's dynamic binding ability to determine at runtime which code to run, given multiple methods with the same name but different operations in the same class or in different classes.

You learned about casting objects among classes in the inheritance hierarchy. You can implicitly cast an object of a subclass to its superclass, since this object is always an instance of the superclass. However, an explicit casting must be used to cast an object of the superclass into a subclass.

You learned how to use an interface. An interface cannot be instantiated. A subclass can only extend one superclass, but it can implement many interfaces to achieve multiple inheritance.

Review Questions

6.1 What is the printout of running the class `C`?

```
class A
{
  public A()
  {
    System.out.println(
      "The default constructor of A is invoked");
  }
}
```

```
class B extends A
{
  public B()
  {
  }
}

public class C
{
  public static void main(String[] args)
  {
    B b = new B();
  }
}
```

6.2 What problem arises in compiling the following program?

```
class A
{
  public A(int x)
  {
  }
}

class B extends A
{
  public B()
  {
  }
}

public class C
{
  public static void main(String[] args)
  {
    B b = new B();
  }
}
```

6.3 Define the following terms: inheritance, superclass, subclass, the keywords `super` and `this`, the modifiers `protected`, `final`, and `abstract`, casting objects, interface.

6.4 Identify the problems in the following classes:

```
public class Circle
{
  private double radius;

  public Circle(double radius)
  {
    radius = radius;
  }

  public double getRadius()
  {
    return radius;
  }

  public double findArea()
  {
```

```
    return radius*radius*Math.PI;
  }
}

class Cylinder extends Circle
{
  private double length;

  Cylinder(double radius, double length)
  {
    Circle(radius);
    length = length;
  }

  // Find the surface area for the cylinder
  public double findArea()
  {
    return findArea()*length;
  }
}
```

6.5 Indicate true or false for the following statements:

- A protected datum or method can be accessed by any class in the same package.
- A protected datum or method can be accessed by any class in different packages.
- A protected datum or method can be accessed by its subclass in any packages.
- A final class can have instances.
- An abstract class can have instances.
- A final class can be extended.
- An abstract class can be extended.
- A final method can be overridden.
- You can always successfully cast a subclass to a superclass.
- You can always successfully cast a superclass to a subclass.
- An interface can be a separate unit and can be compiled into a bytecode file.
- The order in which modifiers appear before a class or a method is important.

6.6 Explain the difference between method overloading and method overriding.

6.7 Does every class have a `toString` method and an `equals` method? Where do they come from? How are they used?

6.8 What modifier should you use on a class so that a class in the same package can access it, but a class in a different package cannot access it?

6.9 What modifier should you use so that a class in a different package cannot access the class, but its subclasses in any package can access it?

6.10 Which of the following class definitions defines a legal abstract class?

a.

```
class A
{
  abstract void unfinished()
  {     }
}
```

b.

```
class A
{
  abstract void unfinished();
}
```

c.

```
abstract class A
{
  abstract void unfinished();
}
```

d.

```
public class abstract A
{
  abstract void unfinished();
}
```

6.11 Given the assumptions

```
Circle circle = new Circle(1);

Cylinder cylinder = new Cylinder(1,1);
```

are the following Boolean expressions true or false?

```
(circle instanceof Cylinder)

(cylinder instanceof Circle)
```

6.12 Are the following statements correct?

```
Cylinder cylinder = new Cylinder(1,1);

Circle circle = cylinder;
```

6.13 Are the following statements correct?

```
Cylinder cylinder = new Cylinder(1,1);

Circle circle = (Circle)cylinder;
```

6.14 Suppose that Fruit, Apple, Orange, Golden Delicious Apple, and Macintosh Apple are declared as shown in Figure 6.14.

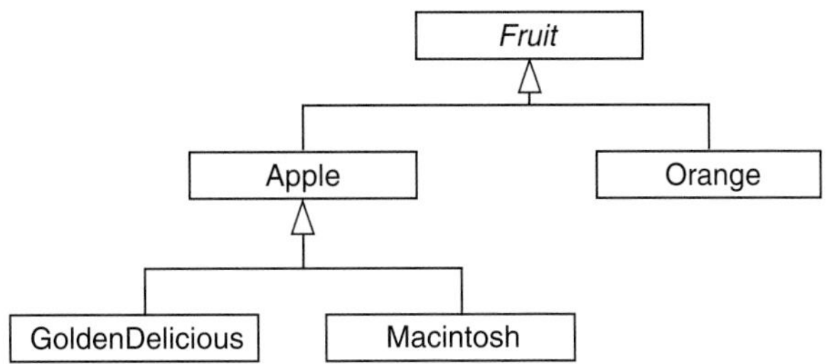

Figure 6.14 *`GoldenDelicious` and `Macintosh` are subclasses of `Apple`, `Apple` and `Orange` are subclasses of `Fruit`.*

Assume the following declaration is given:

```
Fruit fruit = new GoldenDelicious();
Orange orange = new Orange();
```

Answer the following questions:

- Is `fruit instanceof Orange` true?
- Is `fruit instanceof Apple` true?
- Is `fruit instanceof GoldenDelicious` true?
- Is `fruit instanceof Macintosh` true?
- Is `orange instanceof Orange` true?
- Is `orange instanceof Fruit` true?
- Is `orange instanceof Apple` true?
- Suppose the method `makeApple` is defined in the `Apple` class. Can `fruit` invoke this method? Can `orange` invoke this method?
- Suppose the method `makeOrangeJuice` is defined in the `Orange` class. Can `orange` invoke this method? Can `fruit` invoke this method?

6.15 Which of the following is a correct interface?

a.

```
interface A
{
  void print() { };
}
```

b.

```
abstract interface A
{
  print();
}
```

c.

```
abstract interface A extends I1, I2
{
  abstract void print() { };
}
```

d.

```
interface A
{
  void print();
}
```

6.16 What is the output of the following program? This program is the same as the one in Example 6.6 except that one statement is added (see the highlighted line in the code).

```
// TestCloneable.java: Use the TestCloneable interface
// to enable cloning
public class TestCloneable
{
  // Main method
  public static void main(String[] args)
  {
    // Declare and create an instance of CloneableCircle
    CloneableCircle c1 = new CloneableCircle(5);
    CloneableCircle c2 = (CloneableCircle)c1.clone();

    System.out.println("After copying c1 to c2");

    // Check if two variables point to the same object
    if (c1 == c2)
      System.out.println("c1 and c2 reference to the same" +
        "object");
    else
      System.out.println("c1 and c2 don't point to the same" +
        "object");

    // Check if two objects are of identical contents
    if (c1.equals(c2))
      System.out.println("c1 and c2 have the same contents");
    else
      System.out.println("c1 and c2 don't have the same" +
        "contents");

    // Modify c1's radius, name
    c1.setRadius(10);
    c1.setCreator(new Name("Bob", "R", "Smith"));
    c1.getCreator().setFirstname("Michael");
    c1.getCreator().setMi("Z");

    // Display c1 and c2
    System.out.println("\nAfter modifying c1");
    System.out.println("c1 " + c1);
    System.out.println("c2 " + c2);

    System.out.println();
    if (c1 instanceof Cloneable)
    {
      System.out.println("A CloneableCircle object is" +
        "cloneable");
    }
```

```
        else
        {
          System.out.println("A CloneableCircle object is not" +
            "cloneable");
        }

        // Check if a Circle object is cloneable
        Circle c = new Circle();
        if (c instanceof Cloneable)
        {
          System.out.println("A Circle object is cloneable");
        }
        else
        {
          System.out.println("A Circle object is not cloneable");
        }
      }
    }
```

6.17 Can an inner class be used in a class other than the class in which the inner class nests?

6.18 Analyze the following code:

```
class Test extends A
{
  public static void main(String[] args)
  {
    Test t = new Test();
    t.print();
  }
}

class A
{
  String s;

  A(String s)
  {
    this.s = s;
  }

  public void print()
  {
   System.out.println (s);
  }
}
```

a. The program does not compile because Test does not have a constructor `Test()`.
b. The program would compile if the constructor in the class A were removed.
c. The program compiles, but it has a runtime error due to the conflict on the method name `print`.
d. The program runs just fine.

Programming Exercises

6.1 Write a class named `Triangle` that extends `GeometricObject`. The class `Triangle` is defined as follows:

```
public class Triangle extends GeometricObject
{
  private double side1, side2, side3;

  // Construct a triangle with the specified sides
  public Triangle(double side1, double side2, double side3)
  {
    // Implement it
  }

  // Implement the abstract method findArea in
  // GeometricObject
  public double findArea()
  {
    // Implement it
  }

  // Implement the abstract method findPerimeter in
  // GeometricObject
  public double findPerimeter()
  {
    // Implement it
  }
}
```

The formula for computing the area is as follows:

```
s = (side1 + side2 + side3)/2;
```

$$\text{area} = \sqrt{s(s - side1)(s - side2)(s - side3)}$$

6.2 Implement a class named `Person` and two subclasses of `Person`, named `Student` and `Employee`. Make `Faculty` and `Staff` subclasses of `Employee`. A person has a name, address, phone number, and email address. A student has a class status (freshman, sophomore, junior, or senior). Define the status as constants. An employee has an office, salary, and the date-hired. A faculty member has office hours and a rank. A staff member has a title. Override the `toString` method in each class to display the class name and the person's name.

6.3 In Exercise 5.3, the `Account` class was created to model a bank account. An account has properties account number, balance, annual interest rate, and methods to deposit and withdraw. Create two subclasses for checking and saving accounts. A checking account has an overdraft limit, but a savings account cannot go overdrawn.

6.4 Modify the `GeometricObject` class to implement the `Comparable` interface and define the `max` method in the `GeometricObject` class. Write a test program that uses the `max` method to find a maximum circle between two circles and a maximum cylinder between two cylinders.

6.5 Create a class named `ComparableRectangle` that extends `Rectangle` and implements `CompareObject`. Implement the `compareTo` method to compare the rectangles on their areas. Write a test class to find a max between two instances of `ComparableRectangle` objects.

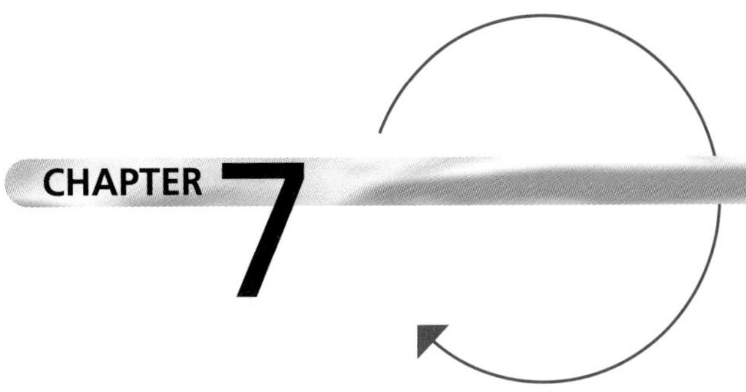

Arrays and Vectors

Objectives

- Understand the concept of arrays.
- Learn the steps involved in using arrays—declaring, creating, initializing, and processing arrays.
- Become familiar with sorting and search algorithms.
- Use objects as array elements.
- Copy arrays.
- Learn how to use multidimensional arrays.
- Become familiar with the numerical wrapper classes and their subclasses.
- Know how to use command-line arguments.
- Design generic classes for matrix operations. (Optional)
- Use the `Vector` class to store unspecified numbers of objects. (Optional)

Introduction

In earlier chapters, you studied examples in which values were overwritten during the execution of a program. In those examples, such as Example 3.2, "Using `while` loops," in Chapter 3, "Control Statements," you did not need to worry about storing former values. However, in some cases, you will have to store a large number of values in memory during the execution of a program. Suppose, for instance, that you want to sort a group of numbers. The numbers must all be stored in memory because later you will have to compare each of them with all of the others.

To store the numbers requires declaring variables in the program. It is practically impossible to declare variables for each number. You need an efficient, organized approach. All of the high-level languages, including Java, provide you with a data structure, array, which stores a collection of the same types of data. Java treats these arrays as objects.

Declaring and Creating Arrays

To use arrays in a program, you need to declare the arrays and the type of elements that can be stored in them. Here is the syntax for declaring an array:

```
datatype[] arrayName;
```

or

```
datatype arrayName[];
```

The following code is an example of this syntax:

```
double[] myList;
```

or

```
double myList[];
```

NOTE

The style `datatype[] arrayName` is preferred. The style `datatype arrayName[]` comes from the C language and was adopted in Java to accommodate C programmers.

Since a Java array is an object, the declaration does not allocate any space in memory for it. You cannot assign elements to an array unless it is already created.

After an array is declared, you can create it by using the `new` operator with the following syntax:

```
arrayName = new datatype[arraySize];
```

Declaration and creation can be combined in one statement, as follows:

```
datatype[] arrayName = new datatype[arraySize];
```

or

```
datatype arrayName[] = new datatype[arraySize];
```

Here is an example of such a statement:

```
double[] myList = new double[10];
```

This statement creates an array of 10 elements of `double` type, as shown in Figure 7.1. When space for the array is allocated, the array size must be given, to specify the number of elements that can be stored in it. After the array is created, its size cannot be changed.

double[ ] myList = new double[10];

myList[0]
myList[1]
myList[2]
myList[3]
myList[4]
myList[5]
myList[6]
myList[7]
myList[8]
myList[9]

Figure 7.1 *The array* `myList` *has 10 elements of* `double` *type and* `int` *indices from 0 to 9.*

Initializing and Processing Arrays

When an array is created, its elements are assigned the default value of `0` for the numeric primitive data type variables, `'\u0000'` for `char` variables, `false` for `boolean` variables, and `null` for object variables. The size of an array is denoted by `arrayObject.length`. After an array is created, the `length` data field is assigned a value that denotes the number of elements in the array.

The array elements are accessed through the index. The array indices are from `0` to `arrayObject.length-1`. In the example in Figure 7.1, `myList` holds 10 `double` values and the indices are from `0` to `9`.

Each element in the array is represented, using the following syntax:

```
arrayName[index];
```

For example, `myList[9]` represents the last element in the array `myList`.

NOTE

In Java, an array index is always an integer that starts with 0. In many other languages, such as Ada and Pascal, the index can be either an integer or another type of value.

Some languages use parentheses to reference an array element, as in `myList(9)`. But Java uses brackets, as in `myList[9]`.

After an array is created, you can enter values into array elements. See, for example, the following loop:

```
for (int i = 0; i < myList.length; i++)
  myList[i] = i;
```

In this example, `myList.length` returns the array size (10) for `myList`.

TIP

The word `length` is a data field belonging to an array object, not to a method. Therefore, using `length()` would result in an error. The `length` property can only be accessed after the array is created. Before the array is created, the array's reference is `null`.

Java has a shorthand notation that creates an array object and initializes it at the same time. The following is an example of its syntax at work:

```
double[] myList = {1.9, 2.9, 3.4, 3.5};
```

This statement creates the array `myList`, which consists of four elements. Therefore, `myList.length` is `4` and `myList[0]` is `1.9`. Note that the `new` operator was not used in the syntax.

When processing array elements, you will often use a `for` loop. Here are the reasons why:

- All of the elements in the array are of the same type and have the same properties. They are even processed in the same fashion—by repeatedly using a loop.
- Since the size of the array is known, it is natural to use a `for` loop.

Example 7.1 Assigning Grades

In this example, a program is written that will read student scores (`int`) from the keyboard, get the best score, and then assign grades based on the following scheme:

Grade is A if score is >= best–10;

Grade is B if score is >= best–20;

Grade is C if score is >= best–30;

Grade is D if score is >= best–40;

Grade is F otherwise.

The program prompts the user to enter the total number of students. Then it prompts the user to enter all of the scores. Finally, it displays the grades.

The output of a sample run of the program is shown in Figure 7.2.

```
// AssignGrade.java: Assign grade
public class AssignGrade
{
  // Main method
  public static void main(String[] args)
  {
    int numOfStudents = 0; // The number of students
    int[] scores; // Array scores
    int best = 0; // The best score
    char grade; // The grade

    // Get number of students
    System.out.println("Please enter number of students");
    numOfStudents = MyInput.readInt();

    // Create array scores
    scores = new int[numOfStudents];

    // Read scores and find the best score
    System.out.println("Please enter " + numOfStudents + " scores");
    for (int i=0; i<scores.length; i++)
    {
      scores[i] = MyInput.readInt();
      if (scores[i] > best)
        best = scores[i];
    }

    // Assign and display grades
    for (int i=0; i<scores.length; i++)
    {
      if (scores[i] >= best - 10)
        grade = 'A';
      else if (scores[i] >= best - 20)
        grade = 'B';
      else if (scores[i] >= best - 30)
        grade = 'C';
      else if (scores[i] >= best - 40)
        grade = 'D';
      else
        grade = 'F';

      System.out.println("Student " + i + " score is " + scores[i] +
        " and grade is " + grade);
    }
  }
}
```

continues

Example 7.1 continued

```
Command Prompt
C:\book>java AssignGrade
Please enter number of students
4
Please enter 4 scores
40
50
60
70
Student 0 score is 40 and grade is C
Student 1 score is 50 and grade is B
Student 2 score is 60 and grade is A
Student 3 score is 70 and grade is A

C:\book>_
```

Figure 7.2 *The program receives the number of students and their scores and then assigns grades.*

Example Review

The `scores` is declared as an array of `int` type in order to store scores. At the time this array is declared, its size is undetermined. After the user enters the number of students into `numOfStudents`, an array with the size of `numOfStudents` is created.

The array is not needed to find the best score, but it is needed to keep all of the scores so that grades can be assigned later on, and it is needed when scores are printed along with the students' grades.

TIP

Accessing an array out of bounds is a common programming error. To avoid it, make sure that you do not use an index beyond `arrayObject.length-1`.

Programmers often mistakenly reference the first element in an array with index 1, so that the index of the tenth element becomes 10. This is called the *off-by-one error*.

Sorting Arrays

Sorting is a common task in computer programming. It would be used, for instance, if you wanted to display the grades from the preceding example in alphabetical order. Many different algorithms are used for sorting. In this section, a simple, intuitive sorting algorithm, *selection sort*, is introduced.

Suppose that you want to sort a list in nondescending order. Selection sort finds the largest number in the list and places it last. It then finds the largest number remaining and places it last, and so on until the remaining list contains only a single number.

Consider the following list:

2 **9** 5 4 8 1 **6**

If you selected 9 (the largest number) and swapped it with 6 (the last in the list), the new list would be:

2 **6** 5 4 8 1 ***9***

The number 9 would now be in the correct position and thus no longer need to be considered. The list is now:

2 6 5 4 **8 1**

If you applied selection sort to the remaining numbers, you would select 8 and swap it with 1. The new list would be:

2 6 5 4 **1** ***8***

Since the number 8 has been placed in the correct position, it would no longer need to be considered. If you continued the same process, eventually the entire list would be sorted.

The algorithm can be described as follows:

```
for (int i=list.length-1; i>=1; i--)
{
  select the largest element in list[1..i];
  swap the largest with list[i], if necessary;
  // list[i] is in place. The next iteration apply on list[1..i-1]
}
```

The code is given in the next example.

Example 7.2 Using Arrays in Sorting

In this example, the `selectionSort` method is used to write a program that will sort a list of double floating-point numbers. The output of the program is shown in Figure 7.3.

```
// SelectionSort.java: Sort numbers using selection sort
public class SelectionSort
{
  // Main method
  public static void main(String[] args)
  {
    // Initialize the list
    double[] myList = {5.0, 4.4, 1.9, 2.9, 3.4, 3.5};

    // Print the original list
    System.out.println("My list before sort is: ");
    printList(myList);

    // Sort the list
    selectionSort(myList);
```

continues

Example 7.2 continued

```
      // Print the sorted list
      System.out.println();
      System.out.println("My list after sort is: ");
      printList(myList);
    }

    // The method for printing numbers
    static void printList(double[] list)
    {
      for (int i=0; i<list.length; i++)
        System.out.print(list[i] + "  ");
      System.out.println();
    }

    // The method for sorting the numbers
    static void selectionSort(double[] list)
    {
      double currentMax;
      int currentMaxIndex;

      for (int i=list.length-1; i>=1; i--)
      {
        // Find the maximum in the list[0..i]
        currentMax = list[i];
        currentMaxIndex = i;

        for (int j=i-1; j>=0; j--)
        {
          if (currentMax < list[j])
          {
            currentMax = list[j];
            currentMaxIndex = j;
          }
        }

        // Swap list[i] with list[currentMaxIndex] if necessary;
        if (currentMaxIndex != i)
        {
          list[currentMaxIndex] = list[i];
          list[i] = currentMax;
        }
      }
    }
  }
```

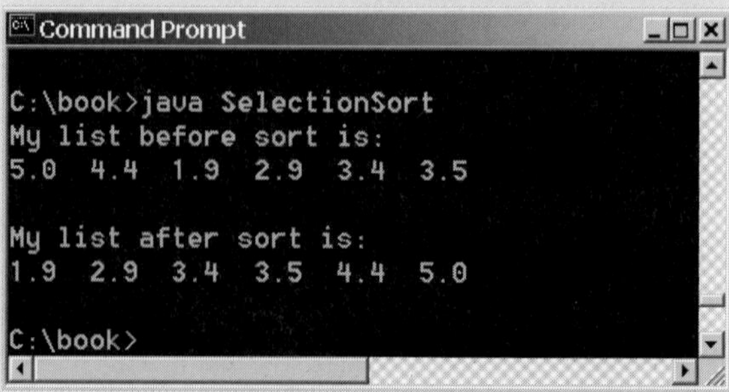

Figure 7.3 *The program invokes* `selectionSort` *in order to sort a list of* `double` *values.*

Example Review

An array `myList` of length 6 was created. Its initial values are listed in the following single statement:

```
double[] myList = {5.0, 4.4, 1.9, 2.9, 3.4, 3.5};
```

The `selectionSort(double[] list)` method sorts any array of double elements. The method is implemented with a nested `for` loop. The outer loop (with the loop control variable `i`) is iterated in order to find the largest element in the list, which ranges from `list[0]` to `list[i]`, and exchange it with the current last element, `list[i]`.

The variable `i` is initially `list.length-1`. After each iteration of the outer loop, `list[i]` is in the right place. Eventually, all the elements are put in the right place; therefore, the whole list is sorted.

Searching Arrays

Searching is the process of looking for a specific element in an array; for example, discovering whether a certain score is included in a list of scores. Searching, like sorting, is a common task in computer programming. There are many algorithms and data structures devoted to searching. In this section, two commonly used approaches are discussed, *linear search* and *binary search*.

The Linear Search Approach

The linear search approach compares the key element, `key`, with each element in the array `list[]`. The method continues to do so until the key matches an element in the list or the list is exhausted without a match being found. If a match is made, the linear search returns the index of the element in the array that matches the key. If no match is found, the search returns `-1`. The algorithm can be simply described as follows:

```
for (int i=0; i<list.length; i++)
{
  if (key == list[i])
    return i;
}

return -1;
```

The example given below demonstrates a linear search.

Example 7.3 Testing Linear Search

In this example, a program is written that will implement and test the linear search method. This program creates an array of 10 random elements of `int` type and then displays it. The program prompts the user to enter a key for testing linear search. The output of a sample run of the program is shown in Figure 7.4.

```
// LinearSearch.java: Search for a number in a list
public class LinearSearch
{
  // Main method
  public static void main(String[] args)
  {
    int[] list = new int[10];

    // Create the list randomly and display it
    System.out.print("The list is  ");
    for (int i=0; i<list.length; i++)
    {
      list[i] = (int)(Math.random()*100);
      System.out.print(list[i]+"  ");
    }
    System.out.println();

    // Prompt the user to enter a key
    System.out.print("Enter a key  ");
    int key = MyInput.readInt();
    int index = linearSearch(key, list);
    if (index != -1)
      System.out.println("The key is found in index "+index);
    else
      System.out.println("The key is not found in the list");
  }

  // The method for finding a key in the list
  public static int linearSearch(int key, int[] list)
  {
    for (int i=0; i<list.length; i++)
      if (key == list[i])
        return i;
    return -1;
  }
}
```

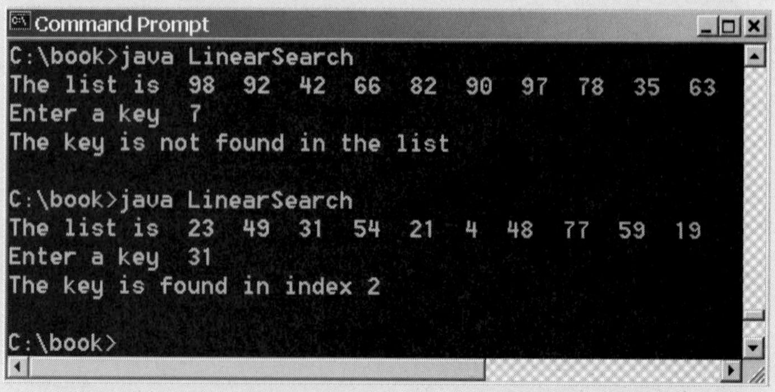

```
Command Prompt
C:\book>java LinearSearch
The list is  98  92  42  66  82  90  97  78  35  63
Enter a key  7
The key is not found in the list

C:\book>java LinearSearch
The list is  23  49  31  54  21  4  48  77  59  19
Enter a key  31
The key is found in index 2

C:\book>
```

Figure 7.4 *The program uses linear search to find a key in a list of* `int` *elements.*

Example Review

`Math.random()` generates a random `double` value greater than or equal to 0.0 and less than 1.0. Therefore, `(int)(Math.random()*100)` is a random integer value greater than or equal to 0.0 and less than 100.0.

In case of a match, the algorithm returns the index of the first element in the array that matches the key. In case of no match, the algorithm returns `-1`.

The linear search method compares the key with each element in the array. The elements in the array can be in any order. On average, the algorithm will have to compare half of the elements in an array. Since the execution time of a linear search increases linearly as the number of array elements increases, linear search is inefficient for a large array.

The Binary Search Approach (Optional)

Binary search is the other common search approach. For binary search to work, the array must already be in the right order. Without loss of generality, assume that the array is in nondescending order. The binary search first compares the key with the element in the middle of the array. Consider the following three cases:

- If the key is less than the middle element, you only need to search the key in the first half of the array.
- If the key is equal to the middle element, the search ends with a match.
- If the key is greater than the middle element, you only need to search the key in the second half of the array.

Clearly, the binary search method eliminates half of the array after each comparison. Suppose that the array has n elements. For convenience, let n be a power of 2. After the first comparison, there are n/2 elements left for further search; after the second comparison, there are (n/2)/2 elements left for further search. After the kth comparison, there are $n/2^k$ elements left for further search. When $k = \log_2 n$, only one element is left in the array, and you only need one more comparison. Therefore, in the worst case, you need $\log_2 n+1$ comparisons to find an element in the sorted array when using the binary search approach. For a list of 1,024 (2^{10}) elements, binary search requires only 11 comparisons in the worst case.

The array being searched shrinks after each comparison. Let `low` and `up` denote, respectively, the first index and the last index of the array that is currently being searched. Initially, `low` is `0` and `up` is `list.length-1`. Let `binarySearch(int key, int[] list, int low, int up)` denote the method that finds the key in the list that has the specified `low` index and `up` index. The algorithm can be described recursively as follows:

```
public static int binarySearch(int key, int[] list, int low, int up)
{
  if (low > up)
    the list has been searched without a match, return -1;
```

```
    // Find mid, the index of the middle element in list[low..up]
    int mid = (low + up)/2;
    if (key < list[mid])
      // Search in list[low..mid-1] recursively.
      return binarySearch(key, list, low, mid-1);
    else if (key == list[mid])
      // A match is found
      return mid;
    else
      // Search in list[mid+1..up] recursively.
      return binarySearch(key, list, mid+1, up);
  }
```

The next example demonstrates the binary search approach.

Example 7.4 Testing Binary Search

In this example, a program is written that will implement and test the binary search method. The program first creates an array of 10 elements of `int` type. It displays this array and then prompts the user to enter a key for testing binary search. The output of a sample run of the program is shown in Figure 7.5.

```
// BinarySearch.java: Search a key in a sorted list
public class BinarySearch
{
  // Main method
  public static void main(String[] args)
  {
    int[] list = new int[10];

    // Create a sorted list and display it
    System.out.print("The list is  ");
    for (int i=0; i<list.length; i++)
    {
      list[i] = 2*i + 1;
      System.out.print(list[i] + "  ");
    }
    System.out.println();

    // Prompt the user to enter a key
    System.out.print("Enter a key  ");
    int key = MyInput.readInt();
    int index = binarySearch(key, list);
    if (index != -1)
      System.out.println("The key is found in index " + index);
    else
      System.out.println("The key is not found in the list");
  }

  // Use binary search to find the key in the list
  public static int binarySearch(int key, int[] list)
  {
    int low = 0;
    int up = list.length - 1;
    return binarySearch(key, list, low, up);
  }
```

```
    // Use binary search to find the key in the list between
    // list[low] list[up]
    public static int binarySearch(int key, int[] list,
      int low, int up)
    {
      if (low > up)  // The list has been exhausted without a match
        return -1;

      int mid = (low + up)/2;
      if (key < list[mid])
        return binarySearch(key, list, low, mid-1);
      else if (key == list[mid])
        return mid;
      else
        return binarySearch(key, list, mid+1, up);

    }
  }
```

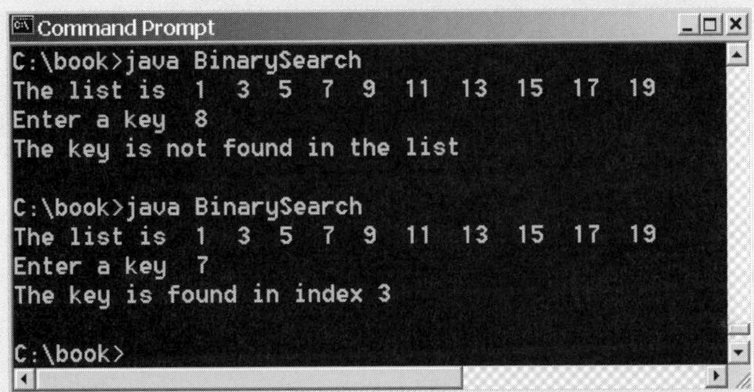

Figure 7.5 *The program uses binary search to find a key in a list of* `int` *elements.*

Example Review

There are two overloaded methods named `binarySearch` in the program: `binarySearch(int key, int[] list)` and `binarySearch(int key, int[] list, int low, int up)`. The first method finds a key in the whole list. The second method finds a key in the list with index from `low` to `up`.

The first `binarySearch` method passes the initial array with `low = 0` and `up = list.length-1` to the second `binarySearch` method. The second method is invoked recursively to find the key in an ever-shrinking subarray. It is a common design technique in recursive programming to choose a second method that can be called recursively.

continues

Example 7.4 continued

This is a good example of using recursion for the following two reasons. First, using recursion enables you to specify a clear, simple solution for the binary search problem, Second, the number of recursive calls is less than the size of the list. So the solution is reasonably efficient. In Exercise 7.4, you will use iterations to rewrite this program.

NOTE
Linear search is useful for finding an element in a small array or an unsorted array, but it is inefficient for large arrays. If the array is sorted, binary search is more efficient.

Array of Objects

In the preceding examples, arrays of primitive type elements were created. You can also create arrays of objects. For example, the following statement declares and creates an array of 10 `Circle` objects:

```
Circle[] circleArray = new Circle[10];
```

To initialize the `circleArray`, you can use a `for` loop like this one:

```
for (int i=0; i<circleArray.length; i++)
{
  circleArray[i] = new Circle();
}
```

The next example demonstrates how to use an array of objects.

Example 7.5 Summarizing the Areas of Circles

In this example, a program is written that will summarize the areas of an array of circles. The program creates `circleArray`—an array composed of 10 `Circle` objects—and initializes circle radii with random values, then display the total area of the circles in the array. The output of a sample run of the program is shown in Figure 7.7.

```
// TotalArea.java: Test passing an array of objects to the method
public class TotalArea
{
  // Main method
  public static void main(String[] args)
  {
    // Declare circleArray
    Circle[] circleArray;

    // Create circleArray
    circleArray = createCircleArray();
```

```
      // Print circleArray and total areas of the circles
      printCircleArray(circleArray);
    }

    // Create an array of Circle objects
    public static Circle[] createCircleArray()
    {
      Circle[] circleArray = new Circle[10];

      for (int i=0; i<circleArray.length; i++)
      {
        circleArray[i] = new Circle(Math.random()*100);
      }

      // Return Circle array
      return circleArray;
    }

    public static void printCircleArray(Circle[] circleArray)
    {
      System.out.println("The radii of the circles are");
      for (int i=0; i<circleArray.length; i++)
      {
        System.out.print("\t\t\t\t" +
          circleArray[i].getRadius() + '\n');
      }

      System.out.println("\t\t\t\t-------------------");

      // Compute and display the result
      System.out.println("The total areas of circles is \t" +
        sum(circleArray));
    }

    // Add circle areas
    public static double sum(Circle[] circleArray)
    {
      // Initialize sum
      double sum = 0;

      // Add areas to sum
      for (int i = 0; i < circleArray.length; i++)
        sum += circleArray[i].findArea();

      return sum;
    }
  }
```

Example Review

The program uses the `createCircleArray` method to create an array of 10 `Circle` objects. The circle radii are randomly generated using the `Math.random()` method. The `createCircleObject` method returns an array of `Circle` objects. The array is passed to the `printCircleArray` method, which displays the radii of the total area of the circles.

The sum of the areas of the circle is computed using the `sum` method, which takes the array of `Circle` objects as the argument and returns a `double` value for the total area.

continues

Example 7.5 continued

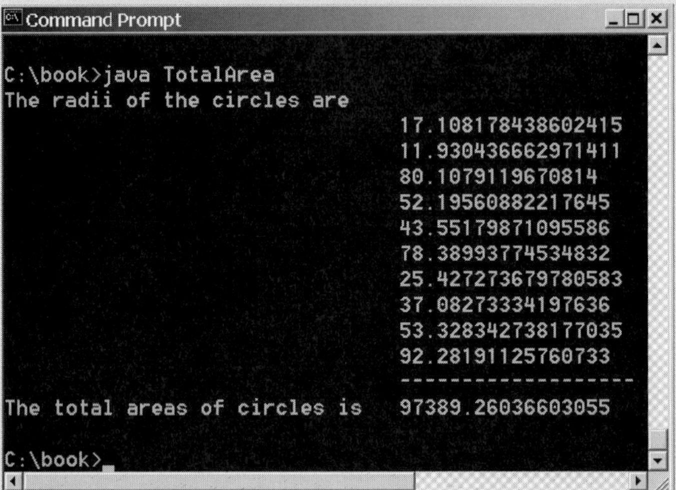

Figure 7.6 *The program creates an array of* `Circle` *objects, displays their radii and total area.*

Several `Circle` classes were introduced in Chapter 5, "Programming with Objects and Classes." You should use the one defined in Example 5.4, "Using the `private` Modifier and Accessor Methods."

Copying Arrays

Often, in a program, you need to duplicate an array or a part of an array. In such cases you could attempt to use the assignment statement (=), as follows:

```
newList = list;
```

It seems to work fine. But if you ran the following program, you would discover that it does not work. The example explains the reason.

Example 7.6 Copying Arrays

In this example, you will see that a simple assignment cannot copy arrays in the following program. The program simply creates two arrays and attempts to copy one to the other, using an assignment statement. The output of the program, shown in Figure 7.7, demonstrates that the two arrays reference the same object after the copy.

```
// TestCopyArray.java: Demonstrate copying arrays
public class TestCopyArray
{
```

```
  // Main method
  public static void main(String[] args)
  {
    // Create an array and assign values
    int[] list1 = {0, 1, 2, 3, 4 ,5};

    // Create an array with default values
    int[] list2 = new int[list1.length];

    // Assign array list1 to array list2
    list2 = list1;

    // Display list1 and list2
    System.out.println("Before modifying list1");
    printList("list1 is ", list1);
    printList("list2 is ", list2);

    // Modify list1
    for (int i=0; i<list1.length; i++)
      list1[i] = 0;

    // Display list1 and list2 after modifying list1
    System.out.println("\nAfter modifying list1");
    printList("list1 is ", list1);
    printList("list2 is ", list2);
  }

  // The method for printing a list
  public static void printList(String s, int[] list)
  {
    System.out.print(s + " ");
    for (int i=0; i<list.length; i++)
      System.out.print(list[i] + " ");

    System.out.print('\n');
  }
}
```

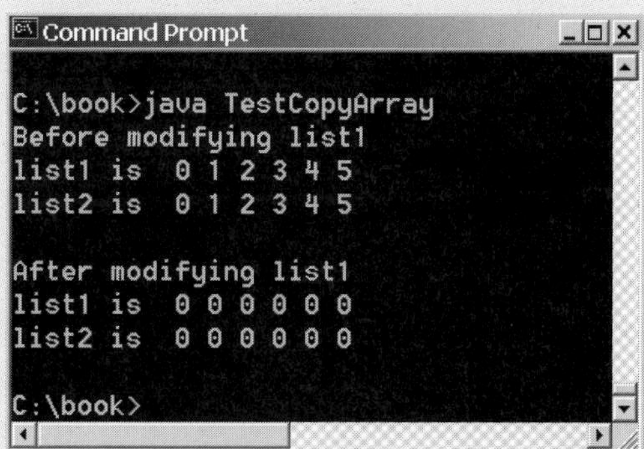

Figure 7.7 *When you are using an assignment statement to copy a source array to a target array, both arrays refer to the same memory location, just as objects do when they are copied using assignment statements.*

continues

Example 7.6 continued

Example Review

The program creates two arrays, `list1` and `list2`; assigns `list1` to `list2`; and displays both `list1` and `list2`. The program then changes the value in `list1` and redisplays `list1` and `list2`. As shown in Figure 7.7, the contents of `list2` were also changed. This occurs because the assignment statement `list2 = list1` makes `list2` point to `list1`'s memory location, as shown in Figure 7.8. Conversely, if you change the value in `list2`, `list1` will see the same change.

In Java, you can use assignment statements to copy primitive data type variables, but not objects, such as arrays. Assigning one object to another object makes both objects point to the same memory location.

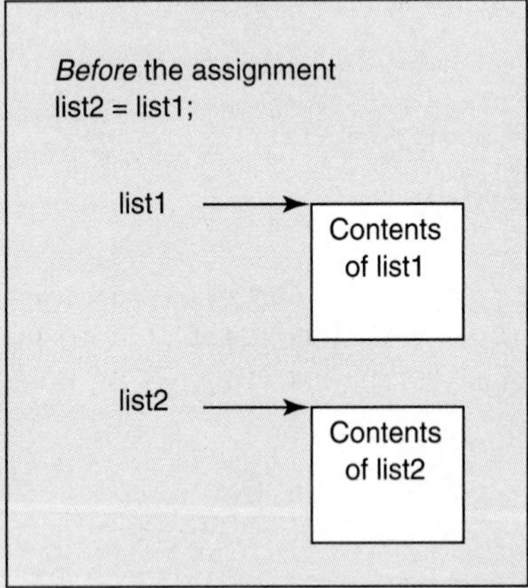

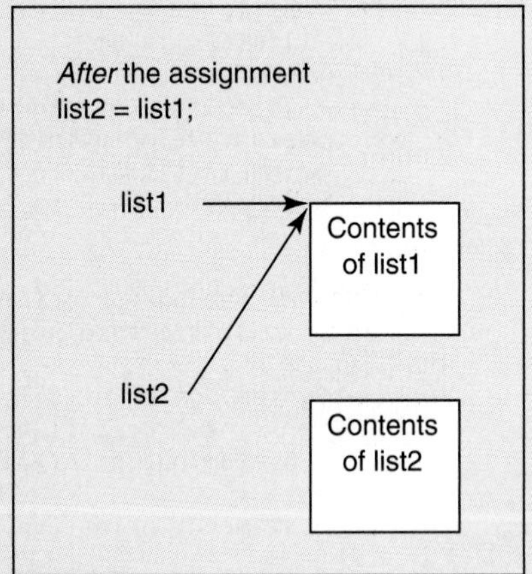

Figure 7.8 *Before the assignment statement,* `list1` *and* `list2` *point to separate memory locations. After the assignment, the reference of the* `list1` *array is passed to* `list2`.

There are three ways to copy arrays:

- Use a loop to copy individual elements.
- Use the `clone` method in the `Object` class.
- Use the static `arraycopy` method in the `System` class.

You can write a loop to copy every element, from the source array to the corresponding element in the target array. The following code, for instance, copies the `sourceArray` to the `targetArray` using a `for` loop.

```
for (int i = 0; i < sourceArray.length; i++)
  targetArray[i] = sourceArray[i];
```

An array is treated as an object in Java and is an instance of the `Object` class. You learned to copy objects using the `clone` method in Chapter 6, "Class Inheritance."

The clone method can also be used to copy arrays. The following statement uses the clone method to copy the sourceArray to the targetArray.

```
int[] targetArray = (int[])sourceArray.clone();
```

Another approach is to use the arraycopy() method in the java.lang.System class to copy arrays instead of using a loop. The syntax for arraycopy is as follows:

```
arraycopy(sourceArray, src pos, targetArray, tar pos, length);
```

The parameters src pos and tar pos indicate the starting positions in sourceArray and targetArray, respectively. The number of elements copied from sourceArray to targetArray is indicated by length. For example, you can rewrite the loop using the following statement:

```
int[] sourceArray = {2, 3, 1, 5, 10};
int[] targetArray = new int[sourceArray.length];
System.arraycopy(sourceArray, 0, targetArray, 0, sourceArray.length);
```

The arraycopy method does not allocate memory space for the target array. The target array must already be created with its memory space allocated. After the copying takes place, targetArray and sourceArray have independent memory locations.

NOTE

All three of these methods provide shallow copies. Therefore, they work fine for arrays of primitive data type elements, but not for arrays of object type elements. To support a deep copy, you have to deal with how to copy individual object elements in the array.

Multidimensional Arrays

Thus far, you have used one-dimensional arrays to model linear collections of elements. To represent a matrix or a table, it is necessary to use a two-dimensional array. In Java, a two-dimensional array is declared as an array of array objects. For example, you can use the following code to declare and create a 5 by 5 matrix:

```
int[][] matrix = new int[5][5];
```

or

```
int matrix[][] = new int[5][5];
```

You can also use a shorthand notation to declare and initialize a two-dimensional array. For example,

```
int[][] matrix =
{
  {1, 2, 3, 4, 5},
  {2, 3, 4, 5, 6},
  {3, 4, 5, 6, 7},
  {4, 5, 6, 7, 8},
  {5, 6, 7, 8, 9}
};
```

Two subscripts are used in a two-dimensional array, one for the row, and the other for the column. To assign a value `7` to a specific element at row 2 and column 0, you can use the following:

```
matrix[2][0] = 7;
```

Occasionally, you will need to represent multidimensional data structures. In Java, you can create `n` dimensional arrays for any integer `n`, as long as your computer has sufficient memory to store the array.

Example 7.7 Adding and Multiplying Two Matrices

In this example, a program is written that uses two-dimensional arrays to create two matrices. The program then adds and multiplies the two matrices.

To add two matrices, they must have the same dimensions and the same or compatible types of elements. As shown below, two matrices are added by adding the two elements of the arrays with the same index:

$$\begin{pmatrix} a_{11} & a_{12} & a_{13} & a_{14} & a_{15} \\ a_{21} & a_{22} & a_{23} & a_{24} & a_{25} \\ a_{31} & a_{32} & a_{33} & a_{34} & a_{35} \\ a_{41} & a_{42} & a_{43} & a_{44} & a_{45} \\ a_{51} & a_{52} & a_{53} & a_{54} & a_{55} \end{pmatrix} + \begin{pmatrix} b_{11} & b_{12} & b_{13} & b_{14} & b_{15} \\ b_{21} & b_{22} & b_{23} & b_{24} & b_{25} \\ b_{31} & b_{32} & b_{33} & b_{34} & b_{35} \\ b_{41} & b_{42} & b_{43} & b_{44} & b_{45} \\ b_{51} & b_{52} & b_{53} & b_{54} & b_{55} \end{pmatrix} =$$

$$\begin{pmatrix} a_{11} + b_{11} & a_{12} + b_{12} & a_{12} + b_{13} & a_{12} + b_{14} & a_{15} + b_{15} \\ a_{21} + b_{21} & a_{22} + b_{22} & a_{23} + b_{23} & a_{24} + b_{24} & a_{25} + b_{25} \\ a_{31} + b_{31} & a_{32} + b_{32} & a_{33} + b_{33} & a_{34} + b_{34} & a_{35} + b_{35} \\ a_{41} + b_{41} & a_{42} + b_{42} & a_{43} + b_{43} & a_{44} + b_{44} & a_{45} + b_{45} \\ a_{51} + b_{51} & a_{52} + b_{52} & a_{53} + b_{53} & a_{54} + b_{54} & a_{55} + b_{55} \end{pmatrix}$$

To multiply matrix `a` by matrix `b`, the number of columns in `a` must be the same as the number of rows in `b`, and the two matrices must have elements of the same or compatible types. Let `c` be the result of the multiplication, and `a`, `b`, and `c` are denoted as follows:

$$\begin{pmatrix} a_{11} & a_{12} & a_{13} & a_{14} & a_{15} \\ a_{21} & a_{22} & a_{23} & a_{24} & a_{25} \\ a_{31} & a_{32} & a_{33} & a_{34} & a_{35} \\ a_{41} & a_{42} & a_{43} & a_{44} & a_{45} \\ a_{51} & a_{52} & a_{53} & a_{54} & a_{55} \end{pmatrix} \times \begin{pmatrix} b_{11} & b_{12} & b_{13} & b_{14} & b_{15} \\ b_{21} & b_{22} & b_{23} & b_{24} & b_{25} \\ b_{31} & b_{32} & b_{33} & b_{34} & b_{35} \\ b_{41} & b_{42} & b_{43} & b_{44} & b_{45} \\ b_{51} & b_{52} & b_{53} & b_{54} & b_{55} \end{pmatrix} = \begin{pmatrix} c_{11} & c_{12} & c_{13} & c_{14} & c_{15} \\ c_{21} & c_{22} & c_{23} & c_{24} & c_{25} \\ c_{31} & c_{32} & c_{33} & c_{34} & c_{35} \\ c_{41} & c_{42} & c_{43} & c_{44} & c_{45} \\ c_{51} & c_{52} & c_{53} & c_{54} & c_{55} \end{pmatrix}$$

Where, $c_{ij} = a_{i1} \times b_{1j}+a_{i2}\times b_{2j}+a_{i3}\times b_{3j}+a_{i4}\times b_{4j}+a_{i5}\times b_{5j}$

Assume that both arrays are 5 by 5 with `int` type elements. The program is given below. The output of the program is shown in Figure 7.9.

```
// TestMatrixOperation.java: Add and multiply two matrices
public class TestMatrixOperation
{
  // Main method
  public static void main(String[] args)
  {
    // Create two matrices as two dimensional arrays
    int[][] matrix1 = new int[5][5];
    int[][] matrix2 = new int[5][5];

    // Assign random values to matrix1 and matrix2
    for (int i=0; i<matrix1.length; i++)
      for (int j=0; j<matrix1[i].length; j++)
      {
        matrix1[i][j] = (int)(Math.random()*10);
        matrix2[i][j] = (int)(Math.random()*10);
      }

    // Add two matrices and print the result
    int[][] resultMatrix  = addMatrix(matrix1, matrix2);
    System.out.println("The addition of the matrices is ");
    printResult(matrix1, matrix2, resultMatrix, '*');

    // Multiply two matrices and print the result
    resultMatrix = multiplyMatrix(matrix1, matrix2);
    System.out.println("\nThe multiplication of the matrices is ");
    printResult(matrix1, matrix2, resultMatrix, '*');
  }

  // The method for adding two matrices
  public static int[][] addMatrix(int[][] m1, int[][] m2)
  {
    int[][] result = new int[m1.length][m1[0].length];
    for (int i=0; i<m1.length; i++)
      for (int j=0; j<m1[0].length; j++)
        result[i][j] = m1[i][j] + m2[i][j];

    return result;
  }

  // The method for multiplying two matrices
  public static int[][] multiplyMatrix(int[][] m1, int[][] m2)
  {
    int[][] result = new int[m1.length][m2[0].length];
    for (int i=0; i<m1.length; i++)
      for (int j=0; j<m2[0].length; j++)
        for (int k=0; k<m1[0].length; k++)
           result[i][j] += m1[i][k]*m2[k][j];

    return result;
  }

  // Print result
  public static void printResult(
    int[][] m1, int[][] m2, int[][] m3, char op)
  {
    for (int i=0; i<m1.length; i++)
    {
      for (int j=0; j<m1[0].length; j++)
        System.out.print(" " + m1[i][j]);
```

continues

Example 7.7 continued

```
        if (i == m1.length/2)
          System.out.print( "  " + op + "  " );
        else
          System.out.print( "     " );

        for (int j=0; j<m2[0].length; j++)
          System.out.print(" " + m2[i][j]);

        if (i == m1.length/2)
          System.out.print( "  =  " );
        else
          System.out.print( "     " );

        for (int j=0; j<m3[0].length; j++)
          System.out.print(" " + m3[i][j]);

        System.out.println();
      }
    }
  }
```

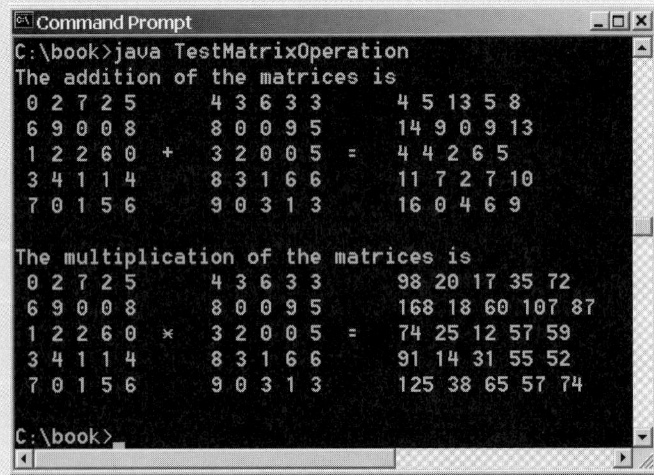

Figure 7.9 *The program adds and multiplies two matrices that are represented in two-dimensional arrays.*

Example Review

The statement `int[][] matrix1 = new int[5][5]` declares and creates a 5 by 5 matrix.

Nested `for` loops are often used to process multidimensional array elements. The matrices `matrix1` and `matrix2` are initialized by using a nested `for` loop with random values.

The `addMatrix(int[][] m1, int[][] m2)` method adds `m1` and `m2` and returns the result matrix.

The `multiplyMatrix(int[][] m1, int[][] m2)` method multiplies `m1` and `m2` and returns the result matrix.

The `printResult(int[][] m1, int m2[][], int[][] m3, char op)` method displays the contents of m1, m2, and m3 in the format `m1 op m2 = m3`.

Processing Primitive Type Values as Objects

Primitive data types are not used as objects in Java. Performance is the reason for this. Because of the overhead of processing objects, the language's performance would be adversely affected if primitive data types were treated as objects. However, many Java methods require the use of objects as arguments. Java offers a convenient way to wrap a primitive data type into an object (for example, wrapping `int` into the class `Integer`). The corresponding class is called a *wrapper class* in Java terminology.

By using wrapper objects instead of a primitive data type variable, you can take advantage of generic programming. An example of generic programming involving numeric values is given in Example 7.9, "Designing Generic Classes for Matrix Operations."

The wrapper classes provide constructors, constants, and conversion methods for manipulating various data types. Java provides `Boolean`, `Character`, `Double`, `Float`, `Byte`, `Short`, `Integer`, and `Long` wrappers for primitive data types. All the wrapper classes are grouped in the `java.lang` package. Their inheritance hierarchy is shown in Figure 7.10.

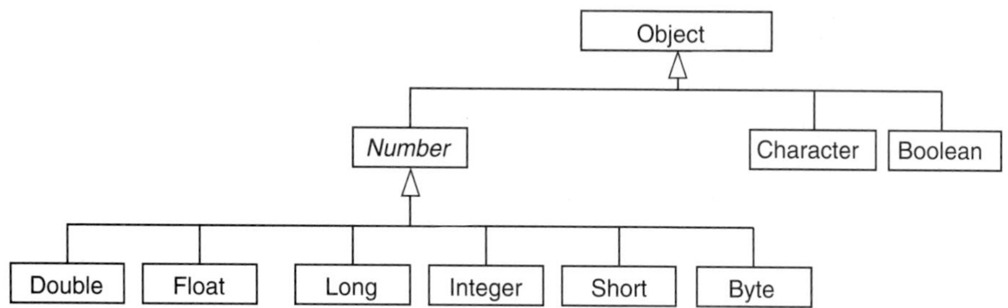

Figure 7.10 *The* `Number` *class is an abstract superclass for* `Double`, `Float`, `Long`, `Integer`, `Short`, *and* `Byte`.

NOTE
The wrapper class name for a primitive type is the same as the primitive data type name with the first letter capitalized. The exceptions are `Integer` and `Character`.

The next section discusses numeric wrapper classes, specifically the `Integer` and `Double` classes. For more detailed information about the wrapper classes, refer to the Java API documentation.

The *Number* Class and Its Subclasses

Because numeric wrapper classes (`Byte`, `Double`, `Float`, `Integer`, `Long`, `Short`) are very similar, their common methods are generalized in an abstract superclass named `Number`. The `Number` class defines abstract methods to convert the represented numeric value to `byte`, `double`, `float`, `int`, `long`, and `short`. These methods are implemented in the subclasses of `Number`:

- `public byte byteValue()`

  This returns the number as a `byte`.

- `public short shortValue()`

  This returns the number as a `short`.

- `public int intValue()`

  This returns the number as an `int`.

- `public long longValue()`

  This returns the number as a `long`.

- `public float floatValue()`

  This returns the number as a `float`.

- `public double doubleValue()`

  This returns the number as a `double`.

Numeric Wrapper Class Constructors

You can construct a numeric wrapper object either from a primitive data type value or from a string representing the numeric value. The constructors for `Integer` and `Double` are:

```
public Integer(int value)

public Integer(String s)

public Double(double value)

public Double(String s)
```

For example, you can construct a wrapper object for `double` value `5.0` using either

```
Double doubleObject = new Double(5.0);
```

or

```
Double doubleObject = new Double("5.0");
```

You can construct a wrapper object for `int` value `5` using either

```
Integer integerObject = new Integer(5);
```

or

```
Integer integerObject = new Integer("5");
```

Numeric Class Constants

Each numerical wrapper class has constants: MAX_VALUE and MIN_VALUE. MAX_VALUE represents the maximum value of the corresponding primitive data type. For Byte, Short, Integer, and Long, MIN_VALUE represents the minimum byte, short, int, and long values. For Float and Double, MIN_VALUE represents the minimum *positive* float and double values. The following statements, for example, display the maximum integer (2,147,483,647), the minimum positive float (1.4E-45), and the maximum double floating-point number (1.79769313486231570e+308d).

```
System.out.println("The maximum integer is " + Integer.MAX VALUE);
System.out.println("The minimum positive float is " +
  Float.MIN VALUE);
System.out.println(
  "The maximum double precision floating-point number is " +
  Double.MAX VALUE);
```

Conversion Methods

Each numeric wrapper class implements the abstract methods doubleValue, floatValue, intValue, longValue, and shortValue, which are defined in the Number class. It also overrides the toString and equals methods defined in the Object class.

For example:

```
long l = doubleObject.longValue();
```

This converts doubleObject's double value to a long variable l.

```
int i = integerObject.intValue();
```

This assigns the int value of integerObject to i.

```
double d = 5.9;
Double doubleObject = new Double(d);
String s = doubleObject.toString();
```

This converts double d to a string s.

The static *valueOf*, *parseInt*, and *parseDouble* Methods

The numeric wrapper classes have a useful class method valueOf(String s). This method creates a new object, initialized to the value represented by the specified string. For example:

```
Double doubleObject = Double.valueOf("12.4");
Integer integerObject = Integer.valueOf("12");
```

The Integer wrapper class has some methods that are not available in Double. The parseInt method, for example, is only available in integer wrappers Integer and Long, but not in Double or Float.

```
public static int parseInt(String s, int radix)
```

This returns the integer value represented in the string s with the specified radix. If radix is omitted, base 10 is assumed.

Since JDK 1.2, the `Double` class supports a static method `parseDouble` with following signature for converting a numeric string into a double value.

```
public static double parseDouble(String s)
```

Command-Line Arguments

Perhaps you have already noticed the unusual declarations for the `main` method, which has parameter `args` of `String[]` type. It is clear that `args` is an array of strings. The `main` method is just like a regular method with parameters. You can call a regular method by passing actual parameters. Can you pass parameters to `main`? This section will discuss how to pass and process arguments from the command line.

Passing Arguments to Java Programs

You can pass arguments to a Java program from the command line when you run the program. The following command line, for example, starts the program `TestMain` with three arguments: `arg0`, `arg1`, and `arg2`:

```
java TestMain arg0 arg1 arg2
```

These arguments are strings, but they don't have to appear in double quotes on the command line. The arguments are separated by a space. If an argument itself contains a space, you must use double quotes to group all of the items in the argument. Consider the following command line:

```
java TestMain "First num" alpha 53
```

It starts the program with three arguments: `"First num"` and `alpha`, which are strings, and `53`, a numeric string. Note that `53` is actually treated as a string. You can use `"53"` instead of `53` in the command line.

Processing Command-Line Parameters

The arguments passed to the main program are stored in `args`, which is an array of strings. The first parameter is represented by `args[0]`, and `args.length` is the number of arguments passed.

Example 7.8 Using Command-Line Parameters

In this example, a program is written that will perform binary operations on integers. The program receives three parameters: an operator and two integers. To add two integers, the following command could be used:

```
java Calculator + 2 3
```

The program will display the following output:

```
2 + 3 = 5
```

The output of sample runs of the program is shown in Figure 7.11.

```
// Calculator.java: Pass parameters from the command line
public class Calculator
{
  // Main method
  public static void main(String[] args)
  {
    // The result of the operation
    int result = 0;

    if (args.length != 3)
    {
      System.out.println(
        "Usage: java Calculator operator operand1 operand2");
      System.exit(0);
    }

    // Determine the operator
    switch (args[0].charAt(0))
    {
      case '+': result = Integer.parseInt(args[1]) +
                         Integer.parseInt(args[2]);
                break;
      case '-': result = Integer.parseInt(args[1]) -
                         Integer.parseInt(args[2]);
                break;
      case '*': result = Integer.parseInt(args[1]) *
                         Integer.parseInt(args[2]);
                break;
      case '/': result = Integer.parseInt(args[1]) /
                         Integer.parseInt(args[2]);
    }

    // Display result
    System.out.println(args[1] + ' ' + args[0] + ' ' + args[2]
      + " = " + result);
  }
}
```

Example Review

The program first tests whether three command-line arguments have been provided. If not, `System.exit(0)` terminates the program.

The arithmetic operations are performed according to `args[0]`, the operator.

`Integer.parseInt(args[1])` converts a digital string into an integer. The string must consist of digits. If not, the program will terminate abnormally.

In the sample run, `"*"` is used instead of `*` for the command

```
java Calculator "*" 4 5
```

In JDK 1.1 and above, the `*` symbol refers to all the files in the current directory when it is used on a command line. The following program displays all the files in the current directory when issuing the command `java Test *`.

continues

Example 7.8 continued

```
C:\book>java Calculator - 63 40
63 - 40 = 23

C:\book>java Calculator + 63 40
63 + 40 = 103

C:\book>java Calculator "*" 63 40
63 * 40 = 2520

C:\book>java Calculator / 63 40
63 / 40 = 1

C:\book>java Calculator / 63
Usage: java Calculator operator operand1 operand2

C:\book>
```

Figure 7.11 *The program takes three parameters (an operator and two operands) from the command line and displays the expression and the result of the arithmetic operation.*

```
public class Test
{
  public static void main(String[] args)
  {
    for (int i=0; i<args.length; i++)
      System.out.println(args[i]);
  }
}
```

Case Studies (Optional)

This section presents a case study on designing classes for matrix operations. The addition and multiplication operations for all the matrices are similar except that their element types differ. Therefore, you can design a superclass that describes the common operations shared by matrices of all types regardless of their element types, and you can create subclasses tailored to specific types of matrices. This case study gives implementations for two types: `int` and `Rational`. For the `int` type, the wrapper class `Integer` should be used to wrap an `int` value into an object, so that the object is passed in the methods for operations.

Example 7.9 Designing Generic Classes for Matrix Operations

This example gives a generic class for matrix arithmetic. This class implements matrix addition and multiplication common for all types of matrices. You use the `Integer` matrix and the `Rational` matrix to test this generic class.

Figure 7.12 describes these classes and illustrates their relationships.

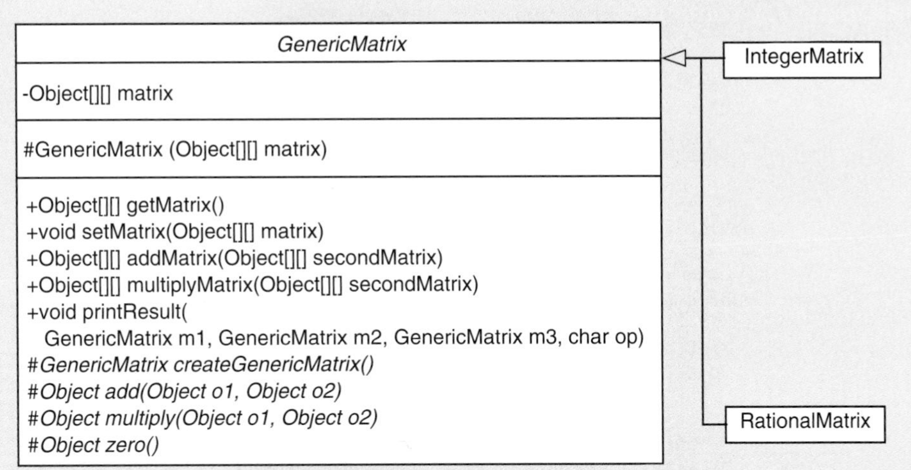

Figure 7.12 *The* `GenericMatrix` *class is an abstract superclass for* `IntegerMatrix`, *and* `RationalMatrix`.

The `GenericMatrix` class provides matrix operations for the matrices of any element type. The data field `matrix` is the internal representation for a generic matrix. The methods `addMatrix` and `multiplyMatrix` add and multiply two matrices of a generic type `Object[][]`. The static method `printResult` displays the matrices, the operations, and their result. The methods `add`, `multiply`, and `zero` are abstract methods, because their implementations are dependent on the specific type of the array elements.

The `IntegerMatrix` and `RationalMatrix` are concrete subclasses of `GenericMatrix`. These two classes implement the `add`, `multiply`, and `zero` methods defined in the `GenericMatrix` class.

Here is the code for classes `GenericMatrix`, `IntegerMatrix`, and `RationalMatrix`:

```
// GenericMatrix.java: Define a matrix and its associated
// operations such as add and multiply
public abstract class GenericMatrix
{
  // Representation of a matrix using a two-dimensional array
  private Object[][] matrix;

  // Construct a matrix
  protected GenericMatrix(Object[][] matrix)
  {
    this.matrix = matrix;
  }

  // Getter method for matrix
  public Object[][] getMatrix()
  {
    return matrix;
  }
```

continues

Example 7.9 continued

```
  // Setter method for matrix
  public void setMatrix(Object[][] matrix)
  {
    this.matrix = matrix;
  }

  public abstract GenericMatrix createGenericMatrix();

  // Add two matrices
  public GenericMatrix addMatrix(GenericMatrix secondGenericMatrix)
  {
    // Create a result matrix
    Object[][] result =
      new Object[matrix.length][matrix[0].length];

    // Obtain the second matrix
    Object[][] secondMatrix =  secondGenericMatrix.getMatrix();

    // Check bounds of the two matrices
    if ((matrix.length != secondMatrix.length) ||
        (matrix[0].length != secondMatrix.length))
    {
      System.out.println(
        "The matrices do not have the same size");
      System.exit(0);
    }

    // Perform addition
    for (int i=0; i<result.length; i++)
      for (int j=0; j<result[i].length; j++)
        result[i][j] = add(matrix[i][j], secondMatrix[i][j]);

    GenericMatrix genericResultMatrix = createGenericMatrix();
    genericResultMatrix.setMatrix(result);
    return genericResultMatrix;
  }

  // Multiply two matrices
  public GenericMatrix multiplyMatrix(
    GenericMatrix secondGenericMatrix)
  {
    // Obtain the second matrix
    Object[][] secondMatrix =  secondGenericMatrix.getMatrix();

    // Create result matrix
    Object[][] result =
      new Object[matrix.length][secondMatrix[0].length];

    // Check bounds
    if (matrix[0].length != secondMatrix.length)
    {
      System.out.println("Bounds error");
      System.exit(0);
    }

    // Perform multiplication of two matrices
    for (int i=0; i<result.length; i++)
      for (int j=0; j<result[0].length; j++)
    {
      result[i][j] = zero();
```

```
        for (int k=0; k<matrix[0].length; k++)
        {
          result[i][j] = add(result[i][j],
            multiply(this.matrix[i][k], secondMatrix[k][j]));
        }
      }

    GenericMatrix genericResultMatrix = createGenericMatrix();
    genericResultMatrix.setMatrix(result);
    return genericResultMatrix;
  }

  // Print matrices, the operator, and their operation result
  public static void printResult(
    GenericMatrix m1, GenericMatrix m2, GenericMatrix m3, char op)
  {
    for (int i=0; i<(m1.getMatrix()).length; i++)
    {
      for (int j=0; j<(m1.getMatrix())[0].length; j++)
        System.out.print(" " + (m1.getMatrix())[i][j]);

      if (i == (m1.getMatrix()).length/2)
        System.out.print( "  " + op + "  " );
      else
        System.out.print( "     " );

      for (int j=0; j<(m2.getMatrix()).length; j++)
        System.out.print(" " + (m2.getMatrix())[i][j]);

      if (i == (m1.getMatrix()).length/2)
        System.out.print( "  =  " );
      else
        System.out.print( "     " );

      for (int j=0; j<(m3.getMatrix()).length; j++)
        System.out.print(" " + (m3.getMatrix())[i][j]);

      System.out.println();
    }
  }

  // Abstract method for adding two elements of the matrices
  protected abstract Object add(Object o1, Object o2);

  // Abstract method for multiplying two elements of the matrices
  protected abstract Object multiply(Object o1, Object o2);

  // Abstract method for defining zero for the matrix element
  protected abstract Object zero();
}

// IntegerMatrix.java:
// Declare IntegerMatrix derived from GenericMatrix
public class IntegerMatrix extends GenericMatrix
{
  // Construct an IntegerMatrix
  public IntegerMatrix(Integer[][] m)
  {
    super(m);
  }
```

continues

Example 7.9 continued

```
    // Implement the createGenericMatrix method
    public GenericMatrix createGenericMatrix()
    {
      Integer[][] matrix =
        new Integer[getMatrix().length][getMatrix().length];
      return new IntegerMatrix(matrix);
    }

    // Implement the add method for adding two matrix elements
    protected Object add(Object o1, Object o2)
    {
      Integer i1 = (Integer)o1;
      Integer i2 = (Integer)o2;
      return new Integer(i1.intValue() + i2.intValue());
    }

    // Implement the multiply method for multiplying two
    // matrix elements
    protected Object multiply(Object o1, Object o2)
    {
      Integer i1 = (Integer)o1;
      Integer i2 = (Integer)o2;
      return new Integer(i1.intValue() * i2.intValue());
    }

    // Implement the zero method to specify zero for Integer
    protected Object zero()
    {
      return new Integer(0);
    }
  }

  // RationalMatrix.java:
  // Declare RationalMatrix derived from GenericMatrix
  public class RationalMatrix extends GenericMatrix
  {
    // Construct a RationalMatrix for a given Rational array
    public RationalMatrix(Rational[][] m1)
    {
      super(m1);
    }

    // Implement the createGenericMatrix method
    public GenericMatrix createGenericMatrix()
    {
      Rational[][] matrix =
        new Rational[getMatrix().length][getMatrix().length];
      return new RationalMatrix(matrix);
    }

    // Implement the add method for adding two rational elements
    protected Object add(Object o1, Object o2)
    {
      Rational r1 = (Rational)o1;
      Rational r2 = (Rational)o2;
      return r1.add(r2);
    }

    // Implement the multiply method for multiplying
    // two rational elements
    protected Object multiply(Object o1, Object o2)
```

```
    {
      Rational r1 = (Rational)o1;
      Rational r2 = (Rational)o2;
      return r1.multiply(r2);
    }

    // Implement the zero method to specify zero for Rational
    protected Object zero()
    {
      return new Rational(0,1);
    }
  }
```

The following is a test program to use the `IntegerMatrix` class. A sample run of the program is shown in Figure 7.13.

```
// TestIntegerMatrix.java: Test matrix operations involving
// integer values
public class TestIntegerMatrix
{
  // Main method
  public static void main(String[] args)
  {
    // Create Integer arrays m1, m2
    Integer[][] m1 = new Integer[5][5];
    Integer[][] m2 = new Integer[5][5];

    // Initialize Integer arrays m1 and m2
    for (int i=0; i<m1.length; i++)
      for (int j=0; j<m1[0].length; j++)
      {
        m1[i][j] = new Integer(i);
      }

    for (int i=0; i<m2.length; i++)
      for (int j=0; j<m2[0].length; j++)
      {
        m2[i][j] = new Integer(i+j);
      }

    // Create instances of IntegerMatrix
    IntegerMatrix im1 = new IntegerMatrix(m1);
    IntegerMatrix im2 = new IntegerMatrix(m2);

    // Perform integer matrix addition, and multiplication
    IntegerMatrix im3 = (IntegerMatrix)im1.addMatrix(im2);
    IntegerMatrix im4 = (IntegerMatrix)im1.multiplyMatrix(im2);

    // Display im1, im2, im3, im4
    System.out.println("m1 + m2 is ...");
    GenericMatrix.printResult(im1, im2, im3, '+');

    System.out.println("\nm1 * m2 is ...");
    GenericMatrix.printResult(im1, im2, im4, '*');
  }
}
```

continues

Example 7.9 continued

```
C:\book>java TestIntegerMatrix
m1 + m2 is ...
 0 0 0 0 0      0 1 2 3 4      0 1 2 3 4
 1 1 1 1 1      1 2 3 4 5      2 3 4 5 6
 2 2 2 2 2  +   2 3 4 5 6  =   4 5 6 7 8
 3 3 3 3 3      3 4 5 6 7      6 7 8 9 10
 4 4 4 4 4      4 5 6 7 8      8 9 10 11 12

m1 * m2 is ...
 0 0 0 0 0      0 1 2 3 4      0 0 0 0 0
 1 1 1 1 1      1 2 3 4 5      10 15 20 25 30
 2 2 2 2 2  *   2 3 4 5 6  =   20 30 40 50 60
 3 3 3 3 3      3 4 5 6 7      30 45 60 75 90
 4 4 4 4 4      4 5 6 7 8      40 60 80 100 120

C:\book>
```

Figure 7.13 *The program creates two* `int` *matrices and performs addition and multiplication on them.*

Next is a test program to use the `RationalMatrix` class. A sample run of the program is shown in Figure 7.14.

```
// TestRationalMatrix.java: Test matrix operations involving
// Rational values
public class TestRationalMatrix
{
  // Main method
  public static void main(String[] args)
  {
    // Declare Rational arrays m1, m2
    Rational[][] m1 = new Rational[4][4];
    Rational[][] m2 = new Rational[4][4];

    // Initialize Rational arrays m1 and m2
    for (int i=0; i<m1.length; i++)
      for (int j=0; j<m1[0].length; j++)
      {
        m1[i][j] = new Rational(i+1,i+3);
        m2[i][j] = new Rational(i+1,i+3);
      }

    // Create RationalMatrix instances
    RationalMatrix rm1 = new RationalMatrix(m1);
    RationalMatrix rm2 = new RationalMatrix(m2);

    // Perform Rational matrix addition, and multiplication
    RationalMatrix rm3 = (RationalMatrix)rm1.addMatrix(rm2);
    RationalMatrix rm4 = (RationalMatrix)rm1.multiplyMatrix(rm2);

    // Display rm1, rm2, rm3, rm4
    System.out.println("m1 + m2 is ...");
    GenericMatrix.printResult(rm1, rm2, rm3, '+');
```

```
      System.out.println("\nm1 * m2 is ...");
      GenericMatrix.printResult(rm1, rm2, rm4, '*');
    }
  }
```

```
Command Prompt
C:\book>java TestRationalMatrix
m1 + m2 is ...
 1/3 1/3 1/3 1/3      1/3 1/3 1/3 1/3      2/3 2/3 2/3 2/3
 1/2 1/2 1/2 1/2      1/2 1/2 1/2 1/2      1 1 1 1
 3/5 3/5 3/5 3/5  +   3/5 3/5 3/5 3/5  =   6/5 6/5 6/5 6/5
 2/3 2/3 2/3 2/3      2/3 2/3 2/3 2/3      4/3 4/3 4/3 4/3

m1 * m2 is ...
 1/3 1/3 1/3 1/3      1/3 1/3 1/3 1/3      7/10 7/10 7/10 7/10
 1/2 1/2 1/2 1/2      1/2 1/2 1/2 1/2      21/20 21/20 21/20 21/20
 3/5 3/5 3/5 3/5  *   3/5 3/5 3/5 3/5  =   63/50 63/50 63/50 63/50
 2/3 2/3 2/3 2/3      2/3 2/3 2/3 2/3      7/5 7/5 7/5 7/5

C:\book>
```

Figure 7.14 *The program creates two matrices of rational numbers and performs addition and multiplication on them.*

Example Review

Because the element type in the `GenericMatrix` class is not specified, the program doesn't know how to add or multiply two matrix elements and doesn't know what the zero value is for the element (for example, 0 for `int` or 0/1 for `Rational`). Therefore, `add`, `multiply`, and `zero` are defined as abstract methods. These methods are implemented in the subclasses in which the matrix element type is specified.

The matrix element type in `GenericMatrix` is `Object`. This enables you to use an object of any class as long as you can implement the abstract `add`, `multiply`, and `zero` methods in subclasses.

The `addMatrix` and `multiplyMatrix` methods are concrete methods, defined and implemented in `GenericMatrix`. They are ready to use as long as the `add`, `multiply`, and `zero` methods are implemented in the subclasses.

The `createGenericMatrix` method creates an instance of `GenericMatrix`. This method is used in the `addMatrix` and `multiplyMatrix` methods for returning instances of the `GenericMatrix` type. Since `GenericMatrix` is an abstract class, the `createGenericMatrix` method must be declared abstract in the `GenericMatrix` class.

The `printResult` method displays the matrix on the console. The `toString` method is used to display the element.

continues

Example 7.9 continued

The `addMatrix` and `multiplyMatrix` methods check the bounds of the matrices before performing operations. If the two matrices have incompatible bounds, the program terminates.

`IntegerMatrix` and `RationalMatrix` are concrete subclasses of `GenericMatrix` for integer matrix arithmetic. These classes extend the `GenericMatrix` class and implement the `add`, `multiply`, and `zero` methods.

Casting the object from type `Object` to type `Integer` in the `IntegerMatrix` class is necessary because the program has to use the `intValue` method for integer addition and multiplication, and it is not available in `Object`. Similar casting is needed from type `Object` to type `Rational` in the `RationalMatrix` class for the same reason.

The `TestIntegerMatrix` program creates and initializes two matrices: `m1` and `m2`. The statement

```
IntegerMatrix im1 = new IntegerMatrix(m1);
IntegerMatrix im2 = new IntegerMatrix(m2);
```

in `TestIntegerMatrix` creates `im1` as an instance of `IntegerMatrix` for matrix `m1`, so you can use `im1.addMatrix(im2)` and `im1.multiplyMatrix(im2)` to perform matrix addition and multiplication for `im1` and `im2`. The variables `rm1` and `rm2` were created for the same reason in `TestRationalMatrix`.

Note

Since the parameters of `add`, `multiply`, and `zero` are of the `Object` type, you can pass any object type to these methods. This is another form of polymorphism in object-oriented programming, known as *generic programming*. Generic programming enables a method to operate on arguments of generic types, making it reusable with multiple types.

Note

The `createGenericMatrix()` method creates an instance of the `GenericMatrix`. Many Java abstract classes provide static methods for creating instances of abstract classes. For instance, the `Calendar` abstract class provides the static method `getInstance()` to create an object of `Calendar`, which is actually an instance of the `GregorianCalendar` class. Classes `Calendar` and `GregorianCalendar` will be introduced in Chapter 12, "Internationalization."

The *Vector* Class (Optional)

Arrays are useful for storing and managing a set of elements of the same type. However, since the length of an array is fixed once the array is created, you need to know the length of the array before you create it. If you don't know the length of the array in advance, you have to estimate the maximum length when creating the array. If the estimate is larger than the actual length, valuable memory space may be wasted; if the estimate is smaller than the actual length, your program could run into trouble.

Obviously, it would be unwise to use an array to store an unspecified number of elements. Instead, use the `Vector` class, provided by Java in the `java.util` package. A vector can grow or shrink dynamically as needed. To create a vector, use its default constructor:

```
Vector vector = new Vector();
```

To add an element to the vector, use the `addElement` method:

```
vector.addElement(anObject);
```

The element in the vector must be an object. The element is appended to the vector.

To retrieve an element, use the `elementAt` method:

```
Object anObject = vector.elementAt(0);
```

This statement returns the *first* element in the vector. The index of the first element is 0. The return value is of the `Object` type.

To find the number of elements in the vector, use the `size` method:

```
int numOfElements = vector.size();
```

To insert an element at a specified index, use the `insertElement` method:

```
vector.insertElement(anObject, 4);
```

This statement inserts the element at index 4. The element formerly at index 4 is moved to index 5, and each object in this vector with an index greater than or equal to 5 is shifted upward to have an index one greater than the value it had previously.

To replace an element at a specified index, use the `setElement` method:

```
vector.setElement(anObject, 4);
```

This statement sets a new element at index 4. The element formerly at index 4 is replaced.

To remove an element at a specified index, use the `removeElement` method:

```
vector.removeElement(4);
```

This statement removes the element at index 4. Each element in this vector with an index greater than or equal to 5 is shifted downward to have an index one smaller than the value it had previously.

Example 7.10 Assigning Grades Using a Vector

This example rewrites Example 7.1 using a vector instead of an array. The program reads student scores from the keyboard, stores the scores in the vector, finds the best scores, and then assigns grades for all the students. A sample run of the program is shown in Figure 7.15.

```
// AssignGradeUsingVector.java: Assign grade
import java.util.*;

public class AssignGradeUsingVector
{
  // Main method
  public static void main(String[] args)
  {
    Vector scoreVector = new Vector(); // Vector to hold scores
    double best = 0; // The best score
    char grade; // The grade

    // Read scores and find the best score
    System.out.println("Please enter scores. " +
      "A negative score terminates input.");
    do
    {
      System.out.print("Please enter a new score: ");
      double score = MyInput.readDouble();

      if (score < 0) break;

      // Add the score into the vector
      scoreVector.addElement(new Double(score));

      // Find the best score
      if (score > best)
        best = score;
    } while (true);

    System.out.println("There are total " + scoreVector.size() +
      " students ");

    // Assign and display grades
    for (int i=0; i<scoreVector.size(); i++)
    {
      // Retrieve an element from the vector
      Double doubleObject = (Double)(scoreVector.elementAt(i));

      // Get the score
      double score = doubleObject.doubleValue();

      if ( score >= best - 10)
        grade = 'A';
      else if (score >= best - 20)
        grade = 'B';
      else if (score >= best - 30)
        grade = 'C';
      else if (score >= best - 40)
        grade = 'D';
      else
        grade = 'F';
```

```
        System.out.println("Student " + i + " score is " + score +
          " and grade is " + grade);
      }
    }
  }
```

```
C:\book>java AssignGradeUsingVector
Please enter scores. A negative score terminates input.
Please enter a new score: 40
Please enter a new score: 50
Please enter a new score: 60
Please enter a new score: 70
Please enter a new score: -2
There are total 4 students
Student 0 score is 40.0 and grade is C
Student 1 score is 50.0 and grade is B
Student 2 score is 60.0 and grade is A
Student 3 score is 70.0 and grade is A

C:\book>
```

Figure 7.15 *The program receives scores, stores them in a vector, and assigns grades.*

Example Review

The `main` method declares and creates `scoreVector` as an instance of `Vector` to store scores. Since the elements in `Vector` are objects, the wrapper class `Double` is used to wrap a `double` value score into an object. The object is added into the vector using the `addElement` method.

The `elementAt` method is used to retrieve the element at a specified index. Since this method returns an element of the `Object` type, you have to cast it into an object of the `Double` type and get the score from the double object using the `doubleValue()` method.

NOTE

You must use the `size()` method to get the size of a vector array, the `length()` method to get the length of the string, and the `length` property to get the length of an array.

TIP

Vectors are less efficient than arrays and are actually implemented with arrays. Use arrays if you know the number of elements in advance.

NOTE

The `Vector` class is part of the Java Collection Framework, which supports such fundamental data structures as `List`, `LinkedList`, `TreeSet`, `HashSet`, `Map`, `Stack`, and `Enumeration`. You will learn these classes in the data structures course.

Chapter Summary

In this chapter, you learned about using array objects to store a collection of data of the same type. You learned how to declare and create arrays and how to access individual elements in an array. Java stores lists of values in arrays, which are contiguous groups of adjacent memory locations. To refer to a particular location or element of an array, you specify the name of the array and then give the index, which is placed in brackets. An index must be an integer or an integer expression.

A Java array is an object. After an array is created, its size becomes permanent and can be obtained using `arrayObject.length`. The index of an array always begins with 0. Therefore, the last index is always `arrayObject.length-1`. An out-of-bounds error would occur if you attempted to reference elements beyond the bounds of an array.

The `for` loop is often used to process all of the elements in an array. You can use `for` loops to initialize arrays, display arrays, and control and manipulate array elements.

Arrays can be passed to a method as actual parameters. An array is an object, so arrays are passed by reference; that is, the called method can modify the elements in the caller's original arrays.

You can use arrays of array objects to form multidimensional arrays. You learned a convenient syntax that can be used to declare multidimensional arrays, and you saw an example of using a multidimensional array.

You learned how to process numeric values as objects. Because most Java methods require the use of objects as arguments, Java provides wrapper classes for modeling primitive data types as objects. You can take advantage of generic programming by using wrapper objects instead of a primitive data type variable.

You learned about passing and processing command-line arguments in the `main` method.

You also learned how to use the `Vector` class to store and process an unspecified number of elements.

Review Questions

7.1 How do you declare and create an array?

7.2 Is an array an object or a primitive type value?

7.3 Is memory allocated when an array is declared? When is the memory allocated for an array?

7.4 Indicate true or false for the following statements:

- Every element in an array has the same type.
- The array size is fixed after it is declared.
- The array size is fixed after it is created.
- The element in the array must be of primitive data type.

7.5 Which of the following statements are valid array declarations?

```
int i = new int(30);

double d[] = new double[30];

Rational[] r = new Rational(1..30);

int i[] = (3, 4, 3, 2);

float f[] = {2.3, 4.5, 5.6};

char[] c = new char();

Rational[][] r = new Rational[2];
```

7.6 What is the array index type? What is the lowest index?

7.7 What is the representation of the third element in an array named a? Write a method to discover whether array a has an element that has a value of 2. If it does, find the index of that element.

7.8 What happens when your program attempts to access an array element with an invalid index?

7.9 What does the following program do?

```
public class Test
{
  public static void main(String[] args)
  {
    Rational[] r = {new Rational(2,3), new Rational(-1, 3),
                    new Rational(3,5)};
    double[] d = new double[r.length];

    for (int i=0; i<r.length; i++)
      d[i] = r[i].getNumerator() / r[i].getDenominator();
  }
}
```

7.10 Use the `arraycopy()` method to copy the following array to a target array `t`.

```
Circle[] source = {new Circle(3), new Circle(4), new Circle(5)};
```

7.11 Declare and create a 4×5 `int` matrix.

7.12 Describe primitive-type wrapper classes. Why do you need these wrapper classes?

7.13 Are the following statements correct?

```
Integer i = new Integer("23");

Integer i = new Integer(23);

Integer i = Integer.valueOf("23");

Integer i = Integer.parseInt("23",8);

Double d = new Double();

Double d = Double.valueOf("23.45");

int i = (Integer.valueOf("23")).intValue();

double d = (Double.valueOf("23.4")).doubleValue();

int i = (Double.valueOf("23.4")).intValue();

String s = (Double.valueOf("23.4")).toString();
```

7.14 How do you create an instance of `Vector`? How do you add or insert a new element in the vector? How do you remove an element from the vector? How do you find the size of the vector?

Programming Exercises

7.1 Write a program that will read 10 integers and display the numbers in reverse order.

7.2 Rewrite Example 4.4 to compute the mean and standard deviation of the numbers using the following formula:

$$mean = \frac{\sum_{i=1}^{n} x_i}{n}$$

$$deviation = \sqrt{\frac{\sum_{i=1}^{n} (x_i - mean)^2}{n - 1}}$$

7.3 Use recursion to rewrite the selection sort used in Example 7.2.

7.4 Use iterations to rewrite the binary search used in Example 7.4.

Hint: You can use a loop to find the key in the list, as follows:

```
public static int binarySearch(int key, int[] list)
{
  int low = 0;
  int up = list.length - 1;

  while (up >= low)
  {
    int mid = (low + up)/2;
    if (key < list[mid])
```

```
        up = mid-1;
      else if (key == list[mid])
        return mid;
      else if (key > list[mid])
        low = mid+1;
    }

    return -1;
  }
```

7.5 Rewrite Example 3.7, "Finding the Sales Amount," using the binary search approach. Since the sales amount is between 1 and `COMMISSION_SOUGHT/0.08`, you can use a binary search to improve Example 3.7.

7.6 Write a program that will summarize an array of rational numbers. The program creates an array called `rationalArray` composed of 10 `Rational` objects, then initializes it with random values and invokes the `sum` method to add all the rational numbers in the list. Print the rational numbers and their summation.

7.7 Write a program that meets the following requirements:

- Create a class for students. The class must contain each student's name (`String`), ID (`int`), and status (`int`). The status indicates the student's class standing: `1` for freshman, `2` for sophomore, `3` for junior, and `4` for senior.
- Create 20 students whose names are Name1, Name2, and so on, to Name20, and whose IDs and status are assigned randomly.
- Find all juniors and print their names and IDs.

7.8 Write a sort method using the bubble-sort algorithm. The bubble-sort algorithm makes several passes through the array. On each pass, neighboring pairs are compared successively. If a pair is in decreasing order, its values are swapped; otherwise, the values remain unchanged. The technique is called a *bubble sort* or *sinking sort* because the smaller values gradually "bubble" their way to the top and the larger values sink to the bottom.

The algorithm can be described as follows:

```
boolean changed = true;
do
{
  changed = false;
  for (int j=0; j<list.length-1; j++)
    if (list[j] > list[j+1])
    {
      swap list[j] with list[j+1];
      changed = true;
    }
}
while (changed);
```

Clearly, the list is in increasing order when the loop terminates. It is easy to show that the `do` loop executes at most `list.length - 1` times.

7.9 Write a program that takes a string from a command-line argument to check whether it is a palindrome.

7.10 Write a program similar to the one in Example 7.8. Instead of using integers, use rationals. You will need to use the `StringTokenizer` class introduced in Chapter 5 to retrieve numerator string and denominator string, and convert strings into integers using the `Integer.parseInt` method.

7.11 Create a new class named `NewRational` that extends `java.lang.Number`. The new class contains all the data fields, constructors, and methods defined in the `Rational` class in Example 5.8, "Using the `Rational` Class." Additionally it must implement the abstract methods defined in the `Number` class. The outline of the `NewRational` class is as follows:

```
public class MyRational extends Number
{
  private int numerator = 0;
  private int denominator = 1;

  public byte byteValue()
  {
    // TODO: override this java.lang.Number method;
  }

  public double doubleValue()
  {
    // TODO: implement this java.lang.Number abstract method;
  }

  public float floatValue()
  {
    // TODO: implement this java.lang.Number abstract method;
  }

  public int intValue()
  {
    // TODO: implement this java.lang.Number abstract method;
  }

  public long longValue()
  {
    // TODO: implement this java.lang.Number abstract method;
  }

  // other methods and constructor from the Rational class
}
```

PART III

Graphics Programming

In Part II, "Object-Oriented Programming," you learned the basics of object-oriented programming. The design of the API for Java graphics programming is an excellent example of how the object-oriented principle is applied. In the chapters that follow in this part of the book, you will learn the architecture of Java graphics programming API and use the user interface components to develop graphics applications and applets.

CHAPTER 8

GETTING STARTED WITH GRAPHICS PROGRAMMING

Objectives

- Describe the Java graphics programming class hierarchy.
- Use frames, panels, and simple UI components.
- Understand the role of layout managers.
- Use the `FlowLayout`, `GridLayout`, and `BorderLayout` managers.
- Become familiar with the `paintComponent` method.
- Become familiar with the classes `Color`, `Font`, and `FontMetrics`.
- Be able to use the drawing methods in the `Graphics` class.
- Understand the concept of event-driven programming.
- Become familiar with the Java event-delegation model: event registration, listening, and handling.

Introduction

Until now, you have only used text-based input and output. You used `MyInput.readInt()` and `MyInput.readDouble()` to read numbers from the keyboard, and `System.out.println` to display results on the console. This is the old-fashioned way to program. Today's client/server and Web-based applications use a graphical user interface known as GUI (pronounced goo-ee).

When Java was introduced, the graphics components were bundled in a library known as the Abstract Window Toolkit (AWT). For every platform on which Java runs, the AWT components are automatically mapped to the platform-specific components through their respective agents, known as *peers*. AWT is fine for developing simple GUI applications, but not for developing comprehensive GUI projects. Besides, AWT is prone to platform-specific bugs because its peer-based approach heavily relies on the underlying platform. With the release of Java 2, the AWT user interface components were replaced by a more robust, versatile, and flexible library known as the *Swing components*. Most Swing components are painted directly on canvases using Java code, except for components that are subclasses of `java.awt.Window` or `java.awt.Panel`, which must be drawn using native GUI on a specific platform. Swing components are less dependent on the target platform and use less of the native GUI resource. For this reason, Swing components that don't rely on native GUI are referred to as *lightweight components*, and AWT components are referred to as *heavyweight components*. Although AWT components are still supported in Java 2, I recommend that you learn to program using the Swing components, because the AWT user interface components will eventually fade away.

Java provides a rich set of classes to help you build graphical user interfaces. You can use various GUI-building classes—frames, panels, labels, buttons, text fields, text areas, combo boxes, check boxes, radio buttons, menus, scroll bars, scroll panes, and tabbed panes—to construct user interfaces. This chapter introduces the basics of Java graphics programming. Specifically, it discusses GUI components and their relationships, containers and layout managers, colors, fonts, and drawing geometric figures, such as lines, rectangles, ovals, arcs, and polygons, and introduces event-driven programming.

NOTE

The Swing components do not replace all the classes in AWT, only the AWT user interface components (`Button`, `TextField`, `TextArea`, etc.). The AWT helper classes (`Graphics`, `Color`, `Font`, `FontMetrics`, and `LayoutManager`) remain unchanged. In addition, the Swing components use the AWT event model.

The Java Graphics API

The design of the Java graphics programming API is an excellent example of the use of classes, inheritances, and interfaces. The graphics API contains the essential classes listed below. Their hierarchical relationships are shown in Figure 8.1.

- **`Component`**: This is a superclass of all user interface classes.

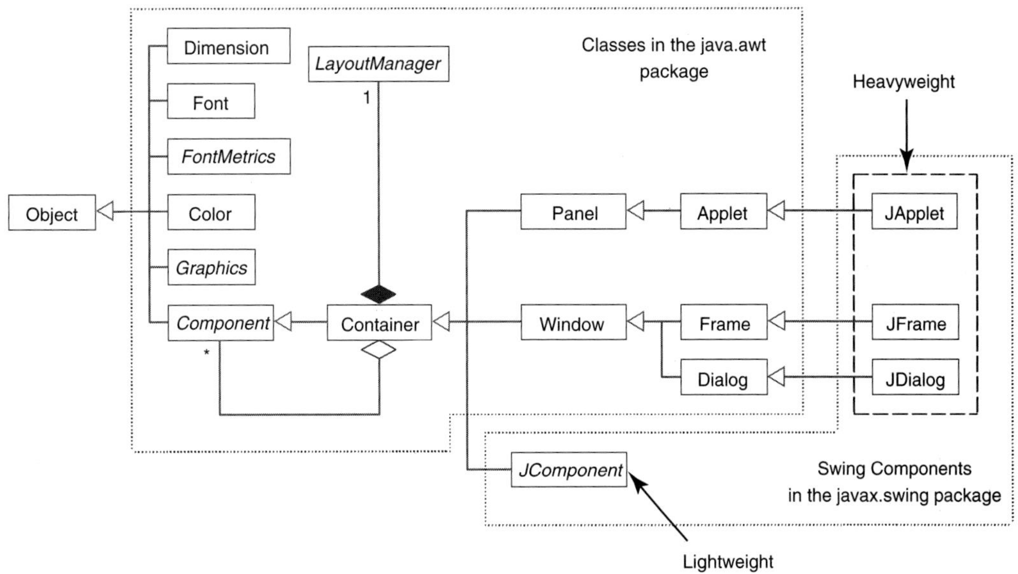

Figure 8.1 *Java graphics programming utilizes the classes shown in this hierarchical diagram.*

- **`Container`:** This is used to group components. A layout manager is used to position and place components in a container in the desired location and style. Frames, panels, and applets are examples of containers.
- **`JComponent`:** This is a superclass of all the lightweight Swing components, which are drawn directly on canvases using Java code, rather than on specific platforms using native GUI. Its subclasses (`JButton`, `JCheckBox`, `JMenu`, `JRadioButton`, `JLabel`, `JList`, `JTextField`, `JTextArea`, `JScrollPane`) are the basic elements for constructing the GUI.
- **`JFrame`:** This is a window not contained inside another window. `JFrame` is the container that holds other Swing user interface components in Java graphical applications.
- **`JDialog`:** This is a popup window generally used as a temporary window to receive additional information from the user or to provide notification that an event has occurred.
- **`JApplet`:** This is a subclass of `Applet`. You must extend `JApplet` to create a Swing-based Java applet.
- **`JPanel`:** This is an invisible container that holds user interface components. Panels can be nested. You can place panels inside panels and in a frame in Java applications or in an applet in Java applets. `JPanel` can also be used as a canvas to draw graphics.
- **`Graphics`:** This is an abstract class that provides a graphical context for drawing strings, lines, and simple shapes.

- `Color`: This deals with the colors of graphics components. For example, you can specify background or foreground colors in a component like `JFrame` and `JPanel`, or you can specify colors of lines, shapes, and strings in drawings.
- `Font`: This is used for drawings in `Graphics`. For example, you can specify the font type (SansSerif), style (bold), and size (24 points) to draw a string.
- `FontMetrics`: This is an abstract class used to get properties of the fonts used in drawings.

The graphics classes can be classified into three groups: the *container classes*, the *component classes*, and the *helper classes*. The container classes, such as `JFrame`, `JPanel`, and `JApplet`, are used to contain other components. The UI component classes, such as `JButton`, `JTextField`, `JTextArea`, `JComboBox`, `JList`, `JRadioButton`, and `JMenu`, are subclasses of `JComponent`. The helper classes, such as `Graphics`, `Color`, `Font`, `FontMetrics`, `Dimension`, and `LayoutManager`, are used by components and containers to draw and place objects.

The `JFrame`, `JApplet`, `JDialog`, and `JComponent` classes and their subclasses are grouped in the package `javax.swing`. All the other classes in Figure 8.1 are grouped in the package `java.awt`. Most Swing components are named with a prefixed *J*. For example, the Swing version of `Button` is called `JButton` to distinguish it from its AWT counterpart.

NOTE

Swing is a comprehensive solution to developing graphic user interface. There are over 250 classes in Swing, some of which are illustrated in Figure 8.2. Since the discussion in this book is only an introduction to Java graphics programming using Swing, the components listed in the dotted rectangle are not covered. For a more detailed treatment of Swing components, including model-view architecture, look and feel, and advanced components, please refer to my *Rapid Java Application Development Using JBuilder 3*, published by Prentice Hall.

TIP

Do not mix Swing user interface components like `JButton` with AWT user interface components like `Button`. Do not place `JButton` in `java.awt.Panel`, and similarly do not place Button in `javax.swing.JPanel`. Mixing them may cause problems. This book uses Swing user interfaces exclusively.

Frames

To create a user interface, you need to create either a frame or an applet to hold the user interface components. Figure 8.3 provides examples of possible user interface layouts in a frame and an applet.

Creating Java applets will be introduced in Chapter 10, "Applets and Advanced Graphics." This section introduces the procedure for creating frames.

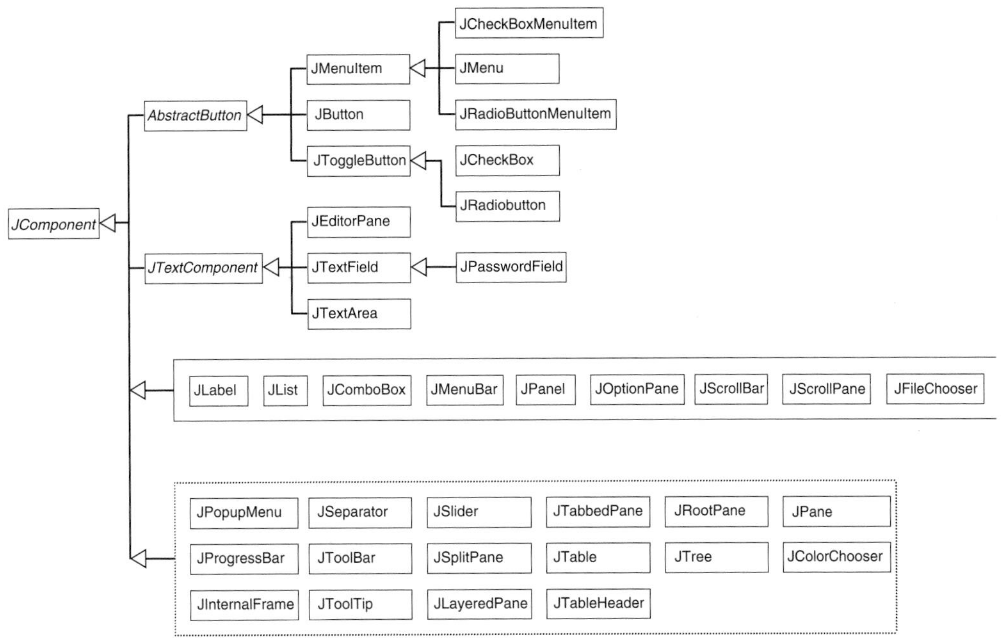

Figure 8.2 `JComponent` *and its subclasses are the basic elements for building graphical user interfaces.*

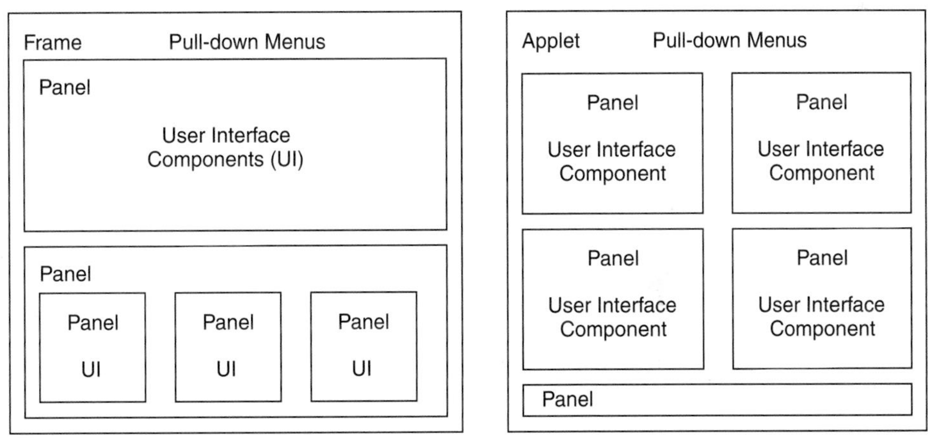

Figure 8.3 *A frame or an applet can contain menus, panels, and user interface components. Panels are used to group user interface components. Panels can contain other panels.*

Creating a Frame

The following program creates a frame:

```
// MyFrame.java: Display a frame
import javax.swing.*;
```

```
public class MyFrame
{
  public static void main(String[] args)
  {
    JFrame frame = new JFrame("Test Frame");
    frame.setSize(400, 300);
    frame.setVisible(true);
    frame.setDefaultCloseOperation(JFrame.EXIT_ON_CLOSE);
  }
}
```

Because `JFrame` is in the package `javax.swing`, the statement `import javax.swing.*` makes available all the classes from the `javax.swing` package, including `JFrame`, so that they can be used in the `MyFrame` class.

The following two constructors are used to create a `JFrame` object.

- `public JFrame();`

  This declares and creates a `JFrame` object that is untitled.

- `public JFrame(String title);`

  This declares and creates a `JFrame` object with a specified title.

The frame is not displayed until the `frame.setVisible(true)` method is applied. `frame.setSize(400, 300)` specifies that the frame is 400 pixels wide and 300 pixels high. If the `setSize` method is not used, the frame will be sized at 0 by 0 pixels, and nothing will be seen except the title bar. Since the `setSize` and `setVisible` methods are both defined in the `Component` class, they are inherited by the `JFrame` class. Later you will see that these methods are also useful in many other subclasses of `Component`.

When you run the `MyFrame` program, the following window will be displayed onscreen (see Figure 8.4) .

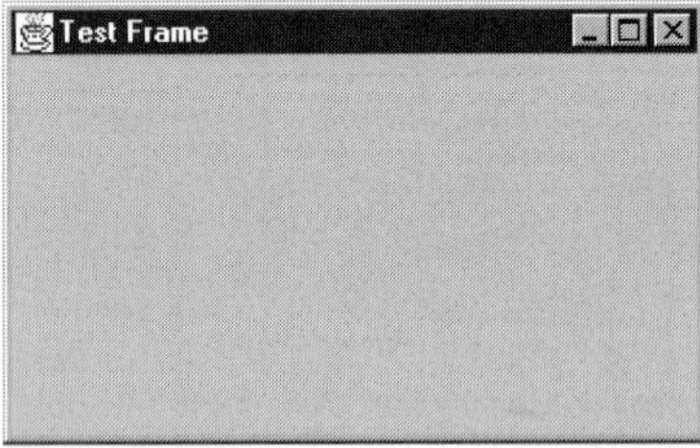

Figure 8.4 *The program creates and displays a frame with the title Test Frame.*

`frame.setDefaultCloseOperation(JFrame.EXIT_ON_CLOSE)` tells the program to terminate when the frame is closed. If this statement is not used, the program does not terminate when the frame is closed. In that case, you have to stop the program by pressing Ctrl+C at the DOS prompt window in Windows or use the kill command to stop the process in Unix.

NOTE

`JFrame.EXIT_ON_CLOSE` is new in Java 2 SDK v1.3. To enable your programs to compile and run in a version prior to v1.3, I will comment this statement in the code from now on. For information on obtaining and installing v1.3, please visit **www.cs.armstrong.edu/liang/intro3e.html**.

Centering a Frame (Optional)

By default, a frame is displayed in the upper-left corner of the screen. To display a frame at a specified location, use the `setLocation(x, y)` method in the `JFrame` class. This method places the upper-left corner of a frame at location (x, y).

To center a frame on the screen, you need to know the width and height of the screen and the frame in order to determine the frame's upper-left coordinates. The screen's width and height can be obtained using the `java.awt.Toolkit` class:

```
Dimension screenSize = Toolkit.getDefaultToolkit().getScreenSize();
int screenWidth = screenSize.width;
int screenHeight = screenSize.height;
```

Therefore, as shown in Figure 8.5, the upper left `x` and `y` coordinates of the centered frame `frame` can be:

```
Dimension frameSize = frame.getSize();
int x = (screenWidth - frameSize.width)/2;
int y = (screenHeight - frameSize.height)/2;
```

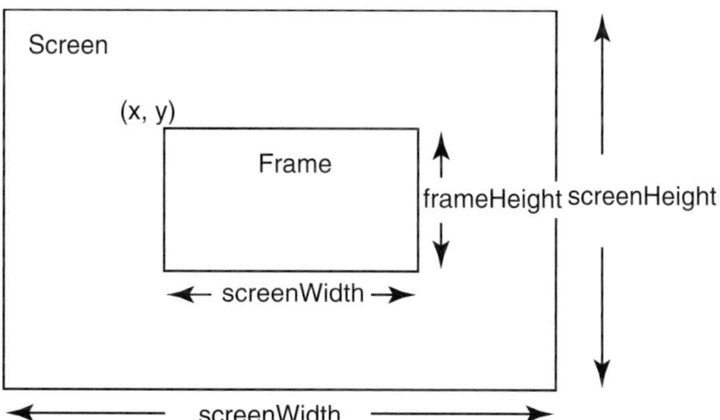

Figure 8.5 *The frame is centered on the screen.*

The `getSize` method is defined in the `Component` class. The `java.awt.Dimension` class encapsulates the width and height of a component (in integer precision) in a single object.

To display a centered frame, the program can be modified as follows:

```
// CenterFrame.java: Display a frame
import javax.swing.*;
import java.awt.*;
```

```
public class CenterFrame
{
  public static void main(String[] args)
  {
    JFrame frame = new JFrame("Centered Frame");
    frame.setSize(400, 300);

    // New in JDK 1.3 to exit the program upon closing
    // frame.setDefaultCloseOperation(JFrame.EXIT_ON_CLOSE);

    // Get the dimension of the screen
    Dimension screenSize = Toolkit.getDefaultToolkit().getScreenSize();
    int screenWidth = screenSize.width;
    int screenHeight = screenSize.height;

    // Get the dimension of the frame
    Dimension frameSize = frame.getSize();
    int x = (screenWidth - frameSize.width)/2;
    int y = (screenHeight - frameSize.height)/2;

    frame.setLocation(x, y);
    frame.setVisible(true);
  }
}
```

Adding Components into a Frame

The frame shown in Figure 8.4 is empty. Using the `add` method, you can add components into the frame's content pane, as follows:

```
// MyFrameWithComponents.java: Add components into a frame
import javax.swing.*;

public class MyFrameWithComponents
{
  public static void main(String[] args)
  {
    JFrame frame = new JFrame("Adding Components into the Frame");

    // Add a button into the frame
    frame.getContentPane().add(new JButton("OK"));

    frame.setSize(400, 300);
    frame.setVisible(true);
    // frame.setDefaultCloseOperation(JFrame.EXIT_ON_CLOSE);
  }
}
```

The `getContentPane` method in the `JFrame` class returns the content pane of the frame. The content pane holds the components in the frame. An object of `JButton` was created using `new JButton("OK")`, and this object was added to the content pane of the frame. When you run the program `MyFrameWithComponents`, the following window will be displayed in Figure 8.6.

The button is always centered in the frame and occupies the entire frame no matter how you resize the frame in Figure 8.6. This is because the content pane uses a layout manager, which is responsible for laying out components in the frame. The default layout manager for the content pane places the button in the center of the frame. In the next section, you will use several different layout managers to place the components in the desired locations.

Figure 8.6 *An OK button is added to the frame.*

Layout Managers

In many other window systems, the user interface components are arranged by using hard-coded pixel measurements. For example, put a button at location (`10, 10`) in the window. Using hard-coded pixel measurements, the user interface might look fine on one system but be unusable on another. Java's layout managers provide a level of abstraction that automatically maps your user interface on all window systems.

The Java GUI components are placed in containers, where they are arranged by the container's layout manager. In the preceding program, you did not specify where to place the OK button in the frame, but Java knows where to place the button because the layout manager works behind the scenes to place components in the correct locations. The five basic layout managers are `FlowLayout`, `GridLayout`, `BorderLayout`, `CardLayout`, and `GridBagLayout`. These classes implement the `LayoutManager` interface.

Layout managers are set in containers. The syntax to set a layout manager is as follows:

```
container.setLayout(new SpecificLayout());
```

To add a component to a container, use the `add` method. To remove a component from a container, use the `remove` method. The following statement adds `jbtOK` to the container.

```
JButton jbtOK = new JButton("OK");
container.add(jbtOK);
```

The container can be the content pane of a frame or an applet, or an instance of `JPanel`.

The following sections introduce the `FlowLayout`, `GridLayout`, and `BorderLayout` managers. The `CardLayout` and `GridBagLayout` are introduced in Chapter 10, "Applets and Advanced Graphics."

FlowLayout

`FlowLayout` is the simplest layout manager. The components are arranged in the container from left to right in the order in which they were added. When one row is filled, a new row is started. You can specify the way the components are aligned by using one of three constants: `FlowLayout.RIGHT`, `FlowLayout.CENTER`, or

FlowLayout.LEFT. You can also specify the gap between components in pixels. FlowLayout has three constructors:

- `public FlowLayout(int align, int hGap, int vGap)`

  This constructs a new FlowLayout with the specified alignment, horizontal gap, and vertical gap. The gaps are the distances in pixels between components.

- `public FlowLayout(int alignment)`

  This constructs a new FlowLayout with a specified alignment and a default gap of five pixels horizontally and vertically.

- `public FlowLayout()`

  This constructs a new FlowLayout with a default center alignment and a default gap of five pixels horizontally and vertically.

Example 8.1 Testing the FlowLayout Manager

This example enables a program to arrange components in a frame by using the FlowLayout manager with a specified alignment and horizontal and vertical gaps. The program uses the following simple code to arrange 10 buttons in a frame. The output is shown in Figure 8.7.

```
// ShowFlowLayout.java: Demonstrate using FlowLayout
import javax.swing.JButton;
import javax.swing.JFrame;
import java.awt.Container;
import java.awt.FlowLayout;

public class ShowFlowLayout extends JFrame
{
  // Default constructor
  public ShowFlowLayout()
  {
    // Get the content pane of the frame
    Container container = getContentPane();

    // Set FlowLayout, aligned left with horizontal gap 10
    // and vertical gap 20 between components
    container.setLayout(new FlowLayout(FlowLayout.LEFT, 10, 20));

    // Add buttons to the frame
    for (int i=1; i<=10; i++)
      container.add(new JButton("Component " + i));
  }

  // Main method
  public static void main(String[] args)
  {
    ShowFlowLayout frame = new ShowFlowLayout();
    frame.setTitle("Show FlowLayout");
    // frame.setDefaultCloseOperation(JFrame.EXIT_ON_CLOSE);
    frame.setSize(200, 200);
    frame.setVisible(true);
  }
}
```

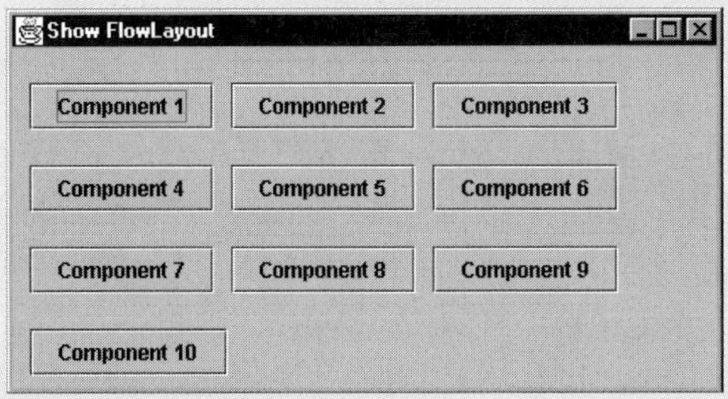

Figure 8.7 *The components are added with the `FlowLayout` manager to fill in the rows in the container one after another.*

Example Review

This example creates a class named `ShowFlowLayout` that extends the `JFrame` class. The constructor of `ShowFlowLayout` constructs and places the components in the frame using the `FlowLayout` manager.

If you resize the frame, the components are automatically rearranged to fit in the frame.

If you replace the `setLayout` statement with `setLayout(new Flow Layout(FlowLayout.LEFT, 0, 0))`, you will see all the buttons left-aligned with no gaps.

An anonymous `FlowLayout` object was created in the statement:

```
container.setLayout(new FlowLayout(FlowLayout.LEFT, 10, 20));
```

This statement is equivalent to the following code:

```
FlowLayout layout = new FlowLayout();
container.setLayout(layout);
```

This code creates an explicit reference to the object `layout` of the `FlowLayout` class. This explicit reference is not necessary, because the object is not directly referenced in the program.

The `setTitle` method is defined in the `java.awt.Frame` class. Since `JFrame` is a subclass of `Frame`, you can use it to set a title for an object of `JFrame`.

TIP

Do not forget to put the `new` operator before a `layout manager` when setting a layout style; for example, `setLayout(new FlowLayout())`.

GridLayout

The `GridLayout` manager arranges components in a grid (matrix) formation with the number of rows and columns defined by the constructor. The components are placed in the grid from left to right, starting with the first row, then the second, and so on, in the order in which they are added. The `GridLayout` manager has three constructors:

- `public GridLayout(int rows, int columns, int hGap, int vGap)`

  This constructs a new `GridLayout` with the specified number of rows and columns, along with specified horizontal and vertical gaps between components in the container.

- `public GridLayout(int rows, int columns)`

  This constructs a new `GridLayout` with the specified number of rows and columns. The horizontal and vertical gaps are zero.

- `public GridLayout()`

  This constructs a new `GridLayout` with one column in a single row.

You can specify the number of rows and columns in the grid. The basic rule is as follows:

- The number of rows or the number of columns can be zero, but not both. If one is zero and the other is nonzero, the nonzero dimension is fixed, while the zero dimension is determined dynamically by the layout manager. For example, if you specify zero rows and three columns for a grid that has 10 components, `GridLayout` creates three fixed columns of four rows, with the last row containing one component. If you specify three rows and zero columns for a grid that has 10 components, `GridLayout` creates three fixed rows of four columns, with the last row containing two components.

- If both the number of rows and the number of columns are nonzero, the number of rows is the dominating parameter; that is, the number of rows is fixed, and the layout manager dynamically calculates the number of columns. For example, if you specify three rows and three columns for a grid that has 10 components, `GridLayout` creates three fixed rows of four columns, with the last row containing two components.

Example 8.2 Testing the `GridLayout` Manager

This example presents a program that arranges components in a frame with `GridLayout`. The program gives the following code to arrange 10 buttons in a grid of four rows and three columns. Its output is shown in Figure 8.8.

```
// ShowGridLayout.java: Demonstrate using GridLayout
import javax.swing.JButton;
import javax.swing.JFrame;
```

```
import java.awt.GridLayout;
import java.awt.Container;

public class ShowGridLayout extends JFrame
{
  // Default constructor
  public ShowGridLayout()
  {
    // Get the content pane of the frame
    Container container = getContentPane();

    // Set GridLayout, 4 rows, 3 columns, and gaps 5 between
    // components horizontally and vertically
    container.setLayout(new GridLayout(4, 3, 5, 5));

    // Add buttons to the frame
    for (int i=1; i<=10; i++)
      container.add(new JButton("Component " + i));
  }

  // Main method
  public static void main(String[] args)
  {
    ShowGridLayout frame = new ShowGridLayout();
    frame.setTitle("Show GridLayout");
    // frame.setDefaultCloseOperation(JFrame.EXIT_ON_CLOSE);
    frame.setSize(200, 200);
    frame.setVisible(true);
  }
}
```

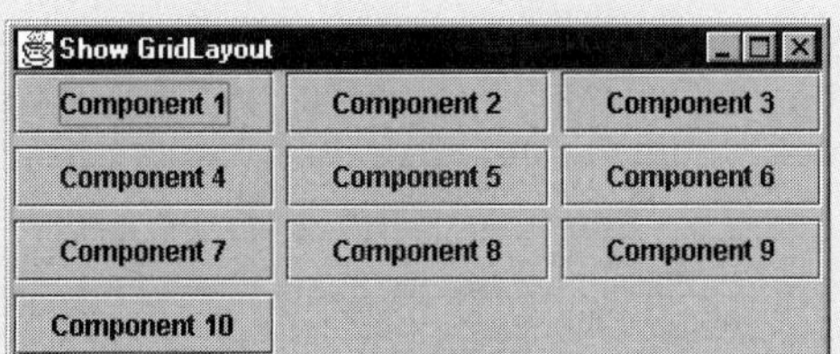

Figure 8.8 *The `GridLayout` manager divides the container into grids, then the components are added to fill in the cells, row by row.*

Example Review

If you resize the frame, the layout of the buttons remains unchanged (that is, the number of rows and columns does not change, and the gaps don't change either).

All components are given equal size in the container of GridLayout.

Replacing the `setLayout` statement with `setLayout(new GridLayout(3, 10))` would yield three rows and *four* columns, with the last row containing two components. The columns parameter is ignored because the rows parameter is nonzero. The actual number of columns is calculated by the layout manager.

continues

Example 8.2 continued

NOTE

In `FlowLayout` and `GridLayout`, the order in which the components are added to the container is important. It determines the location of the components in the container.

BorderLayout

The `BorderLayout` manager divides the window into five areas: East, South, West, North, and Center. Components are added to a `BorderLayout` by using `add(Component, index)`, where `index` is a constant `BorderLayout.EAST`, `BorderLayout.SOUTH`, `BorderLayout.WEST`, `BorderLayout.NORTH`, or `BorderLayout.CENTER`. You can use one of the following two constructors to create a new `BorderLayout`:

- `public BorderLayout(int hGap, int vGap)`

  This constructs a new `BorderLayout` with the specified horizontal and vertical gaps between the components.

- `public BorderLayout()`

  This constructs a new `BorderLayout` without horizontal or vertical gaps.

The components are laid out according to their preferred sizes and where they are placed in the container. The north and south components can stretch horizontally; the east and west components can stretch vertically; the center component can stretch both horizontally and vertically to fill any empty space.

Example 8.3 Testing the `BorderLayout` Manager

The example presents the following code to place East, South, West, North, and Center buttons in the frame by using `BorderLayout`. The output of the program is shown in Figure 8.9.

```
// ShowBorderLayout.java: Demonstrate using BorderLayout
import javax.swing.JButton;
import javax.swing.JFrame;
import java.awt.Container;
import java.awt.BorderLayout;

public class ShowBorderLayout extends JFrame
{
  // Default constructor
  public ShowBorderLayout()
  {
    // Get the content pane of the frame
    Container container = getContentPane();

    // Set BorderLayout with horizontal gap 5 and vertical gap 10
    container.setLayout(new BorderLayout(5, 10));
```

```
    // Add buttons to the frame
    container.add(new JButton("East"), BorderLayout.EAST);
    container.add(new JButton("South"), BorderLayout.SOUTH);
    container.add(new JButton("West"), BorderLayout.WEST);
    container.add(new JButton("North"), BorderLayout.NORTH);
    container.add(new JButton("Center"), BorderLayout.CENTER);
  }

  // Main method
  public static void main(String[] args)
  {
    ShowBorderLayout frame = new ShowBorderLayout();
    frame.setTitle("Show BorderLayout");
    // frame.setDefaultCloseOperation(JFrame.EXIT_ON_CLOSE);
    frame.setSize(300, 200);
    frame.setVisible(true);
  }
}
```

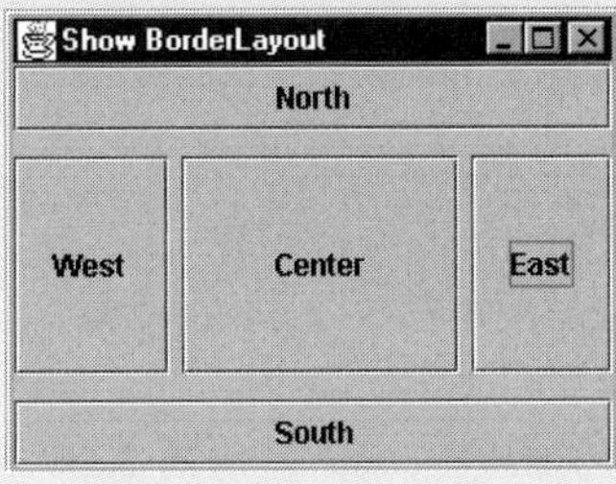

Figure 8.9 `BorderLayout` *divides the container into five areas, each of which can hold a component.*

Example Review

The buttons are added to the frame. Note that the `add` method for `BorderLayout` is different from `FlowLayout` and `GridLayout`. With `BorderLayout` you specify where to put the components.

It is unnecessary to place components to occupy all the areas. If you remove the East button from the program and rerun it, you will see that the center stretches rightward to occupy the East area.

NOTE

For convenience, `BorderLayout` interprets the absence of an index specification as `BorderLayout.CENTER`. For example, `add(component)` is the same as `add(Component, BorderLayout.CENTER)`.

TIP

To avoid mistakes, I recommend that you explicitly set a layout style for a container, even though `BorderLayout` is used by default for the content pane of a `JFrame`.

Using Panels as Containers

Suppose that you want to place 10 buttons and a text field on a frame. The buttons are placed in grid formation, but the text field is placed on a separate row. It is difficult to achieve the desired look by placing all the components in a single container. With Java graphics programming, you can divide a window into panels. Panels act as smaller containers to group user interface components. You add the buttons in one panel, and then add the panel into the frame.

The Swing version of panel is `JPanel`. The constructor in the `JPanel` class is `JPanel()`. To add a button to the panel `p`, for instance, you can use:

```
JPanel p = new JPanel();
p.add(new JButton("ButtonName"));
```

By default, `JPanel` uses `FlowLayout`. Panels can be placed inside a frame or inside another panel. The following statement places panel `p` into frame `f`:

```
f.getContentPane().add(p);
```

NOTE

To add a component to `JFrame`, you actually add it to the content pane of `JFrame`. To add a component to a panel, you add it directly to the panel using the `add` method.

Example 8.4 Testing Panels

This example uses panels to organize components. The program creates a user interface for a microwave oven, as shown in Figure 8.10. The program is given as follows:

```
// TestPanels.java: Use panels to group components
import java.awt.*;
import javax.swing.*;

public class TestPanels extends JFrame
{
  // Default constructor
  public TestPanels()
  {
    // Get the content pane of the frame
    Container container = getContentPane();

    // Set BorderLayout for the frame
    container.setLayout(new BorderLayout());

    // Create panel p1 for the buttons and set GridLayout
    JPanel p1 = new JPanel();
    p1.setLayout(new GridLayout(4, 3));

    // Add buttons to the panel
    for (int i=1; i<=9; i++)
```

```
      {
        p1.add(new JButton(" " + i));
      }

      p1.add(new JButton(" " + 0));
      p1.add(new JButton("Start"));
      p1.add(new JButton("Stop"));

      // Create panel p2 to hold a text field and p1
      JPanel p2 = new JPanel();
      p2.setLayout(new BorderLayout());
      p2.add(new JTextField("Time to be displayed here"),
        BorderLayout.NORTH);
      p2.add(p1, BorderLayout.CENTER);

      // Add p2 and a button to the frame
      container.add(p2, BorderLayout.EAST);
      container.add(new Button("Food to be placed here"),
        BorderLayout.CENTER);
    }

    // Main method
    public static void main(String[] args)
    {
      TestPanels frame = new TestPanels();
      frame.setTitle("The Front View of a Microwave Oven");
      // frame.setDefaultCloseOperation(JFrame.EXIT_ON_CLOSE);
      frame.setSize(400, 250);
      frame.setVisible(true);
    }
  }
```

Figure 8.10 *The program uses panels to organize components.*

Example Review

To achieve the desired layout, the program uses panel `p1` of the `GridLayout` to group the number buttons, the Stop button, and the Start button, uses panel `p2` of `BorderLayout` to hold a text field in the north and `p1` in the center. The button representing the food is placed in the center of frame, and `p2` is placed in the west of the frame.

continues

Example 8.4 continued

The statement

```
p2.add(new JTextField("Time to be displayed here"),
  BorderLayout.NORTH);
```

creates an instance of `JTextField`. Text field is a GUI component that can be used for user input as well as to display values. Text fields will be introduced in Chapter 9, "Creating User Interfaces."

Drawing Graphics in Panels

Panels are invisible and are used as small containers that group components to achieve a desired layout look. Another important use of `JPanel` is for drawing strings and graphics.

To draw in a panel, you create a new class that extends `JPanel` and override the `paintComponent` method to tell the panel how to draw things. You can then display strings, draw geometric shapes, and view images on the panel. Although you can draw things directly in a frame or an applet using the `paint` method, I recommend that you use `JPanel` to draw messages and shapes and to show images; this way your drawing does not interfere with other components.

The signature of the `paintComponent` method is as follows:

```
public void paintComponent(Graphics g)
```

The `Graphics` object `g` is created automatically by the Java runtime system. This object controls how information is drawn. You can use various drawing methods defined in the `Graphics` class to draw strings and geometric figures.

NOTE

The `Graphics` class is an abstract class for displaying figures and images on the screen in different platforms. The `Graphics` class is implemented in the native platform in JVM. When you use the `paintComponent` method to draw things on a graphics context `g`, this `g` is an instance of a concrete subclass of the abstract `Graphics` class for the specific platform. The `Graphics` class encapsulates the platform details and enables you to draw things uniformly without concerning specific platforms.

All the drawing methods have arguments that specify the locations of the subjects to be drawn. The Java coordinate system has x in the horizontal axis and y in the vertical axis, with the origin `(0, 0)` at the upper-left corner of the window. The x coordinate increases to the right, and the y coordinate increases downward. All measurements in Java are made in pixels, as shown in Figure 8.11.

You can draw things using appropriate colors and fonts. The next sections introduce the `Color` class, the `Font` class, the `FontMetrics` class, and drawing methods in the `Graphics` class.

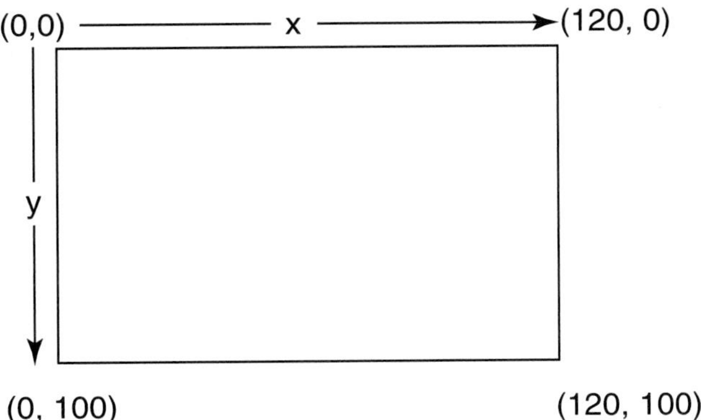

Figure 8.11 *The Java graphics coordinate system is measured in pixels, with* `(0, 0)` *at its upper-left corner.*

The *Color* Class

You can set colors for GUI components by using the `java.awt.Color` class. Colors are made of red, green, and blue components, each of which is represented by a byte value that describes its intensity, ranging from 0 (darkest shade) to 255 (lightest shade). This is commonly known as the RGB model.

The syntax to create a `Color` object is

```
Color color = new Color(r, g, b);
```

in which `r`, `g`, and `b` specify a color by its red, green, and blue components; for example:

```
Color color = new Color(128, 100, 100);
```

You can use the `setBackground(Color c)` and `setForeground(Color c)` methods defined in the `Component` class to set a component's background and foreground colors.

Following is an example of setting the background of a panel by using `Color c`:

```
JPanel myPanel = new JPanel();
myPanel.setBackground(c);
```

Alternatively, you can use one of the 13 standard colors (`black`, `blue`, `cyan`, `darkGray`, `gray`, `green`, `lightGray`, `magenta`, `orange`, `pink`, `red`, `white`, `yellow`) defined as constants in `java.awt.Color`. For example, the following code sets the background color of a panel to yellow.

```
JPanel myPanel = new JPanel();
myPanel.setBackground(Color.yellow);
```

NOTE

The standard color names are constants, but they are named as variables with lowercase for the first word and uppercase for the first letters of subsequent words. Thus the color names violate the Java naming convention.

The *Font* and *FontMetrics* Classes

You can set fonts for the components, or subjects you draw, and use font metrics to measure font size. Fonts and font metrics are encapsulated in the classes `Font` and `FontMetrics`.

Whatever font is current will be used in the subsequent drawing. To set a font, you need to create a `Font` object from the `Font` class. The syntax is:

```
Font myFont = new Font(name, style, size);
```

You can choose a font name from `SansSerif`, `Serif`, `Monospaced`, `Dialog`, or `DialogInput`, and choose a style from `Font.PLAIN`, `Font.BOLD`, and `Font.ITALIC`. The styles can be combined, as in the following code:

```
Font myFont = new Font("SansSerif", Font.BOLD, 16);
Font myFont = new Font("Serif", Font.BOLD+Font.ITALIC, 12);
```

`FontMetrics` can be used to compute the exact length and width of a string, which is helpful for measuring the size of a string in order to display it in the right position. For example, you can center strings in the viewing area with the help of the `FontMetrics` class. A `FontMetrics` is measured by the following attributes (see Figure 8.12):

- **Leading:** Pronounced *ledding*, this is the amount of space between lines of text.
- **Ascent:** This is the height of a character, from the baseline to the top.
- **Descent:** This is the distance from the baseline to the bottom of a descending character, such as *j*, *y*, and *g*.
- **Height:** This is the sum of leading, ascent, and descent.

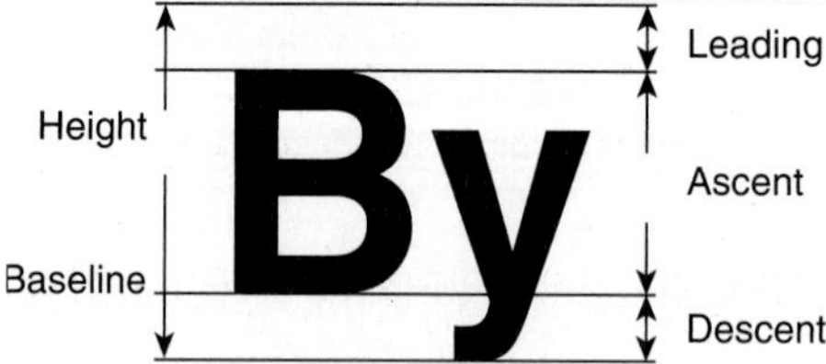

Figure 8.12 *The `FontMetrics` class can be used to determine the font properties of characters.*

`FontMetrics` is an abstract class. To get a `FontMetrics` object for a specific font, use the following `getFontMetrics` methods defined in the `Graphics` class.

- `public FontMetrics getFontMetrics(Font f)`

  This method returns the font metrics of the specified font.

- `public FontMetrics getFontMetrics()`

  This method returns the font metrics of the current font.

You can use the following instance methods in the `FontMetrics` class to obtain font information:

```
public int getAscent()
public int getDescent()
public int getLeading()
public int getHeight()
public int stringWidth(String str)
```

Example 8.5 Using `FontMetrics`

This example presents a program that displays "Welcome to Java" in SansSerif 20-point bold, centered in the frame. The output of the program is shown in Figure 8.13.

```
// TestFontMetrics.java: Draw a message at the center of a panel
import java.awt.Font;
import java.awt.FontMetrics;
import java.awt.Graphics;
import javax.swing.*;

public class TestFontMetrics extends JFrame
{
  // Default constructor
  public TestFontMetrics()
  {
    MessagePanel messagePanel = new MessagePanel("Welcome to Java");

    // Set font SansSerif 20-point bold
    messagePanel.setFont(new Font("SansSerif", Font.BOLD, 20));

    // Center the message
    messagePanel.setCentered(true);

    getContentPane().add(messagePanel);
  }

  // Main method
  public static void main(String[] args)
  {
    TestFontMetrics frame = new TestFontMetrics();
    // frame.setDefaultCloseOperation(JFrame.EXIT_ON_CLOSE);
    frame.setSize(300, 200);
    frame.setTitle("TestFontMetrics");
    frame.setVisible(true);
  }
}

// MessagePanel.java: Display a message on a JPanel
import java.awt.Font;
import java.awt.FontMetrics;
import java.awt.Dimension;
import java.awt.Graphics;
import javax.swing.JPanel;

public class MessagePanel extends JPanel
{
  private String message = "Welcome to Java"; // Message to display
```

continues

Example 8.5 continued

```
// (x, y) coordinates where the message is displayed
private int xCoordinate = 20;
private int yCoordinate = 20;

// Indicating whether the message is displayed in the center
private boolean centered;

// Default constructor
public MessagePanel()
{
}

// Constructor with a message parameter
public MessagePanel(String message)
{
  this.message = message;
}

public String getMessage()
{
  return message;
}

public void setMessage(String message)
{
  this.message = message;
}

public int getXCoordinate()
{
  return xCoordinate;
}

public void setXCoordinate(int x)
{
  this.xCoordinate = x;
}

public int getYCoordinate()
{
  return yCoordinate;
}

public void setYCoordinate(int y)
{
  this.yCoordinate = y;
}

public boolean isCentered()
{
  return centered;
}

public void setCentered(boolean centered)
{
  this.centered = centered;
}
```

```
    public void paintComponent(Graphics g)
    {
      super.paintComponent(g);

      if (centered)
      {
        // Get font metrics for the current font
        FontMetrics fm = g.getFontMetrics();

        // Find the center location to display
        int w = fm.stringWidth(message);  // Get the string width
        // Get the string height, from top to the baseline
        int h = fm.getAscent();
        xCoordinate = (getWidthc)-W)/2;
        yCoordinate = (getHeightc)+h)/2;
      }

      g.drawString(message, xCoordinate, yCoordinate);
    }

    public Dimension getPreferredSize()
    {
      return new Dimension(200, 100);
    }

    public Dimension getMinimumSize()
    {
      return new Dimension(200, 100);
    }
  }
```

Figure 8.13 *The program uses the* `FontMetrics` *class to measure the string width and height, and displays it at the center of the frame.*

Example Review

The example contains two classes: `TestFontMetrics` and `MessagePanel`. The relationship between the two classes is shown in Figure 8.14.

`TestFontMetrics` creates an instance of `MessagePanel` to display a message at the center of the panel. The `setFont` method sets a new font for the message panel. This method is available for all subclasses of `Component`. The new font is created using `new Font("SansSerif", Font.BOLD, 20)`. This new font is used to display the message in the panel.

continues

Example 8.5 continued

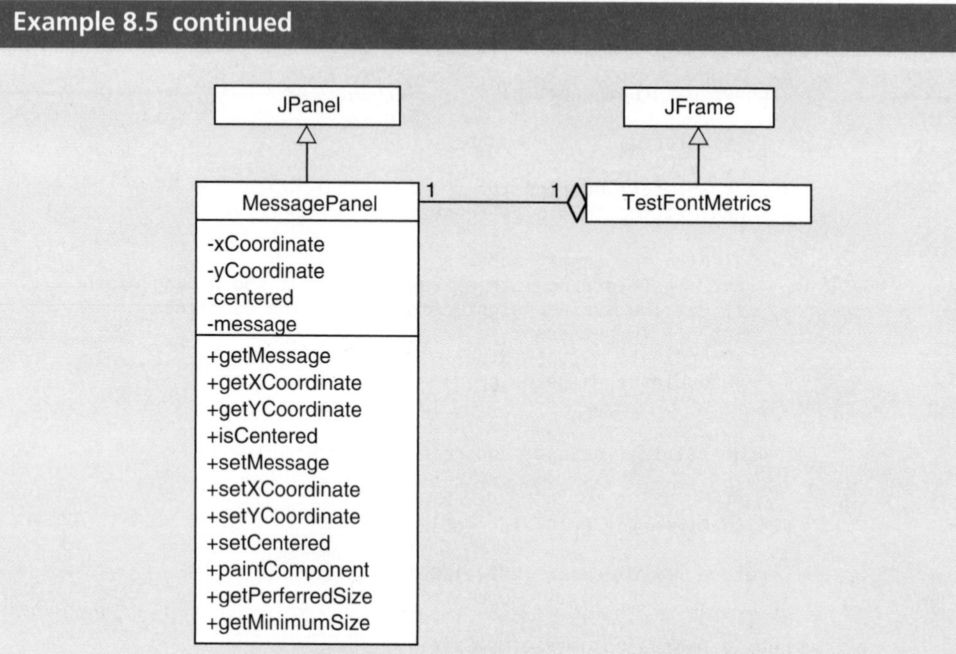

Figure 8.14 *`TestFontMetrics` uses `MessagePanel` to display a message.*

The `MessagePanel` class has the properties `message`, `xCoordinate`, `yCoordinate`, and `centered`. `xCoordinate` and `yCoordinate` specify where the `message` is displayed if `centered` is false. If centered is true, the message is displayed at the center of the panel.

The methods `getWidth()` and `getHeight()`, defined in the `Component` class, return this component's width and height, respectively.

Since the `centered` property is set to `true` in `TestFontMetrics`, the message is displayed in the center of the panel. Resizing the frame results in the message always being displayed in the center of the panel.

`yCoordinate` is height of the baseline for the first character of the string to be displayed. When `centered` is true, `yCoordinate` should be `getSize().height/2 + h/2`, where `h` is the ascent of the string.

The `getPreferredSize()` method, defined in `Component`, is overridden in `MessagePanel` to specify a preferred size for the layout manager to consider when laying out a `MessagePanel` object.

In Example 1.2, "Writing a Simple Applet," you used the `drawString` method to display a string on an applet. In this example, the `drawString` method draws on the panel. The `drawString(s, x, y)` method draws a string `s` whose left end of the baseline starts at `(x, y)`.

The Swing components use the `paintComponent` method to draw things. The `paintComponent` method is invoked to paint the graphics context. This method is invoked when the frame is displayed or whenever you resize the frame. Invoking `super.paintComponent(g)` is necessary to clear the viewing area before a new drawing is displayed. If this method is not invoked, the previous drawings will not be cleared.

NOTE

The `Component` class has the `setBackground`, `setForeground` and `setFont` methods. These methods are for setting colors and fonts for the entire component. Suppose you want to draw several messages in a panel with different colors and fonts, you have to use the `setColor` and `setFont` methods in the `Graphics` class to set the color and font for the current drawing.

Drawing Geometric Figures

This section introduces the methods in the `Graphics` class for drawing lines, rectangles, ovals, arcs, and polygons.

Drawing Lines

You can use the method shown below to draw a straight line:

```
drawLine(x1, y1, x2, y2);
```

The parameters `x1`, `y1`, `x2`, and `y2` represent the starting point (`x1`, `y1`) and the ending point (`x2`, `y2`) of the line, as shown in Figure 8.15.

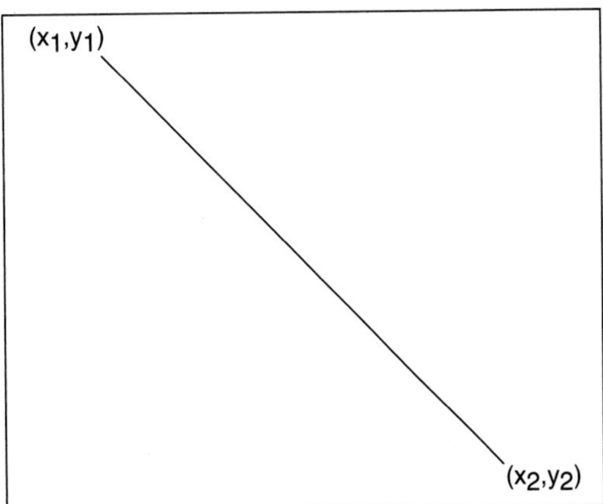

Figure 8.15 *The `drawLine` method draws a line between two specified points.*

Drawing Rectangles

Java provides six methods for drawing rectangles in outline or filled with color. You can draw plain rectangles, rounded rectangles, or 3D rectangles.

To draw a plain rectangle, use:

```
drawRect(x, y, w, h);
```

To draw a rectangle filled with color, use the following code:

```
fillRect(x, y, w, h);
```

The parameters `x`, and `y` represent the upper-left corner of the rectangle, and `w` and `h` are the width and height of the rectangle (see Figure 8.16).

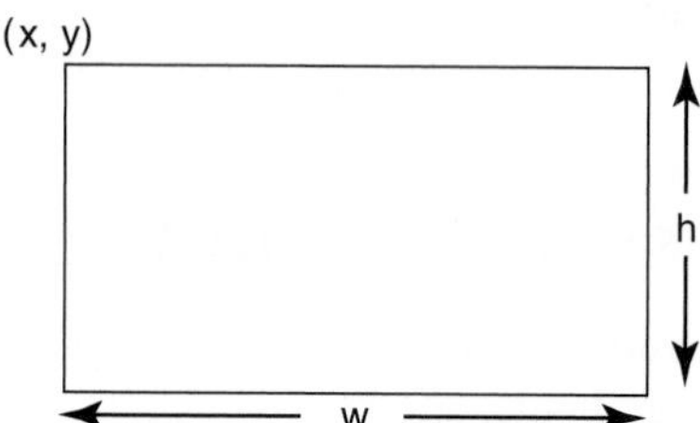

Figure 8.16 *The* `drawRect` *method draws a rectangle with specified upper-left corner* `(x, y)`, *width, and height.*

To draw a rounded rectangle, use the following method:

```
drawRoundRect(x, y, w, h, aw, ah);
```

To draw a rounded rectangle filled with color, use this code:

```
fillRoundRect(x, y, w, h, aw, ah);
```

Parameters `x`, `y`, `w`, and `h` are the same as in the `drawRect` method, parameter `aw` is the horizontal diameter of the arcs at the corner, and `ah` is the vertical diameter of the arcs at the corner (see Figure 8.17).

To draw a 3D rectangle, use

```
draw3DRect(x, y, w, h, raised);
```

in which `x`, `y`, `w`, and `h` are the same as in the `drawRect` method. The last parameter, a Boolean value, indicates whether the rectangle is raised or indented from the surface.

The example given below demonstrates these methods. The output is shown in Figure 8.18.

```
// TestRect.java: Demonstrate drawing rectangles
import java.awt.Graphics;
import java.awt.Color;
import javax.swing.JPanel;
import javax.swing.JFrame;
```

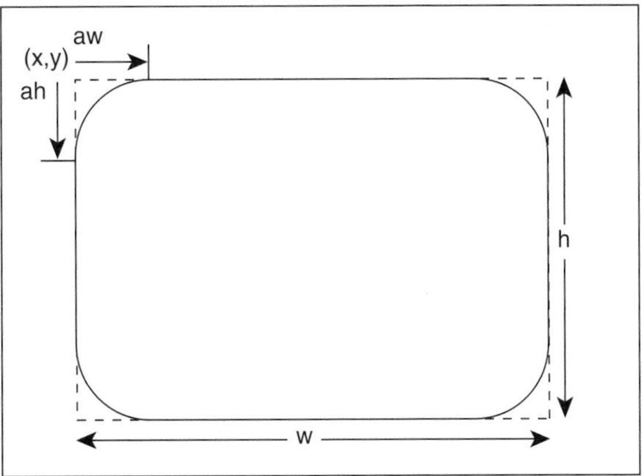

Figure 8.17 *The* `drawRoundRect` *method draws a rounded-corner rectangle.*

```
public class TestRect extends JFrame
{
  // Default constructor
  public TestRect()
  {
    setTitle("Show Rectangles");
    getContentPane().add(new RectPanel());
  }

  // Main method
  public static void main(String[] args)
  {
    TestRect frame = new TestRect();
    // frame.setDefaultCloseOperation(JFrame.EXIT_ON_CLOSE);
    frame.setSize(300,250);
    frame.setVisible(true);
  }
}

class RectPanel extends JPanel
{
  public void paintComponent(Graphics g)
  {
    super.paintComponent(g);

    // Set new color
    g.setColor(Color.red);

    // Draw a rectangle
    g.drawRect(30, 30, 100, 100);

    // Draw a rounded rectangle
    g.drawRoundRect(140, 30, 100, 100, 60, 30);

    // Change the color to cyan
    g.setColor(Color.cyan);

    // Draw a 3D rectangle
    g.fill3DRect(30, 140, 100, 100, true);
```

```
        // Draw a raised 3D rectangle
        g.fill3DRect(140, 140, 100, 100, false);
      }
    }
```

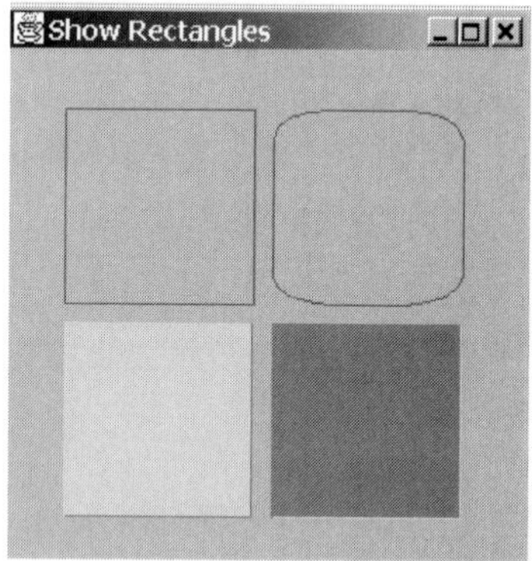

Figure 8.18 *The program draws a rectangle, a rounded rectangle, and a 3D rectangle.*

Drawing Ovals

You can use the methods `drawOval` or `fillOval` to draw an oval in outline or filled solid. In Java, the oval is drawn based on its bounding rectangle; therefore, give the parameters as if you were drawing a rectangle.

Here is the method for drawing an oval:

```
drawOval(x, y, w, h);
```

To draw a filled oval, use the following method:

```
fillOval(x, y, w, h);
```

Parameters `x` and `y` indicate the top-left corner of the bounding rectangle, and `w` and `h` indicate the width and height, respectively, of the bounding rectangle, as shown in Figure 8.19.

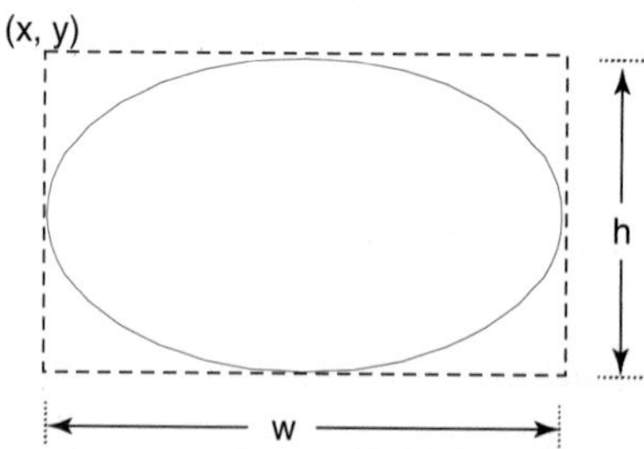

Figure 8.19 *The* `drawOval` *method draws an oval based on its bounding rectangle.*

The following is an example of how to draw ovals, with the output in Figure 8.20.

```
// TestOvals.java: Demonstrate drawing ovals
import javax.swing.JFrame;
import javax.swing.JPanel;
import java.awt.Color;
import java.awt.Graphics;

public class TestOvals extends JFrame
{
  // Default constructor
  public TestOvals()
  {
    setTitle("Show Ovals");
    getContentPane().add(new OvalsPanel());
  }

  // Main method
  public static void main(String[] args)
  {
    TestOvals frame = new TestOvals();
    // frame.setDefaultCloseOperation(JFrame.EXIT_ON_CLOSE);
    frame.setSize(250, 250);
    frame.setVisible(true);
  }
}

// The class for drawing the ovals on a panel
class OvalsPanel extends JPanel
{
  public void paintComponent(Graphics g)
  {
    super.paintComponent(g);

    g.drawOval(10, 30, 100, 60);
    g.drawOval(130, 30, 60, 60);
    g.setColor(Color.yellow);
    g.fillOval(10, 130, 100, 60);
    g.fillOval(130, 130, 60, 60);
  }
}
```

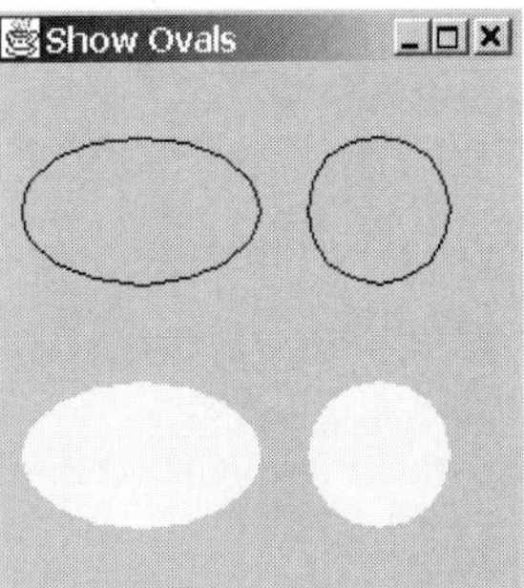

Figure 8.20 *The program draws an oval, a circle, and a filled oval.*

Drawing Arcs

Like an oval, an arc is drawn based on its bounding rectangle. An arc is conceived as part of an oval. The methods to draw or fill an arc are as follows:

```
drawArc(x, y, w, h, angle1, angle2);

fillArc(x, y, w, h, angle1, angle2);
```

Parameters x, y, w, and h are the same as in the drawOval method; parameter angle1 is the starting angle; angle2 is the spanning angle (that is, the angle covered by the arc). Angles are measured in degrees and follow the usual mathematical conventions (that is, 0 degrees is at 3 o'clock, and positive angles indicate counterclockwise rotation; see Figure 8.21).

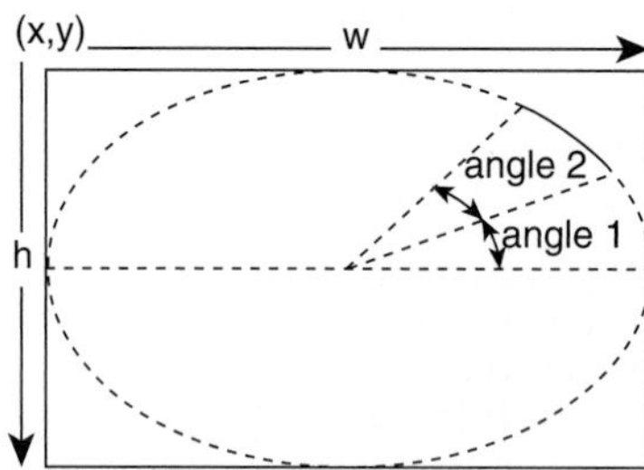

Figure 8.21 *The* drawArc *method draws an arc based on an oval with specified angles.*

Shown below is an example of how to draw arcs; the output is shown in Figure 8.22.

```
// TestArcs.java: Demonstrate drawing arcs
import javax.swing.JFrame;
import javax.swing.JPanel;
import java.awt.Color;
import java.awt.Graphics;

public class TestArcs extends JFrame
{
  // Default constructor
  public TestArcs()
  {
    setTitle("Show Arcs");
    getContentPane().add(new ArcsPanel());
  }

  // Main method
  public static void main(String[] args)
  {
    TestArcs frame = new TestArcs();
    // frame.setDefaultCloseOperation(JFrame.EXIT_ON_CLOSE);
    frame.setSize(250, 300);
    frame.setVisible(true);
  }
}

// The class for drawing arcs on a panel
class ArcsPanel extends JPanel
{
  // Draw four blazes of a fan
  public void paintComponent(Graphics g)
  {
    super.paintComponent(g);
```

```
      int xCenter = getSize().width/2;
      int yCenter = getSize().height/2;
      int radius =
        (int)(Math.min(getSize().width, getSize().height)*0.4);

      int x = xCenter - radius;
      int y = yCenter - radius;

      g.fillArc(x, y, 2*radius, 2*radius, 0, 30);
      g.fillArc(x, y, 2*radius, 2*radius, 90, 30);
      g.fillArc(x, y, 2*radius, 2*radius, 180, 30);
      g.fillArc(x, y, 2*radius, 2*radius, 270, 30);
    }
  }
```

Figure 8.22 *The program draws four filled arcs.*

Drawing Polygons

The `Polygon` class encapsulates a description of a closed, two-dimensional region within a coordinate space. This region is bounded by an arbitrary number of line segments, each of which is one side (or edge) of the polygon. Internally, a polygon comprises a list of `(x, y)` coordinate pairs in which each pair defines a vertex of the polygon, and two successive pairs are the endpoints of a line that is a side of the polygon. The first and final pairs of `(x, y)` points are joined by a line segment that closes the polygon.

Java enables you to draw a polygon in two ways: by using the direct method or by using the `Polygon` object.

The direct method draws a polygon by specifying all the points, using the following two methods:

```
drawPolygon(x, y, n);

fillPolygon(x, y, n);
```

Parameters `x` and `y` are arrays representing x-coordinates and y-coordinates, and `n` indicates the number of points. For example:

```
int x[] = {40, 70, 60, 45, 20};
int y[] = {20, 40, 80, 45, 60};
g.drawPolygon(x, y, x.length);
g.fillPolygon(x, y, x.length);
```

The drawing method opens the polygon by drawing lines between point `(x[i], y[i])` and point `(x[i+1], y[i+1])` for `i = 0, . . . , length-1`; it closes the polygon by drawing a line between the first and last points (see Figure 8.23).

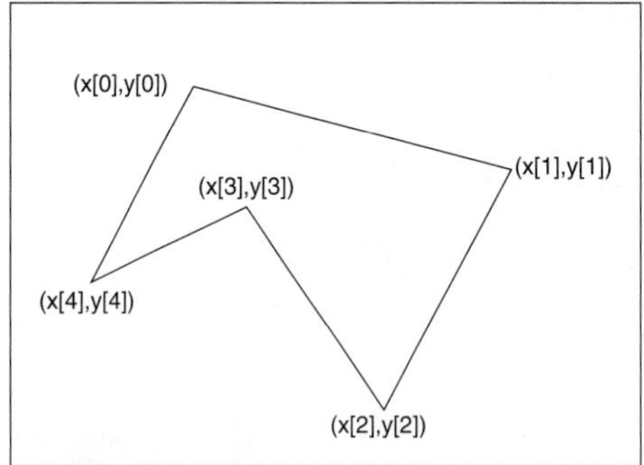

Figure 8.23 *The* `drawPolygon` *method draws a polygon with specified points.*

You can also draw a polygon by first creating a `Polygon` object, then adding points to it, and finally displaying it. To create a `Polygon` object, use

```
Polygon poly = new Polygon();
```

Or

```
Polygon poly = new Polygon(x, y, n);
```

Parameters `x`, `y`, and `n` are the same as in the previous `drawPolygon` method. Here is an example of how to draw a polygon in `Graphics g`:

```
Polygon poly = new Polygon();
poly.addPoint(20, 30);
poly.addPoint(40, 40);
poly.addPoint(50, 50);
g.drawPolygon(poly);
```

The `addPoint` method adds a point to the polygon. The `drawPolygon` method also takes a `Polygon` object as a parameter.

Next is an example of how to draw a polygon with the output shown in Figure 8.24.

```
// TestPolygon.java: Demonstrate drawing polygons
import javax.swing.JFrame;
import javax.swing.JPanel;
import java.awt.Graphics;
import java.awt.Polygon;

public class TestPolygon extends JFrame
{
  // Default constructor
  public TestPolygon()
  {
```

```
    setTitle("Show Polygon");
    getContentPane().add(new PolygonsPanel());
  }

  // Main method
  public static void main(String[] args)
  {
    TestPolygon frame = new TestPolygon();
    // frame.setDefaultCloseOperation(JFrame.EXIT_ON_CLOSE);
    frame.setSize(200, 250);
    frame.setVisible(true);
  }
}

// Draw a polygon in the panel
class PolygonsPanel extends JPanel
{
  public void paintComponent(Graphics g)
  {
    super.paintComponent(g);

    int xCenter = getSize().width/2;
    int yCenter = getSize().height/2;
    int radius =
      (int)(Math.min(getSize().width, getSize().height)*0.4);

    // Create a Polygon object
    Polygon polygon = new Polygon();

    // Add points to the polygon
    polygon.addPoint(xCenter + radius, yCenter);
    polygon.addPoint((int)(xCenter + radius*Math.cos(2*Math.PI/6)),
      (int)(yCenter - radius*Math.sin(2*Math.PI/6)));
    polygon.addPoint((int)(xCenter + radius*Math.cos(2*2*Math.PI/6)),
      (int)(yCenter - radius*Math.sin(2*2*Math.PI/6)));
    polygon.addPoint((int)(xCenter + radius*Math.cos(3*2*Math.PI/6)),
      (int)(yCenter - radius*Math.sin(3*2*Math.PI/6)));
    polygon.addPoint((int)(xCenter + radius*Math.cos(4*2*Math.PI/6)),
      (int)(yCenter - radius*Math.sin(4*2*Math.PI/6)));
    polygon.addPoint((int)(xCenter + radius*Math.cos(5*2*Math.PI/6)),
      (int)(yCenter - radius*Math.sin(5*2*Math.PI/6)));

    // Draw the polygon
    g.drawPolygon(polygon);
  }
}
```

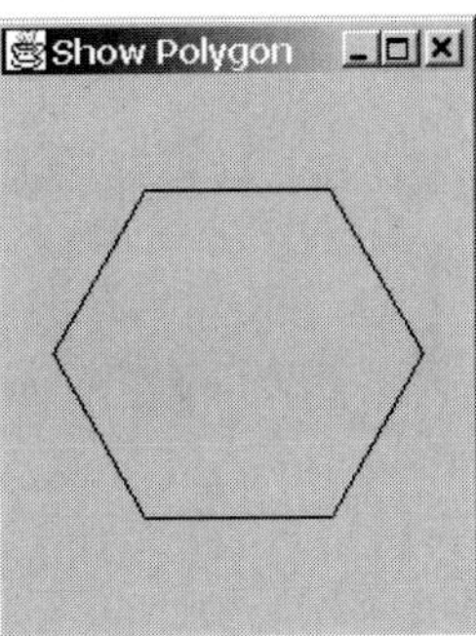

Figure 8.24 *The program uses the* `drawPolygon` *method to draw a polygon.*

NOTE

Prior to JDK 1.1, a polygon was a sequence of lines that were not necessarily closed. But in JDK 1.1, a polygon is always closed. Nevertheless, you can draw a nonclosed polygon by using the `drawPolyline(int[] x, int[] y, int nPoints)` method, which draws a sequence of connected lines defined by arrays of `x` and `y` coordinates. The figure is not closed if the first point differs from the last point.

Case Studies

This case study presents an example that uses several drawing methods and trigonometric methods to draw a clock showing the current time in a frame. To draw a clock, you need to draw a circle and three hands for second, minute, and hour. To draw a hand, you need to specify the two ends of the line. As shown in Figure 8.25, one end is the center of the clock at `(xCenter, yCenter)`, and the other end at `(xEnd, yEnd)` is determined by the following formula:

```
xEnd = xCenter + handLength × sin(π)
yEnd = yCenter - handLength × cos(π)
```

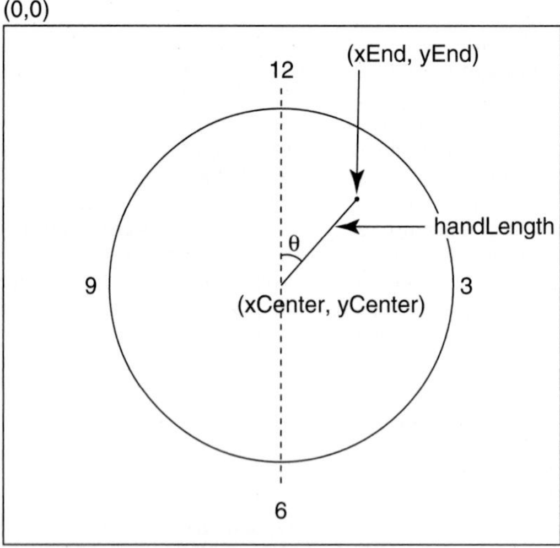

Figure 8.25 *The end point of a clock hand can be determined given the spanning angle, the hand length, and the center point.*

Angle θ is in radians. Let `second`, `minute`, and `hour` denote the current second, minute, and hour.

The angle for the second hand is

```
second × (2π/60)
```

The angle for the minute hand is

```
(minute + second/60) × (2π/60)
```

The angle for hour hand is

```
(hour + minute/60 + second/(60 × 60)) × (2π/12)
```

For simplicity, you can omit the seconds in computing the angles of the minute hand and the hour hand, since they are very small and can be neglected. Therefore the end points for the second hand, minute hand, and hour hand can be computed as:

```
xSecond = xCenter + secondHandLength × sin(second × (2π/60))
ySecond = yCenter - secondHandLength × cos(second × (2π/60))
xMinute = xCenter + minuteHandLength × sin(minute × (2π/60))
yMinute = yCenter - minuteHandLength × cos(minute × (2π/60))
xHour = xCenter + hourHandLength × sin((hour + minute/60) × (2π/60))
yHour = yCenter - hourHandLength × cos((hour + minute/60) × (2π/60))
```

Example 8.6 Drawing a Clock

This example presents a program that displays a clock based on the specified hour, minute, and second. The hour, minute, and second are passed to the program as command-line arguments like this:

```
java DisplayClock hour minute second
```

The program is given next, and its output is shown in Figure 8.26.

```
// DisplayClock.java: Display a clock in a panel
import java.awt.*;
import javax.swing.*;

public class DisplayClock extends JFrame
{
  // Main method with three arguments:
  // args[0]: hour
  // args[1]: minute
  // args[2]: second
  public static void main(String[] args)
  {
    // Declare hour, minute, and second values
    int hour = 0;
    int minute = 0;
    int second = 0;

    // Check usage and get hour, minute, second
    if (args.length > 3)
    {
      System.out.println(
        "Usage: java DisplayClock hour minute second");
      System.exit(0);
    }
    else if (args.length == 3)
    {
      hour = new Integer(args[0]).intValue();
      minute = new Integer(args[1]).intValue();
      second = new Integer(args[2]).intValue();
    }
    else if (args.length == 2)
    {
      hour = new Integer(args[0]).intValue();
```

continues

Example 8.6 continued

```
        minute = new Integer(args[1]).intValue();
      }
      else if (args.length == 1)
      {
        hour = new Integer(args[0]).intValue();
      }

      // Create a frame to hold the clock
      DisplayClock frame = new DisplayClock();
      frame.setTitle("Display Clock");
      frame.getContentPane().add(new DrawClock(hour, minute, second));
      // frame.setDefaultCloseOperation(JFrame.EXIT_ON_CLOSE);
      frame.setSize(300, 350);
      frame.setVisible(true);
    }
  }

  // DrawClock.java: Display a clock in JPanel
  import java.awt.*;
  import javax.swing.*;

  public class DrawClock extends JPanel
  {
    private int hour;
    private int minute;
    private int second;
    protected int xCenter, yCenter;
    protected int clockRadius;

    // Construct a clock panel
    public DrawClock(int hour, int minute, int second)
    {
      this.hour = hour;
      this.minute = minute;
      this.second = second;
    }

    // Draw the clock
    public void paintComponent(Graphics g)
    {
      super.paintComponent(g);

      // Initialize clock parameters
      clockRadius =
        (int)(Math.min(getSize().width, getSize().height)*0.7*0.5);
      xCenter = (getSize().width)/2;
      yCenter = (getSize().height)/2;

      // Draw circle
      g.setColor(Color.black);
      g.drawOval(xCenter - clockRadius,yCenter - clockRadius,
        2*clockRadius, 2*clockRadius);
      g.drawString("12",xCenter-5, yCenter-clockRadius);
      g.drawString("9",xCenter-clockRadius-10,yCenter+3);
      g.drawString("3",xCenter+clockRadius,yCenter+3);
      g.drawString("6",xCenter-3,yCenter+clockRadius+10);

      // Draw second hand
      int sLength = (int)(clockRadius*0.9);
      int xSecond =
```

```
        (int)(xCenter + sLength*Math.sin(second*(2*Math.PI/60)));
      int ySecond =
        (int)(yCenter - sLength*Math.cos(second*(2*Math.PI/60)));
      g.setColor(Color.red);
      g.drawLine(xCenter, yCenter, xSecond, ySecond);

      // Draw minute hand
      int mLength = (int)(clockRadius*0.75);
      int xMinute =
        (int)(xCenter + mLength*Math.sin(minute*(2*Math.PI/60)));
      int yMinute =
        (int)(yCenter - mLength*Math.cos(minute*(2*Math.PI/60)));
      g.setColor(Color.blue);
      g.drawLine(xCenter, yCenter, xMinute, yMinute);

      // Draw hour hand
      int hLength = (int)(clockRadius*0.6);
      int xHour = (int)(xCenter +
        hLength*Math.sin((hour+minute/60.0)*(2*Math.PI/12)));
      int yHour = (int)(yCenter -
        hLength*Math.cos((hour+minute/60.0)*(2*Math.PI/12)));
      g.setColor(Color.green);
      g.drawLine(xCenter, yCenter, xHour, yHour);

      // Display current time in string
      g.setColor(Color.red);
      String time = "Hour: " + hour + " Minute: " + minute +
        " Second: " + second;
      FontMetrics fm = g.getFontMetrics();
      g.drawString(time, (getSize().width -
        fm.stringWidth(time))/2, yCenter+clockRadius+30);
    }
  }
```

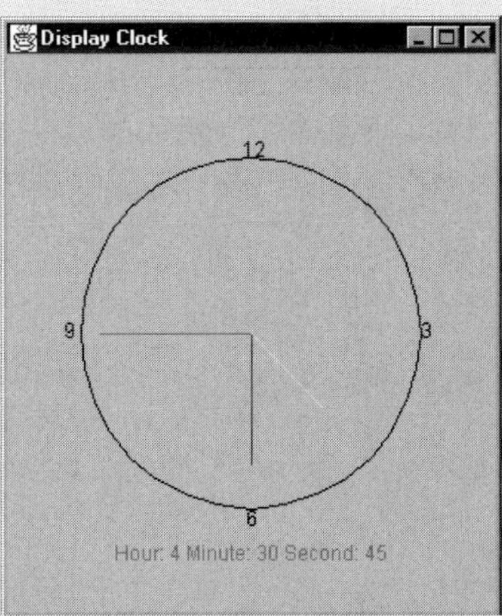

Figure 8.26 *The program displays a clock that shows the time with the specified hour, minute, and second.*

continues

Example 8.6 continued

Example Review

The `DisplayClock` class obtains command-line arguments for hour, minute, and second, and uses this information to create an instance of `DrawClock`. `DrawClock` is responsible for drawing the clock in a panel.

The program enables the clock size to adjust as the frame resizes. Every time you resize the frame, the `paintComponent` method is automatically invoked to paint the new frame. The `paintComponent` method displays the clock in proportion to the frame size.

The numeric time (consisting of hour, minute, and second) is displayed below the clock. The program uses font metrics to determine the size of the time string and display it in the center.

Event-Driven Programming

All the programs you have written so far are object-oriented, but executed in a procedural order. You used decision and loop statements to control the flow of execution, but the program dictated the flow of execution. Java graphics programming is event-driven. In event-driven programming, codes are executed when an event—a button click, perhaps, or a mouse movement—is activated. This section introduces the Java event model.

Event and Event Source

When you run Java graphics programs, the program interacts with the user and the events drive the execution of the program. An *event* can be defined as a signal to the program that something has happened. The event is generated either by external user actions, such as mouse movements, mouse button clicks, and keystrokes, or by the operating system, such as a timer. The program can choose to respond to or ignore the event.

The GUI component on which the event is generated is called a *source object*. For example, a button is the source object for the clicking-button action event. An event is an instance of an event class. The root class of the event classes is `java.util.EventObject`. The hierarchical relationships of the event classes used in this book are shown in Figure 8.27.

An event object contains whatever properties that are pertinent to the event. You can identify the source object of the event using the `getSource()` instance method in the `EventObject` class. The subclasses of `EventObject` deal with special types of events such as button actions, window events, component events, mouse movements, and keystrokes. Table 8.1 lists external user actions, source objects, and event types generated.

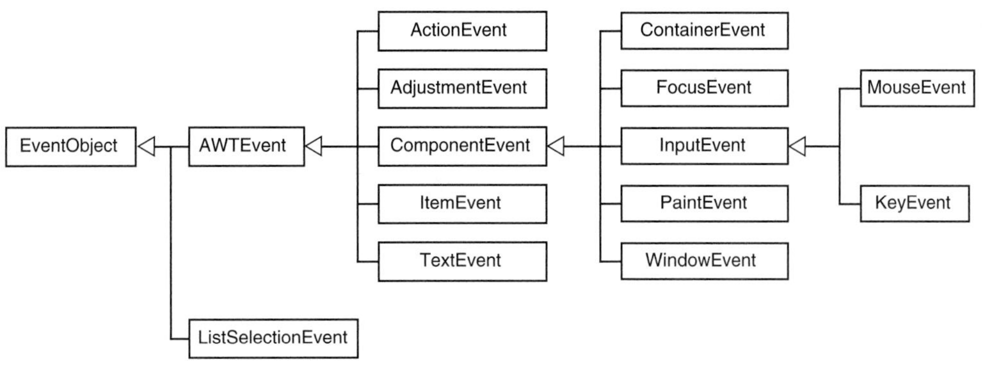

Figure 8.27 *An event is an object of the* `EventObject` *class.*

TABLE 8.1 User Action, Source Object, and Event Type

User Action	*Source Object*	*Event Type Generated*
Click a button	`JButton`	`ActionEvent`
Change text	`JTextComponent`	`TextEvent`
Press return on a text field	`JTextField`	`ActionEvent`
Select a new item	`JComboBox`	`ItemEvent, ActionEvent`
Select item(s)	`JList`	`ListSelectionEvent`
Click a check box	`JCheckBox`	`ItemEvent, ActionEvent`
Click a radio button	`JRadioButton`	`ItemEvent, ActionEvent`
Select a menu item	`JMenuItem`	`ActionEvent`
Move the scroll bar	`JScrollBar`	`AdjustmentEvent`
Window opened, closed, iconified, deiconified, or closing	`Window`	`WindowEvent`
Component added or removed from the container	`Container`	`ContainerEvent`
Component moved, resized, hidden, or shown	`Component`	`ComponentEvent`
Component gained or lost focus	`Component`	`FocusEvent`
Key released or pressed	`Component`	`KeyEvent`
Mouse movement	`Component`	`MouseEvent`

NOTE
If a component can generate an event, any subclass of the component can generate the same type of event. For example, every GUI component can generate `MouseEvent`, `KeyEvent`, `FocusEvent`, and `ComponentEvent`, since `Component` is the superclass of all GUI components.

NOTE
All the event classes in Figure 8.27 are included in the `java.awt.event` package except the `ListSelectionEvent`, which is in the `javax.swing.event` package. The AWT events were originally designed for AWT components, but many Swing components fire them.

Event Registration, Listening, and Handling

Java uses a delegation-based model for event handling: An external user action on a source object triggers an event. An object interested in the event receives the event. Such an object is called a *listener*. Not all objects can receive events. To become a listener, an object must be registered as a listener by the source object. The source object maintains a list of listeners and notifies all the registered listeners by invoking the event-handling method, or *handler*, on the listener object to respond to the event, as shown in Figure 8.28.

For example, if a `JFrame` object is interested in the external events on a `JButton` source object, it must register with the `JButton` object. The registration is done by invoking a method from the `JButton` object to declare that the `JFrame` object is a listener for the `JButton` object. When you click the button, the `JButton` object generates an `ActionEvent` and notifies the listener by invoking a method defined in the listener to handle the event.

NOTE
A source object and a listener object may be the same. A source object may have many listeners. It maintains a queue for all of them.

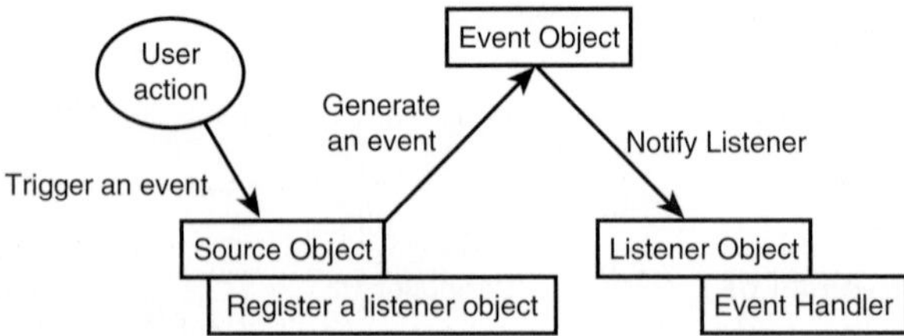

Figure 8.28 *An event is triggered by user actions on the source object; the source object generates the event object and invokes the handler of the listener object to process the event.*

Registration methods are dependent on event type. For `ActionEvent`, the method is `addActionListener`. In general, the method is named `addXListener` for `XEvent`.

To become a listener, the listener must implement the standard handler. The handler is defined in the corresponding event-listener interface. Java provides a listener interface for every type of graphics event. For example, the corresponding listener interface for `ActionEvent` is `ActionListener`; each listener for `ActionEvent` should implement the `ActionListener` interface.

Table 8.2 lists event types, the corresponding listener interfaces, and the methods defined in the listener interfaces.

NOTE

In general, the listener interface is named `XListener` for `XEvent`, except for `MouseMotionListener`.

Handling Events

A listener object must implement the corresponding listener interface. For example, a listener for a `JButton` source object must implement the `ActionListener` interface. The `ActionListener` interface contains the `actionPerformed(ActionEvent e)` method. This method must be implemented in the listener class. Upon receiving notification, it is executed to handle the event.

An event object is passed to the handling method. The event object contains information pertinent to the event type. You can get useful data values from the event object for processing the event. For example, you can use `e.getSource()` to obtain the source object in order to determine whether it is a button, a check box, a radio button, or a menu item.

Two examples of the use of event handling are given below. The first is for the `ActionEvent`, and the second for the `WindowEvent`.

TABLE 8.2 **Events, Event Listeners, and Listener Methods**

Event Class	*Listener Interface*	*Listener Methods (Handlers)*
`ActionEvent`	`ActionListener`	`actionPerformed(ActionEvent e)`
`ItemEvent`	`ItemListener`	`itemStateChanged(ItemEvent e)`
`WindowEvent`	`WindowListener`	`windowClosing(WindowEvent e)`
		`windowOpened(WindowEvent e)`
		`windowIconified(WindowEvent e)`
		`windowDeiconified(WindowEvent e)`
		`windowClosed(WindowEvent e)`
		`windowActivated(WindowEvent e)`
		`windowDeactivated(WindowEvent e)`

TABLE 8.2 Events, Event Listeners, and Listener Methods

Event Class	*Listener Interface*	*Listener Methods (Handlers)*
ContainerEvent	ContainerListener	componentAdded(ContainerEvent e)
		componentRemoved(ContainerEvent e)
ComponentEvent	ComponentListener	componentMoved(ComponentEvent e)
		componentHidden(ComponentEvent e)
		componentResized(ComponentEvent e)
		componentShown(ComponentEvent e)
FocusEvent	FocusListener	focusGained(FocusEvent e)
		focusLost(FocusEvent e)
TextEvent	TextListener	textValueChanged(TextEvent e)
KeyEvent	KeyListener	keyPressed(KeyEvent e)
		keyReleased(KeyEvent e)
		keyTyped(KeyEvent e)
MouseEvent	MouseListener	mousePressed(MouseEvent e)
		mouseReleased(MouseEvent e)
		mouseEntered(MouseEvent e)
		mouseExited(MouseEvent e)
		mouseClicked(MouseEvent e)
	MouseMotionListener	mouseDragged(MouseEvent e)
		mouseMoved(MouseEvent e)
AdjustmentEvent	AdjustmentListener	adjustmentValueChanged (AdjustmentEvent e)

Example 8.7 Handling Simple Action Events

This example presents a program that displays two buttons, OK and Cancel, in the window. A message is displayed on the console to indicate which button is clicked. Figure 8.29 shows a sample run of the program.

```
// TestActionEvent.java: Test action event on buttons.
import javax.swing.*;
import java.awt.*;
import java.awt.event.*;

public class TestActionEvent extends JFrame
  implements ActionListener
{
  // Create two buttons
```

```
  private JButton jbtOk = new JButton("OK");
  private JButton jbtCancel = new JButton("Cancel");

  // Default constructor
  public TestActionEvent()
  {
    // Set the window title
    setTitle("TestActionEvent");

    // Set FlowLayout manager to arrange the components
    // inside the frame
    getContentPane().setLayout(new FlowLayout());

    // Add buttons to the frame
    getContentPane().add(jbtOk);
    getContentPane().add(jbtCancel);

    // Register listeners
    jbtOk.addActionListener(this);
    jbtCancel.addActionListener(this);
  }

  // Main method
  public static void main(String[] args)
  {
    TestActionEvent frame = new TestActionEvent();
    // frame.setDefaultCloseOperation(JFrame.EXIT_ON_CLOSE);
    frame.setSize(100, 80);
    frame.setVisible(true);
  }

  // This method will be invoked when a button is clicked.
  public void actionPerformed(ActionEvent e)
  {
    if (e.getSource() == jbtOk)
    {
      System.out.println("The OK button is clicked");
    }
    else if (e.getSource() == jbtCancel)
    {
      System.out.println("The Cancel button is clicked");
    }
  }
}
```

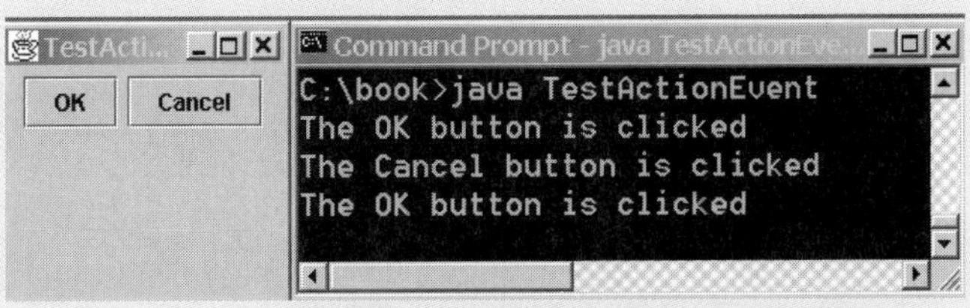

Figure 8.29 *The program responds to the button action events.*

continues

Example 8.7 continued

Example Review

The button objects `jbtOk` and `jbtCancel` are the source of `ActionEvent`. The `TestActionEvent` class is a subclass of `JFrame` and is the listener for the action events. Therefore, `TestActionEvent` implements the `ActionListener` interface.

The statements

```
jbtOk.addActionListener(this);
jbtCancel.addActionListener(this);
```

register `this` (referring to `TestActionEvent`) to listen to `ActionEvent` on `jbtOk` and `jbtCancel`.

Clicking a button causes the `actionPerformed` method to be invoked. The `e.getSource()` method is invoked to determine which button has been clicked.

TIP

Missing listener registration is a common mistake in event handling. Because the source object doesn't notify the listener, the listener cannot act on the event.

Example 8.8 Handling Window Events

This example demonstrates handling window events. Any subclass of the `Window` class can generate the following window events: window opened, closing, closed, activated, deactivated, iconified, and deiconified. This program creates a frame, listens to the window events, and displays a message to indicate the occurring event. Figure 8.30 shows a sample run of the program.

```
// TestWindowEvent.java: Create a frame to test window events
import java.awt.*;
import java.awt.event.*;
import javax.swing.JFrame;

public class TestWindowEvent extends JFrame
  implements WindowListener
{
  // Main method
  public static void main(String[] args)
  {
    TestWindowEvent frame = new TestWindowEvent();
    // frame.setDefaultCloseOperation(JFrame.EXIT_ON_CLOSE);
    frame.setTitle("Test Window Event");
    frame.setSize(100, 80);
    frame.setVisible(true);
  }

  // Default constructor
  public TestWindowEvent()
```

```
{
  super();
  addWindowListener(this);  // Register listener
}

/**
 * Handler for window deiconified event
 * Invoked when a window is changed from a minimized
 * to a normal state.
 */
public void windowDeiconified(WindowEvent event)
{
  System.out.println("Window deiconified");
}

/**
 * Handler for window iconified event
 * Invoked when a window is changed from a normal to a
 * minimized state. For many platforms, a minimized window
 * is displayed as the icon specified in the window's
 * iconImage property.
 * @see Frame#setIconImage
 */
public void windowIconified(WindowEvent event)
{
  System.out.println("Window iconified");
}

/**
 * Handler for window activated event
 * Invoked when the window is set to be the user's
 * active window, which means the window (or one of its
 * subcomponents) will receive keyboard events.
 */
public void windowActivated(WindowEvent event)
{
  System.out.println("Window activated");
}

/**
 * Handler for window deactivated event
 * Invoked when a window is no longer the user's active
 * window, which means that keyboard events will no longer
 * be delivered to the window or its subcomponents.
 */
public void windowDeactivated(WindowEvent event)
{
  System.out.println("Window deactivated");
}

/**
 * Handler for window opened event
 * Invoked the first time a window is made visible.
 */
public void windowOpened(WindowEvent event)
{
  System.out.println("Window opened");
}
```

continues

Example 8.8 Handling Window Events

```
    /**
     * Handler for window closing event
     * Invoked when the user attempts to close the window
     * from the window's system menu.  If the program does not
     * explicitly hide or dispose the window while processing
     * this event, the window close operation will be cancelled.
     */
    public void windowClosing(WindowEvent event)
    {
      System.out.println("Window closing");
    }

    /**
     * Handler for window closed event
     * Invoked when a window has been closed as the result
     * of calling dispose on the window.
     */
    public void windowClosed(WindowEvent event)
    {
      System.out.println("Window closed");
    }
  }
```

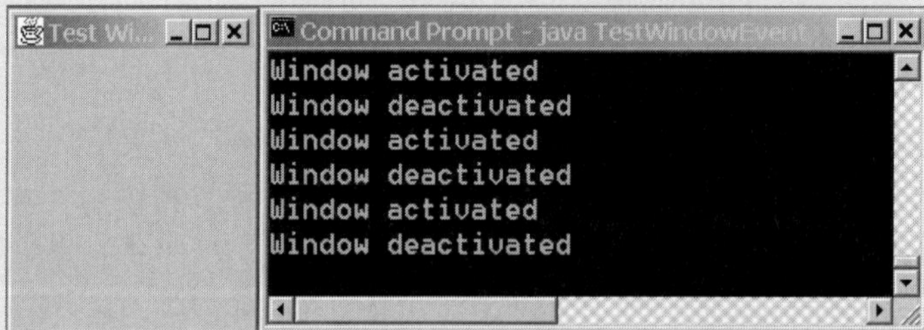

Figure 8.30 *The window events are displayed in the console.*

Example Review

The `WindowEvent` can be generated by the `Window` class or any subclasses of `Window`. Since `JFrame` is a subclass of Window, it can generate `WindowEvent`.

`TestWindowEvent` extends `JFrame` and implements `WindowListener`. The `WindowListener` interface defines several abstract methods (`windowActivated`, `windowClosed`, `windowClosing`, `windowDeactivated`, `windowDeiconified`, `windowIconified`, `windowOpened`) for handling window events when the window is activated, closed, closing, deactivated, deiconified, iconified, or opened.

When a window event, such as activation, occurs, the `windowActivated` method is triggered. You should implement the `windowActivated` method with a concrete response if you want this event to be processed.

Because all these methods in the `WindowListener` interface are abstract, you must implement all of them even if your program does not care about some of the events.

For an object to receive event notification, it must register as an event listener. `addWindowListener(this)` registers the object of `TestWindowEvent` as a window-event listener so that it can receive notification about the window event. `TestWindowEvent` is both a listener and a source object.

Chapter Summary

In this chapter, you learned Java graphics programming using the container classes, UI component classes, and helper classes.

The container classes, such as `JFrame`, `JPanel`, and `JApplet`, are used to contain other components. The UI component classes, such as `JButton`, `JTextField`, `JTextArea`, `JComboBox`, `JList`, `JRadioButton`, and `JMenu`, are subclasses of `JComponent`. They are used to facilitate user interaction. These classes are referred to as Swing UI components and are grouped in the `javax.swing` package.

The helper classes, such as `Graphics`, `Color`, `Font`, `FontMetrics`, `Dimension`, and `LayoutManager`, are used by components and containers to draw and place objects. These classes are grouped in the `java.awt` package.

You learned to override the `paintComponent` method to display graphics and draw strings and simple shapes using the drawing methods in the `Graphics` class.

Java graphics programming is event-driven. The code is executed when events are activated. An event is generated by user actions, such as mouse movements, keystrokes, or clicking buttons. Java uses a delegation-based model to register listeners and handle events. External user actions on the source object generate events. The source object notifies listener objects of events by invoking the handlers implemented by the listener class.

Review Questions

8.1 Describe the Java graphics class hierarchy.

8.2 Describe the methods in `Component`, `Frame`, `JFrame`, `JComponent`, and `JPanel`.

8.3 Explain the difference between the AWT UI components, such as `java.awt.Button`, and the Swing components, such as `javax.swing.JButton`.

8.4 How do you create a frame? How do you set the size for the frame? How do you get the size of a frame? How do you add components to the frame?

8.5 Determine whether the following statements are true or false:

- You can add a component to a button.
- You can add a button to a frame.
- You can add a frame to a panel.
- You can add a panel to a frame.
- You can add any number of components to a panel, a frame, or an applet.
- You can derive a class from `JPanel`, `JFrame`, or `JApplet`.

8.6 Why do you need to use the layout managers?

8.7 Can you use the `setTitle` method in a panel? What is the purpose of using a panel?

8.8 Describe `FlowLayout`. How do you create a `FlowLayout` manager? How do you add a component to a `FlowLayout` container? Is there a limit to the number of components that can be added to a `FlowLayout` container?

8.9 Describe `GridLayout`. How do you create a `GridLayout` manager? How do you add a component to a `GridLayout` container? Is there a limit to the number of components that can be added to a `GridLayout` container?

8.10 Describe `BorderLayout`. How do you create a `BorderLayout` manager? How do you add a component to a `BorderLayout` container? Can you add multiple components in the same section?

8.11 Suppose that you want to draw a new message below an existing message. Should the x, y coordinate increase or decrease?

8.12 How do you set colors and fonts in a graphics context? How do you find the current color and font style?

8.13 Describe the drawing methods for lines, rectangles, ovals, arcs, and polygons.

8.14 Write a statement to draw the following shapes:

- Draw a thick line from (10, 10) to (70, 30). You must draw several lines next to each other to create the effect of one thick line.
- Draw a rectangle of width 100 and height 50 with the upper-left corner at (10, 10).
- Draw a rounded rectangle with width 100, height 200, corner horizontal diameter 40, and corner vertical diameter 20.
- Draw a circle with radius 30.
- Draw an oval with width 50 and height 100.
- Draw the upper half of a circle with radius 50.
- Draw a polygon connecting the following points: (20, 40), (30, 50), (40, 90), (90, 10), (10, 30).
- Draw a 3D cube like the one in Figure 8.31.

8.15 Can a button generate `WindowEvent`? Can a button generate a `MouseEvent`? Can a button generate an `ActionEvent`?

8.16 Explain how to register a listener object and how to implement a listener interface.

8.17 What information is contained in an `AWTEvent` object and the objects of its subclasses? Find the variables, constants, and methods defined in these event classes.

8.18 How do you override a method defined in the listener interface? Do you need to override all the methods defined in the listener interface?

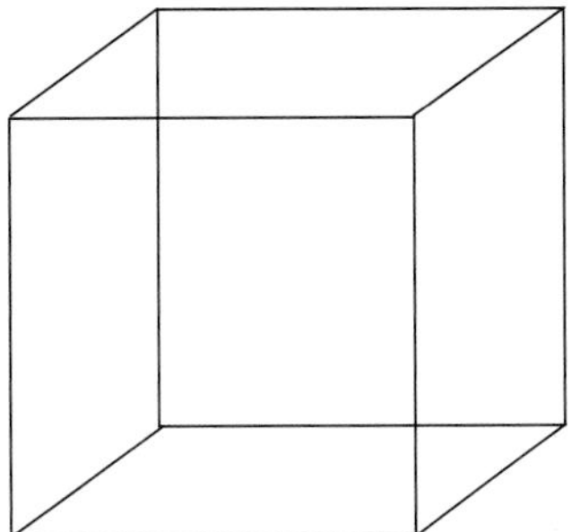

Figure 8.31 *Use the* `drawLine` *method to draw a 3D cube.*

8.19 Describe the `paintComponent` method. Where is it defined? How is it invoked? Can you use the `paintComponent` method to draw things directly on a frame?

Programming Exercises

8.1 Write a program to meet the following requirements (see Figure 8.32):

- Create a frame and set its content pane's layout to `FlowLayout`.
- Create two panels and add the panels to the frame.
- Each panel contains three buttons. The panel uses `FlowLayout`.
- When a button is clicked, display a message on the console indicating that a button has been clicked. (Do this part after finishing the section "Event-driven Programming" in this chapter.)

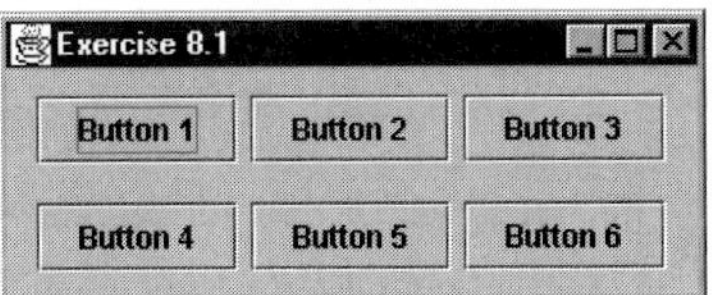

Figure 8.32 *The first three buttons are placed in one panel, and the remaining three buttons are placed in another panel.*

8.2 Rewrite the preceding program to create the same user interface. Instead of using `FlowLayout` for the frame's content pane, use `BorderLayout`. Place one panel in the south of the content pane and the other panel in the center of the content pane.

8.3 Rewrite the preceding program to create the same user interface. Instead of using `FlowLayout` for the panels, use `GridLayout` of two rows and three columns.

8.4 Rewrite the preceding program to create the same user interface. Instead of creating buttons and panels separately, define the panel class that extends the

`JPanel` class. Place three buttons in your panel class, and create two panels from the user-defined panel class.

8.5 Write a program that uses the `MessagePanel` class in Example 8.5 to display a centered message in red, SansSerif, italic, and 20-point size.

8.6 Write a program that displays a multiplication table in a panel using the drawing methods, as shown in Figure 8.33.

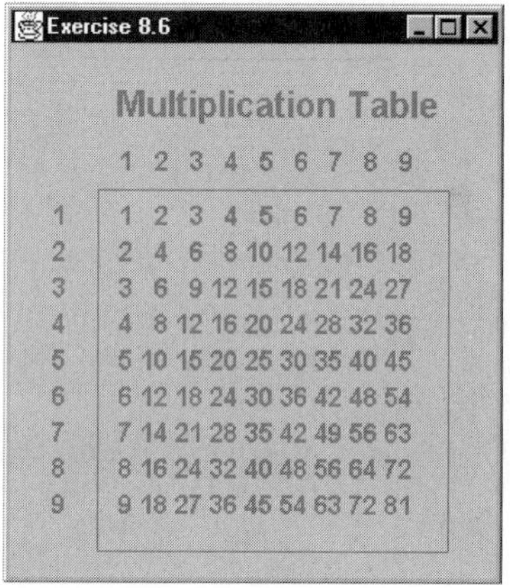

Figure 8.33 *The program displays a multiplication table.*

8.7 Write a program that displays numbers, as shown in Figure 8.34. The number of lines in the display changes to fit the window as the window resizes.

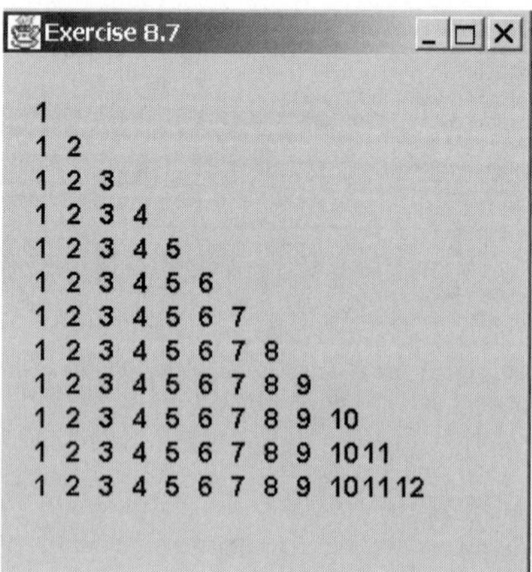

Figure 8.34 *The program displays a multiplication table.*

8.8 Write a program that draws the diagram for the function shown below (see Figure 8.35). (Hint: Create arrays `x[]` and `y[]` for coordinates, and use `drawPolyline` to connect the points.)

$$f(x) = x^2;$$

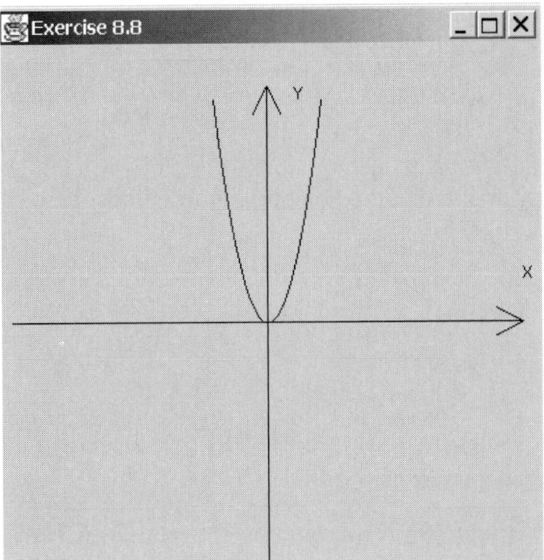

Figure 8.35 *The program draws a diagram for function $f(x) = x^2$.*

8.9 Write a program that draws the diagram for the sin function, as shown in Figure 8.36. (The Unicode for π is \U03C0).

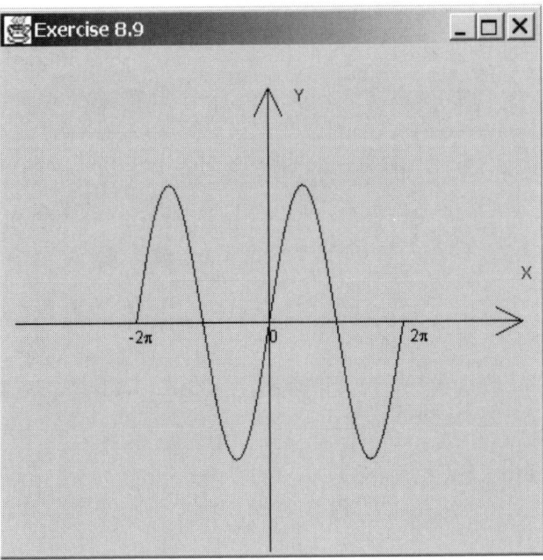

Figure 8.36 *The program draws a diagram for function $f(x) = sin(x)$.*

8.10 Write a generic class that draws the diagram for a function. The class is defined as follows:

```
public abstract class DrawFunction extends JPanel
{
  abstract double f(double x);
```

```
    // Draw the function
    public void drawFunction()
    {
      // Complete the code to draw a diagram for the function f
    }
  }
```

Implement the `drawFunction()` method. Test the class with the following functions:

$$f(x) = x^2;$$

$$f(x) = \cos(x)+5\sin(x);$$

$$f(x) = \log(x) + x^2;$$

For each function, create a class that extends the `DrawFunction` class and implement the `f` method.

8.11 Write a program that draws a fan with four blades, as shown in Figure 8.37. Draw the circle in blue and the blades in red. To make the fan reusable, create a panel to display a fan, and place the panel in the frame. This panel can be reused elsewhere; for example, in Exercise 8.13. (Hint: Use the `fillArc()` method to draw the blades.)

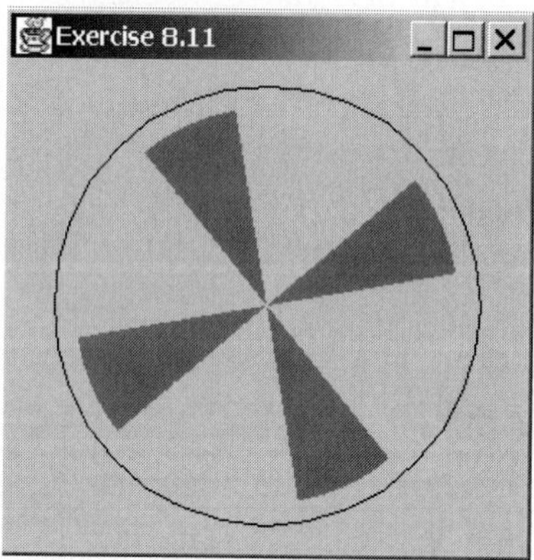

Figure 8.37 *The drawing methods are used to draw a fan with four blades.*

8.12 Modify Example 8.6 to draw the clock with more details on the hours, as shown in Figure 8.38.

8.13 Write a program that places four fans in a frame of `GridLayout` with two rows and two columns, as shown in Figure 8.39.

8.14 Write a program that uses a pie chart to display the percentages of projects, quizzes, midterm exams, and final exam in the overall grade, as shown in Figure 8.40. Suppose that projects take 20% and displayed in red, quizzes take 10% and are displayed in green, midterm exams take 30% and are displayed in blue, and final exam takes 40% and is displayed in orange.

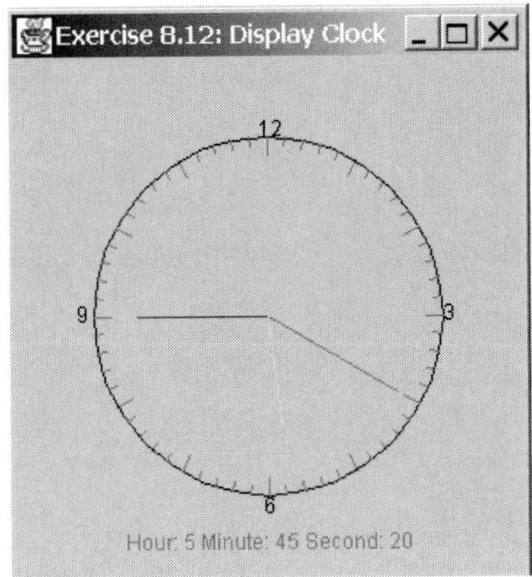

Figure 8.38 *All the hours are displayed on the clock.*

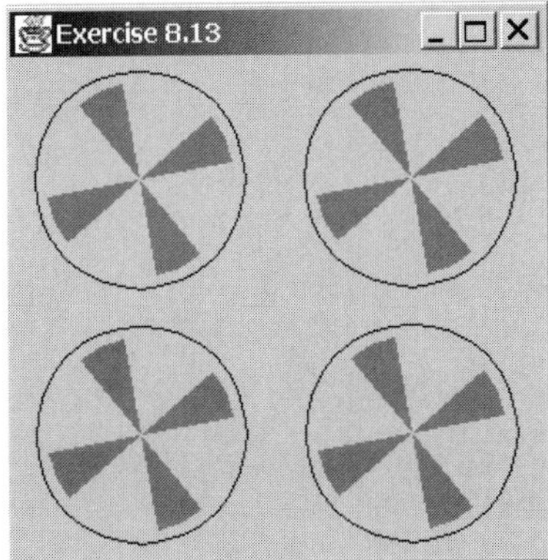

Figure 8.39 *Four fans are placed in a frame.*

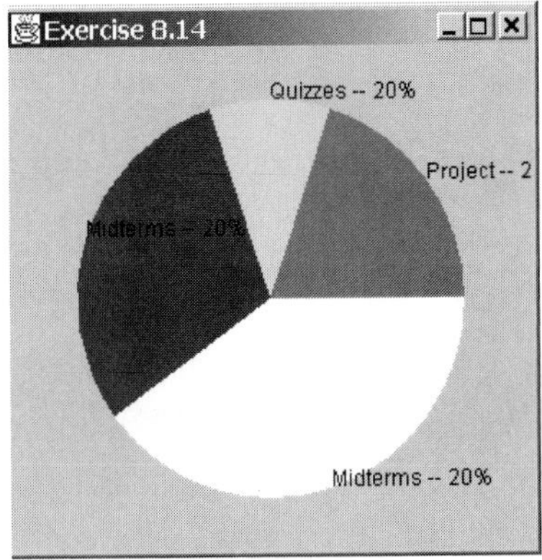

Figure 8.40 *The pie chart displays the percentages of projects, quizzes, midterm exams, and final exam in the overall grade.*

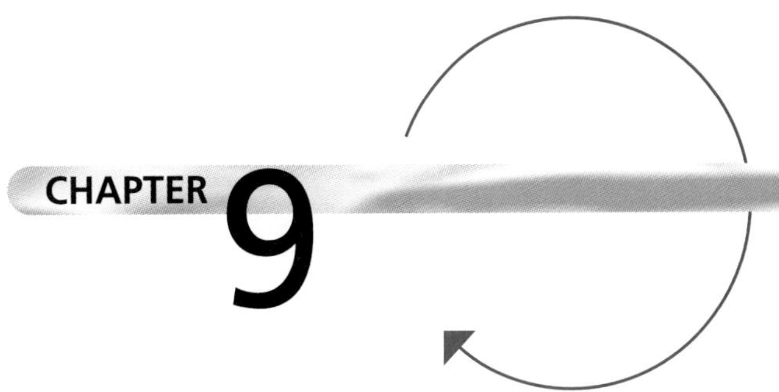

Creating User Interfaces

Objectives

- Become familiar with the JavaBeans concept.
- Know various user interface components: `JButton`, `JLabel`, `JTextField`, `JTextArea`, `JComboBox`, `JList`, `JCheckBox`, `JRadioButton`, `JMenuBar`, `JMenu`, `JMenuItem`, `JCheckBoxMenuItem`, `JRadioButtonMenuItem`, `JScrollBar`, `JScrollPane`, and `JTabbedPane`.
- Use these components to create interactive graphical user interfaces.
- Display images with the `ImageIcon` class.
- Use borders to visually group user interface components.
- Know how to use the message dialog boxes.
- Create multiple windows in an application.
- Implement the listener interface for the user interface components.

Introduction

A graphical user interface (GUI) makes the system easy and fun to use. Creating a GUI requires creativity and knowledge of how the GUI components work. Since the GUI components in Java are very flexible, you can create an extensive array of different user interfaces.

Many Java development tools provide functions for visually designing and programming Java classes. This enables you to rapidly assemble the elements of a user interface (UI) for a Java application or applet with minimum coding. No tools, however, can do everything, so you may have to modify the program they produce. This makes it imperative to understand the basic concepts of Java graphics programming before using the visual tools.

This chapter concentrates on creating user interfaces. In particular, it discusses the various GUI components that make up a user interface and how to make those components work.

JavaBeans

Since all Swing components are JavaBeans, understanding JavaBeans will help you to learn Swing components. JavaBeans is a software component architecture that extends the power of the Java language by enabling well-formed objects to be manipulated visually at design time in a pure Java builder tool, such as JBuilder, Visual Café, or IBM Visual Age for Java. Such well-formed objects are referred to as *JavaBeans* or simply *beans*. The classes that define the beans, referred to as *JavaBeans components* or *bean components*, or simply *components*, conform to the JavaBeans component model with the following requirements:

- A bean must be a public class.
- A bean must have a public default constructor (one that takes no arguments), though it can have other constructors, if needed. For example, a bean named `MyBean` must either have a constructor with the signature

  ```
  public MyBean();
  ```

  or have no constructor if its superclass has a default constructor.
- A bean must implement the `java.io.Serializable` or `java.io.Externalizable` interface to ensure a persistent state. JavaBeans can be used in a wide variety of tools, such as Lotus, Delphi, MS Visual Basic, and MS Word. When JavaBeans are used in other tools, bean persistence may be required. Some tools need to save the beans and restore them later. Bean persistence ensures that the tools can reconstruct the properties and consistent behaviors of the bean to the state when it was saved. For more information on bean persistence and serialization, please refer to my *Rapid Java Application Development Using JBuilder 3*.

- A bean usually has properties with correctly constructed public accessor methods that enable the properties to be seen and updated visually by a builder tool.
- A bean may have events with correctly constructed public registration methods that enable the bean to add and remove listeners. If the bean plays a role as the source of events, it must provide registration methods for registering listeners. For example, you can register a listener for `ActionEvent` using the `addActionListener` method of a `JButton` bean.

The first three requirements must be observed by the beans, and therefore are referred to as *minimum JavaBeans component requirements.* The last two requirements are dependent on implementations. It is possible to write a bean without accessor methods and event registration methods.

A JavaBean component is a special kind of Java class. The relationship between JavaBean components and Java classes is illustrated in Figure 9.1.

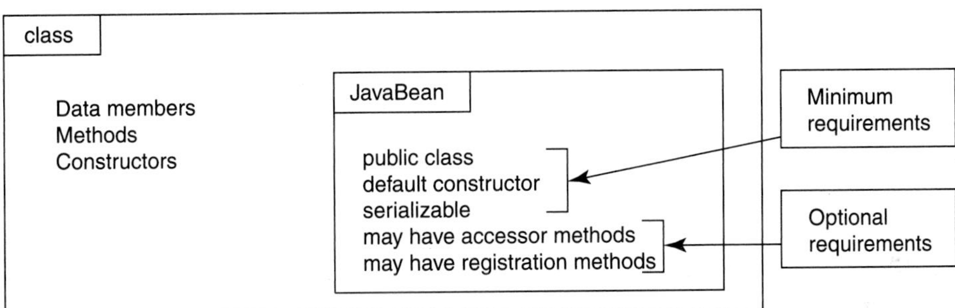

Figure 9.1 *A JavaBean component is a serializable public class with a default constructor.*

The getter method is named `get<PropertyName>()`, which takes no parameters and returns an object of a type identical to the property type. For example, `getContentPane()` is the getter method for the property `contentPane` in the `JFrame` class, which returns an object of the `Container` type. For a property of the `boolean` type, the getter method should be named `is<PropertyName>()`, which returns a `boolean` value. For example, `isVisible()` is the getter method for the `visible` property in the `JFrame` class, which returns `true` if the frame is visible.

The setter method is named `set<PropertyName>`, which takes a single parameter identical to the property type and returns `void`. For example, `setLayout` is the setter method for the `layout` property in the `Container` class for setting the `layout` property value.

Once you understand the basics of Java graphics programming, such as containers, layout managers, and event handling, you will be able to learn new components to explore their properties. The Component class is the root for all the UI components and containers. Here is a list of frequently used properties available in `Component`:

- `font`: The font used to display text on the component.
- `background`: The background color of the component.
- `foreground`: The foreground color of the component.
- `height`: The current height of the component.
- `width`: The current width of the component.
- `locale`: The locale of the component. Locale is introduced in Chapter 12, "Internationalization."
- `preferredSize`: Indicates the ideal size at which the component looks best. This property may or may not be considered by the layout manager, depending on its rules. For example, a component uses its preferred size in a container with a `FlowLayout` manager, but its preferred size may be ignored if it is placed in a container with a `GridLayout` manager.
- `minimumSize`: Specifies the minimum size for the component to be useful. For most of the Swing components, `minimumSize` is the same as `preferredSize`. Layout managers generally respect `minimumSize` more than `preferredSize`.
- `maximumSize`: Specifies the maximum size the component needs so that the layout manager won't waste space by giving it to a component that does not need it. For instance, `BorderLayout` could limit the center component's size to its maximum size, and then either give the space to border components or limit the size of the outer window when resized.

All but a few Swing components, such as `JFrame`, `JApplet`, and `JDialog`, are subclasses of `JComponent`. Many of the properties of the Swing components are defined in the `JComponent` class. Here are some properties available in `JComponent`:

- `toolTipText`: The text displayed when the mouse points on the component without clicking. This text is generally used to give the user a tip about the component's function.
- `doubleBuffered`: Specifies whether the component is painted using double buffering. This is a technique for reducing flickering. In AWT programming, you have to manually implement this technique in the program. With Swing, this capability is automatically supported if the `doubleBuffered` property is set to `true`. By default, it is `true`.
- `border`: Specifies a border of the component. The border types and styles will be introduced in the section "Borders" later in this chapter.

You can retrieve these properties using the getter methods and modify them using the setter methods. The principal benefit of JavaBeans is for use in the Java builder tools for rapid Java application development. As shown in Figure 9.2, you can set the properties of a `JButton` instance in JBuilder's visual designer during design time. For complete coverage of JavaBeans, please refer to my *Rapid Java Application Development Using JBuilder 3*.

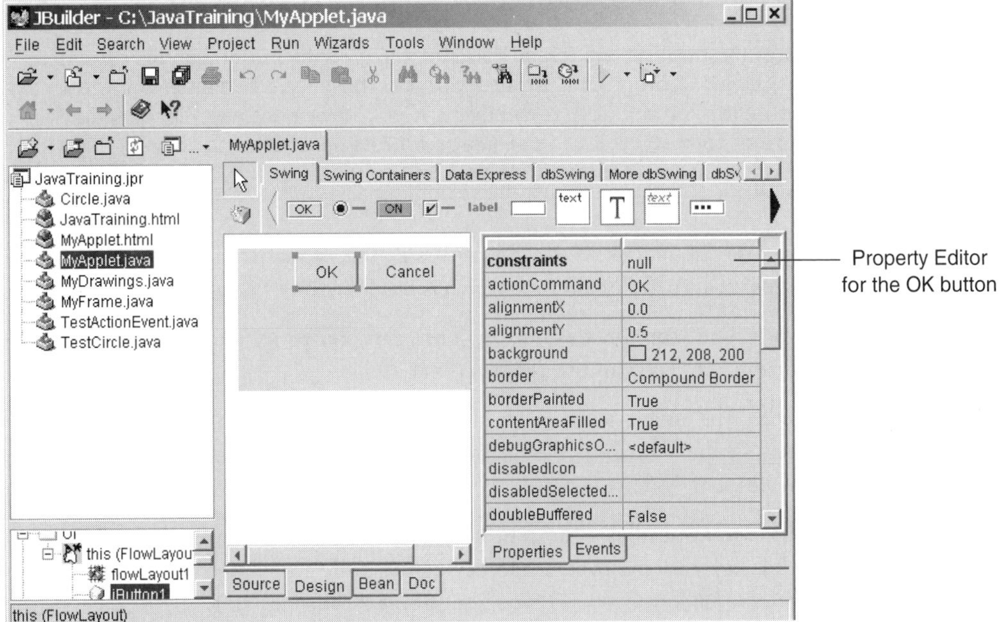

Figure 9.2 *You can set the properties of a JavaBeans instance, such as a* `JButton`*, at design time.*

Buttons

A *button* is a component that triggers an action event when clicked. The Swing version of a button is named `JButton`. Its default constructor creates an empty button. In addition, `JButton` has the following constructors:

- `public JButton(String text)`

  This creates a button labeled with the specified text.

- `public JButton(Icon icon)`

  This creates a button with the specified icon.

- `public JButton(String text, Icon icon)`

  This creates a button with the specified text and icon.

An icon is a fixed-size picture; typically it is small and used to decorate components. An icon can be obtained from an image file by using the `ImageIcon` class, such as

```
Icon icon = new ImageIcon("photo.gif");
```

`javax.swing.ImageIcon` is a subclass of `javax.swing.Icon`.

NOTE
Java currently supports two image formats: GIF (Graphics Interchange Format) and JPEG (Joint Photographic Experts Group). The image filenames for these types end with .gif and .jpg, respectively. If you have a bitmap file, or image files in other formats, you can use image-processing utilities to convert them into GIF or JPEG format for use in Java.

Since `JButton` is a subclass of `JComponent`, all the properties in `JComponent` can be used in `JButton`. Additionally, `JButton` has the following useful properties:

- `text`: The label on the button. For example, to set the label "OK" on the button `jbt`, you can use `jbt.setText("OK")`.
- `icon`: The image icon on the button. For example, to set the icon on `jbt` using the image file smiley.gif, you can use `jbt.setIcon(new ImageIcon("smiley.gif"))`.
- `mnemonic`: Specifies a shortcut key. You can select the button by pressing the ALT key and the mnemonic key at the same time. For example, to set the mnemonic key O on `jbt`, you use `jbt.setMnemonic('O')`.
- `horizontalAlignment`: One of the three values, `SwingConstants.LEFT`, `SwingConstants.CENTER`, and `SwingConstants.RIGHT`, that specify how the icon and label is placed horizontally on a button. The default alignment is `SwingConstants.CENTER`.
- `verticalAlignment`: One of the three values, `SwingConstants.TOP`, `SwingConstants.CENTER`, and `SwingConstants.BOTTOM`, that specify how the label is placed vertically on a button. The default alignment is `SwingConstants.CENTER`.
- `horizontalTextPosition`: One of the three values, `SwingConstants.TOP`, `SwingConstants.CENTER`, and `SwingConstants.BOTTOM`, that specify the horizontal position of the text relative to the icon. The default alignment is `SwingConstants.RIGHT`.
- `verticalTextPosition`: One of the three values, `SwingConstants.TOP`, `SwingConstants.CENTER`, and `SwingConstants.BOTTOM`, that specify the vertical position of the text relative to the icon. The default alignment is `SwingConstants.CENTER`.

Buttons can generate many types of events, but often you need to respond to an `ActionEvent`. In order to make a button responsive to an `ActionEvent`, you must implement the `actionPerformed` method in the `ActionListener` interface. The following code is an example of how to handle a button event. The code prints out "Button clicked" on the console when the button is clicked.

```
public void actionPerformed(ActionEvent e)
{
  // Make sure the event source is a button.
  if (e.getSource() instanceof JButton)
    System.out.println("Button clicked!");
}
```

Example 9.1 Using Buttons

This example gives a program that displays a message on a panel and uses two buttons, <= and =>, to move the message on the panel to the left or right. The output of the program is shown in Figure 9.3.

```
// ButtonDemo.java: Use buttons to move message in a panel
import java.awt.*;
import java.awt.event.ActionListener;
import java.awt.event.ActionEvent;
import javax.swing.*;

public class ButtonDemo extends JFrame implements ActionListener
{
  // Declare a panel for displaying message
  private MessagePanel messagePanel;

  // Declare two buttons to move the message left and right
  private JButton jbtLeft, jbtRight;

  // Main method
  public static void main(String[] args)
  {
    ButtonDemo frame = new ButtonDemo();
    // frame.setDefaultCloseOperation(JFrame.EXIT_ON_CLOSE);
    frame.setSize(200,200);
    frame.setVisible(true);
  }

  public ButtonDemo()
  {
    setTitle("Button Demo");

    // Create a MessagePanel instance and set colors
    messagePanel = new MessagePanel("Welcome to Java");
    messagePanel.setBackground(Color.yellow);

    // Create Panel jpButtons to hold two Buttons "<=" and "right =>"
    JPanel jpButtons = new JPanel();
    jpButtons.setLayout(new FlowLayout());
    jpButtons.add(jbtLeft = new JButton());
    jpButtons.add(jbtRight = new JButton());

    // Set button text
    jbtLeft.setText("<=");
    jbtRight.setText("=>");

    // Set keyboard mnemonics
    jbtLeft.setMnemonic('L');
    jbtRight.setMnemonic('R');

    // Set icons
    //jbtLeft.setIcon(new ImageIcon("images/left.gif"));
    //jbtRight.setIcon(new ImageIcon("images/right.gif"));
    // Set toolTipText on the "<=" and "=>" buttons
    jbtLeft.setToolTipText("Move message to left");
    jbtRight.setToolTipText("Move message to right");

    // Place panels in the frame
    getContentPane().setLayout(new BorderLayout());
    getContentPane().add(messagePanel, BorderLayout.CENTER);
    getContentPane().add(jpButtons, BorderLayout.SOUTH);
```

continues

Example 9.1 continued

```
    // Register listeners with the buttons
    jbtLeft.addActionListener(this);
    jbtRight.addActionListener(this);
  }

  // Handle button events
  public void actionPerformed(ActionEvent e)
  {
    if (e.getSource() == jbtLeft)
    {
      left();
    }
    else if (e.getSource() == jbtRight)
    {
      right();
    }
  }

  // Move the message in the panel left
  private void left()
  {
    int x = messagePanel.getXCoordinate();
    if (x > 10)
    {
      // Shift the message to the left
      messagePanel.setXCoordinate(x-10);
      messagePanel.repaint();
    }
  }

  // Move the message in the panel right
  private void right()
  {
    int x = messagePanel.getXCoordinate();
    if (x < getSize().width - 20)
    {
      // Shift the message to the right
      messagePanel.setXCoordinate(x+10);
      messagePanel.repaint();
    }
  }
}
```

Figure 9.3 *Clicking the <= and => buttons causes the message on the panel to move to the left or right, respectively.*

Example Review

The program displays a message on a panel and places two buttons, <= and =>, on a panel below the message panel. The `MessagePanel` class, created in Example 8.5,

"Using FontMetrics," displays a message on a panel. When you click a button, the handler, `actionPerformed(ActionEvent e)`, determines which button has been clicked and invokes the `left()` or `right()` method to move the message.

Each button has a tool-tip text, which appears when the mouse is set on the button without clicking, as shown in Figure 9.3.

You can set an icon image on the button by using the `setIcon` method. If you replace the `setText` method with the `setIcon` method, as follows:

```
jbtLeft.setIcon(new ImageIcon("images/left.gif"));
jbtRight.setIcon(new ImageIcon("images/right.gif"));
```

the labels are replaced by the icons, as shown in Figure 9.4. "images/left.gif" is located in "c:\book\images\left.gif" in Windows. Note that the back slash is the Windows file path notation. In Java, the forward slash should be used.

You can set both icons and labels on a button at the same time, if you wish. By default, the labels and icons are centered horizontally and vertically.

The button can also be accessed by using the keyboard mnemonics. Pressing ALT+L is equivalent to clicking the <= button, since you set the mnemonic property to 'L' in the left button. If you change the left button text to "Left" and the right button to "Right," the L and R in the captions of these buttons will be underlined, as shown in Figure 9.5.

Figure 9.4 *You can set an icon on a* `JButton`.

Figure 9.5 *The buttons can be accessed by using the keyboard mnemonics.*

The `repaint` method is defined in the `Component` class. Invoking `repaint` causes the `paintComponent` method to be called. The `repaint` method is invoked to refresh the viewing area. Typically, you call it if you have new things to display.

continues

Example 9.1 continued

TIP

The `paintComponent` method should never be invoked directly. It is invoked by the Java runtime system whenever the viewing area changes, or by the `repaint` method. You should override the `paintComponent` method to tell the system how to paint the viewing area, but never override the `repaint` method.

NOTE

The `repaint` method lodges a request to update the viewing area and returns immediately. Its effect is asynchronous, and if several requests are outstanding, it is likely that only the last `paintComponent` will be done.

Labels

A *label* is a display area for a short text, an image, or both. It is often used to label other components (usually text fields). As with other components, the layout managers can place labels inside a container. The default constructor of `JLabel` creates an empty label. Other constructors for `JLabel` are as follows:

- `public JLabel(String text, int horizontalAlignment)`

  This creates a label with the specified string and horizontal alignment (`SwingConstants.LEFT`, `SwingConstants.RIGHT`, or `SwingConstants.CENTER`).

- `public JLabel(String text)`

  This creates a label with a specified text.

- `public JLabel(Icon icon)`

  This creates a label with an icon.

- `public JLabel(Icon icon, int horizontalAlignment)`

  This creates a label with the specified image and horizontal alignment.

- `public JLabel(String text, Icon icon, int horizontalAlignment)`

  This creates a label with the specified text, image, and horizontal alignment.

For example, the following statement creates a label with the string `"Interest Rate"`:

```
JLabel myLabel = new JLabel("Interest Rate");
```

The following statement creates a label with the specified image in the file "images/map.gif":

```
JLabel mapLabel = new JLabel(new ImageIcon("images/map.gif"));
```

`JLabel` inherits all the properties from `JComponent` and has many properties used in `JButton`, such as `text`, `icon`, `horizontalAlignment`, and `verticalAlignment`.

Example 9.2 Using Labels

This example gives a program that uses a label as an area for displaying images. There are 52 images in image files named L1.gif, L2.gif, . . . , L52.gif stored in the images directory under c:\book. You can use two buttons, Prior and Next, to browse the images, as shown in Figure 9.6.

```
// LabelDemo.java: Use label to display images
import java.awt.*;
import java.awt.event.*;
import javax.swing.*;

public class LabelDemo extends JFrame implements ActionListener
{
  // Declare an ImageIcon array. There are total 52 images
  private ImageIcon[] imageIcon = new ImageIcon[52];

  // The current image index
  private int currentIndex = 0;

  // Buttons for browsing images
  private JButton jbtPrior, jbtNext;

  // Label for displaying images
  private JLabel jlblImageViewer = new JLabel();
  final int TOTAL_NUMBER_OF_IMAGES = 52;

  // Main Method
  public static void main(String[] args)
  {
    LabelDemo frame = new LabelDemo();

    // frame.setDefaultCloseOperation(JFrame.EXIT_ON_CLOSE);
    frame.setSize(500, 500);
    frame.setVisible(true);
  }

  // Default Constructor
  public LabelDemo()
  {
    setTitle("Label Demo");

    // Load images into imageIcon array
    for (int i=1; i<=52; i++)
    {
      imageIcon[i-1] = new ImageIcon("images/L" + i + ".gif");
    }

    // Show the first image
    jlblImageViewer.setIcon(imageIcon[currentIndex]);

    // Set center alignment
    jlblImageViewer.setHorizontalAlignment(SwingConstants.CENTER);

    //jlblImageViewer.setVerticalAlignment(SwingConstants.CENTER);
    // Panel jpButtons to hold two buttons for browsing images
    JPanel jpButtons = new JPanel();
    jpButtons.add(jbtPrior = new JButton());
    jbtPrior.setIcon(new ImageIcon("images/left.gif"));
    jpButtons.add(jbtNext = new JButton());
    jbtNext.setIcon(new ImageIcon("images/right.gif"));

    // Add jpButton and the label to the frame
    getContentPane().add(jlblImageViewer, BorderLayout.CENTER);
    getContentPane().add(jpButtons, BorderLayout.SOUTH);
```

continues

Example 9.2 continued

```
      // Register listeners
      jbtPrior.addActionListener(this);
      jbtNext.addActionListener(this);
    }

    // Handle ActionEvent from buttons
    public void actionPerformed(ActionEvent e)
    {
      if (e.getSource() == jbtPrior)
      {
        // Make sure index is nonnegative
        if (currentIndex == 0) currentIndex = TOTAL_NUMBER_OF_IMAGES;
        currentIndex = (currentIndex - 1)%TOTAL_NUMBER_OF_IMAGES;
        jlblImageViewer.setIcon(imageIcon[currentIndex]);
      }
      else if (e.getSource() == jbtNext)
      {
        currentIndex = (currentIndex + 1)%TOTAL_NUMBER_OF_IMAGES;
        jlblImageViewer.setIcon(imageIcon[currentIndex]);
      }
    }
  }
```

Figure 9.6 *You can use the label to display images.*

Example Review

The images are stored in files L1.gif, L2.gif, . . ., and L52.gif, and are loaded to an array of `ImageIcon` in a `for` loop.

By default, the icon is centered vertically, but left aligned horizontally. The following statement ensures that the image is displayed in the center of the viewing area.

```
jlblImageViewer.setHorizontalAlignment(SwingConstants.CENTER);
```

Text Fields

A *text field* is an input area where the user can type in characters. Text fields enable the user to enter variable data, such as names or descriptions. The default constructor of `JTextField` creates an empty text field. Other constructors of `JTextField` are as follows:

- `public JTextField(int columns)`

  This creates an empty text field with the specified number of columns.

- `public JTextField(String text)`

  This creates a text field initialized with the specified text.

- `public JTextField(String text, int columns)`

  This creates a text field initialized with the specified text and the column size.

In addition to such properties as `text` and `horizontalAlignment`, `JTextField` has the following properties:

- `editable`: A `boolean` property indicating whether the text field can be edited by the user.
- `columns`: The width of the text field.

`JTextField` can generate `ActionEvent` and `TextEvent`, among many other events. Pressing Enter in a text field triggers the `ActionEvent`. Changing contents in a text field triggers the `TextEvent`.

Here is an example of how to react to an `ActionEvent` on a text field.

```
public void actionPerformed(ActionEvent e)
{
  // Make sure it is a text field
  if (e.getSource() instanceof JTextField)
    // Process the event
      . . .
}
```

Example 9.3 Using Text Fields

This example gives a program that enters two numbers in two text fields and displays their sum in the third text field when you press the Add button. The output of the program is shown in Figure 9.7.

```
// TextFieldDemo.java: Add two numbers in the text fields
import java.awt.*;
import java.awt.event.*;
import javax.swing.*;

public class TextFieldDemo extends JFrame implements ActionListener
{
  // Declare three text fields
  private JTextField jtfNum1, jtfNum2, jtfResult;
  private JButton jbtAdd; // Declare "Add" button

  // Main method
  public static void main(String[] args)
  {
    TextFieldDemo frame = new TextFieldDemo();
    frame.pack();
    // frame.setDefaultCloseOperation(JFrame.EXIT_ON_CLOSE);
    frame.setVisible(true);
  }

  // Constructor
```

continues

Example 9.3 continued

```
  public TextFieldDemo()
  {
    setTitle("TextFieldDemo");
    setBackground(Color.yellow);
    setForeground(Color.black);

    // Use panel p1 to group text fields
    JPanel p1 = new JPanel();
    p1.setLayout(new FlowLayout());
    p1.add(new JLabel("Number 1"));
    p1.add(jtfNum1 = new JTextField(3));
    p1.add(new JLabel("Number 2"));
    p1.add(jtfNum2 = new JTextField(3));
    p1.add(new JLabel("Result"));
    p1.add(jtfResult = new JTextField(4));
    jtfResult.setEditable(false);   // Set jtfResult noneditable

    // Use panel p2 for the button
    JPanel p2 = new JPanel();
    p2.setLayout(new FlowLayout());
    p2.add(jbtAdd = new JButton("Add"));

    // Set FlowLayout for the frame and add panels to the frame
    getContentPane().setLayout(new BorderLayout());
    getContentPane().add(p1, BorderLayout.CENTER);
    getContentPane().add(p2, BorderLayout.SOUTH);

    // Register listener
    jbtAdd.addActionListener(this);
  }

  // Handle the add operation
  public void actionPerformed(ActionEvent e)
  {
    if (e.getSource() == jbtAdd)
    {
      // Get int values from text fields and use trim() to
      // trim extraneous space in the text field
      int num1 = (Integer.parseInt(jtfNum1.getText().trim()));
      int num2 = (Integer.parseInt(jtfNum2.getText().trim()));
      int result = num1 + num2;

      // Set result in TextField jtfResult
      jtfResult.setText(String.valueOf(result));
    }
  }
}
```

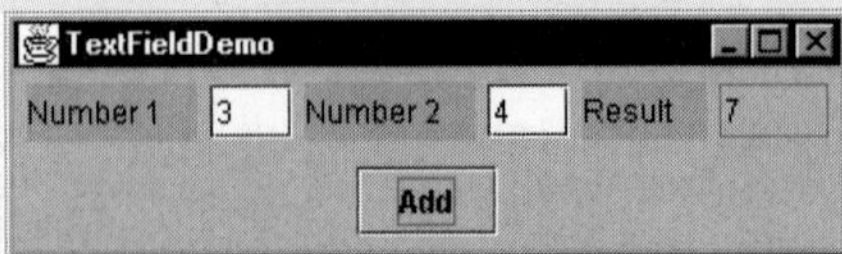

Figure 9.7 *The addition of Number 1 and Number 2 shows in the Result when you click the Add button.*

Example Review

The program uses two panels, p1 and p2, to contain the components. Panel p1 is for the labels and text fields, and p2 is for the Add button. You can place the button directly in the frame instead of in p2, but in this case the button would look very long because it would stretch to fill in the entire south area of the BorderLayout.

Instead of using the setSize method to set the size for the frame, this program uses the pack() method, which automatically sizes up the frame according to the size of the components placed in it.

The jtfNum1.getText() method returns the text in the text field jtfNum1, and jtfResult.setText(s) sets the specified string into text field jtfResult.

The trim() method is useful for removing blank space from both ends of a string. If you run the program without applying trim() to the string, a runtime exception may occur when the string is converted to an integer.

Using jtfResult.setEditable(false) prevents the user from editing the Result text field. By default, editing is enabled on all text fields.

Text Areas

If you want to let the user enter multiple lines of text, you have to create several instances of JTextField. The solution is to use JTextArea, which enables the user to enter multiple lines of text.

The default constructor of JTextArea creates an empty text area. Other constructors of JTextArea are listed below:

- `public JTextArea(int rows, int columns)`

  This creates a text area with the specified number of rows and columns.

- `public JTextArea(String text, int rows, int columns)`

  This creates a text area with the specified text and the number of rows and columns specified.

In addition to text, editable, and columns, JTextArea has the following properties:

- lineWrap: A boolean property indicating whether the line in the text area is automatically wrapped.
- wrapStyleWord: A boolean property indicating whether the line is wrapped on word or character. The default value is false, which indicates that the line is wrapped on character boundaries.
- rows: The number of lines in the text area.
- lineCount: The number of lines in the text.
- tabSize: The number of characters inserted when the Tab key is pressed.

You can use the following methods to insert, append, and replace text:

- `public void insert(String s, int pos)`

  This inserts string s in the specified position in the text area.

- `public void append(String s)`

  This appends string s to the end of the text.

- `public void replaceRange(String s, int start, int end)`

  This replaces partial texts in the range from position `start` to position `end` with string s.

`JTextArea` does not handle scrolling, but you can create a `JScrollPane` object to hold an instance of `JTextArea` and let the `JScrollPane` handle scrolling for `JTextArea`, as follows:

```
// Create a scroll pane to hold text area
JScrollPane scrollPane = new JScrollPane(jta = new JTextArea());
getContentPane().add(scrollPane, BorderLayout.CENTER);
```

`JScrollPane` will be further discussed in the section "Scroll Panes" later in this chapter.

Example 9.4 Using Text Areas

This example gives a program that displays an image in a label, a title in a label, and a text in a text area. A sample run of the program is shown in Figure 9.8.

```
// TextAreaDemo.java: Display an image in a label, the title for
// the image in a label, and the description of the image in a
// text area
import java.awt.*;
import javax.swing.*;

public class TextAreaDemo extends JFrame
{
  // Declare and create a description panel
  private DescriptionPanel descriptionPanel = new DescriptionPanel();

  // Main method
  public static void main(String[] args)
  {
    TextAreaDemo frame = new TextAreaDemo();
    frame.pack();
    // frame.setDefaultCloseOperation(JFrame.EXIT_ON_CLOSE);
    frame.setTitle("Text Area Demo");
    frame.setVisible(true);
  }

  // Constructor
  public TextAreaDemo()
  {
    // Set title, text and image in the description panel
    descriptionPanel.setTitle("Canada");
    String description = "The Maple Leaf flag \n\n" +
      "The Canadian National Flag was adopted by the Canadian " +
      "Parliament on October 22, 1964 and was proclaimed into law " +
      "by Her Majesty Queen Elizabeth II (the Queen of Canada) on " +
      "February 15, 1965. The Canadian Flag (colloquially known " +
      "as The Maple Leaf Flag) is a red flag of the proportions " +
      "two by length and one by width, containing in its center a " +
      "white square, with a single red stylized eleven-point " +
      "mapleleaf centered in the white square.";
    descriptionPanel.setTextDescription(description);
    descriptionPanel.setImageIcon(new ImageIcon("images/ca.gif"));
```

```
    // Add the description panel to the frame
    getContentPane().setLayout(new BorderLayout());
    getContentPane().add(descriptionPanel, BorderLayout.CENTER);
  }
}

// Define a panel for displaying image and text
class DescriptionPanel extends JPanel
{
  // Label for displaying an image icon
  private JLabel jlblImage = new JLabel();

  // Label for displaying a title
  private JLabel jlblTitle = new JLabel();

  // Text area for displaying text
  private JTextArea jtaTextDescription;

  // Default constructor
  public DescriptionPanel()
  {
    // Group image label and title label in a panel
    JPanel panel = new JPanel();
    panel.setLayout(new BorderLayout());
    panel.add(jlblImage, BorderLayout.CENTER);
    panel.add(jlblTitle, BorderLayout.SOUTH);

    // Create a scroll pane to hold text area
    JScrollPane scrollPane = new JScrollPane
      (jtaTextDescription = new JTextArea());

    // Center the title on the label
    jlblTitle.setHorizontalAlignment(JLabel.CENTER);

    // Set the font for the title and text
    jlblTitle.setFont(new Font("SansSerif", Font.BOLD, 16));
    jtaTextDescription.setFont(new Font("Serif", Font.PLAIN, 14));

    // Set lineWrap and wrapStyleWord true for text area
    jtaTextDescription.setLineWrap(true);
    jtaTextDescription.setWrapStyleWord(true);

    // Set preferred size for the scroll pane
    scrollPane.setPreferredSize(new Dimension(200, 100));

    // Set BorderLayout for the whole panel, add panel and scrollpane
    setLayout(new BorderLayout());
    add(scrollPane, BorderLayout.CENTER);
    add(panel, BorderLayout.WEST);
  }

  // Set the title
  public void setTitle(String title)
  {
    jlblTitle.setText(title);
  }

  // Set the image icon
  public void setImageIcon(ImageIcon icon)
  {
    jlblImage.setIcon(icon);
    Dimension dimension = new Dimension(icon.getIconWidth(),
      icon.getIconHeight());
    jlblImage.setPreferredSize(dimension);
  }

  // Set the text description
  public void setTextDescription(String text)
```

continues

Example 9.4 continued

```
    {
      jtaTextDescription.setText(text);
    }
  }
```

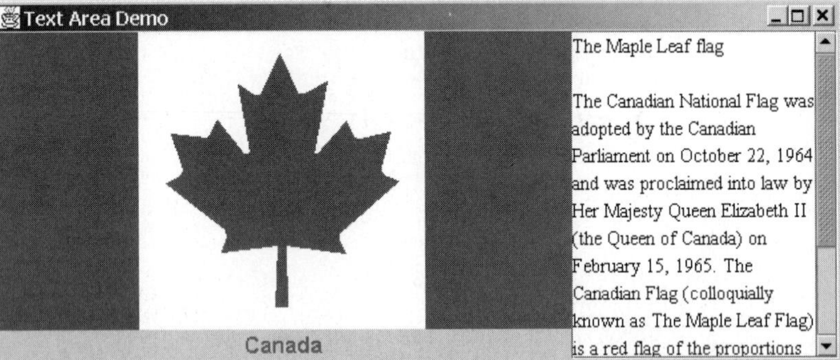

Figure 9.8 *The program displays an image in a label, a title in a label, and a text in the text area.*

Example Review

The program consists of two classes: `TextAreaDemo`, and `DescriptionPanel`. The relationship between the two classes is shown in Figure 9.9.

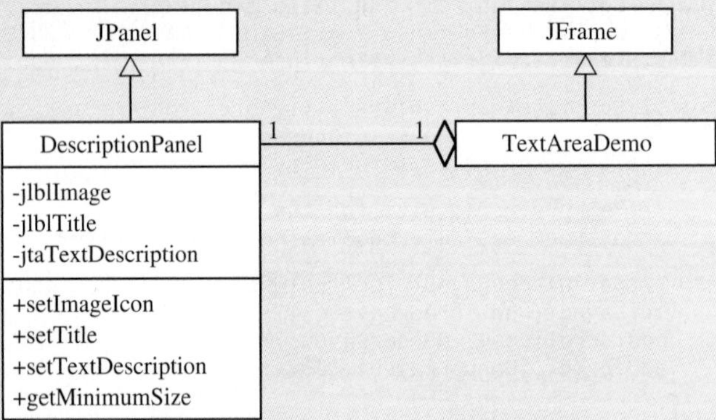

Figure 9.9 `TextAreaDemo` *uses* `DescriptionPanel` *to display image, title, and text description of the national flag.*

`TextAreaDemo` simply creates an instance of `DescriptionPanel`, and sets the title, image, and text in the description panel. `DescriptionPanel` is a subclass of `JPanel`. `DescriptionPanel` contains a label for displaying the image icon, a label for displaying title, and a text area for displaying a description of the image.

It is not necessary to create a separate class for `DescriptionPanel` in this example. Nevertheless, this class was created for reuse in the next example, where you will use it to display a description panel for various images.

The text area is inside a `JScrollPane`, which provides scrolling functions for the text area. Scrollbars automatically appear if there is more text than the physical size of the text area, and disappear if the text is deleted and the remaining text does not exceed the text area size.

The `lineWrap` property is set to true so that the line is automatically wrapped when the text cannot fit in one line. The `wrapStyleWord` property is set to true so that the line is wrapped on words rather than characters.

The text area is editable. It supports editing functions such as cut, paste, and copy.

The `preferredSize` property in `jlblImage` is set to the size of image icon. The `getIconWidth()` and `getIconHeight()` methods obtain the width and height of the icon. The `preferredSize` property in `scrollPane` is set to 200 in width and 100 in height. The `BorderLayout` manager respects the preferred size of the components.

Combo Boxes

A *combo box*, also known as *choice*, is a simple list of items from which the user can choose. It is useful in limiting a user's range of choices and avoids the cumbersome validation of data input.

To create a `JComboBox`, use its default constructor, or use the following constructor to create a list with a set of strings:

```
public JComboBox(Object[] stringItems)
```

where `stringItems` is an array of `String`.

The following properties are often useful:

- `selectedIndex`: An `int` value indicating the index of the selected item in the combo box.
- `selectedItem`: A selected item whose type is `Object`.

The following methods are useful for operating a `JComboBox` object:

- `public void addItem(Object item)`

  This adds the item of any object into the combo box.

- `public Object getItemAt(int index)`

  This gets an item from the combo box at the specified index.

- `public void removeItem(Object anObject)`

  This removes the specified item from the item list.

- `public void removeAllItems()`

  This removes all items from the item list.

Here is an example of how to create a combo box and add items to the object:

```
JComboBox jcb = new JComboBox();
jcb.addItem("Item 1");
jcb.addItem("Item 2");
jcb.addItem("Item 3");
```

This creates a `JComboBox` with three items in the combo box.

To get data from a `JComboBox` menu, you can use `getSelectedItem()` to return the currently selected item, or you can use the `e.getItem()` method to get the item from the `itemStateChanged(ItemEvent e)` handler.

`JComboBox` can generate `ActionEvent` and `ItemEvent`, among many other events. Whenever a new item is selected, `JComboBox` generates `ItemEvent` twice, one for deselecting the previously selected item, and the other for selecting the currently selected item. `JComboBox` generates an `ActionEvent` after generating `ItemEvent`. To respond to an `ItemEvent`, you need to implement the `itemStateChanged(ItemEvent e)` handler for processing a choice. Here is an example of how to get data from the `itemStateChanged(ItemEvent e)` handler:

```
public void itemStateChanged(ItemEvent e)
{
  // Make sure the source is a combo box
  if (e.getSource() instanceof JComboBox)
    String s = (String)e.getItem();
}
```

Example 9.5 Using Combo Boxes

This example gives a program that lets users view an image and description of a country's flag by selecting the country from a combo box. Figure 9.10 shows a sample run of the program.

```
// ComboBoxDemo.java: Use a combo box to select a country and
// display the selected country's flag information
import java.awt.*;
import java.awt.event.*;
import javax.swing.*;

public class ComboBoxDemo extends JFrame implements ItemListener
{
  // Declare an array of Strings for flag titles
  private String[] flagTitle = {"Canada", "China", "Denmark",
    "France", "Germany", "India", "Norway", "United Kingdom",
    "United States of America"};

  // Declare an ImageIcon array for the national flags of 9 countries
  private ImageIcon[] flagImage = new ImageIcon[9];

  // Declare an array of strings for flag descriptions
  private String[] flagDescription = new String[9];

  // Declare and create a description panel
  private DescriptionPanel descriptionPanel = new DescriptionPanel();

  // The combo list for selecting countries
  private JComboBox jcbo;

  // Main Method
  public static void main(String[] args)
```

```
  {
    ComboBoxDemo frame = new ComboBoxDemo();
    frame.pack();
    frame.setTitle("Combo Box Demo");
    // frame.setDefaultCloseOperation(JFrame.EXIT_ON_CLOSE);
    frame.setVisible(true);
  }

  // Default Constructor
  public ComboBoxDemo()
  {
    // Load images info flagImage array
    flagImage[0] = new ImageIcon("images/ca.gif");
    flagImage[1] = new ImageIcon("images/china.gif");
    flagImage[2] = new ImageIcon("images/denmark.gif");
    flagImage[3] = new ImageIcon("images/fr.gif");
    flagImage[4] = new ImageIcon("images/germany.gif");
    flagImage[5] = new ImageIcon("images/india.gif");
    flagImage[6] = new ImageIcon("images/norway.gif");
    flagImage[7] = new ImageIcon("images/uk.gif");
    flagImage[8] = new ImageIcon("images/us.gif");

    // Set text description
    flagDescription[0] = "The Maple Leaf flag \n\n" +
      "The Canadian National Flag was adopted by the Canadian " +
      "Parliament on October 22, 1964 and was proclaimed into law " +
      "by Her Majesty Queen Elizabeth II (the Queen of Canada) on " +
      "February 15, 1965. The Canadian Flag (colloquially known " +
      "as The Maple Leaf Flag) is a red flag of the proportions " +
      "two by length and one by width, containing in its center a " +
      "white square, with a single red stylized eleven-point " +
      "mapleleaf centered in the white square.";
    flagDescription[1] = "Description for China ... ";
    flagDescription[2] = "Description for Denmark ... ";
    flagDescription[3] = "Description for France ... ";
    flagDescription[4] = "Description for Germany ... ";
    flagDescription[5] = "Description for India ... ";
    flagDescription[6] = "Description for Norway ... ";
    flagDescription[7] = "Description for UK ... ";
    flagDescription[8] = "Description for US ... ";

    // Create items into the combo box
    jcbo = new JComboBox(flagTitle);

    // Set the first country (Canada) for display
    setDisplay(0);

    // Add combo box and description panel to the list
    getContentPane().add(jcbo, BorderLayout.NORTH);
    getContentPane().add(descriptionPanel, BorderLayout.CENTER);

    // Register listener
    jcbo.addItemListener(this);
  }

  // Handle item selection
  public void itemStateChanged(ItemEvent e)
  {
    setDisplay(jcbo.getSelectedIndex());
  }

  // Set display information on the description panel
  public void setDisplay(int index)
  {
```

continues

Example 9.5 continued

```
        descriptionPanel.setTitle(flagTitle[index]);
        descriptionPanel.setImageIcon(flagImage[index]);
        descriptionPanel.setTextDescription(flagDescription[index]);
      }
    }
```

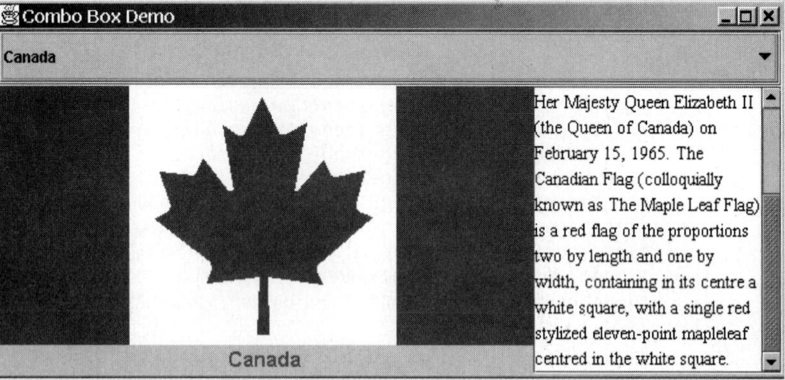

Figure 9.10 *A country's info, including a flag image and a description of the flag, is displayed when the country is selected in the combo box.*

Example Review

The frame listens to `ItemEvent` for the `JComboBox` item, so it implements `ItemListener`. Instead of using the `ItemEvent`, you can rewrite the program to use `ActionEvent` for handling combo box item selection.

The program stores the flag information in three arrays: `flagTitle`, `flagImage`, and `flagDescription`. The array `flagTitle` contains the names of the nine countries, the array `flagImage` contains images of the nine countries' flags, and the array `flagDescription` contains descriptions of the flags.

The program creates an instance of `DescriptionPanel`, which was presented in Example 9.4. The program creates a combo box with initial values from `flagTitle`. When the user selects an item in the combo box, the `ItemStateChanged` handler is executed, which finds the selected index and sets its corresponding flag title, flag image, and flag description on the panel.

Lists

A *list* is a component that basically performs the same function as a combo box but enables the user to choose a single value or multiple values. The Swing `JList` is very versatile. Its advanced features are beyond the scope of this book. This section demonstrates selecting string items from a list.

To create a list with a set of strings, use the following constructor:

```
public JList(Object[] stringItems)
```

where `stringItems` is an array of `String`.

The following properties are often useful:

- `selectedIndex`: An `int` value indicating the index of the selected item in the list.
- `selectedIndices`: An array of `int` values representing the indices of the selected items in the list.
- `selectedValue`: The first selected value in the list.
- `selectedValues`: An array of objects representing selected values in the list.
- `selectionMode`: One of the three values (`SINGLE_SELECTION`, `SINGLE_INTERVAL_SELECTION`, `MULTIPLE_INTERVAL_SELECTION`) that indicate whether a single item, single-interval item, or multiple-interval item can be selected. Single selection allows only one item to be selected. Single-interval selection allows multiple selections, but the selected items must be contiguous. Multiple-interval selection allows selections of multiple contiguous items. The default value is `MULTIPLE_INTERVAL_SELECTION`.
- `visibleRowCount`: The preferred number of rows in the list that can be displayed without a scrollbar. The default value is 8.

Lists do not scroll automatically. To make a list scrollable, create a scroll pane and add the list to it. Text areas are made scrollable in the same way.

`JList` generates `javax.swing.event.ListSelectionEvent` to notify the listeners of the selections. The listener must implement the `valueChanged` handler to process the event. Here is an example of how to get a selected item from the `valueChanged(ListSelectionEvent e)` handler:

```
public void valueChanged(ListSelectionEvent e)
{
  String selectedItem = (String)jlst.getSelectedValue();
}
```

Example 9.6 Using Lists

This example gives a program that lets users select countries in a list and display the flags of the selected countries in the labels. Figure 9.11 shows a sample run of the program.

```
// ListDemo.java: Use list to select a country and display the
// selected country's flag
import java.awt.*;
import java.awt.event.*;
import javax.swing.*;
import javax.swing.event.*;

public class ListDemo extends JFrame implements ListSelectionListener
{
  // Declare an ImageIcon array for the national flags of 9 countries
  private ImageIcon[] imageIcon = new ImageIcon[9];

  // Arrays of labels for displaying images
  private JLabel[] jlblImageViewer = new JLabel[9];
```

continues

Example 9.6 continued

```
// The list for selecting countries
JList jlst;

// Main Method
public static void main(String[] args)
{
  ListDemo frame = new ListDemo();
  frame.setSize(650, 500);
  frame.setTitle("List Demo");
  // frame.setDefaultCloseOperation(JFrame.EXIT_ON_CLOSE);
  frame.setVisible(true);
}

// Default Constructor
public ListDemo()
{
  // Load images into imageIcon array
  imageIcon[0] = new ImageIcon("images/us.gif");
  imageIcon[1] = new ImageIcon("images/ca.gif");
  imageIcon[2] = new ImageIcon("images/uk.gif");
  imageIcon[3] = new ImageIcon("images/germany.gif");
  imageIcon[4] = new ImageIcon("images/fr.gif");
  imageIcon[5] = new ImageIcon("images/denmark.gif");
  imageIcon[6] = new ImageIcon("images/norway.gif");
  imageIcon[7] = new ImageIcon("images/china.gif");
  imageIcon[8] = new ImageIcon("images/india.gif");

  // Create a string of country names
  String[] countries = {"United States of America", "Canada",
    "United Kingdom", "Germany", "France", "Denmark", "Norway",
    "China", "India"};

  // Create a list with the country names
  jlst = new JList(countries);

  // Create a panel to hold nine labels
  JPanel p = new JPanel();
  p.setLayout(new GridLayout(3, 3));

  for (int i=0; i<9; i++)
  {
    p.add(jlblImageViewer[i] = new JLabel());
    jlblImageViewer[i].setHorizontalAlignment
      (SwingConstants.CENTER);
  }

  // Add p and the list to the frame
  getContentPane().add(p, BorderLayout.CENTER);
  getContentPane().add(new JScrollPane(jlst), BorderLayout.WEST);

  // Register listeners
  jlst.addListSelectionListener(this);
}

// Handle list selection
public void valueChanged(ListSelectionEvent e)
{
  // Get selected indices
  int[] indices = jlst.getSelectedIndices();

  int i;

  // Set icons in the labels
  for (i=0; i<indices.length; i++)
  {
```

```
        jlblImageViewer[i].setIcon(imageIcon[indices[i]]);
      }
      // Remove icons from the rest of the labels
      for (; i<9; i++)
      {
        jlblImageViewer[i].setIcon(null);
      }
    }
  }
```

Figure 9.11 *When the countries in the list are selected, corresponding images of their flags are displayed in the labels.*

Example Review

The frame listens to `ListSelectionEvent` for handling the selection of country names in the list, so it implements `ListSelectionListener`. `ListSelectionEvent` and `ListSelectionListener` are defined in the `javax.swing.event` package, so this package is imported in the program.

The program creates an array of nine labels for displaying flag images for nine countries. The program loads the images of the nine countries into an image array and creates a list of the nine countries in the same order as in the image array. Thus the index 0 of the image array corresponds to the first country in the list.

The list is placed in a scroll pane so that it can be scrolled when the number of items in the list extends beyond the viewing area.

By default, the selection mode of the list is multiple-interval, which allows the user to select multiple items from different blocks in the list. When the user selects countries in the list, the `valueChanged` handler is executed, which gets the indices of the selected item and sets their corresponding image icons in the label to display the flags.

The example constructs a list with a fixed set of strings. If you want to add new items to the list or delete existing items, you have to use the list model. The use of list models is explained in *Rapid Java Application Development Using JBuilder 3.*

Check Boxes

A *check box* is a component that enables the user to toggle a choice on or off, like a light switch.

To create a check box, use the following constructor:

- `public JCheckBox()`

  This default constructor creates an unselected empty check box.

- `public JCheckBox(String text)`

  This creates an unselected check box with the specified text.

- `public JCheckBox(String text, boolean selected)`

  This creates a check box with a text and specifies whether the check box is initially selected.

- `public JCheckBox(Icon icon)`

  This creates an unselected check box with an icon.

- `public JCheckBox(Icon icon, boolean selected)`

  This creates a check box with an icon and specifies whether the check box is initially selected.

- `public JCheckBox(String text, Icon icon)`

  This creates an unselected check box with an icon and a text.

- `public JCheckBox(String text, Icon icon, boolean selected)`

  This creates a check box with an icon and a text, and specifies whether the check box is initially selected.

In addition to `text`, `icon`, `mnemonic`, `verticalAlignment`, `horizontalAlignment`, `horizontalTextPosition`, and `verticalTextPosition`, `JCheckBox` has the following property:

- `selected`: Specifies whether the check box is selected.

`JCheckBox` can generate `ActionEvent` and `ItemEvent`, among many other events. The following code shows you how to implement `itemStateChanged` handler to determine whether a box is checked or unchecked in response to an `ItemEvent`:

```
public void itemStateChanged(ItemEvent e)
{
  // Make sure the source is a JCheckBox
  if (e.getSource() instanceof JCheckBox)
    if (jchk1.isSelected())
      // Process the selection for jchk1;
    if (jchk2.isSelected())
      // Process the selection for jchk2;
}
```

Example 9.7 Using Check Boxes

This example gives a program that displays a message in overlapping font styles. The message can be displayed in bold and italic at the same time, or can be displayed in the center of the panel. The output of a sample run of the program is given in Figure 9.12.

```
// CheckBoxDemo.java: Use check boxes to select one or more choices
import java.awt.BorderLayout;
import java.awt.FlowLayout;
import java.awt.Color;
import java.awt.Font;
import java.awt.event.*;
import javax.swing.*;

public class CheckBoxDemo extends JFrame implements ItemListener
{
  // Declare check boxes
  private JCheckBox jchkCentered, jchkBold, jchkItalic;

  // Declare a panel for displaying message
  private MessagePanel messagePanel;

  // Main method
  public static void main(String[] args)
  {
    CheckBoxDemo frame = new CheckBoxDemo();
    // frame.setDefaultCloseOperation(JFrame.EXIT_ON_CLOSE);
    frame.pack();
    frame.setVisible(true);
  }

  // Constructor
  public CheckBoxDemo()
  {
    setTitle("Check Box Demo");

    // Create the message panel
    messagePanel = new MessagePanel();
    messagePanel.setMessage("Welcome to Java!");
    messagePanel.setBackground(Color.yellow);

    // Put three check boxes in panel p
    JPanel p = new JPanel();
    p.setLayout(new FlowLayout());
    p.add(jchkCentered = new JCheckBox("Centered"));
    p.add(jchkBold = new JCheckBox("Bold"));
    p.add(jchkItalic = new JCheckBox("Italic"));

    // Set keyboard mnemonics
    jchkCentered.setMnemonic('C');
    jchkBold.setMnemonic('B');
    jchkItalic.setMnemonic('I');

    // Place messagePanel and p in the frame
    getContentPane().setLayout(new BorderLayout());
    getContentPane().add(messagePanel, BorderLayout.CENTER);
    getContentPane().add(p, BorderLayout.SOUTH);

    // Register listeners on jchkCentered, jchkBold, and jchkItalic
    jchkCentered.addItemListener(this);
    jchkBold.addItemListener(this);
    jchkItalic.addItemListener(this);
  }
```

continues

Example 9.7 continued

```
    // Handle check box selection
    public void itemStateChanged(ItemEvent e)
    {
      if (e.getSource() instanceof JCheckBox)
      {
        // Determine a font style
        int selectedStyle = 0;
        if (jchkBold.isSelected())
          selectedStyle = selectedStyle+Font.BOLD;
        if (jchkItalic.isSelected())
          selectedStyle = selectedStyle+Font.ITALIC;

        // Set font for the message
        messagePanel.setFont(new Font("Serif", selectedStyle, 20));
        if (jchkCentered.isSelected())
          messagePanel.setCentered(true);
        else
          messagePanel.setCentered(false);

        // Make sure the message is repainted
        messagePanel.repaint();
      }
    }
  }
```

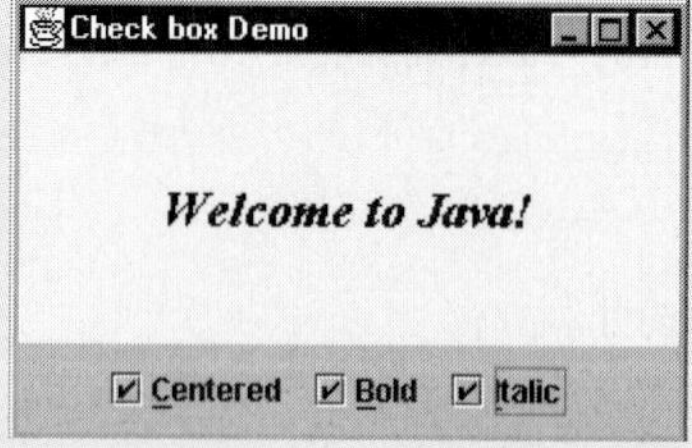

Figure 9.12 *The program uses three* `JCheckBox` *components to let the user choose the font style for the message displayed and specify whether the message is centered.*

Example Review

The program displays the message using the `MessagePanel` class. The check boxes are labeled "Centered," "Bold," and "Italic." The user can toggle a check box on and off to select or deselect it.

Upon selecting a check box, the handler, `itemStateChanged(ItemEvent e)`, is invoked to determine the state of each check box and combines all selected fonts. The font styles are `int` constants: `Font.BOLD` and `Font.ITALIC`. Font styles are combined by adding together the selected integers representing the fonts.

The keyboard mnemonics 'C', 'B', and 'I' are set on the check boxes "Centered," "Bold," and "Italic," respectively. You can use a mouse gesture or a shortcut key to select a check box.

Since invoking the methods `setFont` and `setCentered` in `MessagePanel` does not repaint the viewing area in the panel, you must invoke the `repaint` method to refresh the panel.

Radio Buttons

Radio buttons, also known as *option buttons*, enable you to choose a single item from a list of choices. In appearance radio buttons resemble check boxes, but check boxes display a square that is either checked or blank, whereas radio buttons display a circle that is either filled (if selected) or blank (not selected).

The constructors of `JRadioButton`, shown directly below, are similar to the constructors of `JCheckBox`.

- `public JRadioButton()`

  This default constructor creates an unselected empty radio button.

- `public JRadioButton(String text)`

  This creates an unselected radio button with the specified text.

- `public JRadioButton(String text, boolean selected)`

  This creates a radio button with a text and specifies whether the radio button is initially selected.

- `public JRadioButton(Icon icon)`

  This creates an unselected radio button with an icon.

- `public JRadioButton(Icon icon, boolean selected)`

  This creates a radio button with an icon and specifies whether the radio button is initially selected.

- `public JRadioButton(String text, Icon icon)`

  This creates an unselected radio button with an icon and a text.

- `public JRadioButton(String text, Icon icon, boolean selected)`

  This creates a radio button with an icon and a text, and specifies whether the radio button is initially selected.

Here is how to create a radio button with a text and an icon:

```
JRadioButton jrb = new JRadioButton(
  "My Radio Button", new ImageIcon("imagefile.gif"));
```

The radio buttons are added to a container just like buttons. To group the radio buttons, you need to create an instance of `java.swing.ButtonGroup` and use the `add` method to add them to it, as follows:

```
ButtonGroup btg = new ButtonGroup();
btg.add(jrb1);
btg.add(jrb2);
```

This code creates a radio button group so that `jrb1` and `jrb2` are selected mutually exclusively.

`JRadioButton` has such properties as `text`, `icon`, `mnemonic`, `verticalAlignment`, `horizontalAlignment`, `selected`, `horizontalTextPosition`, and `verticalTextPosition`.

`JRadioButton` can generate `ActionEvent` and `ItemEvent` among many other events. The following code shows you how to implement the `itemStateChanged` handler to determine whether a box is checked or unchecked in response to an `ItemEvent`:

```
public void itemStateChanged(ItemEvent e)
{
  // Make sure the source is a JRadioButton
  if (e.getSource() instanceof JRadioButton)
    if (jrb1.isSelected())
      // Process the selection for jrb1
    else if (jrb2.isSelected())
      // Process the selection for jrb2
}
```

Example 9.8 Using Radio Buttons

This example gives a program that simulates traffic lights. The program lets the user select one of three lights: red, yellow, or green. When a radio button is selected, the light is turned on, and only one light can be on at a time. No light is on when the program starts. Figure 9.13 contains the output of a sample run of the program.

```
// RadioButtonDemo.java: Use radio buttons to select a choice
import java.awt.*;
import java.awt.event.*;
import javax.swing.*;

public class RadioButtonDemo extends JFrame implements ItemListener
{
  // Declare radio buttons
  private JRadioButton jrbRed, jrbYellow, jrbGreen;

  // Declare a radio button group
  private ButtonGroup btg = new ButtonGroup();

  // Declare a traffic light display panel
  private Light light;

  // Main method
  public static void main(String[] args)
  {
    RadioButtonDemo frame = new RadioButtonDemo();
    // frame.setDefaultCloseOperation(JFrame.EXIT_ON_CLOSE);
    frame.setSize(250, 170);
    frame.setVisible(true);
  }

  // Constructor
  public RadioButtonDemo()
  {
    setTitle("RadioButton Demo");

    // Add traffic light panel to panel p1
    JPanel p1 = new JPanel();
    p1.setSize(200, 200);
    p1.setLayout(new FlowLayout(FlowLayout.CENTER));
    light = new Light();
    light.setSize(40, 90);
    p1.add(light);

    // Put the radio button in Panel p2
    JPanel p2 = new JPanel();
```

```
    p2.setLayout(new FlowLayout());
    p2.add(jrbRed = new JRadioButton("Red", false));
    p2.add(jrbYellow = new JRadioButton("Yellow", false));
    p2.add(jrbGreen = new JRadioButton("Green", false));

    // Set keyboard mnemonics
    jrbRed.setMnemonic('R');
    jrbYellow.setMnemonic('Y');
    jrbGreen.setMnemonic('G');

    // Group radio buttons
    btg.add(jrbRed);
    btg.add(jrbYellow);
    btg.add(jrbGreen);

    // Place p1 and p2 in the frame
    getContentPane().setLayout(new BorderLayout());
    getContentPane().add(p1, BorderLayout.CENTER);
    getContentPane().add(p2, BorderLayout.SOUTH);

    // Register listeners for check boxes
    jrbRed.addItemListener(this);
    jrbYellow.addItemListener(this);
    jrbGreen.addItemListener(this);
  }

  // Handle checkbox events
  public void itemStateChanged(ItemEvent e)
  {
    if (jrbRed.isSelected())
      light.turnOnRed(); // Set red light
    if (jrbYellow.isSelected())
      light.turnOnYellow(); // Set yellow light
    if (jrbGreen.isSelected())
      light.turnOnGreen(); // Set green light
  }
}

// Three traffic lights shown in a panel
class Light extends JPanel
{
  private boolean red;
  private boolean yellow;
  private boolean green;

  public Light()
  {
    red = false;
    yellow = false;
    green = false;
  }

  // Set red light on
  public void turnOnRed()
  {
    red = true;
    yellow = false;
    green = false;
    repaint();
  }

  // Set yellow light on
  public void turnOnYellow()
  {
```

continues

Example 9.8 continued

```
    red = false;
    yellow = true;
    green = false;
    repaint();
  }

  // Set green light on
  public void turnOnGreen()
  {
    red = false;
    yellow = false;
    green = true;
    repaint();
  }

  // Display lights
  public void paintComponent(Graphics g)
  {
    super.paintComponent(g);

    if (red)
    {
      g.setColor(Color.red);
      g.fillOval(10, 10, 20, 20);
      g.setColor(Color.black);
      g.drawOval(10, 35, 20, 20);
      g.drawOval(10, 60, 20, 20);
      g.drawRect(5, 5, 30, 80);
    }
    else if (yellow)
    {
      g.setColor(Color.yellow);
      g.fillOval(10, 35, 20, 20);
      g.setColor(Color.black);
      g.drawRect(5, 5, 30, 80);
      g.drawOval(10, 10, 20, 20);
      g.drawOval(10, 60, 20, 20);
    }
    else if (green)
    {
      g.setColor(Color.green);
      g.fillOval(10, 60, 20, 20);
      g.setColor(Color.black);
      g.drawRect(5, 5, 30, 80);
      g.drawOval(10, 10, 20, 20);
      g.drawOval(10, 35, 20, 20);
    }
    else
    {
      g.setColor(Color.black);
      g.drawRect(5, 5, 30, 80);
      g.drawOval(10, 10, 20, 20);
      g.drawOval(10, 35, 20, 20);
      g.drawOval(10, 60, 20, 20);
    }
  }

  // Set preferred size
  public Dimension getPreferredSize()
  {
    return new Dimension(40, 90);
  }
}
```

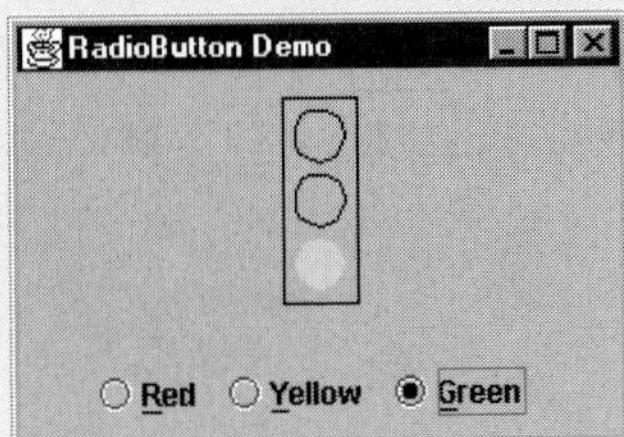

Figure 9.13 *The radio buttons are grouped to let you select one color in the group to control traffic lights.*

Example Review

The lights are displayed on a panel. The program groups the radio buttons in a panel and places it below the traffic light panel. The `BorderLayout` is used to arrange these components.

The `Light` class, a subclass of `JPanel`, contains the methods `turnOnRed()`, `turnOnYellow()`, and `turnOnGreen()` to control the lights. For example, use `light.turnOnRed()` to turn on the red light, where light is an instance of `Light`.

The program creates a `ButtonGroup btg` and puts three `JRadioButton` instances (`jrbRed`, `jrbYellow`, and `jrbGreen`) in the group. When the user checks a box in the group, the handler, `itemStateChanged(ItemEvent e)`, determines which radio button is selected, using the `isSelected()` method, and turns on the corresponding light.

The `getPreferredSize()` method is overridden to set the preferred size to 40 by 90. This is just the right size for displaying the traffic lights.

Borders

Borders are one of the interesting new Swing components features. You can set a border on any object of the `JComponent` class, but often it is useful to set a titled border on a `JPanel` that groups a set of related user interface components.

There are several basic types of borders to choose from. The titled border is the most useful of them. To create a titled border, use the following statement:

```
Border titledBorder = new TitledBorder("A Title");
```

`Border` is the interface for all types of borders. `TitledBorder` is an implementation of `Border` with a title. You can create a border as desired by using the following properties:

- `title`: The title of the border.
- `titleColor`: The color of the title.
- `titleFont`: The font of the title.

- `titleJustification`: Specifies `Border.LEFT`, `Border.CENTER`, or `Border.RIGHT` for left, center, or right title justification.
- `titlePosition`: One of the six values (`Border.ABOVE_TOP`, `Border.TOP`, `Border.BELOW_TOP`, `Border.ABOVE_BOTTOM`, `Border.BOTTOM`, `Border.BELOW_BOTTOM`) that specify the title position above the border line, on the border line, or below the border line.
- `border`: The `TitledBorder` itself has the `border` property for building composite borders.

The other types of borders can be created by using the following classes:

- `BevelBorder`: Creates a 3D-look border that can be lowered or raised. To construct a `BevelBorder`, use the following constructor, which creates a `BevelBorder` with the specified `bevelType` (`BevelBorder.LOWERED` or `BevelBorder.RAISED`)

```
public BevelBorder(int bevelType)
```

- `EtchedBorder`: Creates an etched border that can be etched-in or etched-out. You can use its default constructor to construct an `EtchedBorder` with a lowered border. `EtchedBorder` has a property `etchType` with the value `LOWERED` or `RAISED`.
- `LineBorder`: Creates a line border of arbitrary thickness and a single color. To create a `LineBorder`, use the following constructor:

```
public LineBorder(Color c, int thickness)
```

- `MatteBorder`: Creates a matte-like border padded with the icon images. To create a `MatteBorder`, use the following constructor:

```
public MatteBorder(Icon tileIcon)
```

- `EmptyBorder`: Creates a border with border space but no drawings. To create an `EmptyBorder`, use the following constructor:

```
public EmptyBorder(int top, int left, int bottom, int right)
```

NOTE

All the border classes and interfaces are grouped in the package `javax.swing.border`.

Swing also provides the `javax.swing.BorderFactory` class, which contains static methods for creating borders. Some of the static methods are:

- `public static TitledBorder createTitledBorder(String title)`
- `public static Border createLoweredBevelBorder()`
- `public static Border createRaisedBevelBorder()`
- `public static Border createLineBorder(Color color)`

- `public static Border createLineBorder(Color color, int thickness)`
- `public static Border createEtchedBorder()`
- `public static Border createEtchedBorder(Color highlight, Color shadow)`
- `public static Border createEmptyBorder()`
- `public static Border createEmptyBorder(int top, int left, int bottom, int right)`
- `public static MatteBorder createMatteBorder(int top, int left, int bottom, int right, Color color)`
- `public static MatteBorder createMatteBorder(int top, int left, int bottom, int right, Icon tileIcon)`
- `public static Border createCompoundBorder(Border outsideBorder, Border insideBorder)`

For example, to create an etched border, use the following statement:

```
Border border = BorderFactory.createEtchedBorder();
```

Example 9.9 Using Borders

This example gives a program that creates and displays various types of borders. You can select a border with a title or without a title. For a border without a title, you can choose a border style from Lowered Bevel, Raised Bevel, Etched, Line, Matte, or Empty. For a border with a title, you can specify the title position and justification. You can also embed another border into a titled border. Figure 9.14 displays a sample run of the program.

```
// BorderDemo.java: Use borders for JComponent components
import java.awt.*;
import java.awt.event.ActionListener;
import java.awt.event.ActionEvent;
import javax.swing.*;
import javax.swing.border.*;

public class BorderDemo extends JFrame implements ActionListener
{
  // Declare a panel for displaying message
  private MessagePanel messagePanel;

  // A check box for selecting a border with or without a title
  private JCheckBox jchkTitled;

  // Radio buttons for border styles
  private JRadioButton jrbLoweredBevel, jrbRaisedBevel,
    jrbEtched, jrbLine, jrbMatte, jrbEmpty;

  // Radio buttons for titled border options
  private JRadioButton jrbAboveBottom, jrbBottom,
    jrbBelowBottom, jrbAboveTop, jrbTop, jrbBelowTop,
    jrbLeft, jrbCenter, jrbRight;

  // TitledBorder for the message panel
  private TitledBorder messagePanelBorder = new TitledBorder("");
```

continues

Example 9.9 continued

```
// Main method
public static void main(String[] args)
{
  BorderDemo frame = new BorderDemo();
  // frame.setDefaultCloseOperation(JFrame.EXIT_ON_CLOSE);
  frame.pack();
  frame.setVisible(true);
}

// Constructor
public BorderDemo()
{
  setTitle("Border Demo");

  // Create a MessagePanel instance and set colors
  messagePanel = new MessagePanel("Display the border type");
  messagePanel.setCentered(true);
  messagePanel.setBackground(Color.yellow);
  messagePanel.setBorder(messagePanelBorder);

  // Place title position radio buttons
  JPanel jpPosition = new JPanel();
  jpPosition.setLayout(new GridLayout(3, 2));
  jpPosition.add(
    jrbAboveBottom = new JRadioButton("ABOVE_BOTTOM"));
  jpPosition.add(jrbAboveTop = new JRadioButton("ABOVE_TOP"));
  jpPosition.add(jrbBottom = new JRadioButton("BOTTOM"));
  jpPosition.add(jrbTop = new JRadioButton("TOP"));
  jpPosition.add(
    jrbBelowBottom = new JRadioButton("BELOW_BOTTOM"));
  jpPosition.add(jrbBelowTop = new JRadioButton("BELOW_TOP"));
  jpPosition.setBorder(new TitledBorder("Position"));

  // Place title justification radio buttons
  JPanel jpJustification = new JPanel();
  jpJustification.setLayout(new GridLayout(3,1));
  jpJustification.add(jrbLeft = new JRadioButton("LEFT"));
  jpJustification.add(jrbCenter = new JRadioButton("CENTER"));
  jpJustification.add(jrbRight = new JRadioButton("RIGHT"));
  jpJustification.setBorder(new TitledBorder("Justification"));

  // Create panel jpTitleOptions to hold jpPosition and
  // jpJustification
  JPanel jpTitleOptions = new JPanel();
  jpTitleOptions.setLayout(new BorderLayout());
  jpTitleOptions.add(jpPosition, BorderLayout.CENTER);
  jpTitleOptions.add(jpJustification, BorderLayout.EAST);

  // Create Panel jpTitle to hold a check box and title position
  // radio buttons, and title justification radio buttons
  JPanel jpTitle = new JPanel();
  jpTitle.setBorder(new TitledBorder("Border Title"));
  jpTitle.setLayout(new BorderLayout());
  jpTitle.add(jchkTitled = new JCheckBox("Titled"),
    BorderLayout.NORTH);
  jpTitle.add(jpTitleOptions, BorderLayout.CENTER);

  // Group radio buttons for title position
  ButtonGroup btgTitlePosition = new ButtonGroup();
  btgTitlePosition.add(jrbAboveBottom);
  btgTitlePosition.add(jrbBottom);
  btgTitlePosition.add(jrbBelowBottom);
  btgTitlePosition.add(jrbAboveTop);
  btgTitlePosition.add(jrbTop);
  btgTitlePosition.add(jrbBelowTop);
```

```
    // Group radio buttons for title justification
    ButtonGroup btgTitleJustification = new ButtonGroup();
    btgTitleJustification.add(jrbLeft);
    btgTitleJustification.add(jrbCenter);
    btgTitleJustification.add(jrbRight);

    // Create Panel jpBorderStyle to hold border style radio buttons
    JPanel jpBorderStyle = new JPanel();
    jpBorderStyle.setBorder(new TitledBorder("Border Style"));
    jpBorderStyle.setLayout(new GridLayout(6, 1));
    jpBorderStyle.add(jrbLoweredBevel =
      new JRadioButton("Lowered Bevel"));
    jpBorderStyle.add(jrbRaisedBevel =
      new JRadioButton("Raised Bevel"));
    jpBorderStyle.add(jrbEtched = new JRadioButton("Etched"));
    jpBorderStyle.add(jrbLine = new JRadioButton("Line"));
    jpBorderStyle.add(jrbMatte = new JRadioButton("Matte"));
    jpBorderStyle.add(jrbEmpty = new JRadioButton("Empty"));

    // Group radio buttons for border styles
    ButtonGroup btgBorderStyle = new ButtonGroup();
    btgBorderStyle.add(jrbLoweredBevel);
    btgBorderStyle.add(jrbRaisedBevel);
    btgBorderStyle.add(jrbEtched);
    btgBorderStyle.add(jrbLine);
    btgBorderStyle.add(jrbMatte);
    btgBorderStyle.add(jrbEmpty);

    // Create Panel jpAllChoices to place jpTitle and jpBorderStyle
    JPanel jpAllChoices = new JPanel();
    jpAllChoices.setLayout(new BorderLayout());
    jpAllChoices.add(jpTitle, BorderLayout.CENTER);
    jpAllChoices.add(jpBorderStyle, BorderLayout.EAST);

    // Place panels in the frame
    getContentPane().setLayout(new BorderLayout());
    getContentPane().add(messagePanel, BorderLayout.CENTER);
    getContentPane().add(jpAllChoices, BorderLayout.SOUTH);

    // Register listeners
    jchkTitled.addActionListener(this);
    jrbAboveBottom.addActionListener(this);
    jrbBottom.addActionListener(this);
    jrbBelowBottom.addActionListener(this);
    jrbAboveTop.addActionListener(this);
    jrbTop.addActionListener(this);
    jrbBelowTop.addActionListener(this);
    jrbLeft.addActionListener(this);
    jrbCenter.addActionListener(this);
    jrbRight.addActionListener(this);
    jrbLoweredBevel.addActionListener(this);
    jrbRaisedBevel.addActionListener(this);
    jrbLine.addActionListener(this);
    jrbEtched.addActionListener(this);
    jrbMatte.addActionListener(this);
    jrbEmpty.addActionListener(this);
  }

  // Handle ActionEvents on check box and radio buttons
  public void actionPerformed(ActionEvent e)
  {
    // Get border style
    Border border = new EmptyBorder(2, 2, 2, 2);
```

continues

Example 9.9 continued

```
    if (jrbLoweredBevel.isSelected())
    {
      border = new BevelBorder(BevelBorder.LOWERED);
      messagePanel.setMessage("Lowered Bevel Style");
    }
    else if (jrbRaisedBevel.isSelected())
    {
      border = new BevelBorder(BevelBorder.RAISED);
      messagePanel.setMessage("Raised Bevel Style");
    }
    else if (jrbEtched.isSelected())
    {
      border = new EtchedBorder();
      messagePanel.setMessage("Etched Style");
    }
    else if (jrbLine.isSelected())
    {
      border = new LineBorder(Color.black, 5);
      messagePanel.setMessage("Line Style");
    }
    else if (jrbMatte.isSelected())
    {
      border = new MatteBorder(20, 20, 20, 20,
        new ImageIcon("images/swirl.gif"));
      messagePanel.setMessage("Matte Style");
    }
    else if (jrbEmpty.isSelected())
    {
      border = new EmptyBorder(2, 2, 2, 2);
      messagePanel.setMessage("Empty Style");
    }

    if (jchkTitled.isSelected())
    {
      // Get the title position and justification
      int titlePosition = TitledBorder.DEFAULT_POSITION;
      int titleJustification = TitledBorder.DEFAULT_JUSTIFICATION;

      if (jrbAboveBottom.isSelected())
        titlePosition = TitledBorder.ABOVE_BOTTOM;
      else if (jrbBottom.isSelected())
        titlePosition = TitledBorder.BOTTOM;
      else if (jrbBelowBottom.isSelected())
        titlePosition = TitledBorder.BELOW_BOTTOM;
      else if (jrbAboveTop.isSelected())
        titlePosition = TitledBorder.ABOVE_TOP;
      else if (jrbTop.isSelected())
        titlePosition = TitledBorder.TOP;
      else if (jrbBelowTop.isSelected())
        titlePosition = TitledBorder.BELOW_TOP;

      if (jrbLeft.isSelected())
        titleJustification = TitledBorder.LEFT;
      else if (jrbCenter.isSelected())
        titleJustification = TitledBorder.CENTER;
      else if (jrbRight.isSelected())
        titleJustification = TitledBorder.RIGHT;

      messagePanelBorder = new TitledBorder("A Title");
      messagePanelBorder.setBorder(border);
      messagePanelBorder.setTitlePosition(titlePosition);
      messagePanelBorder.setTitleJustification(titleJustification);
      messagePanelBorder.setTitle("A Title");
```

```
            messagePanel.setBorder(messagePanelBorder);
          }
          else
          {
            messagePanel.setBorder(border);
          }
        }
      }
```

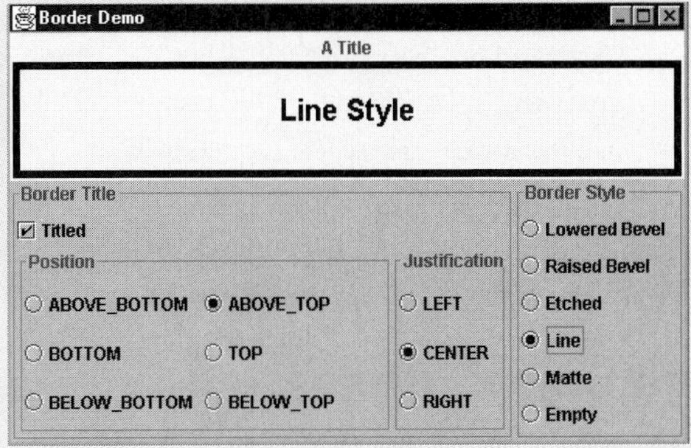

Figure 9.14 *The program demonstrates various types of borders.*

Example Review

This example uses many panels to group UI components to achieve the desired look. Figure 9.14 illustrates the relationship of these panels. The Border Title panel groups all the options for setting title properties. The position options are grouped in the Position panel. The justification options are grouped in the Justification panel. The Border Style panel groups the radio buttons for choosing Lowered Bevel, Raised Bevel, Etched, Line, Matte, and Empty borders.

The `MessagePanel` displays the selected border with or without a title, depending on the selection of the title check box. The `MessagePanel` also displays a message indicating which type of border is being used, depending on the selection of the radio button in the Border Style panel.

The `TitledBorder` can be mixed with other borders. To do so, simply create an instance of `TitledBorder`, and use the `setBorder` method to embed a new border into the `TitledBorder`.

The `MatteBorder` can be used to display icons on the border, as shown in Figure 9.15.

continues

Example 9.9 continued

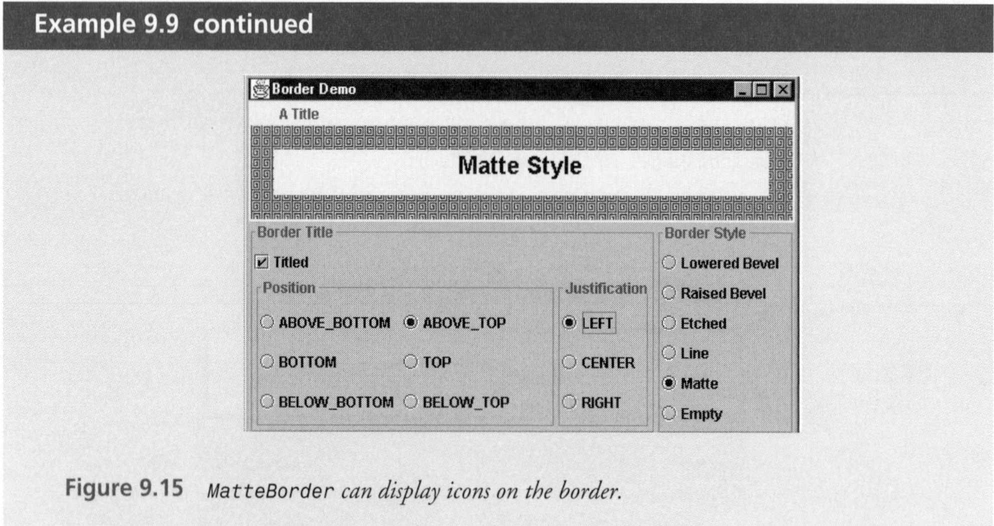

Figure 9.15 `MatteBorder` *can display icons on the border.*

Message Dialog Boxes

A *dialog box* is normally used as a temporary window to receive additional information from the user or to provide notification that some event has occurred. You can build a variety of dialog boxes in Java. This section introduces the *message dialog box*. This simple and frequently used dialog box displays a message to alert the user, as shown in Figure 9.16.

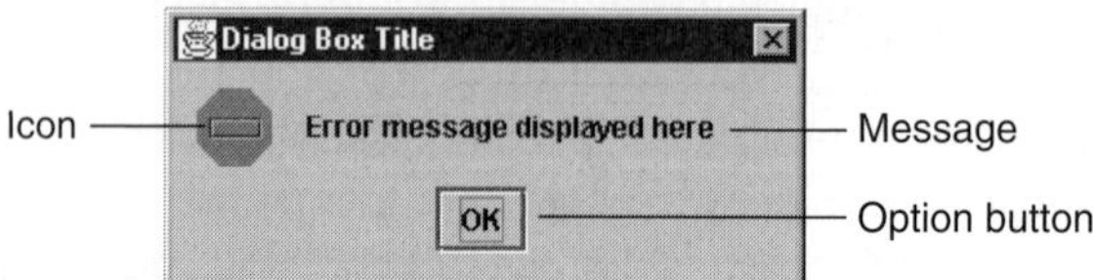

Figure 9.16 *A message dialog box displays a message.*

To display a message dialog box, as shown in Figure 9.16, use the static `showMessageDialog` method in the `JOptionPane` class, as follows:

```
public static void showMessageDialog(Component parentComponent,
                                     Object message,
                                     String title,
                                     int messageType)
```

The `parentComponent` is the parent component of the dialog box, from which the dialog box is launched. The `message` is the object to display. Often you use a string for `message`. The `title` is the title of the dialog box. The `messageType` determines the type of message to be displayed. There are five message types:

- `ERROR_MESSAGE`
- `INFORMATION_MESSAGE`
- `PLAIN_MESSAGE`

- WARNING_MESSAGE
- QUESTION_MESSAGE

Each type, except for the PLAIN_MESSAGE type, has an associated icon. You can use the following method to supply your own icons:

```
public static void showMessageDialog(Component parentComponent,
                                     Object message,
                                     String title,
                                     int messageType,
                                     Icon icon)
```

Example 9.10 Using Message Dialogs

This example gives a program that displays student exam grades. The user enters the SSN and the password, then clicks the Find Score button (see Figure 9.17) to show the student name and the grade. If the SSN is incorrect, a message dialog box displays the message SSN not found, as shown in Figure 9.18. If the password is incorrect, a message dialog box displays Password does not match SSN, as shown in Figure 9.19. In either case, the user must click the OK button in the message dialog box to go back to the main frame.

```
// DialogDemo.java: Use message dialog box to select information
import java.awt.*;
import java.awt.event.*;
import javax.swing.*;

public class DialogDemo extends JFrame implements ActionListener
{
  // Create sample student information in arrays
  // with name, SSN, password, and grade
  private String[][] student =
    {
      {"John Willow", "111223333", "a450", "A"},
      {"Jim Brown", "111223334", "b344", "B"},
      {"Bill Beng", "111223335", "33342csa", "C"},
      {"George Wall", "111223336", "343rea2", "D"},
      {"Jill Jones", "111223337", "34g", "E"}
    };

  // Declare text fields for last name, password, full name and score
  private JTextField jtfSSN;
  private JPasswordField jpfPassword;
  private JTextField jtfName;
  private JTextField jtfGrade;
  private JButton jbtFind;

  // Main method
  public static void main(String[] args)
  {
    DialogDemo frame = new DialogDemo();
    // frame.setDefaultCloseOperation(JFrame.EXIT_ON_CLOSE);
    frame.pack();
    frame.setVisible(true);
  }

  public DialogDemo()
  {
    setTitle("Find The Score");
```

continues

Example 9.10 continued

```
    // Panel jpLabels to hold labels
    JPanel jpLabels = new JPanel();
    jpLabels.setLayout(new GridLayout(4, 1));
    jpLabels.add(new JLabel("Enter SSN"));
    jpLabels.add(new JLabel("Enter Password"));
    jpLabels.add(new JLabel("Name"));
    jpLabels.add(new JLabel("Score"));

    // Panel jpTextFields to hold text fields and password
    JPanel jpTextFields = new JPanel();
    jpTextFields.setLayout(new GridLayout(4, 1));
    jpTextFields.add(jtfSSN = new JTextField(10));
    jpTextFields.add(jpfPassword = new JPasswordField(10));
    jpTextFields.add(jtfName = new JTextField(10));
    jpTextFields.add(jtfGrade = new JTextField(10));
    jtfName.setEditable(false);
    jtfGrade.setEditable(false);

    // Panel p1 for holding jpLabels and jpTextFields
    JPanel p1 = new JPanel();
    p1.setLayout(new BorderLayout());
    p1.add(jpLabels, BorderLayout.WEST);
    p1.add(jpTextFields, BorderLayout.CENTER);

    // Panel p2 for holding the Find button
    JPanel p2 = new JPanel();
    p2.setLayout(new FlowLayout(FlowLayout.RIGHT));
    p2.add(jbtFind = new JButton("Find Score"));

    // Place panels into the frame
    getContentPane().setLayout(new BorderLayout());
    getContentPane().add(p1, BorderLayout.CENTER);
    getContentPane().add(p2, BorderLayout.SOUTH);

    // Register listener for jbtFind
    jbtFind.addActionListener(this);
  }

  public void actionPerformed(ActionEvent e)
  {
    // Find the student in the database
    int index = find(jtfSSN.getText().trim(),
      new String(jpfPassword.getPassword()));

    if (index == -1)
    {
      JOptionPane.showMessageDialog(this, "SSN not found",
        "For Your Information", JOptionPane.INFORMATION_MESSAGE);
    }
    else if (index == -2)
    {
      JOptionPane.showMessageDialog(this,
        "Password does not match SSN",
        "For Your Information", JOptionPane.INFORMATION_MESSAGE);
    }
    else
    {
      // Display name and score
      jtfName.setText(student[index][0]);
      jtfGrade.setText(student[index][3]);
    }
  }

  // Find the student who matched user name and password
```

```
    // return the index if found; return -1 if SSN is not in
    // the database, and return -2 if password does not match SSN
    public int find(String SSN, String pw)
    {
      // Find a student who matches SSN and pw
      for (int i=0; i<student.length; i++)
        if (student[i][1].equals(SSN) && student[i][2].equals(pw))
          return i;

      // Determine if the SSN is in the database
      for (int i=0; i<student.length; i++)
        if (student[i][1].equals(SSN))
          return -2;

      // Return -1 since the SSN and pw do not match
      return -1;
    }
  }
```

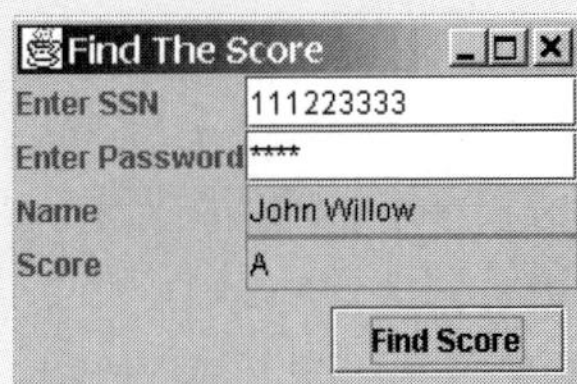

Figure 9.17 *The main frame lets the user enter the SSN and password, and then click the Find Score button to display name and score.*

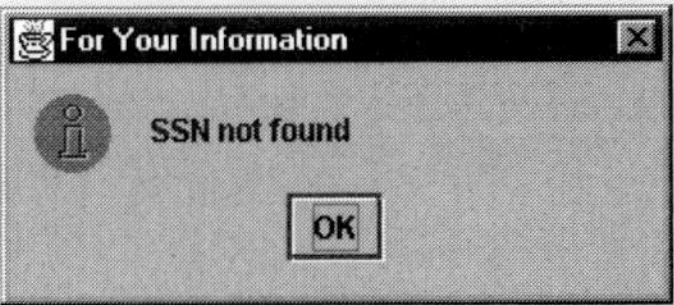

Figure 9.18 *The message box displays the error message* SSN not found.

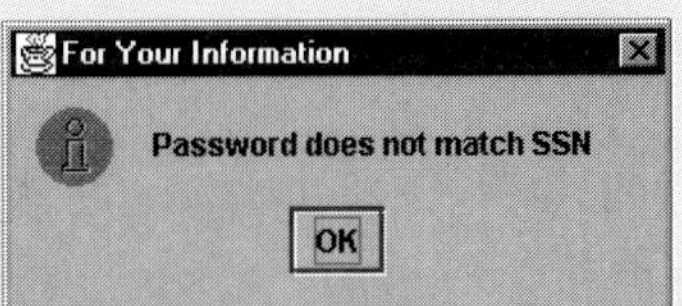

Figure 9.19 *The message box displays the error message* Password does not match SSN.

Example Review

The message dialog box is *modal*, which means that no other window can be accessed before the message dialog is dismissed.

continues

Example 9.10 continued

The student information is stored in the two-dimensional array `student[][]`. Each element in the array consists of name, SSN, password, and grade. If the SSN and password match `student[i][1]` and `student[i][2]` for some `i`, the name (`student[i][0]`) and the grade (`grade[i][3]`) are displayed in the main frame.

When the program starts, the main frame comes up first, as shown in Figure 9.17. If the user enters a wrong SSN, the message SSN not found appears in the dialog box, as shown in Figure 9.18. If the user enters a correct SSN, but a wrong password, the message Password does not match SSN appears in the dialog box, as shown in Figure 9.19. When the correct SSN and password are received, the user's name and grade are displayed in the frame, as shown in Figure 9.17.

The statement

```
JOptionPane.showMessageDialog(this, "SSN not found",
        "For Your Information", JOptionPane.INFORMATION_MESSAGE);
```

displays a message dialog box of the INFORMATION_MESSAGE type with the message "SSN not found" and the title "For Your Information."

The `find(SSN, pw)` method defined in the main frame returns the index of the student array element that matches the SSN and the password, returns -1 if the SSN is not found, and returns -2 if the password does not match the SSN.

The `JPasswordField` component, a subclass of `JTextField`, is specifically designed to receive the password. The characters entered in a `JPasswordField` are echo displayed in * to protect them from being seen by bystanders. To get the password, you need to use the `getPassword()` method, which returns the password in an array of `char`, not a string.

Menus

Menus make selection easier, and are widely used in window applications. Java provides five classes to implement menus: `JMenuBar`, `JMenu`, `JMenuItem`, `JCheckBoxMenuItem`, and `JRadioButtonMenuItem`.

`JMenuBar` is a top-level menu component used to hold the menus. Menus consist of *menu items* that the user can select (or toggle on or off). A menu item can be an instance of `JMenuItem`, `JCheckBoxMenuItem`, or `JRadioButtonMenuItem`.

The sequence of implementing menus in Java is as follows:

1. Create a menu bar and associate it with a frame.

```
JFrame frame = new JFrame();
frame.setSize(300, 200);
frame.setVisible(true);
```

```
JMenuBar jmb = new JMenuBar();
frame.setJMenuBar(jmb);  // Attach a menu bar to a frame
```

This code creates a frame and a menu bar, and sets the menu bar in the frame.

2. Create menus.

   You can use the following constructor to create a menu:

   ```
   public JMenu(String label)
   ```

   The following is an example of creating menus:

   ```
   JMenu fileMenu = new JMenu("File");
   JMenu helpMenu = new JMenu("Help");
   jmb.add(fileMenu);
   jmb.add(helpMenu);
   ```

   This creates two menus labeled `File` and `Help`, as shown in Figure 9.20. The menus will not be seen until they are added to an instance of `JMenuBar`.

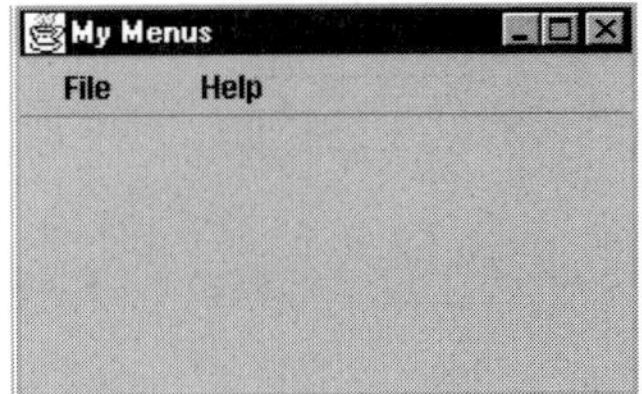

Figure 9.20 *The menu bar appears below the title bar on the frame.*

3. Create menu items and add them to menus.

   ```
   fileMenu.add(new JMenuItem("New"));
   fileMenu.add(new JMenuItem("Open"));
   fileMenu.addSeparator();
   fileMenu.add(new JMenuItem("Print"));
   fileMenu.addSeparator();
   fileMenu.add(new JMenuItem("Exit"));
   ```

   This code adds the menu items New, Open, a separator bar, Print, another separator bar, and Exit, in this order, to the File menu, as shown in Figure 9.21.

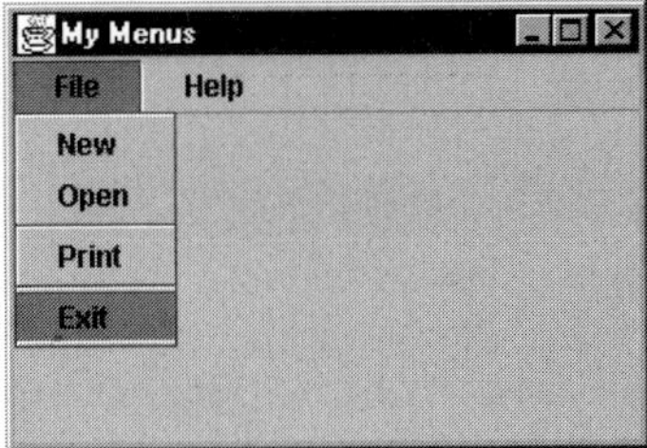

Figure 9.21 *Clicking a menu on the menu bar reveals the items under the menu.*

The `addSeparator()` method adds a separate bar in the menu.

3.1. Creating submenu items.

You can also embed menus inside menus so that the embedded menus become submenus. Here is an example:

```
JMenu softwareHelpSubMenu = new JMenu("Software");
JMenu hardwareHelpSubMenu = new JMenu("Hardware");
helpMenu.add(softwareHelpSubMenu);
helpMenu.add(hardwareHelpSubMenu);
softwareHelpSubMenu.add(new JMenuItem("Unix"));
softwareHelpSubMenu.add(new JMenuItem("NT"));
softwareHelpSubMenu.add(new JMenuItem("Win95"));
```

This code adds two submenus, `softwareSubHelpMenu` and `hardwareHelpSubMenu`, in `helpMenu`. The menu items `Unix`, `NT`, and `Win95` are added to `softwareSubHelpMenu` (see Figure 9.22).

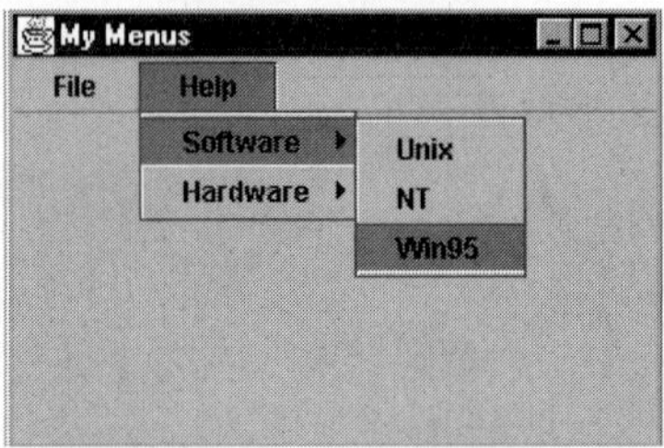

Figure 9.22 *Clicking a menu item reveals the secondary items under the menu item.*

3.2. Creating check box menu items.

You can also add a `JCheckBoxMenuItem` to a `JMenu`. `JCheckBoxMenuItem` is a subclass of `JMenuItem` that adds a Boolean state to the `JMenuItem`, and displays a check when its state is true. You can click the menu item to turn it on and off. For example, the following statement adds the check box menu item `Check it` (see Figure 9.23).

```
helpMenu.add(new JCheckBoxMenuItem("Check it"));
```

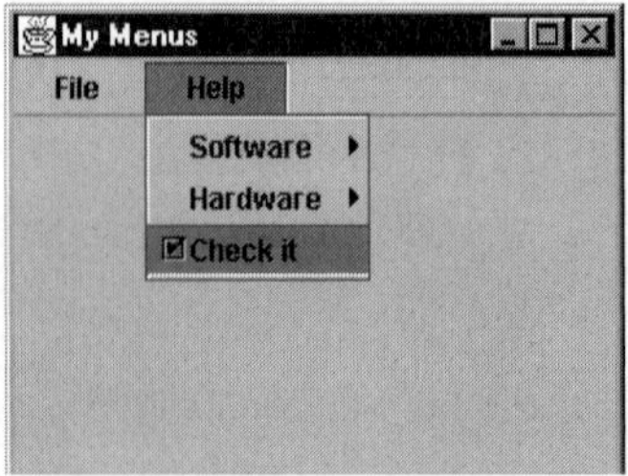

Figure 9.23 *A check box menu item lets you check or uncheck a menu item just like a check box.*

3.3. Creating radio button menu items.

You can also add radio buttons to a menu, using the `JRadioButtonMenuItem` class. This is often useful when you have a group of mutually exclusive choices in the menu. For example, the following statements add a submenu named Color and a set of radio buttons for choosing a color (see Figure 9.24):

```
JMenu colorHelpSubMenu = new JMenu("Color");
helpMenu.add(colorHelpSubMenu);
JRadioButtonMenuItem jrbmiBlue, jrbmiYellow, jrbmiRed;
colorHelpSubMenu.add(jrbmiBlue =
  new JRadioButtonMenuItem("Blue"));
colorHelpSubMenu.add(jrbmiYellow =
  new JRadioButtonMenuItem("Yellow"));
colorHelpSubMenu.add(jrbmiRed =
  new JRadioButtonMenuItem("Red"));
ButtonGroup btg = new ButtonGroup();
btg.add(jrbmiBlue);
btg.add(jrbmiYellow);
btg.add(jrbmiRed);
```

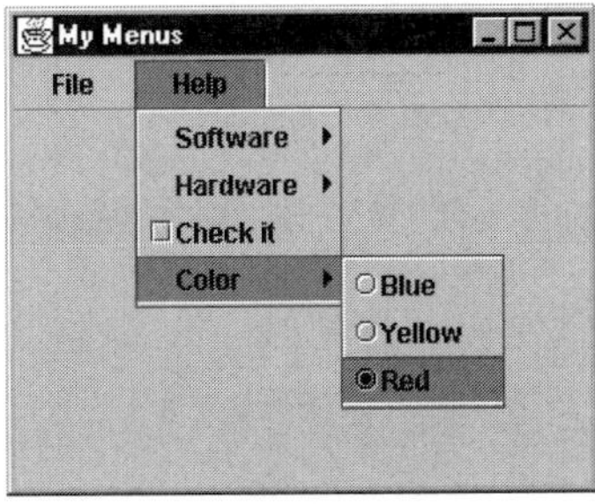

Figure 9.24 *You can use* `JRadioButtonMenuItem` *to choose a mutually exclusive menu choice.*

4. The menu items generate `ActionEvent`. Your program must implement the `actionPerformed` handler to respond to the menu selection. The following is an example:

```
public void actionPerformed(ActionEvent e)
{
  String actionCommand = e.getActionCommand();

  // Make sure the source is JMenuItem
  if (e.getSource() instanceof JMenuItem)
    if ("New".equals(actionCommand))
      respondToNew();
}
```

This code executes the method `respondToNew()` when the menu item labeled `New` is selected.

Image Icons, Keyboard Mnemonics, and Keyboard Accelerators

The menu components `JMenu`, `JMenuItem`, `JCheckBoxMenuItem`, and `JRadioButton-MenuItem` have the `icon` and `mnemonic` properties. For example, using the following code, you can set icons for the New and Open menu items, and set keyboard mnemonic for File, Help, New, and Open:

```
JMenuItem jmiNew, jmiOpen;
fileMenu.add(jmiNew = new JMenuItem("New"));
fileMenu.add(jmiOpen = new JMenuItem("Open"));
jmiNew.setIcon(new ImageIcon("images/new.gif"));
jmiOpen.setIcon(new ImageIcon("images/open.gif"));
helpMenu.setMnemonic('H');
fileMenu.setMnemonic('F');
jmiNew.setMnemonic('N');
jmiOpen.setMnemonic('O');
```

The new icons and mnemonics are shown in Figure 9.25. You can also use `JMenuItem` constructors like the ones that follow to construct and set an icon or mnemonic in one statement.

```
public JMenuItem(String label, Icon icon);

public JMenuItem(String label, int mnemonic);
```

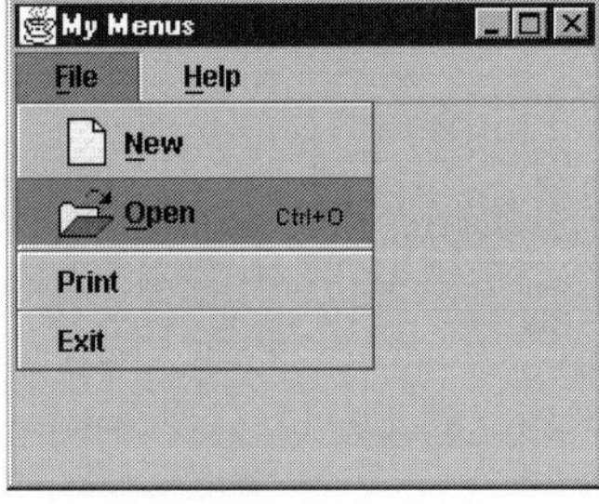

Figure 9.25 *You can set image icons, keyboard mnemonics, and keyboard accelerators in menus.*

To select a menu, you press the ALT key and the mnemonic key. For example, press ALT+F to select the File menu, and then press ALT+O to select the Open menu item. Keyboard mnemonics is useful, but it only lets you select menu items from the currently open menu. Key accelerators, however, let you select a menu item directly by pressing the CTRL and accelerator keys. For example, by using the following code, you can attach the accelerator key CTRL+O to the Open menu item:

```
jmiOpen.setAccelerator(KeyStroke.getKeyStroke
  (KeyEvent.VK_O, ActionEvent.CTRL_MASK));
```

The `setAccelerator` method takes an object `KeyStroke`. The static method `getKeyStroke` in the `KeyStroke` class creates an instance of the key stroke. `VK_O` is a constant representing the `O` key, and `CTRL_MASK` is a constant indicating that the `CTRL` key is associated with the keystroke.

Example 9.11 Using Menus

This example gives a program to create a user interface that does arithmetic. The interface contains labels and text fields for Number 1, Number 2, and Result. The Result text field displays the result of the arithmetic operation between Number 1 and Number 2.

The program has four buttons labeled Add, Subtract, Multiply, and Divide. The program will also create a menu to perform the same operation. The user can choose the operation either from buttons or from menu selections. Figure 9.26 contains a sample run of the program.

```
// MenuDemo.java: Use menus to move message in a panel
import java.awt.*;
import java.awt.event.*;
import javax.swing.*;

public class MenuDemo extends JFrame implements ActionListener
{
  // Text fields for Number 1, Number 2, and Result
  private JTextField jtfNum1, jtfNum2, jtfResult;

  // Buttons "Add", "Subtract", "Multiply" and "Divide"
  private JButton jbtAdd, jbtSub, jbtMul, jbtDiv;

  // Menu items "Add", "Subtract", "Multiply","Divide" and "Close"
  private JMenuItem jmiAdd, jmiSub, jmiMul, jmiDiv, jmiClose;

  // Main Method
  public static void main(String[] args)
  {
    MenuDemo frame = new MenuDemo();
    // frame.setDefaultCloseOperation(JFrame.EXIT_ON_CLOSE);
    frame.pack();
    frame.setVisible(true);
  }

  // Default Constructor
  public MenuDemo()
  {
    setTitle("Menu Demo");

    // Create menu bar
    JMenuBar jmb = new JMenuBar();

    // Set menu bar to the frame
    setJMenuBar(jmb);

    // Add menu "Operation" to menu bar
    JMenu operationMenu = new JMenu("Operation");
    operationMenu.setMnemonic('O');
    jmb.add(operationMenu);

    // Add menu "Exit" in menu bar
    JMenu exitMenu = new JMenu("Exit");
    exitMenu.setMnemonic('E');
    jmb.add(exitMenu);

    // Add menu items with mnemonics to menu "Operation"
    operationMenu.add(jmiAdd= new JMenuItem("Add", 'A'));
    operationMenu.add(jmiSub = new JMenuItem("Subtract", 'S'));
    operationMenu.add(jmiMul = new JMenuItem("Multiply", 'M'));
    operationMenu.add(jmiDiv = new JMenuItem("Divide", 'D'));
    exitMenu.add(jmiClose = new JMenuItem("Close", 'C'));
```

continues

Example 9.11 continued

```
    // Set keyboard accelerators
    jmiAdd.setAccelerator(
      KeyStroke.getKeyStroke(KeyEvent.VK_A, ActionEvent.CTRL_MASK));
    jmiSub.setAccelerator(
      KeyStroke.getKeyStroke(KeyEvent.VK_S, ActionEvent.CTRL_MASK));
    jmiMul.setAccelerator(
      KeyStroke.getKeyStroke(KeyEvent.VK_M, ActionEvent.CTRL_MASK));
    jmiDiv.setAccelerator(
      KeyStroke.getKeyStroke(KeyEvent.VK_D, ActionEvent.CTRL_MASK));

    // Panel p1 to hold text fields and labels
    JPanel p1 = new JPanel();
    p1.setLayout(new FlowLayout());
    p1.add(new JLabel("Number 1"));
    p1.add(jtfNum1 = new JTextField(3));
    p1.add(new JLabel("Number 2"));
    p1.add(jtfNum2 = new JTextField(3));
    p1.add(new JLabel("Result"));
    p1.add(jtfResult = new JTextField(4));
    jtfResult.setEditable(false);

    // Panel p2 to hold buttons
    JPanel p2 = new JPanel();
    p2.setLayout(new FlowLayout());
    p2.add(jbtAdd = new JButton("Add"));
    p2.add(jbtSub = new JButton("Subtract"));
    p2.add(jbtMul = new JButton("Multiply"));
    p2.add(jbtDiv = new JButton("Divide"));

    // Add panels to the frame
    getContentPane().setLayout(new BorderLayout());
    getContentPane().add(p1, BorderLayout.CENTER);
    getContentPane().add(p2, BorderLayout.SOUTH);

    // Register listeners
    jbtAdd.addActionListener(this);
    jbtSub.addActionListener(this);
    jbtMul.addActionListener(this);
    jbtDiv.addActionListener(this);
    jmiAdd.addActionListener(this);
    jmiSub.addActionListener(this);
    jmiMul.addActionListener(this);
    jmiDiv.addActionListener(this);
    jmiClose.addActionListener(this);
  }

  // Handle ActionEvent from buttons and menu items
  public void actionPerformed(ActionEvent e)
  {
    String actionCommand = e.getActionCommand();

    // Handle button events
    if (e.getSource() instanceof JButton)
    {
      if ("Add".equals(actionCommand))
        calculate('+');
      else if ("Subtract".equals(actionCommand))
        calculate('-');
      else if ("Multiply".equals(actionCommand))
        calculate('*');
      else if ("Divide".equals(actionCommand))
        calculate('/');
    }
```

```
    else if (e.getSource() instanceof JMenuItem)
    {
      // Handle menu item events
      if ("Add".equals(actionCommand))
        calculate('+');
      else if ("Subtract".equals(actionCommand))
        calculate('-');
      else if ("Multiply".equals(actionCommand))
        calculate('*');
      else if ("Divide".equals(actionCommand))
        calculate('/');
      else if ("Close".equals(actionCommand))
        System.exit(0);
    }
  }

  // Calculate and show the result in jtfResult
  private void calculate(char operator)
  {
    // Obtain Number 1 and Number 2
    int num1 = (Integer.parseInt(jtfNum1.getText().trim()));
    int num2 = (Integer.parseInt(jtfNum2.getText().trim()));
    int result = 0;

    // Perform selected operation
    switch (operator)
    {
      case '+': result = num1 + num2;
                break;
      case '-': result = num1 - num2;
                break;
      case '*': result = num1 * num2;
                break;
      case '/': result = num1 / num2;
    }

    // Set result in jtfResult
    jtfResult.setText(String.valueOf(result));
  }
}
```

Figure 9.26 *Arithmetic operations can be performed by clicking buttons or by choosing menu items from the Operation menu.*

Example Review

The program creates a menu bar, `jmb`, which holds two menus: `operationMenu` and `exitMenu`. The `operationMenu` contains four menu items for doing arithmetic: Add, Subtract, Multiply, and Divide. The `exitMenu` contains the menu item Close for exiting the program. The menu items in the Operation menu are created with keyboard mnemonics and accelerators.

continues

Example 9.11 continued

The user enters two numbers in the number fields. When an operation is chosen from the menu, its result, involving two numbers, is displayed in the Result field. The user may also click the buttons to perform the same operation.

The private method `calculate(char operator)` retrieves operands from the text fields in Number 1 and Number 2, applies the binary operator on the operands, and sets the result in the Result text field.

Creating Multiple Windows

Occasionally, you may want to create multiple windows in an application. Suppose that your application has two tasks: displaying traffic lights and doing arithmetic calculations. You can design a main frame with two buttons representing the two tasks. When the user clicks one of the buttons, the application opens a new window to perform the specified task. The new windows are called *subwindows,* and the main frame is called the *main window.*

To create a subwindow from an application, you need to create a subclass of `JFrame` that defines the task and tells the new window what to do. You can then create an instance of this subclass in the application and launch the new window by setting the frame instance to be visible.

Example 9.12 Creating Multiple Windows

This example creates a main window with a text area in the scroll pane, and a button named "Show Histogram." When the user clicks the button, a new window appears that displays a histogram to show the occurrence of the letters in the text area. Figure 9.27 contains a sample run of the program.

```
// MultipleWindowsDemo.java: Display histogram in a separate window
import java.awt.*;
import java.awt.event.*;
import javax.swing.*;

public class MultipleWindowsDemo extends JFrame
  implements ActionListener
{
  private JTextArea jta;
  private JButton jbtShowHistogram = new JButton("Show Histogram");
  private Histogram histogram = new Histogram();

  // Create a new frame to hold the histogram panel
  private JFrame histogramFrame = new JFrame();

  // Construct the frame
  public MultipleWindowsDemo()
  {
    // Store text area in a scroll pane
    JScrollPane scrollPane = new JScrollPane(jta = new JTextArea());

    scrollPane.setPreferredSize(new Dimension(300, 200));
```

```
    jta.setWrapStyleWord(true);
    jta.setLineWrap(true);

    // Place scroll pane and button in the frame
    getContentPane().add(scrollPane, BorderLayout.CENTER);
    getContentPane().add(jbtShowHistogram, BorderLayout.SOUTH);

    // Register listener
    jbtShowHistogram.addActionListener(this);

    // Create a new frame to hold the histogram panel
    histogramFrame.getContentPane().add(histogram);
    histogramFrame.pack();
    histogramFrame.setTitle("Histogram");
  }

  // Handle the button action
  public void actionPerformed(ActionEvent e)
  {
    // Count the letters in the text area
    int[] count = countLetters();

    // Set the letter count to histogram for display
    histogram.showHistogram(count);

    // Show the frame
    histogramFrame.setVisible(true);
  }

  // Count the letters in the text area
  private int[] countLetters()
  {
    // Count for 26 letters
    int[] count = new int[26];

    // Get contents from the text area
    String text = jta.getText();

    // Count occurrence of each letter (case insensitive)
    for (int i=0; i<text.length(); i++)
    {
      char character = text.charAt(i);

      if ((character >= 'A') && (character <= 'Z'))
      {
        count[(int)character-65]++; // The ASCII for 'A' is 65
      }
      else if ((character >= 'a') && (character <= 'z'))
      {
        count[(int)character-97]++; // The ASCII for 'a' is 97
      }
    }

    return count; // Return the count array
  }

  // Main method
  public static void main(String[] args)
  {
    MultipleWindowsDemo frame = new MultipleWindowsDemo();
    // frame.setDefaultCloseOperation(JFrame.EXIT_ON_CLOSE);
    frame.setTitle("Multiple Windows Demo");
    frame.pack();
    frame.setVisible(true);
  }
}
```

continues

Example 9.12 continued

```
// Histogram.java: Display a histogram in a panel to show the
// occurrence of the letters
import javax.swing.*;
import java.awt.*;

public class Histogram extends JPanel
{
  // Count the occurrence of 26 letters
  private int count[];

  // Set the count and display histogram
  public void showHistogram(int[] count)
  {
    this.count = count;
    repaint();
  }

  // Paint the histogram
  public void paintComponent(Graphics g)
  {
    if (count == null) return; // No display if count is null

    super.paintComponent(g);

    // Find the panel size and bar width and interval dynamically
    int width = getSize().width;
    int height = getSize().height;
    int interval = (width-40)/count.length;
    int individualWidth = (int)(((width-40)/24)*0.60);

    // Find the maximum count. The maximum count has the highest bar
    int maxCount = 0;
    for (int i=0; i<count.length; i++)
    {
      if (maxCount < count[i])
        maxCount = count[i];
    }

    // x is the start position for the first bar in the histogram
    int x = 30;

    // Draw a horizontal base line
    g.drawLine(10, height-45, width-10, height-45);
    for (int i=0; i<count.length; i++)
    {
      // Find the bar height
      int barHeight =
        (int)(((double)count[i]/(double)maxCount)*(height-55));

      // Display a bar (i.e. rectangle)
      g.drawRect(x, height-45-barHeight, individualWidth,
        barHeight);

      // Display a letter under the base line
      g.drawString((char)(65+i)+"", x, height-30);

      // Move x for displaying the next character
      x += interval;
    }
  }

  public Dimension getPreferredSize()
  {
    return new Dimension(300, 300);
  }
}
```

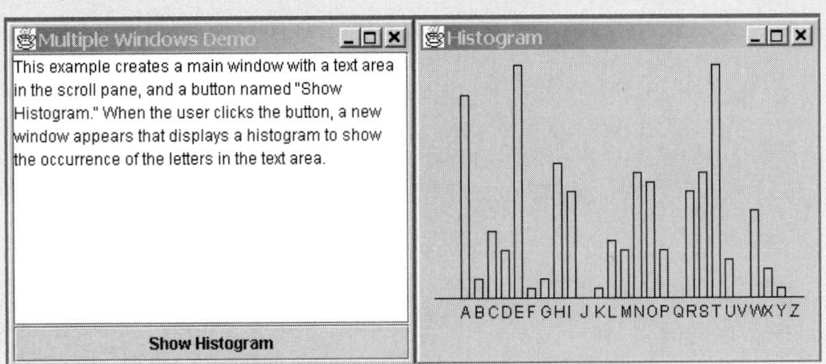

Figure 9.27 *The histogram is displayed in a separate frame.*

Example Review

The program contains two classes: `MultipleWindowsDemo` and `Histogram`. Their relationship is shown in Figure 9.28.

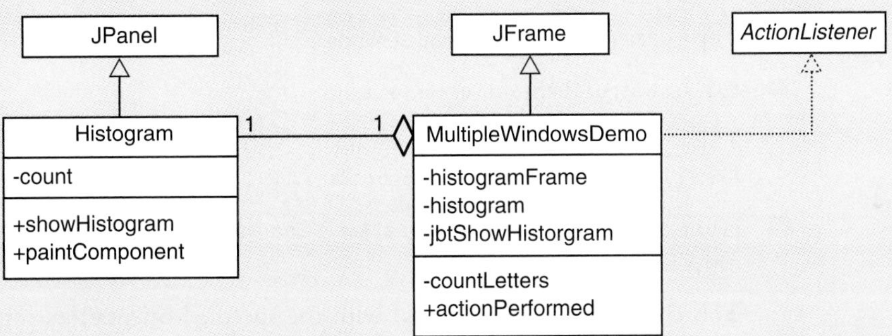

Figure 9.28 *`MultipleWindowsDemo` uses `Histogram` to display a histogram of the occurrence of the letters in a text area in the frame.*

`MultipleWindowsDemo` is a frame that holds a text area in a scroll pane and a button. `Histogram` is a subclass of `JPanel` that displays a histogram for the occurrence of letters in the text area.

When the user clicks the "Show Histogram" button, the handler counts the occurrence of letters in the text area. Letters are counted regardless of their case. Non-letter characters are not counted. The count is stored in an `int` array of 26 elements. The first element stores the count for letter 'a' or 'A', and the last element in the array stores the count for letter 'z' or 'Z'. The count array is passed to histogram for display.

`MultipleWindowsDemo` class also contains an instance of `JFrame`, named `histogramFrame`, which holds an instance of `Histogram`. When the user clicks the "Show Histogram" button, `histogramFrame` is set to visible to display the histogram.

continues

Example 9.12 continued

The `MultipleWindowsDemo` class contains a main method. The main method creates an instance of `MultipleWindowsDemo` and displays the frame. The The height and width of the bars in the histogram are determined dynamically according to the window size of the histogram.

You cannot add an instance of `JFrame` to a container. For example, adding `histogramFrame` to the main frame would cause a runtime exception. However, you can create a frame instance and set it visible to launch a new window.

Scrollbars

A *scrollbar* is a control that enables the user to select from a range of values. Scrollbars appear in two styles, *horizontal* and *vertical.*

You can use the following constructors to create a scrollbar:

- `public JScrollBar()`

  This constructs a new vertical scrollbar.

- `public JScrollBar(int orientation)`

  This constructs a new scrollbar with the specified orientation (`JScrollBar.HORIZONTAL` or `JScrollBar.VERTICAL`).

- `public JScrollbar(int orientation, int value, int visible, int minimum, int maximum)`

  This constructs a new scrollbar with the specified orientation, initial value, visible bubble size, and minimum and maximum values, as shown in Figure 9.29.

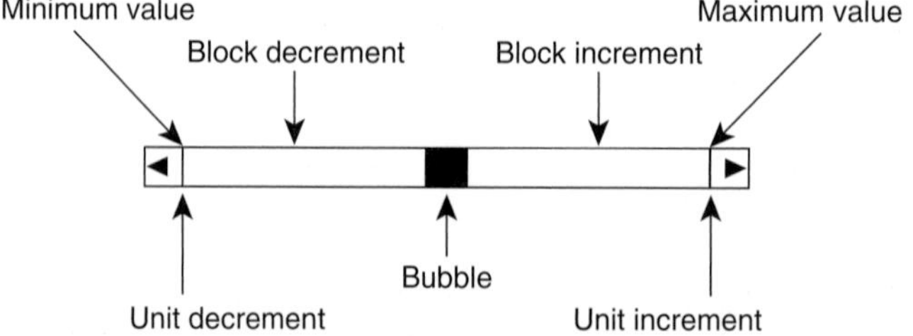

Figure 9.29 *A scrollbar represents a range of values graphically.*

`JScrollBar` has the following properties:

- **`orientation`**: Specifies horizontal or vertical style, with `JScrollBar.HORIZONTAL` (0) for horizontal and `JScrollBar.VERTICAL` (1) for vertical.

- **maximum**: The maximum value the scrollbar represents when the bubble reaches the right end of the scrollbar for horizontal style or the bottom of the scrollbar for vertical style.
- **minimum**: The minimum value the scrollbar represents when the bubble reaches the left end of the scrollbar for horizontal style or the top of the scrollbar for vertical style.
- **visibleAmount:** The relative width of the scrollbar's bubble. The actual width appearing on the screen is determined by the maximum value and the value of `visibleAmount`.
- **value**: Represents the current value of the scrollbar. Normally, a program should change a scrollbar's value by calling the `setValue()` method. The `setValue()` method simultaneously and synchronously sets the minimum, maximum, visible amount, and value properties of a scrollbar, so that they are mutually consistent.
- **blockIncrement**: The value added (subtracted) when the user activates the block increment (decrement) area of the scrollbar, as shown in Figure 9.29. The `blockIncrement` property, which is new in JDK 1.1, supersedes the `pageIncrement` property used in JDK 1.02.
- **unitIncrement**: The value added (subtracted) when the user activates the unit increment (decrement) area of the scrollbar, as shown in Figure 9.29. The `unitIncrement` property, which is new in JDK 1.1, supersedes the `lineIncrement` property used in JDK 1.02.

NOTE

The width of the scrollbar's track corresponds to `maximum+visibleAmount`. When a scrollbar is set to its maximum value, the left side of the bubble is at `maximum`, and the right side is at `maximum+visibleAmount`.

Normally, the user changes the value of the scrollbar by making a gesture with the mouse. For example, the user can drag the scrollbar's bubble up and down, or click in the scrollbar's unit increment or block increment areas. Keyboard gestures can also be mapped to the scrollbar. By convention, the Page Up and Page Down keys are equivalent to clicking in the scrollbar's block increment and block decrement areas.

When the user changes the value of the scrollbar, the scrollbar generates an instance of `AdjustmentEvent`, which is passed to any registered listeners. An object that wishes to be notified of changes to the scrollbar's value should implement `adjustmentValueChanged` method in the `AdjustmentListener` interface defined in the package `java.awt.event`.

Example 9.13 Using Scrollbars

This example uses horizontal and vertical scrollbars to control a message displayed on a panel. The horizontal scrollbar is used to move the message to the left or the right, and the vertical scrollbar to move it up and down. A sample run of the program is shown in Figure 9.30.

```
// ScrollBarDemo.java: Use scrollbars to move the message
import java.awt.*;
import java.awt.event.*;
import javax.swing.*;

public class ScrollBarDemo extends JFrame
  implements AdjustmentListener
{
  // Declare scrollbars
  JScrollBar jscbHort, jscbVert;

  // Declare a MessagePanel
  MessagePanel messagePanel;

  // Main method
  public static void main(String[] args)
  {
    ScrollBarDemo frame = new ScrollBarDemo();
    // frame.setDefaultCloseOperation(JFrame.EXIT_ON_CLOSE);
    frame.pack();
    frame.setVisible(true);
  }

  // Constructor
  public ScrollBarDemo()
  {
    setTitle("ScrollBar Demo");

    // Create a vertical scrollbar
    jscbVert = new JScrollBar();
    jscbVert.setOrientation(Adjustable.VERTICAL);

    // Create a horizontal scrollbar
    jscbHort = new JScrollBar();
    jscbHort.setOrientation(Adjustable.HORIZONTAL);

    // Add scrollbars and message panel to the frame
    messagePanel = new MessagePanel("Welcome to Java");
    getContentPane().setLayout(new BorderLayout());
    getContentPane().add(messagePanel, BorderLayout.CENTER);
    getContentPane().add(jscbVert, BorderLayout.EAST);
    getContentPane().add(jscbHort, BorderLayout.SOUTH);

    // Register listener for the scrollbars
    jscbHort.addAdjustmentListener(this);
    jscbVert.addAdjustmentListener(this);
  }

  // Handle scrollbar adjustment actions
  public void adjustmentValueChanged(AdjustmentEvent e)
  {
    if (e.getSource() == jscbHort)
    {
      // getValue() and getMaximumValue() return int, but for better
      // precision, use double
      double value = jscbHort.getValue();
      double maximumValue = jscbHort.getMaximum();
      double newX =
        (value*messagePanel.getSize().width/maximumValue);
```

```
        messagePanel.setXCoordinate((int)newX);
        messagePanel.repaint();
      }
      else if (e.getSource() == jscbVert)
      {
        // getValue() and getMaximumValue() return int, but for better
        // precision, use double
        double value = jscbVert.getValue();
        double maximumValue = jscbVert.getMaximum();
        double newY =
          (value*messagePanel.getSize().height/maximumValue);
        messagePanel.setYCoordinate((int)newY);
        messagePanel.repaint();
      }
    }
  }
```

Figure 9.30 *The scrollbars move the message on a panel horizontally and vertically.*

Example Review

The program creates an instance of `MessagePanel` (`messagePanel`) and two scrollbars (`jscbVert` and `jscbHort`). `messagePanel` is placed in the center of the frame; `jscbVert` and `jscbHort` are placed in the east and south sections of the frame, respectively.

You can specify the orientation of the scrollbar in the constructor or use the `setOrientation()` method. By default, the property value is 100 for `maximum`, 0 for `minimum`, 10 for `pageIncrement`, and 10 for `visibleAmount`.

When the user drags the bubble, or clicks the increment or decrement unit, the value of the scrollbar changes. An instance of `AdjustmentEvent` is generated and passed to the listener by invoking the `adjustmentValueChanged` handler. Since there are two scrollbars in the frame, the `e.getSource()` method is used to determine the source of the event. The vertical scrollbar moves the message up and down, and the horizontal bar moves the message to right and left.

The maximum value of the vertical scrollbar corresponds to the height of the panel, and the maximum value of the horizontal scrollbar corresponds to the width of the panel. The ratio between current value and the maximum of the horizontal scrollbar is the same as the ratio between the `x` value and the width of the panel. Similarly, the ratio between current value and the maximum of the vertical scrollbar is the same as the ratio between the `y` value and the height of the panel.

Scroll Panes

Often you need to use a scrollbar to scroll the contents of an object that does not fit completely into the viewing area. `JScrollBar` can be used for this purpose, but you have to *manually* write the code to implement scrolling with it. `JScrollPane` is a component that supports *automatic* scrolling without coding. It was used to scroll text area in Example 9.4. In fact, it can be used to scroll any subclass of `JComponent`.

A `JScrollPane` can be viewed as a specialized container with a view port for displaying the contained component. In addition to horizontal and vertical scrollbars, a `JScrollPane` can have a column header, a row header, and corners, as shown in Figure 9.31.

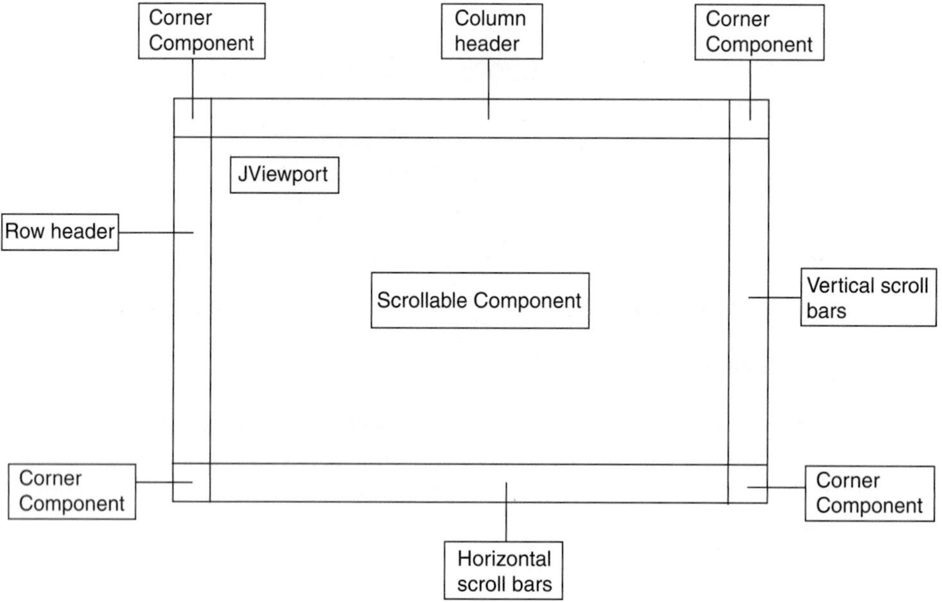

Figure 9.31 *A `JScrollPane` has a view port, optional horizontal and vertical bars, optional column and row headers, and optional corners.*

The view port is an instance of `JViewport` through which a scrollable component is displayed. When you add a component to the scroll pane, you are actually placing it in the scroll pane's view port.

To construct a `JScrollPane` instance, use the following constructors:

- `public JScrollPane()`

  Creates an empty scroll pane with a view port and no viewing component where both horizontal and vertical scrollbars appear when needed.

- `public JScrollPane(Component view)`

  Creates a scroll pane and view port to display the contents of the specified component, where both horizontal and vertical scrollbars appear whenever the component's contents are larger than the view.

- `JScrollPane(Component view, int vsbPolicy, int hsbPolicy)`

  Creates a scroll pane that displays the view component in a view port whose view position can be controlled with a pair of scrollbars.

- `JScrollPane(int vsbPolicy, int hsbPolicy)`

  Creates an empty scroll pane with specified scrollbar policies.

The constructor always creates a view port regardless of whether the viewing component is specified. The `vsbPolicy` parameter can be one of the following three values:

- `JScrollPane.VERTICAL_SCROLLBAR_AS_NEEDED`
- `JScrollPane.VERTICAL_SCROLLBAR_NEVER`
- `JScrollPane.VERTICAL_SCROLLBAR_ALWAYS`

The `hsbPolicy` parameter can be one of the following three values:

- `JScrollPane.HORIZONTAL_SCROLLBAR_AS_NEEDED`
- `JScrollPane.HORIZONTAL_SCROLLBAR_NEVER`
- `JScrollPane.HORIZONTAL_SCROLLBAR_ALWAYS`

The following properties of `JScrollPane` are often useful:

- `horizontalScrollBarPolicy`: Determines when the horizontal scrollbar appears in the scroll pane. The default value is `JScrollPane.HORIZONTAL_SCROLLBAR_AS_NEEDED`.
- `verticalScrollBarPolicy`: Determines when the vertical scrollbar appears in the scroll pane. The default value is `JScrollPane.VERTICAL_SCROLLBAR_AS_NEEDED`.
- `viewportView`: Specifies the component to be viewed in the view port.
- `viewportBorder`: Specifies a border around the view port in the scroll pane.
- `rowHeaderView`: Specifies the row header view component to be used in the scroll pane.
- `columnHeaderView`: Specifies the column header view component to be used in the scroll pane.

To set a corner component, use the following method:

```
public void setCorner(String key, Component corner)
```

The legal values for the key are:

- `JScrollPane.LOWER_LEFT_CORNER`
- `JScrollPane.LOWER_RIGHT_CORNER`
- `JScrollPane.UPPER_LEFT_CORNER`
- `JScrollPane.UPPER_RIGHT_CORNER`

Example 9.14 Using Scroll Panes

This example uses a scroll pane to browse a large map. The program lets you choose a map from a combo box and display it in the scroll pane, as shown in Figure 9.32.

```
// ScrollPaneDemo.java: Use scroll pane to view large maps
import java.awt.*;
import java.awt.event.*;
import javax.swing.*;
import javax.swing.border.*;

public class ScrollPaneDemo extends JFrame implements ItemListener
{
  // Create images in labels
  private JLabel lblIndianaMap =
    new JLabel(new ImageIcon("images/indianaMap.gif"));
  private JLabel lblOhioMap =
    new JLabel(new ImageIcon("images/ohioMap.gif"));

  // Declare a scroll pane to scroll map in the labels
  private JScrollPane jspMap;

  // Main method
  public static void main(String[] args)
  {
    ScrollPaneDemo frame = new ScrollPaneDemo();
    // frame.setDefaultCloseOperation(JFrame.EXIT_ON_CLOSE);
    frame.setSize(300, 300);
    frame.setVisible(true);
  }

  // Default constructor
  public ScrollPaneDemo()
  {
    setTitle("ScrollPane Demo");

    // Create a scroll pane with northern California map
    jspMap = new JScrollPane(lblIndianaMap);

    // Create a combo box for selecting maps
    JComboBox jcboMap = new JComboBox();
    jcboMap.addItem("Indiana");
    jcboMap.addItem("Ohio");

    // Panel p to hold combo box
    JPanel p = new JPanel();
    p.setLayout(new BorderLayout());
    p.add(jcboMap);
    p.setBorder(new TitledBorder("Select a map to display"));

    // Set row header, column header and corner header
    jspMap.setColumnHeaderView(
      new JLabel(new ImageIcon("images/horizontalRuler.gif")));
    jspMap.setRowHeaderView(
      new JLabel(new ImageIcon("images/verticalRuler.gif")));
    jspMap.setCorner(JScrollPane.UPPER_LEFT_CORNER,
      new CornerPanel(JScrollPane.UPPER_LEFT_CORNER));
    jspMap.setCorner(ScrollPaneConstants.UPPER_RIGHT_CORNER,
      new CornerPanel(JScrollPane.UPPER_RIGHT_CORNER));
    jspMap.setCorner(JScrollPane.LOWER_RIGHT_CORNER,
      new CornerPanel(JScrollPane.LOWER_RIGHT_CORNER));
    jspMap.setCorner(JScrollPane.LOWER_LEFT_CORNER,
      new CornerPanel(JScrollPane.LOWER_LEFT_CORNER));
```

```
    // Add the scroll pane and combo box panel to the frame
    getContentPane().add(jspMap, BorderLayout.CENTER);
    getContentPane().add(p, BorderLayout.NORTH);

    // Register listener
    jcboMap.addItemListener(this);
  }

  public void itemStateChanged(ItemEvent e)
  {
    String selectedItem = (String)e.getItem();

    if (selectedItem.equals("Indiana"))
    {
      // Set a new view in the view port
      jspMap.setViewportView(lblIndianaMap);
    }
    else if (selectedItem.equals("Ohio"))
    {
      // Set a new view in the view port
      jspMap.setViewportView(lblOhioMap);
    }

    // Revalidate the scroll pane
    jspMap.revalidate();
  }
}

// A panel displaying a line used for scroll pane corner
class CornerPanel extends JPanel implements ScrollPaneConstants
{
  // Line location
  private String location;

  // Constructor
  public CornerPanel(String location)
  {
    this.location = location;
  }

  // Draw a line depending on the location
  public void paintComponent(Graphics g)
  {
    super.paintComponents(g);

    if (location == "UPPER_LEFT_CORNER")
      g.drawLine(0, getSize().height, getSize().width, 0);
    else if (location == "UPPER_RIGHT_CORNER")
      g.drawLine(0, 0, getSize().width, getSize().height);
    else if (location == "LOWER_RIGHT_CORNER")
      g.drawLine(0, getSize().height, getSize().width, 0);
    else if (location == "LOWER_LEFT_CORNER")
      g.drawLine(0, 0, getSize().width, getSize().height);
  }
}
```

Example Review

The program creates a scroll pane to view image maps. The image maps are created using the `ImageIcon` class and are placed in labels. To view an image, the label that contains the image is placed in the scroll pane's view port.

continues

Example 9.14 continued

Figure 9.32 *The scroll pane can be used to scroll contents automatically.*

The scroll pane has a main view, a header view, a column view, and four corner views. Each view is a subclass of `Component`. Since `ImageIcon` is not a subclass of `Component`, it cannot be directly used as a view in the scroll pane. Instead the program places an `ImageIcon` to a label and uses the label as a view.

The `CornerPanel` is a subclass of `JPanel`, which is used to display a line. How the line is drawn depends on the `location` of the corner. The `location` is a string, passed in as a parameter in the `CornerPanel`'s constructor. The `CornerPanel` class also implements the `ScrollPaneConstants` interface. The constants representing the location of the four corners are available in `CornerPanel`.

Whenever a new map is selected, the label for displaying the map image is set to the scroll pane's view port. The `validate()` method must be invoked to cause the new image to be displayed. The `validate()` method causes a container to lay out its subcomponents again after the components it contains have been added to or modified.

Tabbed Panes

`JTabbedPane` is a useful Swing component that provides a set of mutually exclusive tabs for accessing multiple components. Usually you place the panels inside a `JTabbedPane` and associate a tab with each panel. `JTabbedPane` is easy to use, since the selection of the panel is handled automatically by clicking the corresponding tab. You can switch between a group of panels by clicking a tab with a given title and/or icon.

To construct a `JTabbedPane` instance, use the following constructors:

- `public JTabbedPane()`

  This creates an empty tabbed pane.

- `public JTabbedPane(int tabPlacement)`

This creates an empty `JTabbedPane` with the specified tab placement of either `SwingConstants.TOP`, `SwingConstants.BOTTOM`, `SwingConstants.LEFT`, or `SwingConstants.RIGHT`.

You can also set the tab placement using the following method:

```
public void setTabPlacement(int tabPlacement)
```

By default, the tabs are placed at top.

To add a component to a `JTabbedPane`, use the following `add` method:

```
add(Component component, Object constraints)
```

Where `component` is the component to be displayed when this tab is clicked and `constraints` can be a title for the tab.

Example 9.15 Using Tabbed Panes

This example uses a tabbed pane with four tabs to display four types of figures: Square, Rectangle, Circle, and Oval. You click the corresponding tab to select a figure to be displayed. You can also use the radio buttons to specify the tab placement. A sample run of the program is shown in Figure 9.33.

```
// TabbedPaneDemo.java: Use tabbed pane to select figures
import java.awt.*;
import java.awt.event.*;
import javax.swing.*;
import javax.swing.border.TitledBorder;

public class TabbedPaneDemo extends JFrame implements ItemListener
{
  // Create a tabbed pane to hold figure panels
  private JTabbedPane jtpFigures = new JTabbedPane();

  // Radio buttons for specifying where tab is placed
  private JRadioButton jrbTop, jrbLeft, jrbRight, jrbBottom;

  // Main method
  public static void main(String[] args)
  {
    TabbedPaneDemo frame = new TabbedPaneDemo();
    // frame.setDefaultCloseOperation(JFrame.EXIT_ON_CLOSE);
    frame.setSize(200, 300);
    frame.setVisible(true);
  }

  // Constructor
  public TabbedPaneDemo()
  {
    setTitle("Tabbed Pane Demo");

    jtpFigures.add(new FigurePanel(FigurePanel.SQUARE), "Square");
    jtpFigures.add(
      new FigurePanel(FigurePanel.RECTANGLE), "Rectangle");
    jtpFigures.add(new FigurePanel(FigurePanel.CIRCLE), "Circle");
    jtpFigures.add(new FigurePanel(FigurePanel.OVAL), "Oval");

    // Panel p to hold radio buttons for specifying tab location
    JPanel p = new JPanel();
    p.add(jrbTop = new JRadioButton("TOP"));
    p.add(jrbLeft = new JRadioButton("LEFT"));
```

continues

Example 9.15 continued

```
    p.add(jrbRight = new JRadioButton("RIGHT"));
    p.add(jrbBottom = new JRadioButton("BOTTOM"));
    p.setBorder(new TitledBorder("Specify tab location"));

    // Group radio buttons
    ButtonGroup btg = new ButtonGroup();
    btg.add(jrbTop);
    btg.add(jrbLeft);
    btg.add(jrbRight);
    btg.add(jrbBottom);

    // Place tabbed pane and panel p into the frame
    this.getContentPane().add(jtpFigures, BorderLayout.CENTER);
    this.getContentPane().add(p, BorderLayout.SOUTH);

    // Register listeners
    jrbTop.addItemListener(this);
    jrbLeft.addItemListener(this);
    jrbRight.addItemListener(this);
    jrbBottom.addItemListener(this);
  }

  // Handle radio button selection
  public void itemStateChanged(ItemEvent e)
  {
    if (jrbTop.isSelected())
      jtpFigures.setTabPlacement(SwingConstants.TOP);
    else if (jrbLeft.isSelected())
      jtpFigures.setTabPlacement(SwingConstants.LEFT);
    else if (jrbRight.isSelected())
      jtpFigures.setTabPlacement(SwingConstants.RIGHT);
    else if (jrbBottom.isSelected())
      jtpFigures.setTabPlacement(SwingConstants.BOTTOM);
  }
}

// The panel for displaying a figure
class FigurePanel extends JPanel
{
  final static int SQUARE = 1;
  final static int RECTANGLE = 2;
  final static int CIRCLE = 3;
  final static int OVAL = 4;
  private int figureType = 1;

  // Constructing a figure panel
  public FigurePanel(int figureType)
  {
    this.figureType = figureType;
  }

  // Drawing a figure on the panel
  public void paintComponent(Graphics g)
  {
    super.paintComponent(g);

    // Get the appropriate size for the figure
    int width = getSize().width;
    int height = getSize().height;
    int side = (int)(0.80*Math.min(width, height));

    switch (figureType)
    {
      case 1:
        g.drawRect((width-side)/2, (height-side)/2, side, side);

        break;
```

```
            case 2:
              g.drawRect((int)(0.1*width), (int)(0.1*height),
                (int)(0.8*width), (int)(0.8*height));

              break;
            case 3:
              g.drawOval((width-side)/2, (height-side)/2, side, side);
              break;
            case 4:
              g.drawOval((int)(0.1*width), (int)(0.1*height),
                (int)(0.8*width), (int)(0.8*height));
              break;
          }
        }
      }
```

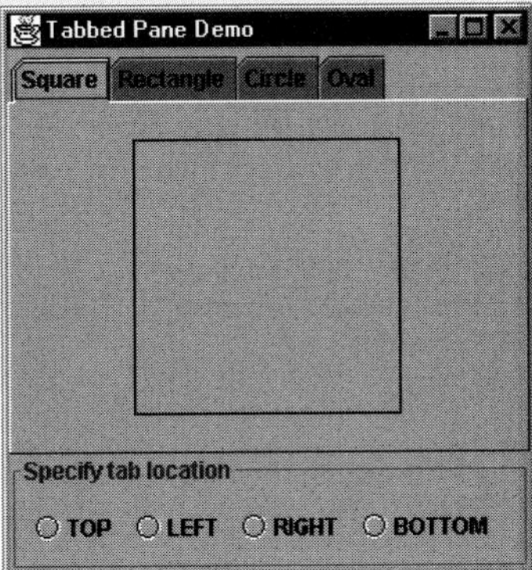

Figure 9.33 *A tabbed pane can be used to access multiple components using tabs.*

Example Review

The program creates a tabbed pane that holds four panels, each of which displays a figure. A panel is associated with a tab. Tabs are created using the `add` method and are titled Square, Rectangle, Circle, and Oval.

By default, the tabs are placed at the top of the tabbed pane. You can use the radio button to select a different placement, as shown in Figure 9.34.

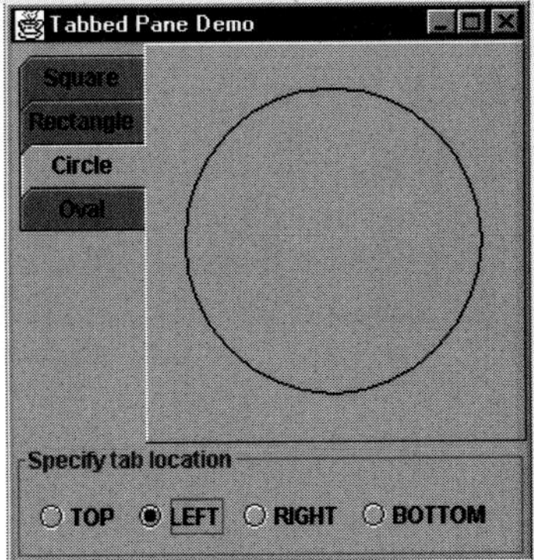

Figure 9.34 *The tabs can be placed at the top, bottom, left, or right of the tabbed pane.*

Chapter Summary

In this chapter, you learned how to create graphical user interfaces using JButton, JLabel, JTextField, JTextArea, JComboBox, JList, JCheckBox, JRadioButton, Border (TitledBorder, BevelBorder, LineBorder, EtchedBorder, MatteBorder, and EmptyBorder), message dialog boxes, JMenuBar, JMenu, JMenuItem, JCheckBoxMenuItem, JRadioButtonMenuItem, JScrollBar, JScrollPane, and JTabbedPane.

JButton is used to activate actions. The user expects something to happen when a button is clicked. Clicking a button generates the ActionEvent and invokes the listener to invoke the actionPerformed method.

JLabel is an area for displaying texts or images, or both. JTextField is used to accept user input into a string. JTextArea can accept multiple lines of strings.

JComboBox is a simple list of values to choose from. JList allows multiple selections. JCheckBox is for specifying whether the item is selected or not. JRadioButton is similar to JCheckBox, but is generally used to select a value exclusively.

A dialog box is commonly used to gather information from the user or show information to the user. This chapter introduced the showMessageDialog method in the JOptionPane class, which can be used to display a simple message box.

Menus can be placed in a frame or an applet. A menu bar is used to hold the menus. You must add a menu bar to the frame or applet using the setJMenuBar method, add menus to the menu bar, and add menu items to a menu.

Scrollbars are the controls for selecting from a range of values. You can create scrollbars using the JScrollBar class and specify horizontal or vertical scrollbars using the setOrientation method. JScrollPane provides automatic scrolling, so using it is convenient in most cases.

JTabbedPane can be used to select multiple panels using tabs. The tabs can be placed at the top, left, right, or bottom. Since tab selection is automatically implemented in JTabbedPane, clicking a tab causes the associated panel to be displayed.

To handle events generated by buttons, combo boxes, check boxes, radio buttons, menus, or scrollbars, you must register the listener object with the source object and implement the corresponding listener interface.

Since you cannot add an instance of the Window class to a container, you cannot put a frame into a frame. However, you can create a frame and set it to visible to launch a separate window in the program.

Review Questions

9.1 How do you create a button labeled "OK"? How do you change a label on a button? How do you set an icon in a button?

9.2 How do you create a label named "Address"? How do you change the name on a label? How do you set an icon in a label?

9.3 How do you create a text field with a width of 10 characters and the default text "Welcome to Java"?

9.4 How do you create a text area with 10 rows and 20 columns? How do you insert three lines into the text area? How do you create a scrollable text area?

9.5 How do you create a combo box, add three items to it, and retrieve a selected item?

9.6 How do you create a check box? How do you determine whether a box is checked?

9.7 How do you create a radio button? How do you group the radio buttons together? How do you determine whether a radio button is selected?

9.8 Can you have a border for any subclass of `JComponent`? How do you set a titled border for a panel?

9.9 How do you create the menus File, Edit, View, Insert, Format, and Help, and add menu items Toolbar, Format Bar, Ruler, Status Bar, and Options to the View menu? (See Figure 9.35.)

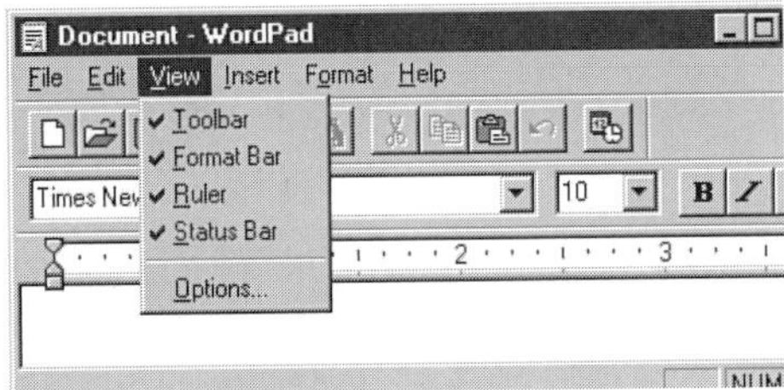

Figure 9.35 *Create a menu like this in WordPad, with menus and menu items.*

9.10 How do you create a vertical scrollbar? What event can a scrollbar generate?

9.11 How do you create a scroll pane to view an image file?

9.12 Describe how to create a simple message dialog box. Describe the message types used in the `JOptionPane` class.

9.13 Explain how to create and show multiple frames in an application.

9.14 What method causes the layout manager to lay out the components in a container again? When should a container be laid out again?

9.15 Suppose you want to display the same component named `c` in the four corners of a scroll pane named `jsp`. What would be wrong using the following statements?

```
jsp.setCorner(JScrollPane.UPPER_LEFT_CORNER, c);

jsp.setCorner(JScrollPane.UPPER_RIGHT_CORNER, c);

jsp.setCorner(JScrollPane.LOWER_RIGHT_CORNER, c);

jsp.setCorner(JScrollPane.LOWER_LEFT_CORNER, c);
```

(Since each corner view is an individual component, you need to create four separate objects.)

Programming Exercises

9.1 Rewrite Example 9.1 to add a group of radio buttons to select background colors. The available colors are red, yellow, white, gray, and green (see Figure 9.36).

Figure 9.36 *The <= and => buttons move the message on the panel, and you can also set the color for the message.*

9.2 Rewrite Example 9.3 to handle double values and perform subtract, multiply, and divide operations in addition to the add operation (see Figure 9.37).

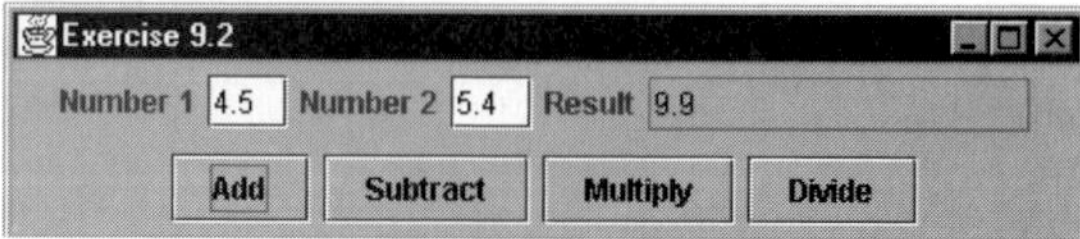

Figure 9.37 *The program does addition, subtraction, multiplication, and division on double numbers.*

9.3 Write a program that meets the following requirements (see Figure 9.38):

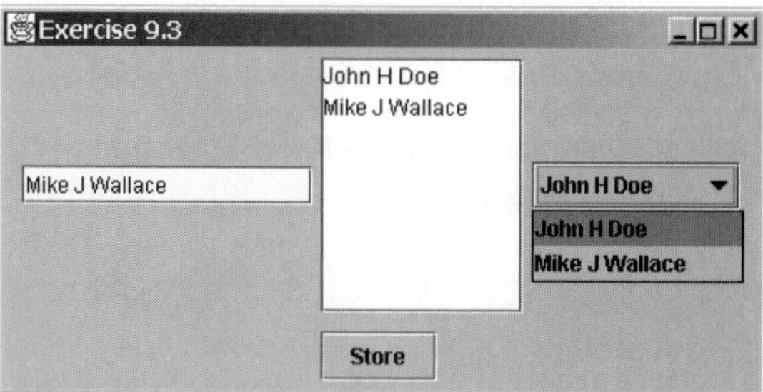

Figure 9.38 *The program stores text from the text field to the text area, and combo box, and displays selected items in the combo box to the text field.*

- Create a text field, a text area, and a combo box in a panel using `FlowLayout`.
- Create a button labeled Store and place it in a panel using `FlowLayout`.
- Place the preceding two panels in a frame of `BorderLayout`. Place the first panel in the center, and the second panel in the south.
- The action of the Store button is to retrieve the item from the text field and store it in a text area and in combo box.
- When an item in the combo box is selected, it is displayed in the text field.

9.4 Write a program that converts Celsius and Fahrenheit temperatures, as shown in Figure 9.39. If you enter a value in the Celsius-degree text field and

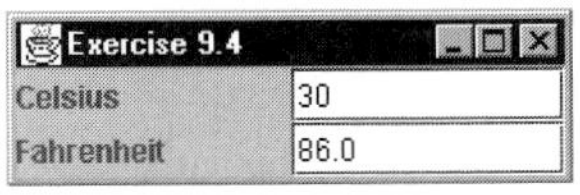

Figure 9.39 *The program converts Celsius to Fahrenheit, and vice versa.*

press the Enter key, the Fahrenheit temperature is displayed in the Fahrenheit text field. Likewise, if you enter a value in the Fahrenheit-degree text field and press the Enter key, the corresponding Celsius degree is displayed in the Celsius text field.

9.5 Write a program that draws various figures on a panel. The user selects a figure from a radio button. The selected figure is then displayed on the panel (see Figure 9.40).

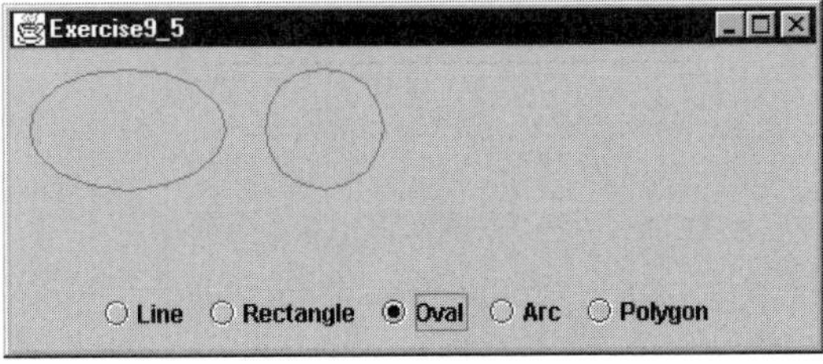

Figure 9.40 *The program displays lines, rectangles, ovals, arcs, or polygons when you select a shape type.*

9.6 Write a program that calculates the future value of an investment at a given interest rate for a specified number of years. The formula for the calculation is as follows:

$$\text{futureValue} = \text{investmentAmount} * (1 + \text{monthlyInterestRate})^{\text{years}*12}$$

Use text fields for interest rate, investment amount, and years. Display the future amount in a text field when the user clicks the Calculate button or chooses Calculate from the Operation menu (see Figure 9.41). Show a message dialog box when the user clicks the About menu item from the Help menu.

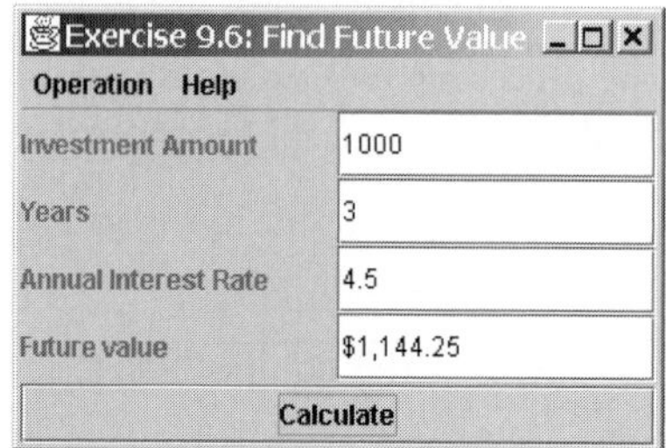

Figure 9.41 *The user enters the investment amount, years, and interest rate to compute future value.*

9.7 Write a program that lets users enter their name, department, university, state, and zip code, and store the information in a text area. The state is a `JComboBox` item. Figure 9.42 shows a sample run of the program.

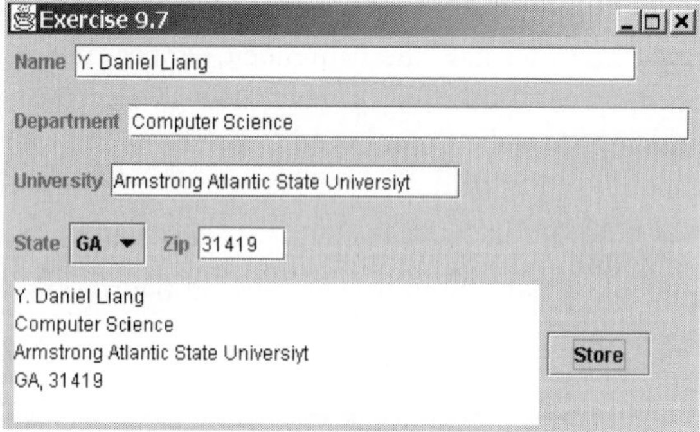

Figure 9.42 *When the Store button is clicked, the name, department, university, state, and zip code are displayed in the text area.*

9.8 Create a main window with two buttons: Simple Calculator and Traffic Lights. When the user clicks Simple Calculator, a new window appears that lets the user perform add, subtract, multiply, and divide operations. When the user clicks Traffic Lights, another window appears that displays traffic lights. (See Figure 9.43.)

The Simple Calculator frame named `MenuDemo` is given in Example 9.11, and the Traffic Lights frame named `RadioButtonDemo` is given in Example 9.8. They can be used directly in this exercise without modification.

When the user clicks the Simple Calculator button, the Calculator window appears and the name of the button changes to Hide Calculator. When the user clicks the Hide Calculator button, the window is closed, and the name

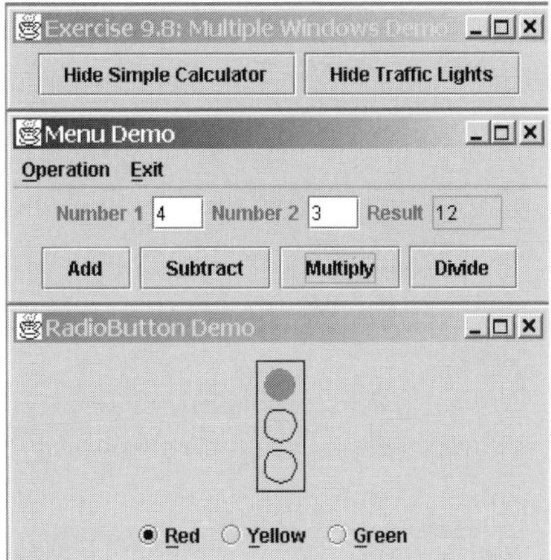

Figure 9.43 *Multiple windows can be displayed simultaneously, as shown in this exercise.*

of the button changes back to Simple Calculator. Implement the function of the Traffic Lights button in the same way.

9.9 Write a program that uses the scrollbars to select the foreground color for a label, as shown in Figure 9.44. Three horizontal scrollbars are used for selecting red, green, and blue components of the color. Use a title border on the panel that holds the scrollbars.

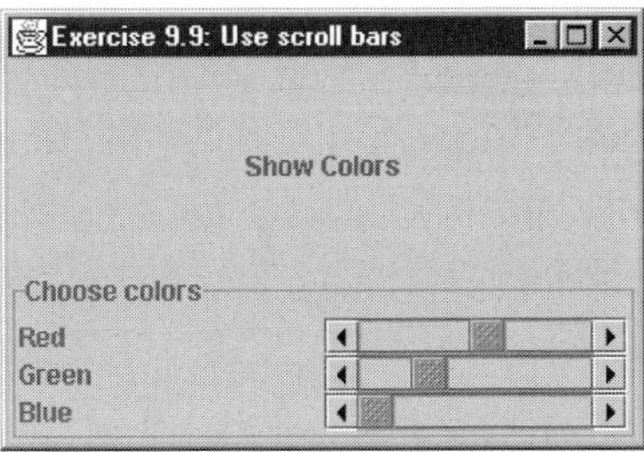

Figure 9.44 *The foreground color changes in the label as you adjust the scrollbars.*

9.10 Write a program that computes sales amount or commission, as shown in Figure 9.45. When the user types a sales amount in the Sales Amount text field and presses the Enter key, the commission is displayed in the Commission text field. Likewise, when the user types a commission, the corresponding sales amount is displayed. The commission rates are the same as in Example 3.7, "Finding Sales Amount." The commission rates are displayed using labels.

9.11 Write a program that sets the alignment and text position properties of a button dynamically, as shown in Figure 9.46.

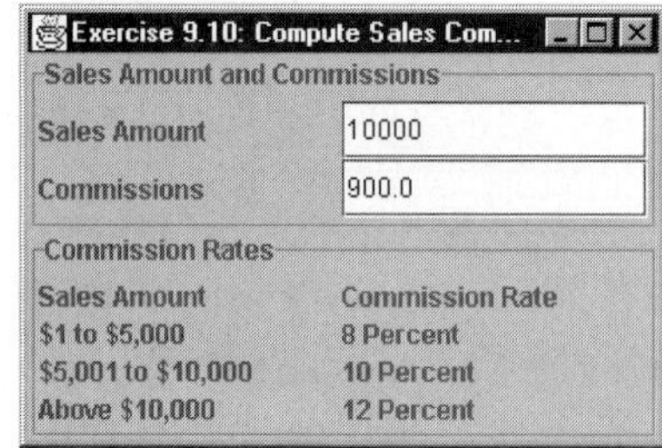

Figure 9.45 *The sales amount and the commission are synchronized. You can compute sales amount given the commission or compute commission given the sales amount.*

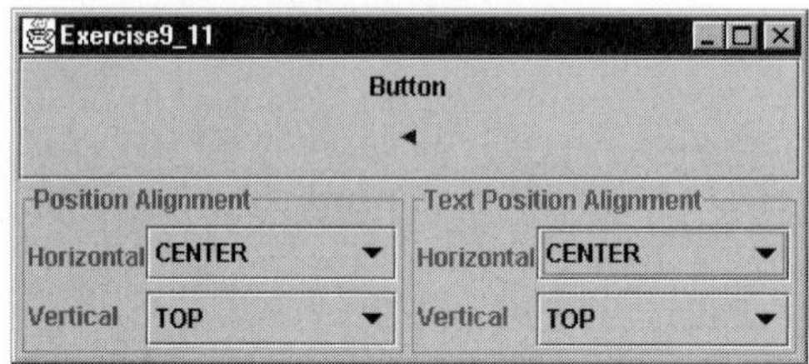

Figure 9.46 *You can set the alignment and text position properties of a button dynamically.*

9.12 Write a program that sets the horizontal alignment and column size properties of a text field dynamically, as shown in Figure 9.47.

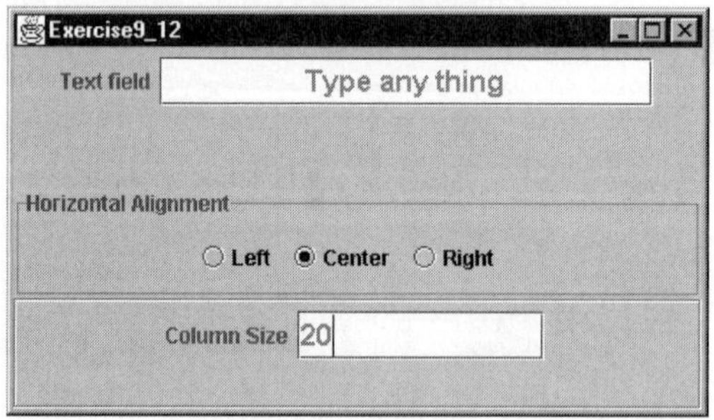

Figure 9.47 *You can set the horizontal alignment and column size properties of a text field dynamically.*

9.13 Write a program that demonstrates the wrapping styles of the text area. The program uses a check box to indicate whether the text area is wrapped. In the case where the text area is wrapped, you need to specify whether it is wrapped by characters or by words, as shown in Figure 9.48.

9.14 Write a program that demonstrates selecting items in a list. The program uses a combo box to specify a selection mode, as shown in Figure 9.49. When you select items, they are displayed in a label below the list.

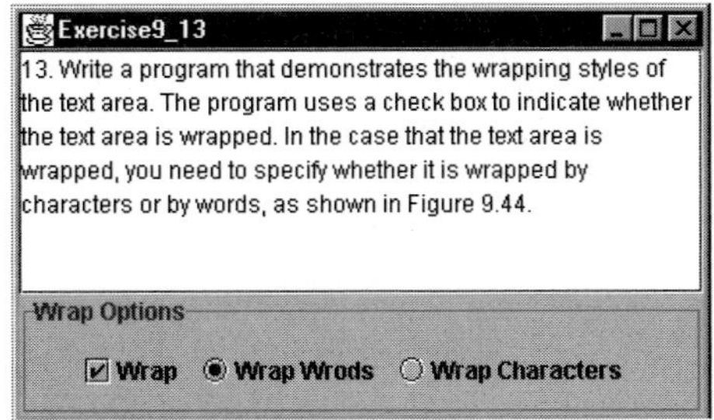

Figure 9.48 *You can set the options to wrap a text area by characters or by words dynamically.*

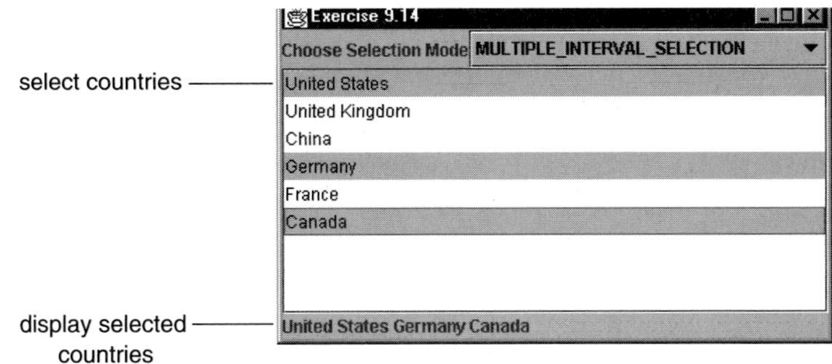

Figure 9.49 *You can choose single selection, single-interval selection, or multiple-interval selection in a list.*

9.15 Create a program that enables the user to set the properties of a `FlowLayout` manager dynamically, as shown in Figure 9.50. The `FlowLayout` manager is used to place 15 components in a panel. You can set the `alignment`, `hgap`, and `vhap` properties of the `FlowLayout` dynamically.

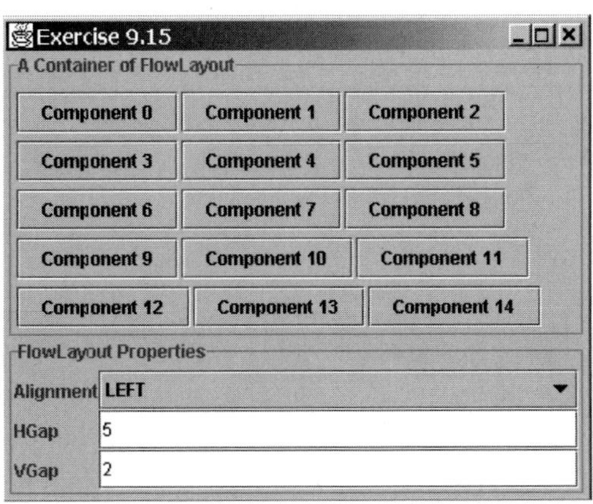

Figure 9.50 *The program enables you to set the properties of a `FlowLayout` manager dynamically.*

9.16. Create a program that enables the user to set the properties of a `GridLayout` manager dynamically, as shown in Figure 9.51. The `GridLayout` manager is used to place 15 components in a panel. You can set the `rows`, `columns`, `hgap`, and `vhap` properties of the `GridLayout` dynamically.

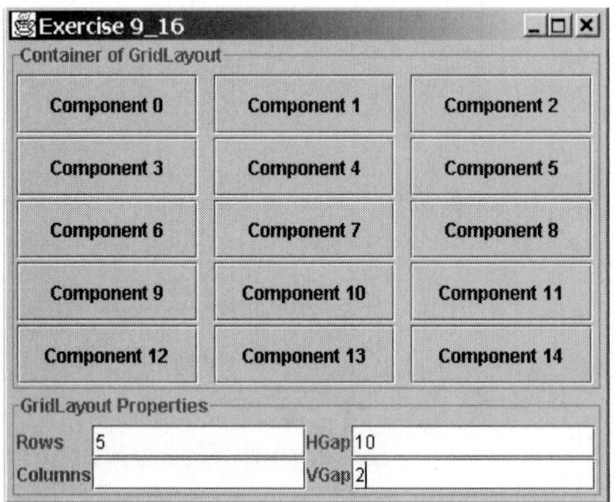

Figure 9.51 *The program enables you to set the properties of a* `GridLayout` *manager dynamically.*

9.17 Use `JTabbedPane` to write a program to display flags for USA, UK, Germany, Canada, China, and India (see Figure 9.52).

Figure 9.52 *You can show the flag by selecting a tab in the tabbed pane.*

CHAPTER 10

APPLETS AND ADVANCED GRAPHICS

Objectives

- Understand how the Web browser controls and executes applets.
- Become familiar with the `init`, `start`, `stop`, and `destroy` methods in the `Applet` class.
- Embed applets in the Web pages.
- Pass parameters to applets from HTML.
- Convert between applications and applets.
- Write a Java program that can run as both an application and an applet.
- Handle mouse events and keystrokes.
- Model dynamic behavior using sequence diagrams and statechart diagrams.
- Package and deploy Java projects.(Optional)
- Know `CardLayout`, `GridBagLayout`, and no layout managers. (Optional)

Introduction

Java's early success has been attributed to applets. Running from a Java-enabled Web browser, applets bring dynamic interaction and live animation to an otherwise static HTML page. It is safe to say that Java would be nowhere today without applets. They make Java appealing, attractive, and popular.

In this book so far, you have mostly used Java applications in examples that introduce Java programming. Everything you have learned about writing applications, however, also applies to writing applets. Because applets are invoked from a Web page, Java provides special features that enable applets to run from a Web browser.

In this chapter, you will learn how to write Java applets, discover the relationship between applets and the Web browser, and explore the similarities and differences between applications and applets. You also will see more complex examples of handling mouse events and keystrokes, and using advanced layout managers.

The *Applet* Class

As shown in Chapter 1, "Introduction to Java," every Java applet extends the `java.applet.Applet` class. The `Applet` class provides the essential framework that enables your applets to be run by a Web browser. Every Java application has a main method that is executed when the application starts. Unlike applications, applets do not have a main method. They depend on the browser to call the methods. Every applet has a structure like the following:

```
public class MyApplet extends java.applet.Applet
{
  ...
  // Called by the browser when the Web page containing
  // this applet is initially loaded, or reloaded
  public void init()
  {
    ...
  }

  // Called by the browser after the init() method, or
  // every time the Web page is visited
  public void start()
  {
    ...
  }

  // Called by the browser when the page containing this
  // applet becomes inactive
  public void stop()
  {
    ...
  }

  // Called by the browser when the Web browser exits
  public void destroy()
  {
    ...
  }

  // Other methods if necessary...
}
```

The browser uses the `init`, `start`, `stop`, and `destroy` methods to control the applets. By default, these methods do nothing. To perform specific functions, they need to be modified in the user's applet so that the browser can call your code properly. Figure 10.1 shows how the browser calls these methods.

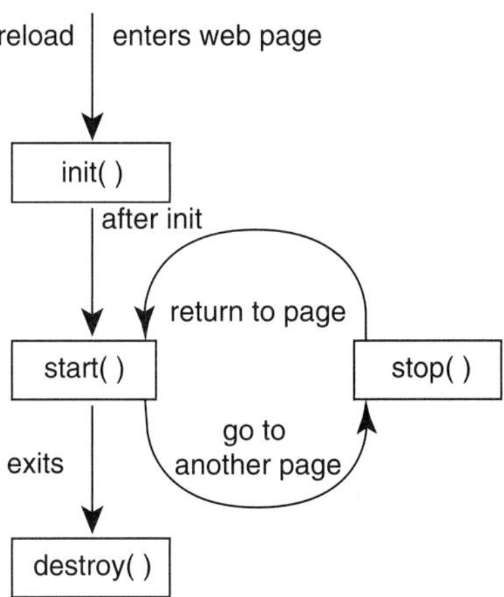

Figure 10.1 *The Web browser uses the* `init`, `start`, `stop`, *and* `destroy` *methods to control the applet.*

The *init* method

The `init` method is invoked when the applet is first loaded and again if it is reloaded.

A subclass of `Applet` should override this method if the subclass has an initialization to perform. The functions usually implemented in this method include creating new threads, loading images, setting up user interface components, and getting parameters from the `<applet>` tag in the HTML page. Chapter 13, "Multithreading," discusses threads in more detail; passing `Applet` parameters is discussed later in this chapter.

The *start* method

The `start` method is invoked after the `init` method. It is also called whenever the applet becomes active again after the page containing the applet is revisited. The `start` method is called, for example, when the user returns to the Web page containing the applet after surfing other pages.

A subclass of `Applet` overrides this method if it has any operation that needs to be performed whenever the Web page containing the applet is visited. An applet with animation, for example, might use the `start` method to resume animation.

The *stop* method

The `stop` method is the opposite of the `start` method. The `start` method is called when the user moves back to the page containing the applet. The `stop` method is invoked when the user leaves the page.

A subclass of `Applet` overrides this method if it has any operation that needs to be performed each time the Web page containing the applet is no longer visible. When the user leaves the page, any threads the applet has started—but not completed—will continue to run. You should override the `stop` method to suspend the running threads so that the applet does not take up system resources when it is inactive.

The *destroy* method

The `destroy` method is invoked when the browser exits normally to inform the applet that it is no longer needed and should release any resources it has allocated. The `stop` method is always called before the `destroy` method.

A subclass of `Applet` overrides this method if it has any operation that needs to be performed before it is destroyed. Usually, you won't need to override this method unless you need to release specific resources, such as threads that the applet created.

The *JApplet* Class

The `Applet` class is an AWT class and does not work well with Swing components. To use Swing components in Java applets, it is necessary to create a Java applet that extends `javax.swing.JApplet`, which is a subclass of `java.applet.Applet`. `JApplet` inherits all the methods from the `Applet` class. In addition, it provides support for laying out Swing components.

To add a component to a `JApplet`, you add it to the content pane of a `JApplet` instance, which is the same as adding a component to a `JFrame` instance. By default, the content pane of `JApplet` uses `BorderLayout`.

Example 10.1 Using Applets

This example shows an applet that computes mortgages. The applet enables the user to enter the interest rate, the number of years, and the loan amount. Clicking the Compute Mortgage button displays the monthly payment and the total payment. The applet and the HTML code containing the applet are provided in the following code. Figure 10.2 contains a sample run of the applet.

```
// MortgageApplet.java: Applet for computing mortgage payments
import java.awt.*;
import java.awt.event.*;
import javax.swing.*;
import javax.swing.border.TitledBorder;

public class MortgageApplet extends JApplet
```

```
  implements ActionListener
{
  // Declare and create text fields for interest rate
  // year, loan amount, monthly payment, and total payment
  private JTextField jtfAnnualInterestRate = new JTextField();
  private JTextField jtfNumOfYears = new JTextField();
  private JTextField jtfLoanAmount = new JTextField();
  private JTextField jtfMonthlyPayment = new JTextField();
  private JTextField jtfTotalPayment = new JTextField();
  // Declare and create a Compute Mortgage button
  private JButton jbtComputeMortgage =
    newJButton("Compute Mortgage");

  // Initialize user interface
  public void init()
  {
    // Set properties on the text fields
    jtfMonthlyPayment.setEditable(false);
    jtfTotalPayment.setEditable(false);

    // Right align text fields
    jtfAnnualInterestRate.setHorizontalAlignment(JTextField.RIGHT);
    jtfNumOfYears.setHorizontalAlignment(JTextField.RIGHT);
    jtfLoanAmount.setHorizontalAlignment(JTextField.RIGHT);
    jtfMonthlyPayment.setHorizontalAlignment(JTextField.RIGHT);
    jtfTotalPayment.setHorizontalAlignment(JTextField.RIGHT);

    // Panel p1 to hold labels and text fields
    JPanel p1 = new JPanel();
    p1.setLayout(new GridLayout(5, 2));
    p1.add(new Label("Annual Interest Rate"));
    p1.add(jtfAnnualInterestRate);
    p1.add(new Label("Number of Years"));
    p1.add(jtfNumOfYears);
    p1.add(new Label("Loan Amount"));
    p1.add(jtfLoanAmount);
    p1.add(new Label("Monthly Payment"));
    p1.add(jtfMonthlyPayment);
    p1.add(new Label("Total Payment"));
    p1.add(jtfTotalPayment);
    p1.setBorder(new
      TitledBorder("Enter interest rate, year and loan amount"));

    // Panel p2 to hold the button
    JPanel p2 = new JPanel();
    p2.setLayout(new FlowLayout(FlowLayout.RIGHT));
    p2.add(jbtComputeMortgage);

    // Add the components to the applet
    getContentPane().add(p1, BorderLayout.CENTER);
    getContentPane().add(p2, BorderLayout.SOUTH);

    // Register listener
    jbtComputeMortgage.addActionListener(this);
  }

  // Handler for the "Compute Mortgage" button
  public void actionPerformed(ActionEvent e)
  {
    if (e.getSource() == jbtComputeMortgage)
    {
      // Get values from text fields
      double interest =
        (Double.valueOf(jtfAnnualInterestRate.getText())).
         doubleValue();
```

continues

Example 10.1 continued

```
        int year =
          (Integer.valueOf(jtfNumOfYears.getText())).intValue();
          (Double.valueOf(jtfLoanAmount.getText())).doubleValue();

        // Create a mortgage object
        Mortgage m = new Mortgage(interest, year, loan);

        // Display monthly payment and total payment
        jtfMonthlyPayment.setText(String.valueOf(m.monthlyPayment()));
        jtfTotalPayment.setText(String.valueOf(m.totalPayment()));
      }
    }
  }

<!-- HTML code, this code is separated from the preceding Java code>
<html>
<head>
<title>Mortgage Applet</title>
</head>
<body>
This is a mortgage calculator, enter your input for interest, year
and loan amount, click the "Compute" button, you will get the payment
information.<p>
<applet
  code = "MortgageApplet.class"
  width = 300
  height = 150
  alt="You must have a JDK1.2-enabled browser to view the applet">
</applet>
</body>
</html>
```

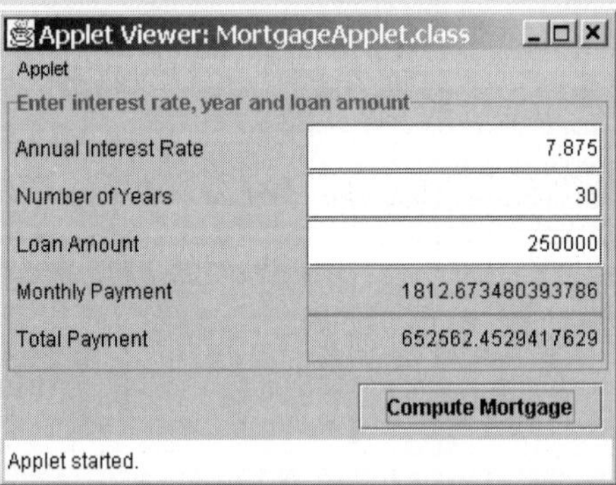

Figure 10.2 *The applet computes the monthly payment and the total payment when provided with the interest rate, number of years, and loan amount.*

Example Review

You need to use the `public` modifier for the `MortgageApplet`; otherwise, the Web browser cannot load it.

`MortgageApplet` implements `ActionListener` because it listens for button actions.

The `init` method initializes the user interface. The program overrides this method to create user interface components (labels, text fields, and a button), and places them in the applet.

The only event handled is the Compute Mortgage button. When this button is clicked, the `actionPerformed` method gets the interest rate, number of years, and loan amount from the text fields. It then creates a `Mortgage` object to obtain the monthly payment and the total payment. Finally, it displays the monthly and total payments in their respective text fields.

The `Mortgage` class is responsible for computing the payments. This class was introduced in Example 5.6, "Borrowing Mortgages" (see Chapter 5, "Programming with Objects and Classes").

The monthly and total payments are not displayed in currency format. To display a number as currency, see Chapter 12, "Internationalization."

Applets are embedded in HTML using the `<applet>` tag, which is discussed in the next section. The `code` parameter specifies the applet bytecode file. The `width` and `height`, both in pixels, specify the initial size of the applet.

Create MortgageApplet.java for the Java source code and MortgaeApplet.html for the HTML file. You can view the applet using the **appletviewer** command at the DOS prompt as follows:

appletviewer MortgageApplet.html

Figure 10.2 shows the applet using the applet viewer.

To make your applet accessible on the Web, you need to store the MortgageApplet.class and MortgageApplet.html on a Web server. You can view the applet from an appropriate URL. For example, I have uploaded these two files on Web server **www.cs.armstrong.edu**. As shown in Figure 10.3, you can access the applet from **www.cs.armstrong.edu /liang/intro3e/MortgageApplet.html.**

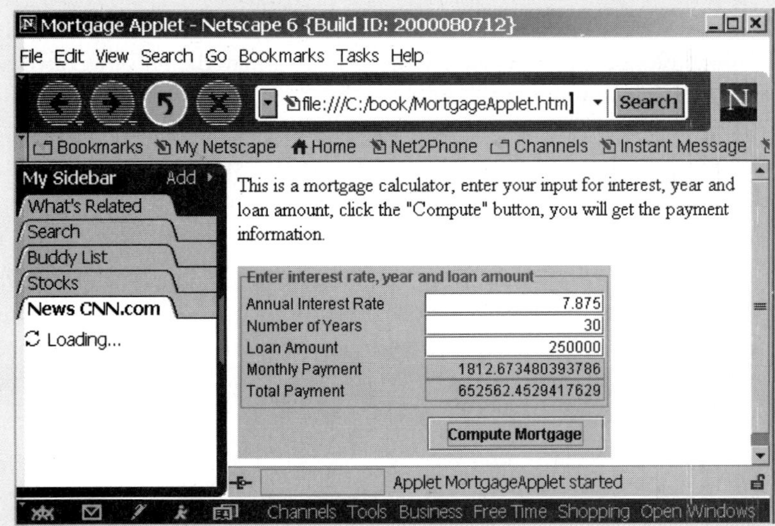

Figure 10.3 *The mortgage applet is downloaded from the Web server.*

continues

Example 10.1 continued

NOTE

You have to view the above applet using a Web browser that supports Java 2. At present, Netscape 6 supports Java 2. To view the applets from other browsers such as IE 5.0 and Netscape 4.7, you have to use the Java Plug-In, which is discussed in the next section.

Running Applets in the Java Plug-In (Optional)

When Java was first introduced in 1995, the only Web browser for viewing Java applets was the HotJava browser by Sun. Netscape quickly updated Navigator 2 to support JDK 1.0. Microsoft followed suit to support JDK 1.0 in Internet Explorer 3. As Java rapidly evolves, browser vendors are falling behind in their effort to keep up with Java updates. Consequently, your Java applets may not be viewable on certain Web browsers. To address this problem, Sun introduced the Java Plug-In technology, which can be installed in browsers so that applets can be viewed consistently on any platform.

To use the Java Plug-In, you have to convert your simple HTML file that uses the `<applet>` tag to a rather complex HTML file that uses the `<object>` tag, using the Java Plug-in HTML Converter supplied by JavaSoft. The converter is packaged in a compressed file named htmlconv1_3.zip, which can be downloaded from

www.javasoft.com/products/plugin/1.3/converter.html

To install the converter, unzip htmlconv1_3.zip and save the files in a directory. To use the converter, change the directory to where the HTMLConvert.class is located and type **`java HTMLConverter`** at the DOS prompt to display a window titled "Java Plug-in HTML Converter," as shown in Figure 10.4. Specify the folder for the HTML files, and select an appropriate conversion template in the Template File text field, as shown in Figure 10.4.

Press the Convert button to process the conversion. The generated HTML file contains the script that prompts you to download and install the Java Plug-In if it is not installed on your machine. You can run it from Netscape or Internet Explorer. Figures 10.5 and 10.6 are sample runs of the `MortgageApplet` running on Netscape and Internet Explorer.

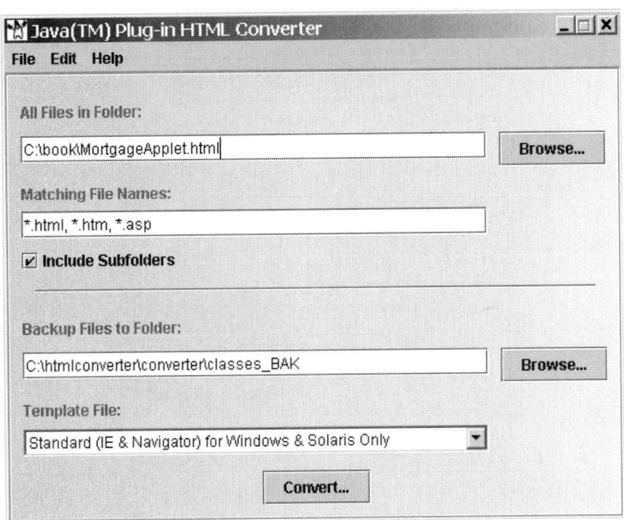

Figure 10.4 *The HTML converter translates a simple HTML file to one that uses the Java Plug-In.*

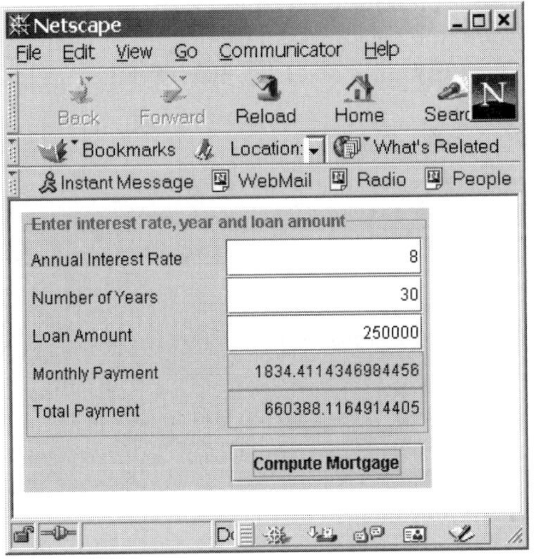

Figure 10.5 *The MortgageApplet runs on Netscape 4.7 using the Java Plug-In.*

NOTE

If you installed JDK 1.3, the Java Plug-In is also installed. The HTML converter is buggy. If you encountered problems, or your HTML files are not converted, please remove all nonessential contents from the HTML, and retain the contents that begin with <applet> and end with </applet>.

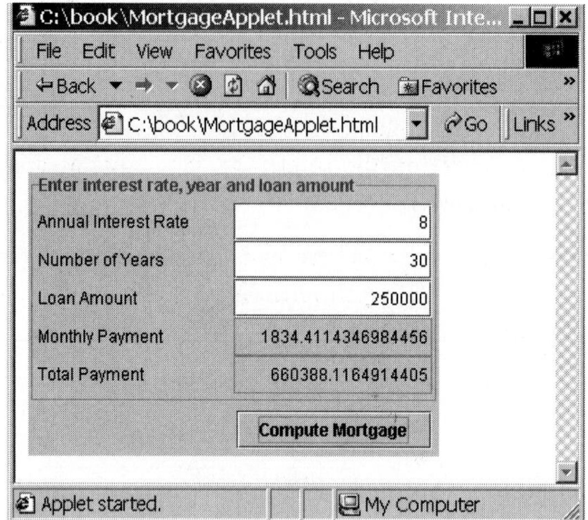

Figure 10.6 *The MortgageApplet runs on Internet Explorer using the Java Plug-In.*

The *<applet>* HTML Tag

To run applets, you must create an HTML file with the `<applet>` tag to specify the applet bytecode file, the applet viewing area dimensions (width and height), and other associated parameters. The syntax of the `<applet>` tag is as follows:

```
<applet
  code=classfilename.class
  width=applet_viewing_width_in_pixels
  height=applet_viewing_height_in_pixels
  [archive=archivefile]
  [codebase=applet_url]
  [vspace=vertical_margin]
  [hspace=horizontal_margin]
  [align=applet_alignment]
  [alt=alternative_text]
>
<param name=param_name1 value=param_value1>
<param name=param_name2 value=param_value2>
...
<param name=param_name3 value=param_value3>
</applet>
```

The `code`, `width`, and `height` attributes are required; all the others are optional. The `<param>` tag is introduced in the section "Passing Parameters to Applets." The meanings of the other attributes are as follows:

- **`archive`**: You can use this attribute to instruct the browser to load an archive file that contains all the class files needed to run the applet. The archiving allows the Web browser to load all the classes from a single compressed file only once, thus reducing loading time and improving performance. To create archives, see the section "Packaging and Deploying Java Projects," later in this chapter.

- **`codebase:`** If this attribute is not used, the Web browser loads the applet from the directory in which the HTML page is located. If your applet is located in a different directory from the HTML page, you must specify the `applet_url` for the browser to load the applet. This attribute enables you to load the class from anywhere on the Internet. The classes used by the applet are dynamically loaded when needed.
- **`vspace`** and **`hspace`**: These two attributes specify the size, in pixels, of the blank margin to leave around the applet vertically and horizontally.
- **`align`**: This attribute specifies how the applet will be aligned in the browser. One of nine values is used: `left`, `right`, `top`, `texttop`, `middle`, `absmiddle`, `baseline`, `bottom`, or `absbottom`.
- **`alt`**: This attribute specifies the text to be displayed in case the browser cannot run Java.

NOTE
The W3 consortium (**www.w3.org**) has introduced the `<object>` tag as a replacement for the <applet> tag. The `<object>` tag has more options and is more versatile than the <applet> tag. Nonetheless, this book will continue to use the <applet> tag, since not all Web browsers support the <object> tag at this time.

Passing Parameters to Applets

In Chapter 7, "Arrays and Vectors," you learned how to pass parameters to Java applications from a command line. The parameters were entered from the Java interpreter and were passed as an array of strings to the `main` method. When the application starts, the `main` method can use these arguments. There is no `main` method in an applet, however, and applets are not run from the command line by the Java interpreter.

How, then, can applets accept arguments? In this section, you will learn how to pass parameters to Java applets.

To be passed to an applet, a parameter must be declared in the HTML file, and must be read by the applet when it is initialized. Parameters are declared using the `<param>` tag. The `<param>` tag must be embedded in the `<applet>` tag and has no end tag. The syntax for the `<param>` tag is as follows:

```
<param name=parametername value=parametervalue>
```

This tag specifies a parameter and its corresponding value.

NOTE
There is no comma separating the parameter name from the parameter value in the HTML code.

Suppose you want to write an applet to display a message. The message is passed as a parameter. In addition, you want the message to be displayed at a specific location. The start location of the message is also passed as a parameter in two values, x coordinate and y coordinate. Assume that the applet is named `DisplayMessage`. The parameters and their values are listed in Table 10.1.

The HTML source file is given as follows:

```
<html>
<head>
<title>Passing Parameters to Java Applets</title>
</head>
<body>
This applet gets a message from the HTML page and displays it.
<p>
<applet
  code = "DisplayMessage.class"
  width = 200
  height = 50
  alt="You must have a JDK 1.2-enabled browser to view the applet"
>
<param name=MESSAGE value="Welcome to Java">
<param name=X value=20>
<param name=Y value=30>
</applet>
</body>
</html>
```

To read the parameter from the applet, use the following method defined in the `Applet` class:

```
public String getParameter("parametername");
```

This returns the value of the specified parameter.

TABLE 10.1 Parameter Names and Values for the `DisplayMessage` Applet

Parameter Name	*Parameter Value*
MESSAGE	"Welcome to Java"
X	20
Y	30

Example 10.2 Passing Parameters to Java Applets

This example shows an applet that displays a message at a specified location. The message and the location (x, y) are obtained from the HTML source. The program creates a Java source file named **DisplayMessage.java**, as shown below. The output of a sample run is shown in Figure 10.7.

```
// DisplayMessage.java: Display a message on a panel in the applet
import javax.swing.*;
```

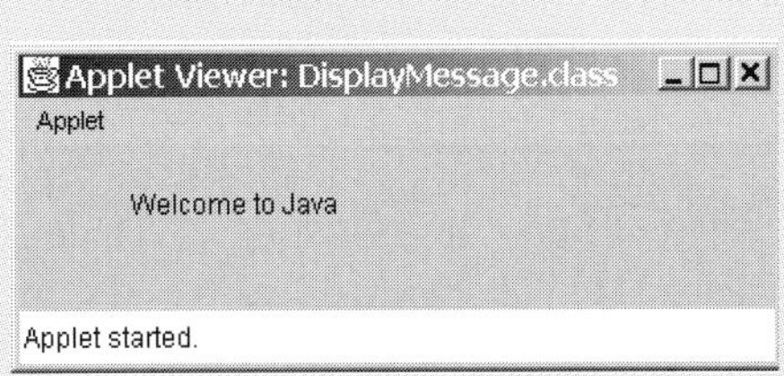

Figure 10.7 *The applet displays the message Welcome to Java passed from the HTML page.*

```
public class DisplayMessage extends JApplet
{
  private String message = "A default message"; // Message to display
  private int x = 20; // Default x coordinate
  private int y = 20; // Default y coordinate

  // Initialize the applet
  public void init()
  {
    // Get parameter values from the HTML file
    message = getParameter("MESSAGE");
    x = Integer.parseInt(getParameter("X"));
    y = Integer.parseInt(getParameter("Y"));

    // Create a message panel
    MessagePanel messagePanel = new MessagePanel(message);
    messagePanel.setXCoordinate(x);
    messagePanel.setYCoordinate(y);

    // Add the message panel to the applet
    getContentPane().add(messagePanel);
  }
}
```

Example Review

The program gets the parameter values from the HTML in the `init` method. The values are strings obtained using the `getParameter` method. Because `x` and `y` are `int`, the program uses `Integer.parseInt(string)` to convert a digital string into an `int` value.

If you change Welcome to Java in the HTML file to Welcome to HTML, and reload the HTML file in the Web browser, you should see Welcome to HTML displayed. Similarly, the `x` and `y` values can be changed to display the message in a desired location.

Conversions between Applications and Applets

The `JFrame` class and the `JApplet` class have a lot in common despite some differences. Since they both are subclasses of the `Container` class, all the user interface components, layout managers, and event-handling features are the same for both classes. Applications, however, are invoked by the Java interpreter, and applets are invoked by the Web browser. In this section, you will learn how to convert between applets and applications.

In general, an applet can be converted to an application. The following are the steps in the conversion:

1. Eliminate the HTML page that invokes the applet. If the applet gets parameters from the HTML page, you can handle them from the command line.
2. Derive the main class named `NewClass`, for instance, from `JFrame` or a subclass of `JFrame` instead of from `JApplet`.
3. Write a constructor in the new class to contain the code in the `init` and `start` methods.
4. Add a main method, as follows:

```
public static void main()
{
  NewClass frame = new NewClass();

  // width and height are from the <applet> tag
  frame.resize(width, height);
  frame.setVisible(true);
}
```

5. Because applets do not have title bars, you can add a title for the window using the `setTitle` method.

NOTE

When using frames in applications, specify an initial size in width and height using the `setSize` method. After the frame is displayed, you can resize it. With applets, the viewing area is fixed on a Web page by the `width` and `height` values in the `<applet>` tag.

Example 10.3 Converting Applets to Applications

This example converts the Java applet `MortgageApplet` (from Example 10.1) to a Java application and displays the frame in the center of the screen. The program is given below, and its sample run is shown in Figure 10.8.

```
// MortgageApplication.java: Application for
// computing mortgage payments
import java.awt.*;
import java.awt.event.*;
import javax.swing.*;
import javax.swing.border.TitledBorder;

public class MortgageApplication extends JFrame
  implements ActionListener
{
  // Declare and create text fields for interest rate
  // year, loan amount, monthly payment, and total payment
  private JTextField jtfAnnualInterestRate = new JTextField(10);
  private JTextField jtfNumOfYears = new JTextField(10);
  private JTextField jtfLoanAmount = new JTextField(10);
  private JTextField jtfMonthlyPayment = new JTextField(10);
  private JTextField jtfTotalPayment = new JTextField(10);
```

```
  // Declare and create a Compute Mortgage button
  private JButton jbtComputeMortgage =
    new JButton("Compute Mortgage");

  // Constructor (replacing the init() method in the applet)
  public MortgageApplication()
  {
    // Set properties on the text fields
    jtfMonthlyPayment.setEditable(false);
    jtfTotalPayment.setEditable(false);

    // Right align text fields
    jtfAnnualInterestRate.setHorizontalAlignment(JTextField.RIGHT);
    jtfNumOfYears.setHorizontalAlignment(JTextField.RIGHT);
    jtfLoanAmount.setHorizontalAlignment(JTextField.RIGHT);
    jtfMonthlyPayment.setHorizontalAlignment(JTextField.RIGHT);
    jtfTotalPayment.setHorizontalAlignment(JTextField.RIGHT);

    // Panel p1 to hold labels and text fields
    JPanel p1 = new JPanel();
    p1.setLayout(new GridLayout(5,2));
    p1.add(new Label("Interest Rate"));
    p1.add(jtfAnnualInterestRate);
    p1.add(new Label("Years "));
    p1.add(jtfNumOfYears);
    p1.add(new Label("Loan Amount"));
    p1.add(jtfLoanAmount);
    p1.add(new Label("Monthly Payment"));
    p1.add(jtfMonthlyPayment);
    p1.add(new Label("Total Payment"));
    p1.add(jtfTotalPayment);
    p1.setBorder(new
      TitledBorder("Enter interest rate, year and loan amount"));

    // Panel p2 to hold the button
    JPanel p2 = new JPanel();
    p2.setLayout(new FlowLayout(FlowLayout.RIGHT));
    p2.add(jbtComputeMortgage);

    // Add the components to the applet
    getContentPane().add(p1, BorderLayout.CENTER);
    getContentPane().add(p2, BorderLayout.SOUTH);

    // Register listener
    jbtComputeMortgage.addActionListener(this);
  }

  // Add a main method
  public static void main(String[] args)
  {
    MortgageApplication frame = new MortgageApplication();
    frame.setTitle("Mortgage Application");
    frame.setSize(400, 200);
    // frame.setDefaultCloseOperation(JFrame.EXIT_ON_CLOSE);
    frame.setVisible(true);
  }

  // Handler for the "Compute" button
  public void actionPerformed(ActionEvent e)
  {
    if (e.getSource() == jbtComputeMortgage)
    {
      // Get values from text fields
      double interest =
```

continues

Example 10.3 continued

```
          (Double.valueOf
           (jtfAnnualInterestRate.getText())).doubleValue();
        int year =
          (Integer.valueOf(jtfNumOfYears.getText())).intValue();
        double loan =
          (Double.valueOf(jtfLoanAmount.getText())).doubleValue();

        // Create a mortgage object
        Mortgage m = new Mortgage(interest, year, loan);

        // Display monthly payment and total payment
        jtfMonthlyPayment.setText(String.valueOf(m.monthlyPayment()));
        jtfTotalPayment.setText(String.valueOf(m.totalPayment()));
      }
    }
  }
```

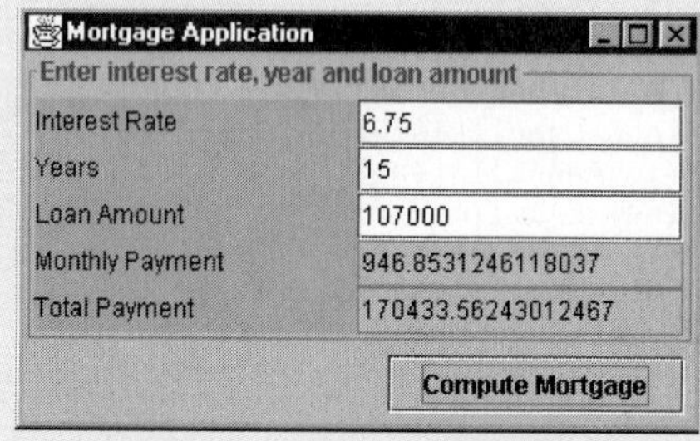

Figure 10.8 *The program is the same as Example 10.1 except that it is written as an application.*

Example Review

The program extends `JFrame` rather than `JApplet`.

The program uses a constructor to initialize the user interface instead of the `init` method. The `setTitle` method is used to set a title for the frame in the constructor.

The program creates a main method to start the program by the Java interpreter.

In Chapter 1, "Introduction to Java," you learned that certain limitations are imposed on applets for security reasons. For example, applets are not allowed to access local files. If the conversion does not violate the security constraints imposed on applets, you can perform the following steps to convert an application to an applet:

1. Create an HTML page with the `<applet>` tag that invokes the applet. If command-line parameters are used in the application, add the parameters in the `<applet>` tag and get the parameters using `getParameter` in the `init` method.

2. Derive the main class from `JApplet` instead of from `JFrame`.

3. Replace the application's constructor by the `init` method.

4. Eliminate the `main` method, which usually contains the method to create and display the frame. The applet is automatically displayed in the size

specified by the width and height in the `<applet>` tag. This step is optional. If you leave the `main` method intact, it is simply ignored.

5. Because applets do not have title bars, eliminate the `setTitle` method (if it is in the application).

Example 10.4 Converting Applications to Applets

This example converts the Java application `MenuDemo`, which performs arithmetic operations using buttons and menus (Example 9.11, "Using Menus," from Chapter 9, "Creating User Interfaces"), into a Java applet.

The following Java applet `AppletMenuDemo` is converted from the application `MenuDemo`. A sample run of the applet is shown in Figure 10.9.

```
// AppletMenuDemo.java: Use menus in an applet
import java.awt.*;
import java.awt.event.*;
import javax.swing.*;

public class AppletMenuDemo extends JApplet
  implements ActionListener
{
  // Text fields for Number 1, Number 2, and Result
  private JTextField jtfNum1, jtfNum2, jtfResult;

  // Buttons "Add", "Subtract", "Multiply" and "Divide"
  private JButton jbtAdd, jbtSub, jbtMul, jbtDiv;

  // Menu items "Add", "Subtract", "Multiply","Divide" and "Close"
  private JMenuItem jmiAdd, jmiSub, jmiMul, jmiDiv, jmiClose;

  // Initialize the applet
  public void init()
  {
    // Create menu bar
    JMenuBar jmb = new JMenuBar();

    // Add menu "Operation" to menu bar
    JMenu operationMenu = new JMenu("Operation");
    operationMenu.setMnemonic('O');
    jmb.add(operationMenu);

    // Add menu "Exit" in menu bar
    JMenu exitMenu = new JMenu("Exit");
    exitMenu.setMnemonic('E');
    jmb.add(exitMenu);

    // Add menu items with mnemonics to menu "Operation"
    operationMenu.add(jmiAdd= new JMenuItem("Add", 'A'));
    operationMenu.add(jmiSub = new JMenuItem("Subtract", 'S'));
    operationMenu.add(jmiMul = new JMenuItem("Multiply", 'M'));
    operationMenu.add(jmiDiv = new JMenuItem("Divide", 'D'));
    exitMenu.add(jmiClose = new JMenuItem("Close", 'C'));

    // Set keyboard accelerators
    jmiAdd.setAccelerator(
      KeyStroke.getKeyStroke(KeyEvent.VK_A, ActionEvent.CTRL_MASK));
    jmiSub.setAccelerator(
      KeyStroke.getKeyStroke(KeyEvent.VK_S, ActionEvent.CTRL_MASK));
    jmiMul.setAccelerator(
      KeyStroke.getKeyStroke(KeyEvent.VK_M, ActionEvent.CTRL_MASK));
    jmiDiv.setAccelerator(
```

continues

Example 10.4 continued

```
      KeyStroke.getKeyStroke(KeyEvent.VK_D, ActionEvent.CTRL_MASK));

    // Panel p1 to hold text fields and labels
    JPanel p1 = new JPanel();
    p1.setLayout(new FlowLayout());
    p1.add(new JLabel("Number 1"));
    p1.add(jtfNum1 = new JTextField(3));
    p1.add(new JLabel("Number 2"));
    p1.add(jtfNum2 = new JTextField(3));
    p1.add(new JLabel("Result"));
    p1.add(jtfResult = new JTextField(4));
    jtfResult.setEditable(false);

    // Panel p2 to hold buttons
    JPanel p2 = new JPanel();
    p2.setLayout(new FlowLayout());
    p2.add(jbtAdd = new JButton("Add"));
    p2.add(jbtSub = new JButton("Subtract"));
    p2.add(jbtMul = new JButton("Multiply"));
    p2.add(jbtDiv = new JButton("Divide"));

    // Add menu bar to the applet
    setJMenuBar(jmb);

    // Add panels to the applet
    getContentPane().add(p1, BorderLayout.CENTER);
    getContentPane().add(p2, BorderLayout.SOUTH);

    // Register listeners
    jbtAdd.addActionListener(this);
    jbtSub.addActionListener(this);
    jbtMul.addActionListener(this);
    jbtDiv.addActionListener(this);
    jmiAdd.addActionListener(this);
    jmiSub.addActionListener(this);
    jmiMul.addActionListener(this);
    jmiDiv.addActionListener(this);
    jmiClose.addActionListener(this);
  }

  // Handle ActionEvent from buttons and menu items
  public void actionPerformed(ActionEvent e)
  {
    String actionCommand = e.getActionCommand();

    // Handle button events
    if (e.getSource() instanceof JButton)
    {
      if ("Add".equals(actionCommand))
        calculate('+');
      else if ("Subtract".equals(actionCommand))
        calculate('-');
      else if ("Multiply".equals(actionCommand))
        calculate('*');
      else if ("Divide".equals(actionCommand))
        calculate('/');
    }
    else if (e.getSource() instanceof JMenuItem)
    {
      // Handle menu item events
      if ("Add".equals(actionCommand))
        calculate('+');
      else if ("Subtract".equals(actionCommand))
        calculate('-');
```

```
        else if ("Multiply".equals(actionCommand))
          calculate('*');
        else if ("Divide".equals(actionCommand))
          calculate('/');
        else if ("Close".equals(actionCommand))
          System.out.println("Can't close applet");
      }
    }

    // Calculate and show the result in jtfResult
    private void calculate(char operator)
    {
      // Obtain Number 1 and Number 2
      int num1 = (Integer.parseInt(jtfNum1.getText().trim()));
      int num2 = (Integer.parseInt(jtfNum2.getText().trim()));
      int result = 0;

      // Perform selected operation
      switch (operator)
      {
        case '+': result = num1 + num2;
                  break;
        case '-': result = num1 - num2;
                  break;
        case '*': result = num1 * num2;
                  break;
        case '/': result = num1 / num2;
      }

      // Set result in jtfResult
      jtfResult.setText(String.valueOf(result));
    }
  }
```

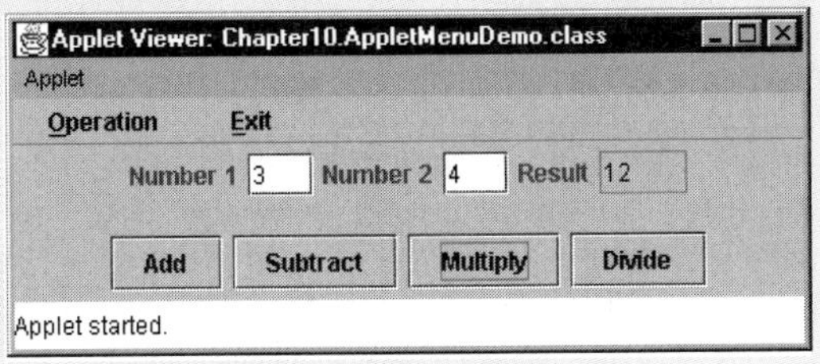

Applet Viewer: Chapter10.AppletMenuDemo.class
Applet
Operation Exit
Number 1 3 Number 2 4 Result 12
Add Subtract Multiply Divide
Applet started.

Figure 10.9 *The* `AppletMenuDemo` *class demonstrates using menus in an applet.*

Example Review

The following changes are made to convert the `MenuDemo` application to `AppletMenuDemo`:

1. Extend `JApplet` rather than `JFrame`.
2. Replace the constructor with the `init` method and eliminate the `setTitle` method.
3. In the `MenuDemo` application, clicking the Close menu item terminates the program. Since the applet cannot be closed in HTML, you cannot terminate the applet by invoking `System.exit(0)`.
4. Create an HTML file to run the applet.

Menus can only be used with applications in AWT programming. In Swing, menus can be used in both applications and applets.

Running a Program as an Applet and an Application

You can implement a main method in an applet that will run as an application or as an applet using the same program. This feature has both theoretical and practical implications. Theoretically, it blurs the difference between applets and applications. You can write a class that is both an applet and an application. Practically, it is convenient to be able to run a program in two ways.

It is not difficult to write such programs on your own. Suppose you have an applet named `TestApplet`. To enable it to run as an application, all you need to do is add a main method in the applet with the implementation, as follows:

```
public static void main(String[] args)
{
  // Create a frame
  JFrame frame = new JFrame(
    "Running a program as applet and frame");

  // Create an instance of TestApplet
  TestApplet applet = new TestApplet();

  // Add the applet instance to the frame
  frame.getContentPane().add(applet, BorderLayout.CENTER);

  // Invoke init and start
  applet.init();
  applet.start();

  // Display the frame
  frame.setSize(300, 300);
  frame.setVisible(true);
}
```

Since the `JApplet` class is a subclass of `Component`, it can be placed in a frame. You can invoke the `init` and `start` methods of the applet to run a `JApplet` object in an application.

Example 10.5 Running a Program as an Applet and as an Application

This example modifies the `DisplayMessage` applet in Example 10.2 to enable it to run both as an applet and as an application. The program is identical to `DisplayMessage` except for the addition of a new main method and of a variable named `isStandalone` to indicate whether it is running as an applet or as an application.

```
// DisplayMessageApp.java:
// The program can run as an applet or application
import javax.swing.*;
import java.awt.BorderLayout;
import java.awt.Font;

public class DisplayMessageApp extends JApplet
{
  private String message = "A default message"; // Message to display
  private int x = 20; // Default x coordinate
  private int y = 20; // Default y coordinate
```

```
// Determine if it is application
private boolean isStandalone = false;

// Initialize the applet
public void init()
{
  if (!isStandalone)
  {
    // Get parameter values from the HTML file
    message = getParameter("MESSAGE");
    x = Integer.parseInt(getParameter("X"));
    y = Integer.parseInt(getParameter("Y"));
  }

  // Create a message panel
  MessagePanel messagePanel = new MessagePanel(message);
  messagePanel.setFont(new Font("SansSerif", Font.BOLD, 20));
  messagePanel.setXCoordinate(x);
  messagePanel.setYCoordinate(y);

  // Add the message panel to the applet
  getContentPane().add(messagePanel);
}

// Main method with three arguments:
// args[0]: x coordinate
// args[1]: y coordinate
// args[2]: message
public static void main(String[] args)
{
  // Create a frame
  JFrame frame = new JFrame("DisplayMessageApp");

  // Create an instance of the applet
  DisplayMessageApp applet = new DisplayMessageApp();

  // It runs as an application
  applet.isStandalone = true;

  // Get parameters from the command line
  applet.getCommandLineParameters(args);

  // Add the applet instance to the frame
  frame.getContentPane().add(applet, BorderLayout.CENTER);

  // Invoke init() and start()
  applet.init();
  applet.start();

  // Display the frame
  frame.setSize(300, 300);
  // frame.setDefaultCloseOperation(JFrame.EXIT_ON_CLOSE);
  frame.setVisible(true);
}

// Get command line parameters
public void getCommandLineParameters(String[] args)
{
  // Check usage and get x, y and message
  if (args.length != 3)
  {
    System.out.println(
      "Usage: java DisplayMessageApp x y message");
    System.exit(0);
  }
  else
```

continues

Example 10.5 continued

```
            x = Integer.parseInt(args[0]);
            y = Integer.parseInt(args[1]);
            message = args[2];
        }
    }
}
```

Example Review

When you run the program as an applet, the main method is ignored. When you run it as an application, the main method is invoked. A sample run of the program as an application and as an applet is shown in Figure 10.10.

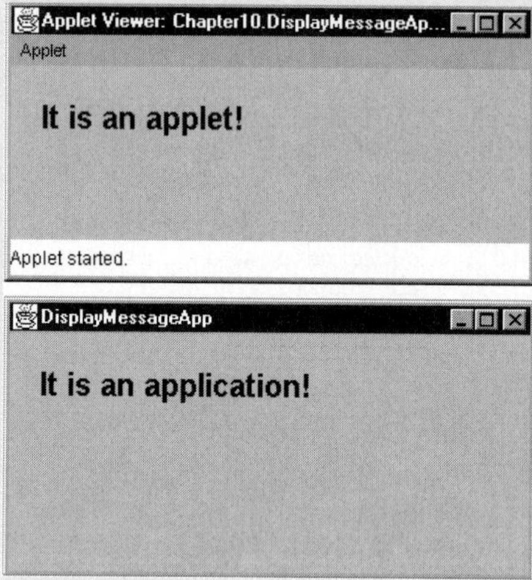

Figure 10.10 *The* `DisplayMessageApp` *class can run as an application and as an applet.*

The main method creates a JFrame object frame and creates applet, an instance of the JApplet. The main method then places the applet applet into the frame frame and invokes its init method. The application runs just like an applet.

The main method sets isStandalone true so that it does not attempt to retrieve HTML parameters when the init method is invoked.

The setVisible(true) method was invoked *after* the components had been added to the applet, and the applet has been added to the frame to ensure that the components will be visible. Otherwise, the components are not shown when the frame starts.

Mouse Events

A mouse event is generated whenever a mouse is clicked, released, moved, or dragged on a component. The mouse event object captures the event, such as the number of clicks associated with it or the location (x and y coordinates) of the mouse. Java provides two listener interfaces, MouseListener and MouseMotionListener, to handle mouse events. Implement the MouseListener interface to listen for such actions as when the mouse is pressed, released, entered, exited, or clicked, and implement the MouseMotionListener interface to listen for such actions as dragging or moving the mouse.

The MouseEvent handlers are listed along with the handlers of other events in Table 8.2 in Chapter 8, "Getting Started with Graphics Programming." They are also explained below.

- The mouseEntered(MouseEvent e) and mouseExit(MouseEvent e) handlers are invoked when a mouse enters a component or exits the component.
- The mousePressed(MouseEvent e) and mouseReleased(MouseEvent e) handlers are invoked when a mouse is pressed or released. The mouseClicked(MouseEvent e) handler is invoked when a mouse is pressed and then released.
- The mouseMoved(MouseEvent e) handler is invoked when the mouse is moved without a button being pressed. The mouseDragged(MouseEvent e) handler is invoked when the mouse is moved with a button pressed.

The Point class is often used for handling mouse events. The Point class encapsulates a point in a plane. The class contains two instance variables, x and y, for coordinates. To create a point object, use the following constructor:

```
Point(int x, int y)
```

This constructs a Point object with the specified x and y coordinates.

You can use the move(int x, int y) method to move the point to the specified x and y coordinates. You can use the following properties from a MouseEvent object when a mouse event occurs:

- public int getClickCount()

  This returns the number of mouse clicks associated with the event.

- public Point getPoint()

  This returns the x and y coordinates of the event relative to the source component.

- public int getX()

  This returns the x coordinate of the event relative to the source component.

- public int getY()

  This returns the y coordinate of the event relative to the source component.

Since the MouseEvent class inherits InputEvent, you can use the methods defined in the InputEvent class on a MouseEvent object. The following methods in InputEvent are often useful for handling mouse events:

- public long getWhen()

  This returns the time stamp indicating when the event occurred.

- `public boolean isAltDown()`

  This returns whether the Alt key is down on the event.

- `public boolean isControlDown()`

  This returns whether the Control key is down on the event.

- `public boolean isMetaDown()`

  This returns `true` if the right mouse button is pressed.

- `public boolean isShiftDown()`

  This returns whether the Shift key is down on the event.

Example 10.6 Moving Message Using Mouse

This example presents a program to display a message in a panel. You can use the mouse to move the message. The message moves as the mouse drags and is always displayed at the mouse point. The output of the program is shown in Figure 10.11.

```
// MoveMessageDemo.java: Move a message in a panel
// by dragging the mouse
import java.awt.*;
import java.awt.event.*;
import javax.swing.*;

public class MoveMessageDemo extends JApplet
{
  // Initialize the applet
  public void init()
  {
    // Create a MoveMessagePanel instance for drawing a message
    MoveMessagePanel p = new MoveMessagePanel("Welcome to Java");

    // Place the message panel in the frame
    getContentPane().setLayout(new BorderLayout());
    getContentPane().add(p);
  }

  // This main method enables the applet to run as an application
  public static void main(String[] args)
  {
    // Create a frame
    JFrame frame = new JFrame("Move Message Using Mouse");

    // Create an instance of the applet
    MoveMessageDemo applet = new MoveMessageDemo();

    // Add the applet instance to the frame
    frame.getContentPane().add(applet, BorderLayout.CENTER);

    // Invoke init() and start()
    applet.init();
    applet.start();

    // Display the frame
    frame.setSize(300, 300);

    // frame.setDefaultCloseOperation(JFrame.EXIT_ON_CLOSE);
    frame.setVisible(true);
  }

  // MoveMessagePanel draws a message
```

```
  // This class is defined as inner class
  class MoveMessagePanel extends MessagePanel
    implements MouseMotionListener
  {
    // Construct a panel to draw string s
    public MoveMessagePanel(String s)
    {
      super(s);
      this.addMouseMotionListener(this);
    }
    // Tell the panel how to draw things
    public void paintComponent(Graphics g)
    {
      // Invoke the paintComponent method in the MessagePanel class
      super.paintComponent(g);
    }
    // Handler for mouse moved event
    public void mouseMoved(MouseEvent e)
    {
    }
    // Handler for mouse dragged event
    public void mouseDragged(MouseEvent e)
    {
      // Get the new location and repaint the screen
      setXCoordinate(e.getX());
      setYCoordinate(e.getY());
      repaint();
    }
  }
}
```

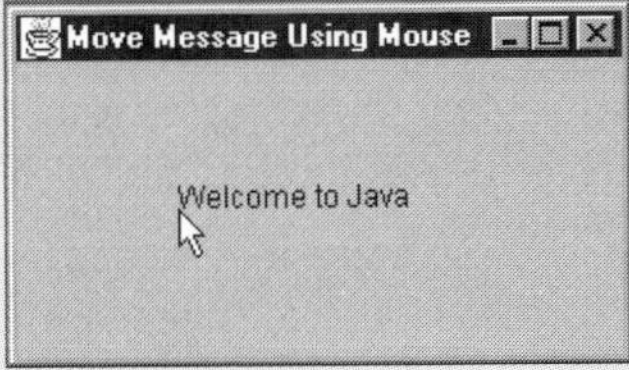

Figure 10.11 *You can move the message by dragging the mouse.*

Example Review

The class `MoveMessagePanel` extends `MessagePanel` and implements `MouseMotionListener`. The `MessagePanel` class was presented in Example 8.5 to display a message in a panel. The `MoveMessagePanel` class inherits all the features from `MessagePanel`. Additionally, it handles redisplaying the message when the mouse is dragged.

The `MouseMotionListener` interface contains two handlers, `mouseMoved` and `mouseDragged`, for handling mouse-motion events. When you move the mouse with the button pressed, the `mouseDragged` method is invoked to repaint the viewing area and display the message at the mouse point. When you move the mouse without pressing the button, the `mouseMoved` method is invoked.

continues

Example 10.6 continued

Because the methods in the `MouseMotionListener` interface are abstract, you must implement all of them even if your program does not care about some of the events. In `MoveMessagePanel`, both `mouseMoved` and `mouseDragged` event handlers are implemented, although only the `mouseDragged` handler is needed.

For an object to receive event notification, it must register as an event listener. `addMouseMotionListener(this)` registers the object of `MoveMessagePanel` as a mouse-motion event listener so that the object can receive notification about the mouse-motion event. `MoveMessagePanel` is both a listener and a source object.

The `mouseDragged` method is invoked when you move the mouse with a button pressed. This method obtains the mouse location using `getX` and `getY` methods in the `MouseEvent` class. This becomes the new location for the message.

Example 10.7 Scribbling with a Mouse

This example shows a program that uses a mouse for scribbling. It can be used to draw things on a panel by dragging with the left mouse button pressed. The drawing can be erased by dragging with the right button pressed. A sample run of the program is shown in Figure 10.12.

```
// ScribbleDemo.java: Scribble using mouse
import java.awt.*;
import javax.swing.*;
import java.awt.event.*;

public class ScribbleDemo extends JApplet
{
  // This main method enables the applet to run as an application
  public static void main(String[] args)
  {
    // Create a frame
    JFrame frame = new JFrame("Scribbling Demo");

    // Create an instance of the applet
    ScribbleDemo applet = new ScribbleDemo();

    // Add the applet instance to the frame
    frame.getContentPane().add(applet, BorderLayout.CENTER);

    // Invoke init() and start()
    applet.init();
    applet.start();

    // Display the frame
    frame.setSize(300, 300);
    // frame.setDefaultCloseOperation(JFrame.EXIT_ON_CLOSE);
    frame.setVisible(true);
  }

  // Initialize the applet
  public void init()
  {
    // Create a PaintPanel and add it to the applet
```

```
    getContentPane().add(new ScribblePanel(), BorderLayout.CENTER);
  }
}

// ScribblePanel for scribbling using the mouse
class ScribblePanel extends JPanel
  implements MouseListener, MouseMotionListener
{
  final int CIRCLESIZE = 20; // Circle diameter used for erasing
  private Point lineStart = new Point(0, 0); // Line start point
  private Graphics g; // Create a Graphics object for drawing

  public ScribblePanel()
  {
    // Register listener for the mouse event
    addMouseListener(this);
    addMouseMotionListener(this);
  }

  public void mouseClicked(MouseEvent e)
  {
  }

  public void mouseEntered(MouseEvent e)
  {
  }

  public void mouseExited(MouseEvent e)
  {
  }

  public void mouseReleased(MouseEvent e)
  {
  }

  public void mousePressed(MouseEvent e)
  {
    lineStart.move(e.getX(), e.getY());
  }

  public void mouseDragged(MouseEvent e)
  {
    g = getGraphics(); // Get graphics context

    if (e.isMetaDown()) // Detect right button pressed
    {
      // Erase the drawing using an oval
      g.setColor(getBackground());
      g.fillOval(e.getX() - (CIRCLESIZE/2),
        e.getY() - (CIRCLESIZE/2), CIRCLESIZE, CIRCLESIZE);
    }
    else
    {
      g.setColor(Color.black);
      g.drawLine(lineStart.x, lineStart.y,
        e.getX(), e.getY());
    }

    lineStart.move(e.getX(), e.getY());

    // Dispose this graphics context
    g.dispose();
  }

  public void mouseMoved(MouseEvent e)
  {
  }
}
```

continues

Example 10.7 continued

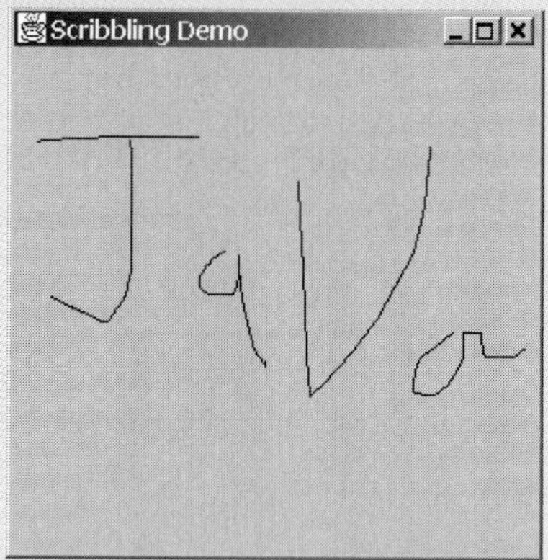

Figure 10.12 *The program enables you to scribble using the mouse.*

Example Review

The program creates a `ScribblePanel` instance to capture mouse movements on the panel. Lines are created or erased by dragging the mouse with the left or right button pressed.

When a button is pressed, the `mousePressed` handler is invoked. This handler sets the `lineStart` to the current mouse point as the starting point. Drawing begins when the mouse is dragged with the left button pressed. In this case, the `mouseDragged` handler sets the foreground color to black, and draws a line along the path of the mouse movement.

When the mouse is dragged with the right button pressed, erasing occurs. In this case, the `mouseDragged` handler sets the foreground color to the background color and draws an oval filled with the background color at the mouse pointer to erase the area covered by the oval.

The program does not use the `paintComponent(Graphics g)` method. Instead, it uses `getGraphics()` to obtain a `Graphics` instance and draws on this.

Because the `mousePressed` handler is defined in the `MouseListener` interface, and the `mouseDragged` handler is defined in the `MouseMotionListener` interface, the program implements both interfaces.

The `dispose` method disposes of this graphics context and releases any system resources it is using. Although the finalization process of the Java runtime system automatically disposes of the object after it is no longer in use, I recommend that you manually free the associated resources by calling this method rather than rely on a finalization process that may not run to completion for a long time. In this program, a large number of `Graphics` objects can be created within a short time. The program would run fine if these objects were not disposed of manually, but it would consume a lot of memory.

Keyboard Events

Keyboard events are generated whenever a key is pressed. They enable the use of the keys to control and perform actions or get input from the keyboard.

The keyboard event object describes the nature of the event (namely, that a key is pressed, released, or typed) and the value of the key. The following handlers from the `KeyListener` interface are used to process keyboard events:

- `public void keyPressed(KeyEvent e)`

  This handler is called when a key is pressed.

- `public void keyReleased(KeyEvent e)`

  This handler is called when a key is released.

- `public void keyTyped(KeyEvent e)`

  This handler is called when a key is pressed and then released.

The keys captured in the event are integers representing Unicode character values, which include alphanumeric characters, function keys, the Tab key, the Enter key, and so on. Every keyboard event has an associated key character or key code that is returned by the `getKeyChar()` or `getKeyCode()` method in `KeyEvent`, respectively.

Java defines many constants for keys, including function keys in the `KeyEvent` class. Table 10.2 shows the most common ones.

TABLE 10.2 Key Constants

Constant	*Description*
`VK_HOME`	The Home key
`VK_End`	The End key
`VK_PGUP`	The Page Up key
`VK_PGDN`	The Page Down key
`VK_UP`	The up-arrow key
`VK_DOWN`	The down-arrow key
`VK_LEFT`	The left-arrow key
`VK_RIGHT`	The right-arrow key
`VK_ESCAPE`	The Esc key
`VK_TAB`	The Tab key

TABLE 10.2 continued

Constant	*Description*
VK_BACK_SPACE	The Backspace key
VK_CAPS_LOCK	The Caps Lock key
VK_NUM_LOCK	The Num Lock key
VK_ENTER	The Enter key
VK_F1 to VK_F12	The function keys from F1 to F12
VK_0 to VK_9	The number keys from 0 to 9
VK_A to VK_Z	The letter keys from A to Z

Example 10.8 Handling Key Events

This example shows a program that displays a user-input character. The user can move the character up, down, left, and right, using arrow keys VK_UP, VK_DOWN, VK_LEFT, and VK_RIGHT. Figure 10.13 contains a sample run of the program.

```
// KeyboardEventDemo.java: Receive key input
import java.awt.*;
import java.awt.event.*;
import javax.swing.*;

public class KeyboardEventDemo extends JApplet
{
  private KeyboardPanel keyboardPanel = new KeyboardPanel();

  // Main method used if run as an application
  public static void main(String[] args)
  {
    // Create a frame
    JFrame frame = new JFrame("KeyboardEvent Demo");

    // Create an instance of the applet
    KeyboardEventDemo applet = new KeyboardEventDemo();

    // Add the applet instance to the frame
    frame.getContentPane().add(applet, BorderLayout.CENTER);

    // Invoke init() and start()
    applet.init();
    applet.start();

    // Display the frame
    frame.setSize(300, 300);
    // frame.setDefaultCloseOperation(JFrame.EXIT_ON_CLOSE);
    frame.setVisible(true);

    // Set focus on the keyboardPanel
    applet.focus();
  }

  // Initialize UI
  public void init()
  {
    // Add the keyboard panel to accept and display user input
    getContentPane().add(keyboardPanel);

    // Request focus
    focus();
```

```
    }

    // Set focus on the panel
    public void focus()
    {
      // It is required for receiving key input
      keyboardPanel.requestFocus();
    }
  }

  // KeyboardPanel for receiving key input
  class KeyboardPanel extends JPanel implements KeyListener
  {
    private int x = 100;
    private int y = 100;
    private char keyChar = 'A'; // Default key

    public KeyboardPanel()
    {
      addKeyListener(this); // Register listener
    }
    public void keyReleased(KeyEvent e)
    {
    }

    public void keyTyped(KeyEvent e)
    {
    }

    public void keyPressed(KeyEvent e)
    {
      switch (e.getKeyCode())
      {
        case KeyEvent.VK_DOWN: y += 10; break;
        case KeyEvent.VK_UP: y -= 10; break;
        case KeyEvent.VK_LEFT: x -= 10; break;
        case KeyEvent.VK_RIGHT: x += 10; break;
        default: keyChar = e.getKeyChar();
      }
      repaint();
    }

    // Draw the character
    public void paintComponent(Graphics g)
    {
      super.paintComponent(g);

      g.setFont(new Font("TimesRoman", Font.PLAIN, 24));
      g.drawString(String.valueOf(keyChar), x, y);
    }
  }
```

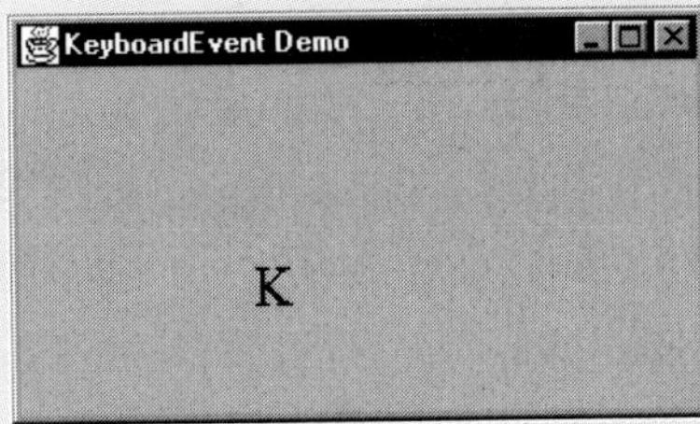

Figure 10.13 *The program responds to the keyboard events by displaying a character and moving it up, down, left, or right.*

continues

Example 10.8 continued

Example Review

When a non-arrow key is pressed, the key is displayed. When an arrow key is pressed, the character moves in the direction indicated by the arrow key.

Because the program gets input from the keyboard, it listens for `KeyEvent` and implements `KeyListener` to handle key input.

When a key is pressed, the `keyPressed` handler is invoked. The program uses `e.getKeyCode()` to obtain the `int` value for the key and `e.getKeyChar()` to get the character for the key. In fact, `(int)e.getKeyChar()` is the same as `e.getKeyCode()`.

Only a focused component can receive `KeyEvent`. When the program runs as an applet, the `keyboardPanel` component receives focus, because it is the last and only component added to the applet. When the program runs as an application, `keyboardPanel` is not focused, since `keyboardPanel` is added to the applet, and the applet is placed inside a frame. Thus you need to set focus to `keyboardPanel` using the `focus()` method defined in the `KeyboardEventDemo`. The `focus()` method sets the focus to `keyboardPanel` using the `requestFocus()` method defined in the `java.awt.Component` class.

Modeling Dynamic Behavior Using Sequence Diagrams and Statecharts

The UML diagrams presented so far describe the properties and methods of a class or the static relationships among classes. This section introduces the sequence diagrams and statechart diagrams that model dynamic behaviors among the objects.

Sequence Diagrams

Sequence diagrams describe interactions among objects by depicting the time ordering of method invocations. A sequence diagram consists of the following elements, as shown in Figure 10.14:

- Class role: Represents the roles the object plays. The objects at the top of the diagram represent class roles.
- Lifeline: Represents the existence of an object over a period of time. A vertical dotted line extending from the object is used to denote a lifeline.
- Activation: Represents the time during which an object is performing an operation. Thin rectangles placed on lifelines are used to denote activations.
- Method invocation: Represents communication between objects. Horizontal arrows labeled with method calls are used to denote method invocations.

The interactions between the `ButtonDemo` object and the `MessagePanel` object in Example 9.1, "Using Buttons," are illustrated in Figure 10.15.

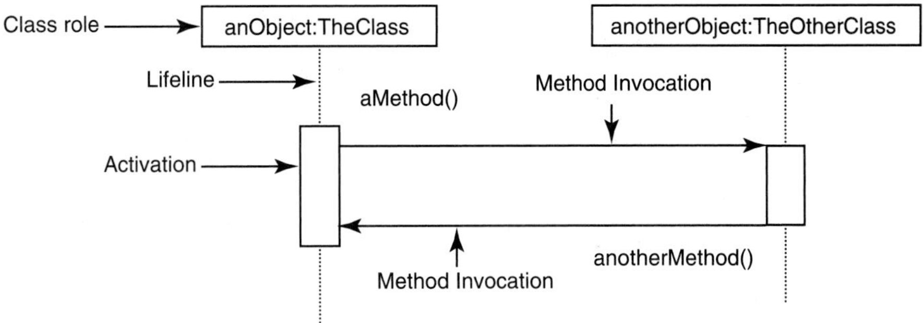

Figure 10.14 *Sequence diagrams describe interactions between objects.*

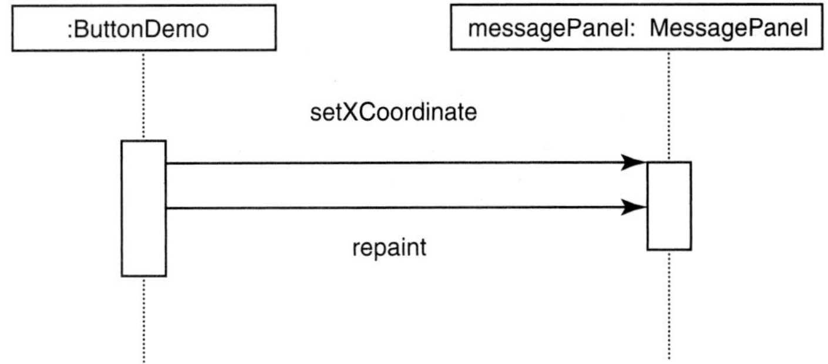

Figure 10.15 *The `ButtonDemo` object invokes the `setXCoordinate` method to move the message on the `MessagePanel` and repaint the message.*

Statechart Diagrams

Statechart diagrams describe the flow of control of the object. A statechart diagram contains the following elements, as shown in Figure 10.16:

- State: Represents a situation during the life of an object in which it satisfies some condition, performs some action, or waits for some event to occur. Each

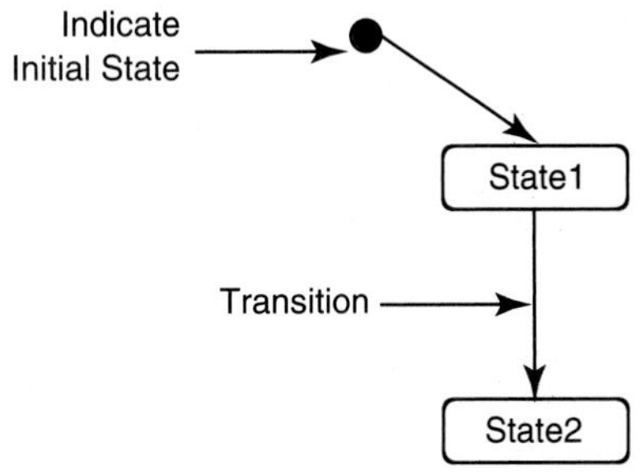

Figure 10.16 *Statechart diagrams describe the flow of control of an object.*

state has a name. Rectangles with rounded corners are used to represent states. The small filled circle is used to denote the initial state.

- Transition: Represents the relationship between two states, indicating that an object will perform some action to transfer from one state to the other. A solid arrow with appropriate method invocation is used to denote a transition.

The statechart diagram in Figure 10.17 can be used to describe the flow of control of an applet. This diagram is much better and clearer than Figure 10.1.

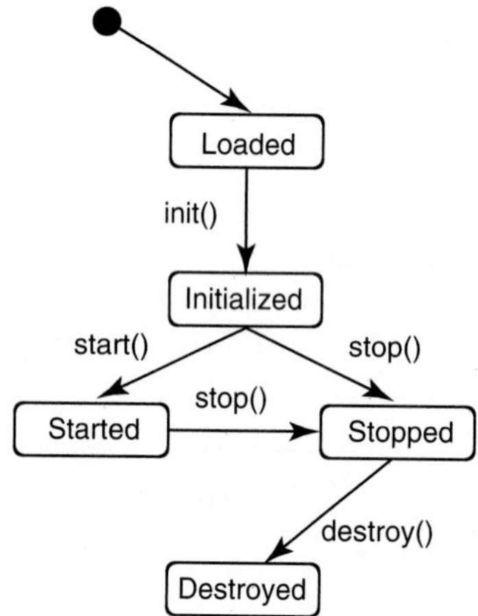

Figure 10.17 *The flow of control of an applet can be described using a statechart diagram.*

Case Studies

You have learned objects, classes, arrays, class inheritance, graphics, event-driven programming, and applets from the many examples in this chapter and the preceding chapters. Now it is time to put what you have learned to work in developing comprehensive projects. In this section, you will develop a Java applet to play the popular game of TicTacToe.

Example 10.9 The TicTacToe Game

This example creates a program for playing TicTacToe. In a game of TicTacToe, two players take turns marking an available cell in a 3 × 3 grid with their respective tokens (either X or O). When one player has placed three tokens in a horizontal, vertical, or diagonal row on the grid, the game is over and that player has won. A draw (no winner) occurs when all the spaces on the grid have been filled with tokens and neither player has achieved a win. Figures 10.18 and 10.19 are representative sample runs of the example.

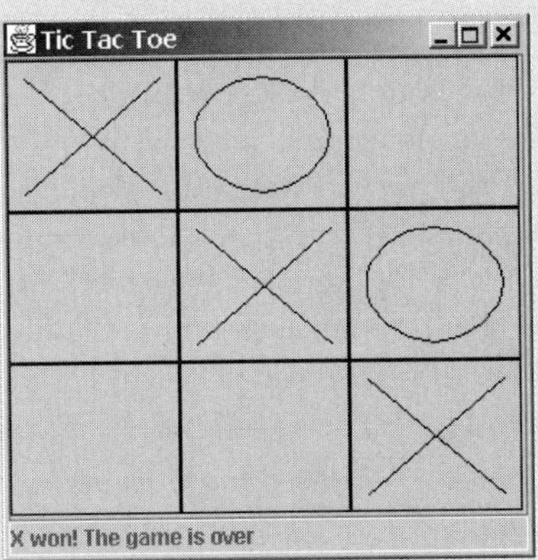

Figure 10.18 *This sample shows that the X player has won.*

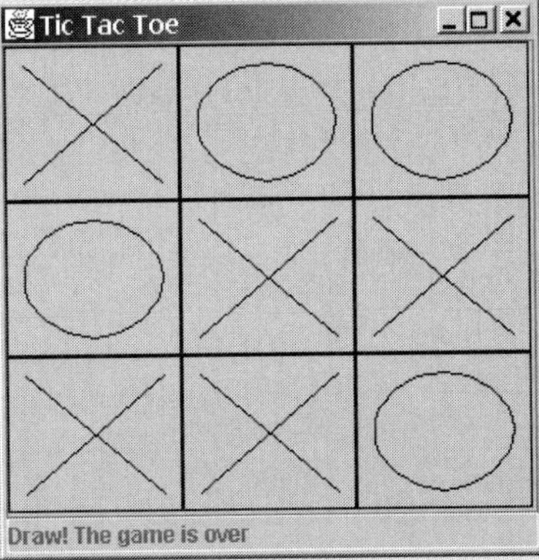

Figure 10.19 *This sample shows a draw with no winner.*

All the examples you have seen so far have simple behaviors that are easy to model with classes. The behavior of the TicTacToe game is somewhat more complex. To create the classes to model the behavior, you need to study and understand the game.

Assume that all the cells are initially empty, and that the first player takes the X token, and the second player takes the O token. To mark a cell, the player points the mouse to the cell and clicks it. If the cell is empty, the token (X or O) is displayed. If the cell is already filled, the player's action is ignored.

From the preceding description, it is obvious that a cell is a GUI object that handles the mouse-click event and displays tokens. Such an object could be either a button or a panel. Drawing on panels is more flexible than on buttons. The token (X or O) can be drawn on a panel in any size, but it only can be displayed on a button as a text label. Therefore, a panel should be used to model a cell.

continues

Example 10.9 continued

Let `Cell` be a subclass of `JPanel`. You can declare the 3 × 3 grid to be an array `new Cell[3][3]` to model the game. How do you know the state of the cell (empty, X, or O)? You simply use a property named `token` of `char` type in the `Cell` class. The `Cell` class is responsible for drawing the token when an empty cell is clicked, so you need to write the code for listening to the `MouseEvent` and for painting the shape for token X and O. To determine which shape to draw, you can introduce a variable named `whoseTurn` of `char` type in the game. `whoseTurn` is initially X, then changes to O, and subsequently changes between X and O whenever a new cell is occupied.

Finally, how do you know whether the game is over with or without a winner and who the winner, if any, is? You can create a method named `isWon(char token)` to check whether a specified token has won and a method named `isFull()` to check whether all the cells are occupied.

Clearly, two classes emerge from the foregoing analysis. One is the `Cell` class, which handles operations for a single cell; and the other is the `TicTacToe` class, which plays the whole game and deals with all the cells. The relationship between these two classes is shown in Figure 10.20.

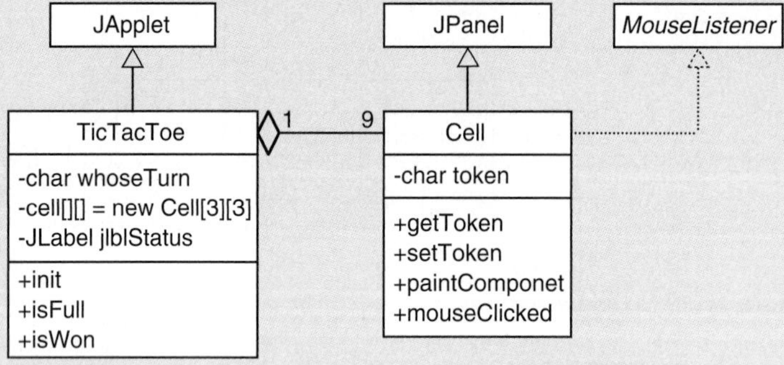

Figure 10.20 *The `TicTacToe` class contains nine cells.*

The `Cell` class has the following data fields and methods:

Data field:

`char token`: Represents the token used in the cell. The initial value is ' ';

Methods:

```
public char getToken()
```

Returns the token of the cell.

```
public void setToken(char token)
```

Sets the token in the cell.

```
public char getToken()
```

Returns the token of the cell.

`public void paintComponent(Graphics g)`

Overrides this method to display the token in the cell.

`public void mouseClicked(MouseEvent e)`

Implements this method in the `MouseListener` to handle a mouse click on the cell.

The `TicTacToe` class has the following data fields and methods:

Data field:

`char whoseTurn`: Indicates which player has the turn. The initial value is 'X', which indicates that the player X has the turn.

`Cell[][] cell`: Represents the cells.

`JLabel jlblStatus`: A label for displaying game status.

Methods:

`public void init()`

Overrides this method to initialize variables and create UI.

`public boolean isFull()`

Determines whether the cells are all filled.

`public boolean isWon(char token)`

Determines whether the player with the specified token wins.

The interaction between the `TicTacToe` object and a `Cell` object is shown in Figure 10.21.

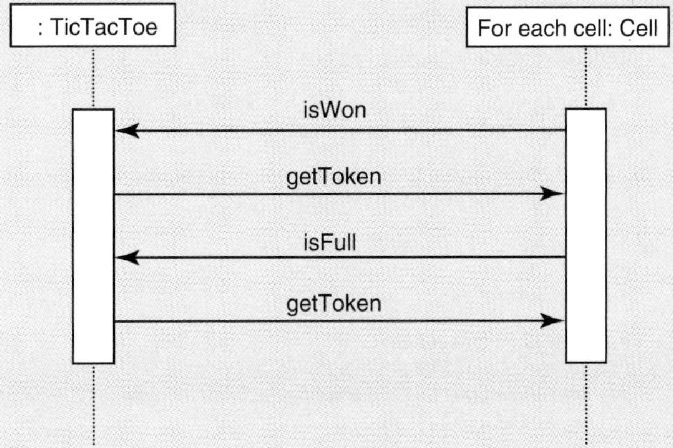

Figure 10.21 *Each Cell object communicates with the `TicTacToe` object to play the game.*

continues

Example 10.9 continued

The program is given below:

```
// TicTacToe.java: Play the TicTacToe game
import java.awt.*;
import java.awt.event.*;
import javax.swing.*;
import javax.swing.border.LineBorder;

public class TicTacToe extends JApplet
{
  // Indicate which player has a turn, initially it is the X player
  private char whoseTurn = 'X';

  // Create and initialize cells
  private Cell[][] cell =  new Cell[3][3];

  // Create and initialize a status label
  private JLabel jlblStatus = new JLabel("X's turn to play");

  // Initialize UI
  public void init()
  {
    // Panel p to hold cells
    JPanel p = new JPanel();
    p.setLayout(new GridLayout(3, 3, 0, 0));
    for (int i=0; i<3; i++)
      for (int j=0; j<3; j++)
        p.add(cell[i][j] = new Cell());

    // Set line borders on the cells panel and the status label
    p.setBorder(new LineBorder(Color.red, 1));
    jlblStatus.setBorder(new LineBorder(Color.yellow, 1));

    // Place the panel and the label to the applet
    this.getContentPane().add(p, BorderLayout.CENTER);
    this.getContentPane().add(jlblStatus, BorderLayout.SOUTH);
  }

  // This main method enables the applet to run as an application
  public static void main(String[] args)
  {
    // Create a frame
    JFrame frame = new JFrame("Tic Tac Toe");

    // Create an instance of the applet
    TicTacToe applet = new TicTacToe();

    // Add the applet instance to the frame
    frame.getContentPane().add(applet, BorderLayout.CENTER);

    // Invoke init() and start()
    applet.init();
    applet.start();

    // Display the frame
    frame.setSize(300, 300);
    // frame.setDefaultCloseOperation(JFrame.EXIT_ON_CLOSE);
    frame.setVisible(true);
  }

  // Determine if the cells are all occupied
  public boolean isFull()
  {
    for (int i=0; i<3; i++)
      for (int j=0; j<3; j++)
```

```
        if (cell[i][j].getToken() == ' ')
          return false;

    return true;
  }

  // Determine if the player with the specified token wins
  public boolean isWon(char token)
  {
    for (int i=0; i<3; i++)
      if ((cell[i][0].getToken() == token)
          && (cell[i][1].getToken() == token)
          && (cell[i][2].getToken() == token))
      {
        return true;
      }

    for (int j=0; j<3; j++)

      if ((cell[0][j].getToken() ==  token)
          && (cell[1][j].getToken() == token)
          && (cell[2][j].getToken() == token))
      {
        return true;
      }

    if ((cell[0][0].getToken() == token)
        && (cell[1][1].getToken() == token)
        && (cell[2][2].getToken() == token))
    {
      return true;
    }

    if ((cell[0][2].getToken() == token)
        && (cell[1][1].getToken() == token)
        && (cell[2][0].getToken() == token))
    {
      return true;
    }

    return false;
  }

  // An inner class for a cell
  public class Cell extends JPanel implements MouseListener
  {
    // Token used for this cell
    private char token = ' ';

    public Cell()
    {
      setBorder(new LineBorder(Color.black, 1)); // Set cell's border
      addMouseListener(this);  // Register listener
    }

    // The getter method for token
    public char getToken()
    {
      return token;
    }

    // The setter method for token
    public void setToken(char c)
    {
      token = c;
      repaint();
    }
```

continues

Example 10.9 continued

```
// Paint the cell
public void paintComponent(Graphics g)
{
  super.paintComponent(g);

  if (token == 'X')
  {
    g.drawLine(10, 10, getSize().width-10, getSize().height-10);
    g.drawLine(getSize().width-10, 10, 10, getSize().height-10);
  }
  else if (token == 'O')
  {
    g.drawOval(10, 10, getSize().width-20, getSize().height-20);
  }
}

// Handle mouse click on a cell
public void mouseClicked(MouseEvent e)
{
  if (token == ' ') // If cell is not occupied
  {
    if (whoseTurn == 'X')  // If it is the X player's turn
    {
      setToken('X');  // Set token in the cell
      whoseTurn = 'O';  // Change the turn
      jlblStatus.setText("O's turn");  // Display status

      if (isWon('X'))
        jlblStatus.setText("X won! The game is over");
      else if (isFull())
        jlblStatus.setText("Draw! The game is over");
    }
    else if (whoseTurn == 'O') // If it is the O player's turn
    {
      setToken('O'); // Set token in the cell
      whoseTurn = 'X';  // Change the turn
      jlblStatus.setText("X's turn"); // Display status

      if (isWon('O'))
        jlblStatus.setText("O won! The game is over");
      else if (isFull())
        jlblStatus.setText("Draw! The game is over");
    }
  }
}

public void mousePressed(MouseEvent e)
{
  // TODO: implement this java.awt.event.MouseListener method;
}

public void mouseReleased(MouseEvent e)
{
  // TODO: implement this java.awt.event.MouseListener method;
}

public void mouseEntered(MouseEvent e)
{
  // TODO: implement this java.awt.event.MouseListener method;
}
```

```
      public void mouseExited(MouseEvent e)
      {
        // TODO: implement this java.awt.event.MouseListener method;
      }
    }
  }
```

Example Review

The `TicTacToe` class initializes the user interface with nine cells placed in a panel of `GridLayout`. A label named `jlblStatus` is used to show the status of the game. The variable `whoseTurn` is used to track the next type of token to be placed in a cell. The methods `isFull()` and `isWon()` are for checking the status of the game.

It is worth noting that the `Cell` class is declared as an inner class for `TicTacToe`. This is because the `mouseClicked()` method in `Cell` references the variable `whoseTurn` and invokes `isFull` and `isWon` in the `TicTacToe` class. Since `Cell` is an inner class in `TicTacToe`, the variable and methods defined in `TicTacToe` can be directly used in it. This approach makes programs simple and concise. If `Cell` were not declared as an inner class of `TicTacToe`, you would have to pass an object of `TicTacToe` to `Cell` for the variables and methods in `TicTacToe` to be used in `Cell`. You will rewrite the program without using an inner class in Exercise 10.6.

The `Cell` class implements `MouseListener` to listen for `MouseEvent`. When a cell is clicked, it draws a shape determined by the variable `whoseTurn`, and then checks whether the game is won or all the cells are occupied.

There is a problem in this program in that the user may continue to mark the cells even after the game is over. You will fix this problem in Exercise 10.6.

This program enables two users to play from the same machine. In Chapter 16, "Networking," you will learn how to develop a distributed TicTacToe applet that will enable two users to play on different machines anywhere on the Internet.

TIP

You should use an incremental approach in developing a Java project of this kind, working one step at a time. The foregoing program can be divided into five steps:

1. Lay out the user interface and display a fixed token X on a cell.
2. Enable the cell to display a fixed token X upon a mouse click.
3. Coordinate between the two players so as to display tokens X and O alternately.
4. Check whether a player wins, or whether all the cells are occupied without a winner.
5. Implement displaying a message on the label upon each move by a player.

Packaging and Deploying Java Projects (Optional)

Your project may consist of many classes and supporting files, such as image files and audio files. To make your programs run on an end-user side, you need to provide end-users with all these files. For convenience, Java supports an archive file that can be used to group all the project files in a compressed file.

The Java archive file format (JAR) is based on the popular ZIP file format. Although JAR can be used as a general archiving tool, the primary motivation for its development was to make it possible for Java applications, applets, and their requisite components (.class files, images, and sounds) to be transported in a single file.

This single file can be deployed on an end-user's machine as an application. It also can be downloaded to a browser in a single HTTP transaction, rather than opening a new connection for each piece. This greatly simplifies application deployment and improves the speed with which an applet can be loaded onto a Web page and begin functioning. The JAR format also supports compression, which reduces the size of the file and improves download time still further. Additionally, individual entries in a JAR file can be digitally signed by the applet author to authenticate their origin.

You can use the JDK **jar** command to create an archive file. The following command creates an archive file named TicTacToe.jar for classes TicTacToe.class and TicTacToe$Cell.class.

```
jar -cf TicTacToe.jar TicTacToe.class TicTacToe$Cell.class
```

The **-c** option is for creating a new archive file, and the **-f** option specifies the archive file's name.

NOTE
You can view the contents of a .JAR file using WinZip32, a popular compression utility for Windows 95 and Windows NT, as shown in Figure 10.22.

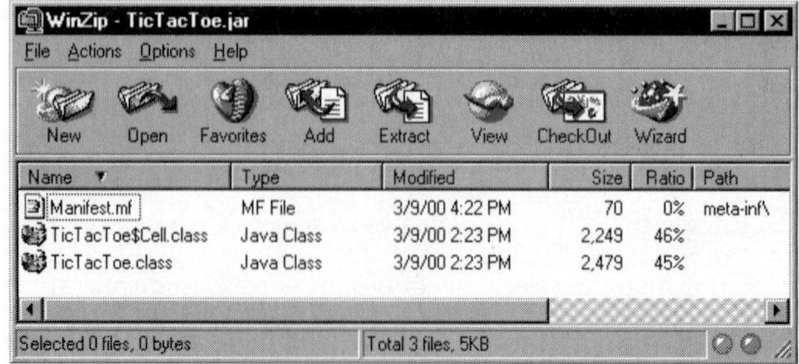

Figure 10.22 *You can view the files contained in the archive file using the WinZip utility.*

The Manifest File

As shown in Figure 10.22, a manifest file was created with the path name `meta-inf\`. The manifest is a special file that contains information about the files packaged in a JAR file. For instance, the manifest file in Figure 10.22 contains the following information:

```
Manifest-Version: 1.0
Name: TicTacToe.class
Java-Bean: True

Name: TioTacToe$Cell.class
Java-Bean: True
```

You can modify the information contained in the manifest file to enable the JAR file to be used for a variety of purposes. For instance, you can add information to specify a main class to run an application using the .jar file.

Running Archived Projects

You can package all the class files and dependent resource files into an archive file, which can be distributed to the end-user. If the project is a Java application, the user should have a Java running environment already installed. If it is not installed, the user can download Java Runtime Environment (JRE) from JavaSoft at **http://www.javasoft.com/** and install it.

NOTE

The Java Runtime Environment is the minimum standard Java platform for running Java programs. It contains the Java interpreter, Java core classes, and supporting files. The JRE does not contain any of the development tools (such as Applet Viewer or javac) or classes that pertain only to a development environment. The JRE is a subset of JDK.

To run `TicTacToe` as an application, take the following steps:

1. Update the manifest file to insert an entry for the main class. You need to create a text file containing the following two lines:

   ```
   Main-Class: TicTacToe
   Sealed: true
   ```

   The first line specifies the main class. The second line is necessary to ensure that the first line can be inserted into an existing manifest file in a jar. Assume that these two lines are contained in the file temp.mf.

2. Execute the `jar` command to insert the main class line to the manifest file in TicTacToe.jar, as follows:

   ```
   jar -uvmf temp.mf TicTacToe.jar
   ```

   The **-u** option is for updating an existing jar file, the **-v** option is for displaying command output, and the **-m** option is for appending the contents in temp.mf to the manifest file in the archive.

3. Run the .jar file using the java command from the directory that contains TicTacToe.jar, as follows:

```
java -jar TicTacToe.jar
```

NOTE

You can write an installation procedure that creates the necessary directories and subdirectories on the end-user's computer. The installation can also create an icon so that the end-user can start the program by double-clicking on the icon.

To run `TicTacToe` as an applet, modify the <APPLET> tag in the HTML file to include an ARCHIVE attribute. The ARCHIVE attribute specifies the archive file in which the applet is contained. For example, the HTML file for running the `TicTacToe` can be modified as follows:

```
<APPLET
  CODE      = "TicTacToe.class"
  ARCHIVE   = "TicTacToe.jar"
  WIDTH     = 400
  HEIGHT    = 300
  HSPACE    = 0
  VSPACE    = 0
  ALIGN     = Middle
>
</APPLET>
```

The *CardLayout* Manager (Optional)

Layout managers arrange components in a container. You have already used the `FlowLayout` manager, `GridLayout` manager, and `BorderLayout` manager. Java has other layout managers like `CardLayout` and `GridBagLayout`. Java also enables you to directly place components in specific positions without using a layout manager. This section discusses the `CardLayout` manager; the following sections discuss the `GridBagLayout` manager and using no layout manager.

The `CardLayout` manager arranges components in a queue of cards. You can only see one card at a time. To construct a `CardLayout`, use the constructor `CardLayout()`.

Cards are usually placed in a container, such as a panel. Components are placed in the card queue in the order in which they are added. To add a component to the `CardLayout` container, use the following method:

```
public void add(Component component, String name)
```

This adds the specified component to the container. The `String` argument of the method, `name`, gives an explicit identity to the component in the queue.

To make a component visible in the container with `CardLayout`, use the following instance methods in the `CardLayout` object:

- `public void first(Container container)`

  This method views the first card in the container.

- `public void last(Container container)`

  This method views the last card in the container.

- `public void next(Container container)`

  This method views the next card in the container.

- `public void previous(Container container)`

  This method views the previous card in the container.

- `public void show(Container container, String name)`

  This method views the component with the specified name in the container. It can be used to directly display the component.

Example 10.10 Testing `CardLayout` Manager

This example shows a program that creates two panels in a frame. The first panel uses `CardLayout` to hold 15 labels for displaying images. The second panel uses `FlowLayout` to group four buttons named First, Next, Previous, and Last, and a combo box labeled `Image`.

These buttons control which image will be shown in the `CardLayout` panel. When the user clicks on the First button, for example, the first image in the `CardLayout` panel appears. The combo box enables the user to directly select an image.

The program follows, and the output of a sample run is shown in Figure 10.23.

```
// ShowCardLayout.java: Using CardLayout to display images
import java.awt.*;
import java.awt.event.*;
import javax.swing.*;

public class ShowCardLayout extends JApplet
  implements ActionListener, ItemListener
{
  private CardLayout queue = new CardLayout();
  private JPanel cardPanel = new JPanel();
  private JButton jbtFirst, jbtNext, jbtPrevious, jbtLast;
  private JComboBox jcboImage;

  public void init()
  {
    // Use CardLayout for cardPanel
    cardPanel.setLayout(queue);

    // Add 15 labels for displaying images into cardPanel
    for (int i=1; i<=15; i++)
      cardPanel.add
        (new JLabel(new ImageIcon("images/L"+i+".gif")),
         String.valueOf(i));

    // Panel p to hold buttons and a combo box
    JPanel p = new JPanel();
    p.add(jbtFirst = new JButton("First"));
    p.add(jbtNext = new JButton("Next"));
    p.add(jbtPrevious= new JButton("Previous"));
    p.add(jbtLast = new JButton("Last"));
    p.add(new JLabel("Image"));
    p.add(jcboImage = new JComboBox());
```

continues

Example 10.10 continued

```
      // Initialize combo box items
      for (int i=1; i<=15; i++)
        jcboImage.addItem(String.valueOf(i));

      // Place panels in the frame
      getContentPane().add(cardPanel, BorderLayout.CENTER);
      getContentPane().add(p, BorderLayout.NORTH);

      // Register listeners with the source objects
      jbtFirst.addActionListener(this);
      jbtNext.addActionListener(this);
      jbtPrevious.addActionListener(this);
      jbtLast.addActionListener(this);
      jcboImage.addItemListener(this);
    }

    // This main method enables the applet to run as an application
    public static void main(String[] args)
    {
      // Create a frame
      JFrame frame = new JFrame("CardLayout Demo");

      // Create an instance of the applet
      ShowCardLayout applet = new ShowCardLayout();

      // Add the applet instance to the frame
      frame.getContentPane().add(applet, BorderLayout.CENTER);

      // Invoke init() and start()
      applet.init();
      applet.start();

      // Display the frame
      frame.setSize(300, 300);
      // frame.setDefaultCloseOperation(JFrame.EXIT_ON_CLOSE);
      frame.setVisible(true);
    }

    // Handle button actions
    public void actionPerformed(ActionEvent e)
    {
      String actionCommand = e.getActionCommand();
      if (e.getSource() instanceof JButton)
        if ("First".equals(actionCommand))
          // Show the first component in queue
          queue.first(cardPanel);
        else if ("Last".equals(actionCommand))
          // Show the last component in queue
          queue.last(cardPanel);
        else if ("Previous".equals(actionCommand))
          // Show the previous component in queue
          queue.previous(cardPanel);
        else if ("Next".equals(actionCommand))
          // Show the next component in queue
          queue.next(cardPanel);
    }

    // Handle selection of combo box item
    public void itemStateChanged(ItemEvent e)
    {
      if (e.getSource() == jcboImage)
        // Show the component at specified index
        queue.show(cardPanel, (String)e.getItem());
    }
  }
```

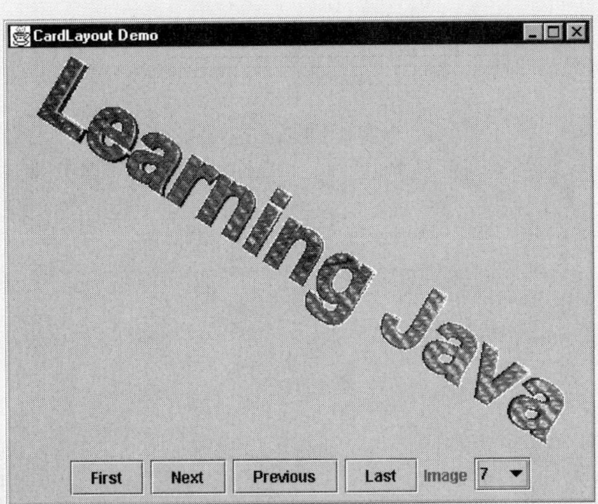

Figure 10.23 *The program shows images in a panel of* `CardLayout`.

Example Review

The program creates an instance of `CardLayout`, `queue = new CardLayout()`. The statement `cardPanel.setLayout(queue)` sets the `cardPanel` with the `CardLayout`; `cardPanel` is an instance of `JPanel`. You have already used such statements as `setLayout(new FlowLayout())` to create an anonymous layout object and set the layout for a container, instead of declaring and creating a separate instance of the layout manager, as in this program. The object `queue`, however, is useful later in the program to show components in `cardPanel`. You have to use `queue.first(cardPanel)`, for example, to view the first component in `cardPanel`.

The statement `cardPanel.add(new JLabel(new ImageIcon ("images/L"+i+".gif")), String.valueOf(i))` adds the image label with identity `String.valueOf(i)`. Later, when the user selects an image with number `i`, the identity `String.valueOf(i)` is used in the `queue.show()` method to view the image with the specified identity.

The *GridBagLayout* Manager (Optional)

The `GridBagLayout` manager is the most flexible and the most complex. It is similar to the `GridLayout` manager in the sense that both layout managers arrange components in a grid. The components of `GridBagLayout` can vary in size, however, and can be added in any order. For example, with `GridBagLayout` you can create the layout shown in Figure 10.24.

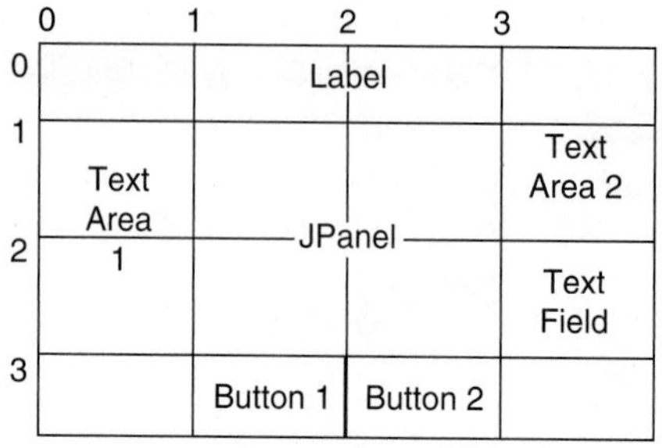

Figure 10.24 *A `GridBagLayout` manager divides the container into cells. A component can occupy several cells.*

The constructor `GridBagLayout()` is used to create a new `GridBagLayout`. In `GridLayout`, the grid size (the number of rows and columns) is specified in the constructor. It is not specified in `GridBagLayout`.

Each `GridBagLayout` uses a dynamic rectangular grid of cells, with each component occupying one or more cells called its *display area*. Each component managed by a `GridBagLayout` is associated with a `GridBagConstraints` instance that specifies how the component is laid out within its display area. How a `GridBagLayout` places a set of components depends on the `GridBagConstraints` and minimum size of each component, as well as the preferred size of the component's container.

To use `GridBagLayout` effectively, you must customize the `GridBagConstraints` of one or more of its components. You customize a `GridBagConstraints` object by setting one or more of its instance variables:

- **`gridx`** and **`gridy`**: Specify the cell at the upper left of the component's display area, where the upper-leftmost cell has the address `gridx=0`, `gridy=0`. Note that `gridx` specifies the column in which the component will be placed, and `gridy` specifies the row in which the component will be placed. In Figure 10.24, Button 1 has a `gridx` value of `1` and a `gridy` value of `3`, and Label has `gridx` value of 0 and a `gridy` value of 0.

- **`gridwidth`** and **`gridheight`**: Specify the number of cells in a row (for `gridwidth`) or column (for `gridheight`) in the component's display area. The default value is `1`. In Figure 10.24, the JPanel in the center occupies two columns and two rows, and Text Area 2 occupies one row and one column.

- **`weightx`** and **`weighty`**: Specify the extra horizontal and vertical space to allocate for the component when the window is resized. Unless you specify a weight for at least one component in a row (`weightx`) and a column (`weighty`), all the components clump together in the center of their container. This is because, when the weight is zero (the default), the `GridBagLayout` puts any extra space between its grid of cells and the edges of the container. You will see the effect of these parameters in Example 10.11.

- **`fill`**: Specifies how the component should be resized if its viewing area is larger than its current size. Valid values are `GridBagConstraints.NONE` (the default), `GridBagConstraints.HORIZONTAL` (makes the component wide enough to fill its display area horizontally, but doesn't change its height), `GridBagConstraints.VERTICAL` (makes the component tall enough to fill its display area vertically, but doesn't change its width), and `GridBagConstraints.BOTH` (makes the component totally fill its display area).

- **`anchor`**: Specifies where in the area the component is placed when it does not fill the entire area. Valid values are as follows:

```
GridBagConstraints.CENTER (the default)

GridBagConstraints.NORTH

GridBagConstraints.NORTHEAST

GridBagConstraints.EAST

GridBagConstraints.SOUTHEAST

GridBagConstraints.SOUTH

GridBagConstraints.SOUTHWEST

GridBagConstraints.WEST

GridBagConstraints.NORTHWEST
```

The `fill` and `anchor` parameters deal with how to fill and place the component when the viewing area is larger than the requested area. The `fill` and `anchor` parameters are class variables, whereas `gridx`, `gridy`, `width`, `height`, `weightx`, and `weighty` are instance variables.

Example 10.11 Testing the `GridBagLayout` Manager

This example shows a program that uses the `GridBagLayout` manager to create a layout for Figure 10.24. The output of the program is shown in Figure 10.25.

```
// ShowGridBagLayout.java: Using GridBagLayout
import java.awt.*;
import java.awt.event.*;
import javax.swing.*;

public class ShowGridBagLayout extends JFrame
{
  private JLabel jlbl;
  private JTextArea jta1, jta2;
  private JTextField jtf;
  private JPanel jp;
  private JButton jbt1, jbt2;
  private GridBagLayout gbLayout;
  private GridBagConstraints gbConstraints;

  // Main method
  public static void main(String[] args)
  {
    ShowGridBagLayout frame = new ShowGridBagLayout();
    frame.setSize(350,200);
    // frame.setDefaultCloseOperation(JFrame.EXIT_ON_CLOSE);
    frame.setVisible(true);
  }
```

continues

Example 10.11 continued

```
  // Add a component to the container
  private void addComp(Component c, GridBagLayout gbLayout,
                       GridBagConstraints gbConstraints,
                       int row, int column, int numRows,
                       int numColumns, int weightx, int weighty)
  {
    // Set parameters
    gbConstraints.gridx = column;
    gbConstraints.gridy = row;
    gbConstraints.gridwidth = numColumns;
    gbConstraints.gridheight = numRows;
    gbConstraints.weightx = weightx;
    gbConstraints.weighty = weighty;

    // Set constraints in the GridBagLayout
    gbLayout.setConstraints(c, gbConstraints);

    // Add component to the container
    getContentPane().add(c);
  }

  // Constructor
  public ShowGridBagLayout()
  {
    setTitle("Show GridBagLayout");

    // Initialize UI components
    jlbl = new JLabel("Resize the Window and Study GridBagLayout",
                JLabel.CENTER);
    jp = new JPanel();
    jta1 = new JTextArea("Text Area", 5, 15 );
    jta2 = new JTextArea("Text Area", 5, 15 );
    jtf = new JTextField("JTextField");
    jbt1 = new JButton("Cancel" );
    jbt2 = new JButton("Ok" );

    // Create GridBagLayout and GridBagConstraints object
    gbLayout = new GridBagLayout();
    gbConstraints = new GridBagConstraints();
    getContentPane().setLayout(gbLayout);

    // Place JLabel to occupy row 0 (the first row)
    gbConstraints.fill = GridBagConstraints.BOTH;
    gbConstraints.anchor = GridBagConstraints.CENTER;
    addComp(jlbl, gbLayout, gbConstraints, 0, 0, 1, 4, 0, 0);

    // Place text area 1 in row 1 and 2, and column 0
    addComp(jta1, gbLayout, gbConstraints, 1, 0, 2, 1, 0, 0);

    // Place Panel in row 1 and 2, and column 1 and 2
    addComp(jp, gbLayout, gbConstraints, 1, 1, 2, 2, 100, 100);
    jp.setBackground(Color.red);

    // Place text area 2 in row 1 and column 3
    addComp(jta2, gbLayout, gbConstraints, 1, 3, 1, 1, 0, 100);

    // Place text field in row 2 and column 3
    addComp(jtf, gbLayout, gbConstraints, 2, 3, 1, 1, 0, 0);

    // Place JButton 1 in row 3 and column 1
    addComp(jbt1, gbLayout, gbConstraints, 3, 1, 1, 1, 0, 0);

    // Place JButton 2 in row 3 and column 2
    addComp(jbt2, gbLayout, gbConstraints, 3, 2, 1, 1, 0, 0);
  }
}
```

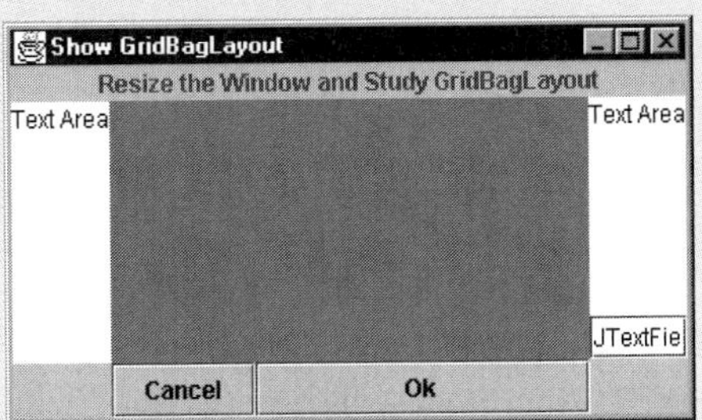

Figure 10.25 *The components are placed in the frame of* `GridBagLayout`.

Example Review

The program defines the `addComp` method to add a component to the `GridBagLayout` with the specified constraint parameters.

Since the program creates a panel with a `weightx` of 100 and a `weighty` of 100, the component has extra space to grow horizontally and vertically up to 100 pixels. If you resize the window, the panel's viewing area will increase or shrink as the window grows or shrinks.

Since the program creates the second text area `jta2` with `weightx` 0 and `weighty` 100, this text area can grow vertically but not horizontally when the window is resized.

The `weightx` and `weighty` for all the other components are 0. Whether the size of these components grows or shrinks depends on the `fill` and `anchor` parameters. The program defines `fill = BOTH` and `anchor = CENTER`.

Because the `fill` and `anchor` parameters are class variables, their values are for all components. Consider this scenario: Suppose that you enlarge the window. The panel is expanded, which causes the display area for text area `jta1` to increase. Because `fill` is `BOTH` for `jta1`, `jta1` fills in its new display area.

Using No Layout Manager (Optional)

Java enables you to place components in a container without using a layout manager. In this case, the component must be placed using the component's instance method `setBounds()`, as follows:

```
public void setBounds(int x, int y, int width, int height);
```

This sets the location and size for the component, as in the following example:

```
JButton jbt = new JButton("Help");
jbt.setBounds(10, 10, 40, 20);
```

The upper-left corner of the Help button is placed at (10, 10); the button width is 40, and the height is 20.

You perform the following steps in order not to use a layout manager:

1. Use the following statement to specify no layout manager:

```
setLayout(null);
```

2. Add the component to the container:

```
add(component);
```

3. Specify the location where the component is to be placed, using the `setBounds()` method, as follows:

```
JButton jbt = new JButton("Help");
jbt.setBounds(10, 10, 40, 20);
```

Example 10.12 Using No Layout Manager

This example shows a program that places the same components in the same layout as in the preceding example, but without using a layout manager. Figure 10.26 contains the sample output.

```
// ShowNoLayout.java: Place components without using a layout manager
import java.awt.*;
import java.awt.event.*;
import javax.swing.*;

public class ShowNoLayout extends JFrame
{
  private JLabel jlbl =
    new JLabel("Resize the Window and Study No Layout",
      JLabel.CENTER);;
  private JTextArea jta1 = new JTextArea("Text Area", 5, 10 );
  private JTextArea jta2 = new JTextArea("Text Area", 5, 10 );
  private JTextField jtf = new JTextField("TextField");
  private JPanel jp = new JPanel();
  private JButton jbt1 = new JButton("Cancel" );
  private JButton jbt2 = new JButton("Ok" );
  private GridBagLayout gbLayout;
  private GridBagConstraints gbConstraints;

  public static void main(String[] args)
  {
    ShowNoLayout frame = new ShowNoLayout();
    frame.setSize(400,200);
    // frame.setDefaultCloseOperation(JFrame.EXIT_ON_CLOSE);
    frame.setVisible(true);
  }

  public ShowNoLayout()
  {
    setTitle("Show No Layout");

    // Set background color for the panel
    jp.setBackground(Color.red);

    // Specify no layout manager
    getContentPane().setLayout(null);

    // Add components to frame
    getContentPane().add(jlbl);
    getContentPane().add(jp);
    getContentPane().add(jta1);
    getContentPane().add(jta2);
```

```
        getContentPane().add(jtf);
        getContentPane().add(jbt1);
        getContentPane().add(jbt2);

        // Put components in the right place
        jlbl.setBounds(0, 10, 400, 40);
        jta1.setBounds(0, 50, 100, 100);
        jp.setBounds(100, 50, 200, 100);
        jta2.setBounds(300, 50, 100, 50);
        jtf.setBounds(300, 100, 100, 50);
        jbt1.setBounds(100, 150, 100, 50);
        jbt2.setBounds(200, 150, 100, 50);
    }
}
```

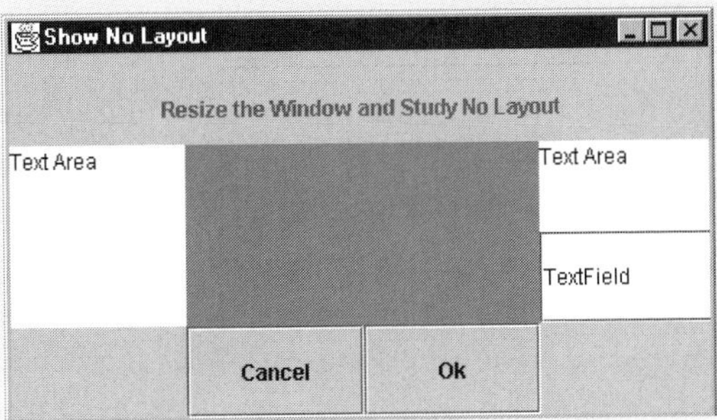

Figure 10.26 *The components are placed in the frame without using a layout manager.*

Example Review

If you run this program on Windows with 640 × 480 resolution, the layout size is just right. When the program is run on Windows with a higher resolution, the components appear very small and clump together. When it is run on Windows with a lower resolution, the components cannot be shown in their entirety.

If you resize the window, you will see that the location and size of the components are not changed, as shown in Figure 10.27.

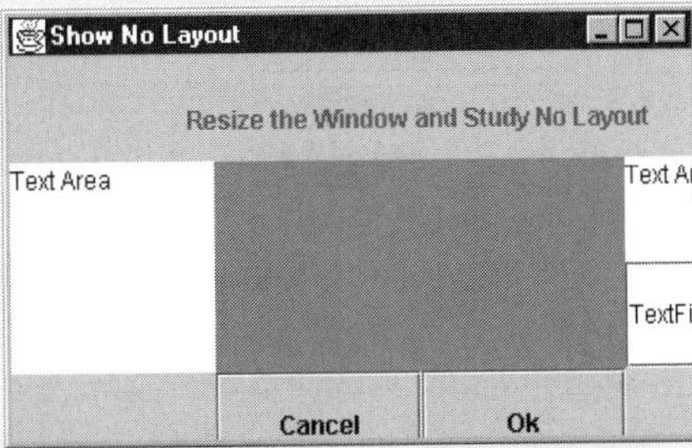

Figure 10.27 *With no layout, the components' size and positions are fixed, and can only be changed in the frame with a layout manager.*

TIP

Do not use the no-layout-manager option to develop platform-independent applications.

Chapter Summary

In this chapter, you learned about applets and advanced graphics programming using mouse and keyboard events, `CardLayout` manager, `GridBagLayout` manager, and using no layout manager. You also learned how to use archive files to efficiently deploy Java projects.

The Web browser controls and executes applets through the `init`, `start`, `stop`, and `destroy` methods in the `Applet` class. Applets always extend the `Applet` class and implement these methods, if applicable, so that they can be run by a Web browser. The applet bytecode must be specified, using the `<applet>` tag in an HTML file to tell the Web browser where to find the applet. The applet can accept parameters from HTML using the `<param>` tag. `JApplet` is a subclass of `Applet`. It should be used for developing Java applets with Swing components.

The procedures for writing applications and writing applets are very similar. An applet can easily be converted into an application, and vice versa. Moreover, an applet can be written with the capability of running, additionally, as an application.

Three examples and a case study demonstrated how to handle mouse events and keyboard events. Mouse events and keyboard events have many uses in graphics programming. Clicking, pressing, or releasing a mouse button generates a `MouseEvent`; dragging or moving a mouse generates a `MouseMotionEvent`. Entering a key generates a `KeyEvent`. `MouseEvent`, `MouseMotionEvent`, and `KeyEvent` are subclasses of `InputEvent`, which contains several common methods useful in processing mouse and keyboard events.

You learned how to use archive files to package Java classes and their associated resource files for efficient deployment of Java projects as applications or applets.

The `CardLayout` manager arranges components in a queue of cards. Only one component can be seen at a time. To add a component to the container, you need to use `add(component, string)`. You can see the components by using the methods `first(container)`, `last(container)`, `next(container)`, `previous(container)`, or `show(container, string)`. The `show(container, string)` method directly displays the component identified by the string.

The `GridBagLayout` manager provides the most flexible way to arrange components. It is similar to `GridLayout` in that the components are placed into cells, but it enables components to occupy multiple cells. Components can vary in size and can be placed in any order.

Components can be placed without using a layout manager. In such cases, they are placed at a hard-coded location. If you use this approach, your program may look fine on one machine and be useless on others. For this reason, it is advisable to use the layout managers to develop a platform-independent graphical user interface.

Review Questions

10.1 How do you run an applet?

10.2 Describe the `init()`, `start()`, `stop()`, and `destroy()` methods in the `Applet` class.

10.3 Where is the `getParameter()` method defined?

10.4 How do you add components to a `JApplet`?

10.5 Describe the `<applet>` HTML tag. How do you pass parameters to an applet?

10.6 Explain the procedure for converting an application to an applet, and vice versa.

10.7 How do you create a frame from an applet?

10.8 Can you place an applet in a frame?

10.9 What is the event type for a mouse movement? What is the event type for getting key input?

10.10 What is the listener interface for move pressed, released, clicked, entered, and exited? What is the listener interface for mouse moved and dragged?

10.11 What method is used to process action event?

10.12 What methods are used in responding to a mouse motion event?

10.13 Describe `CardLayout`. How do you create a `CardLayout`? How do you add a component to a `CardLayout` container? How do you show a card in a `CardLayout` container?

10.14 Describe `GridBagLayout`. How do you create a `GridBagLayout`? How do you create a `GridBagConstraints` object? What are the constraints you learned in this chapter? Describe their functions. How do you add a component to a `GridBagLayout` container?

10.15 Is the order in which the components are added important for certain layout managers? Identify the layout managers.

10.16 Which layout manager allows the components in the container to be moved to other rows when the window is resized?

10.17 Can you place components without using a layout manager? What are the disadvantages of not using a layout manager?

Programming Exercises

10.1 Convert Example 9.7, "Using Radio Buttons," into an applet.

10.2 Rewrite Example 10.2, "Passing Parameters to Java Applets," to display a message with specified color, font, and size. The message, x, y, color, fontname, and fontsize are parameters in the `<applet>` tag, like this:

```
<applet
  code = "Exercise10_2.class"
  width = 200
  height = 50>
  <param name=MESSAGE value="Welcome to Java">
  <param name=X value=40>
  <param name=Y value=50>
```

```
  <param name=COLOR value="red">
  <param name=FONTNAME value="Monospaced">
  <param name=FONTSIZE value=20>
You must have a Java-enabled browser to view the applet
</applet>
```

10.3 Rewrite the `MortgageApplet` in Example 10.1, "Using Applets," to enable it to run as an application as well as an applet.

10.4 Write a program that displays the mouse position when the mouse is pressed (see Figure 10.28).

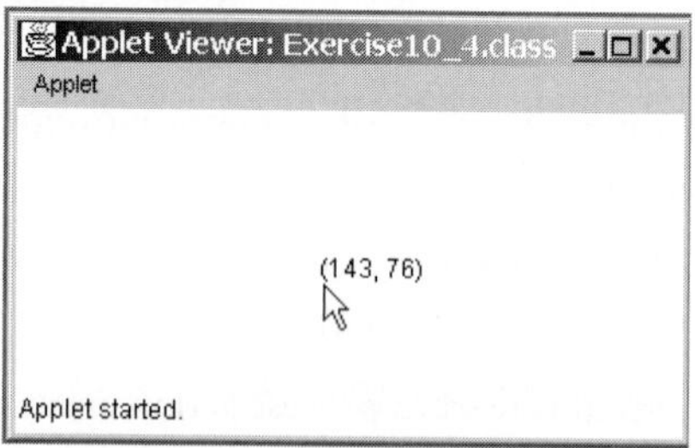

Figure 10.28 *When you click the mouse, the pixel coordinates are shown.*

10.5 Write an applet to find a path in a maze, as shown in Figure 10.29. The applet can also run as an application. The maze is represented by an 8 × 8 board. The path must meet the following conditions:

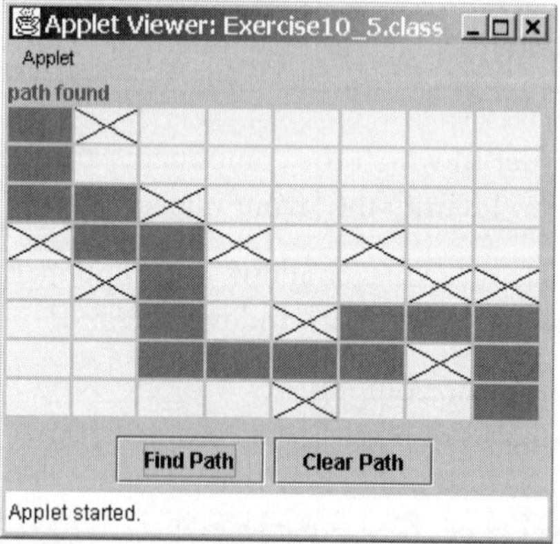

Figure 10.29 *The program finds a path from the upper-left corner to the bottom-right corner.*

- The path is between the upper-left corner cell and the lower-right corner cell in the maze.
- The applet enables the user to insert or remove a mark on a cell. A path consists of adjacent unmarked cells. Two cells are said to be adjacent if they are horizontal or vertical neighbors, but not diagonal neighbors.
- The path does not contain cells that form a square. The path in Figure 10.30, for example, does not meet this condition. (The condition makes a path easy to identify on the board.)

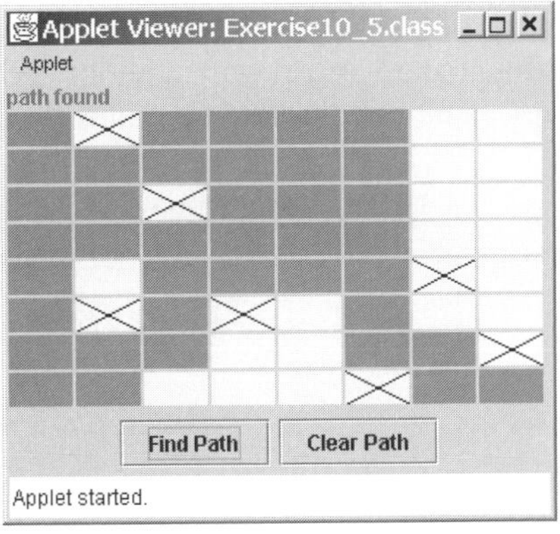

Figure 10.30 *The path does not meet the third condition for this exercise.*

10.6 Rewrite Example 10.9, "The TicTacToe Game," with the following modifications:

- Declare `Cell` as a standalone class rather than an inner class.
- When the game is over, the user cannot click to mark empty cells.

10.7 Write an applet that contains two buttons called Simple Calculator and Mortgage. When you click Simple Calculator, a frame for Example 9.11, "Using Menus," appears in a new window so that you can perform arithmetic (see Chapter 9, "Creating User Interfaces"). When you click Mortgage, a frame for Example 10.4 appears in a separate new window so that you can calculate a mortgage (see Figure 10.31).

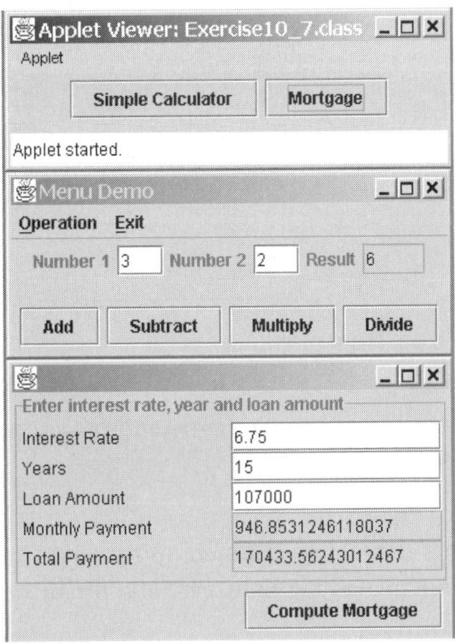

Figure 10.31 *You can show frames in the applets.*

10.8 Use various panels of `FlowLayout`, `GridLayout`, and `BorderLayout` to lay out the following calculator and to implement addition (+), subtraction (–), division (/), square root (sqrt), and modulus (%) functions (see Figure 10.32).

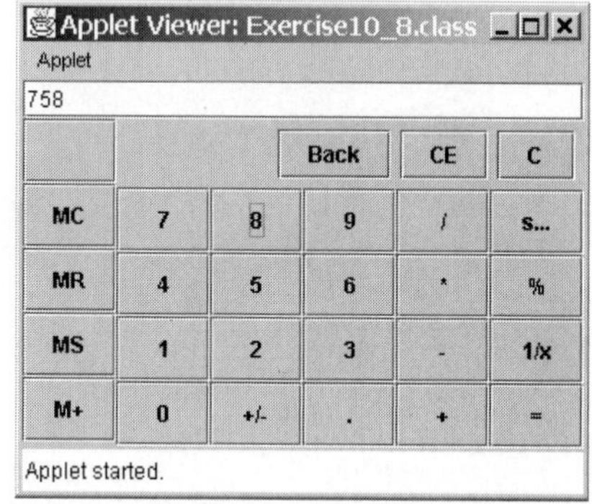

Figure 10.32 *This is a Java implementation of a popular calculator.*

10.9 Use `GridBagLayout` to lay out the preceding calculator.

10.10 Write a program to get character input from the keyboard and put the characters where the mouse points.

10.11 Write an applet to emulate a paint utility. Your program should enable the user to choose options, and to draw shapes or get characters from the keyboard based on the selected options (see Figure 10.33). Enable the applet to run as an application.

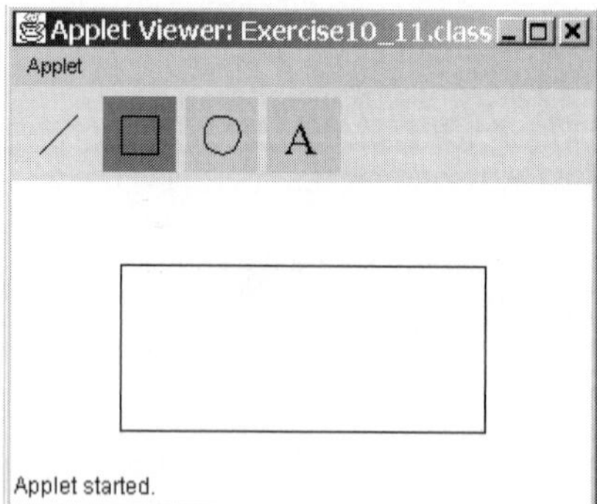

Figure 10.33 *This exercise produces a prototype drawing utility that enables you to draw lines, rectangles, ovals, and characters.*

10.12 Write an applet that does arithmetic on integers and rationals. The program uses two panels in a `CardLayout` manager, one for integer arithmetic and the other for rational arithmetic.

The program provides a menu labeled Operation that has two menu items, Integer and Rational, for selecting the two panels. When the user chooses the Integer menu item from the Operation menu, the integer panel is activated. When the user chooses the Rational menu item, the rational panel is activated. (See Figure 10.34)

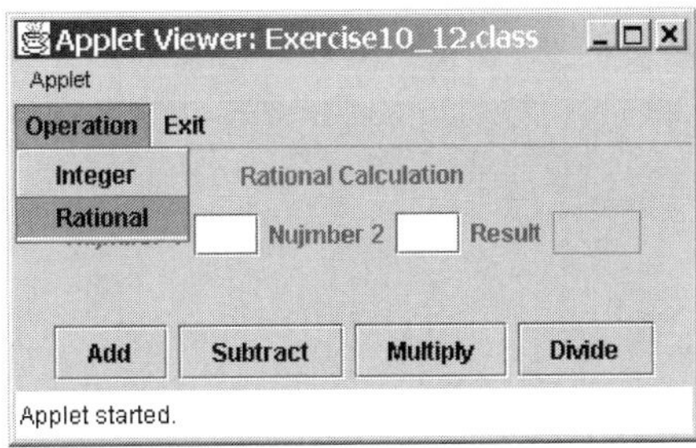

Figure 10.34 *This exercise uses* `CardLayout` *to select panels for performing integer operations or rational number operations.*

10.13 Rewrite the preceding exercise using tabbed panes instead of `CardLayout` (see Figure 10.35).

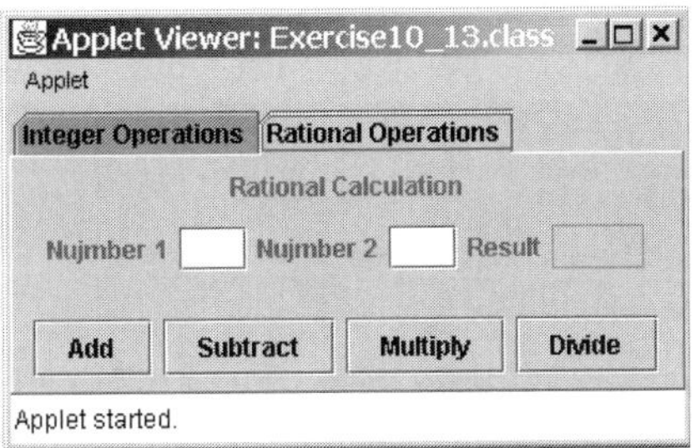

Figure 10.35 *This exercise uses tabbed panes to select panels for performing integer operations or rational number operations.*

PART IV

DEVELOPING COMPREHENSIVE PROJECTS

This part of the book is devoted to several advanced features of Java programming. The subjects treated include the use of exception handling to make programs robust, the use of internationalization support to develop projects for international audiences, the use of multithreading to make programs more responsive and interactive, the incorporation of sound and images to make programs user-friendly, the use of input and output to manage and process large quantities of data, and the creation of client/server applications with Java networking support. You will learn how to use these features to develop comprehensive programs.

CHAPTER 11

EXCEPTION HANDLING

Objectives

- Understand the concept of exception handling.
- Become familiar with exception types.
- Claim exceptions in a method.
- Throw exceptions in a method.
- Use the `try-catch` block to handle exceptions.
- Create your own exception classes.
- Rethrow exceptions in a `try-catch` block.
- Use the `finally` clause in a `try-catch` block.
- Know when to use exceptions.

Introduction

Programming errors are unavoidable, even for experienced programmers. In Chapter 2, "Primitive Data Types and Operations," you learned that there are three categories of errors: compilation errors, runtime errors, and logic errors. *Compilation errors* arise because the rules of the language have not been followed. They are detected by the compiler. *Runtime errors* occur while the program is running if the environment detects an operation that is impossible to carry out. *Logic errors* occur when a program doesn't perform the way it was intended to. In general, syntax errors are easy to find and easy to correct because the compiler indicates where they came from and why they occurred. You can use the debugging techniques introduced in Chapter 2 to find logic errors. This chapter deals with runtime errors.

Runtime errors cause *exceptions*: events that occur during the execution of a program and disrupt the normal flow of control. A program that does not provide the code to handle exceptions may terminate abnormally, causing serious problems. For example, if your program attempts to transfer money from a savings account to a checking account but, because of a runtime error, is terminated *after* the money is drawn from the savings account and *before* the money is deposited in the checking account, the customer will lose money.

Java provides programmers with the capability to handle runtime errors. With this capability, referred to as *exception handling*, you can develop robust programs for mission-critical computing.

For example, the following program terminates abnormally, because the divisor is 0, which causes a numerical error.

```
public class Test
{
  public static void main(String[] args)
  {
    System.out.println(3/0);
  }
}
```

You can handle this error in the following code using a new construct called *the try-catch block* to enable the program to catch the error and continue to execute.

```
public class Test
{
  public static void main(String[] args)
  {
    try
    {
      System.out.println(3/0);
    }
    catch (Exception ex)
    {
      System.out.println("Error: " + ex.getMessage());
    }

    System.out.println("Execution continues");
  }
}
```

This chapter introduces Java's exception-handling model. The chapter covers exception types, claiming exceptions, throwing exceptions, catching exceptions, creating exception classes, rethrowing exceptions, and the `finally` clause.

Exceptions and Exception Types

Runtime errors occur for various reasons. For example, the user may enter an invalid input, or the program may attempt to open a file that doesn't exist, or the network connection may hang up, or the program may attempt to access an out-of-bounds array element. When a runtime error occurs, Java raises an exception.

Exceptions are handled differently from the events of graphics programming. (In Chapter 8, "Getting Started with Graphics Programming," you learned the events used in graphics.) An *event* may be ignored in graphics programming, but an *exception* cannot be ignored. In graphics programming, a listener must register with the source object. External user action on the source object generates an event, and the source object notifies the listener by invoking the handlers implemented by the listener. If no listener is registered with the source object, the event is ignored. However, when an exception occurs, the program may terminate if no handler can be used to deal with the exception.

A Java exception is an instance of a class derived from `Throwable`. The `Throwable` class is contained in the `java.lang` package, and subclasses of `Throwable` are contained in various packages. Errors related to graphics are included in the `java.awt` package; numeric exceptions are included in the `java.lang` package because they are related to the `java.lang.Number` class. You can create your own exception classes by extending `Throwable` or a subclass of `Throwable`. Figure 11.1 shows some of Java's predefined exception classes.

NOTE

The class names `Error`, `Exception`, and `RuntimeException` are somewhat confusing. All the classes are exceptions. `Exception` is just one of these classes, and all the errors discussed here occur at runtime.

The `Error` class describes internal system errors. Such errors rarely occur. If one does, there is little you can do beyond notifying the user and trying to terminate the program gracefully. Examples of subclasses of `Error` are `LinkageError`, `VirtualMachineError`, and `AWTError`. Subclasses of `LinkageError` indicate that a class has some dependency on another class, but that the latter class has changed incompatibly after the compilation of the former class. Subclasses of `VirtualMachineError` indicate that the Java Virtual Machine is broken or has run out of the resources necessary for it to continue operating. `AWTError` is caused by a fatal error in the graphics programs.

The `Exception` class describes errors caused by your program and external circumstances. These errors can be caught and handled by your program. `Exception` has many subclasses. Examples are `ClassNotFoundException`, `CloneNotSupportedException`, `IOException`, `AWTException`, and `RuntimeException`.

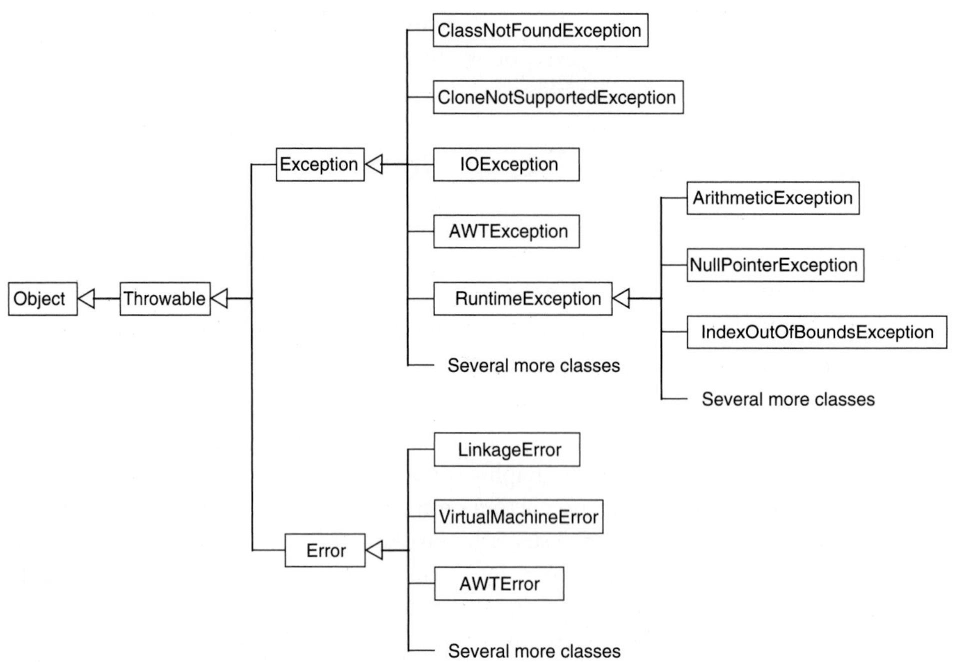

Figure 11.1 *The exceptions are instances of the classes shown in this diagram.*

The `ClassNotFoundException` is raised if you attempt to use a class that does not exist. It would occur, for example, if you tried to run a nonexistent class using the **java** command.

The `CloneNotSupportedException` is raised if you attempt to clone an object whose defining class does not implement the `Cloneable` interface. Cloning objects were introduced in Chapter 6, "Class Inheritance."

The `RuntimeException` class describes programming errors, such as bad casting, accessing an out-of-bound array, and numeric errors. Examples of subclasses of `RuntimeException` are `ArithmeticException`, `NullPointerException`, and `IndexOutOfBoundsException`.

The `IOException` class describes errors related to input/output operations, such as invalid input, reading past the end of a file, and opening a nonexistent file. Examples of subclasses of `IOException` are `InterruptedIOException`, `EOFException`, and `FileNotFoundException`.

The `AWTException` class describes exceptions in graphics programming.

Understanding Exception Handling

Java's exception-handling model is based on three operations: *claiming an exception*, *throwing an exception*, and *catching an exception*, as shown in Figure 11.2.

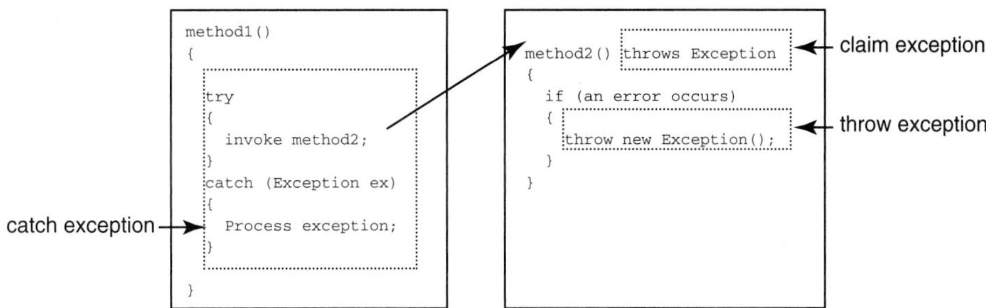

Figure 11.2 *The exception handling in Java consists of claiming exception, throwing exception, and catching and processing exceptions.*

In Java, the statement currently being executed belongs either to the `main` method or to a method invoked by another method. The Java interpreter invokes the `main` method for a Java application, and the Web browser invokes the `init` method for a Java applet. In general, every method must state the types of exceptions it can encounter. This process is called *claiming an exception*, which simply tells the compiler what can go wrong.

When a statement causes errors, the method containing the statement creates an exception object and passes it to the system. The exception object contains information about the exception, including its type and the state of the program when the error occurred. This process is called *throwing an exception.*

After a method throws an exception, the Java runtime system begins the process of finding the code to handle the error. The code that handles the error is called the *exception handler*; it is found by searching backward through a chain of method calls, starting from the current method. The handler must match the type of exception thrown. If no handler is found, the program terminates. The process of finding a handler is called *catching an exception.*

Claiming Exceptions

To claim an exception is to tell the compiler what might go wrong during the execution of a method. Because system errors and runtime errors can happen to any code, Java does not require you to claim `Error` and `RuntimeException` explicitly in the method. However, all the other exceptions must be explicitly claimed in the method declaration if they are thrown by the method.

To claim an exception in a method, you use the `throws` keyword in the method declaration, as in this example:

```
public void myMethod() throws IOException
```

The `throws` keyword indicates that `myMethod` might throw an `IOException`. If the method might throw multiple exceptions, you can add a list of the exceptions, separated by commas, after `throws`:

```
MethodDeclaration throws Exception1, Exception2, ..., ExceptionN
```

Throwing Exceptions

In the method that has claimed the exception, you can throw an object of the exception if the exception arises. The following is the syntax to throw an exception:

```
throw new TheException();
```

Or if you prefer, you can use the following:

```
TheException ex = new TheException();
throw ex;
```

NOTE

The keyword to claim an exception is `throws`, and the keyword to throw an exception is `throw`.

A method can only throw the exceptions claimed in the method declaration or throw `Error`, `RuntimeException`, or subclasses of `Error` and `RuntimeException`. For example, the method cannot throw `IOException` if it is not claimed in the method declaration, but a method can always throw `RuntimeException` or a subclass of it even if it is not claimed by the method.

Catching Exceptions

You now know how to claim an exception and how to throw an exception. Next, you will learn how to handle exceptions.

When calling a method that explicitly claims an exception, you must use the `try-catch` block to wrap the statement, as shown in the next few lines:

```
try
{
  statements;  // Statements that may throw exceptions
}
catch (Exception1 ex)
{
  handler for exception1;
}
catch (Exception2 ex)
{
  handler for exception2;
}
...
catch (ExceptionN ex)
{
  handler for exceptionN;
}
```

If no exceptions arise during the execution of the `try` clause, the `catch` clauses are skipped.

If one of the statements inside the `try` block throws an exception, Java skips the remaining statements and starts to search for a handler for the exception. If the exception type matches one listed in a `catch` clause, the code in the `catch` clause is executed. If the exception type does not match any exception in the `catch` clauses,

Java exits this method, passes the exception to the method that invoked this method, and continues the same process to find a handler. If no handler is found in the chain of methods being invoked, the program terminates and prints an error message on the console.

Consider the scenario in Figure 11.3. Suppose that an exception occurs in the try-catch block that contains a call to method3. If the exception type is Exception3, it is caught by the catch clause for handling exception ex3. If the exception type is Exception2, it is caught by the catch clause for handling exception ex2. If the exception type is Exception1, it is caught by the catch clause for handling exception ex1 in the main method. If the exception type is not Exception1, Exception2, or Exception3, the program immediately terminates.

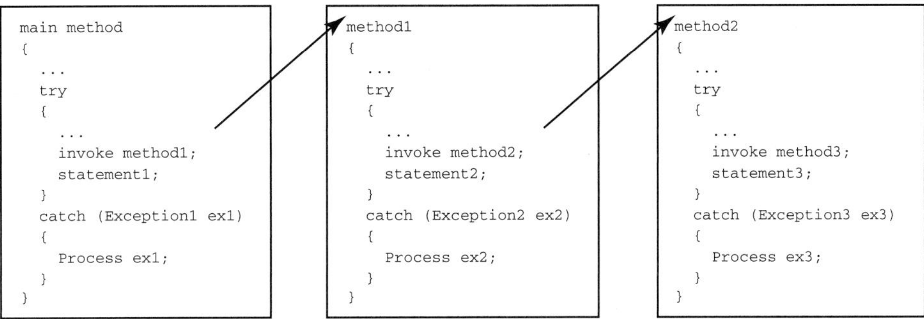

Figure 11.3 *If an exception is not caught in the current method, it is passed to its caller. The process is repeated until the exception is caught or passed to the* main *method.*

If the exception type is Exception3, statement3 is skipped. If the exception type is Exception2, statement2 and statement3 are skipped. If the exception type is Exception1, statement1, statement2, and statement3 are skipped.

NOTE

If an exception of a subclass of Exception occurs in a graphics program, Java prints the error message on the console, but the program goes back to its user-interface-processing loop to run continuously. The exception is ignored.

The exception object contains valuable information about the exception. You may use the following instance methods in the java.lang.Throwable class to get information regarding the exception.

- `public String getMessage()`

  This returns the detailed message of the Throwable object.

- `public String toString()`

  This returns a short description of the Throwable object, whereas getMessage() returns a detailed message.

- `public String getLocalizedMessage()`

  This returns a localized description of the `Throwable` object. Subclasses of `Throwable` can override this method in order to produce a locale-specific message. For subclasses that do not override this method, the default implementation returns the same result as `getMessage()`. Locale-specific issues are addressed in Chapter 12, "Internationalization."

- `public void printStackTrace()`

  This prints the `Throwable` object and its trace information on the console.

NOTE

Various exception classes can be derived from a common superclass. If a `catch` clause catches exception objects of a superclass, it can catch all the exception objects of the subclasses of that superclass.

The order in which the exceptions are specified in a `catch` clause is important. A compilation error will result if you do not specify an exception object of a class before the exception object of the superclass of that class.

NOTE

Java forces you to deal with exceptions. A method that claims an exception other than `Error` or `RuntimeException` must be placed in a `try` statement and be handled to avoid abnormal termination.

Example 11.1 Claiming, Throwing, and Catching Exceptions

This example demonstrates claiming, throwing, and catching exceptions by modifying the `Rational` class defined in Example 5.7, "Using the `Rational` Class" (see Chapter 5, "Programming with Objects and Classes") so that it can handle the zero-denominator exception.

You create a new `Rational` class, which is the same except that the `divide` method throws a zero-denominator exception if the client attempts to call the method with a zero denominator. The new `Rational` class is shown below:

```
// Rational.java: Define a rational number and its associated
// operations such as add, subtract, multiply, and divide
public class Rational
{
  // Data fields for numerator and denominator
  private long numerator = 0;
  private long denominator = 1;

  // Default constructor
  public Rational()
  {
    this(0, 1);
  }

  // Construct a rational with specified numerator and denominator
  public Rational(long numerator, long denominator)
```

```
{
  long gcd = gcd(numerator, denominator);
  this.numerator = numerator/gcd;
  this.denominator = denominator/gcd;
}

// Find GCD of two numbers
private long gcd(long n, long d)
{
  long t1 = Math.abs(n);
  long t2 = Math.abs(d);
  long remainder = t1%t2;

  while (remainder != 0)
  {
    t1 = t2;
    t2 = remainder;
    remainder = t1%t2;
  }

  return t2;
}

// Getter method for numerator
public long getNumerator()
{
  return numerator;
}

public long getDenominator()
{
  return denominator;
}

// Add a rational number to this rational
public Rational add(Rational secondRational)
{
  long n = numerator*secondRational.getDenominator() +
    denominator*secondRational.getNumerator();
  long d = denominator*secondRational.getDenominator();
  return new Rational(n, d);
}

// Subtract a rational number from this rational
public Rational subtract(Rational secondRational)
{
  long n = numerator*secondRational.getDenominator()
    - denominator*secondRational.getNumerator();
  long d = denominator*secondRational.getDenominator();
  return new Rational(n, d);
}

// Multiply a rational number to this rational
public Rational multiply(Rational secondRational)
{
  long n = numerator*secondRational.getNumerator();
  long d = denominator*secondRational.getDenominator();
  return new Rational(n, d);
}

// Divide a rational number from this rational
public Rational divide(Rational secondRational)
  throws RuntimeException
{
  if (secondRational.getNumerator() == 0)
    throw new RuntimeException("Denominator cannot be zero");
```

continues

Example 11.1 continued

```
    long n = numerator*secondRational.getDenominator();
    long d = denominator*secondRational.getNumerator();
    return new Rational(n, d);
  }

  // Override the toString() method
  public String toString()
  {
    if (denominator == 1)
      return numerator + "";
    else
      return numerator + "/" + denominator;
  }
}
```

A test program that uses the new `Rational` class is given as follows. Figure 11.4 shows a sample run of this test program.

```
// TestRationalException.java: Catch and handle exceptions
public class TestRationalException
{
  // Main method
  public static void main(String[] args)
  {
    // Create three rational numbers
    Rational r1 = new Rational(4, 2);
    Rational r2 = new Rational(2, 3);
    Rational r3 = new Rational(0, 1);

    try
    {
      System.out.println(r1+" + "+ r2 +" = " + r1.add(r2));
      System.out.println(r1+" - "+ r2 +" = " + r1.subtract(r2));
      System.out.println(r1+" * "+ r2 +" = " + r1.multiply(r2));
      System.out.println(r1+" / "+ r2 +" = " + r1.divide(r2));
      System.out.println(r1+" / "+ r3 +" = " + r1.divide(r3));
      System.out.println(r1+" + "+ r2 +" = " + r1.add(r2));
    }
    catch(Exception ex)
    {
      System.out.println(ex);
    }

    // Display the result
    System.out.println(r1 + " - " + r2 + " = " + r1.subtract(r2));
  }
}
```

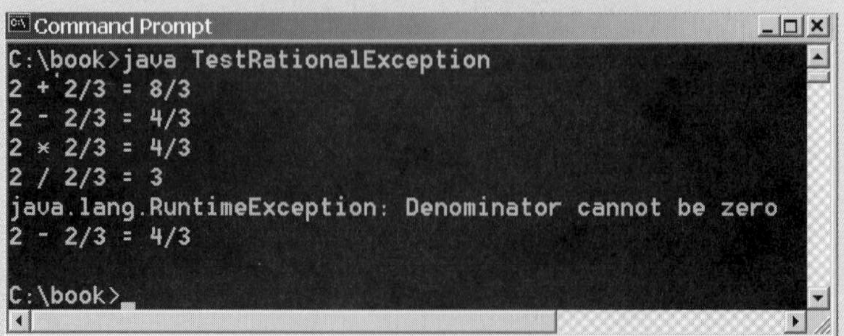

Figure 11.4 *The exception is raised when the divisor is zero.*

Example Review

The original `Rational` class remains intact except for the `divide` method. The `divide` method now claims an exception and throws it if the divisor is zero.

The `divide` method claims the exception to be an instance of `RuntimeException` by using `throws RuntimeException` in the method signature. The method throws the exception by using the following statement:

```
throw new RuntimeException("Denominator cannot be zero");
```

The program creates two `Rational` numbers, `r1` and `r2`, to test numeric methods (`add`, `subtract`, `multiply`, and `divide`) on rational numbers.

Invoking the `divide` method with divisor 0 causes the method to throw an exception object. In the `catch` clause, the type of the object `ex` is `RuntimeException`, which matches the object thrown by the `divide` method. So this exception is caught by the `catch` clause.

The exception handler simply prints a short message, `ex.toString()`, about the exception, using `System.out.println(ex)`.

Note that the execution continues in the event of the zero denominator. If the handlers had not caught the exception, the program would have abruptly terminated.

The test program would still compile if the `try` statement were not used, because the `divide` method throws `RuntimeException`. If a method throws an exception other than `RuntimeException` and `Error`, the method must be invoked within a `try` statement.

Example 11.2 Exceptions in GUI Applications

Here Example 9.11, "Using Menus" (from Chapter 9, "Creating User Interfaces"), is used to demonstrate the effect of exceptions in GUI applications. Run the program and enter any number in the Number 1 field and 0 in the Number 2 field; then click the Divide button (see Figure 11.5). You will see nothing in

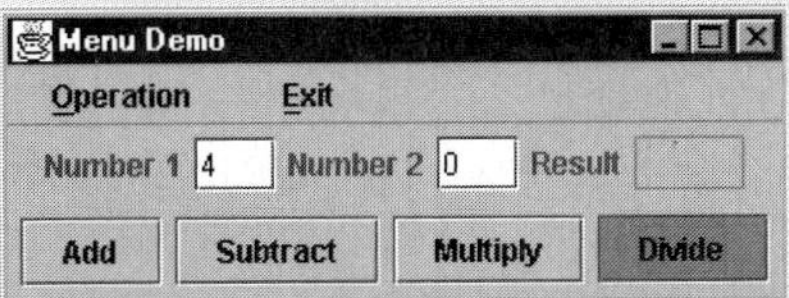

Figure 11.5 *In GUI programs, if an exception of the* `Exception` *class is not caught, it is ignored, and the program continues.*

continues

Example 11.2 continued

the `Result` field, but an error message will appear on the console, as shown in Figure 11.6. The GUI application continues.

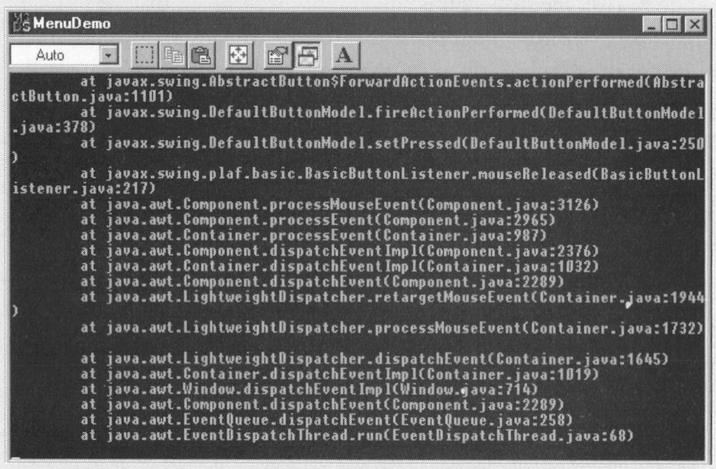

```
MenuDemo
Auto
        at javax.swing.AbstractButton$ForwardActionEvents.actionPerformed(Abstra
ctButton.java:1101)
        at javax.swing.DefaultButtonModel.fireActionPerformed(DefaultButtonModel
.java:378)
        at javax.swing.DefaultButtonModel.setPressed(DefaultButtonModel.java:250
)
        at javax.swing.plaf.basic.BasicButtonListener.mouseReleased(BasicButtonL
istener.java:217)
        at java.awt.Component.processMouseEvent(Component.java:3126)
        at java.awt.Component.processEvent(Component.java:2965)
        at java.awt.Container.processEvent(Container.java:987)
        at java.awt.Component.dispatchEventImpl(Component.java:2376)
        at java.awt.Container.dispatchEventImpl(Container.java:1032)
        at java.awt.Component.dispatchEvent(Component.java:2289)
        at java.awt.LightweightDispatcher.retargetMouseEvent(Container.java:1944
)
        at java.awt.LightweightDispatcher.processMouseEvent(Container.java:1732)

        at java.awt.LightweightDispatcher.dispatchEvent(Container.java:1645)
        at java.awt.Container.dispatchEventImpl(Container.java:1019)
        at java.awt.Window.dispatchEventImpl(Window.java:714)
        at java.awt.Component.dispatchEvent(Component.java:2289)
        at java.awt.EventQueue.dispatchEvent(EventQueue.java:258)
        at java.awt.EventDispatchThread.run(EventDispatchThread.java:68)
```

Figure 11.6 *In GUI programs, if an exception of the* `Exception` *class is not caught, an error message appears on the console.*

Example Review

If an exception of the `Exception` type is not caught when a Java graphics program is running, an error message is displayed on the console, but the program continues to run.

If you rewrite the `calculate` method in the `MenuDemo` program of Example 9.11 with a `try-catch` block to catch `RuntimeException` as follows, the program will display a message dialog box in the case of a numerical error, as shown in Figure 11.7. No errors are shown on the console because they are handled in the program.

```
// Calculate and show the result in jtfResult
private void calculate(char operator)
{
  // Obtain Number 1 and Number 2
  int num1 = (Integer.parseInt(jtfNum1.getText().trim()));
  int num2 = (Integer.parseInt(jtfNum2.getText().trim()));
  int result = 0;

  try
  {
    // Perform selected operation
    switch (operator)
    {
      case '+': result = num1 + num2;
                break;
      case '-': result = num1 - num2;
                break;
      case '*': result = num1 * num2;
                break;
```

```
        case '/': result = num1 / num2;
      }

      // Set result in jtfResult
      jtfResult.setText(String.valueOf(result));
    }
    catch (RuntimeException ex)
    {
      JOptionPane.showMessageDialog(this, ex.getMessage(),
        "Operation error", JOptionPane.ERROR_MESSAGE);
    }
  }
```

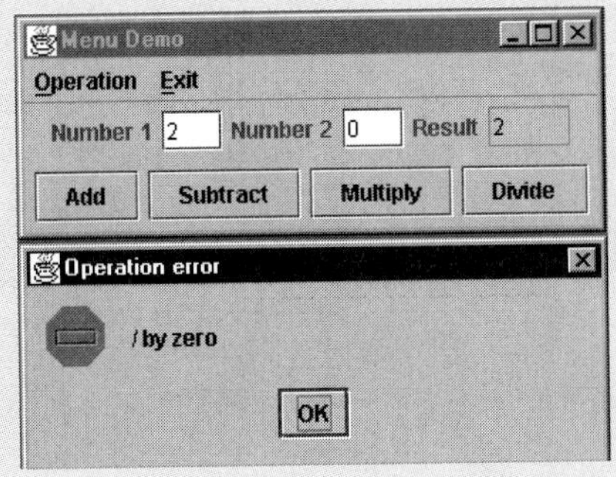

Figure 11.7 *When you click the Divide button to divide a number by 0, a numerical exception occurs. The exception is displayed in the message dialog box.*

Rethrowing Exceptions

When an exception occurs in a method, the method exits immediately if it does not catch the exception. If the method is required to perform some task before exiting, you can catch the exception in the method and then rethrow it to the real handler in a structure like the one given below:

```
try
{
  statements;
}
catch(TheException ex)
{
  perform operations before exits;
  throw ex;
}
```

The statement `throw ex` rethrows the exception so that other handlers get a chance to process the exception `ex`.

The *finally* Clause

Occasionally, you may want some code to be executed regardless of whether the exception occurs or whether it is caught. Java has a `finally` clause that can be used to accomplish this objective. The syntax for the `finally` clause might look like this:

```
try
{
  statements;
}
catch(TheException ex)
{
  handling ex;
}
finally
{
  finalStatements;
}
```

The code in the `finally` block is executed under all circumstances, regardless of whether an exception occurs in the `try` block or whether it is caught. Consider three possible cases:

- If no exception arises in the `try` block, `finalStatements` is executed, and the next statement after the `try` statement is executed.
- If one of the statements causes an exception in the `try` block that is caught in a `catch` clause, the other statements in the `try` block are skipped, the `catch` clause is executed, and the `finally` clause is executed. If the `catch` clause does not rethrow an exception, the next statement after the `try` statement is executed. If it does, the exception is passed to the caller of this method.
- If one of the statements causes an exception that is not caught in any `catch` clause, the other statements in the `try` block are skipped, the `finally` clause is executed, and the exception is passed to the caller of this method.

NOTE
The `catch` clause may be omitted when the `finally` clause is used.

Cautions When Using Exceptions

Exception handling separates error-handling code from normal programming tasks, thus making programs easier to read and to modify. Be aware, however, that exception handling usually requires more time and resources because it requires instantiating a new exception object, rolling back the call stack, and propagating the errors to the calling methods.

Exception handling should not be used to replace simple tests. You should test simple exceptions whenever possible, and let exception handling deal with circumstances that cannot be handled with `if` statements. Do not use exception handling to validate user input. The input can be validated with simple `if` statements.

Creating Custom Exception Classes (Optional)

Java provides quite a few exception classes. Use them whenever possible instead of creating your own exception classes. However, if you run into a problem that cannot be adequately described by the predefined exception classes, you can create your own exception class, derived from `Exception` or from a subclass of `Exception`, such as `IOException`. This section shows how to create your own exception class.

Example 11.3 Creating Your Own Exception Classes

This program creates a Java applet for handling account transactions. The applet displays the account ID and balance, and lets the user deposit to or withdraw from the account. For each transaction, a message is displayed to indicate the status of the transaction: successful or failed. In case of failure, the failure reason is reported. A sample run of the program is shown in Figure 11.8.

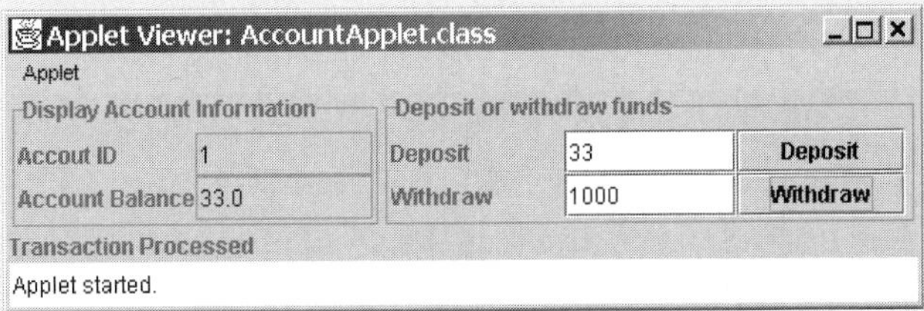

Figure 11.8 *The program lets you deposit and withdraw funds, and displays the transaction status on the label.*

If a transaction amount is negative, the program raises a negative-amount exception. If the account's balance is less than the requested transaction amount, an insufficient-funds exception is raised.

The example consists of four classes: `Account`, `NegativeAmountException`, `InsufficientAmountException`, and `AccountApplet`. The `Account` class provides the information and operations pertaining to the account. `NegativeAmountException` and `InsufficientAmountException` are the exception classes dealing with transactions of negative or insufficient amounts. The `AccountApplet` class utilizes all these classes to perform transactions, transferring funds among accounts. The relationships among these classes are shown in Figure 11.9.

The code for the `Account` class follows. This class contains two data fields: `id` (for account ID) and `balance` (for current balance). The methods for `Account` are `deposit` and `withdraw`. Both methods will throw `NegativeAmountException` if the transaction amount is negative. The `withdraw` method will also throw

continues

Example 11.3 continued

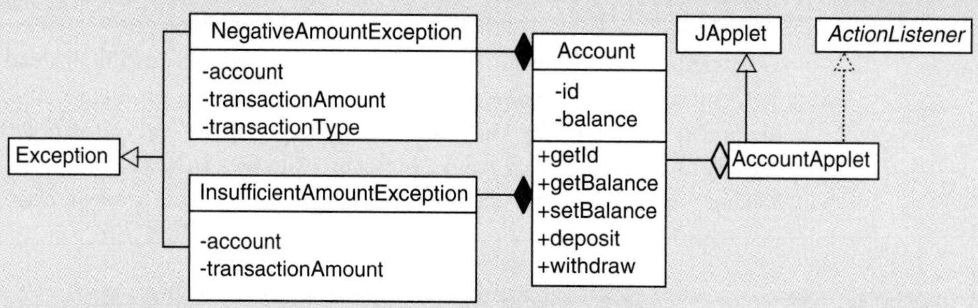

Figure 11.9 `NegativeAmountException` *and* `InsufficientAmountException` *are subclasses of* `Exception` *that contain the account information, transaction amount, and transaction type for the failed transaction.*

`InsufficientFundException` if the current balance is less than the requested transaction amount.

```
// Account.java: The class for describing an account
public class Account
{
  // Two data fields in an account
  private int id;
  private double balance;

  // Construct an account with specified id and balance
  public Account(int id, double balance)
  {
    this.id = id;
    this.balance = balance;
  }

  // Getter method for id
  public int getId()
  {
    return id;
  }

  // Setter method for balance
  public void setBalance(double balance)
  {
    this.balance = balance;
  }

  // Getter method for balance
  public double getBalance()
  {
    return balance;
  }

  // Deposit an amount to this account
  public void deposit(double amount)
    throws NegativeAmountException
  {
    if (amount < 0)
      throw new NegativeAmountException
        (this, amount, "deposit");
    balance = balance + amount;
  }
```

```
    // Withdraw an amount from this account
    public void withdraw(double amount)
      throws NegativeAmountException, InsufficientFundException
    {
      if (amount < 0)
        throw new NegativeAmountException
          (this, amount, "withdraw");
      if (balance < amount)
        throw new InsufficientFundException(this, amount);
      balance = balance - amount;
    }
  }
```

The NegativeAmountException exception class follows. It contains information about the attempted transaction type (deposit or withdrawal), the account, and the negative amount passed from the method.

```
  // NegativeAmountException.java: Negative amount exception
  public class NegativeAmountException extends Exception
  {
    // Information to be passed to the handlers
    private Account account;
    private double amount;
    private String transactionType;

    // Construct an negative amount exception
    public NegativeAmountException(Account account,
                                   double amount,
                                   String transactionType)
    {
      super("Negative amount");
      this.account = account;
      this.amount = amount;
      this.transactionType = transactionType;
    }
  }
```

The InsufficientFundException exception class follows. It contains information about the account and the amount passed from the method.

```
  // InsufficientFundException.java: An exception class for describing
  // insufficient fund exception
  public class InsufficientFundException extends Exception
  {
    // Information to be passed to the handlers
    private Account account;
    private double amount;

    // Construct an insufficient exception
    public InsufficientFundException(Account account, double amount)
    {
      super("Insufficient amount");
      this.account = account;
      this.amount = amount;
    }

    // Override the "toString" method
    public String toString()
    {
      return "Account balance is " + account.getBalance();
    }
  }
```

continues

Example 11.3 continued

The `AccountApplet` class is given as follows:

```
// AccountApplet.java: Use custom exception classes
import java.awt.*;
import java.awt.event.*;
import javax.swing.*;
import javax.swing.border.*;

public class AccountApplet extends JApplet implements ActionListener
{
  // Declare text fields
  private JTextField jtfID, jtfBalance, jtfDeposit, jtfWithdraw;

  // Declare Deposit and Withdraw buttons
  private JButton jbtDeposit, jbtWithdraw;

  // Create an account with initial balance $1000
  private Account account = new Account(1, 1000);

  // Create a label for showing status
  private JLabel jlblStatus = new JLabel();

  // Initialize the applet
  public void init()
  {
    // Panel p1 to group ID and Balance labels and text fields
    JPanel p1 = new JPanel();
    p1.setLayout(new GridLayout(2, 2));
    p1.add(new JLabel("Account ID"));
    p1.add(jtfID = new JTextField(4));
    p1.add(new JLabel("Account Balance"));
    p1.add(jtfBalance = new JTextField(4));
    jtfID.setEditable(false);
    jtfBalance.setEditable(false);
    p1.setBorder(new TitledBorder("Display Account Information"));

    // Panel p2 to group deposit amount and Deposit button and
    // withdraw amount and Withdraw button
    JPanel p2 = new JPanel();
    p2.setLayout(new GridLayout(2, 3));
    p2.add(new JLabel("Deposit"));
    p2.add(jtfDeposit = new JTextField(4));
    p2.add(jbtDeposit = new JButton("Deposit"));
    p2.add(new JLabel("Withdraw"));
    p2.add(jtfWithdraw = new JTextField(4));
    p2.add(jbtWithdraw = new JButton("Withdraw"));
    p2.setBorder(new TitledBorder("Deposit or withdraw funds"));

    // Place panels p1, p2, and label in the applet
    this.getContentPane().add(p1, BorderLayout.WEST);
    this.getContentPane().add(p2, BorderLayout.CENTER);
    this.getContentPane().add(jlblStatus, BorderLayout.SOUTH);

    // Refresh ID and Balance fields
    refreshFields();

    // Register listener
    jbtDeposit.addActionListener(this);
    jbtWithdraw.addActionListener(this);
  }

  // Handle ActionEvent
  public void actionPerformed(ActionEvent evt)
  {
```

```
        String actionCommand = evt.getActionCommand();
        if (evt.getSource() instanceof JButton)
          if ("Deposit".equals(actionCommand))
          {
            try
            {
              double depositValue = (Double.valueOf(
                jtfDeposit.getText().trim())).doubleValue();
              account.deposit(depositValue);
              refreshFields();
              jlblStatus.setText("Transaction Processed");
            }
            catch (NegativeAmountException ex)
            {
              jlblStatus.setText("Negative Amount");
            }
          }
          else if ("Withdraw".equals(actionCommand))
          {
            try
            {
              double withdrawValue = (Double.valueOf(
                jtfWithdraw.getText().trim())).doubleValue();
              account.withdraw(withdrawValue);
              refreshFields();
              jlblStatus.setText("Transaction Processed");
            }
            catch(NegativeAmountException ex)
            {
              jlblStatus.setText("Negative Amount");
            }
            catch (InsufficientFundException ex)
            {
              jlblStatus.setText("Insufficient Funds");
            }
          }
      }

      // Update the display for account balance
      public void refreshFields()
      {
        jtfID.setText(String.valueOf(account.getId()));
        jtfBalance.setText(String.valueOf(account.getBalance()));
      }
    }
```

Example Review

In the `Account` class, the `deposit` method throws `NegativeAmountException` if the amount to be deposited is less than 0. The `withdraw` method throws a `NegativeAmountException` if the amount to be withdrawn is less than 0, and throws an `InsufficientFundException` if the amount to be withdrawn is less than the current balance.

The user-defined exception class always extends `Exception` or a subclass of `Exception`. Therefore, both `NegativeAmountException` and `InsufficientFund-Exception` extend `Exception`.

continues

Example 11.3 continued

Storing relevant information in the exception object is useful, enabling the handler to retrieve the information from the exception object. For example, `NegativeAmountException` contains the account, the amount, and the transaction type.

The `AccountApplet` class creates an applet with two panels (`p1` and `p2`) and a label that displays messages. Panel `p1` contains account ID and balance; panel `p2` contains the action buttons for depositing and withdrawing funds.

With a click of the Deposit button, the amount in the `Deposit` text field is added to the balance. With a click of the Withdraw button, the amount in the `Withdraw` text field is subtracted from the balance.

For each successful transaction, the message `Transaction Processed` is displayed. For a negative amount, the message `Negative Amount` is displayed; for insufficient funds, the message `Insufficient Funds` is displayed.

Chapter Summary

In this chapter, you learned how Java handles exceptions. When an exception occurs, Java creates an object that contains the information for the exception. You can use the information to handle the exception.

A Java exception is an instance of a class derived from `java.lang.Throwable`. You can create your own exception classes by extending `Throwable` or a subclass of `Throwable`. The Java system provides a number of predefined exception classes, such as `Error`, `Exception`, `RuntimeException`, and `IOException`. You can also define your own exception class.

Exceptions occur during the execution of a method. When defining the method, you have to claim an exception if the method might throw that exception, thus telling the compiler what can go wrong.

To use the method that claims exceptions, you need to enclose the method call in the `try` statement. When the exception occurs during the execution of the method, the `catch` clause catches and handles the exception.

Exception handling takes time because it requires the instantiation of a new exception object. Exceptions are not meant to substitute for simple tests. Avoid using exception handling if an alternative solution can be found. Using an alternative would significantly improve the program's performance.

Review Questions

11.1 Describe the Java `Throwable` class, its subclasses, and the types of exceptions.

11.2 What is the purpose of claiming exceptions? How do you claim an exception, and where? Can you claim multiple exceptions in a method declaration?

11.3 How do you throw an exception? Can you throw multiple exceptions in one `throw` statement?

11.4 What is the keyword `throw` used for? What is the keyword `throws` used for?

11.5 What does the Java runtime system do when an exception occurs?

11.6 How do you catch an exception?

11.7 Does the presence of the `try-catch` block impose overhead when no exception occurs?

11.8 Suppose that `statement2` causes an exception in the following `try-catch` block:

```
try
{
  statement1;
  statement2;
  statement3;
}
catch (Exception1 ex1)
{
}
catch (Exception2 ex2)
{
}

statement4;
```

Answer the following questions:

- Will `statement3` be executed?
- If the exception is not caught, will `statement4` be executed?
- If the exception is caught in the catch clause, will `statement4` be executed?
- If the exception is passed to the caller, will `statement4` be executed?

11.9 Suppose that `statement2` causes an exception in the following statement:

```
try
{
  statement1;
  statement2;
  statement3;
}
catch (Exception1 ex1)
{
}
catch (Exception2 ex2)
{
}
catch (Exception3 ex3)
{
  throw ex3;
}
finally
{
  statement4;
};

statement5;
```

Answer the following questions:

- Will `statement5` be executed?

  If the exception is of type `Exception3`, what will happen? Will `statement5` be executed? Will `statement4` be executed?

11.10 What is wrong in the following program?

```
class TestRationalWithException
{
  public static void main(String[] args)
  {
    Rational r1 = new Rational(4,2);
    Rational r2 = new Rational(2,3);
    Rational r3 = new Rational(0,1);

    try
    {
      System.out.println(
        r1 + " + " + r2 + " = " + r1.add(r2));
      System.out.println(
        r1 + " - " + r2 + " = " + r1.subtract(r2));
      System.out.println(
        r1 + " * " + r2 + " = " + r1.multiply(r2));
      System.out.println(
        r1 + " + " + r2 + " = " + r1.add(r2));
    }
  }
}
```

11.11 What is displayed on the console when the following program is run?

```
class Test
{
  public static void main(String[] args)
  {
    try
    {
      System.out.println("Welcome to Java");
    }
    finally
    {
      System.out.println("End of the block");
    }
  }
}
```

11.12 What is displayed on the console when the following program is run?

```
class Test
{
  public static void main(String[] args)
  {
    try
    {
      System.out.println("Welcome to Java");
      return;
    }
    finally
    {
      System.out.println("End of the block");
    }
  }
}
```

11.13 What is displayed on the console when the following program is run?

```
class Test
{
  public static void main(String[] args)
  {
    try
    {
      System.out.println("Welcome to Java");
      int i = 0;
      int y = 2/i;
      System.out.println("Welcome to HTML");
    }
    finally
    {
      System.out.println("End of the block");
    }
  }
}
```

11.14 What is displayed on the console when the following program is run?

```
class Test
{
  public static void main(String[] args)
  {
    try
    {
      System.out.println("Welcome to Java");
      int i = 0;
      double y = 2.0/i;
      System.out.println("Welcome to HTML");
    }
    finally
    {
      System.out.println("End of the block");
    }
  }
}
```

11.15 What is displayed on the console when the following program is run?

```
class Test
{
  public static void main(String[] args)
  {
    try
    {
      System.out.println("Welcome to Java");
      int i = 0;
      int y = 2/i;
      System.out.println("Welcome to Java");
    }
    catch (RuntimeException ex)
    {
      System.out.println("Welcome to Java");
    }
    finally
    {
      System.out.println("End of the block");
    }
  }
}
```

11.16 What is displayed on the console when the following program is run?

```
class Test
{
  public static void main(String[] args)
  {
    try
    {
      System.out.println("Welcome to Java");
      int i = 0;
      int y = 2/i;
      System.out.println("Welcome to Java");
    }
    catch (RuntimeException ex)
    {
      System.out.println("Welcome to Java");
    }
    finally
    {
      System.out.println("End of the block");
    }

    System.out.println("End of the block");
  }
}
```

11.17 What is displayed on the console when the following program is run?

```
class Test
{
  public static void main(String[] args)
  {
    try
    {
      System.out.println("Welcome to Java");
      int i = 0;
      int y = 2/i;
      System.out.println("Welcome to Java");
    }
    finally
    {
      System.out.println("End of the block");
    }

    System.out.println("End of the block");
  }
}
```

In the following questions, assume that the modified `Rational` given in Example 11.1 is used.

11.18 What is wrong with the following code?

```
class Test
{
  public static void main(String[] args)
  {
    try
    {
      Rational r1 = new Rational(3, 4);
      Rational r2   = new Rational(0, 1);
      Rational x = r1.divide(r2);

      int i = 0;
      int y = 2/i;
    }
```

```
        catch (Exception ex)
        {
          System.out.println("Rational operation error ");
        }
        catch (RuntimeException ex)
        {
          System.out.println("Integer operation error");
        }
      }
    }
```

11.19 What is displayed on the console when the following program is run?

```
    class Test
    {
      public static void main(String[] args)
      {
        try
        {
          Rational r1 = new Rational(3, 4);
          Rational r2   = new Rational(0, 1);
          Rational x = r1.divide(r2);

          int i = 0;
          int y = 2/i;
          System.out.println("Welcome to Java");
        }
        catch (RuntimeException ex)
        {
          System.out.println("Integer operation error");
        }
        catch (Exception ex)
        {
          System.out.println("Rational operation error");
        }
      }
    }
```

11.20 What is displayed on the console when the following program is run?

```
    class Test
    {
      public static void main(String[] args)
      {
        try
        {
          method();
          System.out.println("After the method call");
        }
        catch (RuntimeException ex)
        {
          System.out.println("Integer operation error");
        }
        catch (Exception e)
        {
          System.out.println("Rational operation error");
        }
      }

      static void method() throws Exception
      {
        Rational r1 = new Rational(3, 4);
        Rational r2   = new Rational(0, 1);
        Rational x = r1.divide(r2);

        int i = 0;
```

```
      int y = 2/i;
      System.out.println("Welcome to Java");
    }
  }
```

11.21 What is displayed on the console when the following program is run?

```
class Test
{
  public static void main(String[] args)
  {
    try
    {
      method();
      System.out.println("After the method call");
    }
    catch (RuntimeException ex)
    {
      System.out.println("Integer operation error");
    }
    catch (Exception ex)
    {
      System.out.println("Rational operation error");
    }
  }

  static void method() throws Exception
  {
    try
    {
      Rational r1 = new Rational(3, 4);
      Rational r2   = new Rational(0, 1);
      Rational x = r1.divide(r2);

      int i = 0;
      int y = 2/i;
      System.out.println("Welcome to Java");
    }
    catch (RuntimeException ex)
    {
      System.out.println("Integer operation error");
    }
    catch (Exception ex)
    {
      System.out.println("Rational operation error");
    }
  }
}
```

11.22 What is displayed on the console when the following program is run?

```
class Test
{
  public static void main(String[] args)
  {
    try
    {
      method();
      System.out.println("After the method call");
    }
    catch (RuntimeException ex)
    {
      System.out.println("Integer operation error");
    }
    catch (Exception ex)
    {
```

```
      System.out.println("Rational operation error");
    }
  }

  static void method() throws Exception
  {
    try
    {
      Rational r1 = new Rational(3, 4);
      Rational r2   = new Rational(0, 1);
      Rational x = r1.divide(r2);

      int i = 0;
      int y = 2/i;
      System.out.println("Welcome to Java");
    }
    catch (RuntimeException ex)
    {
      System.out.println("Integer operation error");
    }
    catch (Exception ex)
    {
      System.out.println("Rational operation error");
      throw ex;
    }
  }
}
```

11.23 If an exception was not caught in a non-GUI application, what would happen? If an exception was not caught in a GUI application, what would happen?

Programming Exercises

11.1 Example 7.8, "Using Command-Line Parameters," in Chapter 7, "Arrays and Vectors," is a simple command-line calculator. Note that the program terminates if any operand is non-numeric. Write a program with an exception handler to deal with non-numeric operands; then write another program without using an exception handler to achieve the same objective. Your program should display a message to inform the user of the wrong operand type before exiting (see Figure 11.10).

```
MS-DOS Prompt
D:\InstrManual\Exercises>java Exercise11_1 3 4
please use java operator operand1 operand2

D:\InstrManual\Exercises>java Exercise11_1 + 3 4
3+4=7

D:\InstrManual\Exercises>java Exercise11_1 + 3 4/2
Wrong Input: 4/2

D:\InstrManual\Exercises>_
```

Figure 11.10 *The program performs arithmetic operations and detects input errors.*

11.2 Example 9.11, "Using Menus," is a GUI calculator. Note that if `Number 1` or `Number 2` were a non-numeric string, the program would display errors on the console. Modify the program with an exception handler to catch `ArithmeticException` (i.e., divided by 0) and `NumberFormatException` (i.e., input is not an integer) and display the errors in a message dialog box, as shown in Figure 11.11.

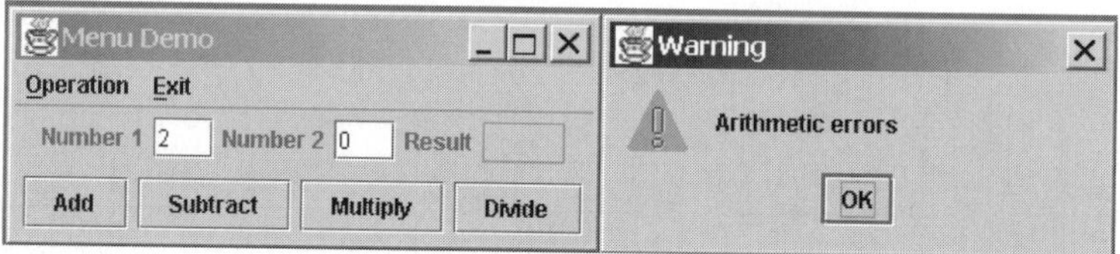

Figure 11.11 *The program displays an error message in the dialog box if the divisor is 0.*

11.3 Write a program that meets the following requirements:

- Create an array with 100 elements that are randomly chosen.
- Create a text field to enter an array index and another text field to display the array element at the specified index (see Figure 11.12).
- Create a Show button to cause the array element to be displayed. If the specified index is out of bounds, display the message Out of Bound.

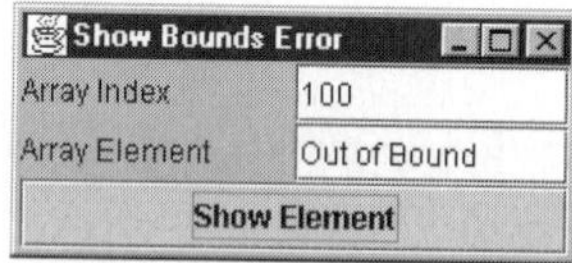

Figure 11.12 *The program displays the array element at the specified index or displays the message Out of Bound if the index is out of bounds.*

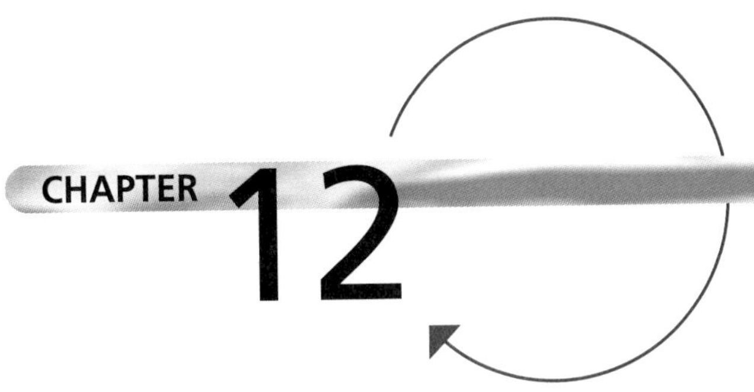

INTERNATIONALIZATION

Objectives

- Understand the concept of Java's internationalization mechanism.
- Know how to construct a locale with language, country, and variant.
- Process date and time based on locales.
- Display numbers, currencies, and percentage based on locales.
- Use resource bundles.

Introduction

Java is an Internet programming language. Since the Internet has no boundaries, your applets may be viewed by people who don't understand English. What is useful for those who can read English may be unusable for those who can only read French. Many Web sites maintain several versions of HTML pages so that readers can choose one written in a language they understand. Because there are so many languages in the world, it would be highly problematic to create and maintain enough different versions to meet the needs of all clients everywhere. Java comes to the rescue. Java is the first language designed from the ground up to support internationalization. In consequence, it allows your programs to be customized for any number of countries or languages without requiring cumbersome changes in the code.

Here are the major Java features that support internationalization:

- Java characters use *Unicode*, a 16-bit encoding scheme established by the Unicode Consortium to support the interchange, processing, and display of written texts in the world's diverse languages. The use of Unicode encoding makes it easy to write Java programs that can manipulate strings in any international language.
- Java provides the `Locale` class to encapsulate information about a specific locale. A locale determines how locale-sensitive information, such as date, time, and number, is displayed, and how locale-sensitive operations, such as sorting strings, are performed. The classes for formatting date, time, and numbers, and for sorting strings are grouped in the `java.text` package.
- Java uses the `ResourceBundle` class to separate locale-specific information, such as status messages and GUI component labels, from the program. The information is stored outside the source code and can be accessed and loaded dynamically at runtime from a `ResourceBundle`, rather than hardcoded into the program.

In this chapter, you will learn how to format date, numbers, currencies, and percentages for different regions, countries, and languages. You will also learn how to use resource bundles to define which images and strings are used by a component, depending on the user's locale and preferences.

The *Locale* Class

A `Locale` object represents a geographical, political, or cultural region in which a specific language or custom is used. For example, Americans speak English, and the Chinese speak Chinese. The conventions for formatting dates, numbers, currencies, and percentages may differ from one country to another. The Chinese, for instance, use year/month/day to represent the date, while Americans use month/day/year. It is important to realize that a locale is not defined only by country. For example, Canadians speak either Canadian English or Canadian French, depending on which region of Canada they reside in.

NOTE
Every Swing user interface class has a `locale` property inherited from the `Component` class.

To create a `Locale` object, use the following constructors in the `java.util.Locale` class:

```
Locale(String language, String country)

Locale(String language, String country, String variant)
```

The `language` should be a valid language code, that is to say, one of the lowercase, two-letter codes defined by ISO-639. For example, zh stands for Chinese, da for Danish, en for English, de for German, and ko for Korean. A complete list can be found at a number of sites, among them:

```
http://www.indigo.ie/egt/standards/iso639/

http://www.ics.uci.edu/pub/ietf/http/related/iso639.txt
```

The country should be a valid ISO country code, that is to say, one of the uppercase, two-letter codes defined by ISO-3166. For example, CA stands for Canada, CN for China, DK for Denmark, DE for Germany, and US for the United States. A complete list can be found at a number of sites, including:

```
ftp://ftp.ripe.net/iso3166-countrycodes

http://userpage.chemie.fu-berlin.de/diverse/doc/ISO_3166.html
```

The argument variant is rarely used and is needed only for exceptional or system-dependent situations to designate information specific to a browser or vendor. For example, the Norwegian language has two sets of spelling rules, a traditional one called *bokmål* and a new one called *nynorsk*. The locale for traditional spelling would be created as follows:

```
new Locale("no", "NO", "B");
```

For convenience, the `Locale` class contains many predefined locale constants. `Locale.CANADA` is for the country Canada and language English; `Locale.CANADA_FRENCH` is for the country Canada and language French.

At present Java supports the locales shown in Table 12.1.

Several useful methods contained in the `Locale` class are listed below (note that the default locale is used if no locale is specified):

- `public static Locale getDefault()`

  This method returns the default locale as stored on the machine where the program is running.

- `public static void setDefault(Locale newLocale)`

  This method sets the default locale.

TABLE 12.1 A List of Supported Locales

Locale	*Language*	*Country*
da_DK	Danish	Denmark
de_AT	German	Austria
de_CH	German	Switzerland
de_DE	German	Germany
el_GR	Greek	Greece
en_CA	English	Canada
en_GB	English	United Kingdom
en_IE	English	Ireland
en_US	English	United States
es_ES	Spanish	Spain
fi_FI	Finnish	Finland
fr_BE	French	Belgium
fr_CA	French	Canada
fr_CH	French	Switzerland
fr_FR	French	France
it_CH	Italian	Switzerland
it_IT	Italian	Italy
ja_JP	Japanese	Japan
ko_KR	Korean	Korea
nl_BE	Dutch	Belgium
nl_NL	Dutch	Netherlands
no_NO	Norwegian (*nynorsk*)	Norway
no_NO_B	Norwegian (*bokmål*)	Norway
pt_PT	Portuguese	Portugal
sv_SE	Swedish	Sweden
tr_TR	Turkish	Turkey
zh_CN	Chinese (Simplified)	China
zh_TW	Chinese (Traditional)	Taiwan

- `public String getLanguage()`

  This method returns a lowercase, two-letter language code.

- `public String getCountry()`

  This method returns an uppercase, two-letter country code.

- `public String getVariant()`

  This method returns the code for the variant.

- `public final String getDisplayLanguage()`

  This method returns the name of the language for the default locale.

- `public String getDisplayLanguage(Locale inLocale)`

  This method returns the name of the language for the specified locale.

- `public final String getDisplayCountry()`

  This method returns the name of the country as expressed in the current locale.

- `public String getDisplayCountry(Locale inLocale)`

  This method returns the name of the country as expressed in the specified locale.

- `public final String getDisplayVariant()`

  This method returns the variant code.

- `public String getDisplayVariant(Locale inLocale)`

  This method returns the variant code for the specified locale.

- `public String getDisplayName(Locale l)`

  This method returns the name for the locale. For example, the name is `Chinese (China)` for the locale `Locale.CHINA`.

- `public String getDisplayName()`

  This method returns the name for the default locale.

An operation that requires a `Locale` to perform its task is called *locale-sensitive*. To display a number as a date or time, for example, is a locale-sensitive operation; the number should be formatted according to the customs and conventions of the user's locale.

Several classes in the Java class libraries contain locale-sensitive methods. `Date`, `Calendar`, `DateFormat`, and `NumberFormat`, for example, are locale-sensitive. All the locale-sensitive classes contain a static method, `getAvailableLocales()`, which returns an array of the locales they support. For example,

```
Locale[] availableLocales = Calendar.getAvailableLocales();
```

returns all the locales for which calendars are installed.

Processing Date and Time

Applications often need to obtain date and time. Java provides a system-independent encapsulation of date and time in the `java.util.Date` class; it also provides `java.util.TimeZone` for dealing with time zones, and `java.util.Calendar` for extracting detailed information from `Date`. Different locales have different conventions for displaying date and time. Should the year, month, or day be displayed first? Should slashes, periods, or colons be used to separate fields of the date? What are the names of the months in the language? The `java.text.DateFormat` class can be used to format date and time in a locale-sensitive way for display to the user.

A `Date` object represents a specific instant in time. You can use its instance method `getTime()` to obtain the number of milliseconds since January 1, 1970, 00:00:00 GMT represented by this date. You can use the `toString()` method to display a string representing this date.

The `Calendar` class contains the overloaded `get` methods to extract year, month, day, hour, minute, and second. For example, you can use `calendar.get(Calendar.YEAR)` to get the year, and `calendar.get(Calendar.MINUTE)` to get the minute from a `Calendar` object `calendar`. You can use the overloaded `set` methods to set year, month, day, hour, minute, and second in this calendar. For example, the following statements set this calendar to December 1, 2000.

```
calendar.set(Calendar.YEAR, year);
calendar.set(Calendar.MONTH, 12-1); // Month starts from 0
calendar.set(Calendar.DATE, 1);
```

Note that month starts from 0 in the `Calendar` class.

Subclasses of `Calendar` interpret a `Date` according to the rules of a specific calendar system. `java.util.GregorianCalendar` is currently supported in Java. Future subclasses could represent other types of calendars used in some parts of the world.

`TimeZone` represents a time zone offset, and also figures out daylight savings. To set a time zone in a `Calendar` object, use the `setTimeZone` method with a time zone ID. For example, `cal.setTimeZone("CST")` sets the time zone to Central Standard Time. To find all the available time zones supported in Java, use the static method `getAvailableIDs()` in the `TimeZone` class. In general, the international time zone ID is a string in the form of continent/city like Europe/Berlin, Asia/Taipei, and America/Washington. You can also use the static method `getDefault()` in the `TimeZone` class to obtain default time zone on the host machine.

The `DateFormat` class can be used to format date and time in a number of styles. The `DateFormat` class supports several standard formatting styles. To format date and time using the `DateFormat` class, simply create an instance of `DateFormat` using one of the following three static methods:

- `public static final DateFormat getDateInstance(int dateStyle, Locale aLocale)`

  This method returns the date formatter with the formatting style for the specified locale.

- `public static final DateFormat getTimeInstance(int timeStyle, Locale aLocale)`

  This method returns the time formatter with the formatting style for the given locale.

- `public static final DateFormat getDateTimeInstance(int dateStyle, int timeStyle, Locale aLocale)`

  This method returns the date/time formatter with the formatting style for the given locale.

If the arguments are not present, the default style or default locale is used. The `dateStyle` and `timeStyle` are one of the following constants: `DateFormat.SHORT`, `DateFormat.MEDIUM`, `DateFormat.LONG`, and `DateFormat.FULL`. The exact result depends on the locale, but generally,

- `SHORT` is completely numeric, such as 7/24/98 (for date) and 4:49 PM (for time);
- `MEDIUM` is longer, such as 24-Jul-98 (for date) and 4:52:09 PM (for time);
- `LONG` is even longer, such as July 24, 1998 (for date) and 4:53:16 PM EST (for time);
- `FULL` is completely specified, such as Friday, July 24, 1998 (for date) and 4:54:13 o'clock PM EST (for time).

The statements given below display current time with a specified time zone (CST), formatting style (full date and full time), and locale (US).

```
GregorianCalendar calendar = new GregorianCalendar();
DateFormat formatter = DateFormat.getDateTimeInstance(
  DateFormat.FULL, DateFormat.FULL, Locale.US);
TimeZone timeZone = TimeZone.getTimeZone("CST");
dateFormat.setTimeZone(timeZone);
System.out.println("The local time is "+
  formatter.format(calendar.getTime()));
```

The date and time formatting subclass, such as `SimpleDateFormat`, enables you to choose any user-defined pattern for date and time formatting. The following constructor can be used to create a `SimpleDateFormat` object, and the object can be used to convert a `Date` object into a string with the desired format:

```
public SimpleDateFormat(String pattern)
```

The parameter `pattern` is a string consisting of characters with special meanings. For example, `y` means year, `M` means month, `d` means day of the month, `G` is for era designator, `h` means hours, `m` means minute of the hour, `s` means second of the minute, and `z` means time zone. Therefore, the following code will display a string like "Current time is 1997.11.12 AD at 04:10:18 PST" because the pattern is "yyyy.MM.dd G 'at' hh:mm:ss z."

```
SimpleDateFormat formatter
  = new SimpleDateFormat ("yyyy.MM.dd G 'at' hh:mm:ss z");
date currentTime = new Date();
String dateString = formatter.format(currentTime);
System.out.println("Current time is " + dateString);
```

The following two examples demonstrate how to display date, time, and calendar based on locale. The first example creates a clock and displays date and time in locale-sensitive format. The second example displays several different calendars with the names of the days shown in the appropriate local language.

Example 12.1 Displaying a Clock

This example presents a program that displays a clock to show current time based on the specified locale and time zone. The language, country, and time zone are passed to the program as parameters. The program can run as an applet or an application. When it runs as an applet, the parameters are passed from HTML tags. When it runs as an application, the parameters are passed as command-line arguments like this:

```
java CurrentTimeApplet en US CST
```

The program is given next, and its sample run is shown in Figure 12.1.

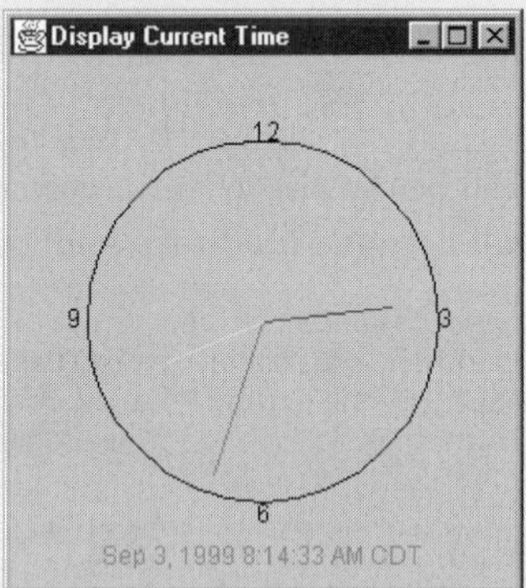

Figure 12.1 *The program displays a clock that shows the current time with specified locale and time zone.*

```
// CurrentTimeApplet.java: Display a still clock on the applet
import java.awt.*;
import java.util.*;
import javax.swing.*;

public class CurrentTimeApplet extends JApplet
{
  protected Locale locale;
  protected TimeZone timeZone;
  protected StillClock stillClock;
  private boolean isStandalone = false;

  // Construct the applet
  public CurrentTimeApplet()
  {
  }

  // Initialize the applet
  public void init()
  {
    // Load native fonts. Uncomment the following two statements,
    // if native fonts such as Chinese fonts are not used
    // GraphicsEnvironment ge =
    //   GraphicsEnvironment.getLocalGraphicsEnvironment();
```

```
    // ge.getAllFonts();

    if (!isStandalone)
    {
      // Get locale and timezone from HTML
      getHTMLParameters();
    }

    // Add the clock to the applet
    createClock();
  }

  // Create a clock and add it to the applet
  public void createClock()
  {
    getContentPane().add(stillClock =
      new StillClock(locale, timeZone));
  }

  public void getHTMLParameters()
  {
    // Get parameters from the HTML
    String language = getParameter("language");
    String country = getParameter("country");
    String timezone = getParameter("timezone");

    // Set default values if parameters are not given
    // in the HTML file
    if (language == null)
      language = "en";

    if (country == null)
      country = "US";

    if (timezone == null)
      timezone = "CST";

    // Set locale and timezone
    locale = new Locale(language, country);
    timeZone = TimeZone.getTimeZone(timezone);
  }

  // Main method with three arguments:
  // args[0]: language such as en
  // args[1]: country such as US
  // args[2]: timezone such as CST
  public static void main(String[] args)
  {
    // Create a frame
    JFrame frame = new JFrame("Display Current Time");

    // Create an instance of the applet
    CurrentTimeApplet applet = new CurrentTimeApplet();

    // It runs as an application
    applet.isStandalone = true;

    // Get parameters from the command line
    applet.getCommandLineParameters(args);

    // Add the applet instance to the frame
    frame.getContentPane().add(applet, BorderLayout.CENTER);

    // Invoke init() and start()
    applet.init();
    applet.start();
```

continues

Example 12.1 continued

```
      // Display the frame
      frame.setSize(300, 300);
      frame.setDefaultCloseOperation(JFrame.EXIT_ON_CLOSE);
      frame.setVisible(true);
    }

    // Get command line parameters
    public void getCommandLineParameters(String[] args)
    {
      // Declare locale and timezone with default values
      locale = Locale.getDefault();
      timeZone = TimeZone.getDefault();

      // Check usage and get language, country and time zone
      if (args.length > 3)
      {
        System.out.println(
          "Usage: java CurrentTimeApplet language country timezone");
        System.exit(0);
      }
      else if (args.length == 3)
      {
        locale = new Locale(args[0], args[1]);
        timeZone = TimeZone.getTimeZone(args[2]);
      }
      else if (args.length == 2)
      {
        locale = new Locale(args[0], args[1]);
        timeZone = TimeZone.getDefault();
      }
      else if (args.length == 1)
      {
        System.out.println(
          "Usage: java DisplayTime language country timezone");
        System.exit(0);
      }
      else
      {
        locale = Locale.getDefault();
        timeZone = TimeZone.getDefault();
      }
    }
  }

  // StillClock.java: Display a clock in JPanel
  import java.awt.*;
  import java.util.*;
  import java.text.*;
  import javax.swing.*;

  public class StillClock extends JPanel
  {
    protected TimeZone timeZone;
    protected int xCenter, yCenter;
    protected int clockRadius;
    protected DateFormat formatter;

    // Default constructor
    public StillClock()
    {
      this(Locale.getDefault(), TimeZone.getDefault());
    }
```

```
// Construct a clock with specified locale and time zone
public StillClock(Locale locale, TimeZone timeZone)
{
  setLocale(locale);
  this.timeZone = timeZone;
}

// Set timezone using a time zone id such as "CST"
public void setTimeZoneID(String newTimeZoneID)
{
  timeZone = TimeZone.getTimeZone(newTimeZoneID);
}

// Override the paintComponent to display a clock
public void paintComponent(Graphics g)
{
  super.paintComponent(g);
  // Initialize clock parameters
  clockRadius =
    (int)(Math.min(getSize().width, getSize().height)*0.7*0.5);
  xCenter = (getSize().width)/2;
  yCenter = (getSize().height)/2;

  // Draw circle
  g.setColor(Color.black);
  g.drawOval(xCenter - clockRadius,yCenter - clockRadius,
    2*clockRadius, 2*clockRadius);
  g.drawString("12",xCenter-5, yCenter-clockRadius);
  g.drawString("9",xCenter-clockRadius-10,yCenter+3);
  g.drawString("3",xCenter+clockRadius,yCenter+3);
  g.drawString("6",xCenter-3,yCenter+clockRadius+10);

  // Get current time using GregorianCalendar
  GregorianCalendar cal = new GregorianCalendar(timeZone);

  // Draw second hand
  int second = (int)cal.get(GregorianCalendar.SECOND);
  int sLength = (int)(clockRadius*0.9);
  int xSecond =
    (int)(xCenter + sLength*Math.sin(second*(2*Math.PI/60)));
  int ySecond =
    (int)(yCenter - sLength*Math.cos(second*(2*Math.PI/60)));
  g.setColor(Color.red);
  g.drawLine(xCenter, yCenter, xSecond, ySecond);

  // Draw minute hand
  int minute = (int)cal.get(GregorianCalendar.MINUTE);
  int mLength = (int)(clockRadius*0.75);
  int xMinute =
    (int)(xCenter + mLength*Math.sin(minute*(2*Math.PI/60)));
  int yMinute =
    (int)(yCenter - mLength*Math.cos(minute*(2*Math.PI/60)));
  g.setColor(Color.blue);
  g.drawLine(xCenter, yCenter, xMinute, yMinute);

  // Draw hour hand
  int hour = (int)cal.get(GregorianCalendar.HOUR_OF_DAY);
  int hLength = (int)(clockRadius*0.6);
  int xHour = (int)(xCenter +
    hLength*Math.sin((hour+minute/60.0)*(2*Math.PI/12)));
  int yHour = (int)(yCenter -
    hLength*Math.cos((hour+minute/60.0)*(2*Math.PI/12)));
  g.setColor(Color.green);
  g.drawLine(xCenter, yCenter, xHour, yHour);
```

continues

Example 12.1 continued

```
        // Set display format in specified style, locale and timezone
        formatter = DateFormat.getDateTimeInstance
          (DateFormat.MEDIUM, DateFormat.LONG, getLocale());
        formatter.setTimeZone(timeZone);

        // Display current date
        g.setColor(Color.red);
        String today = formatter.format(cal.getTime());
        FontMetrics fm = g.getFontMetrics();
        g.drawString(today, (getSize().width -
        fm.stringWidth(today))/2, yCenter+clockRadius+30);
      }
    }
```

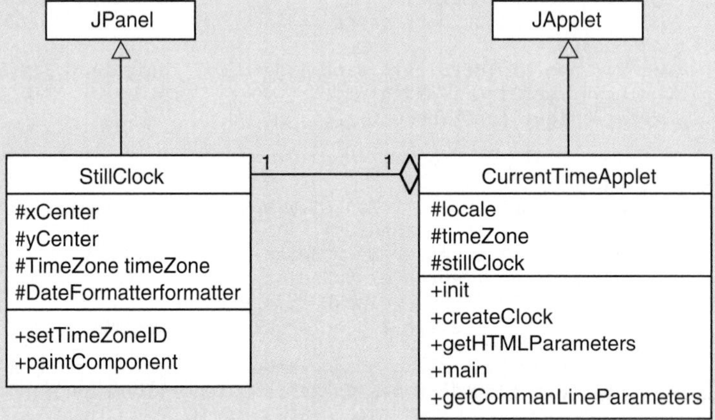

Figure 12.2 *The `CurrentTimeApplet` class displays a clock.*

Example Review

The program consists of two classes: `CurrentTimeApplet` and `StillClock`. Their relationship is shown in Figure 12.2.

The `CurrentTimeApplet` class can run as an applet or as an application. When it runs as an application, it sets `isStandalone true` so that it does not attempt to retrieve HTML parameters.

The program obtains language, country, and time zone as either an HTML parameter or a command-line parameter, and uses this information to create an instance of `StillClock`. `StillClock` is responsible for drawing the clock for the current time. `StillClock` is similar to the `DrawClock` class in Example 8.6, "Drawing a Clock," except that the time (hour, minute, and second) is passed as a parameter to `DrawClock`, but the time in `StillClock` is the current time for the specified locale and time zone.

This program uses the `GregorianCalendar` class to extract the hour, minute, and second from the current time, and the `DateFormat` class to format date and time in a string, with the locale and time zone specified by the user.

The date is displayed below the clock. The program uses font metrics to determine the size of the date/time string and center the display.

The `Component` class has a variable `locale`, which can be accessed through the `getLocale` and `setLocale` methods. Since `StillClock` is a `JPanel`, a subclass of `Component`, you can use these methods to work with the locale in `StillClock`.

The variables are purposely declared as protected so that they can be accessed by `StillClock`'s subclasses in later chapters. The `setTimeZoneID` method defined in `StillClock` is not used here, but it will be used in Example 13.5, "Controlling a Group of Clocks," in Chapter 13, "Multithreading."

The clock is locale-sensitive. If you use the Chinese locale with language (zh) and country (CN), the date and time are displayed in Chinese, as shown in Figure 12.3.

The `CurrentTimeApplet` class is designed for reuse in future chapters. The `createClock` method is purposely defined in such a way as to make it possible to create and add different types of clocks to the applet in Chapter 14, "Multimedia," by overriding this method.

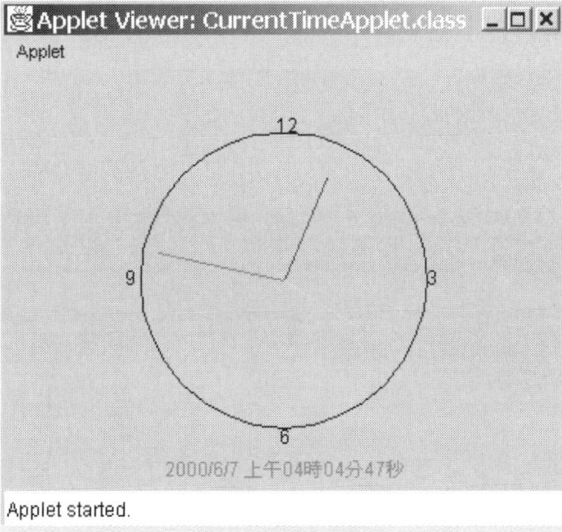

Figure 12.3 *The program displays a clock in the Chinese locale.*

TIP

To enable Asian fonts, you need to install appropriate fonts, and modify the font.properties file in the java\jre\lib directory. For example, to make the Chinese fonts work on Windows, install the MingLiU font, and replace font.properties with font.properties.zh_TW in the jre\lib folder. The MingLiu font can be obtained from the NT4.0 CD.

Example 12.2 Displaying a Calendar

This example presents a program that displays a calendar based on the specified locale, as shown in Figures 12.4 and 12.5. The user can specify a locale from a combo box that consists of a list of all the available locales supported by the system. When the program starts, the calendar for the current month of the year is displayed. The user can use the Prior and Next buttons to browse the calendar.

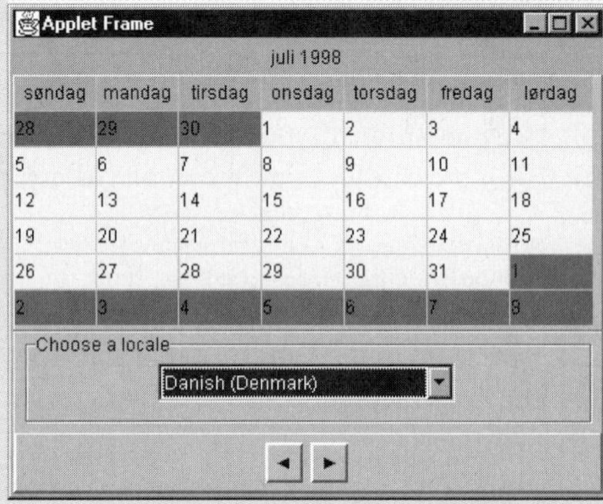

Figure 12.4 *The calendar applet displays a calendar with the Danish locale.*

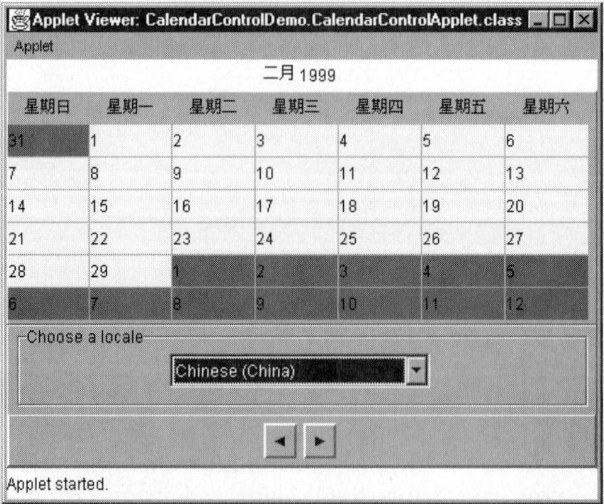

Figure 12.5 *The calendar applet displays a calendar with the Chinese locale.*

```
// CalendarApplet.java: Display a locale-sensitive calendar
import java.awt.*;
import java.awt.event.*;
import javax.swing.*;
import javax.swing.border.*;
```

```
import java.util.*;
import java.text.DateFormat;

public class CalendarApplet extends JApplet
  implements ItemListener, ActionListener
{
  // Create a CalendarPanel for showing calendars
  private CalendarPanel calendarPanel = new CalendarPanel();

  // Combo box for selecting available locales
  private JComboBox jcboLocale = new JComboBox();

  // Declare locales to store available locales
  private Locale locales[] = Calendar.getAvailableLocales();

  // Buttons Prior and Next to displaying prior and next month
  private JButton jbtPrior = new JButton("Prior");
  private JButton jbtNext = new JButton("Next");

  // Initialize the applet
  public void init()
  {
    // Load native fonts. Uncomment the following two statements,
    // if native fonts such as Chinese fonts are not used
    // GraphicsEnvironment ge =
    //  GraphicsEnvironment.getLocalGraphicsEnvironment();
    // ge.getAllFonts();

    // Panel jpLocale to hold the combo box for selecting locales
    JPanel jpLocale = new JPanel();
    jpLocale.setBorder(new TitledBorder("Choose a locale"));
    jpLocale.setLayout(new FlowLayout());
    jpLocale.add(jcboLocale);

    // Initialize the combo box to add locale names
    for (int i=0; i<locales.length; i++)
      jcboLocale.addItem(locales[i].getDisplayName());

    // Panel jpButtons to hold buttons
    JPanel jpButtons = new JPanel();
    jpButtons.setLayout(new FlowLayout());
    jpButtons.add(jbtPrior);
    jpButtons.add(jbtNext);

    // Panel jpCalendar to hold calendarPanel and buttons
    JPanel jpCalendar = new JPanel();
    jpCalendar.setLayout(new BorderLayout());
    jpCalendar.add(calendarPanel, BorderLayout.CENTER);
    jpCalendar.add(jpButtons, BorderLayout.SOUTH);

    // Place jpCalendar and jpLocale to the applet
    this.getContentPane().add(jpCalendar, BorderLayout.CENTER);
    this.getContentPane().add(jpLocale, BorderLayout.SOUTH);

    // Register listeners
    jcboLocale.addItemListener(this);
    jbtPrior.addActionListener(this);
    jbtNext.addActionListener(this);
  }

  // Main method
  public static void main(String[] args)
  {
    // Create a frame
    JFrame frame = new JFrame("Calendar Demo");
```

continues

Example 12.2 continued

```
    // Create an instance of the applet
    CalendarApplet applet = new CalendarApplet();

    // Add the applet instance to the frame
    frame.getContentPane().add(applet, BorderLayout.CENTER);
    // Invoke init() and start()
    applet.init();
    applet.start();

    // Display the frame
    frame.pack();
    frame.setDefaultCloseOperation(JFrame.EXIT_ON_CLOSE);
    frame.setVisible(true);
  }

  // Handle locale selection
  public void itemStateChanged(ItemEvent e)
  {
    // Set a new locale
    calendarPanel.setLocale(locales[jcboLocale.getSelectedIndex()]);
  }

  // Handle the Prior and Next buttons
  public void actionPerformed(ActionEvent e)
  {
    int currentMonth = calendarPanel.getMonth();

    if (e.getSource() == jbtPrior)
    {
      if (currentMonth==1)
      {
        calendarPanel.setMonth(12);
        calendarPanel.setYear(calendarPanel.getYear()-1);
      }
      else
        calendarPanel.setMonth(currentMonth-1);
    }
    else if (e.getSource() == jbtNext)
    {
      if (currentMonth==12)
      {
        calendarPanel.setMonth(1);
        calendarPanel.setYear(calendarPanel.getYear()+1);
      }
      else
        calendarPanel.setMonth(currentMonth+1);
    }
  }
}
// CalendarPanel.java: Display calendar for a month
import java.awt.*;
import javax.swing.*;
import javax.swing.border.LineBorder;
import java.util.*;
import java.text.*;

public class CalendarPanel extends JPanel
{
  private int month;
  private int year;
  private Locale locale = Locale.getDefault();  // Default locale

  // The header label
  private JLabel jlblHeader = new JLabel(" ", JLabel.CENTER);
```

```
// Labels to display day names and days
private JLabel[] jlblDay = new JLabel[49];
// MyCalendar instance
private MyCalendar calendar = new MyCalendar();

// Constructor
public CalendarPanel()
{
  // Panel jpDays to hold day names and days
  JPanel jpDays = new JPanel();
  jpDays.setLayout(new GridLayout(7, 1));
  for (int i=0; i<49; i++)
  {
    jpDays.add(jlblDay[i] = new JLabel());
    jlblDay[i].setBorder(new LineBorder(Color.black, 1));
    jlblDay[i].setHorizontalAlignment(JLabel.RIGHT);
    jlblDay[i].setVerticalAlignment(JLabel.TOP);
  }

  // Place header and calendar body in the panel
  this.setLayout(new BorderLayout());
  this.add(jlblHeader, BorderLayout.NORTH);
  this.add(jpDays, BorderLayout.CENTER);

  // Set current month, and year
  calendar = new MyCalendar();
  month = calendar.get(Calendar.MONTH)+1;
  year = calendar.get(Calendar.YEAR);

  // Show calendar
  showHeader();
  showDayNames();
  showDays();
}

// Update the header based on locale
private void showHeader()
{
  SimpleDateFormat sdf = new SimpleDateFormat("MMMM yyyy", locale);
  String header = sdf.format(calendar.getTime());
  jlblHeader.setText(header);
}

// Update the day names based on locale
private void showDayNames()
{
  DateFormatSymbols dfs = new DateFormatSymbols(locale);
  String dayNames[] = dfs.getWeekdays();

  // Set calendar days
  for (int i=0; i<7; i++)
  {
    jlblDay[i].setText(dayNames[i+1]);
    jlblDay[i].setHorizontalAlignment(JLabel.CENTER);
  }
}

// Display days
public void showDays()
{
  // Set the calendar to the first day of the
  // specified month and year
  calendar.set(Calendar.YEAR, year);
  calendar.set(Calendar.MONTH, month-1);
  calendar.set(Calendar.DATE, 1);
```

continues

Example 12.2 continued

```
    // Get the day of the first day in a month
    int startingDayOfMonth = calendar.get(Calendar.DAY_OF_WEEK);

    // Fill the calendar with the days before this month
    MyCalendar cloneCalendar = (MyCalendar)calendar.clone();
    cloneCalendar.add(Calendar.DATE, -1);
          for (int i=0; i<startingDayOfMonth-1; i++)
    {
      jlblDay[i+7].setForeground(Color.yellow);
      jlblDay[i+7].setText(
        cloneCalendar.daysInMonth()-startingDayOfMonth+2+i+"");
    }

    // Display days of this month
    for (int i=1; i<=calendar.daysInMonth(); i++)
    {
      jlblDay[i-2+startingDayOfMonth+7].setForeground(Color.black);
      jlblDay[i-2+startingDayOfMonth+7].setText(i+"");
    }

    // Fill the calendar with the days after this month
    int j = 1;
    for (int i=calendar.daysInMonth()-1+startingDayOfMonth+7;
      i<49; i++)
    {
      jlblDay[i].setForeground(Color.yellow);
      jlblDay[i].setText(j++ + "");
    }

    showHeader();
  }

  // Getter method for month
  public int getMonth()
  {
    return month;
  }

  // Setter method for month
  public void setMonth(int newMonth)
  {
    month = newMonth;
    showDays();
  }

  // Getter method for year
  public int getYear()
  {
    return year;
  }

  // Setter method for year
  public void setYear(int newYear)
  {
    year = newYear;
    showDays();
  }

  // Set a new locale
  public void setLocale(Locale newLocale)
  {
    locale = newLocale;
    showHeader();
    showDayNames();
  }
}
```

```
// MyCalendar.java: A subclass of GregorianCalendar
import java.awt.*;
import java.util.*;

public class MyCalendar extends GregorianCalendar
{
  // Find the number of days in a month
  public int daysInMonth()
  {
    switch (get(MONTH))
    {
      case 0: case 2: case 4: case 6: case 7: case 9: case 11:
        return 31;
      case 1: if (isLeapYear(get(YEAR))) return 29;
              else return 28;
      case 3: case 5: case 8: case 10: return 30;
      default: return 0;
    }
  }
}
```

Example Review

The program consists of three classes: `CalendarApplet`, `CalendarPanel`, and `MyCalendar`. Their relationships are shown in Figure 12.6.

`MyCalendar` is a subclass of `GregorianCalendar`, which has a new method, `daysInMonth`, that computes the number of days in a month.

`CalendarApplet` creates the user interface and handles the button actions and combo box item selections for locales. The `Calendar.getAvailableLocales()`

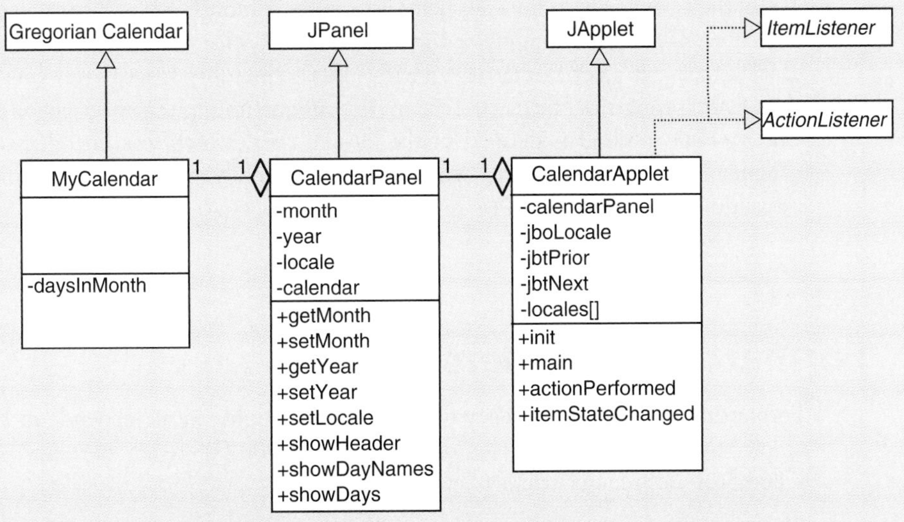

Figure 12.6 *`CalendarApplet` contains `CalendarPanel`, and `CalendarPanel` contains `MyCalendar`.*

continues

Example 12.2 continued

method is used to find all available locales that have calendars. Its `getDisplayName()` method returns the name of each locale, and the name is added to the combo box. When the user selects a locale name in the combo box, a new locale is passed to `calendarPanel`, and a new calendar is displayed based on the new locale.

`CalendarPanel` is created to control and display the calendar. It displays the month and year in the header, and day names and days in the calendar body. The header and day names are locale-sensitive.

The `showHeader` method displays the calendar title in a form like "MMMM yyyy." The `SimpleDateFormat` class used in the `showHeader` method is a subclass of `DateFormat`. `SimpleDateFormat` allows you to customize the date format to display the date in various nonstandard styles.

The `showDayNames` method displays the day names in the calendar. The `DateFormatSymbols` class used in the `showDayNames` method is a class for encapsulating localizable date-time formatting data, such as the names of the months, the names of the days of the week, and the time zone data. The `getWeekdays` method is used to get an array of day names.

The `showDays` method displays the days for the specified month of the year. As you can see in Figure 12.4, the labels before the current month are filled with the last few days of the preceding month, and the labels after the current month are filled with the first few days of the next month.

To fill the calendar with the days before the current month, a clone of `calendar`, named `cloneCalendar`, was created to obtain the days for the preceding month. `cloneCalendar` is a copy of `calendar` with separate memory space. Thus you can change the properties of `cloneCalendar` without corrupting the `calendar` object. The `clone()` method is defined in the `Object` class, which was introduced in Chapter 6, "Class Inheritance." You can clone any object as long as its defining class implements the `Cloneable` interface.

Formatting Numbers

Formatting numbers as currency or percentages is highly locale-dependent. For example, the number 5000.50 is displayed as $5,000.50 in US currency, but as 5 000,50 F in French currency.

Numbers are formatted using the `java.text.NumberFormat` class, an abstract base class that provides the methods for formatting and parsing numbers. With `NumberFormat`, you can format and parse numbers for any locale. Your code can be completely independent of locale conventions for decimal points, thousands-separators, or the particular decimal digits used, and even for whether the number format is decimal.

To format a number for the current locale, use one of the factory class methods to get a formatter. Use `getInstance` or `getNumberInstance` to get the normal number format. Use `getCurrencyInstance` to get the currency number format. And use `getPercentInstance` to get a format for displaying percentages. With this format, a fraction like 0.53 is displayed as 53%.

For example, to display a number in percentages, you can use the following code to create a formatter for the given locale:

```
NumberFormat percentFormatter =
  NumberFormat.getPercentInstance(locale);
```

You can then use `percentFormatter` to format a number into a string like this:

```
String s = percentFormatter.format(0.075);
```

Conversely, if you want to read a number entered or stored with the conventions of a certain locale, use the `parse` method of a formatter to convert the formatted number into an instance of `java.lang.Number`. The `parse` method throws a `ParseException` if parsing fails.

You can also control the display of numbers with such methods as `setMaximumFractionDigits` and `setMinimumFractionDigits`. If you want even more control over the format or parsing, or want to give your users more control, try casting the `NumberFormat` you get from the factory methods to a `DecimalFormat`, which is a subclass of `NumberFormat`. You can then use the `applyPattern` method of the `DecimalFormat` class to specify the patterns for displaying the number.

For example, the following statements create an instance of `DecimalFormat` with the pattern "000.00." A number will be formatted with at least three digits before the decimal point and exactly two digits after the decimal point. If there are more actual digits before the decimal point, all the digits are displayed. If there are more digits after the decimal point, the digits are rounded.

```
NumberFormat numberForm = NumberFormat.getNumberInstance();
DecimalFormat df = (DecimalFormat)numberForm;
df.applyPattern("000.00");
```

For instance, `df.format(30.983)` returns 030.98, `df.format(3000.9856)` returns 3000.99, and `df.format(3.9)` returns 003.90. Note the `format` method returns a string.

For more information about the formation of the patterns for `DecimalFormat`, please browse the online documentation on `java.text.DecimalFormat`.

Example 12.3 Formatting Numbers

This example creates a mortgage calculator similar to the one in Example 10.1, "Using Applets." This new mortgage calculator allows the user to choose locales, and displays numbers in locale-sensitive format. As shown in Figure 12.7, the user enters interest rate, number of years, and loan amount, then clicks the Compute button to display the interest rate in percentage format, the number

continues

Example 12.3 continued

of years in normal number format, and the loan amount, total payment, and monthly payment in currency format.

```
// NumberFormatDemo.java: Demonstrate formatting numbers
import java.awt.*;
import java.awt.event.*;
import javax.swing.*;
import javax.swing.border.*;
import java.util.*;
import java.text.*;

public class NumberFormatDemo extends JApplet
  implements ItemListener, ActionListener
{
  // Combo box for selecting available locales
  JComboBox jcboLocale = new JComboBox();

  // Text fields for interest rate, year, loan amount,
  JTextField jtfInterestRate = new JTextField(10);
  JTextField jtfNumOfYears = new JTextField(10);
  JTextField jtfLoanAmount = new JTextField(10);
  JTextField jtfFormattedInterestRate = new JTextField(10);
  JTextField jtfFormattedNumOfYears = new JTextField(10);
  JTextField jtfFormattedLoanAmount = new JTextField(10);

  // Text fields for monthly payment and total payment
  JTextField jtfTotalPayment = new JTextField();
  JTextField jtfMonthlyPayment = new JTextField();

  // Compute Mortgage button
  JButton jbtCompute = new JButton("Compute");

  // Current locale
  Locale locale = Locale.getDefault();

  // Declare locales to store available locales
  Locale locales[] = Calendar.getAvailableLocales();

  // Initialize the combo box
  public void initializeComboBox()
  {
    // Add locale names to the combo box
    for (int i=0; i<locales.length; i++)
      jcboLocale.addItem(locales[i].getDisplayName());
  }

  // Initialize the applet
  public void init()
  {
    // Load native fonts. Uncomment the following two statements,
    // if native fonts such as Chinese fonts are not used
    // GraphicsEnvironment ge =
    //  GraphicsEnvironment.getLocalGraphicsEnvironment();
    // ge.getAllFonts();

    // Panel p1 to hold the combo box for selecting locales
    JPanel p1 = new JPanel();
    p1.setLayout(new FlowLayout());
    p1.add(jcboLocale);
    initializeComboBox();
    p1.setBorder(new TitledBorder("Choose a Locale"));

    // Panel p2 to hold the input
    JPanel p2 = new JPanel();
```

```
    p2.setLayout(new GridLayout(3, 3));
    p2.add(new JLabel("Interest Rate"));
    p2.add(jtfInterestRate);
    p2.add(jtfFormattedInterestRate);
    p2.add(new JLabel("Number of Years"));
    p2.add(jtfNumOfYears);
    p2.add(jtfFormattedNumOfYears);
    p2.add(new JLabel("Loan Amount"));
    p2.add(jtfLoanAmount);
    p2.add(jtfFormattedLoanAmount);
    p2.setBorder(new TitledBorder("Enter Annual Interest Rate, " +
      "Number of Years, and Loan Amount"));

    // Panel p3 to hold the result
    JPanel p3 = new JPanel();
    p3.setLayout(new GridLayout(2, 2));
    p3.setBorder(new TitledBorder("Payment"));
    p3.add(new JLabel("Monthly Payment"));
    p3.add(jtfMonthlyPayment);
    p3.add(new JLabel("Total Payment"));
    p3.add(jtfTotalPayment);

    // Set text field alignment
    jtfFormattedInterestRate.setHorizontalAlignment(JTextField.RIGHT);
    jtfFormattedNumOfYears.setHorizontalAlignment(JTextField.RIGHT);
    jtfFormattedLoanAmount.setHorizontalAlignment(JTextField.RIGHT);
    jtfTotalPayment.setHorizontalAlignment(JTextField.RIGHT);
    jtfMonthlyPayment.setHorizontalAlignment(JTextField.RIGHT);

    // Set editable false
    jtfFormattedInterestRate.setEditable(false);
    jtfFormattedNumOfYears.setEditable(false);
    jtfFormattedLoanAmount.setEditable(false);
    jtfTotalPayment.setEditable(false);
    jtfMonthlyPayment.setEditable(false);

    // Panel p4 to hold result payments and a button
    JPanel p4 = new JPanel();
    p4.setLayout(new BorderLayout());
    p4.add(p3, BorderLayout.CENTER);
    p4.add(jbtCompute, BorderLayout.SOUTH);

    // Place panels to the applet
    getContentPane().add(p1, BorderLayout.NORTH);
    getContentPane().add(p2, BorderLayout.CENTER);
    getContentPane().add(p4, BorderLayout.SOUTH);

    // Register listeners
    jcboLocale.addItemListener(this);
    jbtCompute.addActionListener(this);
  }

  // Main method
  public static void main(String[] args)
  {
    // Create a frame
    JFrame frame = new JFrame("Number Formatting Demo");

    // Create an instance of the applet
    NumberFormatDemo applet = new NumberFormatDemo();

    // Add the applet instance to the frame
    frame.getContentPane().add(applet, BorderLayout.CENTER);

    // Invoke init() and start()
    applet.init();
```

continues

Example 12.3 continued

```
    applet.start();

    // Display the frame
    frame.setSize(300, 300);
    frame.setDefaultCloseOperation(JFrame.EXIT_ON_CLOSE);
    frame.setVisible(true);
  }

  // Handle locale selection
  public void itemStateChanged(ItemEvent e)
  {
    if (e.getSource() == jcboLocale)
    {
      locale = locales[jcboLocale.getSelectedIndex()];
      computeMortgage();
    }
  }

  // Handle button action
  public void actionPerformed(ActionEvent e)
  {
    if (e.getSource() == jbtCompute)
      computeMortgage();
  }

  // Compute payments and display results locale-sensitive format
  private void computeMortgage()
  {
    // Retrieve input from user
    double loan = new Double(jtfLoanAmount.getText()).doubleValue();
    double interestRate =
      new Double(jtfInterestRate.getText()).doubleValue()/1200;
    int numOfYears = new Integer(jtfNumOfYears.getText()).intValue();

    // Calculate payments
    double monthlyPayment =
        loan*interestRate/
     (1-(Math.pow(1/(1+interestRate),numOfYears*12)));
    double totalPayment = monthlyPayment*numOfYears*12;

    // Get formatters
    NumberFormat percentFormatter =
      NumberFormat.getPercentInstance(locale);
    NumberFormat currencyForm =
      NumberFormat.getCurrencyInstance(locale);
    NumberFormat numberForm = NumberFormat.getNumberInstance(locale);
    percentFormatter.setMinimumFractionDigits(2);

    // Display formatted input
    jtfFormattedInterestRate.setText(
      percentFormatter.format(interestRate*12));
    jtfFormattedNumOfYears.setText(numberForm.format(numOfYears));
    jtfFormattedLoanAmount.setText(currencyForm.format(loan));

    // Display results in currency format
    jtfMonthlyPayment.setText(currencyForm.format(monthlyPayment));
    jtfTotalPayment.setText(currencyForm.format(totalPayment));
  }
}
```

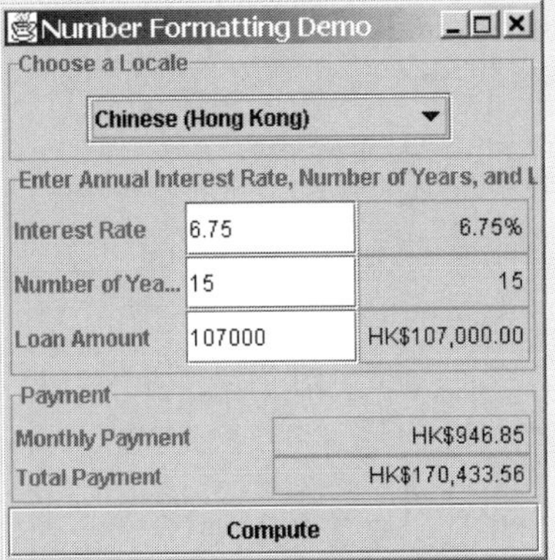

Figure 12.7 *The locale determines the format of the numbers displayed in the mortgage calculator.*

Example Review

The `computeMortgage` method gets the input on interest rate, number of years, and loan amount from the user, computes monthly payment and total payment, and displays annual interest rate in percentage format, number of years in normal number format, and loan amount, monthly payment, and total payment in locale-sensitive format.

The statement `percentFormatter.setMinimumFractionDigits(2)` sets the minimum number of fractional parts to 2. Without this statement, 0.075 would be displayed as 7% rather than 7.5%.

Resource Bundles (Optional)

The `NumberFormatDemo` in Example 12.3 displays the numbers, currencies, and percentages in local customs, but displays all the message strings, titles, and button labels in English. In this section, you will learn how to use resource bundles to localize message strings, titles, button labels, etc.

A *resource bundle* is a Java class file or a text file that provides locale-specific information. This information can be accessed by Java programs dynamically. When a locale-specific resource is needed—a message string, for example—your program can load it from the resource bundle appropriate for the desired locale. In this way, you can write program code that is largely independent of the user's locale, isolating most, if not all, of the locale-specific information in resource bundles.

With resource bundles, you can write programs that separate the locale-sensitive part of your code from the locale-independent part. The programs can easily handle multiple locales, and can be easily modified later to support even more locales.

The resources are placed inside the classes that extend the `ResourceBundle` class or a subclass of `ResourceBundle`. Resource bundles contain *key/value* pairs. Each key uniquely identifies a locale-specific object in the bundle. You can use the key to retrieve the object. `ListResourceBundle` is a convenient subclass of `ResourceBundle` that is often used to simplify the creation of resource bundles. Here is an example of a resource bundle that contains four keys using `ListResourceBundle`:

```
// MyResource.java: resource file
public class MyResource extends java.util.ListResourceBundle
{
  static final Object[][] contents =
  {
    {"nationalFlag", "us.gif"},
    {"nationalAnthem", "us.au"},
    {"nationalColor", Color.red},
    {"annualGrowthRate", new Double(7.8)}
  };

  public Object[][] getContents()
  {
    return contents;
  }
}
```

Keys are case-sensitive strings. In this example, the keys are `nationalFlag`, `nationalAnthem`, `nationalColor`, and `annualGrowthRate`. The values can be any type of `Object`.

If all the resources are strings, they can be placed in a convenient text file with extension .properties. A typical property file would look like this:

```
#Wed Jul 01 07:23:24 EST 1998
nationalFlag=us.gif
nationalAnthem=us.au
```

To retrieve values from a `ResourceBundle` in a program, you first need to create an instance of `ResourceBundle` using one of the following two static methods:

```
public static final ResourceBundle getBundle(String baseName)
  throws MissingResourceException
public static final ResourceBundle getBundle
  (String baseName, Locale locale) throws MissingResourceException
```

The first method returns a `ResourceBundle` for the default locale, and the second method returns a `ResourceBundle` for the specified locale. `baseName` is the base name for a set of classes, each of which describes the information for a given locale. These classes are named in Table 12.2.

TABLE 12.2 **Resource Bundle Naming Conventions**

1. BaseName_language_country_variant.class
2. BaseName_language_country.class
3. BaseName_language.class
4. BaseName.class
5. BaseName_language_country_variant.properties
6. BaseName_language_country.properties
7. BaseName_language.properties
8. BaseName.properties

For example, MyResource_en_BR.class stores resources specific to the United Kingdom, MyResource_en_US.class stores resources specific to the United States, and MyResource_en.class stores resources specific to all the English-speaking countries.

The `getBundle` method attempts to load the class that matches the specified locale by language, country, and variant by searching the file name in the order shown in Table 12.2. The files searched in this order form a *resource chain*. If no file is found in the resource chain, the `getBundle` method raises a `MissingResourceException`.

Once a resource bundle object is created, you can use the `getObject` method to retrieve the value according to the key. For example,

```
ResourceBundle res = ResourceBundle.getBundle("MyResource");
String flagFile = (String)res.getObject("nationalFlag");
String anthemFile = (String)res.getObject("nationalAnthem");
Color color = (Color)res.getObject("nationalColor");
double growthRate =
  (Double)res.getObject("annualGrowthRate").doubleValue();
```

TIP

If the resource value is a string, a convenient `getString` method can be used to replace the `getObject()` method. The `getString` method simply casts the value returned by `getObject` to a string.

What happens if a resource object you are looking for is not defined in the resource bundle? Java employs an intelligent look-up scheme that searches the object in the parent file along the resource chain. This search is repeated until the object is found or all the parent files in the resource chain have been searched. A `MissingResourceException` is raised if the search is unsuccessful.

Example 12.4 Using Resource Bundles

This example modifies the `NumberFormatDemo` program in Example 12.3 so that it displays messages, title, and button labels in English, Chinese, and French, as shown in Figure 12.8.

The source code for ResourceBundleDemo.java is shown below:

```
// ResourceBundleDemo.java: Demonstrate resource bundle
import java.awt.*;
import java.awt.event.*;
import javax.swing.*;
import javax.swing.border.*;
import java.util.*;
import java.text.*;

public class ResourceBundleDemo extends JApplet
  implements ItemListener, ActionListener
{
  // Combo box for selecting available locales
  JComboBox jcboLocale = new JComboBox();
  ResourceBundle res = ResourceBundle.getBundle("MyResource");
```

continues

Example 12.4 continued

```
// Create labels
JLabel jlblInterestRate =
  new JLabel(res.getString("Annual_Interest_Rate"));
JLabel jlblNumOfYears =
  new JLabel(res.getString("Number_Of_Years"));
JLabel jlblLoanAmount = new JLabel(res.getString("Loan_Amount"));
JLabel jlblMonthlyPayment =
  new JLabel(res.getString("Monthly_Payment"));
JLabel jlblTotalPayment = new JLabel(res.getString("Total_Payment"));

// Create titled borders
TitledBorder comboBoxTitle =
  new TitledBorder(res.getString("Choose_a_Locale"));
TitledBorder inputTitle = new TitledBorder
  (res.getString("Enter_Interest_Rate"));
TitledBorder paymentTitle =
  new TitledBorder(res.getString("Payment"));

// Text fields for interest rate, year, loan amount,
JTextField jtfInterestRate = new JTextField(10);
JTextField jtfNumOfYears = new JTextField(10);
JTextField jtfLoanAmount = new JTextField(10);
JTextField jtfFormattedInterestRate = new JTextField(10);
JTextField jtfFormattedNumOfYears = new JTextField(10);
JTextField jtfFormattedLoanAmount = new JTextField(10);

// Text fields for monthly payment and total payment
JTextField jtfTotalPayment = new JTextField();
JTextField jtfMonthlyPayment = new JTextField();

// Compute Mortgage button
JButton jbtCompute = new JButton(res.getString("Compute"));

// Current locale
Locale locale = Locale.getDefault();

// Declare locales to store available locales
Locale locales[] = Calendar.getAvailableLocales();

// Initialize the combo box
public void initializeComboBox()
{
  // Add locale names to the combo box
  for (int i=0; i<locales.length; i++)
    jcboLocale.addItem(locales[i].getDisplayName());
}

// Initialize the applet
public void init()
{
  // Load native fonts. Uncomment the following two statements,
  // if native fonts such as Chinese fonts are not used
  // GraphicsEnvironment ge =
  //  GraphicsEnvironment.getLocalGraphicsEnvironment();
  // ge.getAllFonts();

  // Panel p1 to hold the combo box for selecting locales
  JPanel p1 = new JPanel();
  p1.setLayout(new FlowLayout());
  p1.add(jcboLocale);
  initializeComboBox();
  p1.setBorder(comboBoxTitle);
```

```
    // Panel p2 to hold the input for annual interest rate,
    // number of years and loan amount
    JPanel p2 = new JPanel();
    p2.setLayout(new GridLayout(3, 3));
    p2.add(jlblInterestRate);
    p2.add(jtfInterestRate);
    p2.add(jtfFormattedInterestRate);
    p2.add(jlblNumOfYears);
    p2.add(jtfNumOfYears);
    p2.add(jtfFormattedNumOfYears);
    p2.add(jlblLoanAmount);
    p2.add(jtfLoanAmount);
    p2.add(jtfFormattedLoanAmount);
    p2.setBorder(inputTitle);

    // Panel p3 to hold the payment
    JPanel p3 = new JPanel();
    p3.setLayout(new GridLayout(2, 2));
    p3.setBorder(paymentTitle);
    p3.add(jlblMonthlyPayment);
    p3.add(jtfMonthlyPayment);
    p3.add(jlblTotalPayment);
    p3.add(jtfTotalPayment);

    // Set text field alignment
    jtfFormattedInterestRate.setHorizontalAlignment
      (JTextField.RIGHT);
    jtfFormattedNumOfYears.setHorizontalAlignment(JTextField.RIGHT);
    jtfFormattedLoanAmount.setHorizontalAlignment(JTextField.RIGHT);
    jtfTotalPayment.setHorizontalAlignment(JTextField.RIGHT);
    jtfMonthlyPayment.setHorizontalAlignment(JTextField.RIGHT);

    // Set editable false
    jtfFormattedInterestRate.setEditable(false);
    jtfFormattedNumOfYears.setEditable(false);
    jtfFormattedLoanAmount.setEditable(false);
    jtfTotalPayment.setEditable(false);
    jtfMonthlyPayment.setEditable(false);

    // Panel p4 to hold result payments and a button
    JPanel p4 = new JPanel();
    p4.setLayout(new BorderLayout());
    p4.add(p3, BorderLayout.CENTER);
    p4.add(jbtCompute, BorderLayout.SOUTH);

    // Place panels to the applet
    getContentPane().add(p1, BorderLayout.NORTH);
    getContentPane().add(p2, BorderLayout.CENTER);
    getContentPane().add(p4, BorderLayout.SOUTH);

    // Register listeners
    jcboLocale.addItemListener(this);
    jbtCompute.addActionListener(this);
  }

  // Main method
  public static void main(String[] args)
  {
    // Create an instance of the applet
    ResourceBundleDemo applet = new ResourceBundleDemo();

    // Create a frame with a resource string
    JFrame frame = new JFrame(
      applet.res.getString("Number_Formatting"));
```

continues

Example 12.4 continued

```
    // Add the applet instance to the frame
    frame.getContentPane().add(applet, BorderLayout.CENTER);

    // Invoke init() and start()
    applet.init();
    applet.start();

    // Display the frame
    frame.setSize(300, 300);
    frame.setDefaultCloseOperation(JFrame.EXIT_ON_CLOSE);
    frame.setVisible(true);
  }

  // Handle locale selection
  public void itemStateChanged(ItemEvent e)
  {
    if (e.getSource() == jcboLocale)
    {
      locale = locales[jcboLocale.getSelectedIndex()];
      updateStrings();
      computeMortgage();
    }
  }

  // Handle button action
  public void actionPerformed(ActionEvent e)
  {
    if (e.getSource() == jbtCompute)
      computeMortgage();
  }

  // Compute payments and display results locale-sensitive format
  private void computeMortgage()
  {
    // Retrieve input from user
    double loan = new Double(jtfLoanAmount.getText()).doubleValue();
    double interestRate =
      new Double(jtfInterestRate.getText()).doubleValue()/1200;
    int numOfYears = new Integer(jtfNumOfYears.getText()).intValue();

    // Calculate payments
    double monthlyPayment = loan*interestRate/
      (1-(Math.pow(1/(1+interestRate),numOfYears*12)));
    double totalPayment = monthlyPayment*numOfYears*12;

    // Get formatters
    NumberFormat percentFormatter =
      NumberFormat.getPercentInstance(locale);
    NumberFormat currencyForm =
      NumberFormat.getCurrencyInstance(locale);
    NumberFormat numberForm = NumberFormat.getNumberInstance(locale);
    percentFormatter.setMinimumFractionDigits(2);

    // Display formatted input
    jtfFormattedInterestRate.setText(
      percentFormatter.format(interestRate*12));
    jtfFormattedNumOfYears.setText(numberForm.format(numOfYears));
    jtfFormattedLoanAmount.setText(currencyForm.format(loan));

    // Display results in currency format
    jtfMonthlyPayment.setText(currencyForm.format(monthlyPayment));
    jtfTotalPayment.setText(currencyForm.format(totalPayment));
  }
```

```
    // Update resource strings
    private void updateStrings()
    {
      res = ResourceBundle.getBundle("MyResource", locale);
      jlblInterestRate.setText(res.getString("Annual_Interest_Rate"));
      jlblNumOfYears.setText(res.getString("Number_Of_Years"));
      jlblLoanAmount.setText(res.getString("Loan_Amount"));
      jlblTotalPayment.setText(res.getString("Total_Payment"));
      jlblMonthlyPayment.setText(res.getString("Monthly_Payment"));
      jbtCompute.setText(res.getString("Compute"));
      comboBoxTitle.setTitle(res.getString("Choose_a_Locale"));
      inputTitle.setTitle(res.getString("Enter_Interest_Rate"));
      paymentTitle.setTitle(res.getString("Payment"));

      // Make sure the new labels are displayed
      repaint();
    }
  }
```

The resource bundle for the English language is given as follows:

```
#Thu May 06 07:48:10 EST 1999
Number_Of_Years=Years
Total_Payment=French Total\ Payment
Enter_Interest_Rate=Enter\ Interest\ Rate,\ Years,\ and\ Loan\ Amount
Payment=Payment
Compute=Compute
Annual_Interest_Rate=Interest\ Rate
Number_Formatting=Number\ Formatting\ Demo
Loan_Amount=Loan\ Amount
Choose_a_Locale=Choose\ a\ Locale
Monthly_Payment=Monthly\ Payment
=
```

The resource bundle for the Chinese language is given as follows:

```
#Res_zh.properties for Chinese language
Choose_a_Locale      = \u9078\u64c7\u570b\u5bb6
Enter_Interest_Rate =
  \u8f38\u5165\u5229\u7387,\u5e74\u9650,\u8cb8\u6b3e\u7e3d\u984d
Annual_Interest_Rate  =   \u5229\u7387
Number_Of_Years      =   \u5e74\u9650
Loan_Amount          =   \u8cb8\u6b3e\u984d\u5ea6
Payment              =   \u4ed8\u606f

Monthly_Payment      =   \u6708\u4ed8
Total_Payment        =   \u7e3d\u984d
Compute              =   \u8a08\u7b97\u8cb8\u6b3e\u5229\u606f
=
```

The resource bundle for the French language is given as follows:

```
#Res.properties for French language
#Thu May 06 07:48:10 EST 1999
Number_Of_Years=annees
Annual_Interest_Rate=le taux d'interet
Loan_Amount=Le montant du pret
Enter_Interest_Rate=inscrire le taux d'interet, les annees, et le
montant du pret
Payment=paiement
Compute=Calculer l'hypotheque
```

continues

Example 12.4 continued

```
Number_Formatting=demonstration du formatting des chiffres
Choose_a_Locale=Choisir la localite
Monthly_Payment=versement mensuel
Total_Payment=reglement total
=
```

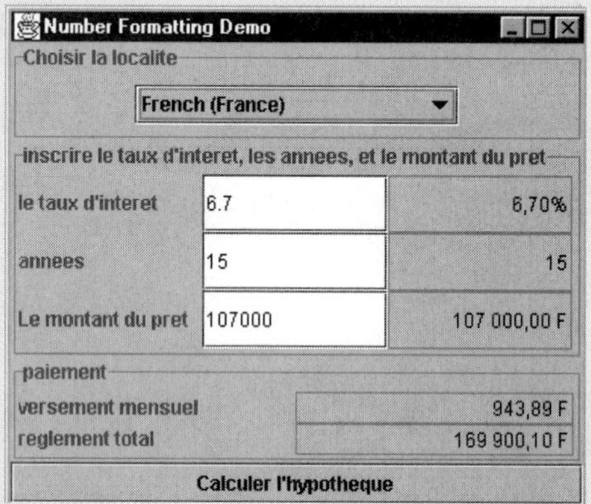

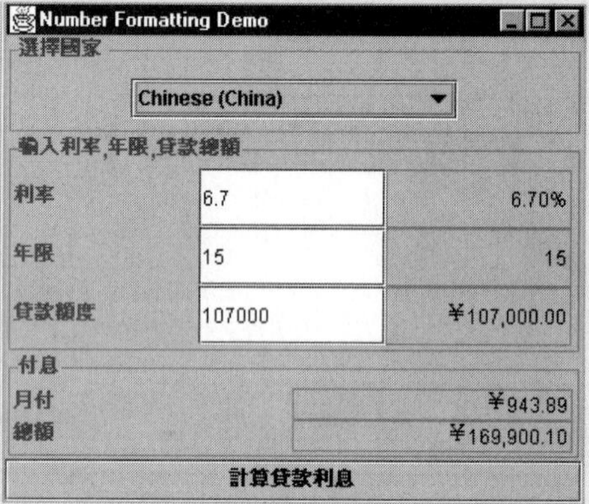

Figure 12.8 *The program displays the strings in French or in Chinese.*

Example Review

Property resource bundles are implemented as text files with a .properties extension, and are placed in the same location as the class files for the application or applet. `ListResourceBundles` are provided as Java source files. Because they are implemented as Java source code, new and modified `ListResourceBundles` need to be recompiled for deployment. With `PropertyResourceBundles`, there is no need for recompilation when translations are modified or added to the application. Nevertheless, `ListResourceBundles` provide considerably better performance than `PropertyResourceBundles`.

If the resource bundle is not found or a resource object is not found in the resource bundle, a `MissingResourceException` is raised. Since `MissingResourceException` is a subclass of `RuntimeException`, you do not need to catch the exception explicitly in the code.

This example is the same as Example 12.3 except that the program contains the code for handling resource strings. The `updateString` method is responsible for displaying the locale-sensitive strings. This method is invoked when a new locale is selected in the combo box. Since the variable `res` of the `ResourceBundle` class is an instance variable in `ResourceBundleDemo`, it cannot be directly used in the `main` method, because the `main` method is static. To fix the problem, create `applet` as an instance of `ResourceBundleDemo` and you will then be able to reference `res` using `applet.res`.

Chapter Summary

This chapter introduced the subject of building Java programs that operate efficiently for an international audience. You learned how to use the `Locale` object to represent a particular locale, how to localize date and time, and how to display numbers in normal format, currency format, and percentage format. You also learned how to create resource bundles and move the locale-specific strings, titles, and labels to them.

Review Questions

12.1 How does Java support international characters in languages like Chinese and Arabic?

12.2 How do you construct a `Locale` object? How do you get all the available locales from a `Calendar` object?

12.3 How do you display current date and time in German?

12.4 How do you format and display numbers and percentages in Chinese?

12.5 How do you limit the number of decimal digits in a fraction number?

12.6 How does the `getBundle` method locate a resource bundle?

12.7 How does the `getObject` method locate a resource?

Programming Exercises

12.1 Develop an applet that displays Unicode characters, as shown in Figure 12.9. The user specifies a Unicode in the text field and presses the Enter key to display a sequence of Unicode characters starting with the specified Unicode. The Unicode characters are displayed in a scrollable text area of 20 lines. Each line contains 16 characters preceded by a Unicode, which is the code for the first character on the line.

Figure 12.9 *The applet displays the Unicode characters.*

12.2 Write a program that displays a calendar for a specified month, using the `Date`, `Calendar`, and `GregorianCalendar` classes. Your program receives the month and year from the command line. For example:

```
java DisplayCalendar 5 1999
```

This displays the calendar shown in Figure 12.10.

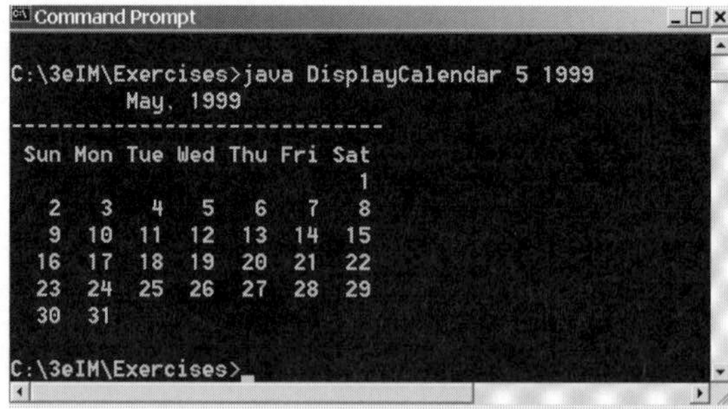

Figure 12.10 *The program displays a calendar for May 1999.*

You also can run the program without the year. In this case, the year is the current year. If you run the program without specifying a month and a year, the month is the current month.

12.3 Modify Example 12.2, "Displaying a Calendar," to localize the labels "Choose a locale" and "Calendar Demo" in French, German, Chinese, or a language of your choice.

12.4 Write a program that converts U.S. dollars to Canadian dollars, German marks, and British pounds, as shown in Figure 12.11. The user enters the U.S. dollar amount and the conversion rate, and clicks the Convert button to display the converted amount.

Exercise 12.4: Exchange Currencies

Enter Dollar Amount

US Dollars 2000 Convert

Display Exchange

	Exchange Rate	Converted Amount
Canadian Dollars	1.5	$3,000.00
German Marks	1.4	¤ 2.800,00
British Pounds	0.5	£1,000.00

Figure 12.11 *The program converts U.S. dollars to Canadian dollars, German marks, and British pounds.*

12.5 Use a tabbed pane to write a program with two tabs. One, labeled Calendar, displays the calendar, and the other, labeled Clock, displays the current time on a clock (see Figure 12.12).

Calendar and Clock

Calendar | Clock

September 1999

Sunday	Monday	Tuesday	Wednesday	Thursday	Friday	Saturday
29	30	31	1	2	3	4
5	6	7	8	9	10	11
12	13	14	15	16	17	18
19	20	21	22	23	24	25
26	27	28	29	30	1	2
3	4	5	6	7	8	9

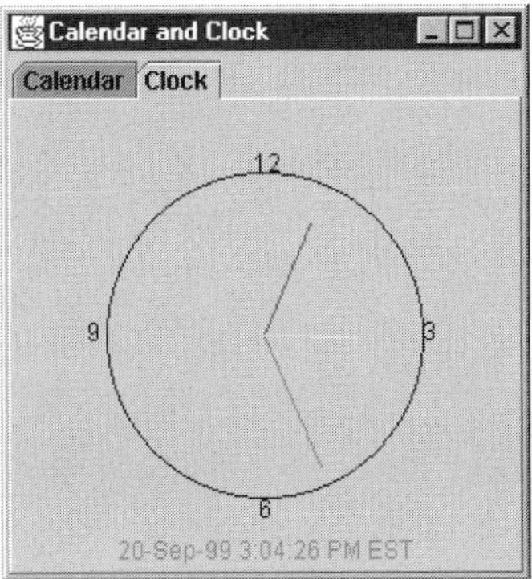

Figure 12.12 *The Calendar tab displays a calendar, and the Clock tab displays a clock.*

12.6 Write a program to display the available locales and time zone ID, as shown in Figure 12.13.

Figure 12.13 *The program displays available locales and time zones.*

12.7 Rewrite Example 2.2 to display the monthly payment and total payment in currency.

12.8 Rewrite Exercise 4.4 to display at most two digits after the decimal point for the temperature.

CHAPTER 13

MULTITHREADING

Objectives

- Understand the concept of multithreading and apply it to develop animation.
- Write threads by extending the `Thread` class.
- Write threads by implementing the `Runnable` interface in cases of multiple inheritance.
- Understand the life-cycle of thread states and set thread priorities.
- Controlling threads.
- Use thread synchronization to avoid resource conflicts.
- Use the `Timer` class to simplify the control of Java animations.

Introduction

A *thread* is a flow of execution, with a beginning and an end, of a task in a program. The programs you have seen so far all run in a single thread; that is, at any given time, a single statement is being executed. With Java, you can launch multiple threads from a program concurrently. These threads can be executed simultaneously in multiprocessor systems, as shown in Figure 13.1.

Figure 13.1 *Here, multiple threads are running on multiple CPUs.*

In single-processor systems, as shown in Figure 13.2, the multiple threads share CPU time, and the operating system is responsible for scheduling and allocating resources to them. This arrangement is practical because most of the time the CPU is idle. For example, it does nothing while waiting for the user to enter data.

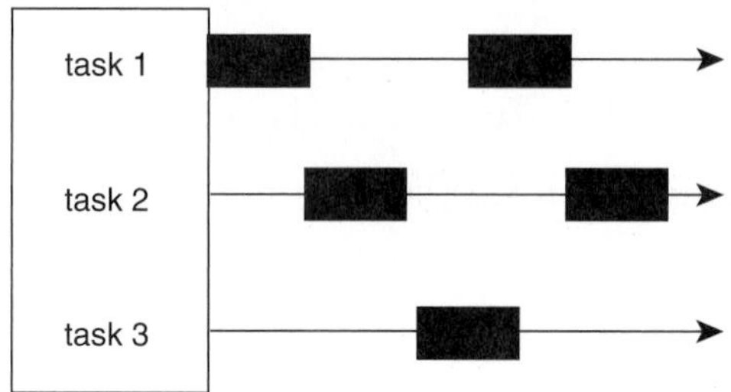

Figure 13.2 *Here, multiple threads share a single CPU.*

Multithreading can make your program more responsive and interactive, as well as enhance performance. For example, a good word processor lets you print or save the file while you are typing. In some cases, multithreaded programs run faster than single-threaded programs even on single-processor systems. Java provides exceptionally good support for programming with multiple threads of execution, including built-in support for creating threads and for locking resources to prevent conflicts.

When your program executes as an application, the Java interpreter starts a thread for the `main` method. When your program executes as an applet, the Web browser starts a thread to run the applet. You can create additional threads to run concurrent tasks in the program. Each new thread is an object of the class that implements the `Runnable` interface or extends a class that implements the `Runnable` interface. This new object is referred to as a *runnable object*.

You can create threads by extending the `Thread` class or implementing the `Runnable` interface. Both `Thread` and `Runnable` are defined in the `java.lang` package. `Thread` actually implements `Runnable`. In this chapter, you will learn how to use the `Thread` class and the `Runnable` interface to write multithreaded programs.

Creating Threads by Extending the *Thread* Class

The `Thread` class contains the constructors for creating threads, as well as many useful methods for controlling threads. To create and run a thread, first define a class that extends the `Thread` class. Your thread class must override the `run()` method, which tells the system how the thread will be executed when it runs. You can then create an object running on the thread.

Figure 13.3 illustrates the key elements of a thread class that extends the `Thread` class, and how to use it to create a thread in a class. The `thread` is a runnable object created from the `CustomThread` class. The `start` method tells the system that the thread is ready to run.

```
// Custom thread class
public class CustomThread extends Thread
{
  ...
  public CustomThread(...)
  {
    ...
  }

  // Override the run method in Thread
  public void run()
  {
    // Tell system how to run custom thread
    ...
  }
  ...
}
```

```
// Client class
public class Client
{
  ...
  public someMethod()
  {
    ...
    // Create a thread
    CustomThread thread = new CustomThread(...);

    // Start a thread
    thread.start();
    ...
  }

  ...
}
```

Figure 13.3 *A thread is defined as a subclass of the* `Thread` *class.*

Example 13.1 Using the `Thread` Class to Create and Launch Threads

This program creates and runs three threads:

- The first thread prints the letter *a* 100 times.
- The second thread prints the letter *b* 100 times.
- The third thread prints the integers 1 through 100.

The program has three independent tasks. To run them concurrently, it needs to create a runnable object for each task. Because the first two threads have similar functionality, they can be defined in one thread class.

continues

Example 13.1 continued

The program is given here, and its output is shown in Figure 13.4.

```
// TestThread.java: Define threads using the Thread class
public class TestThread
{
  // Main method
  public static void main(String[] args)
  {
    // Create threads
    PrintChar printA = new PrintChar('a', 100);
    PrintChar printB = new PrintChar('b', 100);
    PrintNum  print100 = new PrintNum(100);

    // Start threads
    print100.start();
    printA.start();
    printB.start();
  }
}

// The thread class for printing a specified character
// in specified times
class PrintChar extends Thread
{
  private char charToPrint;  // The character to print
  private int times;  // The times to repeat

  // Construct a thread with specified character and number of
  // times to print the character
  public PrintChar(char c, int t)
  {
    charToPrint = c;
    times = t;
  }

  // Override the run() method to tell the system
  // what the thread will do
  public void run()
  {
    for (int i=0; i < times; i++)
      System.out.print(charToPrint);
  }
}

// The thread class for printing number from 1 to n for a given n
class PrintNum extends Thread
{
  private int lastNum;

  // Construct a thread for print 1, 2, ... i
  public PrintNum(int n)
  {
    lastNum = n;
  }

  public void run()
  {
    for (int i=1; i <= lastNum; i++)
      System.out.print(" " + i);
  }
}
```

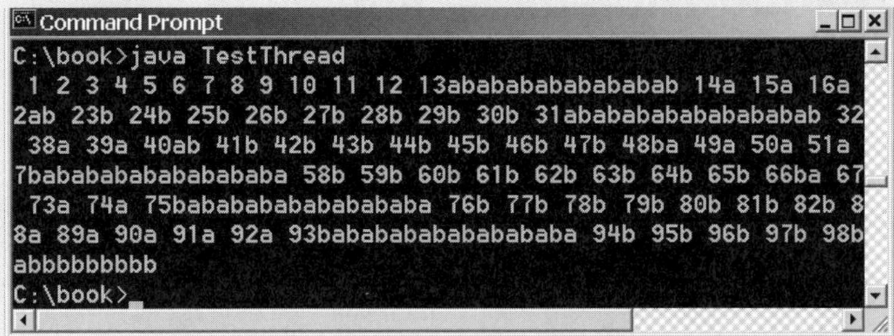

Figure 13.4 *Threads* `printA`, `printB`, *and* `print100` *are executed simultaneously to display the letter a 100 times, the letter b 100 times, and the numbers from 1 to 100.*

Example Review

If you run this program on a multiple-CPU system, all three threads will execute simultaneously. If you run the program on a single-CPU system, the three threads will share the CPU and take turns printing letters and numbers on the console.

The program creates thread classes by extending the `Thread` class. The `PrintChar` class, derived from the `Thread` class, overrides the `run()` method with the print-character action. This class provides a framework for printing any single character a given number of times. The runnable objects `printA` and `printB` are instances of the user-defined thread class `PrintChar`.

The `PrintNum` class overrides the `run()` method with the print-number action. This class provides a framework for printing numbers from *1* to *n*, for any integer *n*. The runnable object `print100` is an instance of the user-defined thread class `printNum`.

In the client program, the program creates a thread, `printA`, for printing the letter *a*, and a thread, `printB`, for printing the letter *b*. Both are objects of the `PrintChar` class. The `print100` thread object is created from the `PrintNum` class.

The `start()` method is invoked to start a thread, which causes the `run()` method to execute. When the `run()` method completes, the threads terminate.

NOTE

On some systems, the program may not terminate or print out all the characters and numbers. The problem has nothing to do with your program. It may be an OS problem or a Java Virtual Machine implementation problem. If the program does not seem to terminate, press Ctrl+C to stop it.

Creating Threads by Implementing the *Runnable* Interface

In the preceding section, you created and ran a thread by declaring a user thread class that extends the `Thread` class. This approach works well if the user thread class inherits only from the `Thread` class, but not if it inherits multiple classes, as in the case of an applet. To inherit multiple classes, you have to implement interfaces. Java provides the `Runnable` interface as an alternative to the `Thread` class.

The `Runnable` interface is rather simple. It contains just the `run` method. You need to implement this method to tell the system how your thread is going to run. Figure 13.5 illustrates the key elements of a thread class that implements the `Runnable` interface, and how to use it to create a thread in a class.

```
// Custom thread class
public class CustomThread
  implements Runnable
{
  ...
  public CustomThread(...)
  {
    ...
  }

  // Implement the run method in Runnable
  public void run()
  {
    // Tell system how to run custom thread
    ...
  }

  ...
}
```

```
// Client class
public class Client
{
  ...
  public someMethod()
  {
    ...
    // Create an instance of CustomThread
    CustomThread customThread
      = new CustomThread(...);

    // Create a thread
    Thread thread = new Thread(customThread);

    // Start a thread
    thread.start();
    ...
  }

  ...
}
```

Figure 13.5 *A thread is defined by implementing the Runnable interface.*

To start a new thread with the `Runnable` interface, you must first create an instance of the class that implements the `Runnable` interface, then use the `Thread` class constructor to construct a thread.

The following example demonstrates how to create threads using the `Runnable` interface.

Example 13.2 Using the `Runnable` Interface to Create and Launch Threads

This program modifies Example 13.1 to create and run the same threads using the `Runnable` interface.

```
// TestRunnable.java: Define threads using the Runnable interface
public class TestRunnable
{
  // Main method
  public static void main(String[] args)
  {
```

```
    // Create threads
    Thread printA = new Thread(new PrintChar('a', 100));
    Thread printB = new Thread(new PrintChar('b', 100));
    Thread print100 = new Thread(new PrintNum(100));

    // Start threads
    print100.start();
    printA.start();
    printB.start();
  }
}

// The thread class for printing a specified character
// in specified times
class PrintChar implements Runnable
{
  private char charToPrint;  // The character to print
  private int times;  // The times to repeat

  // Construct a thread with specified character and number of
  // times to print the character
  public PrintChar(char c, int t)
  {
    charToPrint = c;
    times = t;
  }

  // Override the run() method to tell the system
  // what the thread will do
  public void run()
  {
    for (int i=0; i < times; i++)
      System.out.print(charToPrint);
  }
}

// The thread class for printing number from 1 to n for a given n
class PrintNum implements Runnable
{
  private int lastNum;

  // Construct a thread for print 1, 2, ... i
  public PrintNum(int n)
  {
    lastNum = n;
  }

  public void run()
  {
    for (int i=1; i <= lastNum; i++)
      System.out.print(" " + i);
  }
}
```

Example Review

The program creates thread classes by implementing the `Runnable` interface.

continues

Example 13.2 continued

This example performs the same task as in Example 13.1. The classes `PrintChar` and `PrintNum` are the same as in Example 13.1 except that they implement the `Runnable` interface, instead of extending the `Thread` class.

An instance of the class that extends the `Thread` class is a thread, which can be started using the `start()` method in the `Thread` class. But an instance of the class that implements the `Runnable` interface is not a thread yet. You have to wrap it using the `Thread` class to construct a thread for the instance.

Controlling Threads and Thread States

The `Thread` class contains the following methods for controlling threads:

- `public void run()`

  This method is invoked by the Java runtime system to execute the thread. You must override this method and provide the code you want your thread to execute in your thread class. This method is never directly invoked by the runnable object in the program, although it is an instance method of a runnable object.

- `public void start()`

  This method starts the thread, which causes the `run()` method to be invoked. This method is called by the runnable object in the client class.

- `public void stop()`

  This method stops the thread. As of Java 2, this method is deprecated, because it is known to be inherently unsafe. You should assign `null` to a `Thread` variable to indicate that it is stopped rather than use the `stop()` method.

- `public void suspend()`

  This method suspends the thread. As of Java 2, this method is deprecated, because it is known to be deadlock-prone. You should use the `wait()` method along with a `boolean` variable to indicate whether a thread is suspended rather than use the `suspend()` method. An example of implementing the `suspend()` method is introduced in the next section, "Creating Threads for Applets."

- `public void resume()`

  This method resumes the thread. As of Java 2, this method, along with the `suspend()` method, is deprecated because it is deadlock-prone. You should use the `notify()` method along with a `boolean` variable to indicate whether a thread is resumed rather than use the `resume()` method. An example of implementing the `resume()` method will be introduced in the next section, "The `Runnable` Interface."

- `public static void sleep(long millis) throws InterruptedException`

  This method puts the runnable object to sleep for a specified time in milliseconds. Note that the `sleep` method is a static method.

- `public void interrupt()`

  This method interrupts a running thread.

- `public static boolean isInterrupted()`

  This method tests to see whether the current thread has been interrupted.

- `public boolean isAlive()`

  This method tests to see whether the thread is currently running.

- `public void setPriority(int p)`

  This method sets priority `p` (ranging from `1` to `10`) for this thread.

The `wait()` and `notify()` methods in the `Object` class are often used with threads.

- `public final void wait() throws InterruptedException`

  This method puts the thread to wait for notification by another thread of a change in the object.

- `public final void notify()`

  This method awakens a single thread that is waiting on this object.

Threads can be in one of five states: new, ready, running, blocked, or finished (see Figure 13.6) .

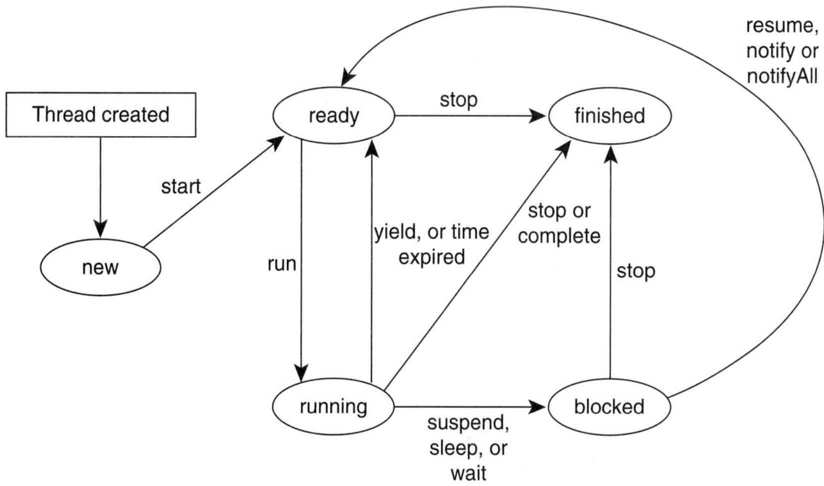

Figure 13.6 *A thread can be in one of five states: new, ready, running, blocked, or finished.*

When a thread is newly created, it enters the *new state*. After a thread is started by calling its `start()` method, it enters the *ready state*. A ready thread is runnable but may not be running yet. The operating system has to allocate CPU time to it.

When a ready thread begins executing, it enters the *running state.* A running thread may enter the ready state if its given CPU time expires or its `yield()` method is called.

A thread may enter the *blocked state* (i.e., inactive) for several reasons. It may have invoked the `sleep()`, `wait()`, or `suspend()` method, or some other thread may have invoked its `sleep()` or `suspend()` method. It may be waiting for an I/O operation to finish. A blocked thread may be reactivated when the action inactivating it is reversed. For example, if a thread has been put to sleep and the sleep time has expired, the thread is reactivated and enters the ready state.

Finally, a thread is *finished* if it completes the execution of its `run()` method or if its `stop()` method is invoked.

The `isAlive()` method is used to find out the state of a thread. It returns `true` if a thread is in the ready, inactive, or running state; it returns `false` if a thread is new and has not started or if it is finished.

Java assigns every thread a priority. By default, a thread inherits the priority of the thread that spawned it. You can increase or decrease the priority of any thread by using the `setPriority` method, and you can get the thread's priority by using the `getPriority` method. Priorities are numbers ranging from 1 to 10. The `Thread` class has `int` constants `MIN_PRIORITY`, `NORM_PRIORITY`, and `MAX_PRIORITY`, representing 1, 5, and 10, respectively. The priority of the main thread is `Thread.NORM_PRIORITY`.

TIP

The priority numbers may be changed in a future version of Java. To minimize the impact of any changes, use the constants in the `Thread` class to specify the thread priorities.

The Java runtime system always picks the currently runnable thread with the highest priority. If several runnable threads have equally high priorities, the CPU is allocated to all of them in a round-robin fashion. A lower-priority thread can run only when no higher-priority threads are running.

Thread Groups

A *thread group* is a set of threads. Some programs contain quite a few threads with similar functionality. For convenience, you can group them together and perform operations on the entire group. For example, you can suspend or resume all of the threads in a group at the same time.

Listed below are the guidelines for using thread groups:

1. Use the `ThreadGroup` constructor to construct a thread group:

   ```
   ThreadGroup g = new ThreadGroup("thread group");
   ```

   This creates a thread group `g` named `"thread group"`. The name is a string and must be unique.

2. Use the `Thread` constructor, place a thread in a thread group:

   ```
   Thread t = new Thread(g, new ThreadClass(), "This thread");
   ```

   The statement `new ThreadClass()` creates a runnable instance for the `ThreadClass`. You can add a thread group under another thread group to form a tree in which every thread group except the initial one has a parent.

3. To find out how many threads in a group are currently running, use the `activeCount()` method. The following statement displays the active number of threads in group `g`.

   ```
   System.out.println("The number of runnable threads in the group "
     + g.activeCount());
   ```

4. Each thread belongs to a thread group. By default, a newly created thread becomes a member of the current thread group that spawned it. To find which group a thread belongs to, use the `getThreadGroup()` method.

NOTE

You have to start each thread individually. There is no `start()` method in `ThreadGroup`. As of Java 2, the `stop()`, `suspend()`, and `resume()` methods are deprecated. You manually implemented the `stop()`, `suspend()`, and `resume()` methods in the `ThreadGroup` class.

In the next section, you will see an example that uses the `ThreadGroup` class.

Synchronization

A shared resource may be corrupted if it is accessed simultaneously by multiple threads. The following example demonstrates the problem.

Example 13.3 Showing Resource Conflict

This program demonstrates the problem of resource conflict. Suppose that you create and launch 100 threads, each of which adds a penny to a piggy bank. Assume that the piggy bank is initially empty. You create a class named `PiggyBank` to model the piggy bank, a class named `AddAPennyThread` to add a penny to the piggy bank, and a main class that creates and launch threads. The relationships of these classes are shown in Figure 13.7.

The program is given as follows. The output of the program is shown in Figure 13.8.

continues

Example 13.3 continued

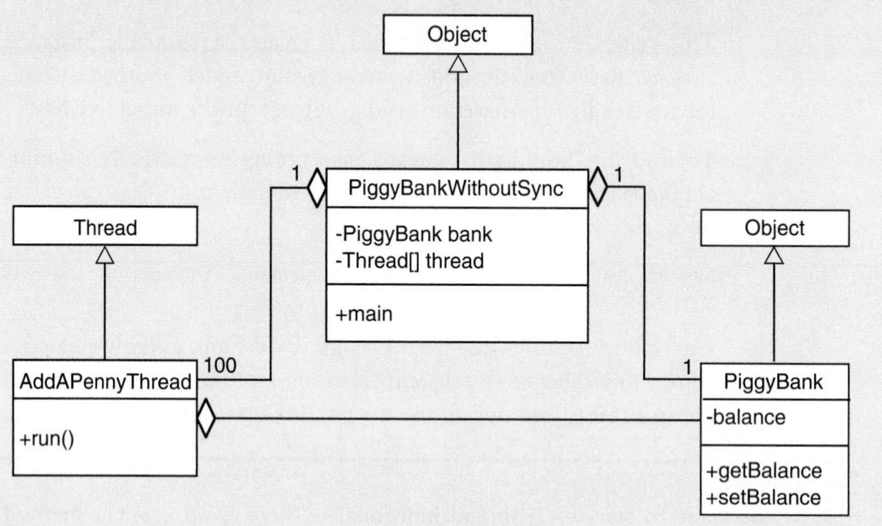

Figure 13.7 *`PiggyBankWithoutSync` contains an instance of `PiggyBank`, and 100 threads of `AddAPennyThread`.*

```
// PiggyBankWithoutSync.java: Demonstrate resource conflict
public class PiggyBankWithoutSync
{
  private PiggyBank bank = new PiggyBank();
  private Thread[] thread = new Thread[100];

  public static void main(String[] args)
  {
    PiggyBankWithoutSync test = new PiggyBankWithoutSync();
    System.out.println("What is balance ? " +
      test.bank.getBalance());
  }

  public PiggyBankWithoutSync()
  {
    ThreadGroup g = new ThreadGroup("group");
    boolean done = false;

    // Create and launch 100 threads
    for (int i=0; i<100; i++)
    {
      thread[i] = new Thread(g, new AddAPennyThread(), "t");
      thread[i].start();
    }

    // Check if all the threads are finished
    while(!done)
      if (g.activeCount() == 0)
        done = true;
  }


  // A thread for adding a penny to the piggy bank
```

```
  class AddAPennyThread extends Thread
  {
    public void run()
    {
      int newBalance = bank.getBalance() + 1;

      try
      {
        Thread.sleep(5);
      }
      catch (InterruptedException ex)
      {
        System.out.println(ex);
      }

      bank.setBalance(newBalance);
    }
  }
}

// A class for piggy bank
class PiggyBank
{
  private int balance = 0;

  public int getBalance()
  {
    return balance;
  }

  public void setBalance(int balance)
  {
    this.balance = balance;
  }
}
```

```
C:\book>java PiggyBankWithoutSync
What is balance ? 7

C:\book>java PiggyBankWithoutSync
What is balance ? 6

C:\book>
```

Figure 13.8 *The `PiggyBankWithoutSync` program causes data inconsistency.*

Example Review

The program creates 100 threads in the array `thread`, and groups all the threads into a thread group `g`. The `activeCount()` method is used to count the active threads. When all the threads are finished, it returns 0.

continues

Example 13.3 continued

The balance of the piggy bank is initially 0. When all the threads are finished, the balance should be 100, but the output is unpredictable. As can be seen in Figure 13.8, the answers are wrong in the sample run. This demonstrates the data-corruption problem that occurs when all the threads have access to the same data source simultaneously.

Interestingly, it is not easy to replicate the problem. The `sleep` method is deliberately added to magnify the data-corruption problem and make it easy to see. If you run the program several times but still do not see the problem, increase the sleep time. This will dramatically increase the chances for resource contention.

So what caused the error in Example 13.3? Here is a possible scenario, as shown in Figure 13.9.

Step	balance	thread[i]	thread[j]
1	0	newBalance = bank.getBalance() + 1;	
2	0		newBalance = bank.getBalance() + 1;
3	1	bank.setBalance(newBalance);	
4	1		bank.setBalance(newBalance);

Figure 13.9 *`Thread[i]` and `thread[j]` both add 1 to the same balance.*

In Step 1, `thread[i]`, for some `i`, gets the balances from the bank. In Step 2, `thread[j]`, for some `j`, gets the same balances from the bank. In Step 3, `thread[i]` writes a new balance to the bank. In Step 4, `thread[j]` writes a new balance to the bank.

The effect of this scenario is that thread `thread[i]` did nothing, because in Step 4 thread `thread[j]` overrides `thread[i]`'s result. Obviously, the problem is that `thread[i]` and `thread[j]` are accessing a common resource in a way that causes conflict.

To avoid resource conflicts, Java uses the keyword `synchronized` to synchronize method invocation so that only one thread can be in a method at a time. To correct the data-corruption problem in Example 13.3, rewrite the program as follows:

```
// PiggyBankWithSync.java: Demonstrate avoiding resource conflict
public class PiggyBankWithSync
{
  private PiggyBank bank = new PiggyBank();
  private Thread[] thread = new Thread[100];

  public static void main(String[] args)
  {
    PiggyBankWithSync test = new PiggyBankWithSync();
    System.out.println("What is balance ? " +
```

```
      test.bank.getBalance());
  }

  public PiggyBankWithSync()
  {
    ThreadGroup g1 = new ThreadGroup("group");
    boolean done = false;

    for (int i=0; i<100; i++)
    {
      thread[i] = new Thread(g1, new AddAPennyThread(), "t");
      thread[i].start();
    }

    while(!done)
      if (g1.activeCount() == 0)
        done = true;
  }

  // Synchronize: add a penny one at a time
  private static synchronized void addAPenny(PiggyBank bank)
  {
    int newBalance = bank.getBalance() + 1;

    try
    {
      Thread.sleep(5);
    }
    catch (InterruptedException ex)
    {
      System.out.println(ex);
    }

    bank.setBalance(newBalance);
  }

  // A thread for adding a penny to the piggy bank
  class AddAPennyThread extends Thread
  {
    public void run()
    {
      addAPenny(bank);
    }
  }
}
```

With the keywords `static synchronized` for the method `addAPenny`, the preceding scenario cannot happen. If thread `thread[j]` starts to enter the method, and thread `thread[i]` is already in the method, thread `thread[j]` is blocked until thread `thread[i]` finishes the method.

A synchronized method acquires a lock before it executes. In the case of an instance method, the lock is on the object for which the method was invoked. In the case of a class (static) method, the lock is on all the objects of the same class.

Creating Threads for Applets

In Example 12.1, "Displaying a Clock," you drew a clock to show the current time in an applet. The clock does not tick after it is displayed. What can you do to let the clock display a new current time every second? The key to making the clock tick is to repaint it every second with a new current time. You can use the code given below to override the `start()` method in `CurrentTimeApplet`:

```
public void start()
{
  while (true)
  {
    stillClock.repaint();
    try
    {
      Thread.sleep(1000);
    }
    catch(InterruptedException ex)
    {
    }
  }
}
```

The `start()` method is called when the applet begins. The infinite loop repaints the clock every 1,000 milliseconds (in other words, at 1-second intervals). This appears to refresh the clock every second, but if you run the program, the browser hangs up. The problem is that as long as the `while` loop is running, the browser cannot serve any other event that might occur. Therefore, the `paintComponent` method is not called. The solution is to move the `while` loop to another thread that can be executed in parallel with the `paintComponent` method.

To create a new thread for the applet, you need to implement the `Runnable` interface in the applet. Here are the implementation guidelines:

1. Add `implements Runnable` in the applet class declaration:

   ```
   public class MyApplet extends JApplet implements Runnable
   ```

2. Declare a thread in `MyApplet`. For example, the following statement declares a thread instance, `thread`, with the initial value `null`:

   ```
   private Thread thread = null;
   ```

   By default, the initial value is `null`, so assigning `null` in this statement is not necessary.

3. Create a new thread in the applet's `init()` method and start it right away in `MyApplet`:

   ```
   public void init()
   {
     thread = new Thread(this);  // Create a thread
     thread.start();  // Start the thread
   }
   ```

   The `this` argument in the `Thread` constructor is required; it specifies that the run function of `MyApplet` should be called when the thread executes an instance of `MyApplet`.

4. Override the `Applet`'s `start()` method in `MyApplet` as follows to resume the thread:

   ```
   public void start()
   ```

```
{
  resume();
}
```

5. Create resume() and suspend() methods as follows:

```
public synchronized void resume()
{
  if (suspended)
  {
    suspended = false;
    notify();
  }
}

public synchronized void suspend()
{
  suspended = true;
}
```

Since the resume() and suspend() methods in the Thread class have been deprecated, you must create new methods for resuming and suspending threads.

The variable suspended should be declared as a data member of the class, which indicates the state of the thread. The synchronized keyword ensures that the resume() and suspend() methods are serialized to avoid race conditions that could result in an inconsistent value for the variable suspended.

6. Write the code you want the thread to execute in the run() method:

```
public void run()
{
  while (true)
  {
    // Repaint the clock to display current time
    stillClock.repaint();

    try
    {
      thread.sleep(1000);
      waitForNotificationToResume();
    }
    catch (InterruptedException ex)
    {
    }
  }
}
```

The run() method is invoked by the Java runtime system when the thread starts. The while loop repeatedly invokes the stillClock.repaint() method every second if the thread is not suspended. If suspended is true, the waitForNotificationToResume() method causes the thread to suspend and wait for notification by the notify() method invoked from the resume() method. The repaint() method runs on the system default thread, which is separate from the thread on which the while loop is running.

7. The waitForNotificationToResume method is implemented as follows:

```
private synchronized void waitForNotificationToResume()
  throws InterruptedException
```

```
{
  while (suspended)
    wait();
}
```

The `synchronized` keyword eliminates potential conflicts that could cause the suspended thread to miss a notification and remain suspended.

8. Override the `stop()` method in the `Applet` class to suspend the running thread:

```
public void stop()
{
  suspend();
}
```

This code suspends the thread so that it does not consume CPU time when the Web page containing this applet becomes inactive.

9. Override the `destroy()` method in the `Applet` class to kill the thread:

```
public void destroy()
{
  thread = null;
}
```

This code releases all the resources associated with the thread when the Web browser exits.

Example 13.4 Displaying a Running Clock in an Applet

The applet presented here displays a clock. To simulate the clock running, a separate thread is used to repaint the clock. The output of the program is shown in Figure 13.10.

```
// ClockApplet.java: Display a running clock on the applet
import java.applet.*;
import java.awt.*;
import java.util.*;

public class ClockApplet extends CurrentTimeApplet
  implements Runnable
{
  // Declare a thread for running the clock
  private Thread thread = null;

  // Determine if the thread is suspended
  private boolean suspended = false;

  // Initialize applet
  public void init()
  {
    super.init();

    // Create the thread
    thread = new Thread(this);

    // Start the thread
    thread.start();
```

```
  }

  // Implement the start() method to resume the thread
  public void start()
  {
    resume();
  }

  // Implement the run() method to dictate what the thread will do
  public void run()
  {
    while (true)
    {
      // Repaint the clock to display current time
      stillClock.repaint();

      try
      {
        thread.sleep(1000);
        waitForNotificationToResume();
      }
      catch (InterruptedException ex)
      {
      }
    }
  }

  private synchronized void waitForNotificationToResume()
    throws InterruptedException
  {
    while (suspended)
      wait();
  }

  // Implement the stop method to suspend the thread
  public void stop()
  {
    suspend();
  }

  // Destroy the thread
  public void destroy()
  {
    thread = null;
  }

  // Resume the suspended thread
  public synchronized void resume()
  {
    if (suspended)
    {
      suspended = false;
      notify(); // Notify the waiting object
    }
  }

  // Suspend the thread
  public synchronized void suspend()
  {
    suspended = true;
  }
}
```

continues

Example 13.4 continued

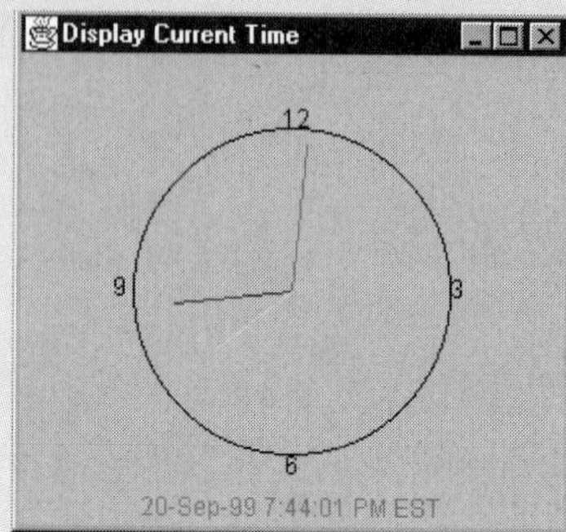

Figure 13.10 *The control of the clock drawing runs a thread separately from the* `paintComponent` *method that draws the clock.*

Example Review

The `CurrentTimeApplet` class is presented in Example 12.1, "Displaying a Clock," to display the current time. The `ClockApplet` class extends `CurrentTimeApplet` with a control loop running on a separate thread to make the clock tick.

The `run` method comes from the `Runnable` interface and is modified to specify what the separate thread will do. The `paintComponent` method is called every second by the `repaint` method to display the current time.

The `init`, `start`, `stop`, and `destroy` methods in the `Applet` class are modified for this program to work with the Web browser. The `init` method is invoked to start the thread when the Web page is loaded. The `stop` method is invoked to suspend the thread when the Web page containing the applet becomes inactive. The `start` method is invoked to resume the thread when the Web page containing the applet becomes active. The `destroy` method is invoked to terminate the thread when the Web browser exits.

The separate thread named `thread` is created and started in the applet's `init` method:

```
thread = new Thread(this);
thread.start();
```

The `ClockApplet`'s `init()` method calls `super.init()` defined in the `CurrentTimeApplet` class, which gets parameters for country, language, and time zone from HTML. Therefore, the `ClockApplet` class can get these parameters from HTML.

The `resume()` method sets the variable `suspended` to `false` and awakens the thread that is waiting on the notification by invoking the `notify()` method. The `suspend()` method sets the variable `suspended` to `true`, which causes the thread to suspend and wait for notification to resume.

NOTE

The `start()` method in `thread.start()` is different from the `start()` method in the applet. The former starts the thread and causes the `run()` method to execute, whereas the latter is executed by the Web browser when the applet starts for the first time or is reactivated.

TIP

I recommend that you suspend the threads in the Applet's `stop` method so that the applet does not consume CPU time when the Web page is inactive.

NOTE

The `ClockApplet` class does not define the main method. But its subclass `CurrentTimeApplet` has a main method. Therefore, you can run `ClockApplet` as an application. But you would not see the clock running, because the main method is for running the `CurrentTimeApplet` class.

Using the *Timer* Class to Control Animation

The previous example creates a thread to run a `while` loop that repaints the clock in a panel every 1,000 milliseconds. Repainting the panel at a predefined rate is frequently used in Java animations. For this reason, Java provides the `javax.swing.Timer` class that can be used to control repainting the panel at a predefined rate. Using the `Timer` class can dramatically simplify the program. A `Timer` object serves as the source of an `ActionEvent`. It fires an `ActionEvent` at a fixed rate. The listeners for the event are registered with the `Timer` object. When you create a `Timer` object, you have to specify the delay and a listener using the following constructor:

```
public Timer(int delay, ActionListener listener)
```

where `delay` specifies the number of milliseconds between two action events. You can add additional listeners using the `addActionListener` method, and adjust the `delay` using the `setDelay` method. To start the timer, use the `start` method. To stop the timer, use the `stop` method. In the action listener class, you can implement the `actionPerformed` handler by invoking the repaint method to repaint the panel. This `actionPerformed` method is invoked at a rate determined by the delay.

Using the `Timer` class, the previous program can be modified as follows:

```
// NewClockApplet.java: Display a running clock on the applet
import java.awt.event.*;
import javax.swing.Timer;

public class NewClockApplet extends CurrentTimeApplet
  implements ActionListener
{
  protected Timer timer;
```

```
    // Initialize applet
    public void init()
    {
      super.init();

      // Create a timer with delay 1000 ms and listener NewClockApplet
      timer = new Timer(1000, this);
    }

    // Override the start method in the Applet class
    public void start()
    {
      timer.start();
    }

    // Override the stop method in the Applet class
    public void stop()
    {
      timer.stop();
    }

    // Handle the action event
    public void actionPerformed(ActionEvent e)
    {
      repaint();
    }
  }
```

NOTE

Using a thread to control animations and using a timer to control animations are two entirely different approaches. The thread approach places the animation control on a separate thread so that it does not interfere with the drawings. The timer approach uses the action event to control the drawing. If your drawings are painted at a fixed rate, use the timer approach, which can greatly simplify programming.

Case Studies

The preceding examples show how to override the `init`, `start`, and `stop` in the `Applet` class to enable threads to work correctly with Java applets using the thread approach and using the timer approach. The `ClockApplet` class and `NewClockApplet` class work correctly to display a running clock. However, reusing these classes is difficult because they are subclasses of `JApplet`, which is a heavyweight component. A heavyweight component is not suitable for placement inside a lightweight container such as `JPanel`. To make reusing it easier, you can create a `Clock` component to be a subclass of `JPanel`. Since the `StillClock` class is a subclass of `JPanel`, you can create `Clock` by extending the `StillClock` class, as follows:

```
// Clock.java: Show a running clock on the panel
import java.util.*;
import java.awt.event.*;
import javax.swing.Timer;
```

```
public class Clock extends StillClock implements ActionListener
{
  protected Timer timer;

  // Default constructor
  public Clock()
  {
    this(Locale.getDefault(), TimeZone.getDefault());
  }

  // Construct a clock with specified locale and time zone
  public Clock(Locale locale, TimeZone timeZone)
  {
    super(locale, timeZone);

    // Create a timer with delay 1000 ms and listener Clock
    timer = new Timer(1000, this);

    // Start the timer
    timer.start();
  }

  // Resume the clock
  public void resume()
  {
    timer.start();
  }

  // Suspend the clock
  public void suspend()
  {
    timer.stop();
  }

  // Handle the action event
  public void actionPerformed(ActionEvent e)
  {
    repaint();
  }
}
```

The `Clock` class extends `StillClock` and implements `ActionListener`. The `Clock` class is the listener for `timer`, which fires an action event every second. When an action event occurs, the `actionPerformed` method is invoked, which invokes the `repaint` method. The `repaint` method causes the `paintComponent` method to be called to redraw the clock with the new current time. The `paintComponent` method is defined in `StillClock`.

The following example uses the `Clock` class to create a group of clocks.

Example 13.5 Controlling a Group of Clocks

This program displays three clocks in a group. Each clock has individual Resume and Suspend control buttons. You can also resume or suspend all the clocks by using the group-control Resume All and Suspend All buttons. Figure 13.11 contains the output of a sample run of the program.

continues

Example 13.5 continued

```
// ClockGroup.java: Display a group of international clocks
import java.awt.*;
import java.awt.event.*;
import java.util.*;
import javax.swing.*;

public class ClockGroup extends JApplet implements ActionListener
{
  // Declare three clock panels
  private ClockPanel clockPanel1, clockPanel2, clockPanel3;

  // Declare group control buttons
  private JButton jbtResumeAll, jbtSuspendAll;

  // This main method enables the applet to run as an application
  public static void main(String[] args)
  {
    // Create a frame
    JFrame frame = new JFrame("Clock Group Demo");

    // Create an instance of the applet
    ClockGroup applet = new ClockGroup();

    // Add the applet instance to the frame
    frame.getContentPane().add(applet, BorderLayout.CENTER);

    // Invoke init() and start()
    applet.init();
    applet.start();

    // Display the frame
    frame.setSize(600, 300);
    frame.setVisible(true);
  }

  // Initialize the applet
  public void init()
  {
    // Panel p1 for holding three clocks
    JPanel p1 = new JPanel();
    p1.setLayout(new GridLayout(1, 3));

    // Create a clock for Berlin
    p1.add(clockPanel1 = new ClockPanel());
    clockPanel1.setTitle("Berlin");
    clockPanel1.clock.setTimeZoneID("ECT");
    clockPanel1.clock.setLocale(Locale.GERMAN);

    // Create a clock for San Francisco
    p1.add(clockPanel2 = new ClockPanel());
    clockPanel2.clock.setLocale(Locale.US);
    clockPanel2.clock.setTimeZoneID("PST");
    clockPanel2.setTitle("San Francisco");

    // Create a clock for Taipei
    p1.add(clockPanel3 = new ClockPanel());
    clockPanel3.setTitle("\u6077\u6079");
    clockPanel3.clock.setLocale(Locale.CHINESE);
    clockPanel3.clock.setTimeZoneID("CTT");
```

```
    // Panel p2 for holding two group control buttons
    JPanel p2 = new JPanel();
    p2.setLayout(new FlowLayout());
    p2.add(jbtResumeAll = new JButton("Resume All"));
    p2.add(jbtSuspendAll = new JButton("Suspend All"));

    // Add panel p1 and p2 into the applet
    getContentPane().setLayout(new BorderLayout());
    getContentPane().add(p1, BorderLayout.CENTER);
    getContentPane().add(p2, BorderLayout.SOUTH);

    // Register listeners
    jbtResumeAll.addActionListener(this);
    jbtSuspendAll.addActionListener(this);
  }

  // Handle group control buttons
  public void actionPerformed(ActionEvent e)
  {
    if (e.getSource() == jbtResumeAll)
    {
      // Start all clocks
      clockPanel1.resume();
      clockPanel2.resume();
      clockPanel3.resume();
    }
    else if (e.getSource() == jbtSuspendAll)
    {
      // Stop all clocks
      clockPanel1.suspend();
      clockPanel2.suspend();
      clockPanel3.suspend();
    }
  }
}

// ClockPanel for holding a header, a clock, and control buttons
class ClockPanel extends JPanel implements ActionListener
{
  // Header title of the clock panel
  private JLabel jlblTitle;

  protected Clock clock  = null;

  // Individual clock Resume and Suspend control buttons
  private JButton jbtResume, jbtSuspend;

  // Constructor
  public ClockPanel()
  {
    // Panel jpButtons for grouping buttons
    JPanel jpButtons = new JPanel();
    jpButtons.add(jbtResume = new JButton("Resume"));
    jpButtons.add(jbtSuspend = new JButton("Suspend"));

    // Set BorderLayout for the ClockPanel
    setLayout(new BorderLayout());

    // Add title label to the north of the panel
    add(jlblTitle = new JLabel(), BorderLayout.NORTH);
    jlblTitle.setHorizontalAlignment(JLabel.CENTER);
```

continues

Example 13.5 continued

```
      // Add the clock to the center of the panel
      add(clock = new Clock(), BorderLayout.CENTER);

      // Add jpButtons to the south of the panel
      add(jpButtons, BorderLayout.SOUTH);

      // Register ClockPanel as a listener to the buttons
      jbtResume.addActionListener(this);
      jbtSuspend.addActionListener(this);
    }

    // Set label on the title
    public void setTitle(String title)
    {
      jlblTitle.setText(title);
    }

    // Handle buttons "Resume" and "Suspend"
    public void actionPerformed(ActionEvent e)
    {
      if (e.getSource() == jbtResume)
      {
        clock.resume();
      }
      else if (e.getSource() == jbtSuspend)
      {
        clock.suspend();
      }
    }

    // Resume the clock
    public void resume()
    {
      if (clock != null) clock.resume();
    }

    // Resume the clock
    public void suspend()
    {
      if (clock != null) clock.suspend();
    }
  }
```

Example Review

The example consists of two new classes: `ClockGroup` and `ClockPanel`.

The `ClockPanel` contains a title, a clock, and its control buttons, Resume and Suspend. You can use these two buttons to resume or suspend an individual clock. The relationship of these classes is shown in Figure 13.12.

The `ClockGroup` class creates and places three clock panels above two group-control buttons, Resume All and Suspend All, in the applet. You can use these two buttons to resume or suspend all the clocks. The three clocks are for Berlin, San Francisco, and Taipei. The titles and times displayed in the panel are locale-sensitive. The Unicode `"\u6077\u6079"` consists of the Chinese characters for

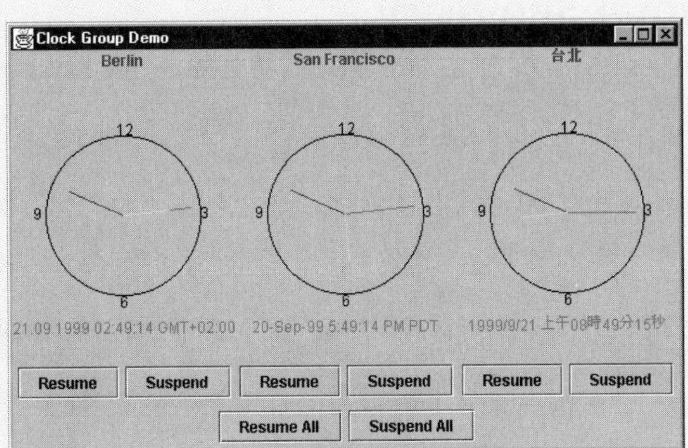

Figure 13.11 *Three clocks run independently with individual control and group control.*

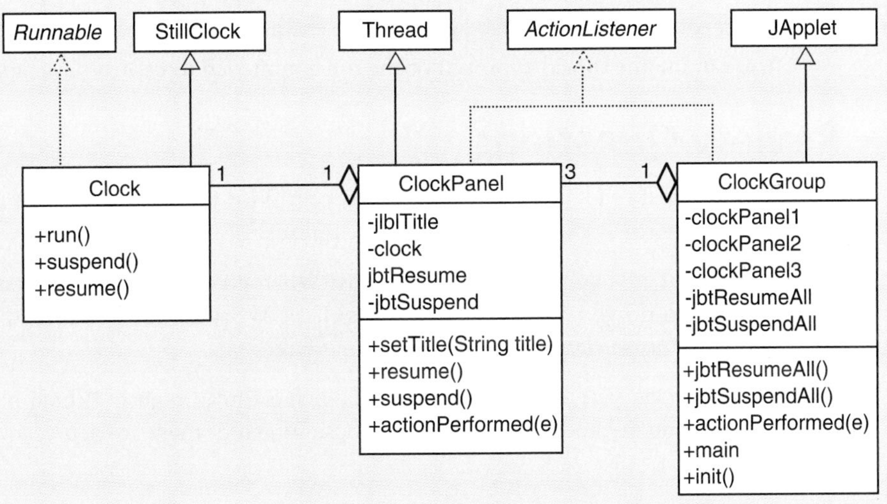

Figure 13.12 `ClockGroup` *contains three instances of* `ClockPanel` *for international clocks with control buttons and titles.*

Taipei, and time is automatically displayed in Chinese because you have set the locale for the clock to `Locale.CHINESE`. If your machine does not support Chinese fonts, you cannot see the Chinese characters.

Chapter Summary

In this chapter, you learned how to develop multithreaded programs, using the `Thread` class and the `Runnable` interface. You can derive your thread class from the `Thread` class and create a thread instance to run a task on a separate thread. If your class needs to inherit multiple classes, you can implement the `Runnable` interface to run multiple tasks in the program simultaneously.

After a thread object is created, you can use the `start method` to start a thread, and the `sleep method` to put a thread to sleep so that other threads get a chance to run. Since the `stop`, `suspend`, and `resume` methods are deprecated in Java 2, you need to implement these methods to stop, suspend, and resume a thread.

A thread object never directly invokes the `run` method. The Java runtime system invokes the `run` method when it is time to execute the thread. Your class must override the `run` method to tell the system what the thread will do when it runs.

Threads can be assigned priorities. The Java runtime system always executes the ready thread with the highest priority. You can use a thread group to put relevant threads together for group control. To prevent threads from corrupting a shared resource, put the `synchronized` keyword into the method that may cause corruption.

You can use the thread approach or the timer approach to control Java animations.

Review Questions

13.1 Why do you need multithreading capability in applications? In a single-processor system, how can multiple threads run simultaneously?

13.2 What are two ways to create threads? When do you use the `Thread` class, and when do you use the `Runnable` interface? What are the differences between the `Thread` class and the `Runnable` interface?

13.3 How do you create a thread and launch a thread object? Which of the following methods are instance methods? Which of them are deprecated in Java 2?

```
run, start, stop, suspend, resume, sleep, isInterrupted
```

13.4 Will the program behave differently if `Thread.sleep(1000)` is replaced by `thread.sleep(1000)` in Example 13.4?

13.5 Explain the life-cycle of a thread object.

13.6 How do you set a priority for a thread? What is the default priority?

13.7 Describe a thread group. How do you create a thread group? Can you control an individual thread in a thread group (suspend, resume, stop, and so on)?

13.8 Give some examples of possible resource corruption when running multiple threads. How do you synchronize conflict threads?

13.9 Why does the following class have a runtime error?

```
class Test extends Thread
{
  public static void main(String[] args)
  {
    Test t = new Test();
    t.start();
    t.start();
  }

  public void run()
  {
    System.out.println("test");
  }
}
```

13.10 Why does the following class have a syntax error?

```
import javax.swing.*;

class Test extends JApplet implements Runnable
{
   public void init() throws InterruptedException
   {
     Thread thread = new Thread(this);
     thread.sleep(1000);
   }

   public synchronized void run()
   {
   }
}
```

13.11 How do you override the methods `init`, `start`, `stop`, and `destroy` in the `Applet` class to work well with the threads in the applets?

13.12 How do you use the `Timer` class to control Java animations?

Programming Exercises

13.1 Write an applet that displays a flashing label. Enable it to run as an application.

Hint: To make the label flash, you need to repaint the window alternately with the label and without the label (blank screen). Use a `boolean` variable to control the alternation.

13.2 Write an applet to display a moving label. The label continuously moves from right to left in the applet's viewing area. Whenever the label disappears from the viewing area, it starts moving again on the right-hand side. The label freezes when the mouse is clicked on it, and moves again when the button is released. Enable it to run as an application.

Hint: Repaint the window with a new x coordinate.

13.3 Rewrite Example 13.1, "Using the `Thread` Class to Create and Launch Threads," to display the output in a text area, as shown in Figure 13.13.

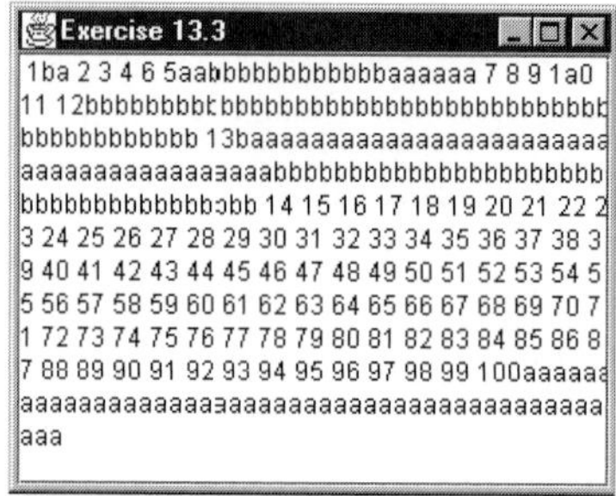

Figure 13.13 *The output from three threads is displayed in a text area.*

13.4 Write a program that launches 100 threads. Each thread adds 1 to a variable `sum` that initially is zero. You need to pass `sum` by reference to each thread. In order to pass it by reference, define an `Integer` wrapper object to hold `sum`. Run the program with and without synchronization to see its effect.

13.5 Modify Example 13.3, "Showing Resource Conflict," as follows:

- Create two panels with the titles "Synchronized Threads" and "Unsynchronized Threads," as shown in Figure 13.14. The Synchronized Threads panel displays a piggy bank balance after a penny has been added 100 times using synchronized threads. The Unsynchronized Thread panel displays a piggy bank balance after a penny has been added 100 times using unsynchronized threads.

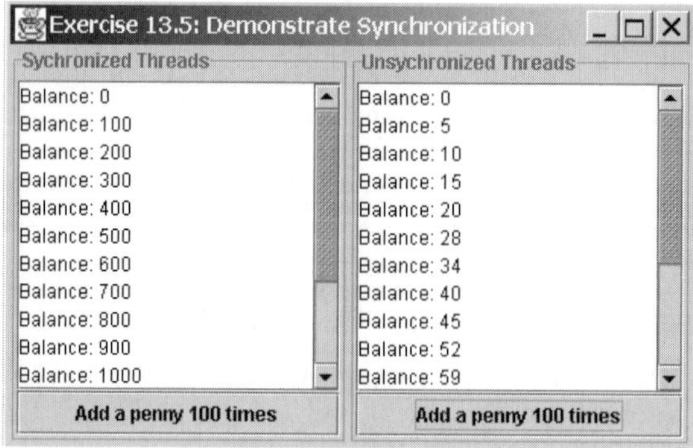

Figure 13.14 *The program shows the effect of executing the threads with synchronization and without synchronization.*

- Since the two panels are very similar, you can create a class to model them uniformly, as shown in Figure 13.15. Use a variable named `mode` to indicate whether synchronized threads or unsynchronized threads are used in the panel. Invoke the method `addAPennyWithSync` or `addAPennyWithoutSync`, depending on the `mode`.

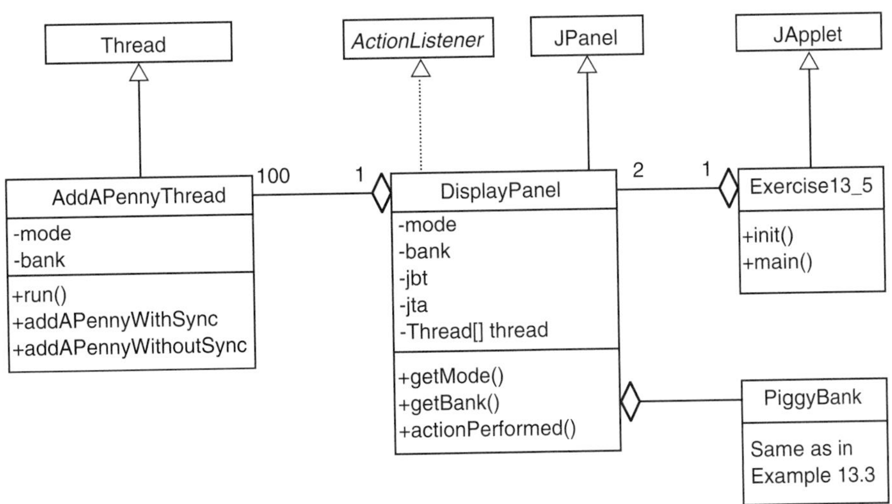

Figure 13.15 `DisplayPanel` *displays the balance in the text area after a penny is added to the balance 100 times.*

13.6 Write a Java applet that displays a stock index ticker (see Figure 13.16). The stock index information is passed from the `<param>` tag in the HTML file. Each index has four parameters: Index Name (for example, S&P 500), Current Time (for example, 15:54), the index from the previous day (for example, 919.01), and Change (for example, 4.54). Enable the applet to run standalone.

Use at least five indexes, such as Dow Jones, S&P 500, NASDAQ, NIKKEI, and Gold & Silver Index. Display positive changes in green, and negative changes in red. The indexes move from right to left in the applet's viewing area. The applet freezes the ticker when the mouse button is pressed; it moves again when the mouse button is released.

Figure 13.16 *The program displays a stock index ticker.*

13.7 Write a Java applet that simulates a running fan, as shown in Figure 13.17. The buttons Start, Stop, and Reverse control the fan. The scrollbar controls the fan's speed. Create a class named `Fan`, a subclass of `JPanel`, to display the

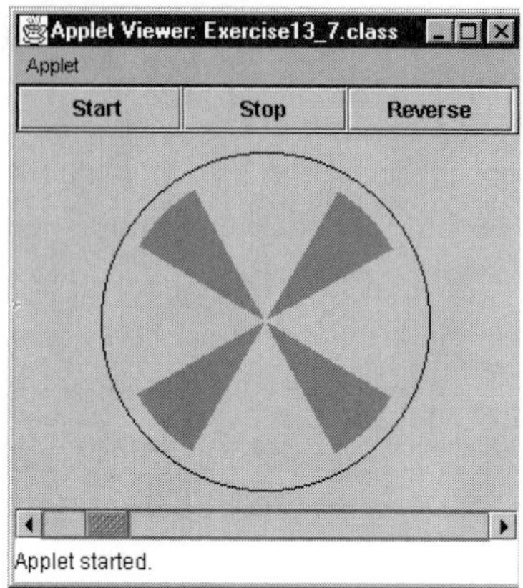

Figure 13.17 *The program simulates a running fan.*

fan. This class also contains the methods to suspend and resume the fan, set its speed, and reverse its direction. Create a class named `FanControlPanel` that contains a fan, and three buttons and a scroll bar to control the fan. Create a Java applet that contains an instance of `FanControlPanel`. Enable the applet to run standalone. The relationships of these classes are shown in Figure 13.18.

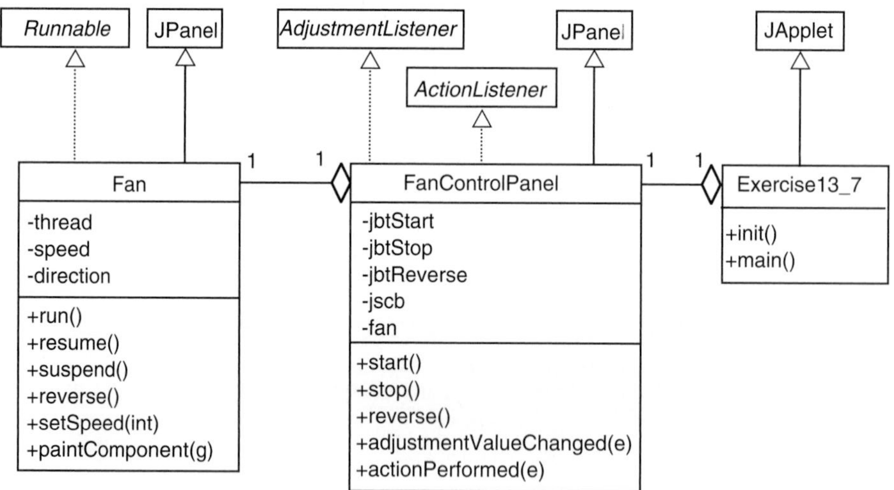

Figure 13.18 *The* `FanControlPanel` *class contains a fan, three buttons, and a scroll bar to control the fan; and the* `Fan` *class displays a running fan.*

13.8 Write a Java applet to display three fans in a group with control buttons to start and stop all of them, as shown in Figure 13.19. Use the `FanControlPanel` to control and display a single fan. Enable the applet to run standalone.

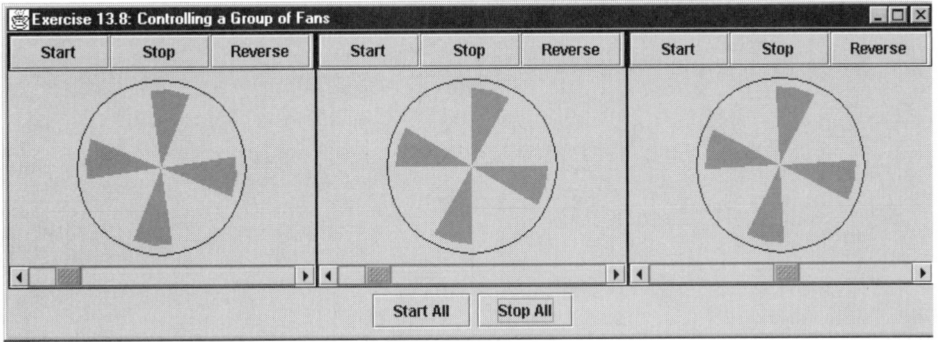

Figure 13.19 *The program runs and controls a group of fans.*

13.9 Write an applet that simulates an elevator going up and down (see Figure 13.20). The buttons on the left indicate the floor where the passenger is now located. The passenger must click a button on the left to request that the elevator move to his or her floor. On entering the elevator, the passenger clicks a button on the right to request that it go to the specified floor. Enable the applet to run standalone.

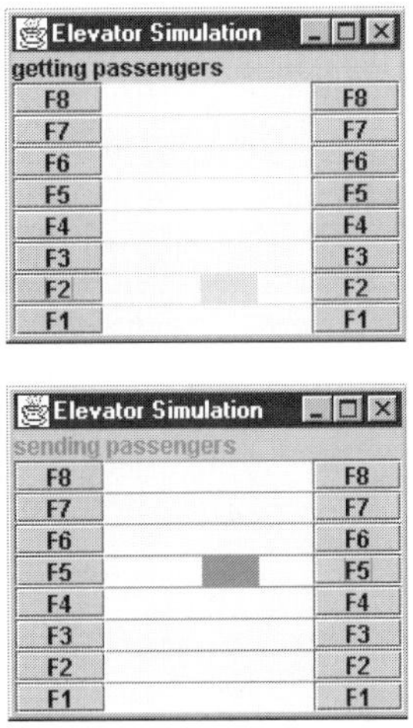

Figure 13.20 *The program simulates elevator operations.*

13.10 The `Clock` class in Case Studies uses the timer approach to redraw the clock. Use the thread approach to rewrite the `Clock` class.

CHAPTER 14

MULTIMEDIA

Objectives

- Develop multimedia applications with audio and images.
- Get audio files and play sound in Java applets.
- Get image files and display graphics in Java applets.
- Display images and play audio in Java applications.
- Use `MediaTracker` to ensure that images are completely loaded before they are displayed.

Introduction

Welcome to the fascinating world of *multimedia*. You have seen computer animation used every day in TV and movies. When surfing the Web, you have seen sites with texts, images, sounds, animation, and movie clips. These are examples of multimedia at work.

Multimedia is a broad term that encompasses making, storing, retrieving, transferring, and presenting various types of information, such as text, graphics, pictures, videos, and sound. Multimedia involves a complex weave of communications, electronics, and computer technologies. It is beyond the scope of this book to cover multimedia in great detail. This chapter concentrates on the presentation of multimedia in Java.

Whereas most programming languages have no built-in multimedia capabilities, Java was designed with multimedia in mind. It provides extensive built-in support that makes it easy to develop powerful multimedia applications. Java's multimedia capabilities include animation that uses drawings, audio, and images.

You have already used animation with drawings in the examples that simulated a clock, and you used the image icons in the Swing components. In this chapter, you will learn how to develop Java programs with audio and images.

Playing Audio

Audio is stored in files. There are several formats of audio files. Prior to Java 2, sound files in the AU format used on the UNIX operating system were the only ones Java was able to play. With Java 2, you can also play sound files in the WAV, AIFF, MIDI, AU, or RMF format with better sound quality.

To play an audio file in an applet, you use the following `play` method in the `Applet` class:

```
public void play(URL url, String filename);
```

This method downloads the audio file from the `url` and plays the audio in the file. Nothing happens if the audio file cannot be found.

The URL (Universal Resource Locator) describes the location of a resource on the Internet. Java provides a class that is used to manipulate URLs: `java.net.URL`. Java's security mechanism restricts all files read via a browser to the directory where the HTML file is stored or to the subdirectory of that location. You can use `getCodeBase()` to get the URL of the applet, or `getDocumentBase()` to get the HTML file that contains the applet. These two methods, `getCodeBase()` and `getDocumentBase()`, are defined in the `Applet` class:

```
play(getCodeBase(), "soundfile.au");

play(getDocumentBase(), "soundfile.au");
```

The former method plays the sound file soundfile.au, which is located in the applet's directory. The latter method plays the sound file soundfile.au, which is located in the HTML file's directory.

The `play(url, filename)` statement downloads the audio file every time you play the audio. If you want to play the audio many times, you can create an *audio clip object* for the file. The audio clip is created once and can be played repeatedly without reloading the file. To create an audio clip, use either of the following methods:

```
public AudioClip getAudioClip(URL url);

public AudioClip getAudioClip(URL url, String name);
```

The former requires an absolute URL address for it to specify a sound file; the latter lets you use a relative URL with the filename. Using the absolute URL address will be introduced in Chapter 16, "Networking." The relative URL is obtained by using `getCodeBase()` or `getDocumentBase()`. For example, the following statement creates an audio clip for the file soundfile.au that is stored in the same directory as the applet that contains the statement.

```
AudioClip ac = getAudioClip(getCodeBase(), "soundfile.au");
```

To manipulate a sound for an audio clip, use the following instance methods of `java.applet.AudioClip`.

- `public void play()`

  Play the clip once. Each time this method is called, the clip is restarted from the beginning.

- `public void loop()`

  Play the clip repeatedly.

- `public void stop()`

  Stop playing the clip.

Example 14.1 Incorporating Sound in Applets

This program displays a running clock, as shown in Example 12.1. In addition, the program plays sound files that announce the time at one-minute intervals. For example, if the current time is 6:30:00, the applet announces, "The time is six-thirty A.M." If the current time is 20:20:00, the applet announces, "The time is eight-twenty P.M." The three audio clips are played in sequence in order to announce a time.

```
// ClockAppletWithAudio.java: Display a running clock on the applet
// with audio
import java.applet.*;
```

continues

Example 14.1 continued

```
public class ClockAppletWithAudio extends CurrentTimeApplet
{
  // Declare audio files
  protected AudioClip[] hourAudio = new AudioClip[12];
  protected AudioClip minuteAudio;
  protected AudioClip amAudio;
  protected AudioClip pmAudio;

  // Declare a clock
  ClockWithAudio clock;

  // Initialize the applet
  public void init()
  {
    super.init();

    // Create audio clips for pronouncing hours
    for (int i=0; i<12; i++)
      hourAudio[i] = getAudioClip(getCodeBase(),
        "timeaudio/hour"+i+".au");

    // Create audio clips for pronouncing am and pm
    amAudio = getAudioClip(getCodeBase(), "timeaudio/am.au");
    pmAudio = getAudioClip(getCodeBase(), "timeaudio/pm.au");
  }

  // Override the createClock method defined in CurrentTimeApplet
  public void createClock()
  {
    getContentPane().add(clock =
      new ClockWithAudio(locale, timeZone, this));
  }

  // Announce the current time at every minute
  public void announceTime(int s, int m, int h)
  {
    if (s == 0)
    {
      // Announce hour
      hourAudio[h%12].play();

      // Load the minute file
      minuteAudio = getAudioClip(getCodeBase(),
        "timeaudio/minute"+m+".au");

      // Time delay to allow hourAudio play to finish
      try
      {
        Thread.sleep(1500);
      }
      catch(InterruptedException ex)
      {
      }

      // Announce minute
      minuteAudio.play();

      // Time delay to allow minuteAudio play to finish
      try
      {
        Thread.sleep(1500);
```

```
        }
        catch(InterruptedException ex)
        {
        }

        // Announce am or pm
        if (h < 12)
          amAudio.play();
        else
          pmAudio.play();
      }
    }

    // Implement Applet's start method to resume the thread
    public void start()
    {
      clock.resume();
    }

    // Implement Applet's stop method to suspend the thread
    public void stop()
    {
      clock.suspend();
    }
  }

  // ClockWithAudio.java: Display a clock and announce time
  import java.awt.*;
  import java.util.*;

  public class ClockWithAudio extends Clock
  {
    protected ClockAppletWithAudio applet;

    // Construct a clock with specified locale, timezone, and applet
    public ClockWithAudio(Locale locale, TimeZone timeZone,
      ClockAppletWithAudio applet)
    {
      // Invoke the Clock class's constructor
      super(locale, timeZone);

      this.applet = applet;
    }

    // Modify the paintComponent() method to play sound
    public void paintComponent(Graphics g)
    {
      // Invoke the paintComponent method in the Clock class
      super.paintComponent(g);

      // Get current time using GregorianCalendar
      GregorianCalendar calendar = new GregorianCalendar(timeZone);

      // Get second, minute and hour
      int s = (int)calendar.get(GregorianCalendar.SECOND);
      int m = (int)calendar.get(GregorianCalendar.MINUTE);
      int h = (int)calendar.get(GregorianCalendar.HOUR_OF_DAY);

      // Announce current time
      applet.announceTime(s, m, h);
    }
  }
```

continues

Example 14.1 continued

Example Review

This example contains two classes named `ClockAppletWithAudio` and `ClockWithAudio`. The `ClockAppletWithAudio` class extends the `CurrentTimeApplet` class with the capability to announce time. `CurrentTimeApplet` was given in Example 12.1, "Displaying a Clock." The `ClockWithAudio` class extends the `Clock` class and invokes the `announceTime` method whenever it repaints the clock. The `Clock` class was given in Example 13.5, "Controlling a Group of Clocks." The relationships of these classes are shown in Figure 14.1.

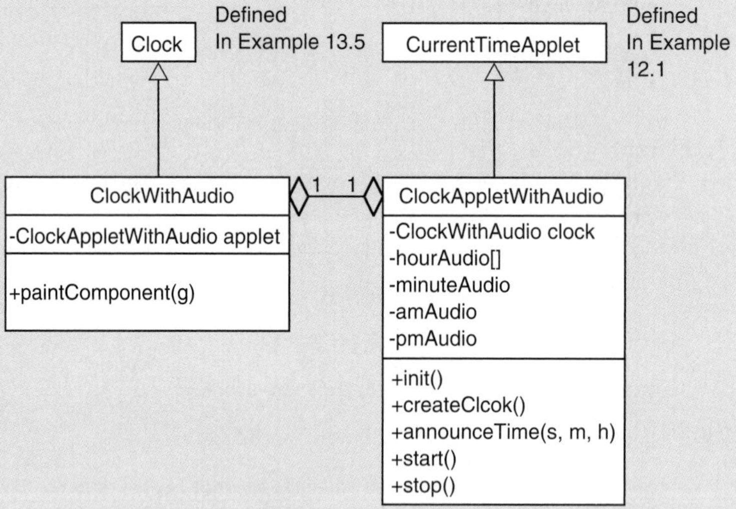

Figure 14.1 *`ClockWithAudio` extends the Clock class with audio, and `ClockAppletWithAudio` is an applet that contains an instance of `ClockWithAudio`.*

The `hourAudio` is an array of 12 audio clips that are used to announce the 12 hours of the day; the `minuteAudio` is an audio clip that is used to announce the minute in an hour. The `amAudio` announces A.M.; the `pmAudio` announces P.M.

The `init()` method invokes `super.init()` defined in the `CurrentTimeApplet` class, and creates audio clips for announcing time. `super.init()` gets country, language, and time zone parameters from HTML, creates a clock, and places it in the applet.

All of the audio files are stored in the directory `timeaudio`, a subdirectory of the applet's directory. The 12 audio clips that are used to announce the hours are stored in the files **hour0.au**, **hour1.au**, and so on, to **hour11.au**. They are loaded using the following loop:

```
for (int i=0; i<12; i++)
  hourAudio[i] = getAudioClip(getCodeBase(),
    "timeaudio/hour" + i + ".au");
```

Similarly, the amAudio clip is stored in the file **am.au**, and the pmAudio clip is stored in the file **pm.au**; they are loaded along with the hour clips in the init() method.

The program created an array of 12 audio clips to announce each of the 12 hours, but did not create 60 audio clips to announce each of the minutes. Instead, the program created and loaded the minute audio clip when needed in the announceTime method. The audio files are very large. Loading all 60 audio clips at once may cause OutOfMemoryError exception.

In the announceTime method, the sleep() method is purposely invoked to ensure that one clip finishes before the next clip starts, so that the clips do not interfere with each other.

The constructor of ClockWithAudio contains an argument that points to ClockAppletWithAudio, which enables the paintComponent method in ClockWithAudio to invoke announceTime defined in ClockAppletWithAudio. This is a common programming technique for an object to reference methods and data from another class. You might declare ClockWithAudio as an inner class inside ClockAppletWithAudio to avoid passing ClockAppletWithAudio as a parameter. This is fine if ClockWithAudio is not reused elsewhere.

The paintComponent method invokes super.paintComponent(g) and announceTime(h, m, s). super.paintComponent(g) defined in Clock draws a clock for the current time. announceTime(h, m, s) announces the current hour, minute, and A.M. or P.M. if the second s is 0.

Running Audio on a Separate Thread

If you ran the preceding program, you noticed that the second hand did not display at the first, second, and third seconds of the minute. This is because sleep(1500) was invoked twice in the announceTime() method, which takes three seconds to announce the time at the beginning of each minute.

As a result of this delay, the paintComponent method does not have time to draw the clock during the first three seconds of each minute. Clearly, the announceTime method for playing audio interferes with repainting the clock. To avoid the conflict, you should announce the time on a separate thread. This problem is fixed in the following program.

Example 14.2 Announcing the Time on a Separate Thread

To avoid the conflict between painting the clock and announcing the time, the program in this example runs these tasks on separate threads.

continues

Example 14.2 continued

```
// ClockAppletWithAudioOnSeparateThread.java: Display a
//  running clock on the applet with audio on a separate thread
import java.applet.*;

public class ClockAppletWithAudioOnSeparateThread
  extends ClockAppletWithAudio
{
  // Declare a thread for announcing time
  AnnounceTime announceTime;

  // Initialize the applet
  public void init()
  {
    super.init();
  }

  // Override this method defined in ClockAppletWithAudio
  // to announce the current time at every minute
  public void announceTime(int s, int m, int h)
  {
    // Load the minute file
    minuteAudio = getAudioClip(getCodeBase(),
      "timeaudio/minute" + m + ".au");

    // Announce current time
    if (s == 0)
    {
      if (h < 12)
        announceTime = new AnnounceTime(hourAudio[h%12],
          minuteAudio, amAudio);
      else
        announceTime = new AnnounceTime(hourAudio[h%12],
          minuteAudio, pmAudio);
      announceTime.start();
    }
  }
}

// Define a thread class for announcing time
class AnnounceTime extends Thread
{
  private AudioClip hourAudio, minuteAudio, amPM;

  // Get Audio clips
  public AnnounceTime(AudioClip hourAudio,
                      AudioClip minuteAudio,
                      AudioClip amPM)
  {
    this.hourAudio = hourAudio;
    this.minuteAudio = minuteAudio;
    this.amPM = amPM;
  }

  public void run()
  {
    // Announce hour
    hourAudio.play();

    // Time delay to allow hourAudio play to finish
    // before playing the clip
```

```
        try
        {
          Thread.sleep(1500);
        }
        catch(InterruptedException ex)
        {
        }

        // Announce minute
        minuteAudio.play();

        // Time delay to allow minuteAudio play to finish
        try
        {
          Thread.sleep(1500);
        }
        catch(InterruptedException ex)
        {
        }

        // Announce am or pm
        amPM.play();
      }
    }
```

Example Review

The program extends `ClockAppletWithAudio` with the capability to announce time without interfering with the `paintComponent` method. The program defines a new thread class, `AnnounceTime`, which is derived from the `Thread` class. This new class plays audio.

To create an instance of the `AnnounceTime` class, you need to pass the three audio clips used to announce the hour, the minute, and A.M. or P.M. This instance is created only when `s` equals 0 at the beginning of each minute.

When running this program, you discover that the audio does not interfere with the clock animation because an instance of `AnnounceTime` starts on a separate thread to announce the current time. This thread is independent of the thread on which the `paintComponent` method runs.

Displaying Images

In Example 9.2, "Using Labels," and Example 9.14, "Using a Scroll Pane," you used the `ImageIcon` class to create an icon from an image file and the `setIcon` method to place the image in a UI component, such as a label. These examples are only applicable to Java applications and are not suitable for Java applets, because the image files are directly accessed from the local file system.

To display an image in Java applets, you need to load an image from an Internet source, using the `getImage` method in the `Applet` class. This method returns a `java.awt.Image` object. Two versions of the `getImage` method are shown below:

- `public Image getImage(URL url)`

  Load the image from the specified URL.

- `public Image getImage(URL url, String filename)`

  Load the image file from the specified file at the given URL.

NOTE
When the *getImage* method is invoked, it launches a separate thread to load the image, which enables the program to continue while the image is being retrieved.

Once you have an `Image` instance for the image file, you can create an `ImageIcon` using the following method:

```
ImageIcon imageIcon = new ImageIcon(image);
```

You can now convert Examples 9.2 and 9.14 to Java applets and use the `getImage` method to load the image files.

Using a label as an area for displaying images is simple and convenient, but you don't have much control over how the image is displayed. A more flexible way to display images is to use the `drawImage` method of the `Graphics` class on a panel.

Here are four versions of the `drawImage` method:

- `drawImage(Image img, int x, int y, Color bgcolor, ImageObserver observer)`

  Draw the image in the specified location. The image's top-left corner is at `(x, y)` in the graphics context's coordinate space. Transparent pixels in the image are drawn in the specified color `bgcolor`. The `observer` is the object on which the image is displayed. The image is cut off if it is larger than the area it is being drawn on.

- `drawImage(Image img, int x, int y, ImageObserver observer)`

  This is the same as the preceding method except that it does not specify a background color.

- `drawImage(Image img, int x, int y, int width, int height, ImageObserver observer)`

  Draw a scaled version of the image that can fill all of the available space in the specified rectangle.

- `drawImage(Image img, int x, int y, int width, int height, Color bgcolor, ImageObserver observer)`

  This is the same as the preceding method except that it provides a solid background color behind the image being drawn.

`ImageObserver` is an asynchronous update interface that receives notifications of image information as the image is constructed. The `Component` class implements `ImageObserver`. Therefore, every GUI component is an instance of `ImageObserver`. To draw images using the `drawImage` method in a Swing component, such as `JPanel`, override the `paintComponent` method to tell the component how to display the image in the panel.

Example 14.3 Displaying Images in an Applet

The program in this example will display an image in an applet. The image is stored in a file located in the same directory as the applet. The user enters the filename in a text field and displays the image on a panel. Figure 14.2 shows a sample run of the program.

```
// DisplayImageApplet.java: Display an image on a panel in the applet
import java.awt.*;
import java.awt.event.*;
import javax.swing.*;
import javax.swing.border.LineBorder;

public class DisplayImageApplet extends JApplet
  implements ActionListener
{
  // The panel for displaying the image  private
  private ImagePanel imagePanel = new ImagePanel();

  // The text field for entering the name of the image file
  private JTextField jtfFilename = new JTextField(20);

  // The button for displaying the image
  private JButton jbtShow = new JButton("Show Image");

  // Initialize the applet
  public void init()
  {
    // Panel p1 to hold a text field and a button
    JPanel p1 = new JPanel();
    p1.setLayout(new BorderLayout());
    p1.add(new JLabel("Image Filename"), BorderLayout.WEST);
    p1.add(jtfFilename, BorderLayout.CENTER);
    p1.add(jbtShow, BorderLayout.EAST);

    // Place an ImagePanel object and p1 in the applet
    getContentPane().add(imagePanel, BorderLayout.CENTER);
    getContentPane().add(p1, BorderLayout.SOUTH);

    // Set line border on the image panel
    imagePanel.setBorder(new LineBorder(Color.black, 1));

    // Register listener
    jbtShow.addActionListener(this);
    jtfFilename.addActionListener(this);
  }

  // Handle the ActionEvent
  public void actionPerformed(ActionEvent e)
  {
    if ((e.getSource() instanceof JButton) ||
      (e.getSource() instanceof JTextField))
      displayImage();
  }

  // Display image on the panel
  private void displayImage()
  {
    // Retrieve image
    Image image = getImage(getCodeBase(),
      jtfFilename.getText().trim());
```

continues

Example 14.3 continued

```
        // Show image in the panel
        imagePanel.showImage(image);
      }
    }

    // Define the panel for showing an image
    class ImagePanel extends JPanel
    {
      // Image instance
      private Image image = null;

      // Default constructor
      public ImagePanel()
      {
      }

      // Set image and show it
      public void showImage(Image image)
      {
        this.image = image;
        repaint();
      }

      // Draw image on the panel
      public void paintComponent(Graphics g)
      {
        super.paintComponent(g);

        if (image != null)
          g.drawImage(image, 0, 0, getWidth(), getHeight(), this);
      }
    }
```

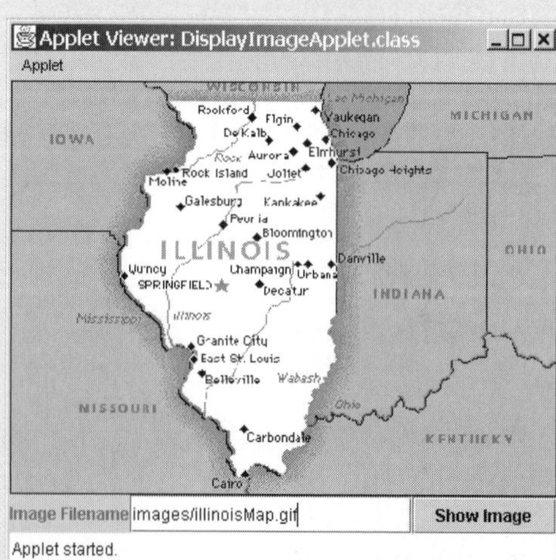

Figure 14.2 *Given the image filename, the applet displays an image.*

Example Review

The image is loaded by using the `getImage` method from the file in the same directory as the applet. The `showImage` method defined in `ImagePanel` sets the image so that it can be drawn in the `paintComponent` method.

The statement `g.drawImage(image, 0, 0, getWidth(), getHeight(), this)` displays the image in the `Graphics` context `g` on the `ImagePanel` object. To display the image, you enter the filename in the text field, then press the Enter key or click the Show Image button. The filename you enter must be located in the same directory or a subdirectory of the applet.

Loading Image and Audio Files in Java Applications

The `getImage` method used in Example 14.3 is defined in the `Applet` class, and thus is only available with the applet. The audio files in Example 14.1, "Incorporating Sound in Applets," are loaded through the URL specified by the `getCodeBase()` method, and thus this method of retrieving audio files cannot be used with Java applications.

When writing a Java application, you can use the `java.lang.Class` class to load an image or audio file. Whenever Java VM loads a class or an interface, it creates an instance of a special class named `Class`. The `Class` class provides access to useful information about the class, such as the data fields and method. It also contains the `getResource(filename)` method, which can be used to obtain the URL of a file name in the same directory with the class or in its subdirectory. Thus, you can use the following code to get the URL of an image or audio file:

```
URL url = this.getClass().getResource(filename);
```

To get an audio clip, use a new static method `newAudioClip()` in the `java.applet.Applet` class in Java 2:

```
AudioClip audioClip = Applet.newAudioClip(url);
```

You might attempt to use the `getImage` method to obtain an `Image` object like this:

```
Image image = getImage(url);
```

This method would work fine for Java applets, but not for Java applications. To get an `Image` object from the URL in a Java application, you may construct an `ImageIcon` object using the new `ImageIcon(url)`, and obtain an image using the `getImage()` method in the `ImageIcon` class, as follows:

```
// Obtain an image icon
ImageIcon imageIcon = new ImageIcon(url);

// Get the image from the image icon
Image image = imageIcon.getImage();
```

Example 14.4 Using Image and Audio in Applications and in Applets

This program uses the `Class` class to obtain the URL of the image and audio resource, which are located in the program's class directory. The program enables you to select a country from a combo box, and then displays the country's flag. You can play the selected country's national anthem by clicking the Play Anthem button, as shown in Figure 14.3.

```
// ResourceLocatorDemo.java: Demonstrate using resource locator to
// load image files and audio files to applets and applications
import java.awt.*;
import java.awt.image.*;
import java.awt.event.*;
import javax.swing.*;
import javax.swing.border.*;
import java.net.URL;
import java.applet.*;

public class ResourceLocatorDemo extends JApplet
  implements ActionListener, ItemListener
{
  // Image panel for displaying an image
  private ImagePanel imagePanel = new ImagePanel();

  // Combo box for selecting a country
  private JComboBox jcboCountry = new JComboBox();

  // Button to play an audio
  private JButton jbtPlayAnthem = new JButton("Play Anthem");

  // Selected country
  private String country = "United States of America";

  // Initialize the applet
  public void init()
  {
    // Panel p to hold a label combo box and a button for play audio
    JPanel p = new JPanel();
    p.add(new JLabel("Select a country"));
    p.add(jcboCountry);
    p.add(jbtPlayAnthem);

    // Initialize the combo box
    jcboCountry.addItem("United States of America");
    jcboCountry.addItem("United Kingdom");
    jcboCountry.addItem("Denmark");
    jcboCountry.addItem("Norway");
    jcboCountry.addItem("China");
    jcboCountry.addItem("India");
    jcboCountry.addItem("Germany");

    // By default, the US flag is displayed
    imagePanel.showImage(createImage("us.gif"));
    imagePanel.setPreferredSize(new Dimension(300, 300));

    // Place p and an image panel in the applet
    getContentPane().add(p, BorderLayout.NORTH);
    getContentPane().add(imagePanel, BorderLayout.CENTER);
    imagePanel.setBorder(new LineBorder(Color.black, 1));

    // Register listener
    jbtPlayAnthem.addActionListener(this);
```

```
    jcboCountry.addItemListener(this);
  }

  // Handle ActionEvent
  public void actionPerformed(ActionEvent e)
  {
    // Get the file name
    String filename = null;

    if (country.equals("United States of America"))
      filename = "us.mid";
    else if (country.equals("United Kingdom"))
      filename = "uk.mid";
    else if (country.equals("Denmark"))
      filename = "denmark.mid";
    else if (country.equals("Norway"))
      filename = "norway.mid";
    else if (country.equals("China"))
      filename = "china.mid";
    else if (country.equals("India"))
      filename = "india.mid";
    else if (country.equals("Germany"))
      filename = "germany.mid";

    // Create an audio clip and play it
    createAudioClip(filename).play();
  }

  // Handle ItemEvent
  public void itemStateChanged(ItemEvent e)
  {
    // Get selected country
    country = (String)jcboCountry.getSelectedItem();

    // Get the file name
    String filename = null;

    if (country.equals("United States of America"))
      filename = "us.gif";
    else if (country.equals("United Kingdom"))
      filename = "uk.gif";
    else if (country.equals("Denmark"))
      filename = "denmark.gif";
    else if (country.equals("Norway"))
      filename = "norway.gif";
    else if (country.equals("China"))
      filename = "china.gif";
    else if (country.equals("India"))
      filename = "india.gif";
    else if (country.equals("Germany"))
      filename = "germany.gif";

    // Load image from the file and show it on the panel
    imagePanel.showImage(createImage(filename));
  }

  // Create an audio from the specified file
  public AudioClip createAudioClip(String filename)
  {
    // Get the URL for the file name

    URL url = this.getClass().getResource("anthems/" + filename);
```

continues

Example 14.4 continued

```
    // Return the audio clip
    return Applet.newAudioClip(url);
  }

  // Create an image from the specified file
  public Image createImage(String filename)
  {
    // Get the URL for the file name
    URL url = this.getClass().getResource("images/" + filename);

    // Obtain an image icon
    ImageIcon imageIcon = new ImageIcon(url);

    // Return the image
    return imageIcon.getImage();
  }

  // Main method
  public static void main(String[] args)
  {
    // Create a frame
    JFrame frame = new JFrame("Display Flags and Play Anthem");

    // Create an instance of the applet
    ResourceLocatorDemo applet = new ResourceLocatorDemo();

    // Add the applet instance to the frame
    frame.getContentPane().add(applet, BorderLayout.CENTER);

    // Invoke init() and start()
    applet.init();
    applet.start();

    // Display the frame
    frame.pack();
    frame.setVisible(true);
  }
}
```

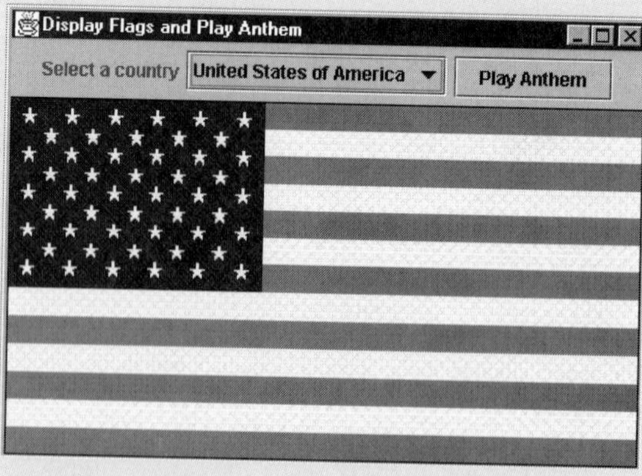

Figure 14.3 *The program displays the flag of the selected country and plays its national anthem.*

Example Review

The program can run as an applet or an application. Obtaining the URL using the `Class` class works not only for standalone applications, but also for Java applets.

The `createAudioClip(filename)` method obtains the `URL` instance for the filename and creates an `AudioClip` for the URL using the `newAudioClip` static method, which is a new method introduced in Java 2 to support playing audio in applications.

The `createImage(filename)` method obtains the URL instance for the filename, creates an image icon for the url, and obtains an `Image` object, using the `getImage` method in the `ImageIcon` class.

The program is not efficient if the user repeatedly chooses the same country and plays the same anthem, because a new `Image` instance is created for every newly selected country, and a new `AudioClip` instance is created every time an audio is played. To improve efficiency, load the image and audio files once and store them in the memory using an array.

Displaying a Sequence of Images

In the preceding section, you learned how to display a single image. Now you will learn how to display a sequence of images that will simulate a movie. As in the clock example in the previous chapter, you can use the thread approach or the timer approach to control the animation. Since the timer approach makes the program shorter and simpler, this example uses a timer to trigger repainting of the viewing area with different images.

Example 14.5 Using Image Animation

This example presents a program that will display a sequence of images in order to create a movie. The images are files stored in the `images` directory that are named **L1.gif**, **L2.gif**, and so on, to **L52.gif**. When you run the program, you will see a phrase entitled "Learning Java" rotate. Figure 14.4 shows a sample run of the program.

```
// ImageAnimation.java: Display a sequence of images
import java.awt.*;
import java.awt.event.*;
import javax.swing.*;
import javax.swing.border.*;

public class ImageAnimation extends JApplet implements ActionListener
{
  private Image imageToDisplay;
  protected Image imageArray[]; // Hold images
  protected int numOfImages = 52, // Total number of images
                currentImageIndex = 0, // Current image subscript
                sleepTime = 100; // Milliseconds to sleep
  protected int direction = 1; // Image rotating direction

  // Image display panel
  protected PlayImage imagePanel = new PlayImage();
```

continues

Example 14.5 continued

```
// Text field for receiving speed
protected JTextField jtfSpeed = new JTextField(5);

// Button for reversing direction
JButton jbtReverse = new JButton("Reverse");

// Initialize the applet
public void init()
{
  // Load the image, the image files are named
  // L1 - L52 in Images directory
  imageArray = new Image[numOfImages];
  for (int i=0; i<imageArray.length; i++ )
  {
    imageArray[i] = getImage(getDocumentBase(),
      "Images/L" + (i+1) + ".gif" );
  }

  // Panel p to hold animation control
  JPanel p = new JPanel();
  p.setLayout(new BorderLayout());
  p.add(new JLabel("Animation speed in millisecond"),
    BorderLayout.WEST);
  p.add(jtfSpeed, BorderLayout.CENTER);
  p.add(jbtReverse, BorderLayout.EAST);

  // Add the image panel and p to the applet
  getContentPane().add(imagePanel, BorderLayout.CENTER);
  getContentPane().add(p, BorderLayout.SOUTH);

  // Register listener
  jtfSpeed.addActionListener(this);
  jbtReverse.addActionListener(this);
}

// Handle ActionEvent
public void actionPerformed(ActionEvent e)
{
  if (e.getSource() == jtfSpeed)
  {
    sleepTime = Integer.parseInt(jtfSpeed.getText());
    imagePanel.setSpeed(sleepTime);
  }
  else if (e.getSource() == jbtReverse)
  {
    direction = -direction;
  }
}

// Override the start method in the Applet class
public void start()
{
  imagePanel.start();
}

// Override the stop method in the Applet class
public void stop()
{
  imagePanel.stop();
}
```

```
protected class PlayImage extends JPanel implements ActionListener
{
  protected Timer timer;

  // Constructor
  public PlayImage()
  {
    // Start with the first image
    currentImageIndex = 0;

    // Set line border on the panel
    setBorder(new LineBorder(Color.red, 1));

    // Create a timer with delay 1000 ms and listener Clock
    timer = new Timer(1000, this);

    // Start the timer
    timer.start();
  }

  public void setSpeed(int sleepTime)
  {
    timer.setDelay(sleepTime);
  }

  public void start()
  {
    timer.start();
  }

  public void stop()
  {
    timer.stop();
  }

  // Choose a new image to display
  public void actionPerformed(ActionEvent e)
  {
    imageToDisplay =
      imageArray[currentImageIndex%numOfImages];

    // Make sure currentImageIndex is nonnegative
    if (currentImageIndex == 0) currentImageIndex = numOfImages;
    currentImageIndex = currentImageIndex + direction;
    repaint();
  }


  // Display an image
  public void paintComponent(Graphics g)
  {
    super.paintComponent(g);

    if (imageToDisplay != null)
    {
      g.drawImage(imageToDisplay, 0, 0, getSize().width,
        getSize().height, this);
    }
  }
}
}
```

continues

Example 14.5 continued

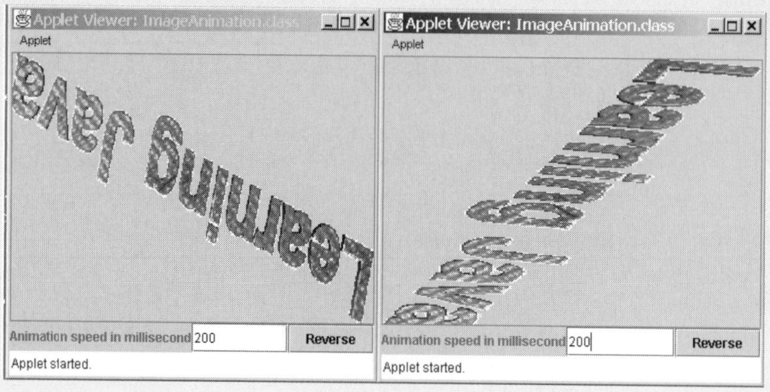

Figure 14.4 *The applet displays a sequence of images.*

Example Review

Fifty-two image files are located in the `images` directory, which is a subdirectory of the `getDocumentBase()` directory. The images in these files are loaded to `imageArray` and then painted continuously on the applet at a fixed rate using a timer.

The image is drawn to occupy the entire applet viewing area in a rectangle. It is scaled to fill in the area.

The `timer` is created and started in the applet's `init()` method. Since it is suspended in the applet's `stop()` method, the images are not displayed when the browser leaves the applet's page. From then on, the thread releases CPU time when it is not active. When the applet becomes active again, the `timer` is resumed in the applet's `start()` method to display images.

You can adjust the `sleepTime` to control animation speed by entering a value in milliseconds and pressing the Enter key for the change to take place.

The display sequence can be reversed by clicking the Reverse button.

You can add a simple function to suspend a timer with the mouse pressed. You can resume a suspended `timer` with the mouse released (see Exercise 14.4).

NOTE
The *JComponent* class has a property named *doubleBuffered*. By default, this property is set to *true*. Double buffering is a technique for reducing animation flickering. It creates a graphics context off-screen and does all the drawings in the off-screen context. When the drawing is complete, it displays the whole context on the real screen. Thus, there is no flickering within an image because all the drawings are displayed at the same time. To see the effect of double buffering, set the *doubleBuffered* property to false. You will see a stunning difference.

Using MediaTracker

One problem you may face if you run the preceding example is that images are only partially displayed while being loaded. This occurs because the image has not yet been loaded completely. The problem is particularly annoying when you are downloading an image over a slow modem.

To resolve the problem, Java provides the `MediaTracker` class to track the status of a number of media objects. Media objects include audio clips as well as images, though currently only images are supported.

You can use `MediaTracker` to determine whether an image has been completely loaded. To use it, you must first create an instance of `MediaTracker` for a specific graphics component. The following is an example of creating a `MediaTracker`:

```
MediaTracker imageTracker = new MediaTracker(this);
```

To enable `imageTracker` (in order to determine whether the image has been loaded), use the `addImage` method to register the image with `imageTracker`. The following statement registers `anImage` of the `Image` type with `imageTracker`:

```
imageTracker.addImage(anImage, id);
```

The second argument, `id`, is an integer ID that controls the priority order in which the images are fetched. Images with a lower ID number are loaded in preference to those with a higher ID number. The ID can be used to query `imageTracker` about the status of the registered image. To query, use the `checkID` method. For example, the following method returns `true` if the image with the `id` is completely loaded:

```
checkID(id)
```

Otherwise, it returns `false`.

You can use the `waitForID(id)` method to force the program to wait until the image registered with the `id` is completely loaded, or you can use the `waitForAll()` method to wait for all of the registered images to be loaded completely. The methods shown below block the program until the image is completely loaded.

```
waitForID(int id) throws InterruptedException

waitForAll() throws InterruptedException
```

TIP

To track multiple images as a group, register them with a media tracker using the same ID.

Example 14.6 Using `MediaTracker`

This example uses `MediaTracker` to improve upon the preceding example. With `MediaTracker`, the user of this program can ensure that all of the images are fully loaded before they are displayed.

```
// ImageAnimationUsingMediaTracker.java: Monitor loading images
// using MediaTracker
import java.awt.*;
import javax.swing.*;

public class ImageAnimationUsingMediaTracker extends ImageAnimation
{
  private MediaTracker imageTracker = new MediaTracker(this);

  // Initialize the applet
  public void init()
  {
    // Load the image, the image files are named
    // L1 - L52 in Images directory
    imageArray = new Image[numOfImages];
    for (int i=0; i<imageArray.length; i++ )
    {
      imageArray[i] = getImage(getDocumentBase(),
        "Images/L" + (i+1) + ".gif" );

      // Register images with the imageTracker
      imageTracker.addImage(imageArray[i], i);
    }

    // Wait for all the images to be completely loaded
    try
    {
      imageTracker.waitForAll();
    }
    catch (InterruptedException ex)
    {
      System.out.println(ex);
    }

    // Dispose of imageTracker since it is no longer needed
    imageTracker = null;
```

```
      // Panel p to hold animation control
      JPanel p = new JPanel();
      p.setLayout(new BorderLayout());
      p.add(new JLabel("Animation speed in millisecond"),
        BorderLayout.WEST);
      p.add(jtfSpeed, BorderLayout.CENTER);
      p.add(jbtReverse, BorderLayout.EAST);

      // Add the image panel and p to the applet
      getContentPane().add(new PlayImage(), BorderLayout.CENTER);
      getContentPane().add(p, BorderLayout.SOUTH);

      // Register listener
      jtfSpeed.addActionListener(this);
      jbtReverse.addActionListener(this);
    }
  }
```

Example Review

The `ImageAnimationUsingMediaTracker` class extends `ImageAnimation`, which was created in Example 14.5. The `ImageAnimationUsingMediaTracker` uses `MediaTracker` to monitor loading images.

The program creates an instance of `MediaTracker`, `imageTracker`, and registers images with `imageTracker` in order to track image loading. The program uses `imageTracker` to ensure that all the images are completely loaded before they are displayed.

The `waitForAll()` method forces the program to wait for all the images to be loaded before displaying any of them. Because the program needs to load 52 images, using `waitForAll()` results in a long delay before images are displayed. You should display something while the image is being loaded in order to keep the user attentive and/or informed. A simple approach is to use the `showStatus()` method in the `Applet` class to display some information on the Web browser's status bar. Here is a possibility:

```
showStatus("Please wait while loading images");
```

Put this statement before the `try-catch` block for `waitForAll()` in the program.

The `imageTracker` object is no longer needed after the images are loaded. The statement `imageTracker = null` notifies the garbage collector of the Java runtime system to reclaim the memory space previously occupied by the `imageTracker` object.

You can rewrite this example to enable it to run as an application (see Exercise 14.4).

Chapter Summary

In this chapter, you learned how to play audio and display images in Java multimedia programming. You also learned how to use the `Class` class to load image and audio files, and the media tracking mechanism to track loading images.

Audio and images files are accessible through a URL. The `getDocumentBase()` method returns the URL of the HTML file that contains the applet. The `getCodeBase()` method returns the URL of the applet. The `Class` class can be used to obtain the URL of an image or audio file for Java applications as well as Java applets. You can obtain an audio clip using `Applet.newAudioClip(url)`. You can construct an image icon using `new ImageIcon(url)` and obtain an image using `getImage()`.

The `MediaTracker` class is used to determine whether one image or all of the images are completely loaded. The `MediaTracker` obtains this information in order to ensure that the images will be displayed fully.

Review Questions

14.1 What types of audio files are used in Java?

14.2 How do you get an audio file? How do you play, repeatedly play, and stop an audio clip?

14.3 The `getAudioClip()` method is defined in the `Applet` class. If you want to use audio in Java applications, what options do you have?

14.4 What is the difference between `getDocumentBase()` and `getCodeBase()`?

14.5 What is the difference between the `getImage` method in the `Applet` class and the `getImage` method in the `ImageIcon` class?

14.6 How do you get the URL of an image or audio file in Java applications?

14.7 Describe the `drawImage` method in the `Graphics` class.

14.8 Can you create image icons and use the `setIcon` method to set an icon in a `JLabel` instance in Java applets?

14.9 Explain the differences between displaying images in a `JLabel` instance and in a `JPanel` instance.

14.10 How do you get an audio clip in Java applications?

14.11 Why do you use `MediaTracker`? How do you add images to a media tracker? How do you know that an image or all of the images are completely loaded? Can you assign images the same ID in order to register them with a media tracker?

Programming Exercises

14.1 Write an applet that meets the following requirements:

- Get an audio file from the URL of the HTML base code.
- Place three buttons labeled Play, Loop, and Stop, as shown in Figure 14.5.
- If you click the Play button, the audio file is played once. If you click the Loop button, the audio file keeps playing repeatedly. If you click the Stop button, the playing stops.
- The applet can run as an application.

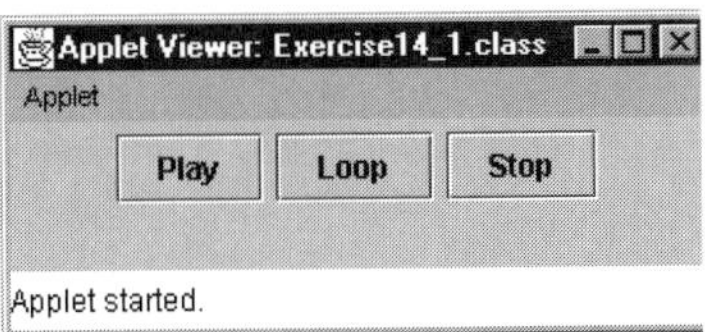

Figure 14.5 *Click Play to play an audio clip once, click Loop to play an audio repeatedly, and click Stop to terminate playing.*

14.2 Sometimes, when you repaint the entire viewing area of a panel, only a tiny portion of the viewing area is changed. You can only improve the performance by repainting the affected area, but do not invoke `super.paintComponent(g)` when repainting the panel, because this will cause the entire viewing area to be cleared. Use this approach to write an applet to display the temperatures of each hour during the last 24 hours in a histogram. Suppose that the temperatures between 50 and 90 degrees Fahrenheit are obtained randomly and are updated every hour. The temperature of the current hour needs to be redisplayed, while others remain unchanged. Use a unique color to highlight the temperature for the current hour (see Figure 14.6).

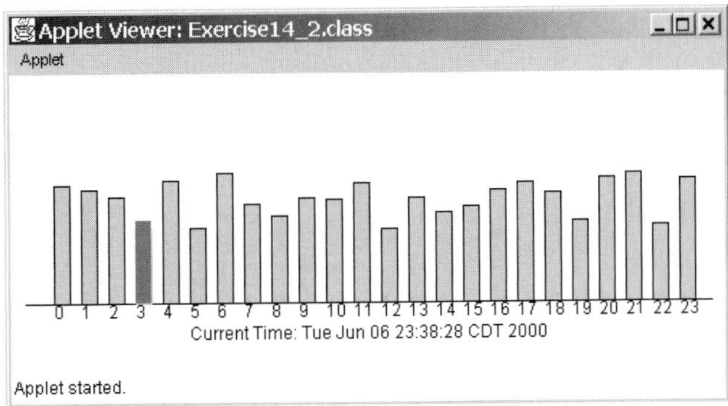

Figure 14.6 *The histogram displays the average temperature of every hour in the last 24 hours.*

14.3 Modify the elevator program in Exercise 13.9 of Chapter 13, "Multithreading," to add sound to the program. When the elevator stops on a floor, announce which floor the elevator is on.

14.4 Rewrite Example 14.6, "Using MediaTracker," to add the following new functions:

- The animation is suspended when the mouse is pressed and resumed when the mouse is released. To implement this feature, add the code in the `PlayImage` inner class of the `ImageAnimation` class to handle the mouse event for `mousePressed` and `mouseReleased` actions.
- Sound is incorporated into the applet so that it is played while images are displayed.
- Enable the applet to run standalone.

14.5 Write an applet that will display a digital clock with a large display panel that shows hour, minute, and second. This clock should allow the user to set an alarm. Figure 14.7 shows an example of such a clock. To turn on the alarm, check the Alarm check box. To specify the alarm time, click the "Set alarm" button to display a new frame, as shown in Figure 14.8. You can set the alarm time in the frame. Enable the applet to run standalone.

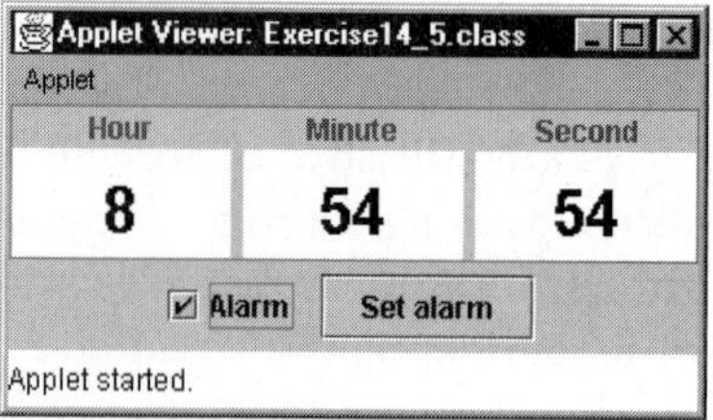

Figure 14.7 *The program displays current hour, minute, and second, and enables you to set an alarm.*

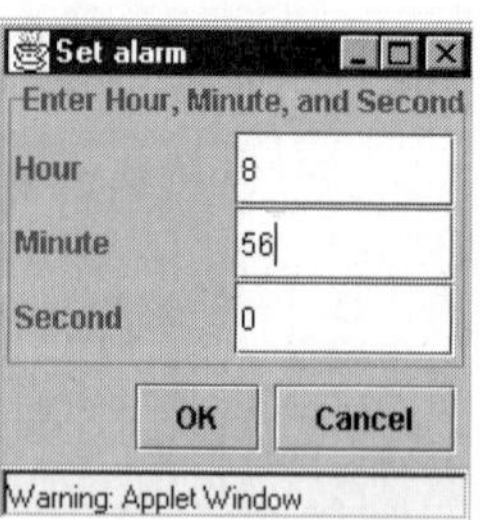

Figure 14.8 *You can set the alarm time by specifying hour, minute, and second.*

14.6 Create animation using the applet (see Figure 14.9) to meet the following requirements:

- Allow the user to specify the animation speed. The user can enter the speed in a text field.

- Get the number of frames and the image filename prefix from the user. For example, if the user enters **n** for the number of frames and **L** for the image prefix, then the files are **L1**, **L2**, and so on, to **Ln**. Assume that the images are stored in the `images` directory, a subdirectory of the applet's directory.
- Allow the user to specify an audio filename. The audio file is stored in the same directory as the applet. The sound is played while the animation runs.
- Enable the applet to run standalone.

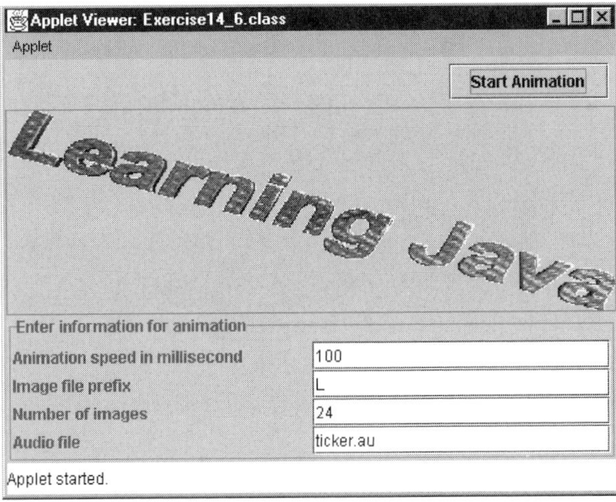

Figure 14.9 *This applet lets the user select image files, audio file, and animation speed.*

14.7 Write an applet that will display a sequence of images for a single image in different sizes. Initially, the viewing area for this image is of 300 width and 300 height. Your program should continuously shrink the viewing area by 1 in width and 10 in height until it reaches a width of 50 and a height of 50. At that point, the viewing area should continuously enlarge by 1 in width and 1 in height until it reaches a width of 300 and a height of 300. The viewing area should shrink and enlarge (alternately) to create animation for the single image. Enable the applet to run standalone.

14.8 Suppose that the instructor asks the students in a Java class to write short paragraphs stating their personal objectives for taking the course. Write an applet that introduces the students, one after the other, by presenting each one's photo, name, and paragraph (see Figure 14.10) along with audio that reads the paragraph.

Suppose there are 10 students in the class. Assume that the audio files, named **a1.au**, **a2.au**, and so on, up to **a10.au**, are stored in a subdirectory named `audio` in the applet's directory, and the photo image files, named **photo1.gif**, **photo2.gif**, and so on, up to **photo10.gif**, are stored in a subdirectory named `photo` in the applet's directory. Assume that the name and paragraph of each student is passed from the HTML. Here is an example for student **a1**.

```
<param name= "paragraph1"
  value="I am taking the class because I want to
    learn to write cool programs like this!">
<param name= "name1"  value = "Michael Liang">
```

Hint: Use the `DescriptionPanel` class to display the image, name, and the text. The `DescriptionPanel` class was introduced in Example 9.4, "Using Text Area,"

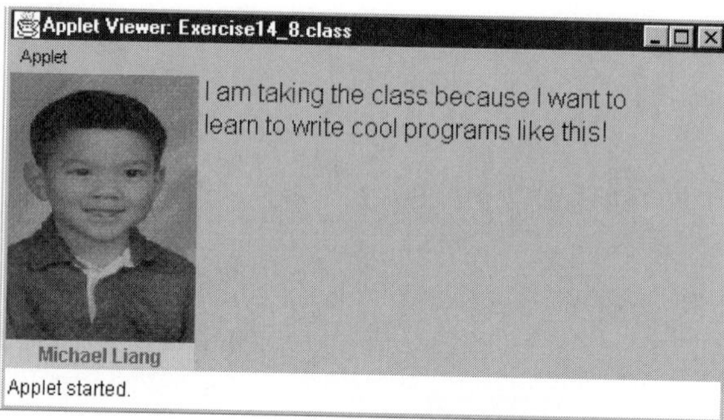

Figure 14.10 *This applet shows each student's photo, name, and paragraph, one after another, and reads the paragraph that is currently shown.*

14.9 Rewrite Example 14.4, "Using Image and Audio in Applications and in Applets." Use the resource bundle to retrieve image and audio files. (Hint: When a new country is selected, set an appropriate locale for the country. Have your program look for the flag and audio file from the resource file for the locale.)

14.10 Rewrite Exercise 14.8 to display an image to fit in a panel of fixed size. In Exercise 14.8, you used the `DescriptionPanel` class to display an image icon in a label. The image icon is not scalable. If the label dimension is smaller than the image icon, you will see only part of the image. In this exercise, use the `ImagePanel` class, introduced in Example 14.3, "Displaying Images in an Applet," to display an image in a panel. You can modify the `DescriptionPanel` class to use `ImagePanel` to replace the label for displaying images.

CHAPTER 15

Input and Output

Objectives

- Understand input and output streams, and learn how to create them.
- Discover the uses of byte and character streams.
- Know how to read from or write to external files using file streams.
- Become familiar with the `File` class.
- Employ data streams for cross-platform data format compatibility.
- Use print streams to output data of primitive types in text format.
- Learn to use `JFileChooser` to display open and save file dialog boxes.
- Use text input and output on the console.
- Store and restore objects using object streams.
- Use `RandomAccessFile` for both read and write.
- Parse text files using `StreamTokenizer`. (Optional)

Introduction

In previous chapters, you used input and output only on the console. In Chapter 2, "Primitive Data Types and Operations," you created the `MyInput` class and used `MyInput.readInt()` and `MyInput.readDouble()` to receive data from the console. You used `System.out.print` to display output on the console. In this chapter, you will learn about many other forms of input and output as well as how they work together.

In Java, all I/Os are handled in streams. A *stream* is an abstraction of the continuous one-way flow of data. Imagine a swimming pool with pipes that connect it to another pool. Let's consider the water in the first pool as the data, and the water in the second pool as your program. The flow of water through the pipes is called a *stream*. If you want input, just open the valve to let water out of the data pool and into the program pool. If you want output, just open the valve to let water out of the program pool and into the data pool.

It's a very simple concept, and a very efficient one. Since Java streams can be applied to any source of data, it is as easy for a programmer to input from a keyboard or output to a console as it is to input from a file or output to a file. Figure 15.1 shows the input and output streams between a program and an external file. Java streams are used liberally. There can even be input and output streams between two programs.

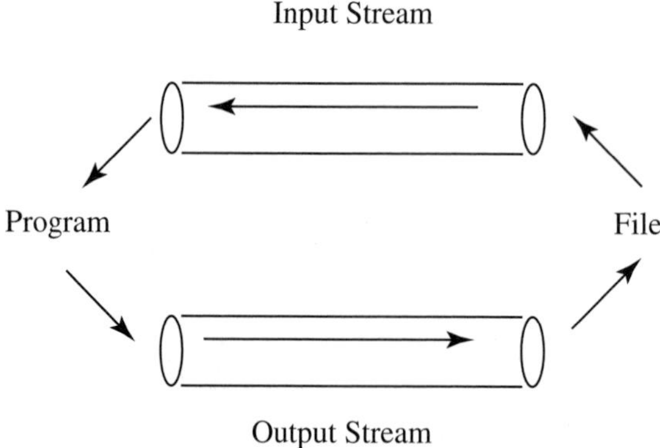

Figure 15.1 *The program receives data through the input stream and sends data through the output stream.*

In general, all streams except random-access file streams flow only in one direction; therefore, if you want to input and output, you need two separate stream objects. In Java, streams can be *layered*—that is, connected to one another in pipeline fashion. The output of one stream becomes the input of another stream.

This layering capability makes it possible to filter data along the pipeline of streams so that you can get data in the desired format. For instance, suppose you want to get integers from an external file. You can use a file input stream to get raw data in binary format, then use a data input stream to extract integers from the output of the input stream.

Streams are objects. Stream objects have methods that read and write data or do other useful things, such as flushing the stream, closing the stream, and counting the number of bytes in the stream.

Stream Classes

Java offers stream classes for processing all kinds of data. Figures 15.2 and 15.3 show the hierarchical relationship of these classes.

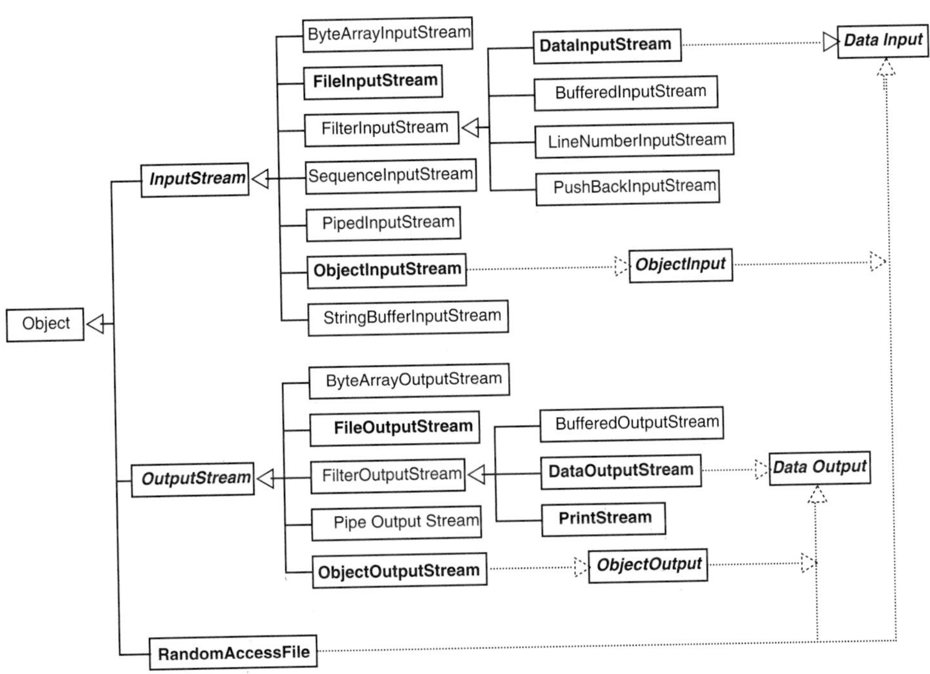

Figure 15.2 `InputStream`, `OutputStream`, `RandomAccessFile`, *and their subclasses deal with streams of bytes.*

NOTE
As shown in Figures 15.2 and 15.3, there are many stream classes in Java. Each stream has its intended application. This chapter introduced the most frequently used streams. These stream classes appear in bold in the figures.

Stream classes can be categorized either as *byte streams* or as *character streams*. The `InputStream`/`OutputStream` class is the root of all byte stream classes, and the `Reader`/`Writer` class is the root of all character stream classes.

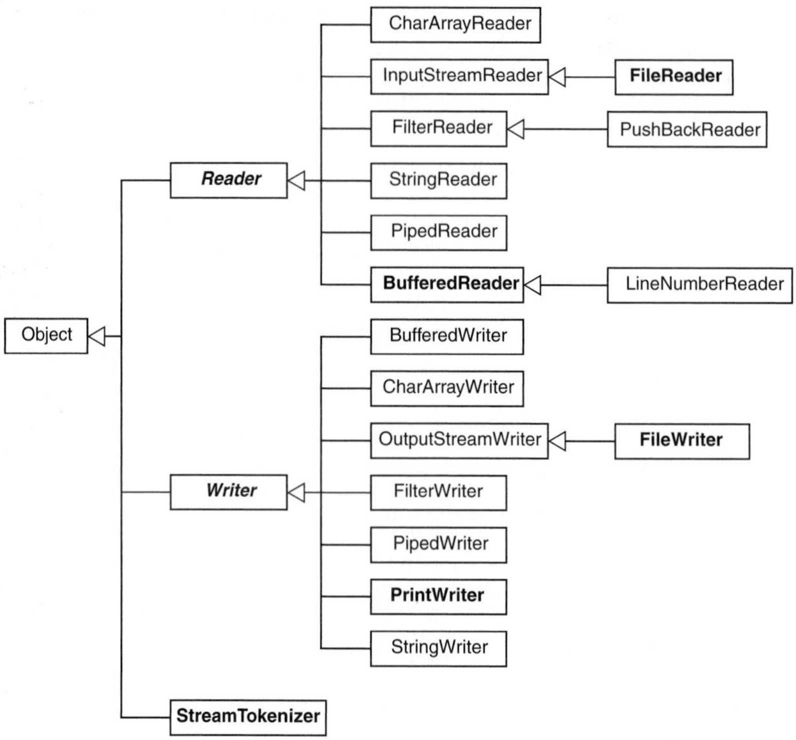

Figure 15.3 *`Reader`, `Writer`, `StreamTokenizer`, and their subclasses are concerned with streams of characters.*

The `RandomAccessFile` class extends `Object` and implements the `DataInput` and `DataOutput` interfaces. It can be used to open a file that allows both reading and writing. The `StreamTokenizer` class that extends `Object` can be used for parsing text files.

InputStream and *Reader*

The abstract `InputStream` and `Reader` classes, extending `Object`, are the base classes for all of the input streams of bytes and characters, respectively. These classes and their subclasses are very similar, except that `InputStream` uses bytes for its fundamental unit of information, and `Reader` uses characters. `InputStream` and `Reader` have many common methods with identical signatures. These methods have similar functionality, but `InputStream` is designed to read bytes, and `Reader` is designed to read characters.

The following methods, defined in `InputStream`, are often useful:

- `public abstract int read() throws IOException`

  This method reads the next byte and returns its value. The value of the byte is returned as an `int` in the range from 0 to 255. At the end of the stream, it returns `-1`. This method blocks the program from executing until input data is available, the end of the stream is detected, or an exception is thrown. A subclass of `InputStream` must provide an implementation of this method.

- `public int read(byte[] b) throws IOException`

  This method reads up to b. length bytes into array `b`, returns `b.length` if the number of available bytes is more than or equal to `b.length`, returns the number of bytes read if the number of available bytes is less than `b.length`, and returns `-1` at the end of the stream.

- `public void close() throws IOException`

  This method closes the input stream.

- `public void int available() throws IOException`

  This method returns the number of bytes that can be read from the input stream without blocking.

- `public long skip(long n) throws IOException`

  This method skips over and discards `n` bytes of data from the input stream. The actual number of bytes skipped is returned.

NOTE
The `read()` method reads a byte from the stream. If no data are available, it blocks the thread from executing the next statement. The thread that invokes the `read()` method is suspended until the data become available.

The `Reader` class contains all of the methods listed previously except `available()`. These methods have the same functionality in `Reader` as in `InputStream`, but they are subject to character stream interpretation. For example, `read()` returns an integer in the range from 0 to 16,383, which represents a Unicode character.

OutputStream and *Writer*

Like `InputStream` and `Reader`, `OutputStream` and `Writer` are counterparts. They are the base classes for all output streams of bytes and characters, respectively. The following instance methods are in both `OutputStream` and `Writer`:

- `public abstract void write(int b) throws IOException`

  This method writes a byte (for `OutputStream`) or a character (for `Writer`).

- `public void write(byte[] b) throws IOException`

  This method writes all bytes in the array `b` to the output stream (for `OutputStream`) or characters in the array of characters (for `Writer`).

- `public void close() throws IOException`

  This method closes the output stream.

- `public void flush() throws IOException`

  This method flushes the output stream (that is, it sends any buffered data in the stream to its destination).

The *File* Class and Processing External Files

The `File` class is intended to provide an abstraction that deals with most of the machine-dependent complexities of files and path names in a machine-independent fashion. The filename is a string. The `File` class is a wrapper class for the file name.

You can create a `File` object using the following statement:

```
File file = new File("in.dat");
```

You can use the `File` class to check properties of files, such as whether the file exists, or is readable, or updateable. You can use the `exists()` method to check whether the file exists, and the `getName()` method to get the name of the file. For example,

```
if (file.exists())
{
  System.out.println("File " + file.getName() + " exists");
}
```

When a filename or a path is used, it is always assumed that the host's file-naming conventions are used. For example, a filename with a path on Windows could be **c:\book\in.dat**, and on UNIX, the path could be **/book/in.dat**.

For example, the following statement creates a file using the full path on Windows:

```
File file = new File("c:\\book\\in.dat");
```

This statement creates a file using the full path on Unix:

```
File file = new File("book/in.dat");
```

You can use the `getPath()` method to get the full path of the file, and the `getParent()` method to get the directory that contains the file. For example,

```
if (file.exists())
{
  System.out.println("The full path is " + file.getPath());
  System.out.println("The directory is " + file.getParent());
}
```

You must use file streams to read from or write to a disk file. `FileInputStream` or `FileOutputStream` is used for byte streams, and `FileReader` or `FileWriter` for character streams. To create a file stream, use the following constructors:

```
public FileInputStream(String filenameString)

public FileInputStream(File file)

public FileOutputStream(String filenameString)

public FileOutputStream(File file)

public FileReader(String filenameString)
```

```
public FileReader(File file)

public FileWriter(String filenameString)

public FileWriter(File file)
```

The following statements create `infile` and `outfile` streams for the input file **in.dat** and the output file **out.dat**, respectively:

```
FileInputStream infile = new FileInputStream("in.dat");

FileOutputStream outfile = new FileOutputStream("out.dat");
```

An abstract method, such as `read(byte b)` in `InputStream`, is implemented in `FileInputStream`, and the abstract `write(int b)` method in the `OutputStream` class is implemented in `FileOutputStream`.

Example 15.1 Processing External Files

This example gives a program that uses `FileInputStream` and `FileOutputStream` to copy files, and the `File` class to check the properties of the file. The user needs to provide a source file and a target file as command-line arguments. The program copies the source file to the target file and displays the number of bytes in the file. A sample run of the program is shown in Figure 15.4.

```
// CopyFileUsingByteStream.java: Copy files
import java.io.*;

public class CopyFileUsingByteStream
{
  // Main method: args[0] for sourcefile and args[1] for target file
  public static void main(String[] args)
  {
    // Declare input and output file streams
    FileInputStream fis = null;
    FileOutputStream fos = null;

    // Check usage
    if (args.length !=2)
    {
      System.out.println(
        "Usage: java CopyFileUsingByteStream fromfile tofile");
      System.exit(0);
    }

    try
    {
      // Create file input stream
      fis = new FileInputStream(new File(args[0]));

      // Create file output stream if the file does not exist
      File file = new File(args[1]);
      if (file.exists())
      {
        System.out.println("file " + args[1] + " already exists");
        return;
      }
      else
        fos = new FileOutputStream(args[1]);
```

continues

Example 15.1 continued

```
        // Display the file size
        System.out.println("The file " + args[0] + " has "+
          fis.available() + " bytes");

        // Continuously read a byte from fis and write it to fos
        int r;
        while ((r = fis.read()) != -1)
        {
          fos.write((byte)r);
        }
      }
      catch (FileNotFoundException ex)
      {
        System.out.println("File not found: " + args[0]);
      }
      catch (IOException ex)
      {
        System.out.println(ex.getMessage());
      }
      finally
      {
        try
        {
          // Close files
          if (fis != null) fis.close();
          if (fos != null) fos.close();
        }
        catch (IOException ex)
        {
          System.out.println(ex);
        }
      }
    }
  }
```

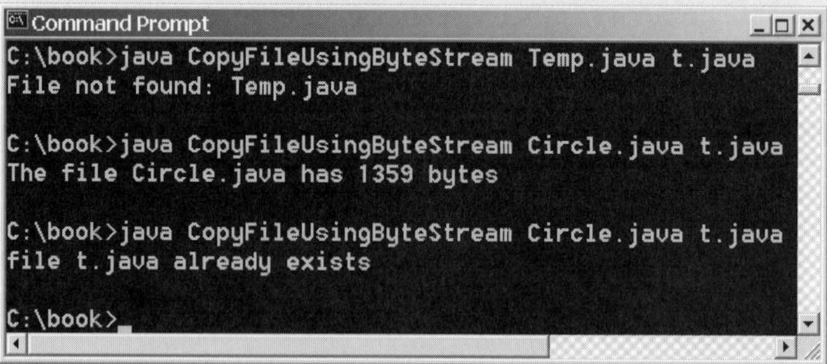

Figure 15.4 *The program copies a file using byte streams.*

Example Review

The program creates the `fis` and `fos` streams for the input file `args[0]` and the output file `args[1]` (see Figure 15.5).

If the input file `args[0]` does not exist, `new FileInputStream(new File(args[0]))` will raise the exception `FileNotFoundException`. By contrast,

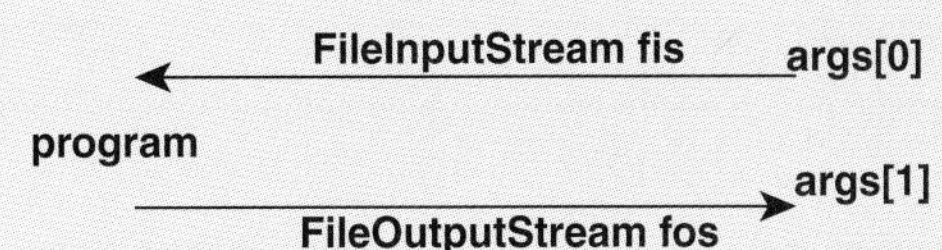

Figure 15.5 *The program uses* `FileInputStream` *to read data from the file and* `FileOutputStream` *to write data to the file.*

`new FileOutputStream(new File(args[1]))` will always create a file output stream, whether or not the file `args[1]` exists.

To avoid writing into an existing file, the program uses the `exists()` method in the `File` class to determine whether `args[1]` exists. If the file already exists, the user would be notified; otherwise, the file should be created.

The program continuously reads a byte from the `fis` stream and sends it to the `fos` stream until all of the bytes have been read. (The condition `(fis.read() == -1)` signifies the end of a file.)

The program closes any open file streams in the `finally` clause. The statements in the `finally` clause are always executed, whether or not exceptions occur.

The program could be rewritten using `FileReader` and `FileWriter`. The new program would be almost exactly the same (see Exercise 15.1).

TIP

Always close files using the `close()` method when the files are no longer needed. In some cases, not closing them will cause programming errors. Files are usually closed in the `finally` clause.

Filter Streams

Filter streams are streams that filter bytes or characters for some purpose. The basic input stream provides a read method that can only be used for reading bytes or characters. If you want to read integers, doubles, or strings, you need a filter class to wrap the input stream. Using a filter class enables you to read integers, doubles, and strings instead of bytes and characters.

When you need to process primitive numeric types, use `FilterInputStream` and `FilterOutputStream` to filter bytes. When you need to process strings, use `BufferedReader` and `PushbackReader` to filter characters. `FilterInputStream` and `FilterOutputStream` are abstract classes; their subclasses (listed below in Tables 15.1 and 15.2) are often used.

Data Streams

The data streams (`DataInputStream` and `DataOutputStream`) read and write Java primitive types in a machine-independent fashion, thereby enabling you to write a

TABLE 15.1 `FilterInputStream` **Subclasses**

Class	*Usage*
`DataInputStream`	Handles binary formats of all the primitive data types.
`BufferedInputStream`	Gets data from the buffer and then reads them from the stream if necessary.
`LineNumberInputStream`	Keeps track of how many lines are read.
`PushbackInputStream`	Allows single-byte lookahead. After the byte is looked at, this stream pushes the byte back to the stream so that the next read can read it.

TABLE 15.2 `FilterOutputStream` **Subclasses**

Class	*Usage*
`DataOutputStream`	Outputs the binary format of all the primitive types, which is useful if another program uses the output.
`BufferedOutputStream`	Outputs to the buffer first and then to the stream if necessary. Programmers can also call the `flush()` method to write the buffer to the stream.
`PrintStream`	Outputs the Unicode format of all the primitive types, which is useful if the format is output to the console.

data file on one machine and read it on another machine that has a different operating system or file structure.

`DataInputStream` extends `FilterInputStream` and implements the `DataInput` interface. `DataOutputStream` extends `FilterOutputStream` and implements the `DataOutput` interface. The `DataInput` and `DataOutput` interfaces are also implemented by the `RandomAccessFile` class, which is discussed in the section "Random Access Files," later in this chapter.

The following methods are defined in the `DataInput` interface:

```
public int readByte() throws IOException

public int readShort() throws IOException

public int readInt() throws IOException

public int readLong() throws IOException

public float readFloat() throws IOException

public double readDouble() throws IOException

public char readChar() throws IOException

public boolean readBoolean() throws IOException

public String readUTF() throws IOException
```

The following methods are defined in the `DataOutput` interface:

```
public void writeByte(byte b) throws IOException

public void writeShort(short s) throws IOException

public void writeInt(int i) throws IOException

public void writeLong(long l) throws IOException

public void writeFloat(float f) throws IOException

public void writeDouble(double d) throws IOException

public void writeChar(char c) throws IOException

public void writeBoolean(boolean b) throws IOException

public void writeBytes(String string) throws IOException

public void writeChars(String string) throws IOException

public void writeUTF(String string) throws IOException
```

Data streams are used as wrappers on existing input and output streams to filter data in the original stream. They are created using the following constructors:

```
public DataInputStream(InputStream instream)

public DataOutputStream(OutputStream outstream)
```

The statements given below create data streams. The first statement creates an input stream for file **in.dat**; the second statement creates an output stream for file **out.dat**.

```
DataInputStream infile =
  new DataInputStream(new FileInputStream("in.dat"));

DataOutputStream outfile =
  new DataOutputStream(new FileOutputStream("out.dat"));
```

Example 15.2 Using Data Streams

This example presents a program that creates 10 random integers, stores them in a data file, retrieves data from the file, and then displays the integers on the console. Figure 15.6 contains a sample run of the program.

```
// TestDataStreams.java: Create a file, store it in binary form, and
// display it on the console
import java.io.*;

public class TestDataStreams
{
  // Main method
  public static void main(String[] args)
  {
    // Declare data input and output streams
    DataInputStream dis = null;
    DataOutputStream dos = null;

    // Construct a temp file
    File tempFile = new File("mytemp.dat");

    // Check if the temp file exists
    if (tempFile.exists())
```

continues

Example 15.2 continued

```
      {
        System.out.println("The file mytemp.dat already exists,"
          + " delete it, rerun the program");
        System.exit(0);
      }

      // Write data
      try
      {
        // Create data output stream for tempFile
        dos = new DataOutputStream(new FileOutputStream(tempFile));
        for (int i=0; i<10; i++)
          dos.writeInt((int)(Math.random()*1000));
      }
      catch (IOException ex)
      {
        System.out.println(ex.getMessage());
      }
      finally
      {
        try
        {
          // Close files
          if (dos != null) dos.close();
        }
        catch (IOException ex)
        {
        }
      }

      // Read data
      try
      {
        // Create data input stream
        dis = new DataInputStream(new FileInputStream(tempFile));
        for (int i=0; i<10; i++)
          System.out.print("  " + dis.readInt());
      }
      catch (FileNotFoundException ex)
      {
        System.out.println("File not found");
      }
      catch (IOException ex)
      {
        System.out.println(ex.getMessage());

      }
      finally
      {
        try
        {
          // Close files
          if (dis != null) dis.close();
        }
        catch (IOException ex)
        {
          System.out.println(ex);
        }
      }
    }
  }
```

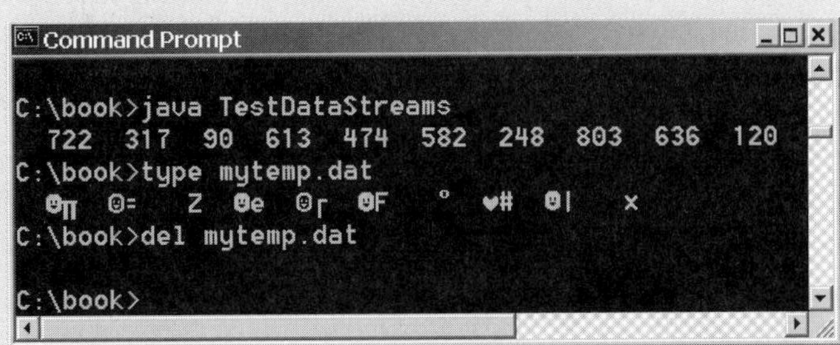

Figure 15.6 *The program creates 10 random numbers and stores them in a file named mytemp.dat. It then reads the data from the file and displays them on the console.*

Example Review

The program creates a `DataInputStream` object `dis` wrapped on `FileInputStream` and creates a `DataOutputStream` object `dos` wrapped on `FileOutputStream` (see Figure 15.7).

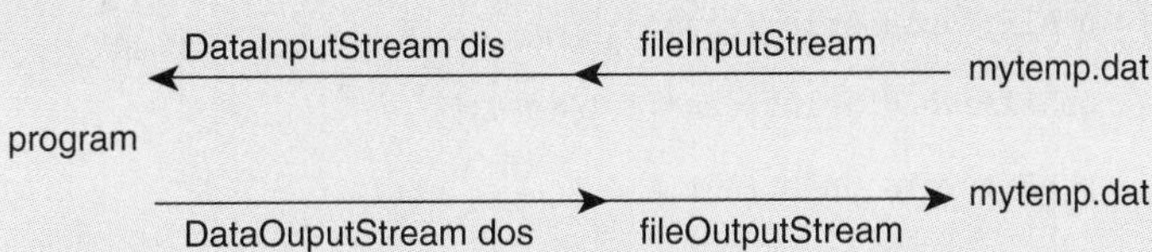

Figure 15.7 *The program uses `DataOutputStream` to write data to a file and `DataInputStream` to read the data from the file.*

The program uses a temporary file to store data. The temporary file is named **mytemp.dat**. The program first creates **mytemp.dat** if it does not exist. Then it writes 10 random integers into **mytemp.dat,** using the data output stream, and closes the stream.

The program creates a data input stream for **mytemp.dat**, reads integers from it, and displays it.

NOTE

The data stored in **mytemp.dat** are in binary format, which is machine-independent and portable. If you need to transport data between different systems, use data input and data output streams.

Print Streams

A data output stream outputs a binary representation of data, so you cannot view its contents as text. As shown in Figure 15.6, when you attempt to view the **mytemp.dat** file on the console, strange symbols are displayed. In Java, you can use print streams to output data into files. These files can be viewed as text.

The PrintStream and PrintWriter classes provide this functionality. You have already used System.out.println to display data on the console. An instance of PrintStream, out, is defined in the java.lang.System class. PrintStream and PrintWriter have similar methods. PrintStream is deprecated in JDK 1.1, but the System.out standard output stream is not, so you can continue to use it for output to the console.

Here are the constructors for PrintWriter:

```
public PrintWriter(Writer out)

public PrintWriter(Writer out, boolean autoFlush)

public PrintWriter(OutputStream out)

public PrintWriter(OutputStream out, boolean autoFlush)
```

The methods in PrintWriter are as follows:

```
public void print(Object o)

public void print(String s)

public void print(char c)

public void print(char[] cArray)

public void print(int i)

public void print(long l)

public void print(float f)

public void print(double d)

public void print(boolean b)
```

You can replace print with println. The println method, which prints the object, is followed by a new line. When an object is passed to print or println, the object's toString() method converts it to a String object.

Example 15.3 Using Print Streams

The program in this example creates 10 random integers and stores them in a text data file. The file can be viewed on the console by using an OS command, such as type on Windows or cat on UNIX. Figure 15.8 contains the output of a sample run of the program.

```
// TestPrintWriters.java: Create a text file using PrintWriter
import java.io.*;

public class TestPrintWriters
{
  // Main method: args[0] is the output file
  public static void main(String[] args)
  {
    // Declare print stream
    PrintWriter pw = null;
```

```
    // Check usage
    if (args.length != 1)
    {
      System.out.println("Usage: java TestPrintWriters file");
      System.exit(0);
    }

    File tempFile = new File(args[0]);

    if (tempFile.exists())
    {
      System.out.println("The file " + args[0] +
        " already exists, delete it, rerun the program");
      System.exit(0);
    }

    // Write data
    try
    {
      // Create data output stream for tempFile
      pw = new PrintWriter(new FileOutputStream(tempFile), true);
      for (int i=0; i<10; i++)
        pw.print(" "+(int)(Math.random()*1000));
    }
    catch (IOException ex)
    {
      System.out.println(ex.getMessage());
    }
    finally
    {
      // Close files
      if (pw != null) pw.close();
    }
  }
}
```

```
Command Prompt
C:\book>java TestPrintWriters
Usage: java TestPrintWriters file

C:\book>java TestPrintWriters t.dat

C:\book>type t.dat
 291 813 6 20 566 475 417 999 299 519
C:\book>
```

Figure 15.8 *The program creates 10 random numbers and stores them in a text file.*

Example Review

The program creates a print stream, `pw`, of `PrintWriter`—wrapped in `FileOutputStream`—for text format (see Figure 15.9).

The program creates the file **args[0]** if that file does not already exist. It writes 10 random integers into the file by using the data output stream, then closes the stream.

continues

Example 15.3 continued

Figure 15.9 *The program uses the `PrintWriter` stream, which is wrapped in `FileOutputStream`, to write data in text format.*

The output into the file is in text format. The data can be seen using the **type** command in DOS.

Buffered Streams

Java introduces buffered streams that speed input and output by reducing the number of reads and writes. Buffered streams employ a buffered array of bytes or characters that acts as a cache. In the case of input, the array reads a chunk of bytes or characters into the buffer before the individual bytes or characters are read. In the case of output, the array accumulates a block of bytes or characters before writing the entire block to the output stream.

The use of buffered streams enables you to read and write a chunk of bytes or characters at once instead of reading or writing the bytes or characters one at a time. The `BufferedInputStream`, `BufferedOutputStream`, `BufferedReader`, and `BufferedWriter` classes provide this functionality.

The following constructors are used to create a buffered stream:

```
public BufferedInputStream(InputStream in)

public BufferedInputStream(InputStream in, int bufferSize)

public BufferedOutputStream(OutputStream in)

public BufferedOutputStream(OutputStream in, int bufferSize)

public BufferedReader(Reader in)

public BufferedReader(Reader in, int bufferSize)

public BufferedWriter(Writer out)

public BufferedWriter(Writer out, int bufferSize)
```

If no buffer size is specified, the default size is 512 bytes or characters. A buffered input stream reads as many data as possible into its buffer in a single read call. By contrast, a buffered output stream calls the write method only when its buffer fills up or when the `flush()` method is called.

The buffered stream classes inherit methods from their superclasses. In addition to using the methods from their superclasses, `BufferedReader` has a `readLine()` method to read a line.

Example 15.4 Displaying a File in a Text Area

This example presents a program that views a file in a text area. The user enters a filename in a text field and clicks the View button; the file is then displayed in a text area. Figure 15.10 contains the output of a sample run of the program.

```
// ViewFile.java: Read a text file and store it in a text area
import java.awt.*;
import java.awt.event.*;
import java.io.*;
import javax.swing.*;

public class ViewFile extends JFrame implements ActionListener
{
  // Button to view view
  private JButton jbtView = new JButton("View");

  // Text field to receive file name
  private JTextField jtfFilename = new JTextField(12);

  // Text area to display file
  private JTextArea jtaFile = new JTextArea();

  // Main method
  public static void main(String[] args)
  {
    ViewFile frame = new ViewFile();
    frame.setTitle("View File");
    frame.setSize(400, 300);
    frame.setVisible(true);
  }

  // Constructor
  public ViewFile()
  {
    // Panel p to hold a label, a text field, and a button
    Panel p = new Panel();
    p.setLayout(new BorderLayout());
    p.add(new Label("Filename"), BorderLayout.WEST);
    p.add(jtfFilename, BorderLayout.CENTER);
    jtfFilename.setBackground(Color.yellow);
    jtfFilename.setForeground(Color.red);
    p.add(jbtView, BorderLayout.EAST);

    // Add jtaFile to a scroll pane
    JScrollPane jsp = new JScrollPane(jtaFile);

    // Add jsp and p to the frame
    getContentPane().add(jsp, BorderLayout.CENTER);
    getContentPane().add(p, BorderLayout.SOUTH);

    // Register listener
    jbtView.addActionListener(this);
  }

  // Handle the "View" button
  public void actionPerformed(ActionEvent e)
  {
    if (e.getSource() == jbtView)
      showFile();
  }

  // Display the file in the text area
  private void showFile()
  {
```

continues

Example 15.4 continued

```
      // Use a BufferedReader to read text from the file
      BufferedReader infile = null;

      // Get file name from the text field
      String filename = jtfFilename.getText().trim();
      String inLine;

      try
      {
        // Create a buffered stream
        infile = new BufferedReader(new FileReader(filename));

        // Read a line and append the line to the text area
        while ((inLine = infile.readLine()) != null)
        {
          jtaFile.append(inLine + '\n');
        }
      }
      catch (FileNotFoundException ex)
      {
        System.out.println("File not found: " + filename);
      }
      catch (IOException ex)
      {
        System.out.println(ex.getMessage());
      }
      finally
      {
        try
        {
          if (infile != null) infile.close();
        }
        catch (IOException ex)
        {
          System.out.println(ex.getMessage());
        }
      }
    }
  }
```

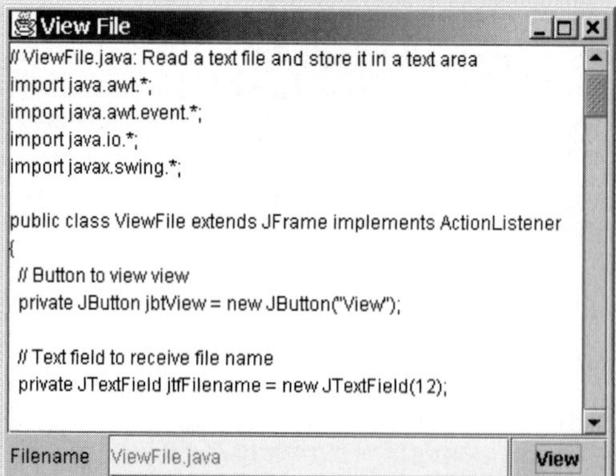

Figure 15.10 *The program displays the specified file in the text area.*

Example Review

The user enters a filename into the Filename text field. When the View button is pressed, the program gets the input filename from the text field; it then creates a data input stream. The data are read one line at a time and appended to the text area for display.

The program uses a `BufferedReader` stream to read lines from a buffer. Instead of using `BufferedReader` and `Reader` classes, the `BufferedInputStream` and `FileInputStream` can also be used in this example.

You are encouraged to rewrite the program without using buffers and then compare the performance of the two programs. This will show you the improvement in performance obtained by using buffers when reading from a large file.

This program reads a file from the local machine, so you have to write it as a Java application. Example 16.6, "Retrieving Remote Files," in Chapter 16, "Networking," gives another program that allows reading from a file on a remote host.

Tip

Since physical input and output involving I/O devices are typically very slow compared with CPU processing speeds, you should use buffered input/output streams to improve performance.

File Dialogs

Swing provides `javax.swing.JFileChooser`, which displays a dialog box from which the user can navigate through the file system and select files to load or save, as shown in Figure 15.11.

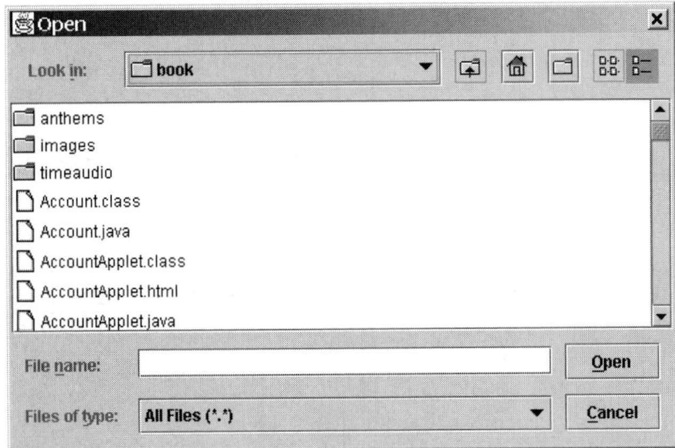

Figure 15.11 *The Swing* `JFileChooser` *shows files and directories, and enables the user to navigate through the file system visually.*

The file dialog box is modal; when displayed, it blocks the rest of the application until it disappears. The file dialog box can appear in two types: *open* and *save*. The *open type* is for opening a file, and the *save type* is for storing a file.

There are several ways to construct a file dialog box. The simplest is to use the `JFileChooser`'s default constructor.

`JFileChooser` is a subclass of `JComponent`. The `JFileChooser` class has the properties inherited from `JComponent`. Additionally, it has the following useful properties:

- `dialogType`: The type of this dialog. Use `OPEN_DIALOG` when you want to bring up a filechooser that the user can use to open a file. Likewise, use `SAVE_DIALOG` to let the user choose a file to save.
- `dialogTitle`: The string displayed in the title bar of the dialog box.
- `currentDirectory`: The current directory of the file. The type of this property is `java.io.File`. If you want the current directory to be used, use `setCurrentDirectory(new File("."))`.
- `selectedFile`: The selected file. You can use `getSelectedFile()` to return the selected file from the dialog box. The type of this property is `java.io.File`. If you have a default file name that you expect to use, use `setSelectedFile(new File(filename))`.
- `selectedFiles`: A list of selected files if the filechooser is set to allow multi-selection. The type of this property is `File[]`.
- `multiSelectionEnabled`: A `boolean` value indicating whether multiple files can be selected. By default, it is `false`.

To display the dialog box, use the following two methods:

```
public int showOpenDialog(Component parent)

public int showSaveDialog(Component parent)
```

The first method displays an "Open" dialog, and the second displays a "Save" dialog. Both methods return an `int` value `APPROVE_OPTION` or `CANCEL_OPTION`, which indicates whether the OK button or the Cancel button was clicked.

Example 15.5 Using File Dialogs

This example gives a program that creates a simple notepad using `JFileChooser` to open and save files. The notepad enables the user to open an existing file, edit the file, and save the note into the current file or to a specified file. You can display and edit the file in a text area.

A sample run of the program is shown in Figure 15.12. When you open a file, a file dialog box with the default title "Open" appears on-screen to let you select a file for loading, as shown in Figure 15.11. When you save a file, a file dialog box with the default title "Save" appears to let you select a file for saving, as shown in Figure 15.13. The status label below the text area displays the status of the file operations.

```
// FileDialogDemo.java: Demonstrate using JFileDialog to display
// file dialog boxes for opening and saving files

import java.awt.*;
import java.awt.event.*;
import java.io.*;
import javax.swing.*;

public class FileDialogDemo extends JFrame
  implements ActionListener
{
  // Menu items Open, Save, exit, and About
  private JMenuItem jmiOpen, jmiSave,jmiExit, jmiAbout;

  // Text area for displaying and editing text files
  private JTextArea jta = new JTextArea();

  // Status label for displaying operation status
  private JLabel jlblStatus = new JLabel();

  // File dialog box
  private JFileChooser jFileChooser = new JFileChooser();

  // Main method
  public static void main(String[] args)
  {
    FileDialogDemo frame = new FileDialogDemo();
    frame.setSize(300, 150);
    frame.setVisible(true);
  }

  public FileDialogDemo()
  {
    setTitle("Test JFileChooser");

    // Create a menu bar mb and attach to the frame
    JMenuBar mb = new JMenuBar();
    setJMenuBar(mb);

    // Add a "File" menu in mb
    JMenu fileMenu = new JMenu("File");
    mb.add(fileMenu);

    //add a "Help" menu in mb
    JMenu helpMenu = new JMenu("Help");
    mb.add(helpMenu);

    // Create and add menu items to the menu
    fileMenu.add(jmiOpen = new JMenuItem("Open"));
    fileMenu.add(jmiSave = new JMenuItem("Save"));
    fileMenu.addSeparator();
    fileMenu.add(jmiExit = new JMenuItem("Exit"));
    helpMenu.add(jmiAbout = new JMenuItem("About"));

    // Set default directory to the current directory
    jFileChooser.setCurrentDirectory(new File("."));

    // Set BorderLayout for the frame
    getContentPane().add(new JScrollPane(jta),
      BorderLayout.CENTER);
    getContentPane().add(jlblStatus, BorderLayout.SOUTH);

    // Register listeners
    jmiOpen.addActionListener(this);
```

continues

Example 15.5 continued

```
    jmiSave.addActionListener(this);
    jmiAbout.addActionListener(this);
    jmiExit.addActionListener(this);
  }

  // Handle ActionEvent for menu items
  public void actionPerformed(ActionEvent e)
  {
    String actionCommand = e.getActionCommand();

    if (e.getSource() instanceof JMenuItem)
    {
      if ("Open".equals(actionCommand))
        open();
      else if ("Save".equals(actionCommand))
        save();
      else if ("About".equals(actionCommand))
        JOptionPane.showMessageDialog(this,
          "Demonstrate Using File Dialogs",
          "About This Demo",
          JOptionPane.INFORMATION_MESSAGE);
      else if ("Exit".equals(actionCommand))
        System.exit(0);
    }
  }

  // Open file
  private void open()
  {
    if (jFileChooser.showOpenDialog(this) ==
      JFileChooser.APPROVE_OPTION)
    {
      open(jFileChooser.getSelectedFile());
    }
  }

  // Open file with the specified File instance
  private void open(File file)
  {
    try
    {
      // Read from the specified file and store it in jta
      BufferedInputStream in = new BufferedInputStream(
        new FileInputStream(file));
      byte[] b = new byte[in.available()];
      in.read(b, 0, b.length);
      jta.append(new String(b, 0, b.length));
      in.close();

      // Display the status of the Open file operation in jlblStatus
      jlblStatus.setText(file.getName() + " Opened");
    }
    catch (IOException ex)
    {
      jlblStatus.setText("Error opening " + file.getName());
    }
  }

  // Save file
  private void save()
  {
    if (jFileChooser.showSaveDialog(this) ==
      JFileChooser.APPROVE_OPTION)
```

```
      {
        save(jFileChooser.getSelectedFile());
      }
    }

    // Save file with specified File instance
    private void save(File file)
    {
      try
      {
        // Write the text in jta to the specified file
        BufferedOutputStream out = new BufferedOutputStream(
          new FileOutputStream(file));
        byte[] b = (jta.getText()).getBytes();
        out.write(b, 0, b.length);
        out.close();

        // Display the status of the save file operation in jlblStatus
        jlblStatus.setText(file.getName()  + " Saved ");
      }
      catch (IOException ex)
      {
        jlblStatus.setText("Error saving " + file.getName());
      }
    }
  }
```

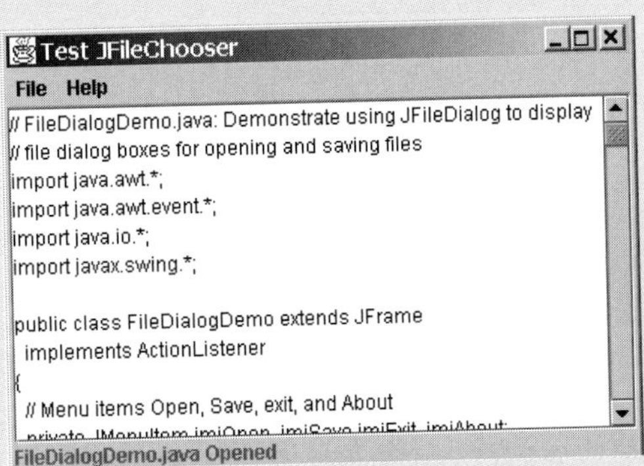

Figure 15.12 *The program enables you to open, save, and edit files.*

Example Review

The program creates the File and Help menus. The File menu contains the menu commands Open for loading a file, Save for saving a file, and Exit for terminating the program. The Help menu contains the menu command About to display a message about the program, as shown in Figure 15.14.

An instance `jFileChooser` of `JFileChooser` is created for displaying the file dialog box to open and save files. The `setCurrentDirectory(new File("."))` method is used to set the current directory to the directory where the class is stored.

continues

Example 15.5 continued

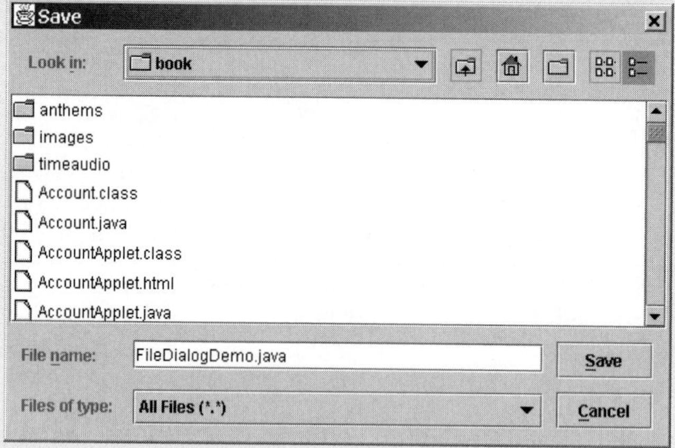

Figure 15.13 *The Save dialog box enables you to save to a new file or an existing file.*

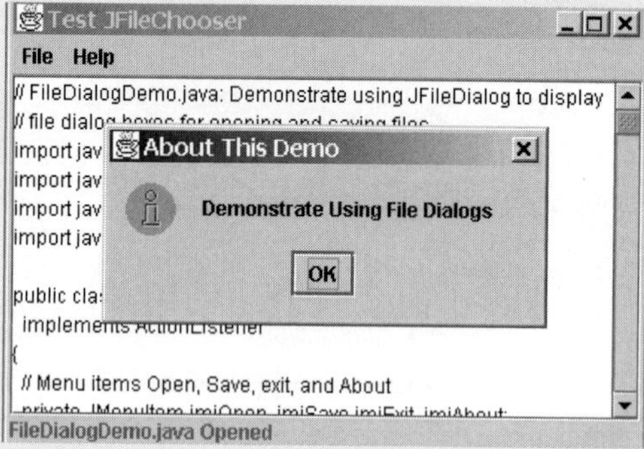

Figure 15.14 *Clicking the About menu item displays a message dialog box.*

The `open()` method is invoked when the user clicks the Open menu command. The `showOpenDialog()` method displays an Open dialog box, as shown in Figure 15.11. Upon receiving the selected file, the method `open(file)` is invoked to load the file to the text area, using a `BufferedInputStream` wrapped on a `FileInputStream`.

The `save()` method is invoked when the user clicks the Save menu command. The `showSaveDialog()` method displays a Save dialog box, as shown in Figure 15.13. Upon receiving the selected file, the method `save(file)` is invoked to save the contents from the text area to the file, using a `BufferedOutputStream` wrapped on a `FileOutputStream`.

Text Input and Output on the Console

There are two types of *interactive I/O*. One involves simple input from the keyboard and simple output in a pure text form. The other involves input and output in a graphical environment. The former is referred to as *text interactive I/O*, and the latter as *graphical interactive I/O*.

Graphical interactive I/O takes an entirely different approach from text interactive I/O. In the graphical environment, input can be received from an UI component, such as a text field, text area, list, combo box, check box, or radio button. It can also be received from a keystroke or a mouse movement. Output is usually displayed in the panel, in text fields, or in text areas.

Now turn your attention to text I/O. In all of the preceding chapters, you used text input and output with the `System` class. The `System` class contains three I/O objects: `System.in`, `System.out`, and `System.err`. The objects `in`, `out`, and `err` are static variables. The variable `in` is of `InputStream` type, and `out` and `err` are of `PrintStream` type. These are the basic objects that all Java programmers use to input from the keyboard, output to the screen, and display error messages.

To perform console output, you can use any of the methods for `PrintStream` in `System.out`. However, keyboard input is not directly supported in Java. In order to get input from the keyboard, you first use the following statements to read a string from the keyboard.

```
BufferedReader br
  = new BufferedReader(new InputStreamReader(System.in), 1);

// Declare and initialize the string
String string = " ";

// Get the string from the keyboard
try
{
  string = br.readLine();
}
catch (IOException ex)
{
  System.out.println(ex);
}
```

You can then parse the string into `byte`, `short`, `int`, `long`, `float`, or `double`.

Chapter 2, "Primitive Data Types and Operations," introduced the `MyInput` class for getting a string, int, and double from the keyboard. The following is an expanded version of the `MyInput` class for reading a string and all types of primitive data values.

```
// MyInput.java: Contain the methods for reading int, double, and
// string values from the keyboard
import java.io.*;

public class MyInput
{
  // Read a string from the keyboard
```

```
  public static String readString()
  {
    BufferedReader br
      = new BufferedReader(new InputStreamReader(System.in), 1);

    // Declare and initialize the string
    String string = " ";

    // Get the string from the keyboard
    try
    {
      string = br.readLine();
    }
    catch (IOException ex)
    {
      System.out.println(ex);
    }

    // Return the string obtained from the keyboard
    return string;
  }

  // Read an int value from the keyboard
  public static int readInt()
  {
    return Integer.parseInt(readString());
  }

  // Read a double value from the keyboard
  public static double readDouble()
  {
    return Double.parseDouble(readString());
  }

  // Read a byte value from the keyboard
  public static byte readByte()
  {
    return Byte.parseByte(readString());
  }

  // Read a short value from the keyboard
  public static short readShort()
  {
    return Short.parseShort(readString());
  }

  // Read a long value from the keyboard
  public static long readLong()
  {
    return Long.parseLong(readString());
  }

  // Read a float value from the keyboard
  public static float readFloat()
  {
    return Float.parseFloat(readString());
  }
}
```

NOTE

JavaSoft knows that some brands of PCs running Windows 95 are prone to cause input problems if the buffer size for the `BufferedReader` stream `br` is not set to 1. Therefore, the buffer size of 1 is purposely chosen to help eliminate input problems.

Object Streams

Thus far, this chapter has covered input and output of bytes, characters, and primitive data types. Object streams enable you to perform input and output at the object level. To enable an object to be read or written, the object's defining class has to implement the `java.io.Serializable` interface or the `java.io.Externalizable` interface. The `Serializable` interface is a marker interface. It has no methods, so you don't need to add additional code in your class that implements `Serializable`. Implementing this interface enables the Java serialization mechanism to automate the process of storing the objects and arrays.

To appreciate this automation feature and understand how an object is stored, consider what you need to do in order to store an object without using this feature. Suppose you want to store an object of the `MessagePanel` class in Example 8.5, "Using `FontMetrics`." To do this you need to store all the current values of the properties in a `MessagePanel` object. The properties defined in `MessagePanel` are `message (String)`, `centered (boolean)`, `xCoordinate (int)`, and `yCoordinate (int)`. Since `MessagePanel` is a subclass of `JPanel`, the property values of `JPanel` have to be stored as well as the properties of all the superclasses of `JPanel`. If a property is of an object type, storing it requires storing all the property values inside this object. As you can see, this is a very tedious process. Fortunately, you don't have to go through this process manually. Java provides a built-in mechanism to automate the process of writing objects. This process is referred to as *object serialization*. In contrast, the process of reading objects is referred to as *object deserialization*.

The `ObjectOutputStream` class is used for storing objects, and the `ObjectInputStream` class is used for restoring objects. These two classes are built upon several other classes. Figure 15.15 shows the hierarchic relationship of these related classes.

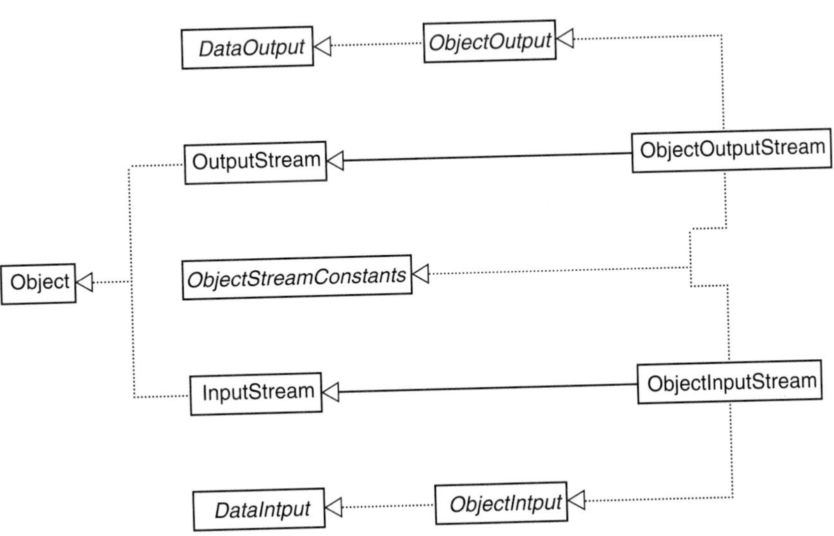

Figure 15.15 *`ObjectOutputStream` extends `OutputStream` and implements `ObjectOutput` and `ObjectStreamConstants`. `ObjectInputStream` extends `InputStream` and implements `ObjectInput` and `ObjectStreamConstants`.*

`ObjectOutputStream` implements `ObjectOutput`, which inherits `DataOutput`. `DataOutput` provides methods for writing Java primitive-data-type values. `ObjectOutput` extends `DataOutput` to include output of objects, arrays, and strings. An `ObjectOutputStream` writes Java primitive-data-type values and objects to an `OutputStream`. Persistent storage can be accomplished using a file for the stream. The format of the output is platform-independent. The `OutputStream` can also be a network socket stream, which will be introduced in Chapter 16, "Networking."

`ObjectInputStream` is an inverse of `ObjectOutputStream`. `ObjectInputStream` implements `ObjectInput`, which inherits `DataInput`. `DataInput` provides methods for reading primitive-data-type values. `ObjectInput` extends `DataInput` to include input of objects, arrays, and strings. An `ObjectInputStream` reads the data previously written using an `ObjectOutputStream` with a file stream or a network socket stream.

Only objects that support the `java.io.Serializable` interface or the `java.io.Externalizable` interface can use `ObjectOutputStream` and `ObjectInputStream`. For information on using the `Externalizable` interface, please refer to *Rapid Java Application Development Using JBuilder 3*.

All the JavaBeans components implement `Serializable`, so they are serializable. The method `writeObject(obj)` is used to write an object to the `ObjectOutputStream`, and `readObject()` is used to read an object from the `ObjectInputStream`. Attempting to store an object that does not support the `Serializable` interface would cause `NotSerializableException`.

When a serializable object is stored, the class of the object is encoded; this includes the class name and the signature of the class, the values of the object's fields and arrays, and the closure of any other objects referenced from the initial object. When a primitive-data-type value is stored, appropriate methods, such as `writeInt()`, `writeBoolean()` in the `DataOuput` interface, are used. Multiple objects or primitives can be written to the stream. The objects must be read back from the corresponding `ObjectInputStream` with the same types and in the same order as they were written. Java's safe casting should be used to get the desired type. For instance, when reading an object of the `MessagePanel` class, the object should be cast to `MessagePanel`.

Here is an example of creating an `ObjectOutputStream` and storing an object `messagePanel` of `MessagePanel` and an `int` value to the file named **object.dat.**

```
ObjectOutputStream out = new ObjectOutputStream(
  new FileOutputStream("object.dat"));
out.writeObject(messagePanel);
out.writeInt(5);
```

The corresponding code to restore the object and the `int` value is shown below.

```
ObjectInputStream in = new ObjectInputStream(new FileInputStream(
  "object.dat"));
MessagePanel c = (MessagePanel)in.readObject();
int x = in.readInt();
```

Example 15.6 Testing Object Streams

This example creates a program to manipulate `MessagePanel`, as shown in Figure 15.16. You will use radio buttons to set the background color, and two buttons, <= and =>, to move the message to left and right. The Store button is provided to save a `MessagePanel` object, and the Restore button is used to reload the saved `MessagePanel` object.

```
// ObjectStreamDemo.java: Demonstrate store and restore objects
import java.awt.*;
import java.awt.event.*;
import javax.swing.*;
import java.io.*;
import java.util.Date;

public class ObjectStreamDemo extends JFrame
  implements ActionListener
{
  // Radio buttons for selecting a color for the message
  JRadioButton jrbRed = new JRadioButton("Red");
  JRadioButton jrbGreen = new JRadioButton("Green");
  JRadioButton jrbYellow = new JRadioButton("Yellow");

  // Buttons for Store, Restore, Left, and Right
  JButton jbtStore = new JButton("Store");
  JButton jbtRestore = new JButton("Restore");
  JButton jbtLeft = new JButton("<=");
  JButton jbtRight = new JButton("=>");

  // Status label to display date when the object is stored
  JLabel jlbStatusBar = new JLabel();

  // Create a MessagePanel instance
  MessagePanel messagePanel = new MessagePanel();

  // Panel for holding radio buttons, message panel, and buttons
  JPanel jpSerialization = new JPanel();

  // Construct the frame
  public ObjectStreamDemo()
  {
    // Create a panel to group radio buttons
    JPanel jpRadioButtons = new JPanel();
    jpRadioButtons.add(jrbRed);
    jpRadioButtons.add(jrbGreen);
    jpRadioButtons.add(jrbYellow);

    // Group radio buttons
    ButtonGroup btg = new ButtonGroup();
    btg.add(jrbRed);
    btg.add(jrbGreen);
    btg.add(jrbYellow);

    // Create a panel to group buttons
    JPanel jpButtons = new JPanel();
    jpButtons.add(jbtStore);
    jpButtons.add(jbtRestore);
    jpButtons.add(jbtLeft);
    jpButtons.add(jbtRight);

    // Group jpRadioButtons, messagePanel, and jpButtons
    jpSerialization.setLayout(new BorderLayout());
```

continues

Example 15.6 continued

```
      jpSerialization.add(jpRadioButtons, BorderLayout.NORTH);
      jpSerialization.add(messagePanel, BorderLayout.CENTER);
      jpSerialization.add(jpButtons, BorderLayout.SOUTH);

      // Set borders
      jpRadioButtons.setBorder(BorderFactory.createEtchedBorder());
      jpButtons.setBorder(BorderFactory.createEtchedBorder());
      messagePanel.setBorder(BorderFactory.createRaisedBevelBorder());

      // Add jpSerializaton and jlbStatusBar to the frame
      Container container = getContentPane();
      container.add(jlbStatusBar, BorderLayout.SOUTH);
      container.add(jpSerialization, BorderLayout.CENTER);

      // Register listeners
      jrbRed.addActionListener(this);
      jrbGreen.addActionListener(this);
      jrbYellow.addActionListener(this);
      jbtStore.addActionListener(this);
      jbtRestore.addActionListener(this);
      jbtLeft.addActionListener(this);
      jbtRight.addActionListener(this);
    }

    // Handle action events
    public void actionPerformed(ActionEvent e)
    {
      if (e.getSource() == jrbRed)
        messagePanel.setBackground(Color.red);
      else if (e.getSource() == jrbGreen)
        messagePanel.setBackground(Color.green);
      else if (e.getSource() == jrbYellow)
        messagePanel.setBackground(Color.yellow);
      else if (e.getSource() == jbtStore)
      {
        try
        {
          ObjectOutputStream out =
            new ObjectOutputStream(new FileOutputStream("object.dat"));
          out.writeObject(messagePanel);
          out.writeObject(new Date());
          out.close();
          jlbStatusBar.setText("The object is stored in object.dat");
        }
        catch (IOException ex)
        {
          System.out.println(ex);
        }
      }
      else if (e.getSource() == jbtRestore)
      {
        try
        {
          ObjectInputStream in =
            new ObjectInputStream(new FileInputStream("object.dat"));
          MessagePanel c = (MessagePanel)in.readObject();
          Date d = (Date)in.readObject();
          jpSerialization.remove(messagePanel);
          messagePanel = c;
          jpSerialization.add(messagePanel, BorderLayout.CENTER);
          jpSerialization.repaint();
          in.close();
          jlbStatusBar.setText("The object saved at " + d.toString()
```

```
            + " is restored");
      }
      catch (IOException ex1)
      {
        System.out.println(ex1);
      }
      catch (ClassNotFoundException ex2)
      {
        System.out.println(ex2);
      }
    }
    else if (e.getSource() == jbtLeft)
      left();
    else if (e.getSource() == jbtRight)
      right();
  }

  // Move the message in the panel left
  private void left()
  {
    int x = messagePanel.getXCoordinate();

    if (x > 10)
    {
      // Shift the message to the left
      messagePanel.setXCoordinate(x-10);
      messagePanel.repaint();
    }
  }

  // Move the message in the panel right
  private void right()
  {
    int x = messagePanel.getXCoordinate();
    if (x < getSize().width - 20)
    {
      // Shift the message to the right
      messagePanel.setXCoordinate(x+10);
      messagePanel.repaint();
    }
  }

  // Main method
  public static void main(String[] args)
  {
    ObjectStreamDemo frame = new ObjectStreamDemo();
    frame.setTitle("Test Object Serialization");

    // frame.setDefaultCloseOperation(JFrame.EXIT_ON_CLOSE);
    frame.pack();
    frame.setVisible(true);
  }
}
```

Example Review

When you click the Store button, the current state of the `messagePanel` and the current time (`new Date()`) are saved to file **object.dat** using `ObjectOutputStream`. When you click the Restore button, these objects are read back from the same file. They must be read back in the same order as they were stored. Explicit type casting must be used to ensure that the objects read are of the right type.

continues

Example 15.6 continued

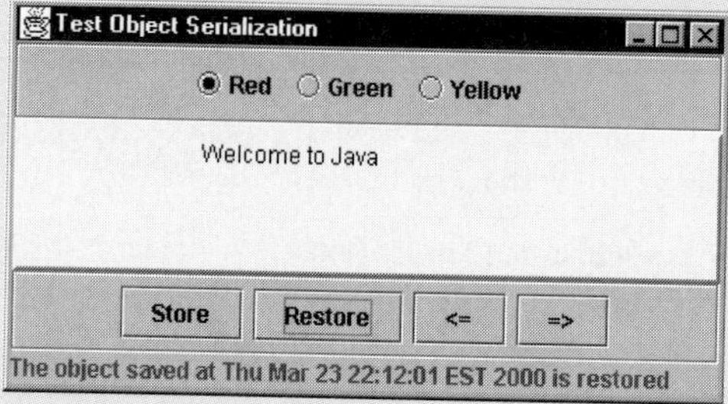

Figure 15.16 *You can use the Store button to save the* `MessagePanel` *object shown in the middle of the window, and the Restore button to reload the saved object later.*

In the handler for the Restore button, `messagePanel` was removed from `jpSerialization`, and then a new `messagePanel` was created and added to `jpSerialization`. This is necessary to ensure that the newly restored `messagePanel` is used in the windows, not the old copy.

Like many Java classes, `java.awt.Component` and `java.util.Date` implement `java.io.Serializable`, so the objects of these classes or their subclasses can be stored using object streams.

By default, all the nonstatic properties of a serialized object are written to the object stream. However, not all the nonstatic properties can be serialized. For example, since the `java.awt.Thread` class does not implement `Serializable`, a `Thread` object cannot be serialized. Interested readers can refer to my *Rapid Java Application Development Using JBuilder 3* for more information on how to deal with nonserializable properties.

Random Access Files

All of the streams you have used so far are known as *read-only* or *write-only* streams. The external files of these streams are sequential files that cannot be updated without creating a new file. It is often necessary to modify files or to insert new records into files. Java provides the `RandomAccessFile` class to allow a file to be read and updated at the same time.

The `RandomAccessFile` class extends `Object` and implements `DataInput` and `DataOutput` interfaces. Because `DataInputStream` implements the `DataInput` interface and `DataOutputStream` implements the `DataOutput` interface, many methods in `RandomAccessFile` are the same as those in `DataInputStream` and `DataOutputStream`. For example, `readInt()`, `readLong()`, `readDouble()`, `readUTF()`, `writeInt()`, `writeLong()`, `writeDouble()`, and `writeUTF()` can be used in data input streams or data output streams as well as in `RandomAccessFile` streams.

Additionally, `RandomAccessFile` provides the following methods to deal with random access:

- `public void seek(long pos) throws IOException`

This method sets the offset from the beginning of the `RandomAccessFile` stream to where the next read or write occurs.

- `public long getFilePointer() throws IOException`

  This method returns the offset, in bytes, from the beginning of the file to where the next read or write occurs.

- `public long length() throws IOException`

  This method returns the length of the file.

- `public final void writeChar(int v) throws IOException`

  This method writes a character to the file as a two-byte Unicode, with the higher byte written first.

- `public final void writeChars(String s) throws IOException`

  This method writes a string to the file as a sequence of characters.

When creating a `RandomAccessFile` stream, you can specify one of two modes (`"r"` or `"rw"`). Mode `"r"` means that the stream is read-only, and mode `"rw"` indicates that the stream allows both read and write. For example, the following statement creates a new stream, `raf`, that allows the program to read from and write to the file **test.dat**:

```
RandomAccessFile raf = new RandomAccessFile("test.dat", "rw");
```

If **test.dat** already exists, `raf` is created to access it; if **test.dat** does not exist, a new file named **test.dat** is created, and `raf` is created to access the new file. The method `raf.length()` indicates the number of bytes in **test.dat** at any given time. If you append new data into the file, `raf.length()` increases.

Note

When you use `writeChar()` to write a character or `writeChars()` to write characters, a character occupies two bytes.

Tip

Open the file with the `"r"` mode if the file is not intended to be modified. This prevents unintentional modification of the file.

Random access files are often used to process files of records. For convenience, fixed-length records are used in random access files so that a record can be located easily. A record consists of a fixed number of fields. A field can be a string or a primitive data type. A string in a fixed-length record has a maximum size. If a string is smaller than the maximum size, the rest of the string is padded with blanks.

Example 15.7 Using Random Access Files

This example presents a program that registers students and displays student information. The user interface consists of a tabbed pane with two tabs: Register Student and View Student. The Register Student tab enables you to store a student in the file, as shown in Figure 15.17. The View Student tab enables you to browse through student information, as shown in Figure 15.18.

The program is given as follows.

```
// TestRandomAccessFile.java: Store and read data
// using RandomAccessFile
import java.io.*;
import java.awt.*;
import java.awt.event.*;
import javax.swing.*;
import javax.swing.border.*;

public class TestRandomAccessFile extends JFrame
{
  // Create a tabbed pane to hold two panels
  private JTabbedPane jtpStudent = new JTabbedPane();

  // Random access file for access the student.dat file
  private RandomAccessFile raf;

  // Main method
  public static void main(String[] args)
  {
    TestRandomAccessFile frame = new TestRandomAccessFile();
    frame.pack();
    frame.setTitle("Test RandomAccessFile");
    frame.setVisible(true);
  }

  // Default constructor
  public TestRandomAccessFile()
  {
    // Open or create a random access file
    try
    {
      raf = new RandomAccessFile("student.dat", "rw");
    }
    catch(IOException ex)
    {
      System.out.print("Error: " + ex);
      System.exit(0);
    }

    // Place buttons in the tabbed pane
    jtpStudent.add(new RegisterStudent(raf), "Register Student");
    jtpStudent.add(new ViewStudent(raf), "View Student");

    // Add the tabbed pane to the frame
    getContentPane().add(jtpStudent);
  }
}

// Register student panel
class RegisterStudent extends JPanel implements ActionListener
{
  // Button for registering a student
  private JButton jbtRegister;

  // Student information panel
```

```
private StudentPanel studentPanel;

// Random access file
private RandomAccessFile raf;

// Constructor
public RegisterStudent(RandomAccessFile raf)
{
  // Pass raf to RegisterStudent Panel
  this.raf = raf;

  // Add studentPanel and jbtRegister in the panel
  setLayout(new BorderLayout());
  add(studentPanel = new StudentPanel(),
    BorderLayout.CENTER);
  add(jbtRegister = new JButton("Register"),
    BorderLayout.SOUTH);

  // Register listener
  jbtRegister.addActionListener(this);
}

// Handle button actions
public void actionPerformed(ActionEvent e)
{
  if (e.getSource() == jbtRegister)
  {
    Student student = studentPanel.getStudent();

    try
    {
      raf.seek(raf.length());
      student.writeStudent(raf);
    }
    catch(IOException ex)
    {
      System.out.print("Error: " + ex);
    }
  }
}
}

// View student panel
class ViewStudent extends JPanel implements ActionListener
{
  // Buttons for viewing student information
  private JButton jbtFirst, jbtNext, jbtPrevious, jbtLast;

  // Random access file
  private RandomAccessFile raf = null;

  // Current student record
  private Student student = new Student();

  // Create a student panel
  private StudentPanel studentPanel = new StudentPanel();

  // File pointer in the random access file
  private long lastPos;
  private long currentPos;

  // Constructor
  public ViewStudent(RandomAccessFile raf)
  {
```

continues

Example 15.7 continued

```
    // Pass raf to ViewStudent
    this.raf = raf;

    // Panel p to hold four navigator buttons
    JPanel p = new JPanel();
    p.setLayout(new FlowLayout(FlowLayout.LEFT));
    p.add(jbtFirst = new JButton("First"));
    p.add(jbtNext = new JButton("Next"));
    p.add(jbtPrevious = new JButton("Previous"));
    p.add(jbtLast = new JButton("Last"));

    // Add panel p and studentPanel to ViewPanel
    setLayout(new BorderLayout());
    add(studentPanel, BorderLayout.CENTER);
    add(p, BorderLayout.SOUTH);

    // Register listeners
    jbtFirst.addActionListener(this);
    jbtNext.addActionListener(this);
    jbtPrevious.addActionListener(this);
    jbtLast.addActionListener(this);
  }

  // Handle navigation button actions
  public void actionPerformed(ActionEvent e)
  {
    String actionCommand = e.getActionCommand();
    if (e.getSource() instanceof JButton)
    {
      try
      {
        if ("First".equals(actionCommand))
        {
          if (raf.length() > 0)
            retrieve(0);
        }
        else if ("Next".equals(actionCommand))
        {
          currentPos = raf.getFilePointer();
          if (currentPos < raf.length())
            retrieve(currentPos);
        }
        else if ("Previous".equals(actionCommand))
        {
          currentPos = raf.getFilePointer();
          if (currentPos > 0)
            retrieve(currentPos - 2*2*Student.RECORD_SIZE);
        }
        else if ("Last".equals(actionCommand))
        {

          lastPos = raf.length();
          if (lastPos > 0)
            retrieve(lastPos - 2*Student.RECORD_SIZE);
        }
      }
      catch(IOException ex)
      {
        System.out.print("Error: " + ex);
      }
    }
  }

  // Retrieve a record at specified position
```

```
  public void retrieve(long pos)
  {
    try
    {
      raf.seek(pos);
      student.readStudent(raf);
      studentPanel.setStudent(student);
    }
    catch(IOException ex)
    {
      System.out.print("Error: " + ex);
    }
  }
}

// This class contains static methods for reading and writing
// fixed length records
class FixedLengthStringIO
{
  // Read fixed number of characters from a DataInput stream
  public static String readFixedLengthString(int size,
    DataInput in) throws IOException
  {
    char c[] = new char[size];

    for (int i=0; i<size; i++)
      c[i] = in.readChar();

    return new String(c);
  }

  // Write fixed number of characters (string s with padded spaces)
  // to a DataOutput stream
  public static void writeFixedLengthString(String s, int size,
    DataOutput out) throws IOException
  {
    char cBuffer[] = new char[size];
    s.getChars(0, s.length(), cBuffer, 0);
    for (int i=s.length(); i<cBuffer.length; i++)
      cBuffer[i] = ' ';
    String newS = new String(cBuffer);
    out.writeChars(newS);
  }
}

// StudentPanel.java: Panel for displaying student information
import javax.swing.*;
import javax.swing.border.*;
import java.awt.*;

public class StudentPanel extends JPanel
{
  JTextField jtfName = new JTextField(32);
  JTextField jtfStreet = new JTextField(32);
  JTextField jtfCity = new JTextField(20);
  JTextField jtfState = new JTextField(2);
  JTextField jtfZip = new JTextField(5);

  // Construct a student panel
  public StudentPanel()
  {
    // Set the panel with line border
    setBorder(new BevelBorder(BevelBorder.RAISED));
```

continues

Example 15.7 continued

```
    // Panel p1 for holding labels Name, Street, and City
    JPanel p1 = new JPanel();
    p1.setLayout(new GridLayout(3, 1));
    p1.add(new JLabel("Name"));
    p1.add(new JLabel("Street"));
    p1.add(new JLabel("City"));

    // Panel jpState for holding state
    JPanel jpState = new JPanel();
    jpState.setLayout(new BorderLayout());
    jpState.add(new JLabel("State"), BorderLayout.WEST);
    jpState.add(jtfState, BorderLayout.CENTER);

    // Panel jpZip for holding zip
    JPanel jpZip = new JPanel();
    jpZip.setLayout(new BorderLayout());
    jpZip.add(new JLabel("Zip"), BorderLayout.WEST);
    jpZip.add(jtfZip, BorderLayout.CENTER);

    // Panel p2 for holding jpState and jpZip
    JPanel p2 = new JPanel();
    p2.setLayout(new BorderLayout());
    p2.add(jpState, BorderLayout.WEST);
    p2.add(jpZip, BorderLayout.CENTER);
    // Panel p3 for holding jtfCity and p2

    JPanel p3 = new JPanel();
    p3.setLayout(new BorderLayout());
    p3.add(jtfCity, BorderLayout.CENTER);
    p3.add(p2, BorderLayout.EAST);

    // Panel p4 for holding jtfName, jtfStreet, and p3
    JPanel p4 = new JPanel();
    p4.setLayout(new GridLayout(3, 1));
    p4.add(jtfName);
    p4.add(jtfStreet);
    p4.add(p3);

    // Place p1 and p4 into StudentPanel
    setLayout(new BorderLayout());
    add(p1, BorderLayout.WEST);
    add(p4, BorderLayout.CENTER);
  }

  // Get student information from the text fields
  public Student getStudent()
  {
    return new Student(jtfName.getText().trim(),
                       jtfStreet.getText().trim(),
                       jtfCity.getText().trim(),
                       jtfState.getText().trim(),
                       jtfZip.getText().trim());
  }

  // Set student information on the text fields
  public void setStudent(Student s)
  {
    jtfName.setText(s.getName());
    jtfStreet.setText(s.getStreet());
    jtfCity.setText(s.getCity());
    jtfState.setText(s.getState());
    jtfZip.setText(s.getZip());
  }
}
```

```
// Student.java: Student class encapsulates student information
import java.io.*;

public class Student
{
  private String name;
  private String street;
  private String city;
  private String state;
  private String zip;

  // Specify the size of five string fields in the record
  final static int NAME_SIZE = 32;
  final static int STREET_SIZE = 32;
  final static int CITY_SIZE = 20;
  final static int STATE_SIZE = 2;
  final static int ZIP_SIZE = 5;

  // the total size of the record in bytes, a Unicode
  // character is 2 bytes size
  final static int RECORD_SIZE =
    (NAME_SIZE + STREET_SIZE + CITY_SIZE + STATE_SIZE + ZIP_SIZE);

  // Default constructor
  public Student()
  {
  }

  // Construct a Student with specified name, street, city, state,
  // and zip
  public Student(String name, String street, String city,
    String state, String zip)
  {
    this.name = name;
    this.street = street;
    this.city = city;
    this.state = state;
    this.zip = zip;
  }

  public String getName()
  {
    return name;
  }

  public String getStreet()
  {
    return street;
  }

  public String getCity()
  {
    return city;
  }

  public String getState()
  {
    return state;
  }

  public String getZip()
  {
    return zip;
  }
```

continues

Example 15.7 continued

```
    // Write a student to a data output stream
    public void writeStudent(DataOutput out) throws IOException
    {
      FixedLengthStringIO.writeFixedLengthString(
        name, NAME_SIZE, out);
      FixedLengthStringIO.writeFixedLengthString(
        street, STREET_SIZE, out);
      FixedLengthStringIO.writeFixedLengthString(
        city, CITY_SIZE, out);
      FixedLengthStringIO.writeFixedLengthString(
        state, STATE_SIZE, out);
      FixedLengthStringIO.writeFixedLengthString(
        zip, ZIP_SIZE, out);
    }

    // Read a student from data input stream
    public void readStudent(DataInput in) throws IOException
    {
      name = FixedLengthStringIO.readFixedLengthString(
        NAME_SIZE, in);
      street = FixedLengthStringIO.readFixedLengthString(
        STREET_SIZE, in);
      city = FixedLengthStringIO.readFixedLengthString(
        CITY_SIZE, in);
      state = FixedLengthStringIO.readFixedLengthString(
        STATE_SIZE, in);
      zip = FixedLengthStringIO.readFixedLengthString(
        ZIP_SIZE, in);
    }
  }
```

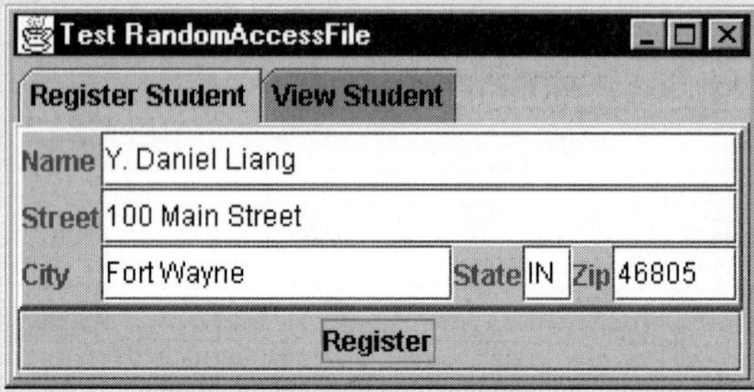

Figure 15.17 *The Register Student tab registers a student.*

Figure 15.18 *The View Student tab displays student information.*

Example Review

A random file, **student.dat**, is created to store student information if the file does not yet exist. If it does exist, the file is opened. The random file object, `raf`, is used in both registration and the viewing part of the program. The user can add a new student record to the file in the Register Student panel and view it immediately in the View Student panel.

Several classes are used in this example. Their relationships are shown in Figure 15.19.

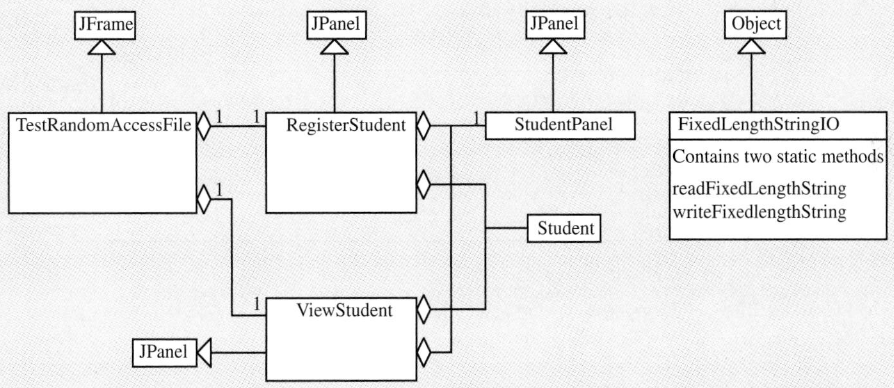

Figure 15.19 *Example 15.7 uses classes* `TestRandomAccessFile`, `RegisterStudent`, `ViewStudent`, `StudentPanel` `Student`, *and* `FixedLengthIO`.

The main class, `TestRandomAccessFile`, is a subclass of `JFrame`, and creates an instance of the `RegisterStudent` class and an instance of the `ViewStudent` class. These two instances are added to a tabbed pane with two tabs: Register Student and View Student. When the Register Student tab is clicked, the registration panel is shown. When the View Student tab is clicked, the viewing panel is shown.

The `RegisterStudent` class and the `ViewStudent` class have many things in common. They both extend the `JPanel` class, and they both use the `StudentPanel` class and the `Student` class.

The student information panels for registering and viewing student information are identical. Therefore, the program creates one class, `StudentPanel`, to lay out the labels and text fields, as shown in Figure 15.20. The `StudentPanel` class also provides the method `getStudent()` for getting text fields and the method `setStudent()` for setting text fields.

The `Student` class defines the student record structure and provides methods for reading and writing a record into the file. Each field in a student record has a

continues

Example 15.7 continued

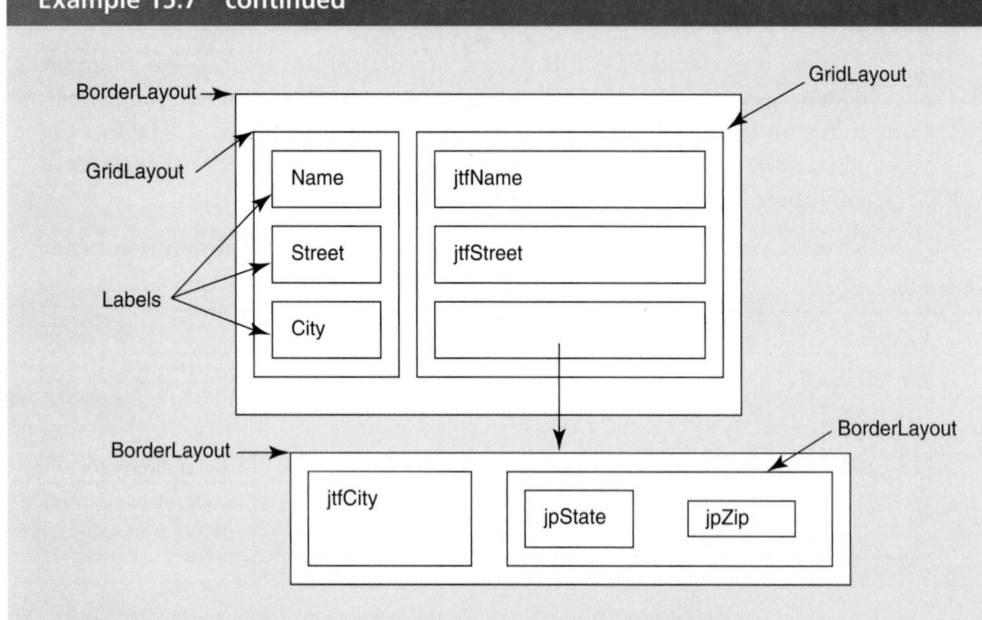

Figure 15.20 *The `StudentPanel` class uses several panels to group components to achieve the desired layout.*

fixed length. The `FixedLengthStringIO` class defines the methods for reading and writing fixed-length strings.

The size of each field in the student record is fixed. For example, zip code is set to a maximum of five characters. If you entered a zip code of more than five characters by mistake, the `ArrayIndexOutofBounds` runtime error would occur when the program attempted to write the zip code into the file using the `writeFixedLengthString` method defined in the `FixedLengthStringIO` class.

Parsing Text Files (Optional)

Occasionally you need to process a text file. For example, the Java source file is a text file. The compiler reads the source file and translates it into bytecode, which is a binary file. Java provides the `StreamTokenizer` class so that you can take an input stream and parse it into words, which are known as *tokens*. The tokens are read one at a time.

To construct an instance of `StreamTokenizer`, you can use `StreamTokenizer(Reader is)` on a given character input stream. The `StreamTokenizer` class contains the useful constants listed in Table 15.3.

The `StreamTokenizer` class also contains the useful variables listed in Table 15.4.

TABLE 15.3 `StreamTokenizer` Constants

Constant	*Description*
`TT_WORD`	The token is a word.
`TT_NUMBER`	The token is a number.
`TT_EOL`	The end of the line has been read.
`TT_EOF`	The end of the file has been read.

TABLE 15.4 `StreamTokenizer` Variables

Variable	*Description*
`int ttype`	Contains the current token type, which matches one of the constants listed previously.
`double nval`	Contains the value of the current token if the token is a number.
`String sval`	Contains a string that gives the characters of the current token if the token is a word.

Typically, the `nextToken()` method is used to retrieve tokens one by one in a loop until `TT_EOF` is returned. The following method parses the next token from the input stream of a `StreamTokenizer`:

```
public int nextToken() throws IOException
```

The type of the next token is returned in the `ttype` field. If `ttype == StreamTokenizer.TT_WORD`, the token is stored in `sval`; if `ttype == StreamTokenizer.TT_NUMBER`, the token is stored in `nval`.

Example 15.8 Using `StreamTokenizer`

The program in this example demonstrates parsing text files. The program reads a text file containing students' exam scores. Each record in the input file consists of a student's name, two midterm exam scores, and a final exam score. The program reads the fields for each record and computes the total score. It then stores the result in a new file. The formula for computing the total score is:

```
total score = midterm1*30% + midterm2*30% + final*40%;
```

Each record in the output file consists of a student's name and total score. Figure 15.21 contains the output of a sample run of the program.

```
// ParsingTextFile.java: Process text file using StreamTokenizer
import java.io.*;

public class ParsingTextFile
{
  // Main method
  public static void main(String[] args)
  {
```

continues

Example 15.8 continued

```
    // Declare file reader and writer streams
    FileReader frs = null;
    FileWriter fws = null;

    // Declare streamTokenizer
    StreamTokenizer in = null;

    // Declare a print stream
    PrintWriter out = null;

    // Four input file fields: student name, midterm1,
    // midterm2, and final exam score
    String sname = null;
    double midterm1 = 0;

    double midterm2 = 0;
    double finalScore = 0;

    // Computed total score
    double total = 0;

    try
    {
      // Create file input and output streams
      frs = new FileReader("in.dat");
      fws = new FileWriter("out.dat");

      // Create a stream tokenizer wrapping file input stream
      in = new StreamTokenizer(frs);
      out = new PrintWriter(fws);

      // Read first token
      in.nextToken();

      // Process a record
      while (in.ttype != StreamTokenizer.TT_EOF)
      {
        // Get student name
        if (in.ttype == StreamTokenizer.TT_WORD)
          sname = in.sval;
        else
          System.out.println("Bad file format");

        // Get midterm1
        if (in.nextToken() == StreamTokenizer.TT_NUMBER)
          midterm1 = in.nval;
        else
          System.out.println("Bad file format");

        // Get midterm2
        if (in.nextToken() == StreamTokenizer.TT_NUMBER)
          midterm2 = in.nval;
        else
          System.out.println("Bad file format");

        // Get final score
        if (in.nextToken() == StreamTokenizer.TT_NUMBER)
          finalScore = in.nval;

        total = midterm1*0.3 + midterm2*0.3 + finalScore*0.4;
        out.println(sname + " " +total);

        in.nextToken();
      }
    }
    catch (FileNotFoundException ex)
```

```
      {
        System.out.println("File not found: in.dat");
      }
      catch (IOException ex)
      {
        System.out.println(ex.getMessage());
      }
      finally
      {
        try
        {
          if (frs != null) frs.close();
          if (fws != null) fws.close();
        }
        catch (IOException ex)
        {
          System.out.println(ex);
        }
      }
    }
  }
```

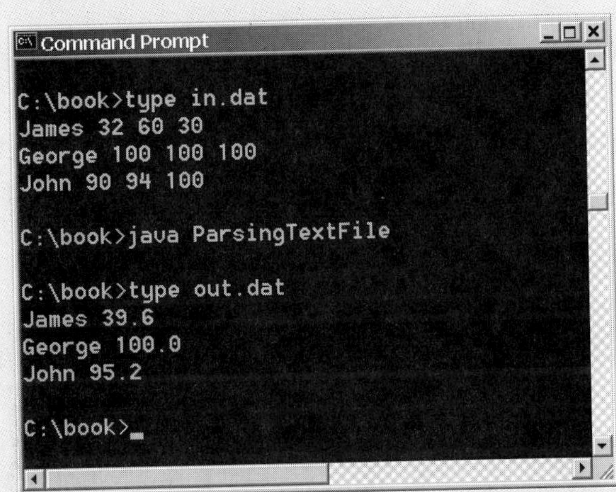

Figure 15.21 *The program uses* `StreamTokenizer` *to parse the text file into strings and numbers.*

Example Review

Before running this program, make sure you have created the text file **in.dat**. To parse the text file **in.dat**, the program uses `StreamTokenizer` to wrap a `FileReader` stream. The `nextToken()` method is used on a `StreamTokenizer` object to get one token at a time. The token value is stored in the `nval` field if the token is numeric, and in the `sval` field if the token is a string. The token type is stored in the `ttype` field.

continues

Example 15.8 continued

For each record, the program reads the name and the three exam scores and then computes the total score. A `FileWriter` stream is used to store the name and the total score in the text file **out.dat** (see Figure 15.22).

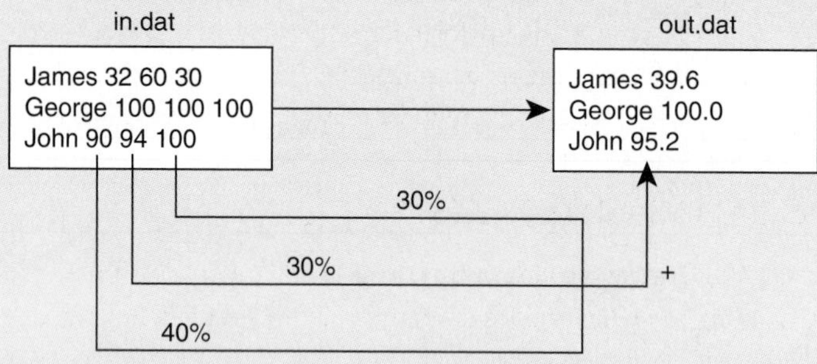

Figure 15.22 *The program reads two midterm scores and a final exam score, and then computes a total score.*

Array Streams, Piped Streams, String Streams, Pushback Streams, and Line Number Streams (Optional)

You have learned many I/O streams in this chapter. Each stream has its intended application. Streams were first used for file input/output in the C language, but Java streams are not limited to this function. There are several other stream classes that you might find useful. A brief discussion of them follows:

- **Array streams:** Array streams like `ByteArrayInputStream`, `CharArrayReader`, `ByteArrayOutputStream`, and `CharArrayWriter` are used to read and write bytes or characters from arrays.
- **Piped streams:** A piped stream can be thought of as the two ends of a pipe that connects two processes. One process sends data out through the pipe, and the other receives data from the pipe. Piped streams are used in inter-process communication (IPC). Two processes running on separate threads can exchange data. Java provides `PipedInputStream`, `PipedOutputStream`, `PipedReader`, and `PipedWriter` to support piped streams.
- **String streams:** String streams (`StringReader` and `StringWriter`) are exactly like character array streams, except that the source of a string stream is a string, and the destination of a string stream is a string buffer.
- **Pushback streams:** These are commonly used in parsers to "push back" a single byte or character in the input stream after reading from the input stream. A pushback stream previews the input to determine what to do next.

The number of bytes or characters pushed can be specified when the stream is constructed. By default, a single byte or a single character is pushed back. Java provides the classes `PushbackInputStream` and `PushbackReader` to support pushback streams.

- **Line-number streams:** These allow you to track the current line number of an input stream. Java provides the `LineNumberReader` class for this purpose. This class is useful for such applications as editing and debugging. You can use the `getLineNumber()` method to get the current line number of the input, and the `getLine()` method to retrieve a line into a string.

Chapter Summary

In this chapter, you learned about Java input and output. In Java, all I/O is handled in streams. Java offers many stream classes for processing all kinds of data.

Streams can be categorized as byte streams and character streams. The `InputStream` and `OutputStream` classes are the root of all byte stream classes, and the `Reader` and `Writer` classes are the root of all character stream classes. The subclasses of `InputStream` and `OutputStream` are analogous to the subclasses of `Reader` and `Writer`. Many of them have similar method signatures, and you can use them in the same way.

File streams (`FileInputStream` and `FileOutputStream` for byte streams, `FileReader` and `FileWriter` for character streams) are used to read from or write data to external files. Data streams (`DataInputStream` and `DataOutputStream`) read or write Java primitive-data-type values in machine-independent fashion, which enables you to write a data file on one machine and read it on a machine that has a different OS or file structure.

Since the data output stream outputs a binary representation of data, you cannot view its content as text. The `PrintStream` and `PrintWriter` classes allow you to print streams in text format. `System.out`, `System.in`, and `System.err` are examples of `PrintStream` objects.

The `BufferedInputStream`, `BufferedOutputStream`, `BufferedReader`, and `BufferedWriter` classes can be used to speed input and output by reducing the number of reads and writes. Typical physical input/output involving I/O devices is very slow compared with CPU processing, so using buffered I/O can greatly improve performance.

You can use the `JFileChooser` class to display standard file dialog boxes from which the user can navigate through the file systems and select files to load or save.

You can use the `ObjectOutputStream` and `ObjectInputStream` classes to store and restore objects. To enable object serialization, the object's defining class must implement the `java.io.Serializable` marker interface.

The `RandomAccessFile` class enables you to read and write data to a file at the same time. You can open a file with the `"r"` mode to indicate that the file is read-only, or you can open a file with the `"rw"` mode to indicate that the file is updateable. Since the `RandomAccessFile` class implements `DataInput` and `DataOutput` interfaces, many methods in `RandomAccessFile` are the same as those in `DataInputStream` and `DataOutputStream`.

The StreamTokenizer class is useful in processing text files. This class enables you to parse an input stream into tokens and read them one at a time.

Review Questions

15.1 Which streams must always be used to process external files?

15.2 What type of data is read or written by InputStream and OutputStream? Can you use read() or write(byte b) in these streams?

15.3 InputStream reads bytes. Why does the read() method return an int instead of a byte?

15.4 What type of data is read or written by Reader and Writer? Can you use read() or write(char c) in these streams?

15.5 What are the differences between byte streams and character streams?

15.6 What type of data are read or written by file streams? Can you use read() or write(byte b) in file streams?

15.7 How are data input and output streams used to read and write data?

15.8 What are the differences between DataOutputStream and PrintStream?

15.9 Is JFileChooser modal? What is the return type for getSelectedFile() and getSelectedDirectory()? How do you set the current directory as the default directory for a JFileChooser dialog?

15.10 What are the data types for System.in, System.out, and System.err?

15.11 What types of objects can be stored using the ObjectOutput stream? What is the method for writing an object? What is the method for reading an object? What is the return type of the method that reads an object from the ObjectInputStream?

15.12 Can RandomAccessFile streams read a data file that is created by DataOutputStream?

15.13 Create a RandomAccessFile stream for the file **student.dat** to allow the updating of student information in the file. Create a DataOutputStream for the file **student.dat**. Explain the differences between these two statements.

15.14 What happens if the file **test.dat** does not exist when you attempt to compile and run the following code?

```
import java.io.*;
class Test
{
  public static void main(String[] args)
  {
    try
    {
      RandomAccessFile raf =
        new RandomAccessFile("test.dat", "r");
      int i = raf.readInt();
```

```
        }
        catch(IOException ex)
        {
          System.out.println("IO exception");
        }
      }
    }
```

15.15 Answer the following questions regarding `StreamTokenizer`:

- When do you use StreamTokenizer?
- How do you read data using StreamTokenizer?
- Where is the token stored when you are using the `nextToken()` method?
- How do you find the data type of the token?

15.16 Can you close a `StreamTokenizer`?

Programming Exercises

15.1 Rewrite Example 15.1, "Processing External Files," using `FileReader` and `FileWriter` streams. Write another program with buffered streams to boost performance. Test the performance of these two programs (one with buffered streams and the other without buffered streams), as shown in Figure 15.23.

15.2 Write a program that will count the number of characters, including blanks, words, and lines, in a file. The filename should be passed as a command-line argument, as shown in Figure 15.24.

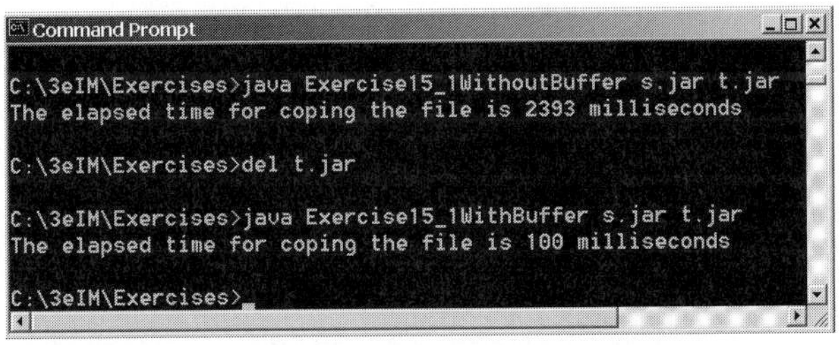

```
Command Prompt

C:\3eIM\Exercises>java Exercise15_1WithoutBuffer s.jar t.jar
The elapsed time for coping the file is 2393 milliseconds

C:\3eIM\Exercises>del t.jar

C:\3eIM\Exercises>java Exercise15_1WithBuffer s.jar t.jar
The elapsed time for coping the file is 100 milliseconds

C:\3eIM\Exercises>_
```

Figure 15.23 *Buffered streams can significantly boost performance.*

```
Command Prompt

C:\3eIM\Exercises>java Exercise15_2 Exercise15_2.java
File Exercise15_2.java has
1691 characters,
223 words, and
74 lines.

C:\3eIM\Exercises>_
```

Figure 15.24 *The program displays the number of characters, words, and lines in the given file.*

15.3 Suppose a text file **score.txt** contains an unspecified number of scores. Write a program that reads the scores from the file, displays the scores in a text area, and displays the average of the scores. Scores are separated by blanks. (Hint: Read the scores one line at a time until all lines are read. For each line, use the `StringTokenizer` to extract the scores, and convert the scores into double values using the `Double.parseDouble` method.)

15.4 Example 9.5, "Using Combo Boxes," gives a program that lets users view a country's flag image and description by selecting the country from a combo box. The description is a string coded in the program. Rewrite the program to read the text description from a file. Suppose the descriptions are stored in the file **description0.txt**, . . . , and **description8.txt** for the nine countries Canada, China, Denmark, France, Germany, India, Norway, the United Kingdom, and the United States, in this order.

15.5 Rewrite Example 15.4, "Displaying a File in a Text Area," to enable the user to view the file by opening it from a file open dialog box, as shown in Figure 15.25. A file open dialog box is displayed when the Browse button is clicked. The file is displayed in the text area, and the filename is displayed in the text field when the OK button is clicked in the file open dialog box. You can also enter the filename in the text field and press the Enter key to display the file in the text area.

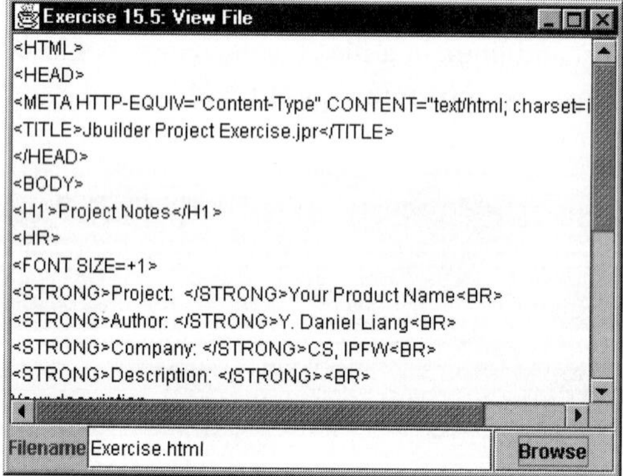

Figure 15.25 *The program enables the user to view a file by selecting it from a file open dialog box.*

15.6 Write a program to select an audio file using the file dialog box, and use three buttons, "Play," "Loop," and "Stop," to control the audio, as shown in Figure 15.26. If you click the Play button, the audio file is played once. If you click the Loop button, the audio file keeps playing repeatedly. If you click the Stop button, the playing stops.

15.7 Write a Java application that will display a stock index ticker, as shown in Figure 13.13 for Exercise 13.6. In that exercise, the stock index information is passed from the <param> tag in the HTML file.

Your program will get index information from an external text file. The first line in the file contains an integer that indicates the number of stock indices

Figure 15.26 *The program allows you to choose an audio file from a dialog box, and play, repeatedly play, or stop the audio using the buttons.*

given in the file. Each subsequent line should consist of four fields: Index Name, Current Time, Previous Day Index, and Index Change. The fields are separated by the pound sign (#). The file could contain two lines, such as the following:

```
2
S&P 500#15:54#919.01#4.54
NIKKEI#04:03#1865.17#-7.00
```

15.8 In Example 9.12, "Creating Multiple Windows," you developed a program that displays a histogram to show the occurrence of each letter in a text area. Reuse the `Histogram` class created in Example 9.12 to write a program that will display a histogram on a panel. The histogram should show the occurrence of each letter in a text file, as shown in Figure 15.27. Assume that the letters are not case-sensitive.

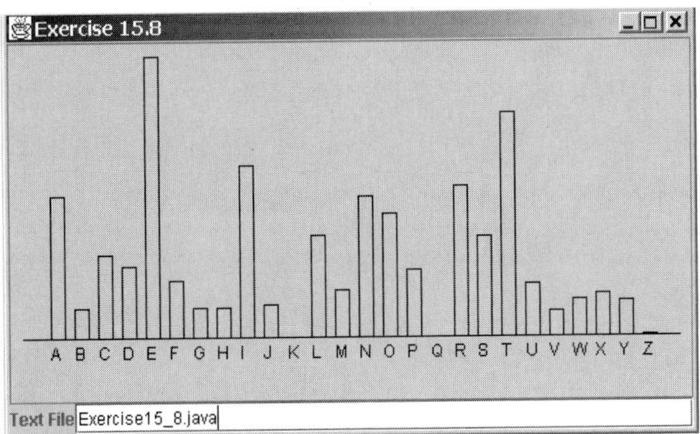

Figure 15.27 *The program displays a histogram that shows the occurrence of each letter in the file.*

- Place a panel that will display the histogram in the center of the frame.
- Place a label and a text field in a panel, and put the panel in the south side of the frame. The text file will be entered from this text field.

- Pressing the Enter key on the text field causes the program to count the occurrences of each letter and display the count in a histogram.

15.9 Modify the View Student panel in Example 15.7, "Using Random Access Files," to add an Update button for updating the student record that is being displayed, as shown in Figure 15.28. The Tab "View Student" is now changed to "View and Update Student."

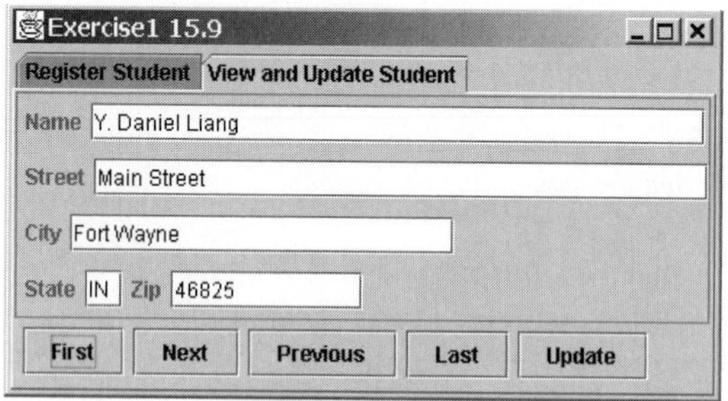

Figure 15.28 *You can browse student records and update the student record that is currently displayed.*

15.10 Use `StreamTokenizer` to write a program that will add all of the integers in a data file. Suppose that the integers are delimited by spaces. Display the result on the console. Rewrite the program, assuming this time that the numbers are `double`.

15.11 Rewrite Example 15.8, "Using `StreamTokenizer`," so that it reads a line as a string in a `BufferedReader` stream, and then use `StringTokenizer` to extract the fields.

CHAPTER 16

NETWORKING

Objectives

- Comprehend socket-based communication in Java.
- Understand client/server computing.
- Implement Java networking programs.
- Produce servers for multiple clients.
- Send and receive objects on the network.
- Develop applets that communicate with the server.
- Use the `URL` class and view Web pages from the applet.
- Create applications or applets to retrieve files from the network.
- View HTML files from the `JEditorPane` class.

Introduction

Networking is tightly integrated in Java. *Socket-based communication* is provided that enables programs to communicate through designated sockets. A *socket* is an abstraction that facilitates communication between a server and a client. Java treats socket communications much as it treats I/O operations; thus programs can read from or write to sockets as easily as they can read from or write to files.

Java supports *stream sockets* and *datagram sockets*. Stream sockets use TCP (Transmission Control Protocol) for data transmission, whereas datagram sockets use UDP (User Datagram Protocol). Since TCP can detect lost transmissions and resubmit them, transmissions are lossless and reliable. UDP, in contrast, cannot guarantee lossless transmission. Because of this, stream sockets are used in most areas of Java programming, and that is why the discussion in this chapter is based on stream sockets.

Client/Server Computing

Network programming usually involves a server and one or more clients. The client sends requests to the server, and the server responds to the requests. The client begins by attempting to establish a connection to the server. The server can accept or deny the connection. Once a connection is established, the client and the server communicate through sockets.

The server must be running when a client starts. The server waits for a connection request from a client. The statements needed to create a server and a client are shown in Figure 16.1.

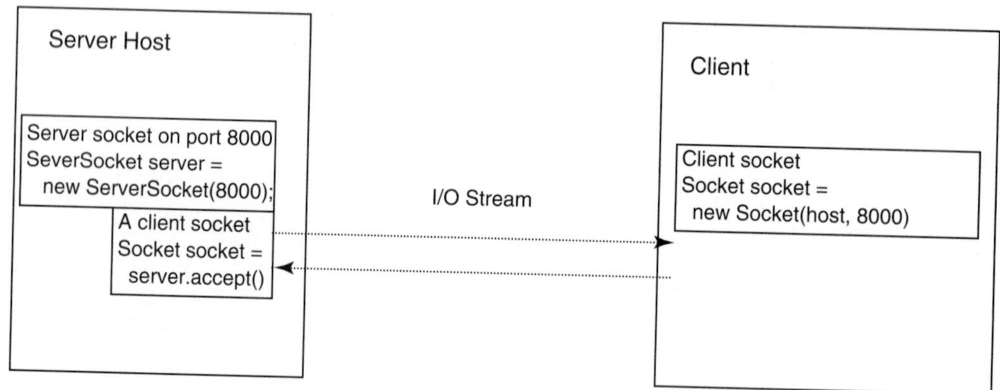

Figure 16.1 *The server creates a server socket and, once a connection to the client is established, connects to a client with a client socket.*

To establish a server, you need to create a server socket and attach it to a port, which is where the server listens for connections. The port identifies the TCP service on the socket. Port numbers between 0 and 1023 are reserved for privileged processes. For instance, the e-mail server runs on port 25, and the Web server usually runs on port 80. You can choose any port number that is not currently used by any other process. The following statement creates a server socket s:

```
ServerSocket s = new ServerSocket(port);
```

NOTE
Attempting to create a server socket on a port already in use would cause the `java.net.BindException` runtime exception.

After a server socket is created, the server can use the following statement to listen for connections:

```
Socket connectToClient = s.accept();
```

This statement waits until a client connects to the server socket. The client issues the following statement to request a connection to a server:

```
Socket connectToServer = new Socket(ServerName, port);
```

This statement opens a socket so that the client program can communicate with the server. *ServerName* is the server's Internet host name or IP address. The following statement creates a socket at port 8000 on the client machine to connect to the host `liang.armstrong.edu`:

```
Socket connectToServer = new Socket("liang.armstrong.edu", 8000);
```

Alternatively, you can use the IP address to create a socket, as follows:

```
Socket connectToServer = new Socket("130.254.190.237", 8000)
```

An IP address, consisting of four dotted decimal numbers between 0 and 255, such as 130.254.190.237, is a computer's unique identity on the Internet. Since it is not easy to remember so many numbers, they are often mapped to meaningful names called *host names*, such as `liang.armstrong.edu`.

NOTE
There are special servers on the Internet that translate host names into IP addresses. These servers are called Domain Name Servers (DNS). The translation is done behind the scenes. When you create a socket with the host name, the Java Runtime System asks the DNS to translate the host name into the IP address.

After the server accepts the connection, communication between the server and the client is conducted the same as for I/O streams. The statements needed to create the streams and to exchange data between them are shown in Figure 16.2.

To get an input stream and an output stream, use the `getInputStream()` and `getOutputStream()` methods on a socket object. For example, the following statements create an `InputStream` stream, `isFromServer`, and an `OutputStream` stream, `osToServer`, from the socket `connectToServer`:

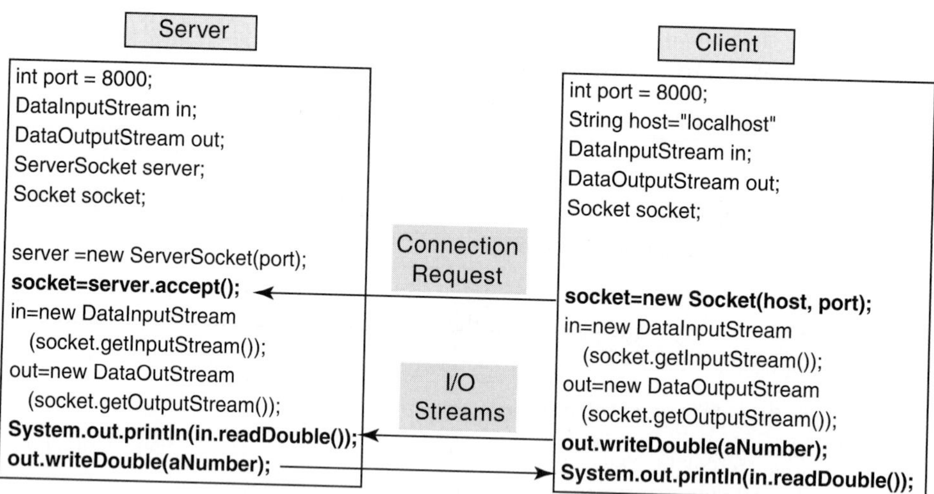

Figure 16.2 *The server uses I/O streams to establish a server socket that facilitates communication between the server and the client.*

```
InputStream isFromServer = connectToServer.getInputStream();

OutputStream osToServer = connectToServer.getOutputStream();
```

The `InputStream` and `OutputStream` streams are used to read or write bytes. You can use `DataInputStream`, `DataOutputStream`, `BufferedReader`, and `PrintWriter` to wrap on the `InputStream`, and `OutputStream` to read or write values of data, such as `int`, `double`, or `String`. The following statements, for instance, create a `DataInputStream` stream, `isFromClient`, and a `DataOutput` stream, `osToClient`, to read and write primitive data values:

```
DataInputStream isFromClient = new DataInputStream
  (connectToClient.getInputStream());
DataOutputStream osToClient = new DataInputStream
  (connectToClient.getOutputStream());
```

The server can use `isFromClient.read()` to receive data from the client, and `osToClient.write()` to send data to the client.

Example 16.1 A Client/Server Example

This example presents a client program and a server program. The client sends data to a server. The server receives the data, uses them to produce a result, and then sends the result back to the client. The client displays the result on the console. In this example, the data sent from the client is the radius of a circle, and the result produced by the server is the area of the circle (see Figure 16.3).

The server program follows. A sample run of the program is shown in Figure 16.4.

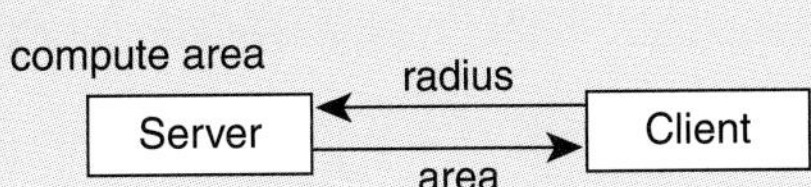

Figure 16.3 *The client sends the radius to the server; the server computes the area and sends it to the client.*

```
// Server.java: The server accepts data from the client, processes it
// and returns the result back to the client
import java.io.*;
import java.net.*;

public class Server
{
  // Main method
  public static void main(String[] args)
  {
    try
    {
      // Create a server socket
      ServerSocket serverSocket = new ServerSocket(8000);

      // Start listening for connections on the server socket
      Socket connectToClient = serverSocket.accept();

      // Create an input stream to get data from the client
      DataInputStream isFromClient = new DataInputStream(
        connectToClient.getInputStream());

      // Create an output stream to send data to the client
      DataOutputStream osToClient = new DataOutputStream(
        connectToClient.getOutputStream());

      // Continuously read from the client and process it,
      // and send result back to the client
      while (true)
      {
        // Read a string from the input stream
        double radius = isFromClient.readDouble();

        // Display radius on console
        System.out.println("radius received from client: " + radius);

        // Compute area
        double area = radius*radius*Math.PI;

        // Send the result to the client
        osToClient.writeDouble(area);
        osToClient.flush();

        // Print the result to the console
        System.out.println("Area found: " + area);
      }
    }
    catch(IOException ex)
    {
      System.err.println(ex);
    }
  }
}
```

continues

Example 16.1 continued

The client program follows. A sample run of the program is shown in Figure 16.5.

```
// Client.java: The client sends the input to the server and receives
// result back from the server
import java.io.*;
import java.net.*;

public class Client
{
  // Main method
  public static void main(String[] args)
  {
    try
    {
      // Create a socket to connect to the server
      Socket connectToServer = new Socket("localhost", 8000);
      // Socket connectToServer = new Socket("130.254.32.8", 8000);

      // Create an input stream to receive data from the server
      DataInputStream isFromServer = new DataInputStream(
        connectToServer.getInputStream());

      // Create an output stream to send data to the server
      DataOutputStream osToServer =
        new DataOutputStream(connectToServer.getOutputStream());

      // Continuously send radius and receive area from the server
      while (true)
      {
        // Read the radius from the keyboard
        System.out.print("Please enter a radius: ");
        double radius = MyInput.readDouble();

        // Send the radius to the server
        osToServer.writeDouble(radius);
        osToServer.flush();

        // Get area from the server
        double area = isFromServer.readDouble();

        // Print area on the console
        System.out.println("Area received from the server is "
          + area);
      }
    }
    catch (IOException ex)
    {
      System.err.println(ex);
    }
  }
}
```

Example Review

You should start the server program first, then start the client program. The client program prompts the user to enter a radius, which is sent to the server. The server computes the area and sends it back to the client. This process is repeated until one of the two programs terminates. To terminate a program, press Ctrl+C on the console.

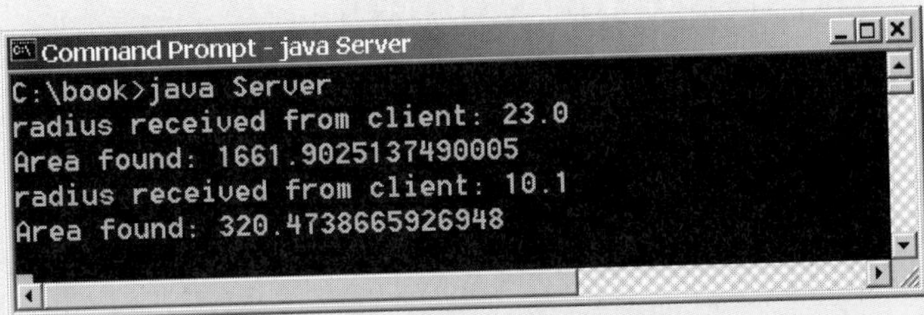

Figure 16.4 *The server receives a radius from the client, computes the area, and sends the area to the client.*

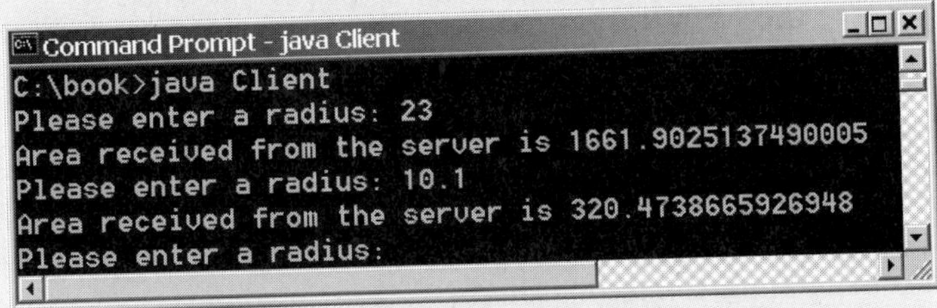

Figure 16.5 *The client sends the radius to the server and receives the area from the server.*

The networking classes are in the package `java.net`. This should be imported when writing Java network programs.

The `Server` class creates a `ServerSocket serverSocket` and attaches it to port 8000, using the following statement:

```
ServerSocket serverSocket = new ServerSocket(8000);
```

The server then starts to listen for connection requests, using the following statement:

```
Socket connectToClient = serverSocket.accept();
```

The server waits until a client requests a connection. After it is connected, the server reads radius from the client through an input stream, computes area, and sends the result to the client through an output stream.

The `Client` class uses the following statement to create a socket that will request a connection to the server at port 8000.

```
Socket connectToServer = new Socket("localhost", 8000);
```

The host name `localhost` refers to the machine on which the client is running. If you run the server and the client on different machines, replace `localhost` with the server machine's host name or IP address. In this example, the server and the client are running on the same machine.

If the server is not running, the client program terminates with a `java.net.ConnectException`. After it is connected, the client gets input and output streams—wrapped by data input and output streams—in order to receive and send data to the server.

Serving Multiple Clients and the *InetAddress* class

Multiple clients are quite often connected to a single server at the same time. Typically, a server runs constantly on a server computer, and clients from all over the Internet may want to connect to it. You can use threads to handle the server's multiple clients simultaneously. Simply create a thread for each connection. Here is how the server handles the establishment of a connection:

```
while (true)
{
  Socket connectToClient = serverSocket.accept();
  Thread thread = new ThreadClass(connectToClient);
  thread.start();
}
```

The server socket can have many connections. Each iteration of the `while` loop creates a new connection. Whenever a connection is established, a new thread is created to handle communication between the server and the new client; and this allows multiple connections to run at the same time.

Occasionally, you would like to know who is connecting to the server. You can use the `InetAddress` class to find the client's host name and IP address. The `InetAddress` class models an IP address. You can use the following statement to create an instance of `InetAddress` for the client on the socket `connectToClient`.

```
InetAddress clientInetAddress = connectToClient.getInetAddress();
```

You can then display the client's host name and IP address as follows:

```
System.out.println("Client's host name is " +
  clientInetAddress.getHostName());
System.out.println("Client's IP Address is " +
  clientInetAddress.getHostAddress());
```

Example 16.2 Serving Multiple Clients

This example shows how to serve multiple clients simultaneously. For each connection, the server starts a new thread. This thread continuously receives input (the radius of a circle) from a client and sends the result (the area of the circle) back to the client (see Figure 16.6).

The new server program follows. A sample run of the server is shown in Figure 16.7, and sample runs of two clients are shown in Figures 16.8 and 16.9.

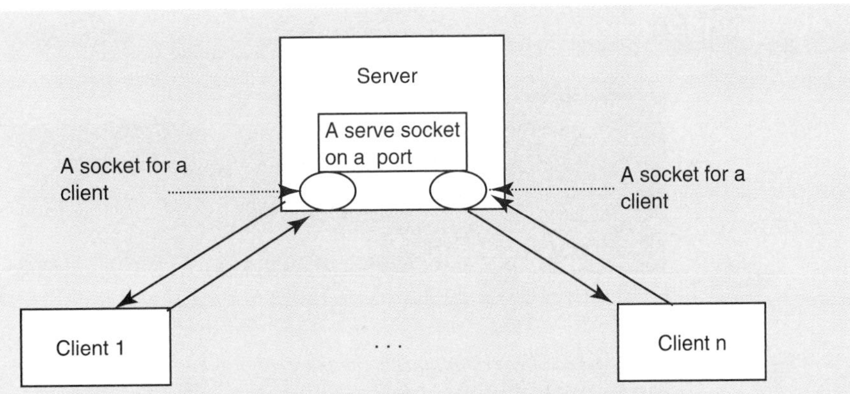

Figure 16.6 *Multithreading enables a server to handle multiple independent clients.*

```
Command Prompt - java MultiThreadServer
C:\book>java MultiThreadServer
Start thread for client 1
Client 1's hostname is 127.0.0.1
Client 1's IP Address is 127.0.0.1
radius received from client 1: 2.5
Area found: 19.634954084936208
Start thread for client 2
Client 2's hostname is 127.0.0.1
Client 2's IP Address is 127.0.0.1
radius received from client 2: 100.0
Area found: 31415.926535897932
radius received from client 2: 20.1
Area found: 1269.2348479768125
radius received from client 1: 3.5
Area found: 38.48451000647496
```

Figure 16.7 *The server spawns a thread in order to serve a client.*

```
Command Prompt - java Client
C:\book>java Client
Please enter a radius: 2.5
Area received from the server is 19.634954084936208
Please enter a radius: 3.5
Area received from the server is 38.48451000647496
Please enter a radius:
```

Figure 16.8 *The first client communicates to the server on thread 1.*

continues

Example 16.2 continued

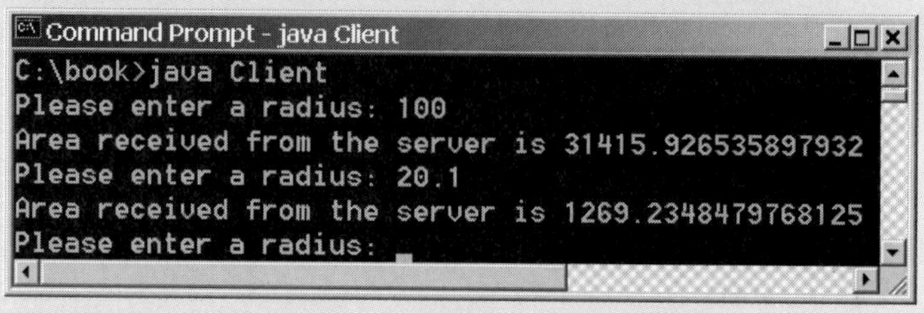

```
C:\book>java Client
Please enter a radius: 100
Area received from the server is 31415.926535897932
Please enter a radius: 20.1
Area received from the server is 1269.2348479768125
Please enter a radius:
```

Figure 16.9 *The second client communicates to the server on thread 2.*

```
// MultiThreadServer.java: The server can communicate with
// multiple clients concurrently using the multiple threads
import java.io.*;
import java.net.*;

public class MultiThreadServer
{
  // Main method
  public static void main(String[] args)
  {
    try
    {
      // Create a server socket
      ServerSocket serverSocket = new ServerSocket(8000);

      // To number a client
      int clientNo = 1;

      while (true)
      {
        // Listen for a new connection request
        Socket connectToClient = serverSocket.accept();

        // Print the new connect number on the console
        System.out.println("Start thread for client " + clientNo);

        // Find the client's host name, and IP address
        InetAddress clientInetAddress =
          connectToClient.getInetAddress();
        System.out.println("Client " + clientNo + "'s host name is "
          + clientInetAddress.getHostName());
        System.out.println("Client " + clientNo + "'s IP Address is "
          + clientInetAddress.getHostAddress());

        // Create a new thread for the connection
        HandleAClient thread = new HandleAClient(connectToClient);

        // Start the new thread
        thread.start();

        // Increment clientNo
        clientNo++;
      }
    }
    catch(IOException ex)
    {
      System.err.println(ex);
    }
  }
}
```

```
// Define the thread class for handling a new connection
class HandleAClient extends Thread
{
  private Socket connectToClient; // A connected socket

  // Construct a thread
  public HandleAClient(Socket socket)
  {
    connectToClient = socket;
  }

  // Implement the run() method for the thread
  public void run()
  {
    try
    {
      // Create data input and output streams
      DataInputStream isFromClient = new DataInputStream(
        connectToClient.getInputStream());
      DataOutputStream osToClient = new DataOutputStream(
        connectToClient.getOutputStream());

      // Continuously serve the client
      while (true)
      {
        // Receive radius from the client
        double radius = isFromClient.readDouble();
        System.out.println("radius received from client: " + radius);

        // Compute area
        double area = radius*radius*Math.PI;

        // Send area back to the client
        osToClient.writeDouble(area);
        System.out.println("Area found: " + area);
      }
    }
    catch(IOException ex)
    {
      System.err.println(ex);
    }
  }
}
```

Example Review

The server creates a server socket at port 8000 and waits for a connection. When a connection with a client is established, the server creates a new thread to handle the communication. It then waits for another connection.

The threads, which run independently of one another, communicate with designated clients. Each thread creates buffered reader and writer streams that receive and send data to the client.

This server accepts an unlimited number of clients. To limit the number of concurrent connections, you can use a thread group to monitor the number of active threads and modify the `while` loop, as follows:

```
ThreadGroup group = new ThreadGroup("serving clients");

while (group.activeCount() < maxThreadLimit)
{
```

continues

Example 16.2 continued

```
        // Listen for a new connection request
        Socket connectToClient = serverSocket.accept();

        // Print the new connect number on the console
        System.out.println("Starting thread " + i);

        // Create a new thread for the connection
        Thread thread = new Thread(group, new HandleAClient(
          connectToClient, i));

        // Start the new thread
        thread.start();

        // Increment i to label the next connection
        i++;
      }
```

Applet Clients

Due to security constraints, applets can only connect to the host from which they were loaded. Therefore, the HTML file must be located on the machine on which the server is running. Below is an example of how to use an applet to connect to a server.

Example 16.3 Creating Applet Clients

This example, which is similar to Example 15.7, "Using Random Access Files," in Chapter 15, "Input and Output," shows how to use an applet to register students. The client collects and sends registration information to the server. The server appends the information to a data file using a random-access file stream. The server program follows. A sample run of this program is shown in Figure 16.10.

```
// RegistrationServer.java: The server for the applet responsible for
// writing on the server side
import java.io.*;
import java.net.*;
import javax.swing.*;
import java.awt.*;
import java.util.Date;

public class RegistrationServer extends JFrame
{
  private static JTextArea jtaLog;

  // The file to store the records
  private static RandomAccessFile raf = null;

  // Main method
  public static void main(String[] args)
  {
    RegistrationServer server = new RegistrationServer();
  }

  public RegistrationServer()
  {
```

```
    // Create a scroll pane to hold text area
    JScrollPane scrollPane = new JScrollPane(
      jtaLog = new JTextArea());

    // Add the scroll pane to the frame
    getContentPane().add(scrollPane, BorderLayout.CENTER);

    setSize(300, 300);
    setTitle("Registration Server");
    setVisible(true);

    // Open the local file on the server side
    try
    {
      // Open the file if the file exists, create a new file
      // if the file does not exist
      raf = new RandomAccessFile("student.dat", "rw");
    }
    catch(IOException ex)
    {
      jtaLog.append(new Date() + ": Error: " + ex);
      System.exit(0);
    }

    // Establish server socket
    try
    {
      // Create a server socket
      ServerSocket serverSocket = new ServerSocket(8000);
      jtaLog.append(new Date() + ": Start a new server\n");

      // Count the number of threads started
      int count = 1;
      while (true)

      {
        // Connect to a client
        Socket socket = serverSocket.accept();

        jtaLog.append(new Date() + ": A client at " +
          socket.getInetAddress().getHostAddress() + " connected\n");

        // Start a new thread to register a client
        new RegistrationThread(socket, count++).start();
      }
    }
    catch (IOException ex)
    {
      jtaLog.append(new Date() + ": " + ex);
    }
  }

  // Write student information to the file
  private synchronized static void writeToFile(Student student)
  {
    try
    {
      // Append it to "student.dat"
      raf.seek(raf.length());
      student.writeStudent(raf);

      // Display data saved
      jtaLog.append("The following info saved in the file\n");
      jtaLog.append(student.toString());
    }
```

continues

Example 16.3 continued

```
      catch (Exception ex)
      {
        jtaLog.append(new Date() + ": " + ex);
      }
    }

    // Define a thread to process the client registration
    class RegistrationThread extends Thread
    {
      // The socket to serve a client
      private Socket socket;
      private int clientNo; // The thread number

      // Buffered reader to get input from the client

      private BufferedReader in;
      // Create a registration thread

      public RegistrationThread(Socket socket, int clientNo)
      {
        this.socket = socket;
        this.clientNo = clientNo;

        jtaLog.append(new Date() + ": Thread " + clientNo
          + " started\n");

        // Create an input stream to receive data from a client
        try
        {
          in = new BufferedReader
            (new InputStreamReader(socket.getInputStream()));
        }
        catch(IOException ex)
        {
          jtaLog.append(new Date() + ": " + ex);
        }
      }

      public void run()
      {
        String name;
        String street;
        String city;
        String state;
        String zip;

        try
        {
          // Receive data from the client
          name = new String(in.readLine());
          street = new String(in.readLine());
          city = new String(in.readLine());
          state = new String(in.readLine());
          zip = new String(in.readLine());

          // Create a student instance
          Student student =
            new Student(name, street, city, state, zip);

          writeToFile(student);
        }
        catch (IOException ex)
        {
          System.out.println(ex);
```

```
        }
      }
    }
  }
```

The applet client follows, and its sample run is shown in Figure 16.11.

```
// RegistrationClient.java: The applet client for gathering student
// informationthe and passing it to the server
import java.io.*;
import java.net.*;
import java.awt.BorderLayout;
import java.awt.event.*;
import javax.swing.*;

public class RegistrationClient extends JApplet
  implements ActionListener
{
  // Button for registering a student in the file
  private JButton jbtRegister = new JButton("Register");

  // Create student information panel
  private StudentPanel studentPanel = new StudentPanel();

  // Indicate if it runs as application
  private boolean isStandAlone = false;

  public void init()
  {
    // Add the student panel and button to the applet
    getContentPane().add(studentPanel, BorderLayout.CENTER);
    getContentPane().add(jbtRegister, BorderLayout.SOUTH);

    // Register listener
    jbtRegister.addActionListener(this);
  }

  // Handle button action
  public void actionPerformed(ActionEvent e)
  {
    if (e.getSource() == jbtRegister)
    {
      try
      {
        // Establish connection with the server
        Socket socket;
        if (isStandAlone)
          //  socket = new Socket("url", 8000);
          socket = new Socket("localhost", 8000);
        else
          socket = new Socket(getCodeBase().getHost(), 8000);

        // Create an output stream to the server
        PrintWriter toServer =
          new PrintWriter(socket.getOutputStream(), true);

        // Get text field
        Student s = studentPanel.getStudent();

        // Get data from text fields and send it to the server
        toServer.println(s.getName());
        toServer.println(s.getStreet());
        toServer.println(s.getCity());
        toServer.println(s.getState());
        toServer.println(s.getZip());
```

continues

Example 16.3 continued

```
        }
        catch (IOException ex)
        {
          System.err.println(ex);
        }
      }
    }

    // Run the applet as an application
    public static void main(String[] args)
    {
      // Create a frame
      JFrame frame = new JFrame("Register Student Client");

      // Create an instance of the applet
      RegistrationClient applet = new RegistrationClient();
      applet.isStandAlone = true;

      // Add the applet instance to the frame
      frame.getContentPane().add(applet, BorderLayout.CENTER);

      // Invoke init() and start()
      applet.init();
      applet.start();

      // Display the frame
      frame.pack();
      frame.setVisible(true);
    }
  }
```

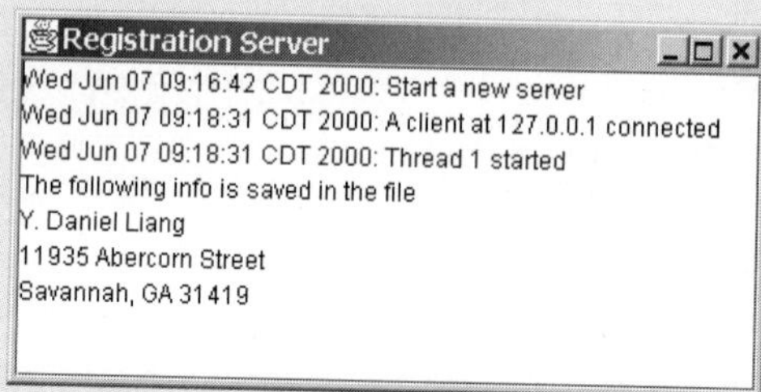

Figure 16.10 *The server receives information (name, street, city, state, and zip code) from the client, and stores it in a file.*

Figure 16.11 *The client gathers the name and address and sends them to the server.*

Example Review

The server handles multiple clients. It waits for a connection request from the client in the `while` loop. After a connection with a client is established, the server creates a thread to serve the client. The server then stays in the `while` loop to listen for the next connection request.

The server passes `socket` (connection socket) and `clientNo` (thread number) to the thread. The `clientNo` argument is nonessential; its only use is to identify the thread. The thread receives student information from the client through the `BufferedReader` stream and appends a student record to **student.dat**, using the random access file stream `raf`.

The `StudentPanel` and `Student` classes are defined in Example 15.7. The statement given below creates an instance of `Student`:

```
Student s = new Student(name, street, city, state, zip);
```

The next code writes the student record into the file:

```
s.writeStudent(raf);
```

The client is an applet and can run standalone. When it runs as an applet, it uses `getCodeBase().getHost()` to return the IP address for the server. When it runs as an application, it passes the URL from the command line. If the URL is not passed from the command line, by default "localhost" is used for the URL.

The data are entered into text fields (name, street, city, state, and zip). When the Register button is clicked, the data from the text fields are collected and sent to the server. Each time the Register button is clicked from a client, the server creates a new thread to store the student information. Obviously, this is not efficient. In Exercise 16.3, you will modify the program to enable one thread to handle all registration requests from a client.

When multiple clients register students simultaneously, data may be corrupted. To avoid this, the `writeToFile()` method is synchronized and defined as a static method. The synchronization is at the class level, meaning that only one object of the `RegistrationThread` at a time can execute the `writeToFile()` method to write a student to the file.

NOTE

Student information is stored in a data file in this example. In real-world applications, data are usually stored in a database. In the database course, you will learn how to develop Java programs to access data from a database. Interested readers may refer to Part IV, "Java Database Programming," in my *Rapid Java Application Development Using JBuilder 3.*

Sending and Receiving Objects

In the preceding examples, you learned to pass data of primitive types. You can also pass objects. To enable passing, the objects must be serializable. The following example demonstrates passing objects.

Example 16.4 Passing Objects in Network Programs

This example rewrites Example 16.3, "Creating Applet Clients," using object streams on the socket. Instead of passing name, street, state, and zip separately, the program passes the student object as a whole object. The client uses `writeObject` method in the `ObjectOutputStream` class to send a student to the server, and the server receives the student using the `readObject` method in the `ObjectInputStream` class. The server and client programs are given as follows:

```
// RegistrationServerUsingObjectStream.java: The server for the
// applet responsible for writing on the server side
import java.io.*;
import java.net.*;
import javax.swing.*;
import java.awt.*;
import java.util.Date;

public class RegistrationServerUsingObjectStream extends JFrame
{
  private static JTextArea jtaLog;

  // The file to store the records
  private static RandomAccessFile raf = null;

  // Main method
  public static void main(String[] args)
  {
    RegistrationServerUsingObjectStream server =
      new RegistrationServerUsingObjectStream();
  }

  public RegistrationServerUsingObjectStream()
  {
    // Create a scroll pane to hold text area
    JScrollPane scrollPane = new JScrollPane(
      jtaLog = new JTextArea());

    // Add the scroll pane to the frame
    getContentPane().add(scrollPane, BorderLayout.CENTER);

    setSize(300, 300);
    setTitle("Registration Server Using Object Streams");
    setVisible(true);

    // Open the local file on the server side
    try
    {
      // Open the file if the file exists, create a new file
      // if the file does not exist
      raf = new RandomAccessFile("student.dat", "rw");
    }
    catch(IOException ex)
    {
      jtaLog.append(new Date() + ": Error: " + ex);
```

```
      System.exit(0);
    }

    // Establish server socket
    try
    {
      // Create a server socket
      ServerSocket serverSocket = new ServerSocket(8000);
      jtaLog.append(new Date() + ": Start a new server\n");

      // Count the number of threads started
      int count = 1;

      while (true)
      {
        // Connect to a client
        Socket socket = serverSocket.accept();
        jtaLog.append(new Date() + ": A client at " +
          socket.getInetAddress().getHostAddress() + " connected\n");

        // Start a new thread to register a client
        new RegistrationThread(socket, count++).start();
      }
    }
    catch (IOException ex)
    {
      jtaLog.append(new Date() + ": " + ex);
    }
  }

  // Write student information to the file
  private synchronized static void writeToFile(Student student)
  {
    try
    {
      // Append it to "student.dat"
      raf.seek(raf.length());
      student.writeStudent(raf);

      // Display data saved
      jtaLog.append("The following info is saved in the file\n");
      jtaLog.append(student.toString());
    }
    catch (Exception ex)
    {
      jtaLog.append(new Date() + ": " + ex);
    }
  }

  // Define a thread to process the client registration
  class RegistrationThread extends Thread
  {
    // The socket to serve a client
    private Socket socket;

    private int clientNo; // The thread number

    // Object input stream to get input from the client
    private ObjectInputStream in;

    // Create a registration thread
    public RegistrationThread(Socket socket, int clientNo)
    {
      this.socket = socket;
      this.clientNo = clientNo;
```

continues

Example 16.4 continued

```
        jtaLog.append(new Date() + ": Thread " + clientNo
          + " started\n");

        // Create an input stream to receive data from a client
        try
        {
          in = new ObjectInputStream(socket.getInputStream());
        }
        catch(IOException ex)
        {
          jtaLog.append(new Date() + ": " + ex);
        }
      }

      public void run()
      {
        try
        {
          // Receive data from the client
          Student student = (Student)in.readObject();

          writeToFile(student);
        }
        catch (Exception ex)
        {
          System.out.println(ex);
        }
      }
    }
  }

  // RegistrationClientUsingObjectStream.java: The applet client for
  // gathering student informationthe and passing it to the server
  import java.io.*;
  import java.net.*;
  import java.awt.BorderLayout;
  import java.awt.event.*;
  import javax.swing.*;

  public class RegistrationClientUsingObjectStream extends JApplet
    implements ActionListener
  {
    // Button for registering a student in the file
    private JButton jbtRegister = new JButton("Register");

    // Create student information panel
    private StudentPanel studentPanel = new StudentPanel();

    // Indicate if it runs as application
    private boolean isStandAlone = false;

    // IP address of the server
    String serverIP = "localhost";

    public void init()
    {
      // Add the student panel and button to the applet
      getContentPane().add(studentPanel, BorderLayout.CENTER);
      getContentPane().add(jbtRegister, BorderLayout.SOUTH);

      // Register listener
      jbtRegister.addActionListener(this);

      // Find the IP address of the Web server
      if (!isStandAlone)
```

```
      serverIP = getCodeBase().getHost();
  }

  // Handle button action
  public void actionPerformed(ActionEvent e)
  {
    if (e.getSource() == jbtRegister)
    {
      try
      {
        // Establish connection with the server
        Socket socket = new Socket(serverIP, 8000);

        // Create an output stream to the server
        ObjectOutputStream toServer =
          new ObjectOutputStream(socket.getOutputStream());

        // Get text field
        Student s = studentPanel.getStudent();

        // Get data from text fields and send it to the server
        toServer.writeObject(s);

      }
      catch (IOException ex)
      {
        System.err.println(ex);
      }
    }
  }

  // Run the applet as an application
  public static void main(String[] args)
  {
    // Create a frame
    JFrame frame = new JFrame("Register Student Client");

    // Create an instance of the applet
    RegistrationClientUsingObjectStream applet =
      new RegistrationClientUsingObjectStream();
    applet.isStandAlone = true;

    // Add the applet instance to the frame
    frame.getContentPane().add(applet, BorderLayout.CENTER);

    // Invoke init() and start()
    applet.init();
    applet.start();

    // Display the frame
    frame.pack();
    frame.setVisible(true);
  }
}
```

Example Review

The client collects student information from the text fields and creates an instance of the `Student` class. The client then serializes the object and sends it to the server using the object output stream through the socket. The server restores the object using the object input stream on the socket.

The `Student` class in Example 15.7 implements the `Serializable` interface. Therefore, it can be sent and received using the object output and input streams.

The *URL* Class and Viewing Web Pages from Applets

Given a URL, a Web browser can view an HTML page, for example, **http://www.sun.com**. HTTP is the common standard used for communication between Web servers and the Internet. You can open a URL and view a Web page in a Java applet. A URL is a description of a resource location on the Internet. Java provides a class, `java.net.URL`, to manipulate URLs. The following code can be written to create a URL:

```
try
{
  URL url = new URL(URLString);
}
catch(MalformedURLException ex)
{
}
```

The following statement creates a Java URL object:

```
try
{
  URL url = new URL("http://www.sun.com");
}
catch(MalformedURLException ex)
{
}
```

A `MalformedURLException` is thrown if the URL string has a syntax error. For example, the URL string `"http:/www.sun.com"` would cause the `MalformedURLException` runtime error because two slashes (`//`) are required.

To actually view the contents of an HTML page, you would need to write the following code:

```
AppletContext context = getAppletContext();
context.showDocument(url);
```

The `java.applet.AppletContext` class provides the environment for displaying Web page contents. The `showDocument` method displays the Web page in the environment.

Example 16.5 Viewing HTML Pages from Java

This example demonstrates an applet that views Web pages. The Web page's URL is entered, the Go button is clicked, and the Web page is displayed (see Figures 16.12 and 16.13).

```
// ViewWebPage.java: Access HTML pages through applets
import java.net.*;
import java.awt.*;
import java.awt.event.*;
import javax.swing.*;
import java.applet.*;
```

continues

```
public class ViewWebPage extends JApplet implements ActionListener
{
  // Button to display an HTML page on the applet
  private JButton jbtGo = new JButton("Go");

  // Text field for receiving the URL of the HTML page
  private JTextField jtfURL = new JTextField(20);

  // Initialize the applet
  public void init()
  {
    // Add URL text field and Go button
    getContentPane().setLayout(new FlowLayout());
    getContentPane().add(new JLabel("URL"));
    getContentPane().add(jtfURL);
    getContentPane().add(jbtGo);

    // Register listener
    jbtGo.addActionListener(this);
  }

  // Handle the ActionEvent
  public void actionPerformed(ActionEvent evt)
  {
    if (evt.getSource() == jbtGo)
      try
      {
        AppletContext context = getAppletContext();

        // Get the URL from text field
        URL url = new URL(jtfURL.getText());
        context.showDocument(url);
      }
      catch(Exception ex)
      {
        showStatus("Error " + ex);
      }
  }
}
```

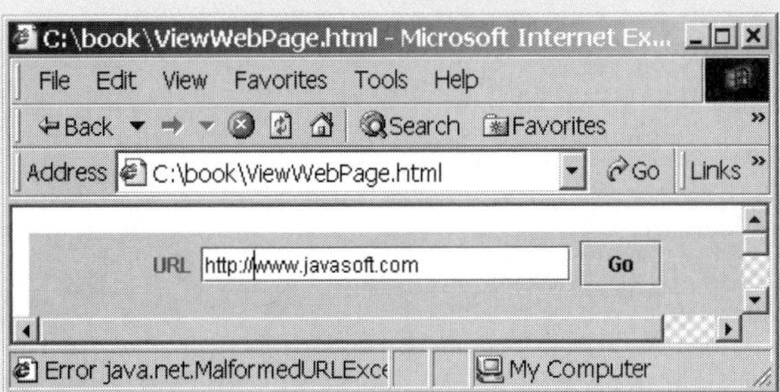

Figure 16.12 *Given the URL, the applet can display a Web page.*

continues

Example 16.5 continued

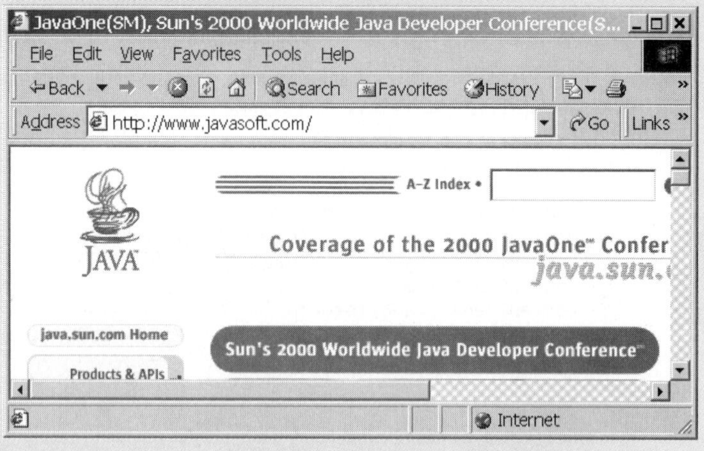

Figure 16.13 *The Web page specified in the applet is displayed in the browser.*

Example Review

When the URL of a publicly available HTML file is entered and the Go button is clicked, a new HTML page is displayed. The page containing the applet becomes the preceding page. A user could return to the preceding page to enter a new URL and then view the new page.

Anyone using this program would have to run it from a Web browser, not from the Applet Viewer utility.

Retrieving Files from Web Servers

You can display an HTML page from an applet, as shown in the preceding section. But sometimes you need the Web server to give you access to the contents of a file. This access allows you to pass dynamic information from the server to the applet clients or the standalone application clients, as shown in Figure 16.14. To access the file, you would use the `openStream()` method defined in the URL class to open a stream to the file's URL.

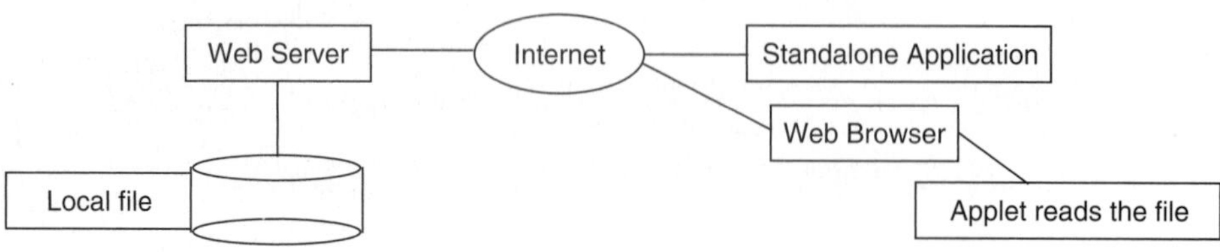

Figure 16.14 *The applet client or application client retrieves files from a Web server.*

The following method opens a connection to the file's URL and returns an `InputStream` so that you can read from the connection:

```
public final InputStream openStream() throws IOException
```

The following statements, for example, open an input stream for the URL **http://www.cs.armstrong.edu/liang/index.html** for the file **index.html**, which is stored on the author's Web server.

```
try
{
  String urlString = "http://www.cs.armstrong.edu/liang/index.html";
  url = new URL(urlString);
  InputStream is = url.openStream();
}
catch (MalformedURLException ex)
{
  System.out.println("Bad URL : " + url);
}
catch (IOException ex)
{
  System.out.println("IO Error : " + ex.getMessage());
}
```

Example 16.6 Retrieving Remote Files

This example, which is similar to Example 15.4, "Displaying a File in a Text Area," in Chapter 15, "Input and Output," demonstrates how to retrieve a file from a Web server. The program can run as an application or an applet. The user interface includes a text field in which to enter the URL of the filename, a text area in which to show the file, and a button that can be used to submit an action. A label is added at the bottom of the applet to indicate the status, such as File loaded successfully or Network connection problem. A sample run of the program is shown in Figure 16.15.

```
// ViewRemoteFile.java: Retrieve remote files
import java.awt.*;
import java.awt.event.*;
import java.io.*;
import java.net.*;
import javax.swing.*;

public class ViewRemoteFile extends JApplet
  implements ActionListener
{
  // Button to view the file
  private JButton jbtView = new JButton("View");

  // Text field to receive file name
  private JTextField jtfURL = new JTextField(12);

  // Text area to store file
  private JTextArea jtaFile = new JTextArea();

  // Label to display status
  private JLabel jlblStatus = new JLabel();
```

continues

Example 16.6 continued

```
  // Initialize the applet
  public void init()
  {
    // Create a panel to hold a label, a text field, and a button
    Panel p1 = new Panel();
    p1.setLayout(new BorderLayout());
    p1.add(new JLabel("Filename"), BorderLayout.WEST);
    p1.add(jtfURL, BorderLayout.CENTER);
    p1.add(jbtView, BorderLayout.EAST);

    // Place text area and panel p to the applet
    getContentPane().setLayout(new BorderLayout());
    getContentPane().add(new JScrollPane(jtaFile),
      BorderLayout.CENTER);
    getContentPane().add(p1, BorderLayout.NORTH);
    getContentPane().add(jlblStatus, BorderLayout.SOUTH);

    // Register listener
    jbtView.addActionListener(this);
  }

  // Handle the "View" button
  public void actionPerformed(ActionEvent e)
  {
    if (e.getSource() == jbtView)
      showFile();
  }

  private void showFile()
  {
    // Declare buffered stream
    BufferedReader infile = null;

    // Get file name from the text field
    String inLine;

    URL url = null;

    try
    {
      // Sample URL
      String urlString =
        "http://www.cs.armstrong.edu/liang/index.html";
        //"file:/C:\\Book\\ViewRemoteFile.java";
        //"http://www.cs.armstrong.edu/liang/intro3e" + filename;

      urlString = jtfURL.getText().trim();
      url = new URL(urlString);
      InputStream is = url.openStream();

      // Create a buffered stream
      infile = new BufferedReader(new InputStreamReader(is));

      // Read a line and append the line to the text area
      while ((inLine = infile.readLine()) != null)
      {
        jtaFile.append(inLine + '\n');
      }

      jlblStatus.setText("File loaded successfully");
    }
    catch (FileNotFoundException e)
    {
      jlblStatus.setText("URL not found: " + url);
```

```
      }
      catch (IOException e)
      {
        jlblStatus.setText(e.getMessage());
      }
      finally
      {
        try
        {
          if (infile != null) infile.close();
        }
        catch (IOException e) {}
      }
    }

    // Main method
    public static void main(String[] args)
    {
      // Create a frame
      JFrame frame = new JFrame("View File From a Web Server");

      // Create an instance of MortgageApplet
      ViewRemoteFile applet = new ViewRemoteFile();

      // Add the applet instance to the frame
      frame.getContentPane().add(applet, BorderLayout.CENTER);

      // Invoke init() and start()
      applet.init();
      applet.start();

      // Display the frame
      frame.setSize(300, 300);
      frame.setVisible(true);
    }
  }
```

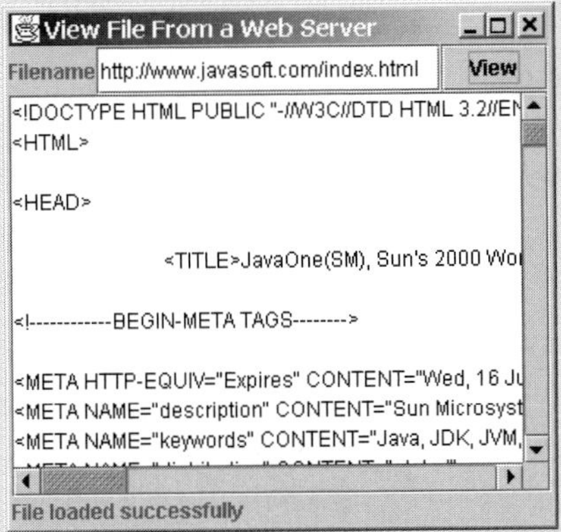

Figure 16.15 *The program displays the contents of a specified file on the Web server.*

Example Review

This program can run either as an applet or as an application. In order for it to run as an applet, the user would need to place two files on the Web server:

```
ViewRemoteFile.class
ViewRemoteFile.html
```

continues

Example 16.6 continued

ViewRemoteFile.html can be browsed from any JDK 1.2-enabled Web browser.

The `url = new URL(urlString)` statement creates a URL. The `InputStream is = url.openStream()` opens an input stream to read the remote file. After the input stream is established, reading data from the remote file is just like reading data locally.

Viewing HTML Files Using *JEditorPane*

Swing provides a new component named `javax.swing.JEditorPane` that can be used to display HTML files. `JEditorPane` is a subclass of `JTextComponent`. Thus it inherits all the behavior and properties of `JTextComponent`. Additionally, it is capable of rendering an HTML file with a given URL. The URL is specified in the `page` property, whose setter method is defined as follows:

```
public void setPage(URL url) IOException
```

`JEditorPane` generates `javax.swing.event.HyperlinkEvent` when a hyperlink in the editor pane is clicked. Through this event, you can get the URL of the hyperlink and display the content again using the `setPage(url)` method.

Example 16.7 Creating a Web Browser

This example creates a simple Web browser to render HTML files. The program lets the user enter an HTML file in a text field and press the Enter key to display the HTML file in an editor pane, as shown in Figure 16.16.

```
// WebBrowser.java: Display HTML file in JEditorPane
import java.awt.*;
import java.awt.event.*;
import java.applet.*;
import javax.swing.*;
import java.net.URL;
import javax.swing.event.*;
import java.io.*;

public class WebBrowser extends JApplet
  implements ActionListener, HyperlinkListener
{
  // JEditor pane to view HTML files
  private JEditorPane jep = new JEditorPane();

  // Label for URL
  private JLabel jlblURL = new JLabel("URL");

  // Text field for entering URL
  private JTextField jtfURL = new JTextField();

  // Initialize the applet
  public void init()
  {
```

```
    // Create a panel jpURL to hold the label and text field
    JPanel jpURL = new JPanel();
    jpURL.setLayout(new BorderLayout());
    jpURL.add(jlblURL, BorderLayout.WEST);
    jpURL.add(jtfURL, BorderLayout.CENTER);

    // Create a scroll pane to hold JEditorPane
    JScrollPane jspViewer = new JScrollPane();
    jspViewer.getViewport().add(jep, null);

    // Place jpURL and jspViewer in the applet
    this.getContentPane().add(jspViewer, BorderLayout.CENTER);
    this.getContentPane().add(jpURL, BorderLayout.NORTH);

    // Set jep noneditable
    jep.setEditable(false);

    // Register listener
    jep.addHyperlinkListener(this);
    jtfURL.addActionListener(this);
  }

  public void actionPerformed(ActionEvent e)
  {
    // TODO: Implement this java.awt.event.ActionListener method
    try
    {
      // Get the URL from text field
      URL url = new URL(jtfURL.getText().trim());

      // Display the HTML file
      jep.setPage(url);
    }
    catch (IOException ex)
    {
      System.out.println(ex);
    }
  }

  public void hyperlinkUpdate(HyperlinkEvent e)
  {
    // TODO: Implement HyperlinkListener method
    try
    {
      jep.setPage(e.getURL());
    }
    catch (IOException ex)
    {
      System.out.println(ex);
    }
  }

  // Main method
  public static void main(String[] args)
  {
    // Create a frame
    JFrame frame = new JFrame("Web Browser");

    // Create an instance of the applet
    WebBrowser applet = new WebBrowser();

    // Add the applet instance to the frame
    frame.getContentPane().add(applet, BorderLayout.CENTER);

    // Invoke init() and start()
    applet.init();
    applet.start();
```

continues

Example 16.7 continued

```
        // Display the frame
        frame.setSize(600, 600);
        // frame.setDefaultCloseOperation(JFrame.EXIT_ON_CLOSE);
        frame.setVisible(true);
      }
    }
```

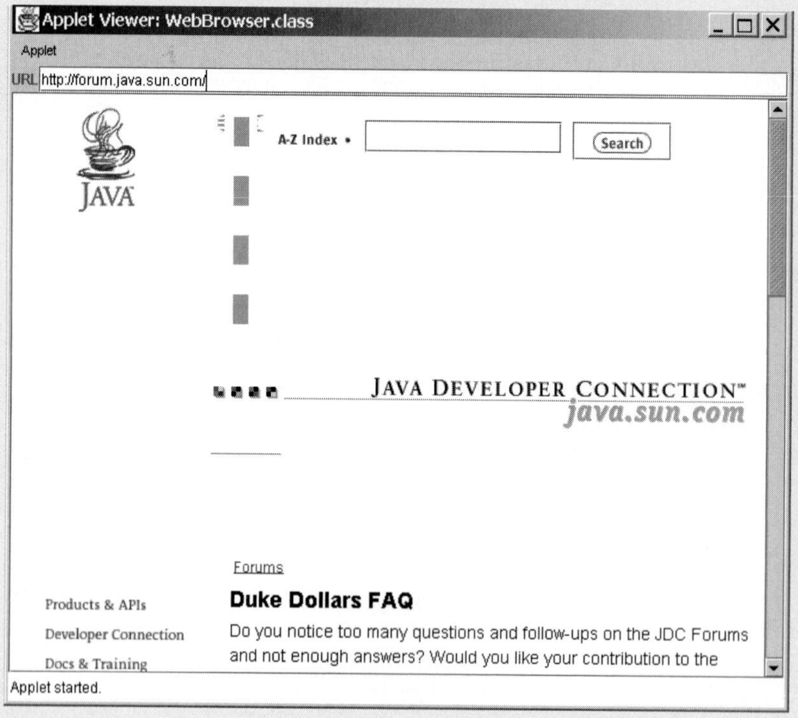

Figure 16.16 *You can specify a URL in the text field and display the HTML file in an editor pane.*

Example Review

In this example, a simple Web browser is created using the `JEditorPane` class. `JEditorPane` is capable of displaying files in the HTML format or in the RTF format. To enable scrolling, the editor pane is placed inside a scroll pane.

The user enters a URL of the HTML file in the text field and presses the Enter key to fire an action event to display the URL in the editor pane. To display the URL in the editor pane, simply set the URL in the `page` property of the editor pane.

The editor pane does not have all the functions of a commercial Web browser, but it is convenient for displaying HTML files, including embedded images.

This program cannot view a local HTML file. To view a remote HTML file, you have to enter a URL beginning with http://. In Exercise 16.8, you will modify the program so that it can also view an HTML file from the local host and accept URLs beginning with either http:// or www.

TIP

In JDK 1.2.2 or above, you have to take the following steps to cross security checks to run this applet using applet viewer:

1. Create a policy file named java.policy, as follows:

```
grant
{
  // Allow everything for now
  permission java.security.AllPermission;
};
```

2. Use the following command to run the applet:

```
appletviewer -J-Djava.security.policy=java.policy WebBrowser.html
```

Cases Studies (Optional)

In the Case Studies section in Chapter 10, "Applets and Advanced Graphics," you developed an applet for the TicTacToe game that enables two players to play from the same machine. In this section, you will learn to develop a distributed TicTacToe game using multithreads and networking with socket streams.

Example 16.8 Distributed TicTacToe Game

This example creates a distributed TicTacToe game that enables users to play on different machines from anywhere on the Internet. The example consists of a server for multiple clients. The server creates a server socket, and accepts connections from every two players to form a session. Each session is a thread that communicates with the two players and determines the status of the game. The server can establish any number of sessions, as shown in Figure 16.17.

For each session, the first client connecting to the server is identified as player 1 with token 'X', and the second client connecting to the server is identified as player 2 with token 'O'. The server notifies the players of their respective tokens. Once two clients are connected to the server, the server starts a thread to facilitate the game between the two players by performing the steps repeatedly, as shown in Figure 16.18.

The server does not have to be a graphical component, but creating it as a frame in which game information can be viewed is user-friendly. You can create a scroll pane to hold a text area in the frame, and display game information in the text area. The server creates a thread to handle a game session when two players are connected to the server.

continues

Example 16.8 continued

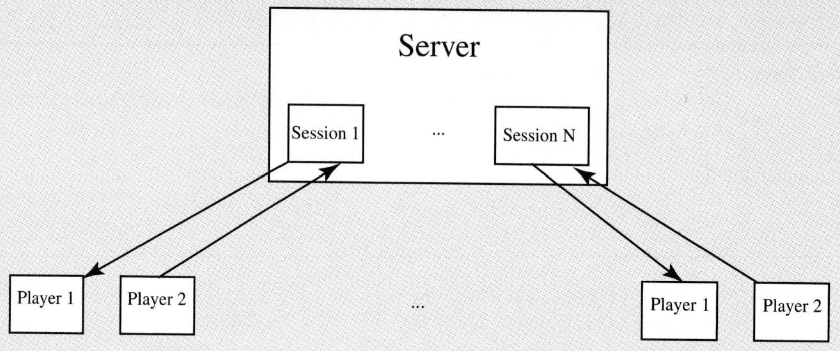

Server

Session 1 ... Session N

Player 1 Player 2 ... Player 1 Player 2

Figure 16.17 *The server can create many sessions, each of which facilitates a TicTacToe game for two players.*

The client is responsible for interacting with the players. It creates a user interface with nine cells, and displays the game title and status to the players in the labels. The client class is very similar to the TicTacToe class presented in Example 10.9, "The TicTacToe Game." However, the client in this example does not determine the game status (win or draw), it simply passes the moves to the server and receives game status from the server.

Based on the foregoing analysis, you can create the following classes:

- `TicTacToeServer` to serve all the clients.
- `HandleASession` to facilitate the game for two players.
- `TicTacToeClient` to model a player.
- `Cell` to model a cell in the game.
- `TicTacToeConstants` is an interface that defines the constants shared by all the classes in this example.

The relationships of these classes are shown in Figure 16.19.

The program is given as follows:

```
// TicTacToeConstants.java: Define constants for the classes
public interface TicTacToeConstants
{
  public static int PLAYER1 = 1; // Indicate player 1
  public static int PLAYER2 = 2; // Indicate player 2
  public static int PLAYER1_WON = 1; // Indicate player 1 won
  public static int PLAYER2_WON = 2; // Indicate player 2 won
  public static int DRAW = 3; // Indicate a draw
  public static int CONTINUE = 4; // Indicate to continue
}

// TicTacToeServer.java: Server for the TicTacToe game
import java.io.*;
import java.net.*;
```

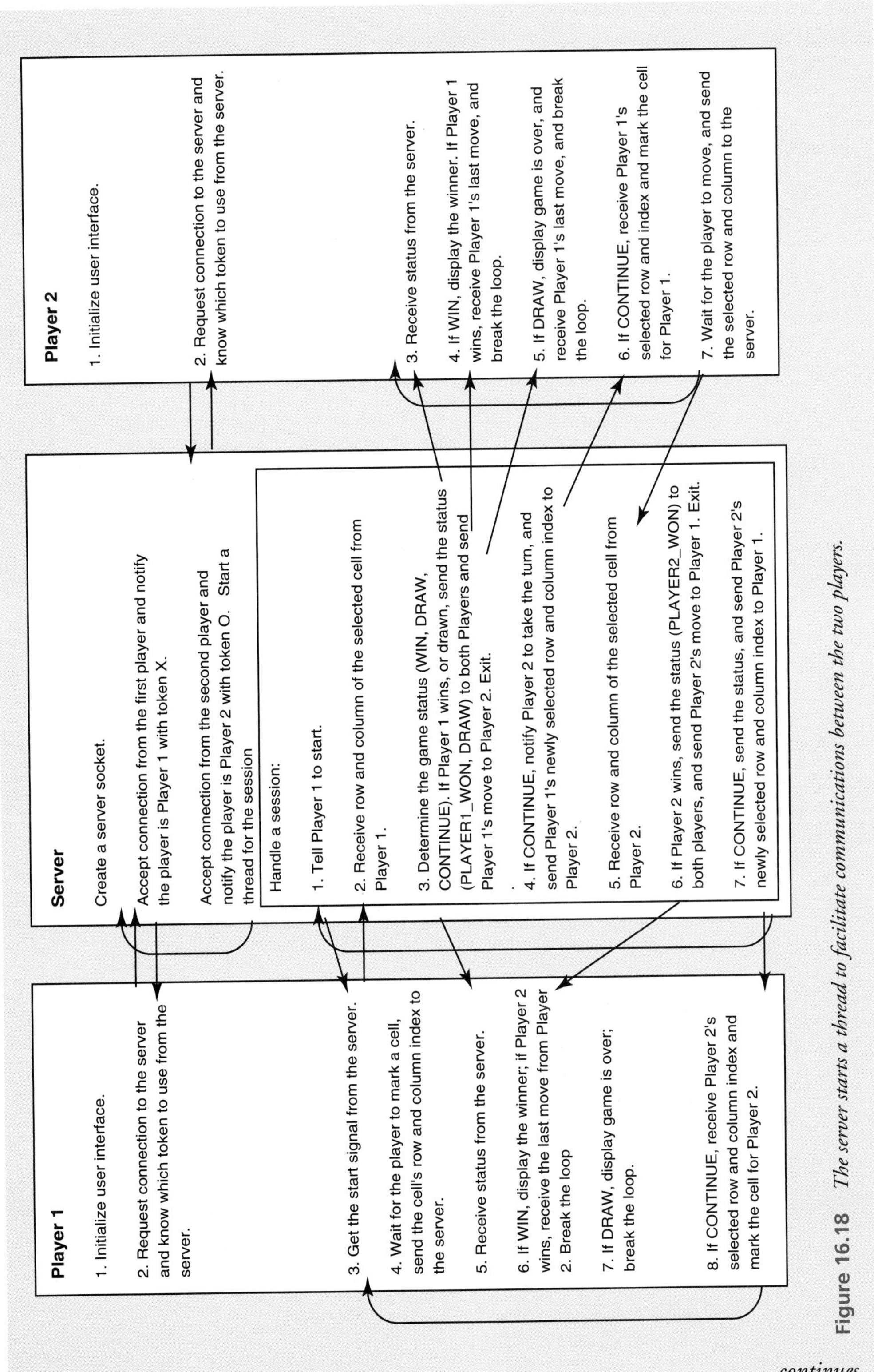

Figure 16.18 *The server starts a thread to facilitate communications between the two players.*

continues

Example 16.8 continued

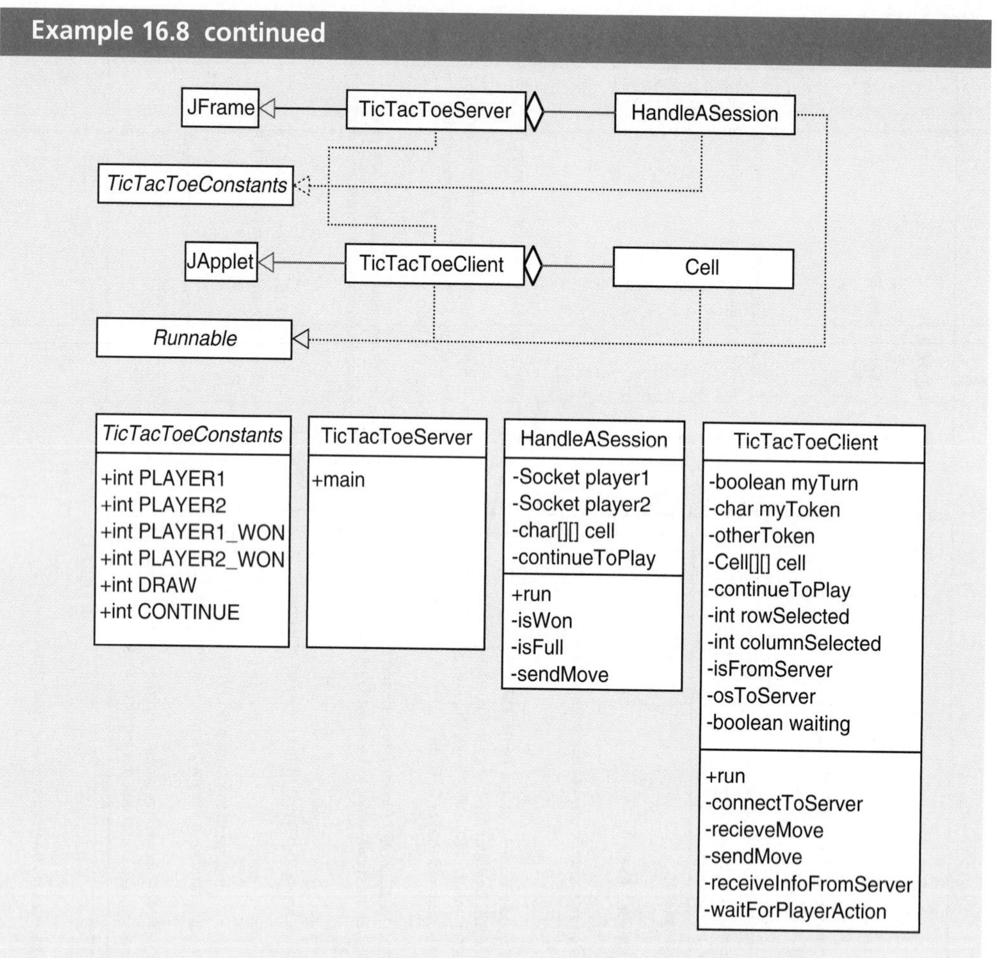

Figure 16.19 *`TicTacToeServer` creates an instance of `HandleASession` for each session of two players. `TicTacToeClient` creates nine cells in the UI.*

```
import javax.swing.*;
import java.awt.*;
import java.util.Date;

public class TicTacToeServer extends JFrame
  implements TicTacToeConstants
{
  // Main method
  public static void main(String[] args)
  {
    TicTacToeServer frame = new TicTacToeServer();
  }

  public TicTacToeServer()
  {
    JTextArea jtaLog;

    // Create a scroll pane to hold text area
    JScrollPane scrollPane = new JScrollPane(
      jtaLog = new JTextArea());
```

```
      // Add the scroll pane to the frame
      getContentPane().add(scrollPane, BorderLayout.CENTER);

      setSize(300, 300);
      setTitle("TicTacToeServer");
      setVisible(true);

      try
      {
        // Create a server socket
        ServerSocket serverSocket = new ServerSocket(8000);
        jtaLog.append(new Date() +
          ": Server started at socket 8000\n");

        // Number a session
        int sessionNo = 1;

        // Ready to create a session for every two players
        while (true)
        {
          jtaLog.append(new Date() +
            ": Wait for players to join session " + sessionNo + '\n');

          // Connect to player 1
          Socket player1 = serverSocket.accept();

          jtaLog.append(new Date() + ": Player 1 joined session " +
            sessionNo + '\n');
          jtaLog.append("Player 1's IP address" +
            player1.getInetAddress().getHostAddress() + '\n');

          // Notify that the player is Player 1
          new DataOutputStream(
            player1.getOutputStream()).writeInt(PLAYER1);

          // Connect to player 2
          Socket player2 = serverSocket.accept();

          jtaLog.append(new Date() +
            ": Player 2 joined session " + sessionNo + '\n');
          jtaLog.append("Player 2's IP address" +
            player2.getInetAddress().getHostAddress() + '\n');

          // Notify that the player is Player 2
          new DataOutputStream(
            player2.getOutputStream()).writeInt(PLAYER2);

          // Display this session and increment session number
          jtaLog.append(new Date() + ": Start a thread for session " +
            sessionNo++ + '\n');

          // Create a new thread for this session of two players
          HandleASession thread = new HandleASession(player1, player2);

          // Start the new thread
          thread.start();
        }
      }
      catch(IOException ex)
      {
        System.err.println(ex);
      }
    }
  }
```

continues

Example 16.8 continued

```
// Define the thread class for handling a new session for two players
class HandleASession extends Thread implements TicTacToeConstants
{
  private Socket player1;
  private Socket player2;

  // Create and initialize cells
  private char[][] cell =  new char[3][3];

  private DataInputStream isFromPlayer1;
  private DataOutputStream osToPlayer1;
  private DataInputStream isFromPlayer2;
  private DataOutputStream osToPlayer2;

  // Continue to play
  private boolean continueToPlay = true;

  // Construct a thread
  public HandleASession(Socket player1, Socket player2)
  {
    this.player1 = player1;
    this.player2 = player2;

    // Initialize cells
    for (int i=0; i<3; i++)
      for (int j=0; j<3; j++)
        cell[i][j] = ' ';
  }

  // Implement the run() method for the thread
  public void run()
  {
    try
    {
      // Create data input and output streams
      DataInputStream isFromPlayer1 = new DataInputStream(
        player1.getInputStream());
      DataOutputStream osToPlayer1 = new DataOutputStream(
        player1.getOutputStream());
      DataInputStream isFromPlayer2 = new DataInputStream(
        player2.getInputStream());
      DataOutputStream osToPlayer2 = new DataOutputStream(
        player2.getOutputStream());

      // Write anything to notify player 1 to start
      // This is just to let player 1 know to start
      osToPlayer1.writeInt(1);

      // Continuously serve the players and determine and report
      // the game status to the players
      while (true)
      {
        // Receive a move from player 1
        int row = isFromPlayer1.readInt();
        int column = isFromPlayer1.readInt();
        cell[row][column] = 'X';

        // Check if Player 1 wins
        if (isWon('X'))
        {
          osToPlayer1.writeInt(PLAYER1_WON);
          osToPlayer2.writeInt(PLAYER1_WON);
          sendMove(osToPlayer2, row, column);
```

```
          break; // Break the loop
        }
        else if (isFull()) // Check if all cells are filled
        {
          osToPlayer1.writeInt(DRAW);
          osToPlayer2.writeInt(DRAW);
          sendMove(osToPlayer2, row, column);
          break;
        }
        else
        {
          // Notify player 2 to take the turn
          osToPlayer2.writeInt(CONTINUE);

          // Send player 1's selected row and column to player 2
          sendMove(osToPlayer2, row, column);
        }

        // Receive a move from Player 2
        row = isFromPlayer2.readInt();

        column = isFromPlayer2.readInt();
        cell[row][column] = 'O';

        // Check if Player 2 wins
        if (isWon('O'))
        {
          osToPlayer1.writeInt(PLAYER2_WON);
          osToPlayer2.writeInt(PLAYER2_WON);
          sendMove(osToPlayer1, row, column);
          break;
        }
        else
        {
          // Notify player 1 to take the turn
          osToPlayer1.writeInt(CONTINUE);

          // Send player 2's selected row and column to player 1
          sendMove(osToPlayer1, row, column);
        }
      }
    }
    catch(IOException ex)
    {
      System.err.println(ex);
    }
  }

  // Send the move to other player
  private void sendMove(DataOutputStream out, int row, int column)
    throws IOException
  {
    out.writeInt(row); // Send row index
    out.writeInt(column); // Send column index
  }

  // Determine if the cells are all occupied
  private boolean isFull()
  {
    for (int i=0; i<3; i++)
      for (int j=0; j<3; j++)
        if (cell[i][j] == ' ')
          return false; // At least one cell is not filled
```

continues

Example 16.8 continued

```
      // All cells are filled
      return true;
    }

    // Determine if the player with the specified token wins
    private boolean isWon(char token)
    {
      // Check all rows
      for (int i=0; i<3; i++)
        if ((cell[i][0] == token)
            && (cell[i][1] == token)
            && (cell[i][2] == token))
        {
          return true;
        }

      // Check all columns
      for (int j=0; j<3; j++)
        if ((cell[0][j] == token)
            && (cell[1][j] == token)
            && (cell[2][j] == token))
        {
          return true;
        }

      // Check major diagonal
      if ((cell[0][0] == token)
          && (cell[1][1] == token)
          && (cell[2][2] == token))
      {
        return true;
      }

      // Check subdiagonal
      if ((cell[0][2] == token)
          && (cell[1][1] == token)
          && (cell[2][0] == token))
      {
        return true;
      }

      // All checked, but no winner
      return false;
    }
  }

// TicTacToeClient.java: Play the TicTacToe game
import java.awt.*;
import java.awt.event.*;
import javax.swing.*;
import javax.swing.border.LineBorder;
import java.io.*;
import java.net.*;

public class TicTacToeClient extends JApplet
  implements Runnable, TicTacToeConstants
{
  // Indicate whether the player has the turn
  private boolean myTurn = false;

  // Indicate the token for the player
  private char myToken = ' ';

  // Indicate the token for the other player
```

```
private char otherToken = ' ';

// Create and initialize cells
private Cell[][] cell =  new Cell[3][3];

// Create and initialize a title label
private JLabel jlblTitle = new JLabel();

// Create and initialize a status label
private JLabel jlblStatus = new JLabel();

// Indicate selected row and column by the current move
private int rowSelected;
private int columnSelected;

// Input and output streams from/to server
private DataInputStream isFromServer;
private DataOutputStream osToServer;

// Continue to play?
private boolean continueToPlay = true;

// Wait for the player to mark a cell
private boolean waiting = true;

// Initialize UI
public void init()
{
  // Panel p to hold cells
  JPanel p = new JPanel();
  p.setLayout(new GridLayout(3, 3, 0, 0));
  for (int i=0; i<3; i++)
    for (int j=0; j<3; j++)
      p.add(cell[i][j] = new Cell(i, j));

  // Set properties for labels and borders for labels and panel
  p.setBorder(new LineBorder(Color.black, 1));
  jlblTitle.setHorizontalAlignment(JLabel.CENTER);
  jlblTitle.setFont(new Font("SansSerif", Font.BOLD, 16));
  jlblTitle.setBorder(new LineBorder(Color.black, 1));
  jlblStatus.setBorder(new LineBorder(Color.black, 1));

  // Place the panel and the labels to the applet
  this.getContentPane().add(jlblTitle, BorderLayout.NORTH);
  this.getContentPane().add(p, BorderLayout.CENTER);
  this.getContentPane().add(jlblStatus, BorderLayout.SOUTH);

  // Connect to the server
  connectToServer();
}

private void connectToServer()
{
  try
  {
    // Create a socket to connect to the server
    Socket connectToServer = new Socket("localhost", 8000);

    // Create an input stream to receive data from the server
    isFromServer = new DataInputStream(
      connectToServer.getInputStream());

    // Create an output stream to send data to the server
    osToServer =
      new DataOutputStream(connectToServer.getOutputStream());
```

continues

Example 16.8 continued

```
    }
    catch (Exception ex)
    {
      System.err.println(ex);
    }

    // Control the game on a separate thread
    Thread thread = new Thread(this);
    thread.start();
  }

  // This main method enables the applet to run as an application
  public static void main(String[] args)
  {
    // Create a frame
    JFrame frame = new JFrame("Tic Tac Toe Client");

    // Create an instance of the applet
    TicTacToeClient applet = new TicTacToeClient();

    // Add the applet instance to the frame
    frame.getContentPane().add(applet, BorderLayout.CENTER);

    // Invoke init() and start()
    applet.init();
    applet.start();

    // Display the frame
    frame.setSize(320, 300);
    // frame.setDefaultCloseOperation(JFrame.EXIT_ON_CLOSE);
    frame.setVisible(true);
  }

  public void run()
  {
    try
    {
      // Get notification from the server
      int player = isFromServer.readInt();

      // Am I player 1 or 2?
      if (player == PLAYER1)
      {
        myToken = 'X';
        otherToken = 'O';
        jlblTitle.setText("Player 1 with token 'X'");
        jlblStatus.setText("Waiting for player 2 to join");

        // Receive startup notification from the server
        isFromServer.readInt(); // Whatever read is ignored

        // The other player has joined
        jlblStatus.setText("Player 2 has joined. I start first");

        // It is my turn
        myTurn = true;
      }
      else if (player == PLAYER2)
      {
        myToken = 'O';
        otherToken = 'X';
        jlblTitle.setText("Player 2 with token 'O'");
        jlblStatus.setText("Waiting for player 1 to move");
      }
```

```
      // Continue to play
      while (continueToPlay)
      {
        if (player == PLAYER1)
        {
          waitForPlayerAction(); // Wait for player 1 to move
          sendMove(); // Send the move to the server
          receiveInfoFromServer(); // Receive info from the server
        }
        else if (player == PLAYER2)
        {
          receiveInfoFromServer(); // Receive info from the server
          waitForPlayerAction(); // Wait for player 2 to move
          sendMove(); // Send player 2's move to the server
        }
      }
    }
    catch (Exception ex)
    { }
  }

  // Wait for the player to mark a cell
  private void waitForPlayerAction() throws InterruptedException
  {
    while (waiting)
    {
      Thread.sleep(100);
    }

    waiting = true;
  }

  // Send this player's move to the server
  private void sendMove() throws IOException
  {
    osToServer.writeInt(rowSelected); // Send the selected row
    osToServer.writeInt(columnSelected); // Send the selected column
  }

  // Receive info from the server
  private void receiveInfoFromServer() throws IOException
  {
    // Receive game status
    int status = isFromServer.readInt();

    if (status == PLAYER1_WON)
    {
      // Player 1 won, stop playing

      continueToPlay = false;
      if (myToken == 'X')
      {
        jlblStatus.setText("I won! (X)");
      }
      else if (myToken == 'O')
      {
        jlblStatus.setText("Player 1 (X) has won!");
        receiveMove();
      }
    }
    else if (status == PLAYER2_WON)
    {
      // Player 2 won, stop playing
      continueToPlay = false;
      if (myToken == 'O')
```

continues

Example 16.8 continued

```
        {
          jlblStatus.setText("I won! (O)");
        }
        else if (myToken == 'X')
        {
          jlblStatus.setText("Player 2 (O) has won!");
          receiveMove();
        }
      }
      else if (status == DRAW)
      {
        // No winner, game is over
        continueToPlay = false;
        jlblStatus.setText("Game is over, no winner!");

        //
        if (myToken == 'O')
        {
          receiveMove();
        }
      }
      else
      {
        receiveMove();
        jlblStatus.setText("My turn");
        myTurn = true; // It is my turn
      }
    }

    private void receiveMove() throws IOException
    {
      // Get the other player's move
      int row = isFromServer.readInt();
      int column = isFromServer.readInt();
      cell[row][column].setToken(otherToken);
    }

    // An inner class for a cell
    public class Cell extends JPanel implements MouseListener
    {
      // Indicate the row and column of this cell in the board
      private int row;
      private int column;

      // Token used for this cell
      private char token = ' ';

      public Cell(int row, int column)
      {
        this.row = row;
        this.column = column;
        setBorder(new LineBorder(Color.black, 1)); // Set cell's border
        addMouseListener(this);  // Register listener
      }

      // The getter method for token
      public char getToken()
      {
        return token;
      }

      // The setter method for token
      public void setToken(char c)
      {
```

```
        token = c;
        repaint();
      }

      // Paint the cell
      public void paintComponent(Graphics g)
      {
        super.paintComponent(g);

        if (token == 'X')
        {
          g.drawLine(10, 10, getSize().width-10, getSize().height-10);
          g.drawLine(getSize().width-10, 10, 10, getSize().height-10);
        }
        else if (token == 'O')
        {
          g.drawOval(10, 10, getSize().width-20, getSize().height-20);
        }
      }

      // Handle mouse click on a cell
      public void mouseClicked(MouseEvent e)
      {
        // If cell is not occupied and the player has the turn
        if ((token == ' ') && myTurn)
        {
          setToken(myToken);  // Set the player's token in the cell
          myTurn = false;
          rowSelected = row;
          columnSelected = column;
          jlblStatus.setText("Waiting for the other player to move");
          waiting = false; // Just completed a successful move
        }
      }

      public void mousePressed(MouseEvent e)
      {
        // TODO: implement this java.awt.event.MouseListener method;
      }

      public void mouseReleased(MouseEvent e)
      {
        // TODO: implement this java.awt.event.MouseListener method;
      }

      public void mouseEntered(MouseEvent e)
      {
        // TODO: implement this java.awt.event.MouseListener method;
      }

      public void mouseExited(MouseEvent e)
      {
        // TODO: implement this java.awt.event.MouseListener method;
      }
    }
  }
```

Example Review

The server can serve any number of sessions. Each session takes care of two players. The client can be a Java applet or a Java application. To run a client as a Java applet from a Web browser, the server must run from a Web server. Figures 16.20 and 16.21 show sample runs of the server and the clients.

continues

Example 16.8 continued

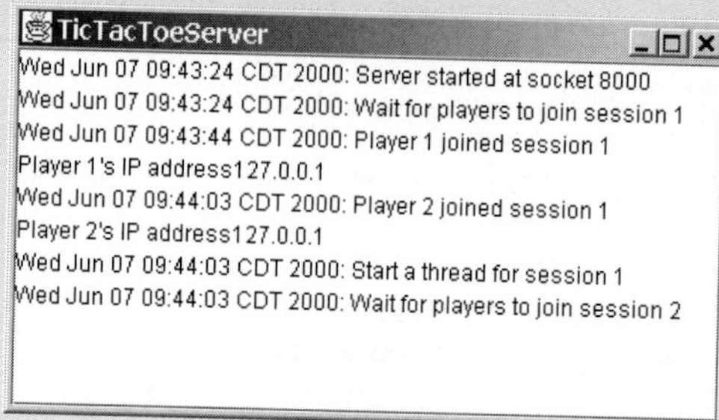

Figure 16.20 `TicTacToeServer` *accepts connection requests and creates sessions to serve pairs of players.*

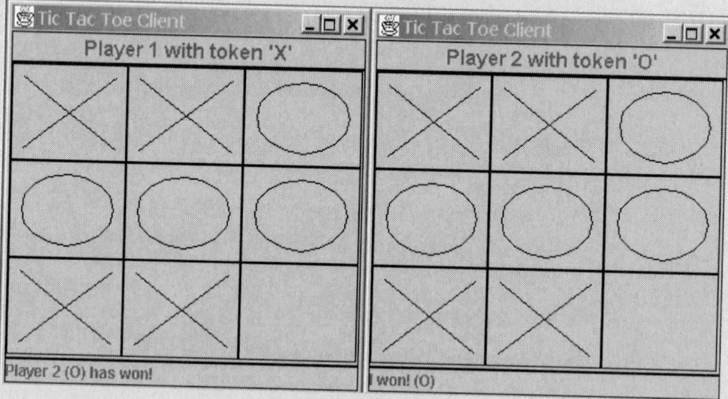

Figure 16.21 `TicTacToeClient` *can run as an applet or an application.*

The `TicTacToeConstants` interface defines the constants shared by all the classes in the project. Centrally defining constants in an interface is a common practice in Java. For example, all the constants shared by Swing classes are defined in `java.swing.SwingConstants`.

Once a session is established, the server receives moves from the players in alternation. Upon receiving a move from a player, the server determines the status of the game. If the game is not finished, the server sends the status (CONTINUE) and the player's move to the other player. If the game is won or drawn, the server sends the status (PLAYER1_WON, PLAYER2_WON, or DRAW) to both players.

The implementation of Java network programs at the socket level is tightly synchronized. An operation to send data from one machine requires an operation to receive data from the other machine. As shown in this example, the server and the client are tightly synchronized to send or to receive data.

Note
There are several techniques for developing Java network programs. Socket-level programming is very primitive. Another technique is known as Remote Method Invocation (RMI). RMI is the Java Distributed Object Model for facilitating communications among distributed objects. RMI is a higher-level API built on top of sockets. Socket-level programming allows you to pass data through sockets among computers. RMI enables you not only to pass data among objects on different systems, but also to invoke methods in a remote object. For more information, please refer to my *Rapid Java Application Development Using JBuilder 3.*

Chapter Summary

This chapter introduced socket-level network programming in Java. You learned how to write client/server applications.

To create a server, you must first obtain a server socket, using `new ServerSocket(port)`. After a server socket is created, the server can start to listen for connections, using the `accept()` method on the server socket. The client requests a connection to a server by using `new socket(ServerName, port)` to create a client socket.

Stream socket communication is very much like input/output stream communication after the connection between a server and a client is established. You can obtain an input stream using the `getInputStream` method and obtain an output stream using the `getOutputStream` method on the socket.

A server must often work with multiple clients at the same time. You can use threads to handle the server's multiple clients simultaneously by creating a thread for each connection.

Applets are good for deploying multiple clients. They can be run anywhere with a single copy of the program. However, an applet client can only connect to the server where the applet is loaded, due to security restrictions.

Java programs can get HTML pages through HTTP by directly connecting with a Web server. The URL can be used to view a Web page in a Java applet. To retrieve data files on the Web server from applets, you can open a stream on the file's URL on the Web server.

Review Questions

16.1 How do you create a server socket? What port numbers can be used? What happens if a requested socket number is already in use? Can a port connect to multiple clients?

16.2 What are the differences between a server socket and a client socket?

16.3 How does a client program initiate a connection?

16.4 How does a server accept a connection?

16.5 How are data transferred between a client and a server? Can objects be transferred?

16.6 How do you make a server serve multiple clients?

16.7 Can an application retrieve a file from a remote host? Can an application update a file on a remote host?

Programming Exercises

16.1 Rewrite Example 16.1 using buffered reader for input and print stream for output. Use the `readLine()` method to read a string from the input stream, and use the `Double.parseDouble(string)` to convert the string into a double value. Name the client Exercise16_1Client and the server Exercise16_1Server.

16.2 Rewrite Example 16.2 using GUI for the server and the client rather than console input and output. Display a message in the text area on the server side when the server receives a message from a client, as shown in Figure 16.22. On the client side, you can use a text field to enter the radius, as shown in Figure 16.23. Name the client Exercise16_2Client and the server Exercise16_2Server.

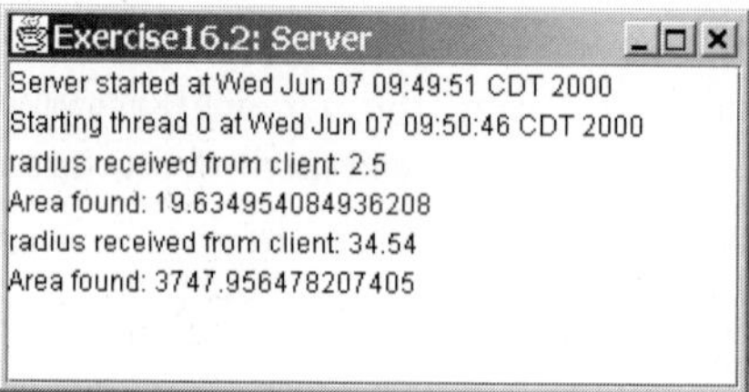

Figure 16.22 *The server receives a radius from a client, computes the area, and sends the area to the client.*

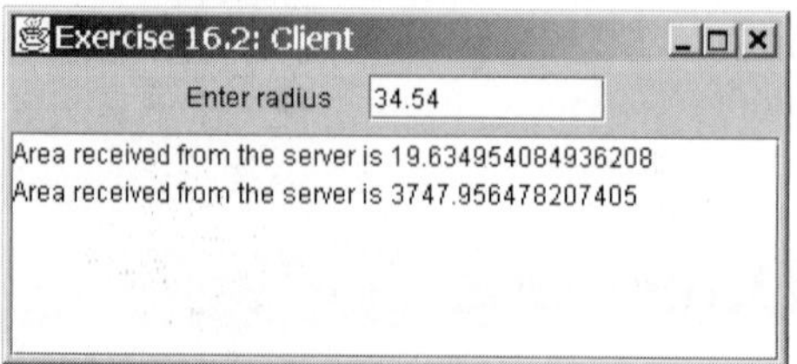

Figure 16.23 *The client sends the radius to the server and receives the area from the server.*

16.3 Modify Example 16.3, "Creating Applet Clients," by adding the following features:

- Add a View button to the user interface that allows the client to view a record for a specified name. The user will be able to enter a name in the Name field and click the View button to display the record for the student, as shown in Figure 16.24.
- Limit the concurrent connections to two clients.
- Display the status of the submission (Successful or Failed) on a label.
- Use one thread to handle all requests from a client. The thread terminates when the client exits.
- Name the client Exercise16_3Client and the server Exercise16_3Server.

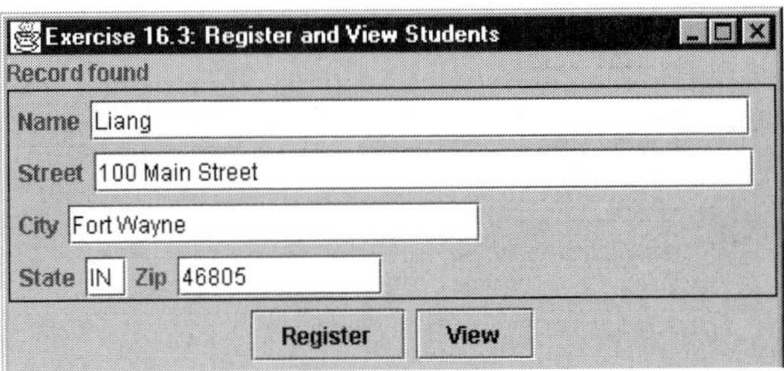

Figure 16.24 *You can view or register students in this applet.*

16.4 Example 15.8, "Using `StreamTokenizer`," in Chapter 15, "Input and Output," computes total scores from exam scores stored in a text file. Rewrite this example as an applet to read the file from a Web server. The exercise reads the file from a Web server rather than from the local system. The file contains student exam scores. Each record in the input file consists of a student name, two midterm exam scores, and a final exam score. The program reads the fields for each record, computes the total score, and displays the result in a text area. Figure 16.25 contains the output of a sample run of the program.

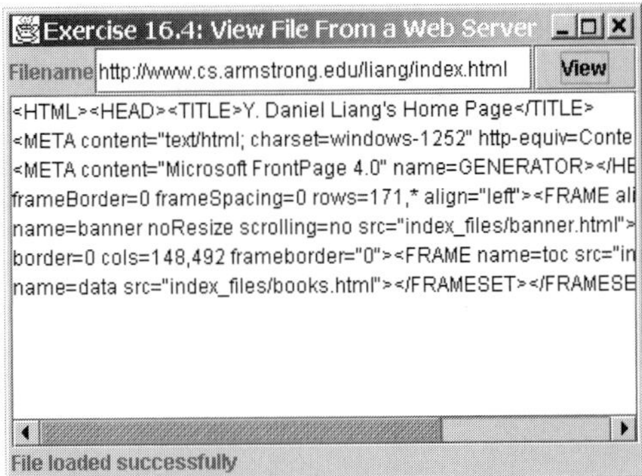

Figure 16.25 *The applet retrieves the file from the Web server and processes it.*

16.5 Rewrite Example 16.6, "Retrieving Remote Files," to use `JEditorPane` to replace `JTextArea`.

16.6 Write an applet that shows the number of visits made to a Web page. The count should be stored in a file on the server side. Every time the page is visited or reloaded, the applet should send a request to the server, and the server should increase the count and send it to the applet. The applet should then display the new count in a message, such as You are visitor number: 1000, as shown in Figure 16.26. Name the client Exercise16_6Client and the server Exercise16_6Server.

(Hint: Use a random-access file stream to read or write the count to the file. To improve performance, read the count from the file when the server starts and save the count to the file when the server exits. When the server is alive, use a variable to store the count. When a client applet starts, it connects to the server; the server increases the count by 1 and sends it to the client for display.)

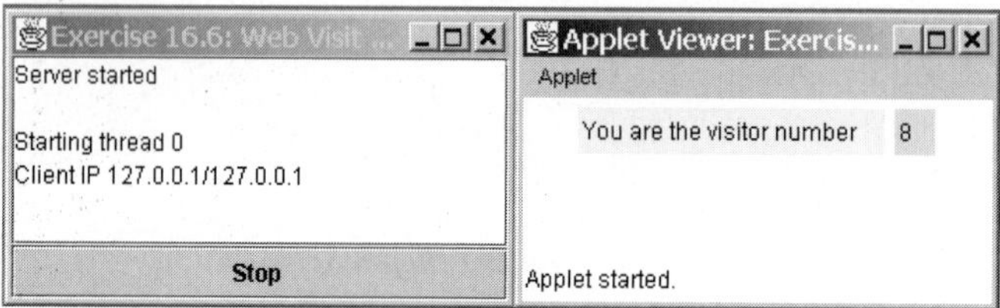

Figure 16.26 *The applet displays how many times this Web page has been accessed. The server stores the count.*

16.7 Write an applet like the ones in Exercise 15.7. Ensure that the applet gets the stock index from a file stored on the Web server. Enable the applet to run standalone.

16.8 Modify Example 16.7, "Creating a Web Browser," as follows:

- It accepts an HTML file from a local host. Assume that a local HTML filename begins neither with http:// nor with www.
- It accepts a remote HTML file. A remote HTML filename begins with either http:// or www.

APPENDIXES

The appendixes cover a mixed bag of topics. Appendix A lists Java keywords. Appendix B gives tables of ASCII characters and their associated codes in decimal and in hex. Appendix C shows the operator precedence. Appendix D summarizes Java modifiers and their usage. Appendix E introduces number systems and conversions among binary, decimal, and hex numbers. Appendix F introduces HTML basics. Appendix G lists UML Graphical Notations for describing classes and their relationships. Appendix H introduces packages for grouping classes. Appendix I gives a JBuilder 3.5 tutorial. Finally, Appendix J provides a glossary of key terms used in the text.

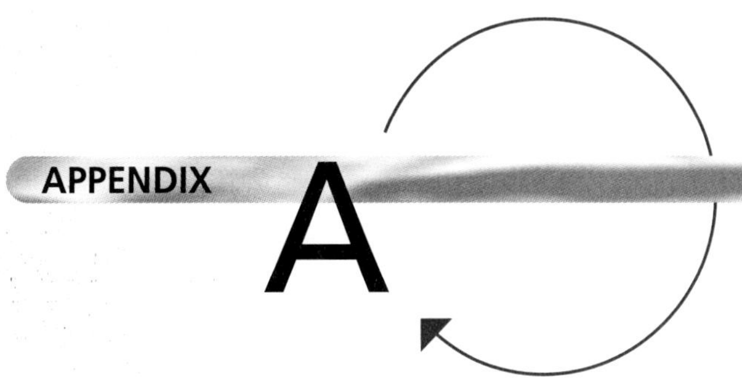

Java Keywords

The following 47 keywords are reserved for use by the Java language:

```
abstract       finally        public
boolean        float          return
break          for            short
byte           goto           static
case           if             super
catch          implements     switch
char           import         synchronized
class          instanceof     this
const          int            throw
continue       interface      throws
default        long           transient
do             native         try
double         new            void
else           package        volatile
extends        private        while
final          protected
```

The keywords `goto` and `const` are C++ keywords reserved, but not currently used, in Java. This enables Java compilers to identify them and to produce better error messages if they appear in Java programs.

The Boolean literal values `true` and `false` are not keywords. Similarly, the `null` object value is not classified as a keyword. You cannot use them for other purposes, however.

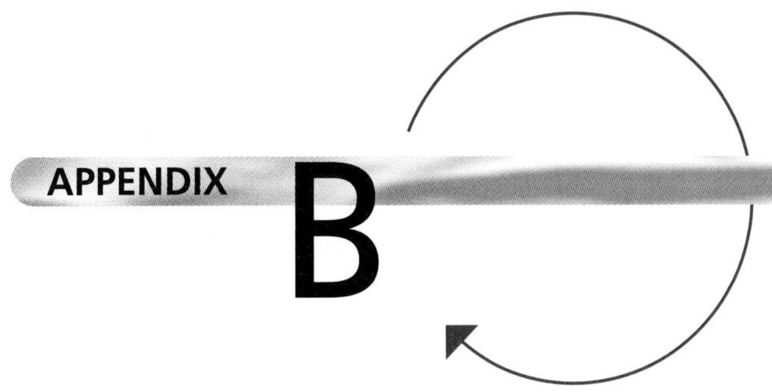

The ASCII Character Set

Tables B.1 and B.2 show ASCII characters and their respective decimal and hexadecimal codes. The decimal or hexadecimal code of a character is a combination of its row index and column index. For example, in Table B.1, the letter A is at row 6 and column 5, so its decimal equivalent is 65; in Table B.2, letter A is at row 4 and column 1, so its hexadecimal equivalent is 41.

TABLE B.1 ASCII Character Set in the Decimal Index

	0	*1*	*2*	*3*	*4*	*5*	*6*	*7*	*8*	*9*
0	nul	soh	stx	etx	eot	enq	ack	bel	bs	ht
1	nl	vt	ff	cr	so	si	dle	dcl	dc2	dc3
2	dc4	nak	syn	etb	can	em	sub	esc	fs	gs
3	rs	us	sp	!	”	#	$	%	&	’
4	(	)	*	+	,	-	.	/	0	1
5	2	3	4	5	6	7	8	9	:	;
6	<	=	>	?	@	A	B	C	D	E
7	F	G	H	I	J	K	L	M	N	O
8	P	Q	R	S	T	U	V	W	X	Y
9	Z	[	\	]	^	_	‘	a	b	c
10	d	e	f	g	h	i	j	k	l	m
11	n	o	p	q	r	s	t	u	v	w
12	x	y	z	{	|	}	~	del		

TABLE B.2 ASCII Character Set in the Hexadecimal Index

	0	*1*	*2*	*3*	*4*	*5*	*6*	*7*	*8*	*9*	*A*	*B*	*C*	*D*	*E*	*F*
0	nul	soh	stx	etx	eot	enq	ack	bel	bs	ht	nl	vt	ff	cr	so	si
1	dle	dcl	dc2	dc3	dc4	nak	syn	etb	can	em	sub	esc	fs	gs	rs	us
2	sp	!	“	#	$	%	&	’	(	)	*	+	,	-	.	/
3	0	1	2	3	4	5	6	7	8	9	:	;	<	=	>	?
4	@	A	B	C	D	E	F	G	H	I	J	K	L	M	N	O
5	P	Q	R	S	T	U	V	W	X	Y	Z	[	\	]	^	_
6	‘	a	b	c	d	e	f	g	h	i	j	k	l	m	n	o
7	p	q	r	s	t	u	v	w	x	y	z	{	|	}	~	del

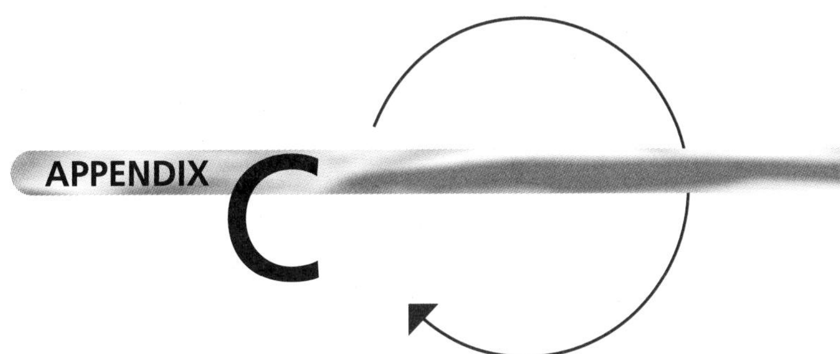

OPERATOR PRECEDENCE CHART

The operators are shown in decreasing order of precedence from top to bottom. Operators in the same group have the same precedence.

<table>
<tr><th>Operator</th><th>Name</th></tr>
<tr><td>()</td><td>Parentheses</td></tr>
<tr><td>()</td><td>Function call</td></tr>
<tr><td>[]</td><td>Array subscript</td></tr>
<tr><td>.</td><td>Object member access</td></tr>
<tr><td>++</td><td>Prefix increment</td></tr>
<tr><td>--</td><td>Prefix decrement</td></tr>
<tr><td>+</td><td>Unary plus</td></tr>
<tr><td>-</td><td>Unary minus</td></tr>
<tr><td>!</td><td>Unary logical negation</td></tr>
<tr><td>(type)</td><td>Unary casting</td></tr>
<tr><td>new</td><td>Creating object</td></tr>
<tr><td>*</td><td>Multiplication</td></tr>
<tr><td>/</td><td>Division</td></tr>
<tr><td>%</td><td>Integer modulus</td></tr>
<tr><td>+</td><td>Addition</td></tr>
<tr><td>-</td><td>Subtraction</td></tr>
<tr><td><</td><td>Less than</td></tr>
<tr><td>>=</td><td>Less than or equal to</td></tr>
<tr><td>></td><td>Greater than</td></tr>
<tr><td>>=</td><td>Greater than or equal to</td></tr>
<tr><td>instanceof</td><td>Checking object type</td></tr>
<tr><td>==</td><td>Equal comparison</td></tr>
<tr><td>!=</td><td>Not equal</td></tr>
<tr><td>&</td><td>(Unconditional AND)</td></tr>
<tr><td>^</td><td>(Exclusive OR)</td></tr>
<tr><td>|</td><td>(Unconditional OR)</td></tr>
<tr><td>&&</td><td>Boolean AND</td></tr>
<tr><td>||</td><td>Boolean OR</td></tr>
<tr><td>?:</td><td>Ternary condition (Conditional expression)</td></tr>
</table>

Operator	*Name*
=	Assignment
+=	Addition assignment
-=	Subtraction assignment
*=	Multiplication assignment
/=	Division assignment
%=	Modulus assignment

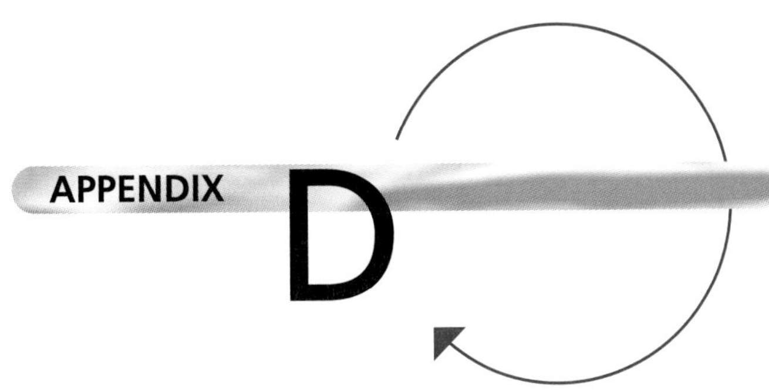

JAVA MODIFIERS

Modifiers are used on classes and class members (methods and data), but the `final` modifier can also be used on local variables in a method. A modifier that can be applied to a class is called a *class modifier*. A modifier that can be applied to a method is called a *method modifier*. A modifier that can be applied to a data field is called a *data modifier*. The following table gives a summary of the Java modifiers.

Modifier	*class*	*method*	*data*	*Explanation*
`(default)`	✓	✓	✓	A class, method, or data field is visible in this package.
`public`	✓	✓	✓	A class, method, or data field is visible to all the programs in any package.
`private`		✓	✓	A method or data field is only visible in this class.
`protected`		✓	✓	A method or data field is visible in this package and in subclasses of this class in any package.
`static`		✓	✓	Defines a class method or a class data field.
`final`	✓	✓	✓	A final class cannot be extended. A final method cannot be modified in a subclass. A final data field is a constant.
`abstract`	✓	✓		An abstract class must be extended. An abstract method must be implemented in a concrete subclass.
`native`		✓		A native method indicates that the method is implemented using a language other than Java.
`synchronized`		✓		Only one thread at a time can execute this method.

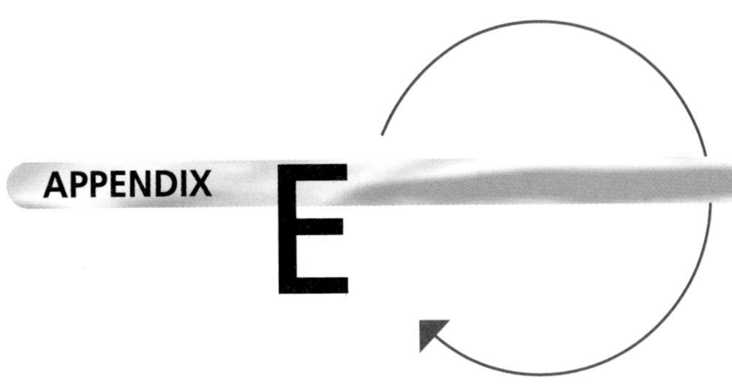

Number Systems

Introduction

This appendix introduces binary numbers, decimal numbers, and hexadecimal numbers, and the methods for converting among them.

The binary number system has two digits, 0 and 1. Computers use binary numbers internally because storage devices like memory and disk are made to store 0s and 1s. A number inside a computer is stored as a sequence of 0s and 1s. Each 0 and 1 is called a *bit*, short for binary digit.

Binary numbers are not intuitive, since we use decimal numbers in our daily life. When you write a number like 20 in a Java program, it is assumed to be a decimal number. The digits in the decimal number system are 0, 1, 2, 3, 4, 5, 6, 7, 8, and 9. Internally, computer software is used to convert decimal numbers into binary numbers, and vice versa.

In this book you write programs using decimal number systems. However, if you write programs to deal with a system like an operating system, you need to use binary numbers to reach down to the "machine-level." Binary numbers tend to be very long and cumbersome. Hexadecimal numbers are often used to abbreviate binary numbers. The hexadecimal number system has 16 digits: 0, 1, 2, 3, 4, 5, 6, 7, 8, 9, A, B, C, D, E, and F. The letters A, B, C, D, E, and F correspond to the decimal numbers 10, 11, 12, 13, 14, and 15.

Conversions between Binary Numbers and Decimal Numbers

Given a binary number $b_n b_{n-1} b_{n-2} \ldots b_2 b_1 b_0$, its equivalent decimal value is simply $b_n \times 2^n + b_{n-1} \times 2^{n-1} + b_{n-2} \times 2^{n-2} + \ldots + b_2 \times 2^2 + b_1 \times 2^1 + b_0 \times 2^0$.

For example, the binary number 10101001 is 169 in decimal, since $1\times2^7 + 0\times2^6 + 1\times2^5 + 0\times2^4 + 1\times2^3 + 0\times2^2 + 0\times2^1 + 1\times2^0 = 169$.

To convert a decimal number *d* to a binary number is to find the bits b_n, b_{n-1}, b_{n-2}, ... , b_2, b_1, and b_0 such that $d = b_n \times 2^n + b_{n-1} \times 2^{n-1} + b_{n-2} \times 2^{n-2} + ... + b_2 \times 2^2 + b_1 \times 2^1 + b_0 \times 2^0$. These bits can be found by successively dividing d by 2 until the quotient is 0. The remainders are b_0, b_1, b_2, ... , b_{n-2}, b_{n-1}, and b_n.

For example, the decimal number 123 is 1111011 in binary. The conversion is conducted as follows:

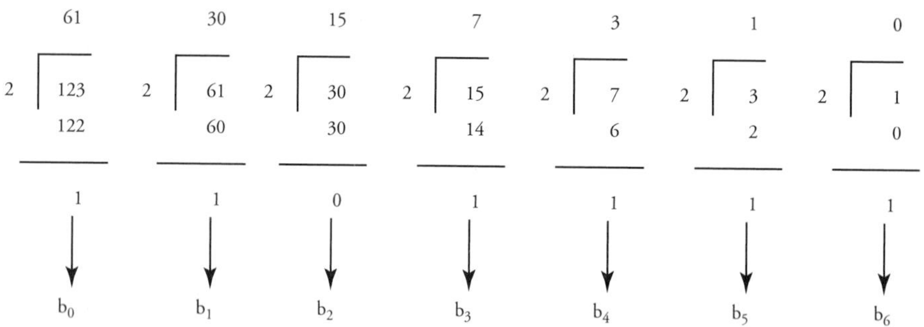

1. 123%2 = 1 (b_0)
2. The quotient of 123 divided by 2 is 61. 61%2 = 1 (b_1)
3. The quotient of 61 divided by 2 is 30. 30%2 = 0 (b_2)
4. The quotient of 30 divided by 2 is 15. 15%2 = 1 (b_3)
5. The quotient of 15 divided by 2 is 7. 7%2 = 1 (b_4)
6. The quotient of 7 divided by 2 is 3. 3%2 = 1 (b_5)
7. The quotient of 3 divided by 2 is 1. 1%2 = 1 (b_6)
8. The quotient of 1 divided by 2 is 0. The conversion is completed.

Conversions Between Hexadecimal Numbers and Decimal Numbers

Given a hexadecimal number $h_n h_{n-1} h_{n-2} \ldots h_2 h_1 h_0$, its equivalent decimal value is simply $h_n \times 16^n + h_{n-1} \times 16^{n-1} + h_{n-2} \times 16^{n-2} + ... + h_2 \times 16^2 + h_1 \times 16^1 + h_0 \times 16^0$.

For example, the hexadecimal number 43A is 1082 in decimal, since $4 \times 16^2 + 3 \times 16^1 + 10 = 1082$.

To convert a decimal number *d* to a hexadecimal number is to find the hexadecimal digits h_n, h_{n-1}, h_{n-2}, ... , h_2, h_1, and h_0 such that $d = h_n \times 16^n + h_{n-1} \times 16^{n-1} + h_{n-2} \times 16^{n-2} + ... + h_2 \times 16^2 + h_1 \times 16^1 + h_0 \times 16^0$. These numbers can be found by successively dividing d by 16 until the quotient is 0. The remainders are h_0, h_1, h_2, ... , h_{n-2}, h_{n-1}, and h_n.

For example, the decimal number 123 is 7B in hexadecimal. The conversion is conducted as follows:

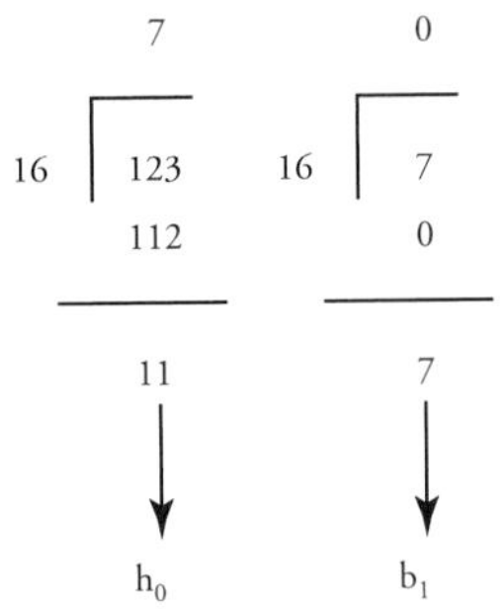

```
        7            0
     ______       ______
16 | 123     16 |  7
     112           0
   ______       ______
      11           7
      |            |
      v            v
     h0           b1
```

1. 123%16 = 11 (b_0)
2. The quotient of 123 divided by 16 is 7. 7%16 = 7 (b_1)
3. The quotient of 7 divided by 16 is 0. The conversion is completed.

Conversions Between Binary Numbers and Hexadecimal Numbers

To convert a hexadecimal number to a binary number, simply convert each digit in the hexadecimal number into a four-digit binary number using the following table:

Hexadecimal	*Binary*	*Decimal*
0	0	0
1	1	1
2	10	2
3	11	3
4	100	4
5	101	5
6	110	6
7	111	7
8	1000	8
9	1001	9
A	1010	10
B	1011	11
C	1100	12
D	1101	13
E	1110	14
F	1111	15

For example, the hexadecimal number 7B is 1111011, where 7 is 111 in binary, and B is 1011 in binary.

To convert a binary number to a hexadecimal, convert every four binary digits from left to right in the binary number into a hexadecimal number.

For example, the binary number 1110001101 is 38D, since 1101 is D, 1000 is 8 and 11 is 3 as shown below.

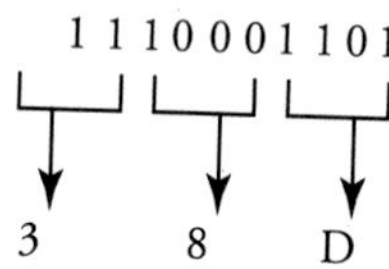

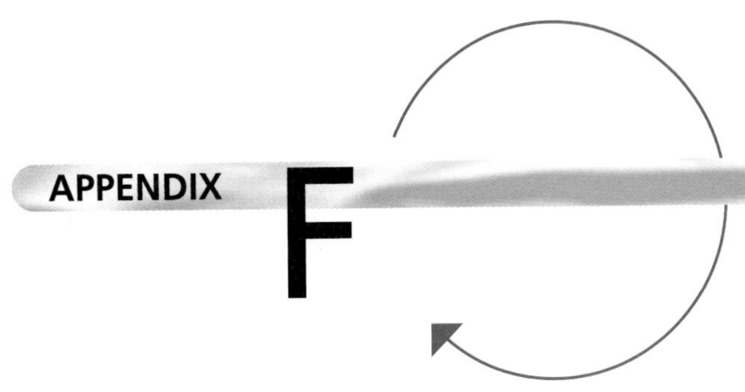

An HTML Tutorial

Java applets are embedded in HTML files. HTML (HyperText Markup Language) is a markup language used to design Web pages for creating and sharing multimedia-enabled, integrated electronic documents over the Internet. HTML allows documents on the Internet to be hyperlinked and presented using fonts and image and line justification appropriate for the systems on which they are displayed. The World Wide Web is a network of static and dynamic documents, including texts, sound, and images. The Internet has been around for more than 30 years, but has only recently become popular. The Web is the major reason for its popularity.

HTML documents are displayed by a program called a *Web browser*. When a document is coded in HTML, a Web browser interprets the HTML to identify the elements of the document and render it. The browser has control over the document's look-and-feel. At present there are no absolute, unifying HTML standards. Different vendors have rushed to introduce their own features, interpretable by their proprietary browsers. However, the differences aren't significant. This tutorial introduces some frequently used HTML features that have been adopted by most browsers.

There are many easy-to-use authoring tools for creating Web pages. For example, you can create HTML files using Microsoft Word. The Internet Explorer and Netscape Navigator have simple authoring tools to let you create and edit HTML files. Microsoft FrontPage is a comprehensive and fully loaded tool that enables you to design more sophisticated Web pages. Authoring tools greatly simplify the task of creating Web pages but do not support all features of HTML. Since you will probably end up editing the source text produced by whatever tool you adopt, it is imperative to know the basic concept of HTML. In this tutorial, you will learn how to use HTML to create your own Web pages.

Getting Started

Let us begin with an example that demonstrates the structure and syntax of an HTML document.

Example F.1 An HTML Example

The following HTML document displays a message and a list of Web browsers: Netscape, Internet Explorer, and Mosaic. You may use any text editor, such as Microsoft NotePad on Windows, to create HTML documents, as long as it can save the file in ACSII text format.

```
<html>
<head>
<title>My First Web Page</title>
</head>
<body>
<i>Welcome to</i> <b>HTML</b>. Here is a list of popular Web
browsers.
<ul>
  <li>Netscape
  <li>Internet Explorer
  <li>Mosaic
</ul>
<hr size=3>
Created by <A HREF=www.cs.armstrong.edu/liang>Y. Daniel Liang</A>.
</body>
</html>
```

Assume that you have created a file named **ExampleF1.html** for this HTML document. You may use any Web browser to view the document. To view it on Internet Explorer, start up your browser and choose Open from the File menu. A popup window opens to accept the filename. Type the full name of the file (including path), or click the Browser button to locate the file. Click OK to load and display the HTML file. Your document should be displayed as shown in Figure F.1.

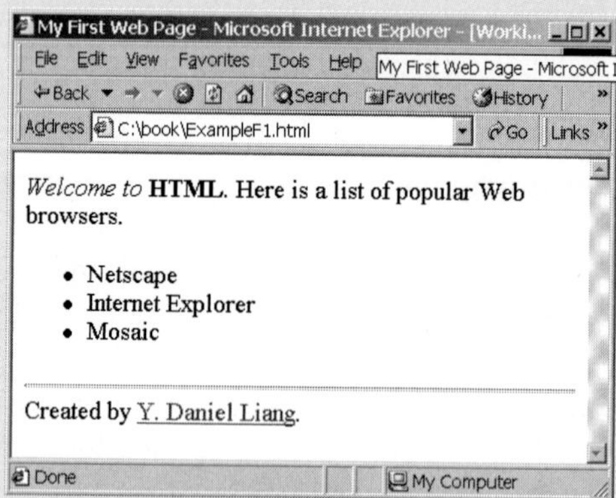

Figure F.1 *The HTML page is rendered by a Web browser.*

NOTE

HTML filenames are case-sensitive on UNIX but not on other operating systems. HTML files end with .html or .htm.

NOTE
The same document may be rendered differently depending on the capabilities of the Web browser. Regardless of the differences, the power of HTML is that your document can be viewed on a variety of browsers and on most platforms, and can be formatted to suit any reader. This tutorial uses Internet Explorer 5.0 for illustrations.

What makes *Welcome to* appear in italic in Figure F.1? What makes the document appear in a desired style? HTML is a document-layout and hyperlink-specification language; that is, it tells the Web browser how to display the contents of the document, including text, images, and other media, using instructions called *tags*. The browser interprets the tags and decides how to display or otherwise treat the subsequent contents of the HTML document. Tags are enclosed in brackets; `<html>`, `<i>`, `<b>`, and `</html>` are tags that appear in the preceding HTML example. The first word in a tag, called the *tag name*, describes tag functions. Tags may have additional attributes, sometimes with a value after an equals sign, which further define their action. For example, in Example F.1, the attribute size in the tag `<hr>` defines the size of the bar as 3 inches.

Most tags have a *start tag* and a corresponding *end tag*. A tag has a specific effect on the region between the start tag and the end tag. For example, `<b>text</b>` advises the browser to display the word "text" in bold. `<b>` and `</b>` are the start and end tags for displaying boldface text. An end tag is always the start tag's name preceded by a forward slash (`/`). A few tags do not have end tags. For example, `<hr>`, a tag to draw a line, has no corresponding end tag.

A tag can be embedded inside another tag; for example, all tags are embedded within `<html>` and `</html>`. However, tags cannot overlap; it would be wrong, for instance, to use `<b>bold and <i>italic</b></i>`; the correct use should be `<b><i>bold and italic</i></b>`.

TIP
Tags are not case-sensitive, but it is good practice to use case consistently for clarity and readability. This tutorial uses lowercase for tags.

The following types of tags are introduced in the upcoming sections:

- **Structure tags**: Define the structure of documents.
- **Text appearance tags:** Define the appearance of text.
- **Paragraph tags**: Define headings, paragraphs, and line breaks.
- **Font tags**: Specify font sizes and colors.
- **List tags**: Define ordered or unordered lists and definition lists.
- **Table tags**: Define tables.
- **Link tags**: Specify navigation links to other documents.
- **Image tags**: Specify where to get images and how to display them.

Structure Tags

An HTML document begins with the `<html>` tag, which declares that the document is written with HTML. Every document has two parts, a *head* and a *body*, defined, respectively, by a `<head>` tag and a `<body>` tag. The head part contains the document title (using the `<title>` tag) and other parameters the browser may use when rendering the document; the body part contains the actual contents of the document. An HTML document may have the following structure:

```
<html>
<head>
<title>My First Web Page</title>
</head>
<body>
<!-- document body-->
</body>
</html>
```

Here the special starting tag `<!--` and ending tag `-->` are used to enclose comments in the HTML documents. The comments are not displayed.

NOTE

Your documents may be displayed properly even if you don't use `<html>`, `<head>`, `<title>`, and `<body>` tags. However, use of these tags is strongly recommended because they communicate certain information to the browser about the properties of a document; the information they provide helps in using the document effectively.

Text Appearance Tags

HTML provides tags to advise about the appearance of text. At present, some text tags have the same effect. For example, `<em>`, `<cite>`, and `<i>` will all display the text in italic. However, a future version of HTML may make these tags distinct. Text tag names are fairly descriptive. Text tags can be classified into two categories: *content-based tags* and *physical tags*.

Content-Based Tags

Content-based tags inform the browser to display the text based on semantic meaning, such as citation, program code, and emphasis. Here is a summary of the content-based tags:

- **`<cite>`**: Indicates that the enclosed text is a bibliographic citation, displayed in italic.
- **`<code>`**: Indicates that the enclosed text is a programming code, displayed in monospace font.
- **`<em>`**: Indicates that the enclosed text should be displayed with emphasis, displayed in italic.

- **<strong>**: Indicates that the enclosed text should be strongly emphasized, displayed in bold.
- **<var>**: Indicates that the enclosed text is a computer variable, displayed in italic.
- **<address>**: Indicates that the enclosed text is an address, displayed in italic.

Table F.1 lists the content-based tags and provides examples of their use.

TABLE F.1 **Using Content-Based Tags**

Tag	*Example*	*Display*
`<cite> . . . </cite>`	`<cite>bibliographic </cite>`	*bibliographic*
`<code> . . . </code>`	`<code>source code </code>`	source code
`<em> . . . </em>`	`<em>emphasis</em>`	*emphasis*
`<strong> . . . </strong>`	`<strong>strongly emphasized</strong>`	**strongly emphasized**
`<var> . . . </var>`	`<var>programming variable</var>`	*programming variable*
`<address> . . . </address>`	`<address>Computer Dept</address>`	*Computer Dept*

Physical Tags

Physical tags explicitly ask the browser to display text in bold, italic, or other ways. Following are six commonly used physical tags:

- **<i>** (italic)
- **<b>** (bold)
- **<u>** (underline)
- **<tt>** (monospace)
- **<strike>** (strike-through text)
- **<blink>** (blink)

Table F.2 lists the physical tags and provides examples of their use.

Paragraph-Style Tags

There are many tags in HTML for dealing with paragraph styles. There are six heading tags (<h1>, <h2>, <h3>, <h4>, <h5>, <h6>) for different sizes of headings, a

TABLE F.2 Using Physical Tags

Tag	*Example*	*Display*
<i> . . . </i>	<i>italic</i>	*italic*
<b> . . . </b>	<b>bold</b>	**bold**
<u> . . . </u>	<u>underline</u>	underline
<tt> . . . </tt>	<tt>monospace</tt>	monospace
<strike> . . . </strike>	<strike>strike </strike>	~~strike~~
<blink> . . .</blink>	<blink>blink </blink>	blink (causes it to blink)

line-break tag (<br>), a paragraph start tag (<p>), a preformat tag (<pre>), and a block-quote tag (<blockquote>).

The six heading tags indicate the highest (<h1>) and lowest (<h6>) precedence a heading may have in the document. Heading tags may be used with an align attribute to place the heading toward *left*, *center*, or *right*. The default alignment is left. For example, <h3 align=right>Heading</h3> tells the browser to right-align the heading.

The line-break tag <br> tells the browser to start displaying from the next line. This tag has no end tag.

The paragraph-start tag <p> signals the start of a paragraph. This tag has an optional end tag </p>.

The <pre> tag and its required end tag (</pre>) define the enclosed segment to be displayed in monospaced font by the browser.

The <blockquote> tag is used to contain text quoted from another source. The quote will be indented from both left and right.

Example F.2 HTML Source Code Using Structure Tags

The following HTML source code illustrates the use of paragraph tags. The text the code creates is displayed in Figure F.2.

```
<html>
<head>
<title>Demonstrating Paragraph Tags</title>
</head>
<body>
<!-- Example F.2 -->
<h1 align=right>h1: Heading 1</h1>
<h3 align=center>h3: Heading 3</h3>
<h6 align=left>h6: Heading 6</h6>
<p>
<pre>preformat tag</pre>
```

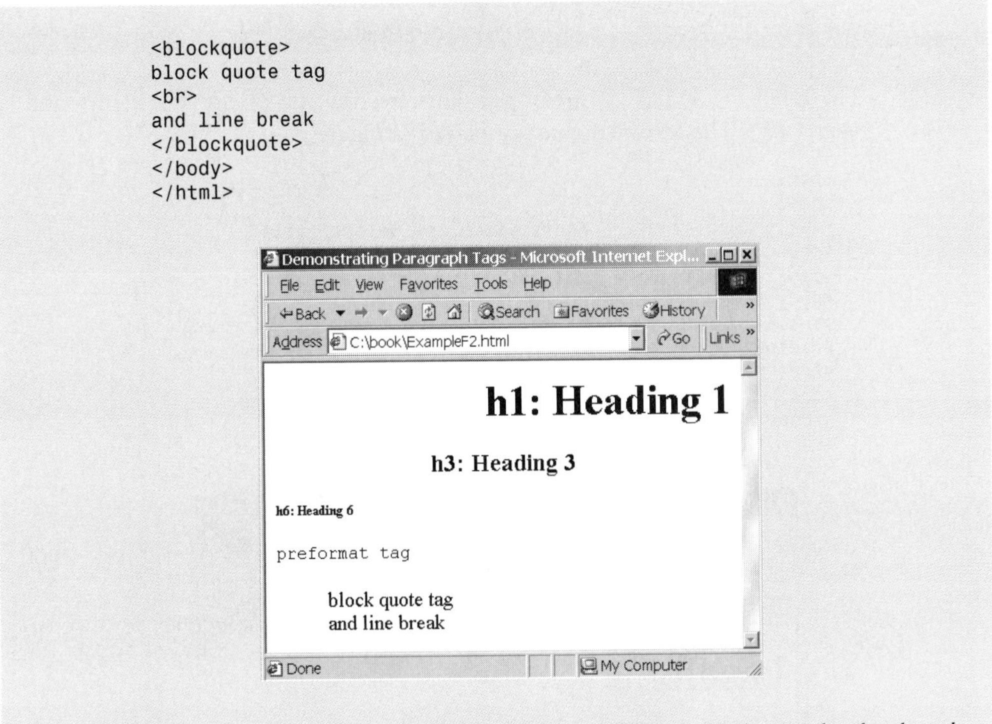

```
<blockquote>
block quote tag
<br>
and line break
</blockquote>
</body>
</html>
```


Figure F.2 *Paragraph tags specify heading styles, paragraph format, block quote, line break, and so on.*

Font, Size, and Color Tags

With HTML you can specify font size and colors using font tags. There are two font tags: `<basefont>` and `<font>`.

The `<basefont>` tag is typically placed in the head of an HTML document, where it sets the base font size for the entire document. However, it may appear anywhere in the document, and it may appear many times, each time with a new size attribute. Many browsers use a relative model for sizing fonts, ranging from 1 to 7; the default base font size is 3. Each successive size is 20 percent larger than its predecessor in the range.

The `<font>` tag allows you to specify the size and color of the enclosed text, using size and color attributes. The size attribute is the same as the one for `<basefont>` tag. The color attribute sets the color for the enclosed text between `<font>` and `</font>`. The value of the attribute is a six-digit hex number preceded by a pound sign (#). The first two digits are the red component, the next two digits are the green component, and the last two digits are the blue component. The digits are from 00 to FF. Alternatively, you may set the color by using standard names like red, yellow, blue, or orange.

Example F.3 Testing Font Tags

The following HTML source code illustrates the use of the `<basefont>` and `<font>` tags. The text it creates is displayed in Figure F.3.

```
<html>
<head>
<title>Demonstrating Fonts, Size and Color</title>
</head>
<basefont size=6>
<body bgcolor=white>
<!-- Example F.3 -->
basefont<br>
<font size=7 color=blue>blue7</font><br>
<font size=3 color=#FF0000>red3</font><br>
</body>
</html>
```

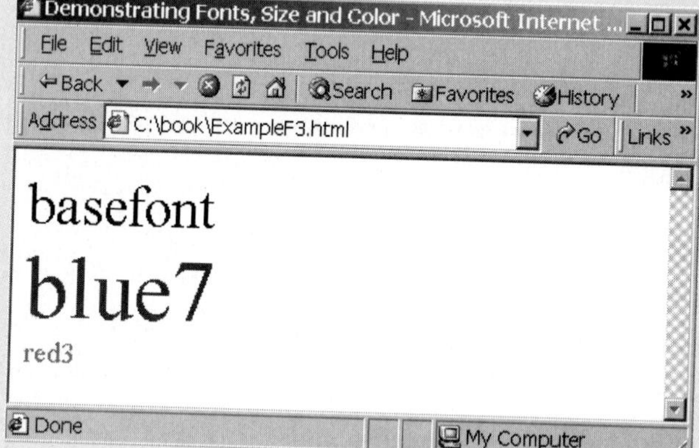

Figure F.3 *Font and color tags specify fonts and colors in HTML pages.*

List Tags

HTML allows you to define three kinds of lists: *ordered lists, unordered lists,* and *definition lists*. You can also build nested lists. Example F.1 contains an unordered list of three Web browsers.

Ordered Lists

Ordered lists label the items they contain. An ordered list is used when the sequence of the listed items is important. For example, chapters are listed in order. An ordered list starts with the tag `<ol>` and ends with `</ol>`, and items are placed in between. Each item begins with an `<li>` tag. The browser automatically numbers list items, starting from numeric 1. Instead of using the default numeric numbers for labeling, you may associate the tag `<ol>` with a type attribute. The value of the type determines the style of the label.

- Type value `A` for uppercase letter labels A, B, C, . . .

- Type value a for lowercase letter labels a, b, c, . . .
- Type value I for capital roman numerals I, II, III, . . .
- Type value i for lowercase roman numerals i, ii, iii, . . .
- Type value 1 for arabic numerals 1, 2, 3, . . .

Unordered Lists

When the sequence of the listed items is not important, use an unordered list. For example, a list of Web browsers can be given in any order. An unordered list starts with the tag `<ul>` and ends with `</ul>`. Inside, you use `<li>` tags for items. By default, the browser uses bullets to mark each item. You may use `disc`, `circle`, or `square` as type values to indicate the use of markers other than bullets.

Definition Lists

A definition list is used to define terms. The list is enclosed between `<dl>` and `</dl>` tags. Inside the tags are the terms and their definitions. The term and definition have the leading tags `<dt>` and `<dd>`, respectively. Browsers typically render the term name at the left margin and the definition below it and indented.

Example F.4 Using Various List Tags

This example illustrates the use of tags for ordered lists, unordered lists, definition lists, and nested lists. The output of the following code is displayed in Figure F.4.

```
<html>
<head>
<title>Demonstrating List Tags</title>
</head>
<body bgcolor=white>
<!-- Example F.4 List Tags -->
<center><b>List Tags</b></center>
An ordered List
<ol type=A>
  <li>Chapter 1: Introduction to Java
  <li>Chapter 2: Java Building Elements
  <li>Chapter 3: Control Structures
</ol>
An unordered List
<ul type=square>
  <li>Apples
  <li>Oranges
  <li>Peaches
</ul>
Definition List
<dl>
   <dt>What is Java?
   <dd>An Internet programming language.
</dl>
</body>
</html>
```

continues

Example F.4 continued

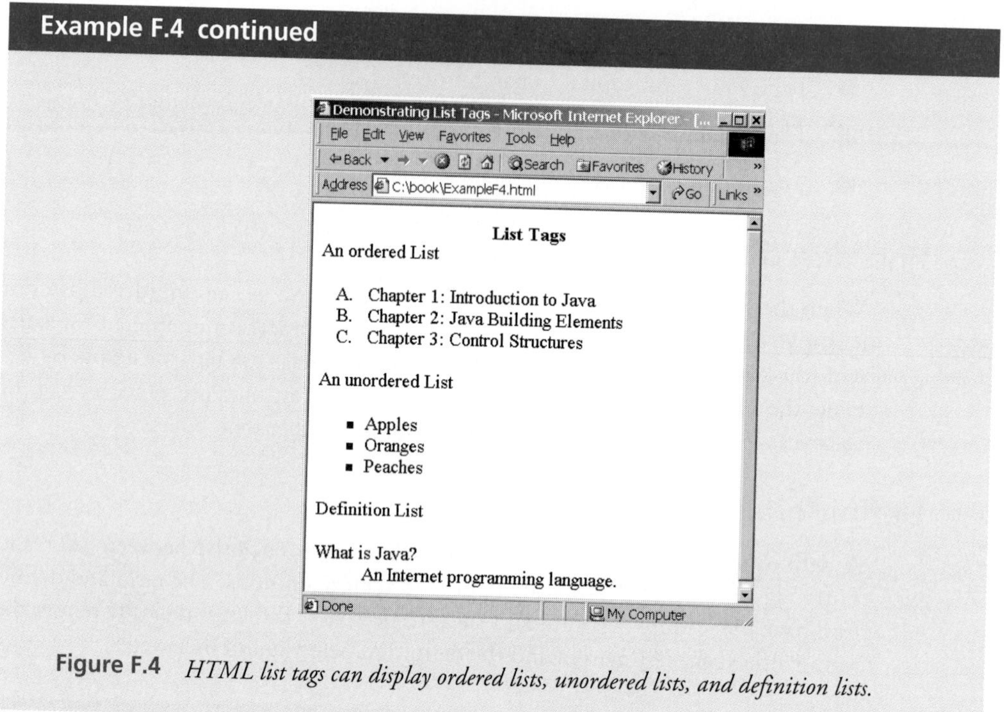

Figure F.4 *HTML list tags can display ordered lists, unordered lists, and definition lists.*

Table Tags

Tables are useful features supported by many browsers. Tables are collections of numbers and words arranged in rows and columns of cells. In HTML, table elements, including data items, row and column headers, and captions, are enclosed between `<table>` and `</table>` tags. Several table tags may be used to specify the layout of a table. Each row in the table is wrapped by `<tr>` and `</tr>`. Inside the row, data or words in a cell are enclosed by `<td>` and `</td>`. You may use `<caption>...</caption>` to display a caption for the table, and `<th>...</th>` to display column headers.

Table tags may be used with attributes to obtain special effects. Here are some useful attributes:

- **`border`**: Can appear in the `<table>` tag to specify that all cells are surrounded with a border.
- **`align`**: Can appear in the `<caption>`, `<tr>`, `<th>`, or `<td>` tag. If it appears in `<caption>`, it specifies whether the caption appears above or below the table, using the values `top` or `bottom`. The default is `align=top`. If it appears in `<tr>`, `<th>`, or `<td>`, `align` specifies whether the text is aligned to the left, the right, or centered inside the table cell(s).
- **`valign`**: Can appear in `<tr>`, `<th>`, or `<td>`. The values of the attribute are `top`, `middle`, and `bottom` to specify whether the text is aligned to the top, the bottom, or centered inside the table cell(s).

- **colspan**: Can appear in any table cell to specify how many columns of the table the cell should span. The default value is 1.
- **rowspan**: Can appear in any column to specify how many rows of the table the cell should span. The default value is 1.

Example F.5 Illustration of Table Tags

This example creates an HTML table. The output of the code is displayed in Figure F.5.

```
<html>
<head>
<title>Demonstrating Table Tags</title>
</head>
<body bgcolor=white>
<!-- Example F.5 Table Tags -->
<center>Table Tags</center>
<br>
<table border=2>
<caption>This is a Table</caption>
<tr>
  <th>Table heading</th>
  <td>Table data</td>
</tr>
<tr>
  <th valign=bottom>Second row
  <td>Embedded Table
      <table border=3>
      <tr>
        <th>Table heading</th>
        <td align=right>Table data</td>
      </tr>
      </table>
  </td>
</tr>
</table>
</body>
</html>
```

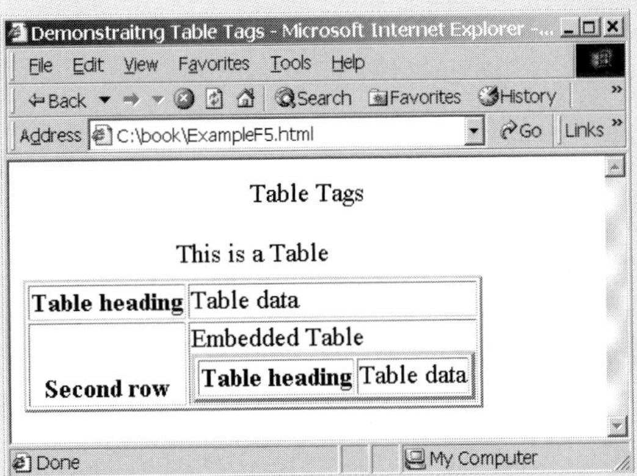

Figure F.5 *Table tags are useful for displaying tables in HTML pages.*

Hyperlink Tags

The true power of HTML lies in its capability to join collections of documents together into a full electronic library of information, and to link documents with other documents over the Internet. This is called *hypertext linking*, which is the key feature that makes the Web appealing and popular. By adding hypertext links, called *anchors*, to your HTML document, you create a highly intuitive information flow and guide users directly to the information they want. You can link documents on different computers or on the same computer, and can jump within the same document using anchor tags.

Linking Documents on Different Computers

Every document on the Web has a unique address, known as its *Uniform Resource Locator* (URL). To navigate from a source document to a target document, you need to reference the target's URL inside the anchor tags `<a>` and `</a>` using attribute `href`. The following example displays a list of database vendors:

```
<ul>
 <li><a href="http://www.oracle.com">Oracle</a>
 <li><a href="http://www.sybase.com">Sybase</a>
 <li><a href="http://www.informix.com">Informix</a>
</ul>
```

In this example, clicking on Oracle will display the Oracle homepage. The URL of Oracle's home page Internet address is **http://www.oracle.com**. The general format of a URL is:

```
method://servername:port/pathname/fullfilename
```

method is the name of the operation that is performed to interpret this URL. The most common methods are `http`, `ftp`, and `file`.

- **`http`**: Accesses a page over the network using the HTTP protocol. For example, **http://www.microsoft.com** links to Microsoft's homepage. **http://** can be omitted.
- **`ftp`**: Downloads a file using anonymous FTP service from a server; for example, **ftp://hostname/directory/fullfilename**.
- **`File`**: Reads a file from the local disk. For example, `file://home/liang/liang.html` displays the file **liang.html** from the directory `/home/liang` on the local machine.

servername is a computer's unique Internet name or Internet Protocol (IP) numerical address on the network. For example, **www.sun.com** is the hostname of Sun Microsystem's Web server. If a server name is not specified, it is assumed that the file is on the same server.

port is the TCP port number that the Web server is running on. Most Web servers use port number 80 by default.

pathname is optional and indicates the directory under which the file is located.

fullfilename is optional and indicates the target filename. Web servers generally use **index.html** on UNIX and **default.htm** on Windows for a default filename. For example, `<a href="http://www.oracle.com">Oracle</a>` is equivalent to `<a href="http://www.oracle.com/index.html">Oracle</a>`.

Linking Documents on the Same Computer

To link documents on the same computer, use the `file` method rather than the `http` method in the target URL. There are two types of links: *absolute links* and *relative links*.

When linking to a document on a different machine, you must use an absolute link to identify the target document. An absolute link uses a URL to indicate the complete path to the target file.

When you are linking to a document on the same computer, it is better to use a relative link. A relative URL omits method and server name and directories. For instance, assume that the source document is under directory `liang/teaching` on the server `www.cs.armstrong.edu`. The URL

```
file://www.cs.armstrong.edu/liang/teaching/teaching.html
```

is equivalent to

```
file://teaching.html
```

Here, `file://` can be omitted. An obvious advantage of using a relative URL is that you can move the entire set of documents to another directory or even another server and never have to change a single link.

Jumping Within the Same Document

HTML offers navigation within the same document. This is helpful for direct browsing of interesting segments of the document.

Example F.6 Navigation Within the Same Document

This example shows a document with three sections. The output of the following code is shown in Figure F.6. When the user clicks Section 1: Introduction on the list, the browser jumps to Section 1 of the document. The `name` attribute within the `<a>` tag labels the section. The label is used as a link to the section. This feature is also known as *using bookmarks.*

When you test this example, make the window small so that you can see the effects of jumping to each reference through the link tags.

```
<html>
<head>
<title>Demonstrating Link Tags</title>
</head>
<body>
```

continues

Example F.6 continued

```
<ol>
  <li><a href="#introduction">Section 1: Introduction</a>
  <li><a href="#methodology">Section 2: Methodology</a>
  <li><a href="#summary">Section 3: Summary</a>
</ol>

<h3><a name="introduction"><b>Section 1</b>: Introduction</a></h3>
an introductory paragraph

<h3><a name="methodology"><b>Section 2</b>: Methodology</a></h3>
a paragraph on methodology

<h3><a name="summary"><b>Section 3</b>: Summary</a></h3>
a summary paragraph
</body>
</html>
```

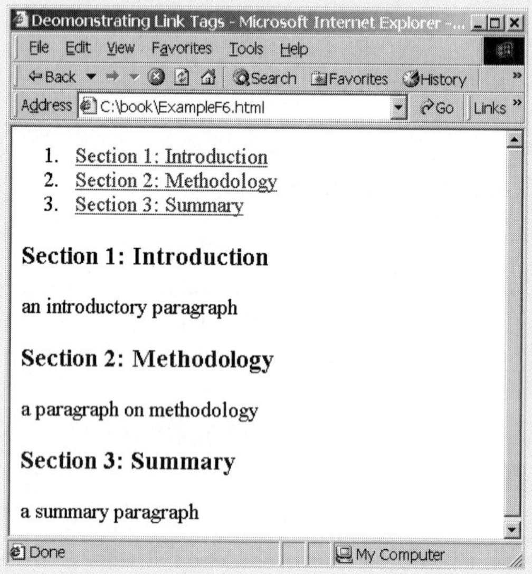

Figure F.6 *Hyperlink tags link documents.*

Embedding Graphics

One of the most compelling features of the Web is its ability to embed graphics in a document. Graphics can be used for icons, pictures, illustrations, drawings, and so on. They bring a live dimension to your documents. You may use an image as a visual map of hyperlinks. This section introduces the use of *horizontal bar tags* and *image tags*.

Horizontal Bar Tags

The horizontal bar tag (`<hr>`) is used to display a rule. It is useful in separating sections of your document with horizontal rules. The attributes `size`, `width`, and `align` can be associated to achieve the desired effect. The rule can be thickened using the `size` attribute with values in pixels. The `width` attribute specifies the length of the bar with values in either absolute number of pixels or extension across a certain percentage of the page. The `align` attribute specifies whether the bar is `left`, `centered`, or `right` aligned.

Example F.7 Illustration of Horizontal Bar Tags

This example illustrates the use of the `size`, `width`, and `align` attributes in horizontal bar tags. The output of the following code is shown in Figure F.7.

```
<html>
<head>
<title>Demonstrating Horizontal Rules</title>
</head>
<body bgcolor=white>
<!-- Example F.7 Horizontal Rule -->
<center>Horizontal Rules</center>
<hr size=3 width=80% align=left>
<hr size=2 width=20% align=right noshade>
<hr>
</body>
</html>
```

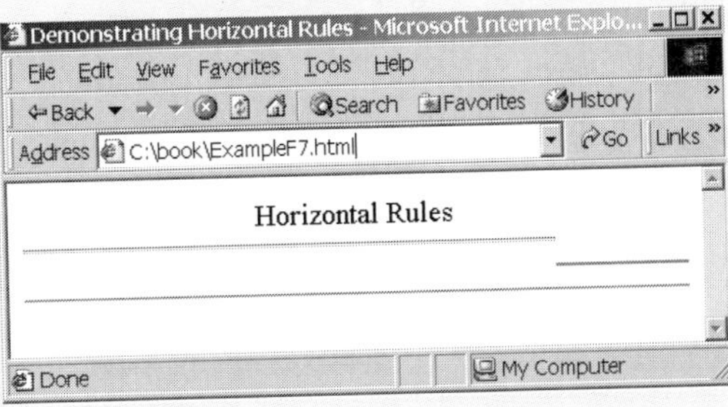

Figure F.7 *Horizontal bar tags are often used to separate contents in documents.*

Image Tags

The image tag, `<img>`, lets you reference and insert images into the current text. The syntax for the tag is:

```
<img src=URL alt=text align = [top ¦ middle ¦ bottom ¦ texttop ]>
```

Most browsers support GIF and JPEG image format. Format is an encoding scheme to store images. The attribute `src` specifies the source of the image. The attribute `alt` specifies an alternative text message to be displayed in case the client's browser cannot display the image. The attribute `alt` is optional; if it is omitted, no message is displayed. The attribute `align` tells the browser where to place the image.

Example F.8 Illustration of Image Tags

This example creates a document with image tags. The output of the code is shown in Figure F.8.

```
<html>
<head>
<title>Demonstrating Image Tags</title>
</head>
<body bgcolor=white>
<!-- Example F.8 Image Tags -->
<center>Image Tags</center>
<img src="illinoisMap.gif" align=middle>
</body>
</html>
```

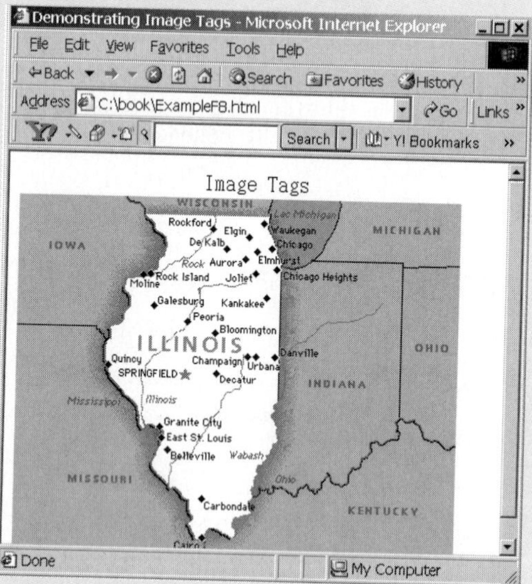

Figure F.8. *Image tags display images in HTML pages.*

More on HTML

This tutorial is not intended to be a complete reference manual on HTML. It does not mention many interesting features, such as *forms* and *frames*. You will find dozens of books on HTML in your local bookstore. *Special Edition Using HTML* by Mark Brown and John Jung, published by QUE, is a comprehensive reference; it covers all the new HTML features supported by Netscape Navigator and Microsoft Internet Explorer. *HTML Quick Reference* by Robert Mullen, also published by QUE, contains all the essential information you need to build Web pages with HTML in 100 pages. Please refer to these and other books for more information. You can also get information online at the following Web sites:

www.ncsa.uiuc.edu/General/Internet/WWW/HTMLPrimer.html
www.w3.org/pub/WWW/MarkUp/
www.mcli.dist.maricopa.edu/tut/lessons.html
www.netscape.com/assist/net_sites/frames.html

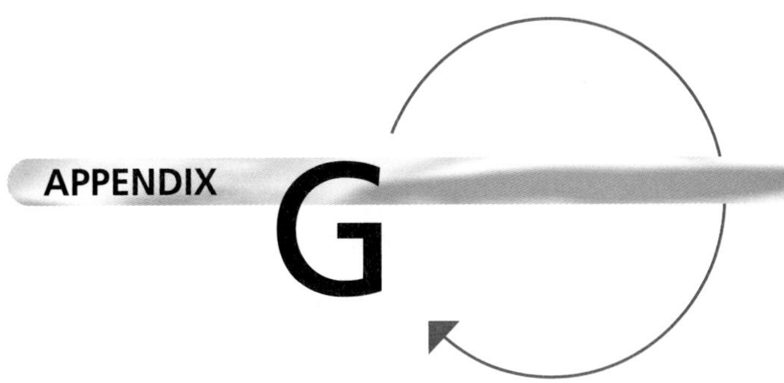

UML Graphical Notations

This appendix summarizes the UML notations used in this book.

Classes and Objects

A class is described using a rectangle box with three sections.

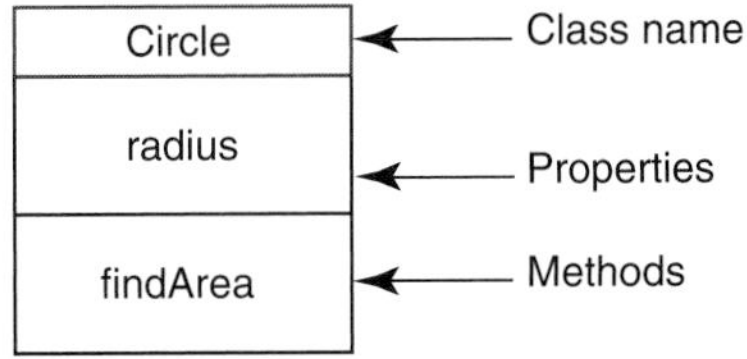

The top section gives the class name, the middle section describes the properties, and the bottom section describes the methods. The middle and bottom sections are optional, but the top section is required.

An object is described using a rectangle box with two sections.

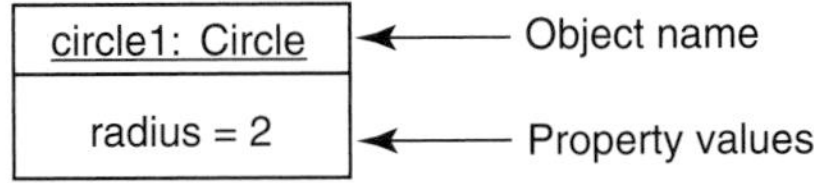

The top section is required. It gives the object's name and its defining class. The second section is optional; it indicates the object's property values.

The Modifiers *public, private, protected,* and *static*

The symbols +, -, and # are used to denote, respectively, `public`, `private`, and `protected` modifiers in the UML. The static properties and methods are underlined.

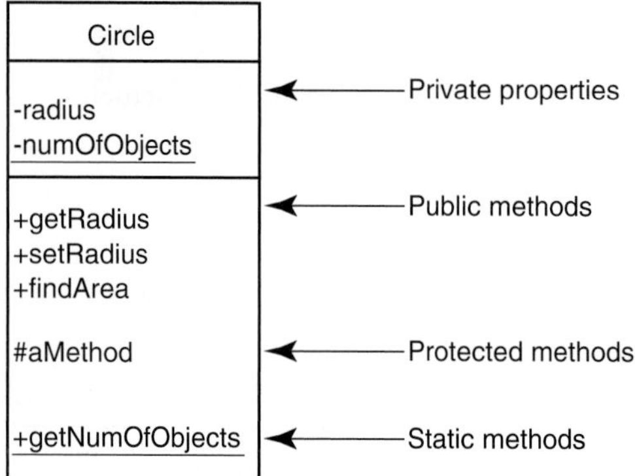

Class Relationships

The relationships of the classes are association, aggregation, and inheritance.

An association is illustrated using a solid line between the two classes with an optional label that describes the relationship.

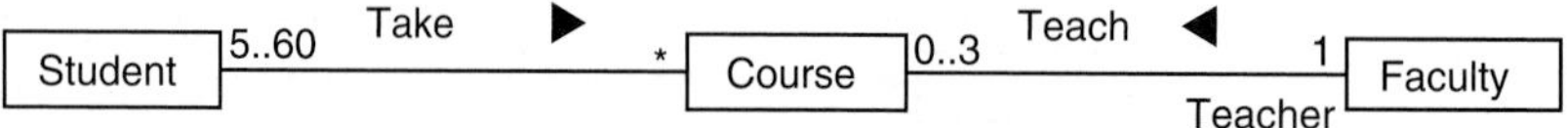

Each class involved in the relationship has a role name that describes the role played by the class in the relationship.

Each class involved in the association may specify a multiplicity. A multiplicity is a number or an interval that specifies the number of objects of the class that are involved in the relationship. The character * means that the number of objects is unlimited, and an interval `l..u` means that the number of objects should be between `l` and `u`, inclusive.

A filled diamond is attached to the composed class to denote the composition relationship, and a hollow diamond is attached to the aggregated class to denote the aggregation relationship, as shown below.

Inheritance models the is-a relationship between two classes, as shown below. An open triangle pointing to the superclass is used to denote the inheritance relationship between the two classes involved.

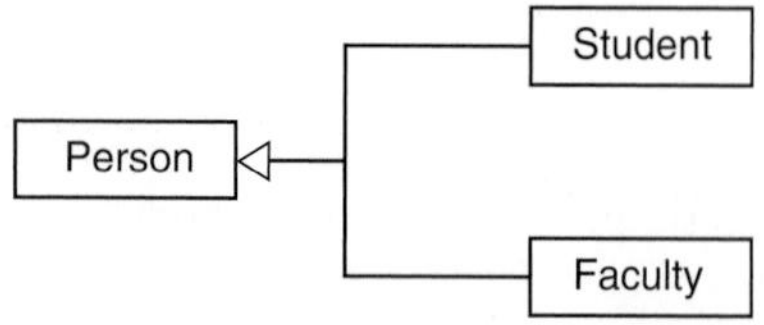

Abstract Classes and Interfaces

Abstract class names, interface names, and abstract methods are italicized. Dashed lines and dashed open triangles are used to point to the interface, as shown below:

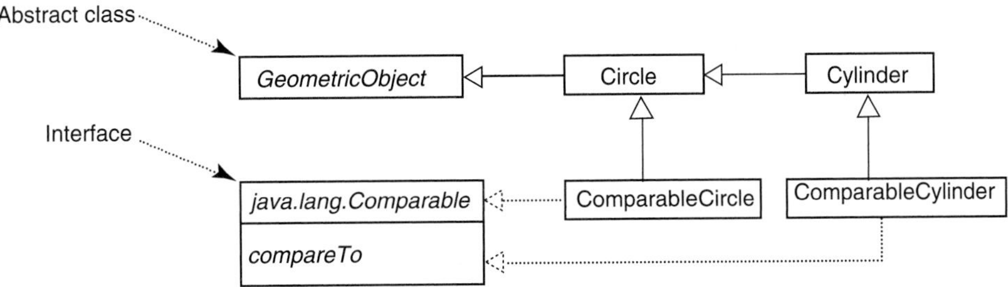

Sequence Diagrams

Sequence diagrams describe interactions among objects by depicting the time ordering of method invocations. The sequence diagram shown below consists of the following elements:

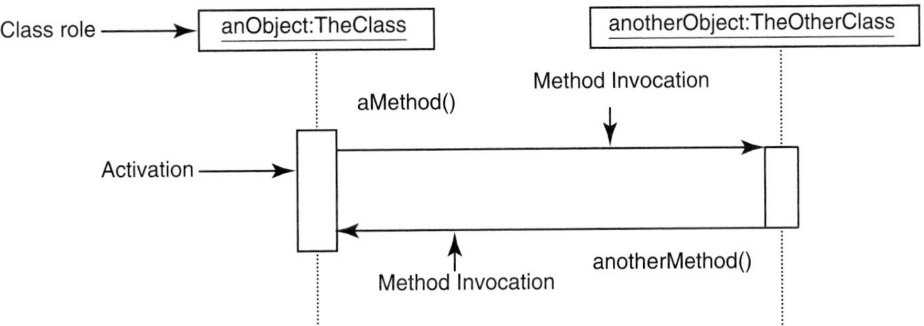

- Class role: Represents the role an object plays. The objects at the top of the diagram represent class roles.
- Lifeline: Represents the existence of an object over a period of time. A vertical dashed line extending from the object is used to denote a lifeline.
- Activation: Represents the time during which an object is performing an operation. Thin rectangles placed on lifelines are used to denote activations.
- Method invocation: Represents communications between objects. Horizontal arrows labeled with method calls are used to denote method invocations.

Statechart Diagrams

Statechart diagrams describe the flow of control of the object. The statechart diagram shown below contains the following elements:

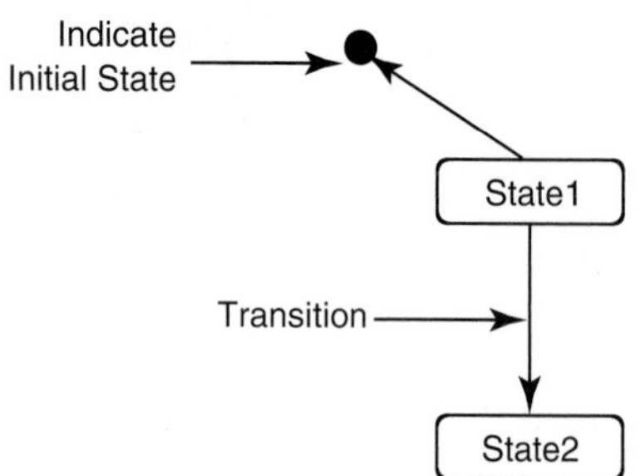

- State: Represents a situation during the life of an object in which it satisfies some condition, performs some action, or waits for some event to occur. Each state has a name. Rectangles with rounded corners are used to represent states. The small filled circle is used to denote the initial state.
- Transition: Represents the relationship between two states, indicating that an object will perform some action to transfer from one state to the other. A solid arrow with appropriate method invocation is used to denote a transition.

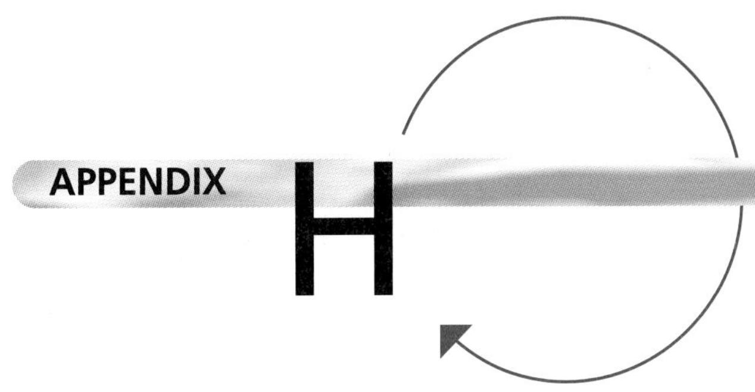

Java Packages

This appendix introduces Java package-naming conventions, creating packages, and using packages.

Package-Naming Conventions

Packages are hierarchical, and you can have packages within packages. For example, `java.lang.Math` indicates that `Math` is a class in the package `lang` and that `lang` is a package within the package `java`. Levels of nesting can be used to ensure the uniqueness of package names.

Choosing a unique name is important because your package might be used on the Internet by other programs. Java designers recommend that you use your Internet domain name in reverse order as a package prefix. Since Internet domain names are unique, this avoids naming conflicts. Suppose you want to create a package named `mypackage.io` on a host machine with the Internet domain name `liangy.ipfw.indiana.edu`. To follow the naming convention, you would name the entire package `edu.indiana.ipfw.liangy.mypackage.io`.

Java expects one-to-one mapping of the package name and the file system directory structure. For the package named `edu.indiana.ipfw.liangy.mypackage.io`, you must create a directory, as shown in Figure H.1. In other words, a package is actually a directory that contains the bytecode of the classes.

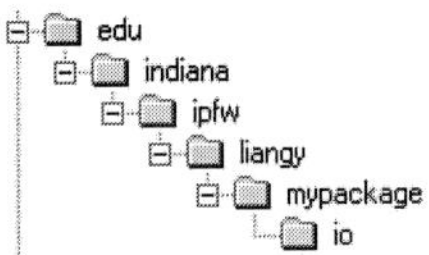

Figure H.1 *The package* `edu.indiana.ipfw.liangy.mypackge.io` *is mapped to a directory structure in the file system.*

The *classpath* Environment Variable

The edu directory does not have to be the root directory. In order for Java to know where your package is in the file system, you must modify the environment variable classpath so that it points to the directory in which your package resides. For example, the following line defines three directories in classpath.

```
classpath=.;c:\edu\ipfw\indiana\liangy;
```

The period (.) indicating the current directory is always in classpath. The directory c:\edu\ipfw\indiana\liangy is in classpath so that you can use the package mypackage.io in the program.

You can add as many directories as necessary in classpath. The order in which the directories are specified is the order in which the classes are searched. If you have two classes of the same name in different directories, Java uses the first one it finds.

The classpath variable is set differently in Windows and UNIX, as follows:

- **Windows 95 and Windows 98:** Edit **autoexec.bat** using a text editor, such as Microsoft Notepad.
- **Windows NT and Windows 2000:** Go to the Start button and choose Control Panel, select the System icon, then modify classpath in the environment.
- **UNIX:** Use the setenv command to set classpath, such as

```
setenv classpath .:/home/edu/indiana/ipfw/liangy
```

If you insert this line into the .cshrc file, the classpath variable will be automatically set when you log on.

NOTE

You must restart the system for the classpath variable to take effect on Windows 95 and Windows 98. On Windows NT and Windows 2000, however, the settings are stored permanently, and affect any new command-line windows, but not the existing command-line windows.

Putting Classes into Packages

Every class in Java belongs to a package. The class is added to the package when it is compiled. All the classes that you have used so far in this book were placed in the current directory (a default package) when the Java source programs were compiled. To put a class in a specific package, you need to add the following line as the first non-comment and non-blank statement in the program:

```
package packagename;
```

Example H.1 Putting Classes into Packages

This example creates the class `MyInput` and stores it in the package `mypackage.io`.

```
// Class with methods to read integers and doubles
package mypackage.io;

import java.io.*;

public class MyInput
{
  // Read a string from the keyboard
  public static String readString()
  {
    BufferedReader br
      = new BufferedReader(new InputStreamReader(System.in), 1);

    // Declare and initialize the string
    String string = " ";

    // Get the string from the keyboard
    try
    {
      string = br.readLine();
    }
    catch (IOException ex)
    {
      System.out.println(ex);
    }

    // Return the string obtained from the keyboard
    return string;
  }

  // Read an int value from the keyboard
  public static int readInt()
  {
    return Integer.parseInt(readString());
  }

  // Read a double value from the keyboard
  public static double readDouble()
  {
    return Double.parseDouble(readString());
  }
}
```

Example Review

A class must be defined as public in order to be accessed by other programs. Since the directory for the package is not automatically created using the **javac** compiler in JDK, you have to manually create it before compiling it.

If you use the **javac** compiler in JDK to compile this program, you must use the following command with the `-d` option to specify the destination of the bytecode file in order for the bytecode file to be placed in the `\edu\indiana\ipfw\liangy\mypackage\io` directory:

continues

Example H.1 continued

```
javac MyInput.java -d c:\edu\indiana\ipfw\liangy\mypackage\io
```

NOTE
If you want to put several classes into the package, you have to create separate source files for them because one file can have only one public class.

NOTE
The class files can be archived into a single file for convenience. For instance, you may compress all the class files in the folder mypackage into a single zip file named mypackage.zip with subfolder information kept as shown in Figure H.2. To make the classes in the zip file available for use, add the zip file to the classpath like this:

```
classpath=%classpath%;c:\mypackage.zip
```

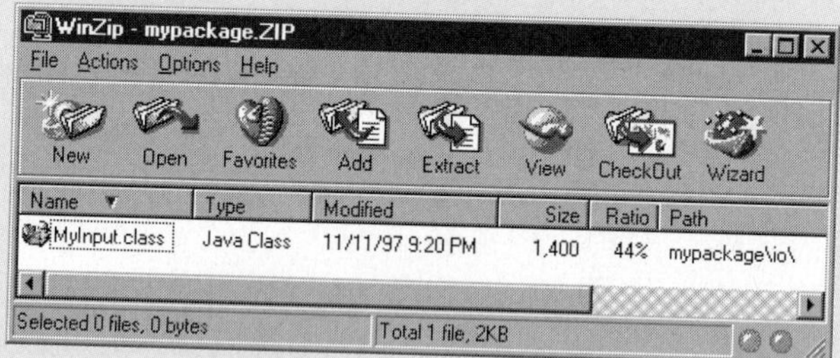

Figure H.2 *The class files can be archived into a single compressed file.*

Using Packages

To use a class from a package in your program, add an `import` statement to the top of the program; for example:

```
import mypackage.io.MyInput;
```

If you have many classes to use from the same package, use the asterisk (*) to indicate use of all the classes in the package, for example:

```
import mypackage.io.*;
```

This statement imports all the classes in the `mypackage.io` package.

Example H.2 Using Your Own Packages

This example shows a program that uses the `MyInput` class in the `mypackage.io` package. The program reads data and echo prints it. The output of the program is shown in Figure H.3.

```
import mypackage.io.MyInput;

public class TestMyInput
{
  public static void main(String[] args)
  {
    System.out.println("Enter an integer");
    int i = MyInput.readInt();
    System.out.println("You entered " + i);

    System.out.println("Enter a double");
    double d = MyInput.readDouble();
    System.out.println("You entered "+d);
  }
}
```

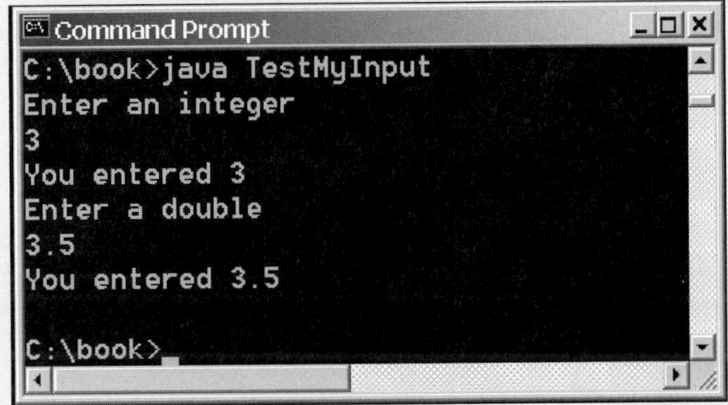

Figure H.3 *The program uses the* `MyInput` *class to read an* `int` *value and* `double` *value, and echo prints the values.*

Example Review

Before compiling this program, make sure the environment variable `classpath` is properly set so that the `MyInput` class can be found. Also, please note that `MyInput` is defined as public so that it can be used by classes in other packages.

The program uses the `import` statement to get the class `MyInput`. You have been using this class since Chapter 2, "Primitive Data Types and Operations." You did not use the `import` statement, however, because it was included in the same directory with these examples.

You cannot import entire packages, such as `mypackage.*.*`. Only one asterisk (*) can be used in the `import` statement.

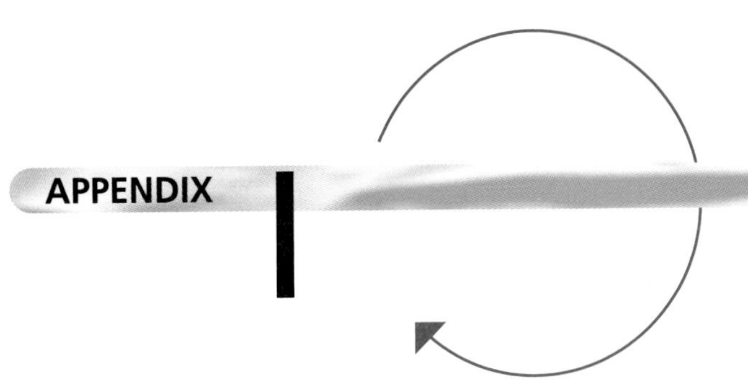

A JBuilder 3.5 Tutorial

Introduction

This tutorial is intended for students who want to create, compile, and run Java programs using JBuilder 3.5 Foundation rather than the command-line JDK 1.3. Please skip this appendix if you want to use JDK 1.3. For information on obtaining and installing JDK 1.3, please visit **`www.cs.armstrong.edu/liang/intro3e.html`**.

This tutorial covers the following topics:

1. What is JBuilder 3.5?
2. Obtain and install JBuilder 3.5
3. Get started with JBuilder 3.5
4. Create a new project
5. Set project properties
6. Create a Java application
7. Compile a Java program
8. Run a Java application
9. Create a Java applet
10. Compile and view Java applets in JBuilder 3.5
11. Use the `MyInput` class in JBuilder 3.5
12. Some known problems of JBuilder 3.5

What Is JBuilder 3.5?

JDK consists of a set of separate programs, such as compiler, interpreter, and appletviewer, each of which is invoked from a command line. JBuilder 3.5 provides an *integrated development environment* (IDE) for developing Java programs. Editing, compiling, building, debugging, and online help are integrated in one graphical user interface. Just enter source code in one window or open an existing file in a window, then click a button, menu item, or function key to compile the source code. The use of JBuilder makes developing Java programs easy and productive.

JBuilder 3.5 is written completely in Java. It uses the Swing component library, provided by JavaSoft (Sun Microsystems), as its foundation. This pure Java component library allows JBuilder to have a complex UI and remain 100% Java. The Swing library also gives the added benefit of a pluggable look-and-feel, which allows JBuilder to adjust its appearance to match the computer's native operating system UI without sacrificing the power and flexibility of the JBuilder UI. JBuilder 3.5 runs on the Windows 98, NT, and 2000, Linux, and Solaris platforms.

Functionally, JBuilder 3.5 Foundation is almost equivalent to JBuilder 3 Standard Edition. The functionalities of menus, wizards, and dialog boxes are retained in JBuilder 3.5 Foundation, but some of the wizards and many of the dialog boxes have been redesigned. It is safe to say that you can cruise through JBuilder 3.5 if you know JBuilder 3.

Obtaining and Installing JBuilder 3.5

The companion CD-ROM of this book contains JBuilder 3.5 Foundation.

You can also download JBuilder 3.5 from the Inprise Web site at

`www.inprise.com/jbuilder/foundation/`

JBuilder 3.5 Foundation can run on Linux, Solaris, and Windows. Download the one that matches your platform.

Read the installation instructions from setup_windows.html, and follow them to install JBuilder 3.5 Foundation and obtain the authorization key.

NOTE

JBuilder 4 will be released in September 2000. The UI interface of JBuilder 4 is almost the same as in JBuilder 3.5. I will post a tutorial for JBuilder 4 at **`www.cs.armstrong.edu/liang/intro3e.html`**.

Getting Started with JBuilder 3.5

Assume that you have successfully installed JBuilder 3.5 Foundation on your machine. Start JBuilder 3.5. The JBuilder user interface appears, as shown in Figure I.1. If you don't see the Welcome project, choose Welcome Project (Sample) from the Help menu.

NOTE

When you start JBuilder 3.5 Foundation for the first time, the License Manager dialog box will be displayed. Enter your name and your company name, and click Add to enter serial number and license key. Click OK to exit the License Manager. JBuilder will start immediately.

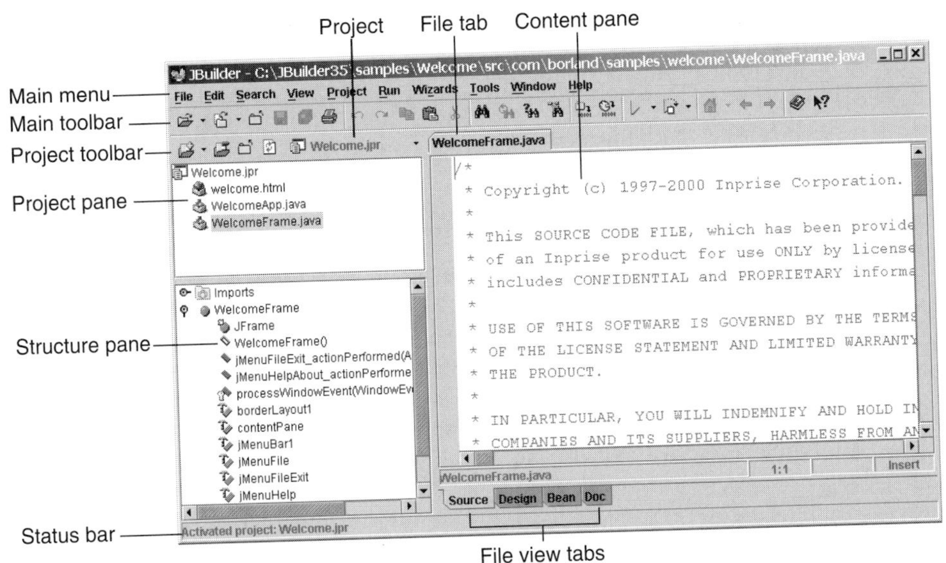

Figure I.1 *The JBuilder user interface is a single window that performs functions for editing, compiling, debugging, and running programs.*

The JBuilder user interface presents a single window for managing Java projects, browsing files, compiling, running, and debugging programs. This user interface is called *AppBrowser* in JBuilder 3.5. Note that the AppBrowser window and the main window are two separate windows in JBuilder 3, but are combined into one window in JBuilder 3.5.

Traditional IDE tools use many windows to accommodate various development tasks, such as editing, debugging, and browsing information. As a result, finding the window you need is often difficult. Because it is easy to get lost, beginners may be intimidated. For this reason, some new programmers prefer to use separate utilities, such as the JDK command line tools, for developing programs.

Borland is aware of the usability problem and has made significant efforts to simplify the JBuilder user interface. JBuilder introduces the AppBrowser window, which enables you to explore, edit, design, and debug projects all in one unified window.

The AppBrowser window primarily consists of the main menu, main toolbar, project pane, structure pane, content pane, and status bar.

The Main Menu

The main menu is similar to that of other Windows applications and provides most of the commands you need to use JBuilder, including those for creating, editing, compiling, running, and debugging programs. The menu items are enabled and disabled in response to the current context.

The Toolbar

The toolbar provides buttons for several frequently used commands on the menu bar. Clicking a toolbar is faster than using the menu bar. For some commands, you also can use function keys or keyboard shortcuts. For example, you can save a file in three ways:

- Select File, Save from the menu bar.
- Click the "save" toolbar button.
- Use the keyboard shortcut Ctrl+S.

TIP

You can display a label, known as *ToolTip*, for a button by pointing the mouse to the button without clicking.

The Status Bar

The status bar displays a message to alert users to the operation status, such as file saved for the Save file command and compilation successful for the Compilation command.

The Project Pane

The project pane displays the contents of one or more projects opened in the App-Browser. It consists of the following items, as shown in Figure I.2:

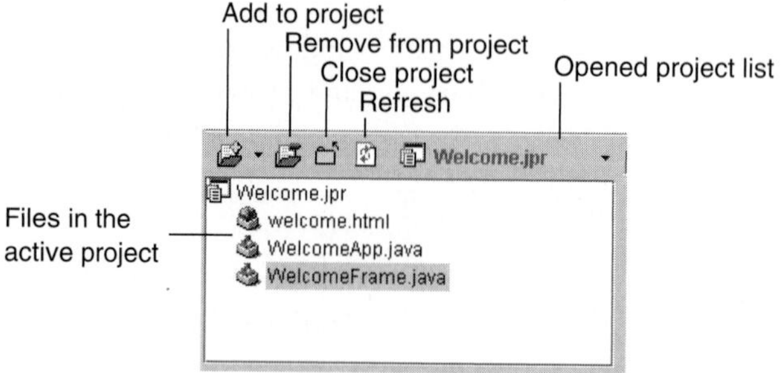

Figure I.2 *The JBuilder project pane holds manages the files in the project.*

- A small toolbar with four buttons (Add To Project, Remove From Project, Close Project, and Refresh).
- A drop-down list of all opened projects.
- A tree view of all the files that make up the active project.

The project pane shows a list of one or more files. In the case of the Project browser, you will see the project (.jpr) file first. Attached to that is a list of the files in the project. The list can include .java, .html, text, or image files. You select a file in the project pane by clicking it. The content pane and the structure pane display information about the selected file. As you select different files in the project pane, each one will be represented in the content and structure panes.

The project pane shown in Figure I.2 contains three files. The Add button is used to add new files to the project, and the Remove button to remove files from the project. For example, you can remove WelcomeFrame.java by selecting the file in the project pane and clicking the Remove button. You can then add the file back to the project as follows:

1. Click the Add button to display the Open dialog box shown in Figure I.3.
2. Open WelcomeFrame.java. You will see WelcomeFrame.java displayed in the project pane.

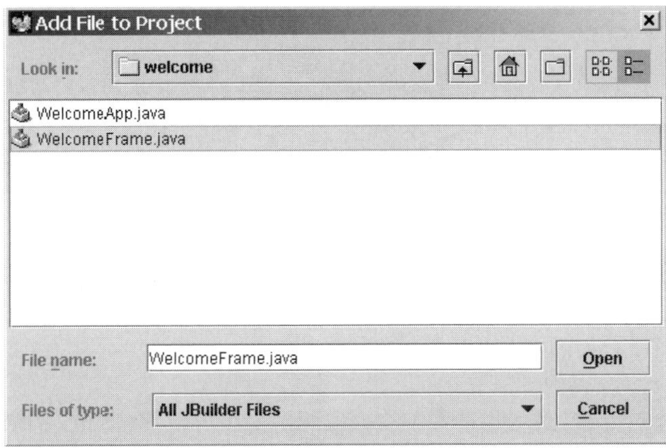

Figure I.3 *The Open dialog box enables you to open an existing file.*

NOTE

Due to a bug in the Swing's `JFileChooser` component, you cannot select multiple files from the file dialog box in JBuilder 3.5.

The Content Pane

The content pane displays all opened files as a set of tabs. To open a file in the content pane, double-click it in the project pane. The content pane displays the detailed content of the selected file. The editor or viewer used is determined by the file's extension. If you click the WelcomeFrame.java file in the project pane, for example, you will see four tabs (Source, Design, Bean, and Doc) at the bottom of the content pane (see Figure I.1). If you select the Source tab, you will see the JBuilder Java source code editor. This is a full-featured, syntax-highlighted programming editor.

If you select Welcome.html in the project pane, you will see the content pane become an HTML browser, as shown in Figure I.4. If you choose the Source tab, you can view and edit the HTML code in the content pane, as shown in Figure I.5.

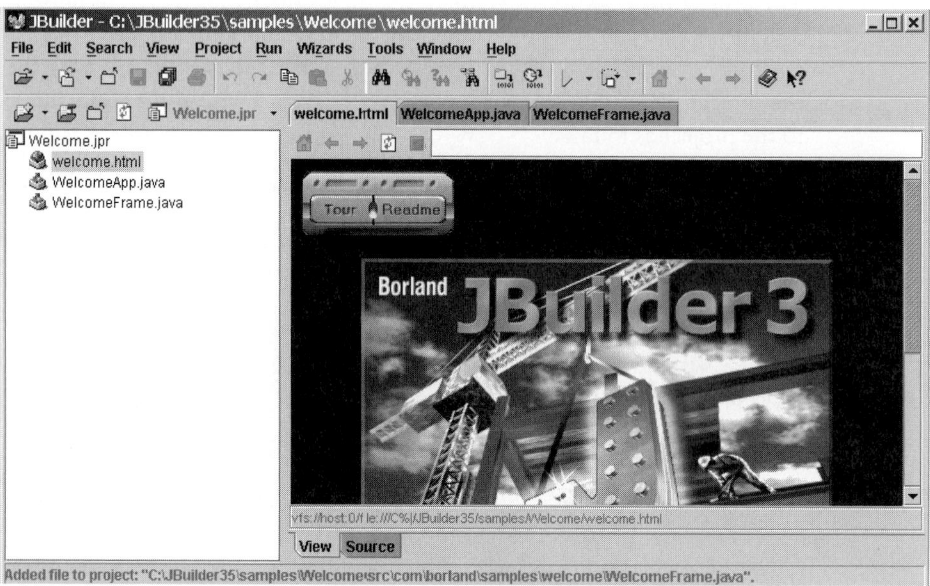

Figure I.4 *The content can display HTML files.*

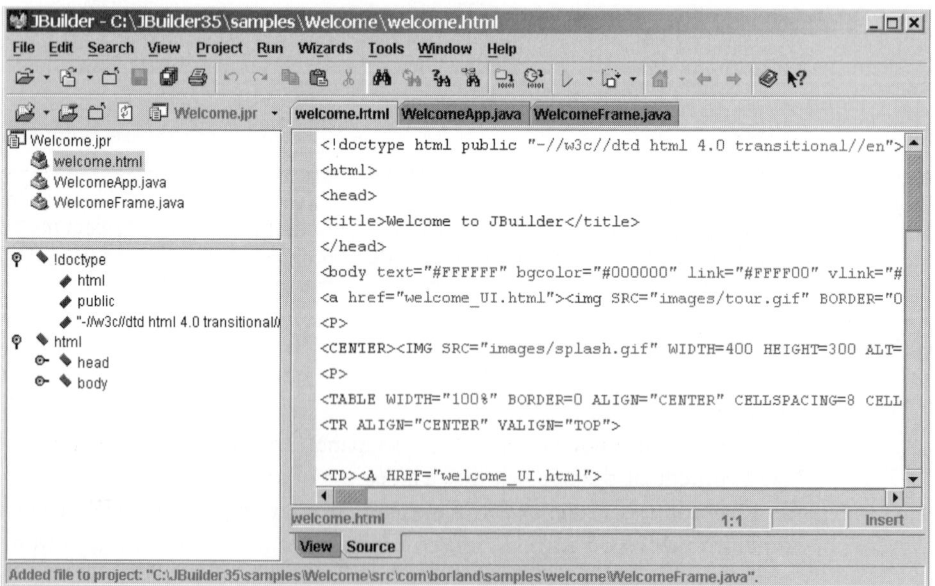

Figure I.5 *You can edit HTML files in the content pane.*

The Structure Pane

The structure pane displays the structural information about the files you selected in the project pane. All the items displayed in the structure pane are in the form of a hierarchical indexed list. The expand symbol in front of an item indicates that it contains subitems. You can see the subitems by clicking on the expand symbol.

You also can use the structure pane as a quick navigational tool to the various structural elements in the file. If you select the WelcomeFrame.java file, for example, you see classes, variables, and methods in the structure pane. If you then click on any of those elements in the structure pane, the content pane will move to and highlight it in the source code.

If you click on the `jMenuFile` item in the structure pane, as shown in Figure I.6, the content pane moves to and highlights the statement that defines the `jMenuFile` data field. This provides a much faster way to browse and find the elements of a .java file than scrolling through it.

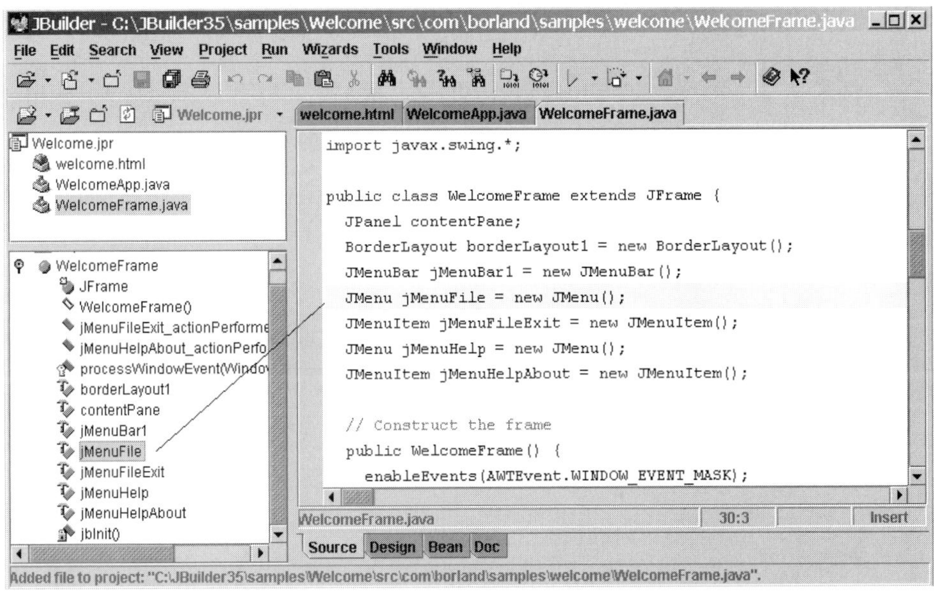

Figure I.6 *You can cruise through the source code from the structure pane.*

Creating a Project

A project is like a holder that ties all the files together. The information about each JBuilder project is stored in a project file with a .jpr file extension. The project file contains a list of all the files and project settings and properties. JBuilder uses this information to load and save all the files in the project and compile and run the programs.

To match the code used in this book, I recommend that you create a project to hold all your Java source files and class files, as follows:

1. Choose File, New Project to bring up the Project Wizard dialog box, as shown in Figure I.7.
2. Type "c:\book\book.jpr" in the Project File field. Check Make project notes file. Click Next to display Project Wizard Step 2 of 2 as shown in Figure I.8.
3. Fill in the title, author, company, and description fields. These optional fields provide a description for the project.
4. Click Finish. The new project is displayed in the project pane, as shown in Figure I.9. The Project Wizard created the project file (.jpr) and an HTML file (.html), and placed them in c:\book .

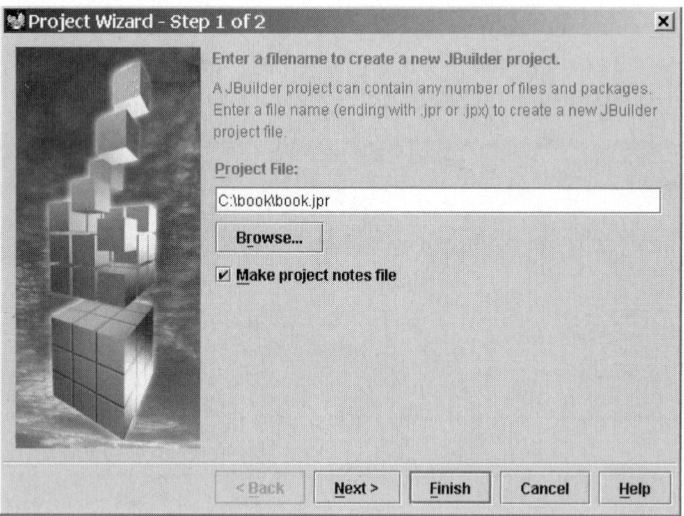

Figure I.7 *The Project Wizard dialog box enables you to specify the project file with other optional information.*

TIP

I recommend that new users of JBuilder put all the files in one package to avoid the hassle of managing projects.

Setting Project Properties

JBuilder uses a project file to store project information, such as where the source files are located, and where the output files are stored. You cannot edit the project file manually; it is modified automatically, however, whenever you add or remove files from the project or set project options. You can see the project file as a node at the top of the project tree in the project pane. JBuilder uses a Project Properties dialog box for setting project properties and provides a Project Wizard to facilitate creating projects.

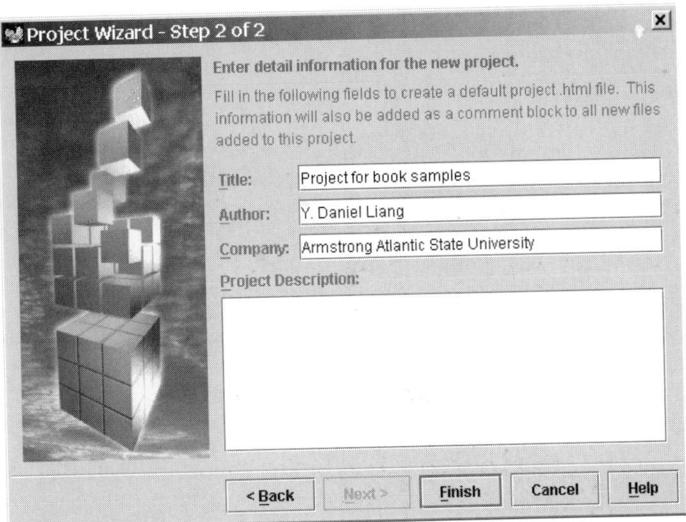

Figure I.8 *Project Wizard Step 2 of 2 collects optional information for the project.*

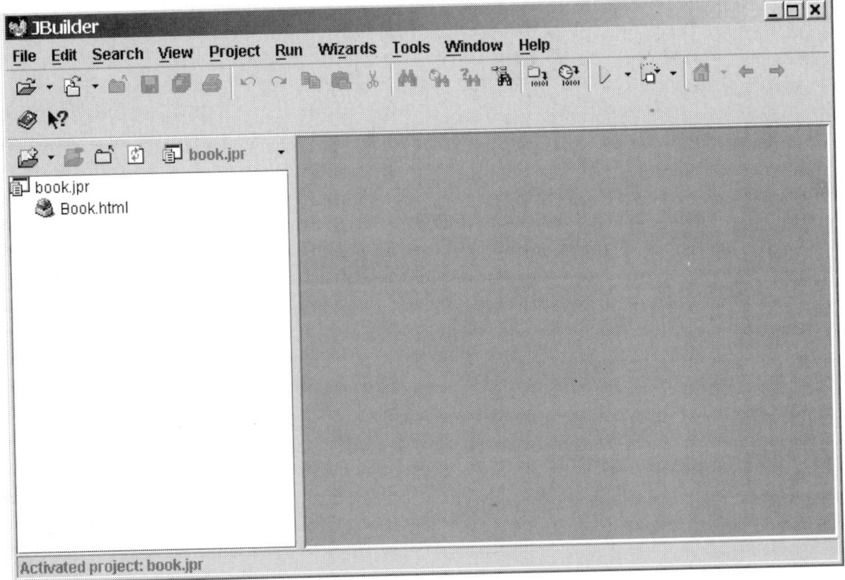

Figure I.9 *A new project is created with the .jpr file and .html file.*

JBuilder uses the Default Project Properties dialog box to set default environment properties for all the projects. An individual project has its own Project Properties dialog box, which can be used to set project-specific properties.

To display the default Project Properties dialog box, select Project, Default Properties, as shown in Figure I.10. To display the Project Properties dialog box, select Project, Properties, as shown in Figure I.11. You can also right-click the project file in the project pane and choose the Properties command to display the Project Properties dialog box.

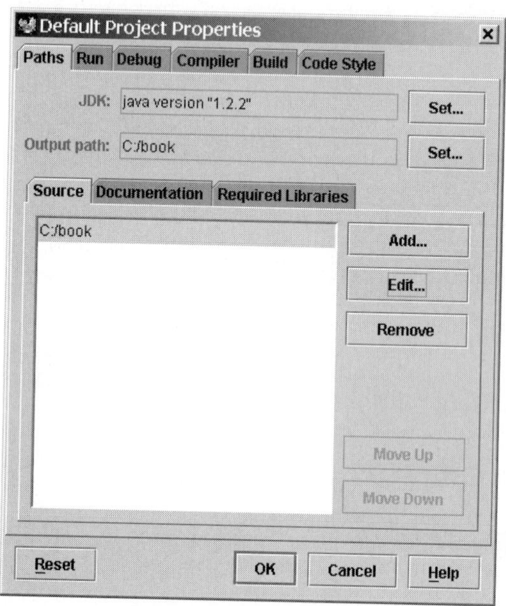

Figure I.10 *The Default Project Properties dialog box enables you to set default properties to cover all the projects.*

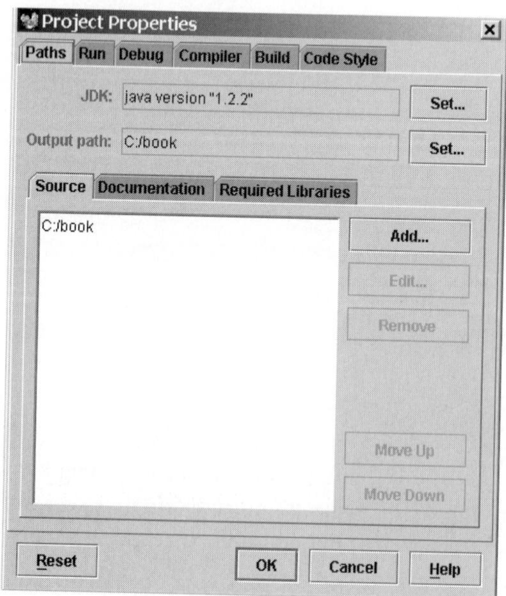

Figure I.11 *Each project keeps its own project properties.*

The Default Project Properties dialog box (Figure I.10) and the Project Properties dialog box (Figure I.11) look the same but have different titles. Both dialog boxes contain Paths, Run, Debug, Compiler, Build, and Code Style. You can set options in these pages for the current project or the default project, depending on whether the dialog box is for the current project or the default project.

To make your project work, you must set the output path and source path properties correctly. Setting proper paths is necessary for JBuilder to locate the associated files in the right directory for compiling and running the programs in the project. The source path specifies one or more paths for the source file. The output root directory specifies the path where the compiler places the .class files. Files are placed in a directory tree that is based on the Output root directory and the package name. For example, if the output root directory is **c:\book** and the package name is **chapter1** in the source code, the .class file is placed in **c:\book\chapter1**.

> **NOTE**
> For simplicity at this point, please do not use the `package` statement in your program.

Creating a Java Application

You have created a project and set the appropriate properties for it. You can create a Java application in the project. There are many ways to create a Java program in JBuilder. You can use various wizards to create certain types of Java programs.

Here are the steps in creating the file for Example 1.1 without using a wizard:

1. Click the Add to project button in the project pane to the Open dialog box, as shown in Figure I.12.

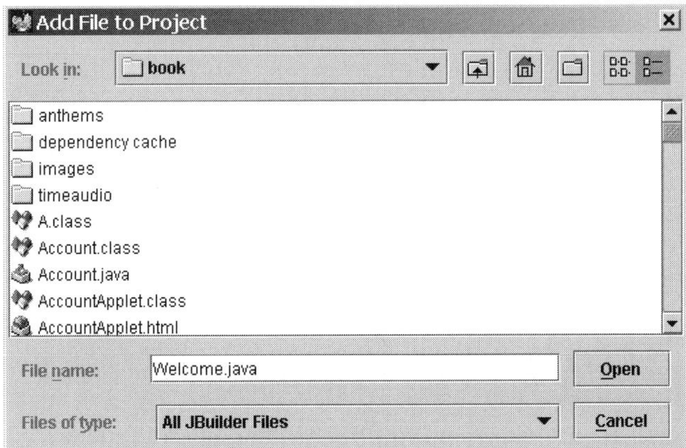

Figure I.12 *The Open dialog box allows you to open files from a file directory or a package or to create a new file.*

2. Type Welcome.java in the File name field and click Open. Since the file does not exist, the File Does Not Exist dialog box is displayed. Click OK in this dialog box to create the file. By convention, Java program source files must end with the extension .java. You should see Welcome.java added to the project and currently selected in the project pane.

3. Double-click Welcome.java in the project pane to open it. Type the Java source code in Example 1.1 in the content pane, as shown in Figure I.13.

4. Select File, Save All to save all your work. You should see a confirmation message in the status bar indicating that the files are saved.

NOTE

As you type, the code completion assistance automatically comes up to give you suggestions for completing the code. For instance, when you type a dot (.) after System and pause for a second, JBuilder displays a popup menu with suggestions to complete the code, as shown in Figure I.14. You can then select from the menu to complete the code.

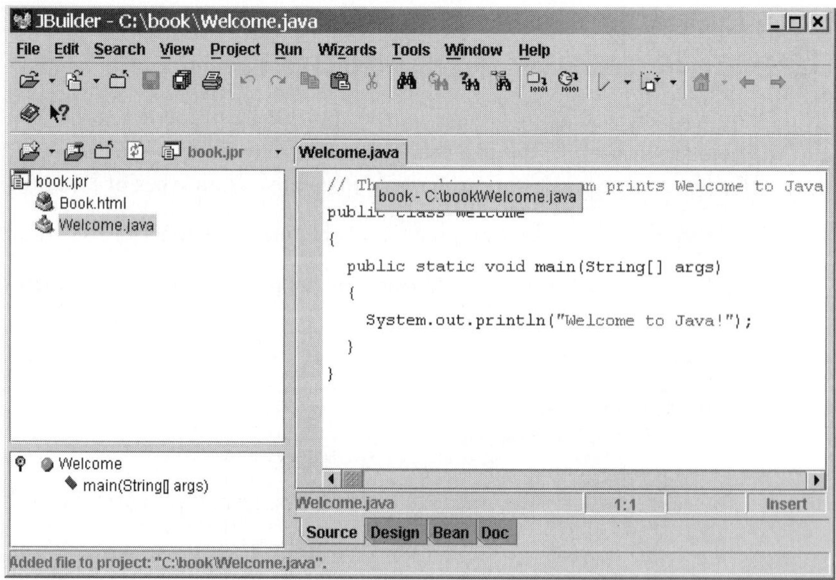

Figure I.13 *The program Welcome is typed in the content pane.*

Compiling a Java Program

To execute the program, you have to compile it first, using one of the following methods. (Be sure that Welcome.java is selected on the project page.)

- Select Project, Make "Welcome.java" from the menu bar.
- Click the Make toolbar button ( ).

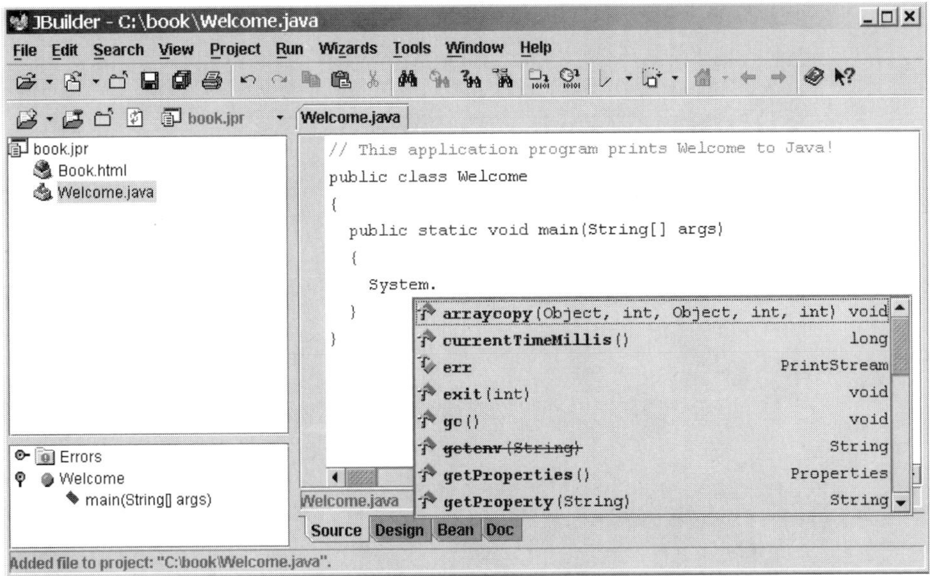

Figure I.14 *The Code Insight popup menu is automatically displayed to help you complete the code.*

- Point to Welcome.java in the project pane, right-click the mouse button to display a popup menu (see Figure I.15), and choose Make from the menu.

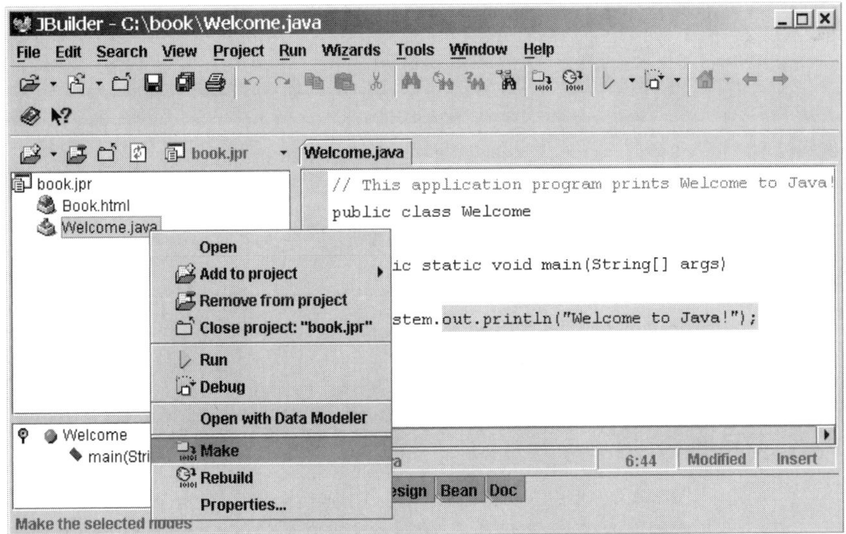

Figure I.15 *Point the mouse to the file in the project pane and right-click it to display a popup menu that contains the commands for processing the file.*

The compilation status is displayed on the status bar. If there are no syntax errors, the compiler generates a file named Welcome.class. This file is stored in outputpath\package (i.e., **c:\book** in this case, since outputpath is **c:\book** and the `package` statement is not used in the source code).

Executing a Java Application

To run Welcome.class, simply point to Welcome.java in the project pane and right-click the mouse button to display a popup menu. Choose Run from the popup menu.

When this program executes, JBuilder displays the output in the message pane, as shown in Figure I.16.

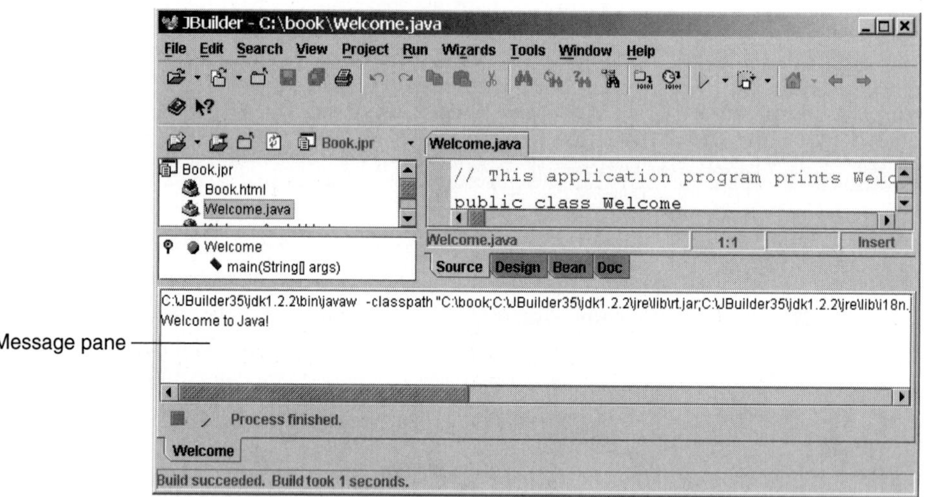

Figure I.16 *The execution result is shown in the message pane.*

Creating a Java Applet

You can create and compile an applet the same way you created and compiled an application in the preceding section. The JBuilder Applet Wizard enables you to quickly create templates for the applet and its associated HTML file.

The following are the steps in creating the applet for Example 1.2 using the Applet Wizard:

1. Open project book.jpr if it is not opened. To open it, choose File, Reopen to display a submenu consisting of the most recently opened projects and files, as shown in Figure I.17. Select the project if it is in the menu. Otherwise, choose File, Open to locate and open **book.jpr.** The project file is the one with the icon.

2. Choose File, New to display Object Gallery, as shown in Figure I.18. Object Gallery contains the wizards for creating many types of Java classes.

3. Click the Applet icon in the Object Gallery to display the Applet Wizard, as shown in Figure I.19. Leave the Package field blank and type **WelcomeApplet** in the Class field. Click Finish to close the dialog box. JBuilder automatically created **WelcomeApplet.java** and **WelcomeApplet.html,** as shown in Figure I.20.

4. **WelcomeApplet.java** contains a lot of code we are not interested in at this time. Therefore, replace the code with Example 1.2, as shown in Figure I.21. Note that a new statement g.setColor(Color.red) was added to this program to display the message in red.

5. Choose File, Save All to preserve your work.

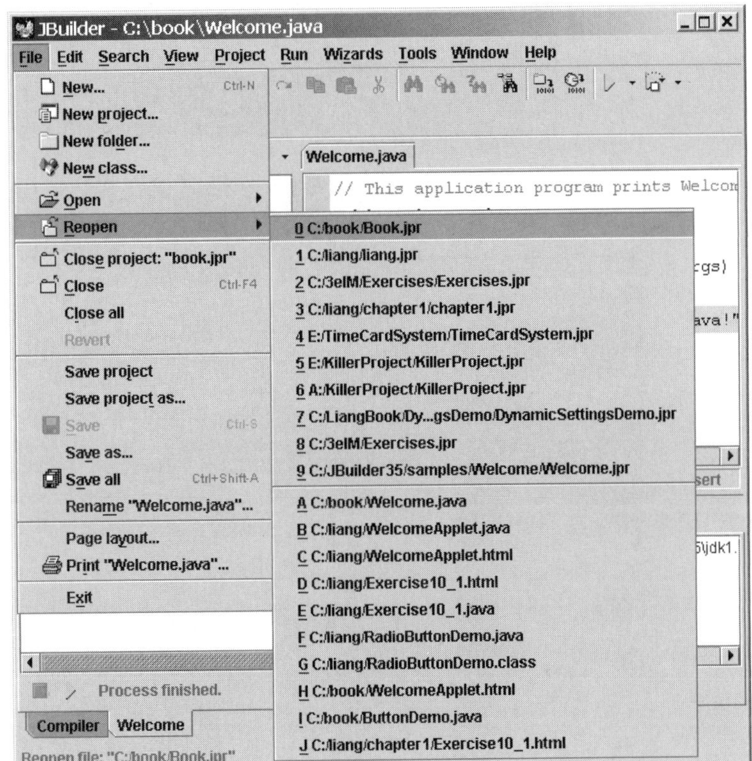

Figure I.17 *Recently used projects can be reopened by choosing File, Reopen.*

Compiling and Viewing Applets in JBuilder 3.5

Compile the program by pointing to WelcomeApplet.java in the project pane and right-clicking the mouse button to display a popup menu. Select Make to compile the program in the popup menu.

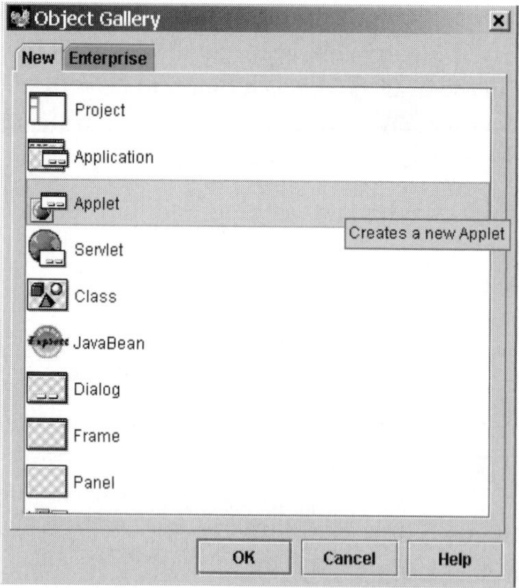

Figure I.18 *The Object Gallery box contains wizards for creating various types of Java programs.*

Figure I.19 *The Applet Wizard enables you to create an applet and its associated HTML file.*

To view this applet, double-click WelcomeApplet.html in the project pane and choose the View tab, if this tab has not been selected. You will see the applet in the content pane, as shown in Figure I.22.

NOTE

Due to a bug in JB 3.5, the `WelcomeApplet` applet will not be displayed in the content pane if `g.setColor()` method is not used.

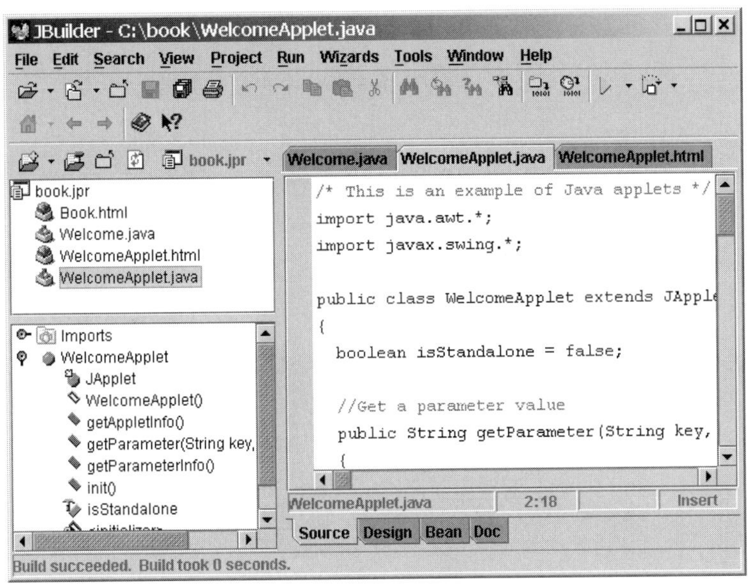

Figure I.20 *The Applet Wizard generated WelcomeApplet.java and WelcomeApplet.html.*

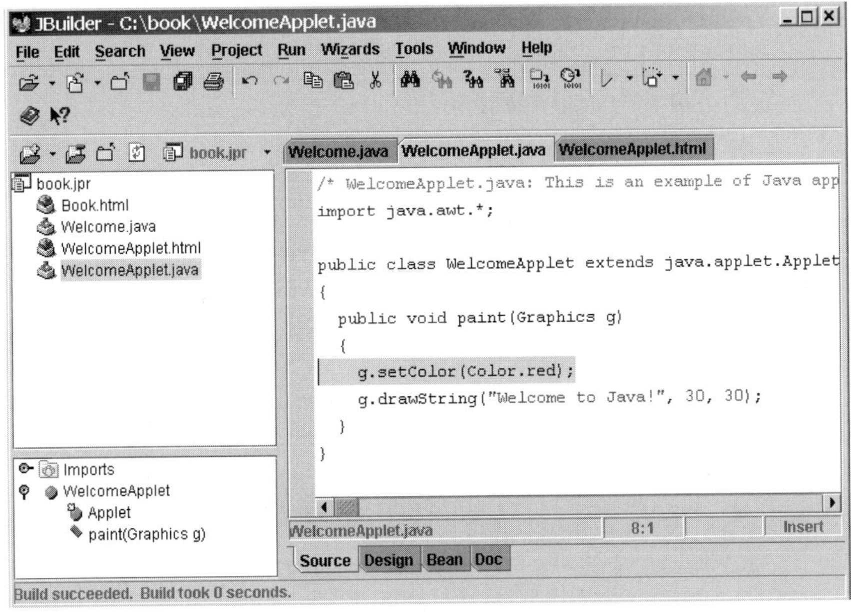

Figure I.21 *You typed the code in Example 1.2 for WelcomeApplet.java in the Content pane.*

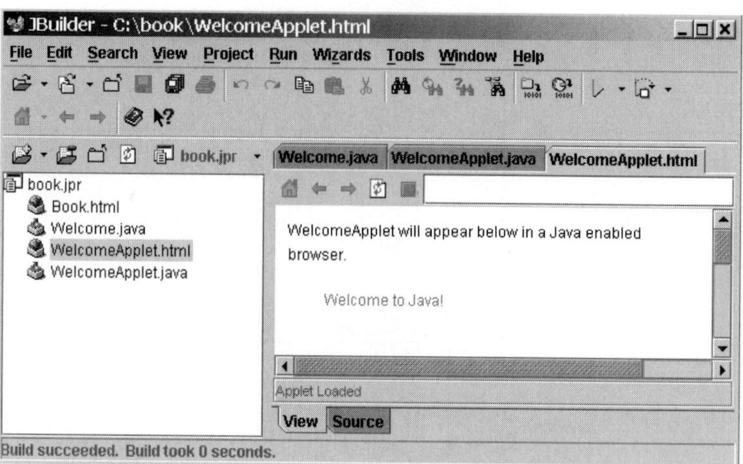

Figure I.22 *You can view a Java applet in the content pane in JBuilder 3.5.*

You can also view the applet by running WelcomeApplet.html. JB 3.5 displays an applet viewer to show the applet, as shown in Figure I.23.

Using the *MyInput* Class in JBuilder 3.5

The `MyInput` class, introduced in Chapter 2, "Primitive Data Types and Operations," enables your Java programs to read integer, floating-point, and string values from the keyboard. In JBuilder 3.5, the output is displayed in the message pane, and input from the keyboard is also echo displayed in the message pane. Here is an example of using `MyInput`:

- Open project **book.jpr**.
- Create **MyInput.java**.
- Create **ComputeMortgage.java**, as shown in Example 1.2.
- Select **ComputeMortgage.java** in the project pane. Right-click it to display a popup menu. Choose Run from the menu to run the program. Click the mouse in the message pane.
- Enter the yearly interest rate and click Enter. Enter the number of years and click Enter. Enter the loan amount, and click Enter. You will see the result displayed in the message pane, as shown in Figure I.24.

Some Known Problems of JBuilder 3.5

Q: Why can't I choose multiple files from the File dialog box?

A: This problem is due to a bug in `JFileChooser`. New versions of the Swing component library will fix it. It is fixed in JBuilder 4.

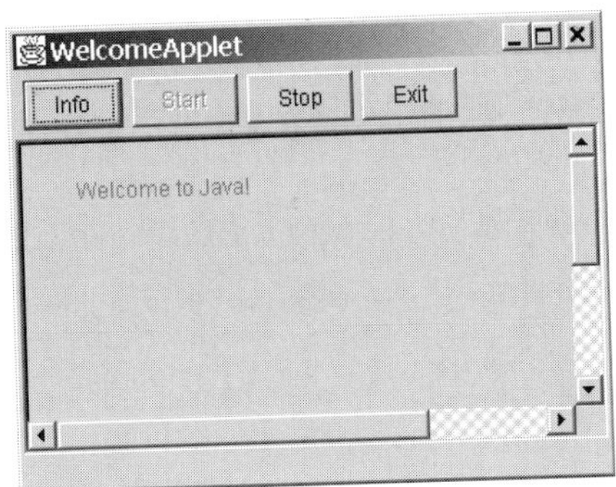

Figure I.23 *You can view a Java applet using applet viewer.*

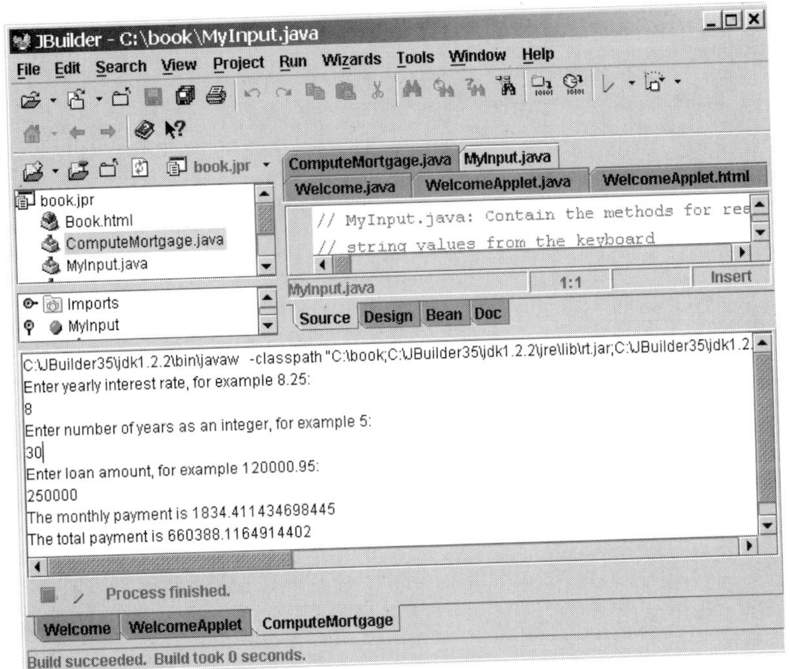

Figure I.24 *The keyboard input is echo displayed in the message pane.*

Q: JBuilder 3.5 can't find the current working directory for the files. The problem occurs when a `FileNotFoundException` is raised while reading a file from a relative path—for example, images\us.gif.

A: There are two ways to fix this problem. One fix is to use the absolute path, such as **c:\book\images\us.gif**.

The other fix is as follows:

1. Invoke the program using

   -Duser.dir=c:\someDir\someOtherDir in the java command, or set this in the VM parameters.

2. In the program, you have to use

   ```
   String baseDirectory = System.getProperty("user.dir");
   ```

   to get base directory.

3. Replace the statement, such as

```
ImageIcon = new ImageIcon("image/us.gif");
```

with

```
ImageIcon = new ImageIcon(baseDirectory + "image/us.gif");
```

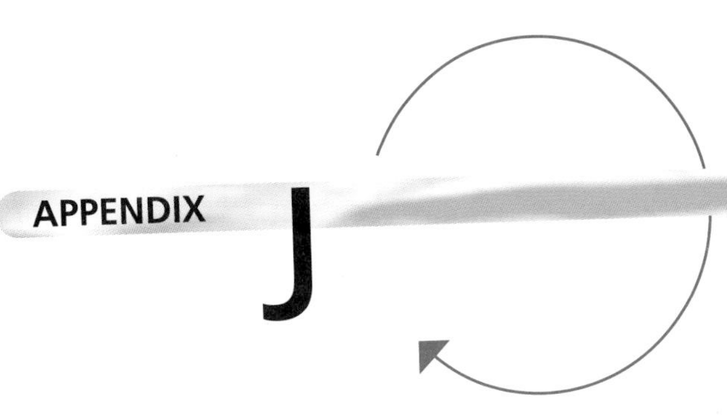

GLOSSARY

This glossary lists and defines the key terms used in the book.

abstract class When you are designing classes, a superclass should contain common features that are shared by subclasses. Sometimes the superclass is so abstract that it cannot have any specific instances. These classes are called *abstract classes* and are declared using the `abstract` modifier. Abstract classes are like regular classes with data and methods, but you cannot create instances of abstract classes using the `new` operator.

abstraction A technique in software development that hides detailed implementation. Java supports method abstraction and class abstraction. *Method abstraction* is defined as separating the use of a method from its implementation. The client can use a method without knowing how it is implemented. If you decide to change the implementation, the client program will not be affected. Similarly, class abstraction hides the implementation of the class from the client.

abstract method A method signature without implementation. Its implementation is provided by its subclasses. An abstract method is denoted with an `abstract` modifier and must be contained in an abstract class. In a nonabstract subclass extended from an abstract class, all abstract methods must be implemented, even if they are not used in the subclass.

Abstract Window Toolkit (AWT) The set of components for developing simple graphics applications that was in use before the introduction of Swing components. The AWT user interface components have now been replaced by the Swing components, but other AWT classes such as helper classes, layout manage classes, and event-handling classes are still used.

accessor method The getter and setter methods for retrieving and setting private fields in an object.

actual parameter The value passed to a method when it is invoked. Actual parameters should match formal parameters in type, order, and number.

algorithm Pseudocode that describes how a problem is solved in terms of the actions to be executed, and specifies the order in which these actions should be executed. Algorithms can help the programmer plan a program before writing it in a programming language.

aggregation A special form of association that represents an ownership relationship between two classes.

applet A special kind of Java program that can run directly from a Web browser or an applet viewer. Various security restrictions are imposed on applets. For example, they cannot perform input/output operations on a user's system and therefore cannot read or write files or transmit computer viruses.

application A standalone program, such as any program written using a high-level language. Applications can be executed from any computer with a Java interpreter. Applications are not subject to the security restrictions imposed on Java applets. An application class must contain a main method.

argument Same as actual parameter.

array A container object that stores an indexed sequence of the same types of data. Typically, the individual elements are referenced by an index value. The index is an `int` value starting with 0 for the first element, 1 for the second, and so on.

assignment statement A simple statement that assigns a value to a variable.

association A general binary relationship that describes an activity between two classes.

block A sequence of statements enclosed in braces ({}).

bytecode The result of compiling Java source code. Bytecode is machine-independent and can run on any machine that has a Java running environment.

casting The process of converting a primitive data type value into another primitive type or converting an object of one object type into another object type. For example, `(int)3.5` converts 3.5 into an `int` value, and `(Cylinder)c` converts an object `c` into the Cylinder type. For the object casting to be successful, the object to be casted must be an instance of the target class.

child class Same as subclass.

class An encapsulated collection of data and methods that operate on data. A class may be instantiated to create an object that is an instance of the class.

class hierarchy A collection of classes organized in terms of superclass and subclass relationships.

class method A method that can be invoked without creating an instance of the class. To define class methods, put the modifier `static` in the method declaration.

class variable A data member declared using the `static` modifier. A class variable is shared by all instances of that class. Class variables are used to communicate between different objects of the same class and to handle global states among these objects.

comment Comments document what a program is and how it is constructed. They are not programming statements and are ignored by the compiler. In Java, comments are preceded by two slashes (`//`) in a line or enclosed between `/*` and `*/` in multiple lines.

compiler A software program that translates Java source code into bytecode.

composition A form of relationship that represents exclusive ownership of the class by the aggregated class.

constant A variable declared `final` in Java. Since a class constant is usually shared by all objects of the same class, a class constant is often declared `static`. A local constant is a constant declared inside a method.

constructor A special method for initializing objects when creating objects using the `new` operator. The constructor has exactly the same name as its defining class. Constructors can be overloaded, making it easier to construct objects with different initial data values.

data type Data type is used to define variables. Java supports primitive data types and object data types.

debugging The process of finding and fixing errors in a program.

declaration Defines variables, methods, and classes in a program.

default constructor A constructor that has no parameters. A default constructor is required for a JavaBeans component.

definition Alternative term for a declaration.

deserialization The process of restoring an object that was previously serialized.

design To plan how a program can be structured and implemented by coding.

double buffering A technique to reduce flickering in image animation in Java.

encapsulation Combining of methods and data into a single data structure. In Java, this is known as a *class*.

event A signal to the program that something has happened. Events are generated by external user actions, such as mouse movements, mouse button clicks, and keystrokes, or by the operating system, such as a timer. The program can choose to respond to an event or to ignore it.

event adapter A class used to filter event methods and only handle specified ones.

event delegation In Java event-driven programming, events are assigned to the listener object for processing. This is referred to as event delegation.

event-driven programming Java graphics programming is event-driven. In event-driven programming, codes are executed upon the activation of events, such as clicking a button or moving the mouse.

event handler A method in the listener's object that is designed to do some specified processing when a particular event occurs.

event listener The object that receives and handles the event.

event listener interface An interface implemented by the listener class to handle the specified events.

event registration To become a listener, an object must be registered as a listener by the source object. The source object maintains a list of listeners and notifies all the registered listeners when an event occurs.

event source The object that generates the event.

exception An unexpected event indicating that a program has failed in some way. Exceptions are represented by exception objects in Java. Exceptions can be handled in a `trycatch` block.

`final` A modifier for classes, data, methods, and local variables. A final class cannot be extended, a final data or local variable is a constant, and a final method cannot be overridden in a subclass.

formal parameter The parameters defined in the method signature.

garbage collection A JVM feature that automatically detects and reclaims the space occupied by unreferenced objects.

getter method For retrieving private data in a class.

graphical user interface (GUI) An interface to a program that is implemented using AWT or Swing components, such as frames, buttons, labels, text fields, and so on.

HTML (Hypertext Markup Language) A markup language to design Web pages for creating and sharing multimedia-enabled, integrated electronic documents over the Internet.

Identifier A name of a variable, method, class, interface, or package.

information hiding A software engineering concept for hiding and protecting an object's internal features and structure.

inheritance In object-oriented programming, the use of the `extends` keyword to derive new classes from existing classes.

inner class A class embedded in another class. Inner classes enable you to define small auxiliary objects and pass units of behavior, thus making programs simple and concise.

instance An object of a class.

instance method A nonstatic method in a class. Instance methods belong to instances and can only be invoked by them.

instance variable A nonstatic data member of a class. An instance variable belongs to an instance of the class

instantiation The process of creating an object of a class.

Integrated Development Environment (IDE) Software that helps programmers write code efficiently. IDE tools integrate editing, compiling, building, debugging, and online help in one graphical user interface.

interface An interface is treated like a special class in Java. Each interface is compiled into a separate bytecode file, just like a regular class. You cannot create an instance for an interface. The structure of a Java interface is similar to that of an abstract class in that it can have data and methods. The data, however, must be constants, and the methods can have only declarations without implementation. Single inheritance is the Java restriction wherein a class can inherit from a single superclass. This restriction is eased by the use of an interface.

interpreter Software for interpreting and running Java bytecode.

JavaBean A public class that has a default constructor and is serializable.

Java Development Toolkit (JDK) Defines the Java API and contains a set of command-line utilities, such as `javac` (compiler) and `java` (interpreter). With Java 2, Sun renamed JDK 1.2 to Java 2 SDK v 1.2. SDK stands for Software Development Toolkit.

Just-in-Time compiler Capable of compiling each bytecode once, and then reinvoking the compiled code repeatedly when the bytecode is executed.

keyword A reserved word defined as part of the Java language. (See Appendix A, "Java Keywords," for a full list of keywords.)

local variable A variable defined inside a method.

main class A class that contains a main method.

marker interface An empty interface that is used to signify that all the classes implementing the interface share certain properties.

method A collection of statements grouped together to perform an operation. *See* class method; instance method.

method overloading Method overloading means that you can define methods with the same name in a class as long as there is enough difference in their parameter profiles.

method overriding Method overriding means that you can modify a method in a subclass that was originally defined in a superclass.

method signature The combination of the name of a method and the list of its parameters.

modal dialog box A dialog box that prevents the user from using other windows before it is dismissed.

modifier A Java keyword that specifies the properties of data, methods, and classes and how they can be used. Examples of modifiers are `public`, `private`, and `static`.

multithreading The capability of a program to perform several tasks simultaneously within a program.

narrowing (of types) Casting a variable of a type with a larger range to a variable of a type with a smaller range.

object Same as instance.

object-oriented programming (OOP) An approach to programming that involves organizing objects and their behavior into classes of reusable components.

operator Operations for primitive data type values. Examples of operators are `+`, `-`, `*`, `/`, and `%`.

operator precedence Defines the order in which operators will be evaluated in an expression.

package A collection of classes.

parent class Same as superclass.

pass-by-value A term used when a copy of a primitive data type variable is passed as a method parameter. The actual variable outside the method is not affected, regardless of the changes made to the formal parameter inside the method.

primitive data type The primitive data types are `byte`, `short`, `int`, `long`, `float`, `double`, `boolean`, and `char`.

private A modifier for members of a class. A private member can only be referenced inside the class.

protected A modifier for members of a class. A protected member of a class can be used in the class in which it is declared or any subclass derived from that class.

public A modifier for classes, data, and methods that can be accessed by all programs.

recursive method A method that invokes itself, directly or indirectly.

reserved word Same as keyword.

sequence diagram A UML diagram that describes interactions among objects by depicting the time-ordering of method invocations.

serialization The process of writing an object to a stream.

setter method For updating private data in a class.

socket The facilitation of communication between a server and a client.

statechart A UML diagram that describes the flow of control of an object.

statement A unit of code that represents an action or a sequence of actions.

static method Same as class method.

static variable Same as class variable.

stream The continuous one-way flow of data between a sender and a receiver.

subclass A class that inherits from or extends a superclass.

superclass A class inherited from a subclass.

Swing component The Swing GUI components are painted directly on canvases using Java code except for components that are subclasses of `java.awt.Window` or `java.awt.Panel`, which must be drawn using native GUI on a specific platform. Swing components are less dependent on the target platform and use less resources of the native GUI. Swing components are more flexible and versatile than their AWT counterparts.

tag An HTML instruction that tells a Web browser how to display a document. Tags are enclosed in brackets, such as `<html>`, `<i>`, `<b>`, and `</html>`.

thread A flow of execution of a task, with a beginning and an end, in a program.

Unicode A code system for international characters managed by the Unicode Consortium. Java supports Unicode.

Unified Modeling Language (UML) A graphical notation for describing classes and their relationships.

Universal Resource Locator (URL) A mechanism that uniquely identifies resources on the Internet.

widening (of types) Casting a variable of a type with a smaller range to a variable of a type with a larger range.

INDEX

SYMBOLS